GERM RAILWAYS

PART 2. PRIVATE OPERATORS, MUSEUMS AND MUSEUM LINES

FIFTH EDITION

The complete guide to all Locomotives and Multiple Units of Private Railway Companies and Operators in Germany

Brian Garvin

Published by Platform 5 Publishing Ltd.,
52 Broadfield Road, Sheffield, S8 0XJ, England.

Printed in England by Berforts Information Press, Eynsham, Oxford.

ISBN 978 1 909431 18 8

Above: Osthannoversche Eisenbahn 92 80 1273 005, running number V1001-033, passes Hammerstein with a steel train from Georgsmarienhütte to Bendorf on 28 March 2014. This is an original version Vossloh G2000 with asymmetrical cabs. **Matthias Müller**

Front cover: On 26 September 2012, A convoy of locomotives owned by Lokomotion Gesellschaft für Schienentraktion (LM) is passing Terfens on its way from Brennero to München. The consist comprises 91 80 6139 133, 6139 555, 6186 286, 6185 663 and 6185 664. **Matthias Müller**

Back cover: Keolis Deutschland - Eurobahn (ERB) EMU 94 80 0428 126, running number ET6.02, is a Stadler FLIRT 4-section articulated unit. It is seen at the company's Hamm depot in the company of shunter 98 80 3332 090, running number V 249, on 2 July 2009. **David Haydock**

CONTENTS

FOREWORD

This new edition of German Railways Part 2 has been a long time coming! More than ten years have passed since the last edition, during which time the changes on German Railways have been tremendous. Quite a few of the operators mentioned in the last edition have ceased to exist, others have been created and in some cases they too have ceased to exist! It is not the intention to go into detail of these companies but to outline the situation in mid 2015.

One of the biggest problems has been the continual change with operators coming and going and rolling stock swapping between operators as, in the case of passenger train operators, franchises are won or lost. Then there are locomotives belonging to the leasing companies which can stay with an operating company for years or be on short term loan and have several different operators each year and in some cases each month! So there may be some instances of incorrect information but your compiler has worked hard to provide the best available information.

Generally though, the advent of open access private operators has led to a more interesting railway scene. Whilst the passenger operators have specific routes and services, the private freight operators can work on various routes and there tend to be many special ad hoc or spot services. One only has to think of a place like Bremen Hbf where freight trains roll through to and from the docks producing locomotives of various types from numerous operators in different liveries; even the passenger scene is enlivened by the appearance of Nord West Bahn, Metronom and erixx alongside DB Fernverkehr and DB Regio.

So, go now and enjoy the railway scene, taking along this book which hopefully will answer many of your questions!

Brian Garvin

INTRODUCTION

BACKGROUND

Railway fans from the UK often went to Germany via the Harwich–Hook of Holland route and entered Germany via Bad Bentheim. At this very first town in Germany some private railway shunting locomotives could be seen with the logo *BE* on them – *Bentheimer Eisenbahn*. But how many more such lines were there? The answer is many. For many years they were in decline but are now having a renaissance.

Latterly the private railways in Germany have been known as the "Nichtbundeseigene Eisenbahnen" – literally "non-state-owned railways" i.e. private lines. Germany has always had private railways, the format of which was laid down by law. Besides the state run lines other railways were built as feeder lines or simple railways connecting some local communities. There were four main types:

Nebenbahnen: Standard gauge secondary railways normally with a top speed of 50 km/h. Some of the state railway's secondary lines were called Nebenbahnen as they came into this category.

Kreisbahnen/Lokalbahnen: These could be of 1435 mm, 1000 mm or 750 mm gauge but with a lower speed than Nebenbahnen.

Kleinbahnen: In addition to the above gauges a Kleinbahn could be of 600 mm gauge.

Examples of some railway names are:

Augsburger Localbahn	AL
Bentheimer Eisenbahn	BE
Rügensche Bäderbahn	RüBB
Dürener Kreisbahn	DKB
Hohenzollerische Landesbahn	HzL
Nebenbahn Nürtingen–Neuffen	NN

Note that each railway company has its own official abbreviation.

Until a few years ago the number of private railways was declining but this has changed now because of regionalisation and open access arrangements brought about by European Union legislation.

Regionalisation. Local passenger train service levels have always been decided by local authorities and run by DB. The change in railway legislation and the need for savings allowed the local authorities to tender for the supply of rail passenger services. It was found that DB prices were quite high compared to new local operators. Consequently local operators have taken over passenger trains in many areas that were once run by DB.

Open Access. The European Union has directed that track and signalling should be accounted for separately to show the costs of operating railways against roads. Consequently in several countries "Track Authorities" have been set up. The precise manner varies between countries but the result is that in the EU there should be open access for any train company to run trains over railway networks.

Train Operators. The changes mentioned above have led to a surge in new operators, both passenger and freight. In the latter category the freight operators can be sub-divided into commercial freight operators and track contractors – the latter hauling their own equipment and supplies around the national network. All locomotives and rolling stock have to conform to certain norms laid down by the Eisenbahnbundesamt (EBA – see later). The growth in the number of operators has meant a booming market in second hand locomotives. These operators have snapped up redundant locomotives, being thwarted for a while by DB. Many got hold of locomotives that had been sold to preservation groups who were glad to have the cash (the loco after all is still available to preserve later) or imported locomotives that had "grandfather" rights on the DB. In this category come Polish ST44, CD 781 which were the same as DB class 220 (ex-DR). These could not be refused an operating licence as the safety case already existed!

Contractors and Dealers. The growth in the private sector has led to the creation of smaller back up organisations and quite a few entrepreneurs. Track renewal contractors have mushroomed with more and more track work being contracted out. Locomotive dealers have emerged who are quite adept at finding spare locomotives should someone be short. This has led to locomotives being imported as previously mentioned. Not to be outdone the major manufacturers have seen the opportunities and have set up hire fleets for short term hire for particular flows. In a case of "if you cannot beat them join them" the DB diesel overhaul works at Stendal (DB Regio) started selling or hiring out reconditioned Class 202 diesels before being taken over by Alstom. However under the new regime the work continues with ex-DB 212s also being overhauled and hired out or even sold.

Eisenbahn Bundesamt (EBA). This organisation is where the German Railways differ from the UK. The track authority in Germany is DB Netz. It owns the tracks and provides the signalling and signallers etc. However the safety case for the equipment is done by the EBA which has a supervisory role. Locomotives and rolling stock in Germany must comply with certain laid down safety and operating criteria (e.g. being fitted with ATP systems, proper braking systems etc.). Imported locomotives have to meet these criteria and the locomotives will be inspected to ensure they do. DB itself has to get its locomotives and rolling stock passed by the EBA and each locomotive, unit or carriage will have stamped into the frame somewhere its EBA authorisation number. On new locomotives only the prototypes will be fully inspected and once agreed to run authority is granted for a fleet of similar locomotives etc. Should there be an incident where EBA standards have not been complied with there will be severe penalties.

Industrial Railways. These operate to different standards and locomotives are not normally allowed on to DB tracks. Usually they can work into exchange sidings only. Some industrial operators have always had special concessions for running over part of DB (Auf DB Gleis zugelassen); in particular this applies to industrial operators in the Ruhr area where firms would take traffic from a mine to a steelworks which would include a short section of DB track. A few of these railways have been included as their locomotives are often to be seen when passing through the Ruhr area.

European Vehicle Number. As part of the interoperability arrangements all rolling stock has to display its European vehicle number. The system is explained at the beginning of the fleet lists.

Vehicle Keeper Marking. In addition to the European number a vehicle has to have a coded suffix showing the country where the vehicle is based and who owns it; e.g. D-DISPO in the case of MRCE Dispolok. These abbreviations have been used in the listing of Train Operating Companies.

USING THIS BOOK

The style has been changed compared to the first edition. Open access has led to vast numbers of similar locomotives working for different operators. The adoption of the European Vehicle Number (EVN) system by all open access operators now allows all these locomotives to be listed together. Consequently all the operators are listed together; there then follows a section dealing with leasing companies and after that are comprehensive fleet lists for all the different types and that is where an explanation of the European Vehicle Number will be found.

There are a few problem areas: Some narrow gauge lines such as the Insel Borkum line and the Zugspitzbahn do not fit into the system as they are isolated lines and no EVNs have been issued for the stock on those lines. Consequently for these few lines their stock is shown under the operator details, as in the previous edition. Again the major narrow gauge operators such as the Harzer Schmalspur Bahn present a similar problem. But for these lines their stock has been listed at the end of the various sections as if they had EVNs!

ACKNOWLEDGEMENTS

The data has been collated over many years dating back in some cases to early visits to Germany in the 1960s when the Bentheimer Eisenbahn was met as soon as the border was passed! In recent years observations at particular stations or just generally travelling around has meant many discoveries. Additionally many friends have sent in details of their observations.

The German magazines Bahn Report, Drehscheibe, Eisenbahn Kurier, and LOK-Report carry good reports on private operators whilst the Swiss magazine Eisenbahn Revue International gives good coverage of the European scene as of course does *Today's Railways Europe* magazine from Platform 5.

Internet sites can be very useful but some are not updated regularly and thus information shown can soon be out of date but they can be a useful start. Some of the sites consulted in the preparation of this book are:

www.drehscheibe-online.de
www.deutschekleinloks.de
www.lok-report.de
www.loks-aus-kiel.de
www.mainlinediesels.net
www.privat-bahn.de
www.railcolor.net
www.rangierlok.de
www.revisionsdaten.de
www.v100.de (DB V100)
www.v100-online.de (DR V100)

The following individuals have been helpful either by sending in reports or answering questions: D. Haydock, G. Kelsey, J. Merte, J. Miller, K.A. Richter. Thanks are also due to all the photographers that have provided illustrations whose names appear with the photos.

MAPS OF THE GERMAN RAILWAY NETWORK

KEY TO MAPS

Notes:

The maps on pages 8–16 are not to scale and are a guide both to railways of DB Netz and those of private operators whose stock is detailed in the second part of this book. They should not be used to determine the exact location of any particular line or station.

Whilst we hope these maps will prove very useful to readers of this book, we would refer readers looking for more detailed maps to the comprehensive atlases produced by Schweers and Wall, details of which are below.

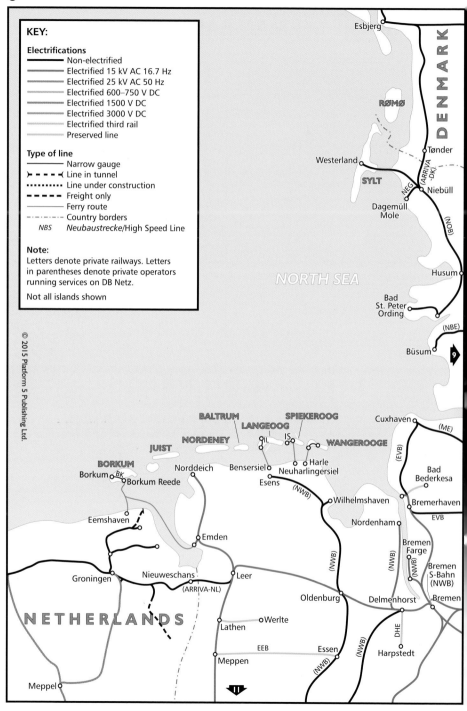

KEY:

Electrifications
- Non-electrified
- Electrified 15 kV AC 16.7 Hz
- Electrified 25 kV AC 50 Hz
- Electrified 600–750 V DC
- Electrified 1500 V DC
- Electrified 3000 V DC
- Electrified third rail
- Preserved line

Type of line
- Narrow gauge
-)— — —(Line in tunnel
- ·········· Line under construction
- — — — Freight only
- Ferry route
- ·—··—··— Country borders
- *NBS* *Neubaustrecke*/High Speed Line

Note:
Letters denote private railways. Letters in parentheses denote private operators running services on DB Netz.

Not all islands shown

© 2015 Platform 5 Publishing Ltd.

DENMARK

Esbjerg

RØMØ

Tønder

Westerland

SYLT

(ARRIVA -DK)

NEG

Niebüll

Dagemüll Mole

(BON)

NORTH SEA

Husum

Bad St. Peter Ording

(NBE)

Büsum

9

BALTRUM

SPIEKEROOG

LANGEOOG

Cuxhaven

(ME)

NORDENEY

IL

IS

WANGEROOGE

JUIST

(EVB)

BORKUM

Norddeich

Benersiel

Harle

Bad Bederkesa

Borkum BK Borkum Reede

Neuharlingersiel

Esens

(NWB)

Wilhelmshaven

Bremerhaven

Eemshaven

Nordenham

EVB

Emden

Bremen Farge

(NWB)

(NWB)

(NWB)

Bremen S-Bahn (NWB)

Groningen

Nieuweschans

Leer

(ARRIVA-NL)

Oldenburg

Delmenhorst

Bremen

NETHERLANDS

Lathen

Werlte

(NWB)

DHE

EEB

Essen

Harpstedt

Meppen

(NWB)

(NWB)

Meppel

Malmö
Simrishamn
Ystad
Trelleborg

BALTIC SEA

© 2015 Platform 5 Publishing Ltd.

Sassnitz
RÜGEN
Sassnitz Fährhafen
Bergen
Ostseebad Binz
Barth
Pütbus RüKB
(UBB)
Stralsund
Lauterbach Mole
Göhren
Velgast
Peenemünde
9
Greifswald
USEDOM
UBB
Wolgast
Seebad Heringsdorf
UBB
Swinoujście Centrum
Tessin
Demmin
Züssow
Swinoujście
Ueckermünde Stadthafen
Lalendorf
Friedland
Trzebież Szczecińskie
Jatznick
Police
Waren (Müritz)
Neubrandenburg
Pasewalk
(HANS)
POLAND
(ODEG)
Malchow
Prenzlau
Szczecin
Meyenburg
Neustrelitz
(HANS)
(EGP)
Mirow
Fürstenberg
Passow
Poznan
Wittstock
Rheinsberg (Mark)
Templin
Schwedt (Oder)
Angermünde
(EGP)
Gross Schönebeck
Joachimsthal
(NEBB)
(ODEG)
Neuruppin
Löwenberg (Mark)
Eberswalde
(NEBB)
Neustadt-(Dosse)
(ODEG)
(NEBB)
13
Kostrzyn

Kampen
Zwolle
Mariënberg
Almelo
Deventer
Hengelo
Zutphen
Enschede
N E T H E R L A N D S
Arnhem
Zevenaar
B
Emmerich
Kleve
Winterswijk
Bocholt
Borken
Xanten
Millingen
Venlo
Krefeld
Dalheim
MÖ
Rheydt
WTC
Linnich
Julich
Alsdorf
Herzogenrath
Düren
AA
Stolberg
Eupen
Heimbach

Meppen
(EEB)
8
Essen
Vechta
Lingen
(Ems)
Quakenbrück
Diepholz
Uchta
Rahden
Bramsche
Bad Bentheim
(WFB)
RVM
Rheine
Gronau
(WFB)
Ibbenbüren
Osnabrück
(WFB)
Minden
(ERB)
Ahaus
Lengerich
Dissen-Bad
Rothenfelde
Löhne
(NWB)
Coesfeld
Münster
TWE
(NWB)
Bielefeld
(ERB)
Lage
(Lippe)
Gütersloh
TWE
(NWB)
NWB
Rheda–
Wiedenbrück
Altenbeken
Haltern
Lünen
Hamm
WLE
(ERB)
Paderborn
Neubeckum
DO
Bochum
Unna
(ERB)
Soest
Lippstadt
WLE
Warstein
Hagen
Bestwig
Brilon Wald
DU
WU
Neuenrade
(ABRN)
Korbach
ES
RB
MS
Winterberg
RB
RB
DÜ
Neuss
Solingen
Brügge
Lüdenscheid
Finnentrop
Marienheide
GR
Frankenberg
BG
Gummersbach
Olpe
Bad
Berleburg
KÖLN
Troisdorf
Siegen
Marburg
Bonn
Au
WEBA
HTB
Dillenburg
Daaden
Euskirchen
(TRD)
Altenkirchen
NBS
(HLB)
Wetzlar
Giessen
(HLB)
Bad
Münstereifel
Remagen
Siershahn
(HLB)
Brandoberndorf
Brohl
BSEG
Ahrbrück
Andernach
Montabaur
Limburg
FKE
Friedberg
Engeln
KO
Gerolstein
Kaisersesch
Boppard
(HLB)
Niedernhamsen
HA
(VEN)
Bullay
Emmelshausen
Wiesbaden
(VAS)
Rüdesheim
(TRD)
FFM
Traben-
Trarbach
(VEN)
Bingen
M
Bad
Kreuznach
14
DA
(Vlexx)

12

© 2015 Platform 5 Publishing Ltd.

AA   Aachen
BG   Bergisch
        Gladbach
DA   Darmstadt
DO   Dortmund
DU   Duisburg
DÜ   Düsseldorf
ES   Essen
FFM Frankfurt (Main)
GR   Grevenbroich
HA   Hanau
KO   Koblenz
M   Mainz
MÖ   Mönchengladbach
MS   Mettmann
        Stadtwald
WU   Wuppertal
B   Betuweroute
WTC   Wildenrath test circuit
        (Multi voltage)

12

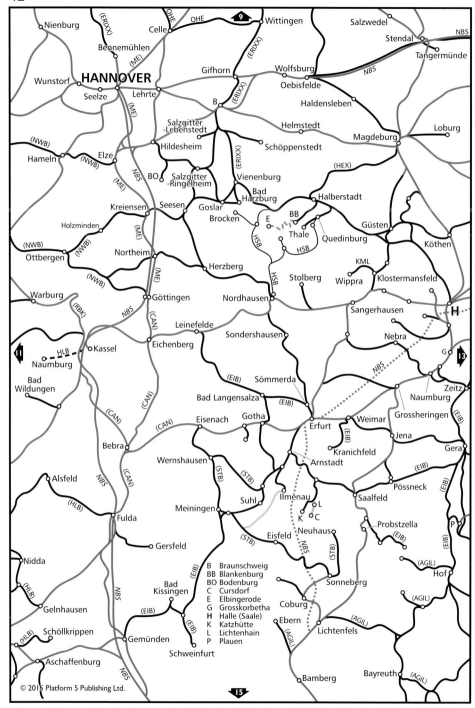

© 2015 Platform 5 Publishing Ltd.

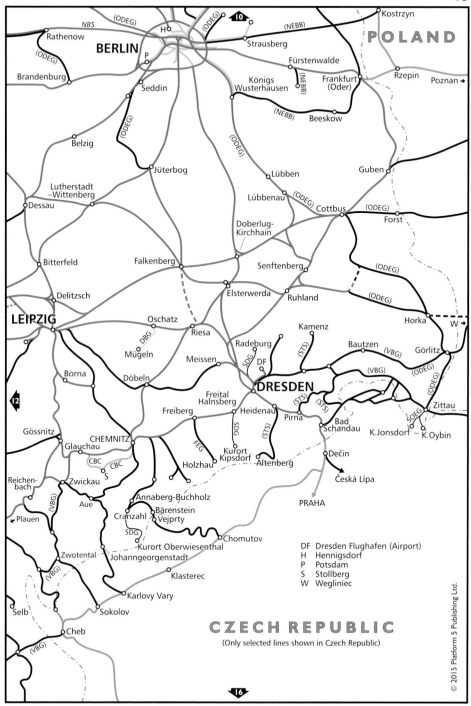

DF Dresden Flughafen (Airport)
H   Hennigsdorf
P   Potsdam
S   Stollberg
W   Wegliniec

CZECH REPUBLIC
(Only selected lines shown in Czech Republic)

© 2015 Platform 5 Publishing Ltd.

14

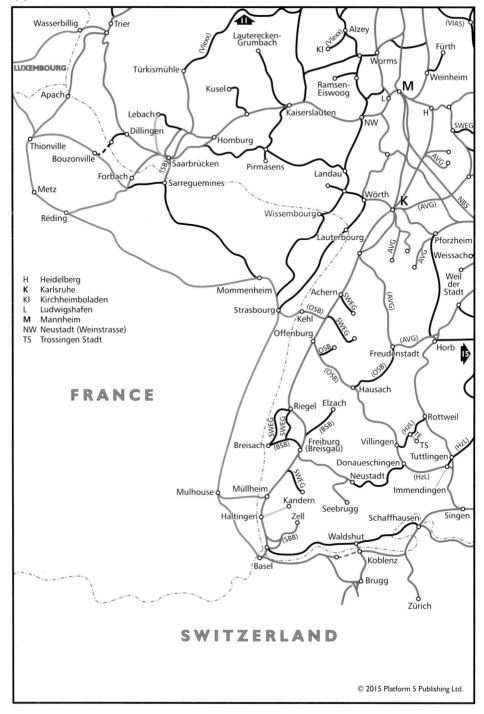

H   Heidelberg
K   Karlsruhe
KI Kirchheimboladen
L   Ludwigshafen
M   Mannheim
NW Neustadt (Weinstrasse)
TS Trossingen Stadt

FRANCE

SWITZERLAND

© 2015 Platform 5 Publishing Ltd.

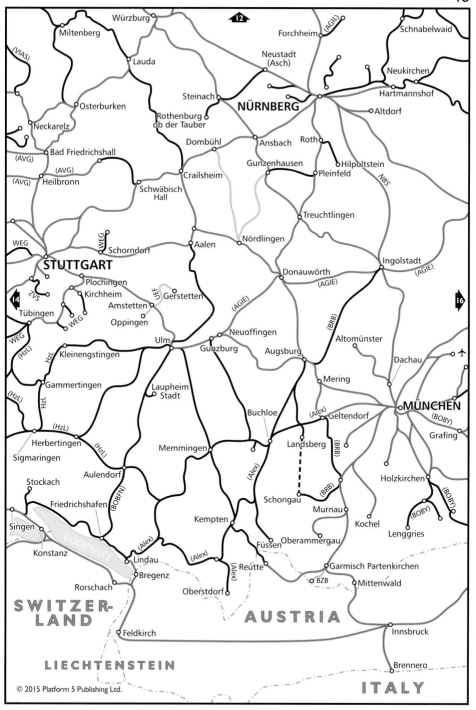

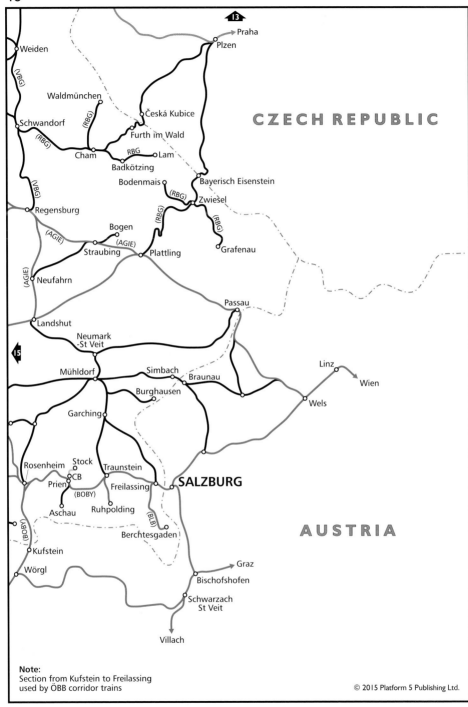

Note:
Section from Kufstein to Freilassing
used by ÖBB corridor trains

© 2015 Platform 5 Publishing Ltd.

1. TRAIN OPERATING COMPANIES

Train operating companies in Germany are known as Eisenbahn Verkehrs Unternehmen (EVU), not to be confused with Eisenbahn Infrastrukture Unternehmen (EIU) companies that own the tracks. Most former private railways owned their own tracks but with the advent of open access arrangements, tracks are now owned mostly by DB Netz. Consequently most of the train operating companies listed are purely train operators; in many cases these firms own very little apart from the staff.

The lists below include the names of most companies that have applied for an operating licence whether they have started operating or not. It should be noted that not all companies with operating licences are shown; some operating companies only provide drivers – a sort of driver leasing company. These companies generally have not been included in the lists. The companies have been listed in alphabetical order of company name, with the Vehicle Keeper Marking (VKM) shown to the right. Please note that the VKM often corresponds to the initials of the company but this is not always the case.

ABELLIO RAIL MITTELDEUTSCHLAND Gmbh   ABRM

Halle (Saale), Sachsen-Anhalt.

EVU Licence: Passenger, 19/06/2013–30/06/2028.
Routes: The Saale-Thüringen-Südharz network covers many services in the area such as RE trains Halle–Kassel, Halle–Erfurt via Nordhausen, Leipzig–Erfurt, Leipzig–Saalfeld, Halle–Eisenach and some RB services in the area.
Depot: A new depot is being built in Sangerhausen.

In 2012 Abellio won a 15 year contract to provide the trains for the Saale-Thüringen-Südharz network commencing with the winter timetable in December 2015. Thus, later in 2012, 20 3-car and 15 5-car Talent 2 EMUs were ordered from Bombardier. In 2013 Abellio was successful in winning another major contract when it was awarded the Mitteldeutsche S-Bahn Netz II to start in December 2015, but later backed out of the deal.

ABELLIO RAIL NRW Gmbh   ABRN

Essen, Nordrhein-Westfalen.

EVU Licence: Passenger, 15/03/2005–31/03/2020.
Routes: RB40 "Ruhr Lenne Bahn" Essen–Bochum–Witten–Hagen; RB46 "Nokia Bahn" Bochum–Wanne Eicke–Gelsenkirchen; RE16 "Ruhr Sieg Express" Essen–Bochum–Witten–Hagen–Siegen; RB91 "Ruhr-Sieg Bahn" Hagen–Finnentrop–Siegen; RB56 "Der Iserlohner" Hagen–Letmathe–Iserlohne; RB40 "Ruhe Lenne Bahn" Essen–Bochum–Hagen; RB 47 Solingen Hbf–Wuppertal Hbf; RB 33 Mönchengladbach–Wesel and RB 35 Düsseldorf–Arnhem.
Depot: Hagen.

Formed 01/01/2004 as Abellio GmbH, Abellio Beteiligungsgesellschaft mbH out of Essener Verkehrs AG Betriebs-gesellschaft. 85% Essener Versorgungs und Verkehrsgesellschaft mbH and 15% Essener Ominbusunternehmer Bernd Mesenhall. Subsidiary companies are Kraftverkehrsgesellschaft Dreiländereck GmbH KVG (94.9%); Abellio Rail NRW GmbH (100%); Westfalen Bahn Gmbh (25%). In 2005 75% was sold to the British investment group Star capital. The Abellio Rail NRW title was adopted 11/12/2005. In 2008 Abellio became a subsidiary of the Dutch railway company NS! In the Ruhr area RB 40 and RB46 are now worked by EMUs after an initial period of loco-hauled working.

Abellio having obtained these franchises then started bidding for more and was successful in obtaining the franchises for the Westfalenbahn (q.v.) and for the Ruhr-Sieg Netz (until 2019) for which 17 FLIRT EMUs were ordered from Stadler financed via CB Rail. Further contracts have been won, that for RB 47 running 08/12/2013 to 09/12/2028 whilst RB 33 and RB 35 will run for 12 years from December 2016.

AGILIS EISENBAHNGESELLSCHAFT mbH & Co. KG.   AGIE

Regensburg, Bayern.

EVU Licence: Passenger & Freight, 18/08/2014–15/07/2029.
Routes: Plattling–Regensburg–Neumarkt (Opf), Ingolstadt–Regensburg–Landshut plus since December 2011 Ingolstadt–Ulm.
Depot: Regensburg - a new depot near to the sugar factory.
Rolling Stock: 18 3-car and eight 4-car Alstom Coradia EMUs of Class 440.

Agilis was formed as a joint venture by BeNEX GmbH and Hamburger Hochbahn AG (HHA) to bid for contracts in Bayern. In 2007 it was awarded the contract for electric train services radiating from Regensburg, services starting in 2010.

AGILIS VERKEHRSGESELLSCHAFT mbH & Co. KG.   AGIL

Regensburg, Bayern.

EVU Licence: Passenger & Freight, 10/06/2009–10/06/2024.
Routes: A large number of non-electrified lines in northern Bayern including Hof–Bad Steben, Hof–Selb Stadt, Bayreuth–Marktredwitz, Bayreuth–Weiden, Bayreuth–Kulmbach–Lichtenfels, Forchheim–Ebermannstadt, Lichtenfels–Coburg–Bad Rodach, Bamberg–Ebern.
Rolling Stock: 38 Stadler Regio Shuttles of Class 650.
Depot: A new depot at Marktredwitz.

Having won the contract for the Dieselnetz Oberfranken, Agilis formed a separate company to operate these services and build another new depot, this time at Marktredwitz.

▲ Agilis Eisenbahngesellschaft (AGIE) operates a network of electric services based on Regensburg, using 3-secton Coradia Continental articulated EMUs from Alstom. Unit 94 80 0440 414 (440 914 nearest the camera) waits in the snow at Regensburg on an exceptionally cold day in February 2012.   **Brian Denton**

AHG INDUSTRY GmbH & Co. KG   AHG

Cottbus, Brandenburg.
EVU Licence: Freight & Passenger, 21/08/2009–31/12/2023.

This is a Lausitz based building contractor that started getting involved in railway infrastructure work and acquired its first locomotive in mid 2001. It operates local freight trips from Cottbus. From 01/06/2005 AHG took over servicing of the Heizkraftwerk Küchwald on behalf of Stadtwerke Chemnitz and presumably inherited its locos.

AKN EISENBAHN AG   AKN

Kaltenkirchen, Schleswig-Holstein.
EVU Licence: Freight & Passenger, 15/12/1997–31/12/2024.
Traction: One G1100, 15 VT2E, 18 VTA (some Electro-diesel), three railbuses.
Depot: Kaltenkirchen.

This company operates over lines north of Hamburg totalling some 120 km and runs a busy commuter service into Hamburg. Besides covering the area denoted by its name the company also operates over lines Ulzburg to Elmshorn and Hamburg-Bergedorf to Geesthacht. Services operated are: Hamburg-Eidelstedt–Ulzburg Süd–Kaltenkirchen–Neumünster; Norderstedt Mitte–Ulzburg Süd; Ulzburg Süd–Elmshorn. In recent years freight traffic has been handled by DB Schenker whilst the AKN depot at Billbrook has been sold to Northrail Technical Service (NTS). AKN is part owner of Nordbahn (NBE) q.v. During 2015 AKN will start to receive new DMUs to replace existing stock.

ALBTAL-VERKEHRS-GESELLSCHAFT mbH   AVG

Karlsruhe, Baden-Württemberg.
EVU Licence: Freight & Passenger 10/05/1995–30/04/2024.
Depots: Ettlingen, Bad Herrenalb, Hochstetten, Ittersbach, Menzingen, Eppingen, Freudenstadt.
Electrical Systems: 750 V DC and 15 kV AC.

The AVG network has undergone great changes in recent years. Originally parts were 1000mm gauge but today all lines are standard gauge. The principal line from which the company gets its name is Karlsruhe Albtalbahnhof–Bad Herrenalb. The big changes came about in the 1990s when AVG was linked up to the Karlsruhe tramway system and a connection built to DB. AVG trains then started to run to destinations on the DB network and the "Karlsruhe Tram/Train Model" was born. Now AVG operates S-Bahn services over DB to Baden-Baden, Bretten, Bruchsal, Gölshausen, Pforzheim, Wörth and Heilbronn. At Heilbronn the AVG line has been extended through the town and then back onto DB on the line to Crailsheim as far as Öhringen. All the 800/900 series railcars are dual-voltage for working over DB. The introduction of the new S-Bahn services have been a great success with passenger numbers continuing to climb. The system of trains/trams running along main lines and then into the streets of the cities being served is being followed by other places. Note that four units also have DB numbers. This dates from the period before open access when DB and AVG shared some costs so that DB provided some units. With open access this was discontinued. In fact all the units that are dual voltage should now have EVNs! Late in 2000 it was announced that AVG was to take over the passenger service from Karlsruhe to Freudenstadt and electrify Rastatt to Freudenstadt for which services more railcars were ordered. A further extension of the S-Bahn services has now opened from Heilbronn to Sinsheim for which more units have been built but the supplier was changed to Bombardier after years of Siemens/Duewag providing the trains. AVG uses its locomotives for various local freight flows which tend to be trips from DB yards to local sidings.

AMMENDORFER TRANSPORT und LOGISTIK GmbH ATL

Halle, Sachsen-Anhalt.
EVU Licence: Freight, 29/03/2010–28/02/2025.

This small company is in effect an industrial railway registered as an EVU and is only allowed to operate over sidings at Halle Ammendorf. It has just one shunting locomotive.

ANHALTINISCH–BRANDENBURGISCHE
EISENBAHNGESELLSCHAFT mbH ABEG

Halle, Sachsen-Anhalt.
EVU Licence: Freight, 19/07/2012–18/07/2027.

Established in 2011, this company has amongst its owners ENON, whilst some of its directors are also involved in other firms such as EGP. Consequently it has no locomotives of its own but uses hired-in locos from these companies for container trains to and from Hamburg and Bremerhaven.

ARCELORMITTAL EISEHÜTTENSTADT TRANSPORT GmbH EKO

Eisenhüttenstadt, Brandenburg.
EVU Licence: Freight & Passenger, 21/10/2003–31/12/2017.
Traction: Numerous diesel locomotives.
Depot: ArcelorMittal Steelworks, Eisenhüttenstadt.

ArcelorMittel took over the former EKO Transport in 2011. EKO Transport began running its own trains in 1997 and has grown since then. Besides handling internal traffic in the works at Eisenhüttenstadt from the interchange yards at Ziltendorf it has many long distance workings many of which originate from nearby Poland. Most are connected with the steel industry. Note that the old VKM of EKO is still in use.

ARCO TRANSPORTATION GmbH ARCO

Tröglitz, Sachsen-Anhalt.
EVU Licence: Freight & Passenger, 02/03/2005–28/02/2020.
Traction: Two DH240B, one DH500C, two 228, seven V60D.

This company acquired parts of the financially troubled Karsdorfer Eisenbahn Gesellschaft, taking over its depots and workshops in Tröglitz and Karsdorf. It appears to have a Hungarian backer. The company has a licence for passenger work but so far it appears to be mainly involved in spot hire work, engineering trains etc. All the old DMUs have been scrapped or sold. It too is experiencing difficulties with many locomotives stored but still struggles on with trip workings around Tröglitz.

AUGSBURGER LOCALBAHN GmbH AULOC

Augsburg, Bayern.
EVU Licence: Freight & Passenger, 04/08/1995–31/12/2025.
Traction: Six ML440C, six V100DR.
Depot: Augsburg Ring (Friedbergstrasse).

As the name suggests this railway serves local destinations around Augsburg. Open access brought along new opportunities resulting in the locomotive fleet being increased several times with modernised DR V100s.

A.V.G. ASCHERSLEBENER VERKEHRSGESELLSCHAFT mbh
ASLVG

Aschersleben, Sachsen-Anhalt.

EVU Licence: Freight, 28/09/2005–31/08/2020 and passenger, 24/04/2008–31/08/2020.
Traction: One DG 1200BBM.

This company was founded 01/08/2001 but had a slow start, only obtaining an EVU licence four years later. Once located in the old DB depot at Aschersleben it is now understood to be based in Westeregeln and undertakes traffic movements local to the area.

BALTIC PORT RAIL MUKRAN GmbH   BPRM

Founded in 2011, this company took over the broad gauge network at Mukran port and with it the three DB broad gauge Class 347 diesel shunters. Their idea is to offer services to all operators wishing to use Mukran. During 2014 the standard gauge operations were also taken over. The locomotives actually belong to the port of Mukran FHS – Fahr Hafen Sassnitz GmbH. For the standard gauge sidings locos are hired in from companies such as WFL.

BAHN TOURISTIK EXPRESS GmbH   BTEX

Nürnberg, Bayern.

EVU Licence: Freight & Passenger, 26/02/2014–29/01/2029.

A small company running charter passenger trains around the country and into adjoining countries. The main depot is in Nürnberg where a former DB Class 360 shunts. Main line trains are hauled by another former DB loco 217 001. With 26 carriages some are often leased to other companies for use on extra trains e.g. football specials.

BAHNEN DER STADT MONHEIM GmbH   BSM

Monheim, Nordrhein-Westfalen.

EVU Licence: Freight & Passenger, 11/10/1995–31/12/2023.
Routes: Langenfeld–Monheim-Blee–Hitdorfer Kapelle 6.1 km; Wasserwerk–Monheim Nord 3.0 km.
Length: 9.5 km.
Depot: Daimlerstrasse, Monheim.

This local railway has recently closed down. It had three locos of its own, an ex DB 333 and two OK MC700C which are up for sale.

BASF AG   BASF

Ludwigshafen, Baden-Württemberg.

EVU Licence: Freight & Passenger, 26/05/2008–31/05/2023.
Traction: In the process of being re-equipped with new locos with Vossloh providing 16 G6, four DE12 and two DE18.
Depot: Ludwigshafen.

BASF (Badische Anilin und Soda Fabrik) has a large chemical works in Ludwigshafen. It moves about five million tonnes of traffic by rail each year. Open access gave the firm the opportunity to run its own trains which it now does, tripping to Mannheim, Germersheim and Kaiserslautern.

22

BAYERISCHE CARGOBAHN GmbH   BCB

Neu Ulm, Bayern.
EVU Licence: Freight & Passenger, 14/03/2002–01/12/2016.

This is a Captrain (q.v.) company and an offshoot of BOBY. Freight activities are being sought in Bayern and in 2002 the firm started getting involved in container movements as well as occasional freight trips. V146 was received from RBB early in 2003 for oil train trips at Ingolstadt in connection with new flows worked by HGK and KEG.

BAYERISCHE OBERLANDBAHN GmbH   BOBY

Holzkirchen, Bayern.
EVU Licence: Passenger & Freight, 10/03/1998–01/03/2028.
Routes: Holzkirchen–Bayrischzell, Holzkirchen–Lenggries, Schaftlach–Tegernsee. The first two are DB Netz tracks whilst the last is the former Tegernseebahn.
Length: 12.3 km (being the former Tegernseebahn).
Depot: Lenggries.

This company was set up to run the local services from München to Lenggries, Tegernsee and Bayerischzell. It is a subsidiary of Veolia (q.v.) and has recently had its contract renewed. The Tegernseebahn (TAG) was taken over as part of the reorganisation and its stock has been sold. It started with 17 "INTEGRAL" 5-car articulated DMU sets (Class 609.1) but with increasing traffic some Talent DMUs have also been obtained. It also owns two ex-DB V100 diesels for winter snowplough work.

In 2010 Veolia won the contract for "E-Netz Rosenheim" (München–Salzburg/Kufstein including the route via Holzkirchen to Rosenheim). The operating contract was passed to BOBY under the trading name of "Meridian". 28 6-car (Class 1430) and seven 3-car (Class 1427) FLIRT EMUs were ordered for this service. A depot for the Meridian units was to be built in München but there are planning problems. Consequently some temporary arrangements are having to be made with some units going to Regensburg for attention at the Agilis depot. Meanwhile all the Meridian units have been sold to Alpha Trains and leased back!

BAYERISCHE REGIOBAHN GmbH   BRB

Augsburg, Bayern.
EVU Licence: Passenger & Freight, 05/05/2003–01/05/2018.
Routes: Augsburg–Ingolstadt–Eischstätt Stadt; Augsburg–Weilheim–Schongau.
Rolling Stock: 28 Alstom LINT 41 DMUs leased from Société Générale.
Depot: Augsburg.

This is another Veolia company. It was formed in 2002 but was only awarded its first contract in 2006, by winning the Augsburger Diesel Netzes II. It had a difficult start, having to rent space in the railway museum in Augsburg (Bahnpark – the old DB depot) until it could establish its own depot.

BAYERISCHE ZUGSPITZBAHN BERGBAHN AG   BZB

Garmisch-Partenkirchen, Bayern.
EVU Licence: Freight & Passenger, 23/12/2010–31/12/2025.
Routes: Garmisch-Partenkirchen–Grainau(valley section)–Eibsee–Höllental–Schneefernerhaus Gletscherbhf Zugspitzplatt.
Length: 18.7 km.
Electrical System: 1650 V DC.
Depot: Grainau.
Gauge: 1000 mm.

The BZB is a typical mountain railway of metre gauge having a valley section before the real climb starts with Riggenbach rack assistance. The starting point at Garmisch Partenkirchen is 705 metres above sea level and the top station at Schneefernerhaus is 2649 metres a.s.l. There is talk of closing the existing terminus at Garmisch with a new connection be installed to allow trains to terminate at or alongside the DB station. Note: there is no Number 13!

No.	Builder, No. & Year	kW	Details	Comments
1	AEG 4268/1929	2 x 112	Bo E	Valley loco
4	AEG 4271/1929	2 x 112	Bo E	Valley loco
14	AEG 4263/1929	3 x 370	Bo E	Rack fitted
15	AEG 4264/1929	3 x 370	Bo E	Rack fitted
ET 1	MAN 140874/1954	4 x 117	Bo-Bo ER	Rack fitted, stored
ET 2	MAN 141470/1956	4 x 117	Bo-Bo ER	Rack fitted
ET 5	SLM 5132/1978	4 x 117	Bo-Bo ER	Rack fitted
ET 6	SLM 5133/1978	4 x 117	Bo-Bo ER	Rack fitted
ET 7	SLM/BBC/1979	4 x 250	Bo-Bo ER	Ex Swiss BOB ABeh4/4 309
ET 10	SLM 5316/1987	4 x 216	Bo-Bo ER	Rack fitted
ET 11	SLM 5317/1987	4 x 216	Bo-Bo ER	Rack fitted
ET 12	Stadler 2006	6 x 300	Bo-Bo-Bo ER	Rack Fitted
ET 14	Stadler 2006	6 x 300	Bo-Bo-Bo ER	Rack Fitted
ET 15	Stadler 2006	6 x 300	Bo-Bo-Bo ER	Rack Fitted
ET 16	Stadler 2006	6 x 300	Bo-Bo-Bo ER	Rack Fitted

BAYERNBAHN BETRIEBSGESELLSCHAFT mbH   BYB

Nördlingen, Bayern.

EVU Licence: Freight & Passenger, 23/12/2010–31/12/2025.

This organisation is the operating arm of the Bayerisches Eisenbahn Museum in Nördlingen. The EVU was set up so that trains can be run over the DB Netz lines from Nördlingen to Dombühl and Gunzenhausen for which BYB has now become the EIU for some 90 km of track. Then along came open access and with it the opportunity to move freight, some of which originates on its own lines. The operating locos are from the Bayerisches Eisenbahn Museum in Nördlingen; some are preserved locos but most were acquired specially for freight work.

BBL LOGISTIK GmbH   BBL

Lüneburg, Niedersachsen.

EVU Licence: Freight, 17/02/2006–10/02/2021.

This company was founded in 2005 and issued with an EVU licence in 2006. Their main activity is providing engineering and infrastructure work trains, BBL standing for Bahn Bau Lüneburg. Some spot traffic has been sought. BBL has about 16 locos in its fleet of former DB Class 202, 212, and 215 types, some of which are the modernised versions of Classes 203 and 214.

BEHALA BERLINER HAFEN & LAGERHAUSGESELLSCHAFT mbh   BHL

Berlin.

EVU Licence: Freight & Passenger, 06/07/2007–31/07/2022.

This company is a long established industrial railway in Berlin that has now acquired an EVU licence, so perhaps bigger things are in store. The main depot and yard is at Westhafen. Traffic is mainly over its own networks to and from DB yards.

BENTHEIMER EISENBAHN · BE

Nordhorn, Niedersachsen.

EVU Licence: Freight & Passenger, 26/10/1995–25/10/2025.
Routes: Coevorden (NL)–Neuenhaus–Nordhorn–Bad Bentheim–Ochtrup–Brecht.
Length: 75.7 km.
Traction: The locomotive fleet comprises several former DB locos and others normally associated with private railways.
Depots: Nordhorn Süd, Nordhorn, Bad Bentheim.

This is a well established private railway, having opened between Bentheim and Nordhorn in 1895. Its line into the Netherlands serves Coevorden which has a growing logistics centre. Consqunetly BE can trip trains there that have arrived at Bad Bentheim behind electric traction. It is also involved with container trains from Coevorden to Rotterdam and has purchased former NS 1835 for this work. Bad Bentheim–Neuenhaus may be reopened to passenger services.

BERCHTESGADENER LAND BAHN Gmbh · BLB

Freilassing, Bayern.

EVU Licence: Covered by that issued to Regentalbahn.
Depot: Salzburg.

In 2006 a joint venture of Regentalbahn and Salzburger Lokalbahn won the passenger service contract for the local trains from Freilassing to Berchtesgaden. A separate operating company (BLB) was set up in 2009. The service got off to a bad start as the EBA refused to certify the units as they did not conform to regulations. (The regulations changed whilst they were under construction!). The service has now settled down. The five Class 427 FLIRT3 units are maintained at the SLB depot in Salzburg.

BERGBAHNEN IM SIEBENGEBIRGE AG, DRACHENFELSBAHN

Königswinter, Nordrhein-Westfalen.

EVU Licence: Passenger, 10/05/1994–31/12/2030.
Routes: Königswinter–Plateau Drachenfels 1.5 km.
Electrical System: 900 V DC.
Depot: Königswinter.
Gauge: 1000 mm.

At Königswinter, just south of Bonn, lies the Drachenfelsbahn. The metre gauge Riggenbach rack line runs for just 1.5 km. Originally steam worked it was electrified in the 1950s and still uses stock from this period. One of the line's steam locos is plinthed outside Königswinter station.

No.	Builder, No. & Year	Type	kW	Details	Comments
II	Rastatt/1955	88		Bo ER	Rack fitted
III	Rastatt/1957	88		Bo ER	Rack fitted
IV	Rastatt/1959	88		Bo ER	Rack fitted
V	Rastatt/1960	88		Bo ER	Rack fitted
VI	Drachenfels/1979	88		Bo ER	Rack fitted

BLG RAILTEC GmbH · BLGRT

Falkenberg/Elster, Brandenburg.

EVU Licence: Freight, 08/10/2012–31/12/2026.

BLG Logistics formed this company to take over the former DB marshalling yard at Fakenberg/Elster (Oberebahnhof) to receive and sort train loads of motor cars from various centres, making up fresh train loads to go forward. Two diesel locos were acquired and besides doing the shunting these also work car trains to a distribution terminal at Recknitz, north of Leipzig.

BLP WIEBE LOGISTIK GmbH   BLP

Achim, Niedersachsen.

EVU Licence: Freight, 02/06/2005–01/06/2020.
Traction: 12 locomotives, mostly ex DB of types V100 and V160 but including the unique V320.
Depot: Nienburg.

The Wiebe company is a well known track maintenance firm which for many years only owned on-track machines. The change in circumstances on Germany's railways has allowed the company to run its own locomotives. Based in Nienburg and Achim, both near Bremen, the locos can be found anywhere in Germany where the firm gets a contract. Whilst the VKM is BLP, the biggest name on the locomotives is Wiebe!

BOCHOLTER EISENBAHNGESELLSCHAFT mbH   BOEG

Dinslaken, Nordrhein-Westfalen.

EVU Licence: Passenger & Freight, 16/02/2005–28/02/2020.

Formed by members of Verein zur Erhaltung und Förderung des Schienenverkehrs e.V. (VEFS). After use was made of their locomotives for local shunting and trip working they could see that an EVU could be the easy answer. Current duties involve various trips in the Emmerich area; usually last mile workings into the harbour but there are also workings from Dormagen and Oberhausen West.

BODENSEE-OBERSCHWABEN-BAHN GmbH   BOBFN

Friedrichshafen, Baden-Württemberg.

EVU Licence: Passenger, 27/11/2013–31/12/2028.
Routes: Friedrichshafen Hafen–Friedrichshafen Hbf–Ravensburg–Aulendorf.
Length: 42 km.
Depot: Friedrichshafen Stadt.

The BOB took over local passenger services between Friedrichshafen Stadt and Ravensburg from DB in 1993, reopening several stations in the process. Until its two NE 81 DMUs were delivered, Regio Sprinter sets were hired from the DKB. Services went from strength to strength, far exceeding expectations, so soon a third unit was acquired. In September 1997 further growth took place when BOB extended operations to include the Friedrichshafen Hafen branch and services to Ravensburg were extended to Aulendorf. For these new services some Regio Shuttles were obtained. In 2005 BOB acquired three further RS1 railcars in order to standardise its fleet and sold its NE81 units to HzL. In 2011 a further two RS1 units were ordered to cope with traffic growth.

BOLAY & MOSER EVU Gbr

Öhringen, Baden-Württemberg.

EVU Licence: Freight and Passenger, 18/05/2009–31/05/2024.

This company has a contract to move sand from the Karlsruhe area to Stuttgart-Untertürkheim in connection with the rebuilding of the Stuttgart Hbf area – a project known as "Stuttgart 21". It has acquired one Maxima 30CC for this traffic.

BORKUMER KLEINBAHN UND DAMPFSCHIFFART GmbH BK

Borkum, Niedersachsen.
EVU Licence: Freight & Passenger, 24/01/1996–30/05/2026.
Routes: Borkum Bhf–Borkum Reede.
Length: 7.4 km.
Depot: Borkum Stadtbahnhof.
Gauge: 900 mm.

This 900 mm gauge line on the Ostfriesland island of Borkum connects the harbour with the town. Freight finished in 1968 but the line is very busy in the summer season when steam hauled trains complement the usual diesel hauled service. Note that most locomotives have no numbers–only names–how splendid! The line is 7.4 km long and has 3.2 km of double track.

No.	Builder, No. & Year	Type	kW	Details	Comments
Emden	Schöma 3222/1970	CFL200DA	169	B DM	Ex Faxe, Denmark
Leer	DWK 551/1934		40	B DM	
Münster II	Schöma 1989/1957		82	B DM	
Hannover	Schöma 5342/1993	CFL150DCL	180	B DH	
Berlin	Schöma 5343/1993	CFL150DCL	180	B DH	
Münster III	Schöma 5385/1994	CFL150DCL	180	B DH	
Aurich	Schöma 6073/2007	CFL150DCL	180	B DH	
Borkum	OK 13571/1940	Steam		0-4-0T	
T 1	Wismar 21145/1940			10A DMR	

boxXpress.de GmbH BOXX

Hamburg.
EVU Licence: Freight, 07/05/2003–31/05/2018.

This company is involved in the movement of containers from the North Sea ports to the south of Germany and on into Austria and Hungary. It founded its own transport company on 29/05/2002 made up as follows:

European Rail Shuttle B.V. (ERS) 47% (involving Maersk and P&O Nedlloyd)
Eurogate Intermodal 38%
Net Log Netzwerklogistik (Now TX Logistic) 15%

Some 24 locos are hired in from MRCE (Classes 182, 185, 189) and over 600 wagons from several leasing companies. The company operates the main line runs; last mile work and shunting is contracted out to any convenient operator including DB Schenker.

BRÄUNERT EISENBAHNVERKEHR GmbH & Co. K.G. BEV

Albisheim, Rheinland-Pfalz.
EVU Licence: Freight & Passenger, 05/12/2006–30/11/2021.

This small company uses Class 185 locos leased from Railpool and Class 193s from MRCE to operate trains on a programmed basis on behalf of its parent company, Transpetrol. It is also involved the movement of aluminium from Nievenheim to destinations in Germany (e.g. Göttingen). This traffic originates in Ditton (UK)!

BREISGAU S-BAHN Gmbh   BSB

Endingen, Baden-Württemberg.
EVU Licence: Freight & Passenger, 24/01/1996–28/02/2026.
Route: Freiburg Hbf–Gottenheim–Breisach (DB Netz).
Length: 22.5 km.
Depot: Endingen (with SWEG).

This company was jointly owned by SWEG (50%) and Freiburger Verkehrs AG (50%) but the latter sold out to SWEG at the end of 2012. The company operates passenger services from Freiburg to Breisgau and revolutionised the service with modern rolling stock leased initially from Rail Charter GmbH which later became Fahrzeugbeteitstellung Baden-Württemberg GmbH (FBBW). Maintenance is carried out at the SWEG depot in Endingen. In 2000 BSB won a contract to run the services between Freiburg and Elzach which entailed ordering some more units, delivered in 2002. These units differ from the earlier examples in having air-conditioning and a WC. Increasing traffic saw another two units added to stock in 2005. There is now talk of electrification of these routes by the end of the current decade.

BROHLTAL-SCHMALSPUR EISENBAHN BETRIEBS-Gmbh   BEG

Brohl–Lützing, Rheinland-Pfalz.
EVU Licence: Freight & Passenger, 22/12/2010–31/12/2025.
Routes: Brohl–Brohl Hafen (Dual gauge) 2.0 km; Brohl–Engeln 17.6 km.
Length: 19.6 km.
Depot: Brohl.
Gauge: 1000 mm/1435 mm.

This 19.6 km metre-gauge line is located to the south of Bonn and its main depot is a short walk from the DB station. There is a branch down to a harbour on the Rhein which is dual-gauge. The line has had mixed times with freight traffic finishing some years ago. The railway kept going by running regular tourist trains at the top end of the line which is quite scenic. To improve the attraction some steam locos were imported from Poland which have since been sold and the money used to overhaul the line's own Mallet locomotive; this is due to return to traffic in May 2015. A metre gauge diesel has been acquired from Spain along with some container flat wagons for the transport of freight on an as required basis. The company has also gone into main line work using its docks facility to handle traffic. Consequently some standard gauge locomotives have been obtained since 2005 and now various trip workings often take place as "last mile" work for long distance operators (e.g. Koblenz–Limburg). The principal standard gauge locos are a V60, V65, V90 and a V200.

No.	Builder, No. & Year	Type	kW	Details	Comments
D 1	OK 26528/1965	MV10S		C DM	
D 2	OK 26529/1965	MV10S		C DM	
D 3	OK 26623/1966	MV10S		C DM	
D 5	Hens 31004/1966	DHG1200BB	883	B-B DH	Ex FEVE 1405
7	LKM 250349/1967	V10C	75	C DM	Ex Mansfeld
VT 30	Fuchs 9053/1956		4 x 125	Bo-Bo DER	Ex WEG T30

BUG VERKEHRSBAU AG, BERLIN   BUG

Berlin.
Livery: Green and black.

Founded in 1990 as Bug Bau und Unterhaltung von Gleisanlagen GmbH this firm is owned by several Berlin area companies including HVLE. There are two ex DR V100 which are used on ballast trains.

CANTUS VERKEHRSGESELLSCHAFT mbH   CAN
Kassel, Hessen.

EVU Licence: Passenger, 13/07/2006–31/01/2021.
Routes: Göttingen–Eichenberg–Kassel–Bebra–Fulda; Göttingen–Eschwege–Bebra; Bebra–Eisenach.
Depot: Kassel Wilhelmshöhe

This is a joint company set up by HLB and HHA to operate the so called "Nordhessen Netz". Having won the concession, a fleet of 3-car and 4-car FLIRT EMUs were ordered from Stadler Berlin, Classes 427 and 428. In 2014 the franchise was extended to run until 2031.

CAPTRAIN DEUTSCHLAND GmbH   CTD
Dortmund, Nordrhein-Westfalen.

A complicated story. First there was Connex, then in 2000 its freight arm became Connex Cargo Logistics and later Veolia Cargo Deutschland. In 2009 Veolia sold off its freight activities to SNCF which formed Captrain Deutschland in 2010. In the period between 2000 and 2010 many other undertakings were acquired; these are listed below and each retains its own identity under the Captrain banner. Refer to the individual companies for more information.

Bayerische CargoBahn GmbH	(BCB)
Dortmunder Eisenbahn GmbH	(DE)
Farge-Vegesacker Eisenbahn-Gesellschaft mbH	(FVE)
Hörseltalbahn GmbH	(HTB)
Industriebahn Geschellschaft Berlin mbH (25.1%)	(IGB)
ITL Cargo Gmbh (From 2011).	(ITL)
Rail4Chem GmbH	(R4C)
Regiobahn Bitterfeld Berlin GmbH	(RBB)
Teutoburger Wald Eisenbahn (53.9%)	(TWE)
Württembergische Eisenbahn Gesellschaft (96.9%)	(WEG)

The individual companies have their own locomotive fleets but long distance traction is taken from a general pool run by Captrain centrally.

CARGO LOGISTIK RAIL SERVICE GmbH   CLR
Barleben, Sachsen-Anhalt.

Founded in 2008 with links to Magdeburger Hafenbahn where the depot is located, the company is involved in infrastructure trains and often leases locos to other operators as required. No EVU licence can be traced so presumably the operations are carried out under another operator's banner. Two DR V60D shunting locos and a V180 are available as well as two former DSB Nohab diesels.

CARGO RAIL GmbH   CR
Dillingen, Saarland.

EVU Licence: Freight, 02/07/1999–31/12/2013.

Cargo Rail is a subsidiary of the Dillinger Hüttenwerke AG having been founded in 1998 to service several factories: Dillinger Hüttenwerke; Roheisen Gesellschaft Saar mbH (ROGESA, also in Dillingen); Zentralkokerei Saar GmbH(ZKS) and some other private sidings. In 1999 Cargo Rail seems to have become a fully fledged EVU and started tripping from the various works to the exchange sidings with DB at Dillingen. In 2002 it took over from DB the servicing of the Dillingen–Limbach line and by the year end had obtained locomotives D23/24 with a view to acquiring more main line work. All of their locos are listed although some of them might not venture out of their old haunts. Note that the official VKM for the locomotives is DH – Dillingen Hüttenwerkwerke AG. Loco numbers are prefixed by a letter denoting where they normally work: D = Dillingen; R = Roheisen Gesellschaft Saar mbH (ROGESA); Z = Zentralkokerei Saar GmbH (ZKS).

▲ The metre gauge Brohtal-Schmalspur Eisenbahn Betriebs (BEG) has acquired some standard gauge locomotives for traffic to and from their docks, most notably former DB Class V200, 92 80 1220 053. Here it is seen at Leutersdorf in charge of a train of aluminium from Spellen to Koblenz harbour on 27 September 2013. **Matthias Müller**

▼ Centralbahn (CBB) is the operating arm of German railway magazine Eisenbahn Kurier; it uses a small fleet made up of interesting locomotive types. Here, 91 80 0010 008 & 019, the former SBB Class Re4/4^{I} 10008 and 10019 are seen between Linz and Erpel with the "Hetzerather" special from Wittlich to Rheine on 5 May 2013. **Matthias Müller**

CENTRALBAHN AG CBB

This is the operating arm of the German railway magazine Eisenbahn Kurier, primarily for running excursion trains but also any other work that comes their way. The RHEB is understood to be the EVU. The depot is believed to be the old postal depot in Freiburg. The main line locomotives can turn up anywhere in Germany. Because many excursion trains now start from the Ruhr area, Centralbahn also uses the former DB depot in Mönchengladbach.

CFL CARGO DEUTSCHLAND GmbH CFLDE

Niebüll, Schleswig-Holstein.

EVU Licence: Freight & Passenger, 19/03/2007–31/12/2021.
Route: Uetersen Hafen–Tornesch.
Length: 4.5 km.
Depot: Uetersen Ost.

In 2001 Luxembourg Railways (CFL) established Euro Lux Cargo and subsequently acquired the operating rights of Norddeutsche Eisenbahn Gesellschaft mbH (NEG), thus giving itself operating rights in Germany. Some trip workings around Trier took place but further developments were put on the back burner to allow a settling in period. It soon became clear that the best way forward was to declare their full intention and thus the present firm became established. Later it took over the Nordfriesische Verkehrsbetriebe AG (NVAG) now renamed NEG Niebüll. CFL Cargo is now involved in miscellaneous freight workings nationwide, many linked to Luxembourg. CFL Cargo also has subsidiaries in Denmark and the Czech Republic which also produce traffic for Germany and Luxembourg. The locomotive fleet is principally hired-in electric locomotives from MRCE (Class 185s) whilst last mile work is handed over to local operators. Quite often electric locomotives from the parent CFL company are used in Germany (CFL Class 4000).

CHEMION LOGISTIK GmbH - BAHNBETRIEBE CLG

Leverkusen, Nordrhein-Westfalen.

EVU Licence: Freight, 22/02/2002–30/09/2025.
Routes: Köln-Mülheim–Köln-Stammheim–Köln-Flittard–Leverkusen Bayerwerk; and to/from factories at Leverkusen, Dormagen and Uerdingen.
Length: 5.5 km.
Depot: Leverkusen Bayerwerk.
Traction: Locomotives are mostly hired in from Alpha Trains or Alstom Locomotive Service.

This railway title dates from 01/07/2001, prior to which it was known as the Eisenbahn Köln–Mülheim–Leverkusen (EKML). It is in effect another idustrial server that now has main line access having obtained the status of an EVU on 22/02/2002. In this case the customer is the large chemical works of Bayer AG at Leverkusen which is the parent company. Instead of DB delivering some traffic to the works, Chemion goes and collects it itself. As EKML it has been running over DB since at least 1985. Besides shuttles between the various chemical plants, long distance traffic is tripped to electrified yards on behalf of various operators.

CHIEMSEEBAHN

Prien, Bayern.

EVU Licence: Freight & Passenger, 21/12/2010–31/12/2025.
Routes: Prien–Hafen Stock.
Length: 1.8 km.
Depot: Hafen Stock.

This charming little railway continues to provide the link between the DB station at Prien and the landing stage on the Chiemsee. The steam loco and coaching stock were all original to the line. The loco had a new boiler some years back and until quite recently was the sole motive power on the line. It was decided a standby loco was needed so a suitable diesel loco was found and adapted to look like a replica of the steam loco. The line has had mixed fortunes recently and was facing possible closure but has been reprieved. If you have not been there please go and see this gem of a line!

No.	Builder, No. & Year	Type	kW	Details	Comments
–	KrMu 1813/1887	44		0-4-0T	Steam tram engine
–	Deutz 57499/1962	KG125BS	92	B DM	replica

CITY BAHN CHEMNITZ Gmbh   CB

Chemnitz, Sachsen.

EVU Licence: Passenger, 04/12/1997–31/12/2027.
Routes: Chemnitz Hbf–Chemnitz Süd–Stollberg (1998); Chemnitz–Burgstadt (2002); Stollberg–Glauchau (2003); Chemnitz–Hainichen (2004).
Depot: Stolberg.

The passenger service on the former DB line from Chemnitz to Stolberg was privatised as City Bahn Chemnitz. Chemnitz is following Karlsruhe and having a Stadtbahn (or Citybahn!) with the line to Stolberg being connected in to the city transport system via a new chord line in Altchemnitz. Six Variobahn Stadtbahn railcars (trams) and six Stadler RS1 railcars make up the present stock. In connection with the project Chemnitz Hbf has been completely rebuilt linking the railway with the city tramway system.

CTL LOGISTICS Gmbh   CTL

Berlin.

EVU Licence: Passenger & Freight, 28/06/2006–30/06/2021.
Traction: Some 15 electric and diesel locomotives are leased mostly from MRCE, mainly of Classes 185 and 189.

This company began life as Rent a Train based in Hamburg but was then taken over by Chem Trans Logistic Holding Polska S.A. CTL Logistics is thus the German arm of this Polish operator which concentrates on freight flows between Poland and Germany, mostly connected with the chemical industry.

D & D EISENBAHNGESELLSCHAFT mbH   DUD

Hagenow Land, Mecklenburg-Vorpommern.

EVU Licence: Freight & Passenger, 10/02/2000–31/01/2015.
Traction: Two 203.1, three 203.2 and a 323.
Depot: Former DB depot at Hagenow Land.

This company dates from 1999/2000 and is based in the old depot at Hagenow Land. It takes advantage of any engineering contracts that are going and also spot hires its locos.

DAMPFLOKWERK MEININGEN   DLW

Meiningen, Thüringen.

Surprisingly this steam locomotive works has two main line locomotives. One is a steam locomotive available as a replacement for locomotives sent to Meiningen for overhaul, whilst the other is a Class 202 diesel used for transporting locomotives to and from the works.

DELMENHORST–HARPSTEDTER EISENBAHN GmbH   DHE

Harpstedt, Niedersachsen.
EVU Licence: Freight & Passenger, 26/10/1995–25/10/2025.
Routes: Delmenhorst Süd–Harpstedt.
Length: 27.1/32.2 km.
Depot: Harpstedt.

This short line lost its passenger service in the 1960s and since then has quietly served a few private sidings along the line. More recently passenger trains were reintroduced as tourist trains at weekends in the summer using at first the line's own diesel railcar and more recently a steam locomotive.

DELTARAIL GmbH   DELTA

Frankfurt/Oder, Brandenburg.
EVU Licence: Freight, 07/04/2005–31/12/2019.
Traction: Two locomotives leased from Northrail, an electric locomotive being ex-ÖBB!

This small company was founded in 2004 but taken over in 2011 by Polish Via Cargo S.A. Based in Frankfurt/Oder on the border with Poland the company provides transport into Germany for trains originating in Poland, many of which work through with Polish locomotives.

DEUTSCHE PRIVATBAHN GmbH   DP

Altenbeken, Nordrhein-Westfalen.
EVU Licence: Freight & Passenger, 19/04/2007–28/02/2020.
Traction: Various former DB and DR shunting locos, the main line fleet being former DR Class 142s acquired from Switzerland.
Depot: Altenbeken.

The origins of this company can be traced back to several others, all founded by the same person but many now closed down (e.g. Eisenbahn Betriebs Gesellschaft EBG). What remains now is a much slimmed down concern. Some freight trafic is still moved by DP but many locomotives have been leased out to EGP. Some shunting turns remain with DP.

DIE LEI GmbH   DLI

Kassel, Hessen.
EVU Licence: Freight & Passenger, 26/10/2010–31/01/2016.
Depot: Kassel.
Traction: Mostly former DR V60 shunting locos and DB Class 701 OHLE maintenance units, but for main line work there is one former DR Class 142 and several rebuilt V100DR.

This organisation is another one specialising in providing locomotives and stock etc. for engineering work.

DÖLLNITZBAHN GmbH — DBGM
Mügeln, Sachsen.
EVU Licence: Passenger & Freight, 15/02/1999–31/07/2025.
Routes: Oschatz–Mügeln–Glossen/Kemmlitz (Kemmlitz no longer served).
Length: 21 km.
Gauge: 750 mm.
Depot: Mügeln.

This short 750 mm gauge line had great beginnings, being all that is left of a network of narrow gauge lines radiating from Mügeln. It was notable in DR days as being the last line using Sachsen Meyer type 0-4-4-0T locos, three of which remained on the books when the line was privatised in 1993. Freight traffic has disappeared in recent years but the line has a contract to run passenger trains for school children. It is expected in the future that the line will come under the umbrella of the Sachsische Schmalspurbahnen. See also the museum line section.

DORTMUNDER EISENBAHN GmbH — DE
Dortmund, Nordrhein-Westfalen.
EVU Licence: Freight, 29/04/2005–30/04/2020.
Routes: Dortmund Nord–Dortmund Stadthafen–Dortmund-Westerholz–Dortmund-Obereving Süd–Dortmund-Stockheide–Dortmund-Körne–Dortmund-Remberg; branch to Dortmund-Hardeberghafen; also works railways of Krupp Hoesch Stahl AG in Dortmund and in Bochum.
Length: 20.3 km (275 km including the steelworks lines and sidings!).
Traction: About 30 miscellaneous locomotives mostly of industrial types including some G1203, G1206, G1600 BBs from MaK.
Depot: Westfalenhütte.

The DE serves numerous industries in the Dortmund area. Starting off as a basic industrial railway it has grown over the years as industrial take-overs and contraction gave it more work. In 1980 it took over the railway needs of the Hoesch steelworks and as late as 1994 the railway network at the Krupp steelworks in Bochum was added to the DE empire. It had some 241 km of track and handled 30 million tonnes of traffic in 1999! This had risen to 39 million tonnes in 2000.

In 2005 Connex acquired the Thyssen Krupp Stahl shares of DE and split the company into DE Transport GmbH (29/03/2005) and DE Infrastructure GmbH. DE Transport thus became 65% Connex and 35% Dortmunder Hafen AG. The Infrastructure is 81% Dortmunder Hafen AG and 19% Connex. In 2006 DE Transport was again named plain Dortmunder Eisenbahn which it remains to this day, however Connex has become Captrain. DE continues to serve all the traditional industries in the area but long distance work tends to be handled by Captrain.

No.	Builder, No. & Year	Type	kW	Details	Comments	
VT 13	Dessau 2423/1938		132		A-1 DMR	Ex RBG

DUISPORT RAIL GmbH — DPR
Duisburg, Nordrhein-Westfalen.
EVU Licence: Freight, 18/01/2001–31/12/2015.
Traction: Some 15 locos, mostly ex DB V60C but also some Alstom modernised V100DR and Vossloh G1206 supplemented by leased locomotives.
Depot: Duisburg-Diessern.

This company was set up in 2001 and received its EVU licence during the summer of that year. It is a 100% subsidiary of Duisburger Hafen AG. Apart from work on the harbour lines there is much trip work in the form of "last mile" operations. Duisburg-Rheinhausen yard is perhaps the best place to see the locomotives.

EfW–VERKEHRSGESELLSCHAFT mbH   EFW

Frechen, Nordrhein-Westfalen.
EVU Licence: Freight & Passenger, 29/06/2001–30/06/2016.
Traction. Several former DB V100, V200, and V60 diesels (15 in total).
Depot: Was once at the Worms Hafenbahn but most maintenance is now carried out at DB depots. Refuelling takes place anywhere convenient.

EfW stands for Eisenbahnfreunde Westerwald, whose company formed for running railtours (EfW-Tours) went bankrupt in early 2002, but their other company remains as an EVU and operates ballast trains etc. Initially locomotives were all hired in from the Bombardier pool but late in 2002 EfW started to acquire former DB locos. Being formed by railway fans, most locomotives have been restored to old DB liveries.

EHB EISENBAHN UND HAFENBETRIEBSGESELLSCHAFT Gmbh
REGION OSNABRÜCK mbH   EHB/HABA

Osnabrück, Niedersachsen.
EVU Licence: None, appears to run under auspices of Nord West Bahn.
Traction: Six diesels of types V60C, V90 and V100DR.
Depot: Osnabrück Hafen.

Osnabrück has a harbour connected with the Mittellandkanal. The locomotives are used to trip traffic from the harbour lines to Osnabrück marshalling yard.

EICHHOLZ EIVEL GmbH   EIVEL

Berlin.
EVU Licence: Freight & Passenger, 02/02/2007–31/12/2022.
Depot: Haldensleben (former DR depot).

This company was originally Eicholz Verkehr und Logistik GmbH which was founded in 2002 but became insolvent and was subsequently sold to Strabag of Austria. The company was renamed to the present title 31/08/2006. The original company obtained the batch of Nohab diesels that had been operating with Eurotrac and Gamma Leasing but most have been sold on. Eicholz now works infrastructure trains on a spot basis but seems to have retained one Nohab loco.

EISENBAHN & VERKEHRSBETRIEBE ELBE–WESER GmbH   EVB

Zeven, Niedersachsen.
EVU Licence: Freight & Passenger, 28/12/1995–27/12/2025.
Routes: Bremervörde Süd–Osterholz-Scharmbeck; Wilstedt–Zeven Süd–Tostedt; Rotenburg–Bremervörde–Hollenstedt; Hesedorf–Stade; Harsefeld–Buxtehude; Rotenburg–Brockel.
Length: 286 km.
Traction: DMUs of Classes 628 and 648; locos of types 140, 211, 223, G1000, G1206, and leased 185s etc.
Depots: Bremervörde Süd, Zeven Süd, Harsefeld Süd.

EVB was formed in 1981 by the fusion of Bremervörde–Osterholzer Eisenbahn GmbH (BOE) and the Wilstedt–Zeven–Tostedter Eisenbahn GmbH (WZTE). Passenger traffic on these lines had finished in the 1970s so on formation EVB was freight only. In 1991 it took over from DB the passenger services Bremerhaven–Stade–Bremervörde–Brockel and Hesedorf–Hollenstedt, later acquiring several Class 628.2 DMUs diverted from the DB order. In 1993 operations were extended further when the passenger traffic between Buxtehude and Harsefeld came to EVB. EVB now also operates the passenger services between Bremerhaven and Cuxhaven using DMUs leased from LNVG. Freight traffic is principally container trains to and from the nearby ports with some longer runs to central and southern Germany. Shunting is also undertaken in the ports. EVB has recently merged with MWB, certainly for freight allowing resources to be pooled. MWB however still retains its own fleet.

No.	Builder, No. & Year	Type	kW	Details	Comments
164	Talbot 97213/1955		2 x 107	1A-A1 DMR	Ex BOE
170	LHW 1936/1959		2 x 107	B-2 DHR	Ex BOE, ex DB VT51 104

Note: The internal numbering system starts with a figure denoting the number of axles followed by the power rating in thousands. A running number over 50 denotes a radio controlled locomotive.

EISENBAHN GESELLSCHAFT POTSDAM mbH   EGP

Potsdam, Brandenburg.

EVU Licence: Freight & Passenger, 11/04/2005–31/12/2019.
Routes: RB 74 Pritzwalk–Meyenburg (December 2012–December 2014); R6 Mirow–Neustrelitz.
Traction: Over 50 items, many of which are former DR types – V22B, V60D, V100DB.
Depots: Potsdam Rehbrücke, Wittenberge.

This firm seems to have been founded in 2004/05, initially finding traffic and getting others to move it whilst it awaited an EVU licence. On 01/01/2006 it took over the branch line and sidings at Potsdam Rehbrücke which it also hires out to other companies wanting sidings and stabling space close to Berlin. On 01/09/2006 it took over the freight operations of PE Cargo from Arriva which wanted the passenger side of PE and the OMB workshops at Neustrelitz. Since then EGP has gained strength and is continually increasing its locomotive fleet. Besides those listed EGP also hires electric locos from DP. In recent years EGP has branched out into passenger work operating several branch lines in the greater Berlin area as noted above. Most of the freight work is in the former East Germany but there are some long listance flows to North Sea ports. Since 2010 the major part of EGP is owned by ENON (80%), a company which has its roots in the former PEG! ENON also owns Hanseatische Eisenbahn (q.v.).

EISENBAHN LOGISTIK GESELLSCHAFT – ELG GmbH   ELG

Essen, Nordrhein-Westfalen.

EVU Licence: Freight, 21/06/2007–30/06/2020.
Traction: Does not appear to own any locos but hires in as required.

This is another company dealing with infrastructure trains etc. Although it hires in locos it does in fact have several engineering trollies on its books.

EISENBAHN LOGISTIK LEIPZIG GmbH   ELL

Leipzig, Sachsen.

EVU Licence: Freight & Passenger, 19/07/2005–31/07/2020.
Traction: One V100DR and three Class 701s.

Originally set up as Aus und Weiterbildungszentrum Verkehrsgewerbe, Leipzig (AWV) the organisation changed its name in March 2006 to that shown above. Although holding freight and passenger licences, the rolling stock suggests the company is involved in infrastructure work!

EISENBAHN LOGISTIK UND SERVICE GmbH   ELS

Neustrelitz, Mecklenburg-Vorpommern.

EVU Licence: Freight, 24/03/2005–22/03/2020.
Traction: One V18B owned; other locos hired in as necessary.

A small company which is the EIU for several lines in north east Germany. Presumably handles traffic on a spot-hire basis.

EISENBAHN LOGISTIK VIENENBURG
(WILLRICH & MÜHLBERG Gbr)   ELV
Vienenburg, Niedersachsen.

EVU Licence: Operates under the licence of MBB.
Traction: Four locos - two V60C and two V100DB.

Willrich and Mühlberg were two people involved with the museum group in Vienenberg who circa 2007 decided to get on the open access band wagon. Main work is infrastructure trains.

EISENBAHN SERVICE GESELLSCHAFT mbH   ESGBI
Vaihingen/Enz, Baden-Württemberg.

EVU Licence: Freight & Passenger, 24/03/2004–15/04/2019.
Traction: 13 locomotives of types Köf, V60C, G1205, G1206 and Austrian 1142.
Depot: Bietigheim-Bissingen.

Founded in 1998, the main work of this company centres on infrastructure trains and shunting duties in the greater Stuttgart area. However its locos can turn up anywhere as they are often leased out on a spot-hire basis.

EISENBAHN UND HÄFEN GmbH   EH
EH GÜTERVERKEHR GmbH   EHG
THYSSENKRUPP STEEL EUROPE AG
Duisburg, Nordrhein-Westfalen.

EVU Licence: Freight, 17/11/1998–30/11/2028.
Routes: This company operates a vast system of branch lines and sidings around Dinslaken, Duisburg, Krefeld, Mülheim and Oberhausen.
Length: 572 km of which 234 km electrified.
Electric System: 600 V DC.
Traction. Main line EHG locomotives are MaK G1205 and Vossloh G1206. The locos listed below are in effect internal user locos.
Depots: Duisburg-Hamborn, Duisburg-Ruhrort, Duisburg-Beeckerwerth, Oberhausen.
Workshop: Duisburg-Hamborn.

EH started off as an industrial railway in the Ruhr but over the years has taken over other operations and is now quite a big business, perhaps the busiest of all the German private railways. It has 572 km of tracks and interchanges with DB at nine locations. Some 70 million tonnes of freight are handled each year. EHG is owned by Thyssen Stahl (100%). The previous firm of Eisenbahn und Hafen has now been absorbed into ThyssenKrupp Steel Europe AG (circa 2011) which now appears to have kept the "internal" locomotives. If passing through Duisburg, Krefeld, Mülheim, Oberhausen or Witten areas a visitor is likely to catch sight of mysterious green locos darting about with freight trips. Note that the VKM EH is now used for ThyssenKrupp Steel Europe and EHG for EH Güterverkehr.

No.	Builder, No. & Year	Type	kW	Details	Comments
144	Jung 14073/1969	EDL	592/169	Bo-Bo ED	
147	Jung 14076/1969	EDL	592/169	Bo-Bo ED	
148	Jung 14077/1969	EDL	592/169	Bo-Bo ED	
171	Jung 14078/1969	EDL	592/169	Bo-Bo ED	Ex 149
317	Wind 2291/1976		70	A-A DMR	OHLE vehicle
320	Wind 2281/1976		70	A-A DMR	OHLE vehicle
385	Jung 14120/1971	EDL	592/169	Bo-Bo ED	Ex 162
387	Jung 14116/1971	EDL	592/169	Bo-Bo ED	Ex 16x
651	OK 26876/1976	MBB1200N	552	B-B DH	Ex HKM 05
652	OK 26877/1976	MBB1200N	552	B-B DH	Ex HKM 06
701	Hens 32564/1983	DE500C	500	C DE	Ex TEW Witten 1

702	Hens 32563/1983	DE500C	500	C DE	Ex TEW Witten 3
703	Hens 32567/1983	DE500C	500	C DE	Ex TEW Witten 4
711	Hens 32750/1987	DHG700C	565	C DH	Ex TEW Witten 2
751	JW 3680059/1965	MG530C	397	C DH	Ex HKM 61
752	JW 3680060/1965	MG530C	397	C DH	Ex HKM 62
754	JW 3680062/1965	MG530C	397	C DH	Ex HKM 64
757	OK 26894/1978	MC700N	397	C DH	Ex HKM 67
801	Jung 13350/1961	EDL	592/375	Bo-Bo ED	Ex 119
802	Jung 13850/1964	EDL	592/375	Bo-Bo ED	Ex 140
803	Jung 13348/1961	EDL	592/375	Bo-Bo ED	Ex 117
804	Jung 13583/1962	EDL	592/375	Bo-Bo ED	Ex 129
805	Jung 13585/1963	EDL	592/375	Bo-Bo ED	Ex 131
806	Jung 13352/1961	EDL	592/375	Bo-Bo ED	Ex 121
807	Jung 13586/1963	EDL	592/375	Bo-Bo ED	Ex 132
808	Jung 13393/1961	EDL	592/375	Bo-Bo ED	Ex 124
809	Jung 13394/1961	EDL	592/375	Bo-Bo ED	Ex 125
812	Jung 13351/1961	EDL	592/375	Bo-Bo ED	Ex 120

EISENBAHN-BAU- UND BETRIEBSGESELLSCHAFT
PRESSNITZTALBAHN mbH   PRESS

Jöhstadt, Sachsen.

EVU Licence: Freight & Passenger, 07/06/2000–07/06/2015.
Traction: Over 40 locos of types V60C, V60D, V100DR, ER20, 110, 140 and 145.
Depots: Espenhain, Lübbenau.

The preservation society that runs the Jöhstadt–Steinbach line formed its own EVU and started out obtaining work on infrastructure trains or simply hiring out its locos to other agencies. Since then it has got into the big time and operates many services all over Germany with quite a lot of activity in the old eastern parts. Locos are numbered with the DB style classification but the last three digits represent the PRESS numerical order e.g. 145 023 is not the DB locomotive of that number, but the 23rd in the PRESS fleet which just happens to be a 145; its EVN is 145 085. PRESS also operates the Rügensche BäderBahn which is listed separately. PRESS also takes on infrastructure work on narrow gauge lines and hires in narrow gauge diesel locomotives from the Jöhstadt preservation group.

EISENBAHNBETRIEB MITTLERER NECKAR GmbH   EMN

Kornwestheim, Baden-Württemberg.

EVU Licence: Freight & Passenger, 15/03/2006–31/03/2021.
Depot: Kornwestheim Rbf.
Livery: Red.

This organisation was founded in 1999 and is believed to be the operating arm of the Stuttgart area preservation group Gesellschaft zur Erhaltung von Schienenfahrzeugen.

EISENBAHNBETRIEBSGESELLSCHAFT MITTELRHEIN mbH –
EBM CARGO   EBM

Gummersbach, Nordrhein-Westfalen.

EVU Licence: Freight, 07/05/2012–31/12/2027.
Traction: Eight locomotives with more expected. Classes 140, 202, 203, 225 and 363.

This company was founded in 2010 and could easily be confused with another company with the same initials that went bankrupt some years earlier. Traffic appears to be infrastructure trains and last mile work in the Ruhr area.

EISENBAHNGESELLSCHAFT OSTFRIESLAND-OLDENBURG mbH
EGOO

Aurich, Niedersachsen.

EVU Licence: Freight & Passenger 18/07/2013–31/07/2028.
Traction: Four diesels of Classes 203 and 223 plus others hired in as necessary.

This company is part of ENERCOM GmbH and is in the business of supplying and transporting wind turbine blades but now also deals with general freight transport.

ELBA LOGISTIK GmbH   ELBA

Backnang, Baden-Württemberg.

EVU Licence: Freight, 18/10/2005–31/10/2020.
Traction: Two locos, a V18B and a V60C.

This small firm dates from 2004 and is involved in infrastruture train operation in the Stuttgart area.

EMSLÄNDISCHE EISENBAHN GmbH   EEB

Meppen, Niedersachsen.

EVU Licence: Freight & Passenger, 11/09/1998–11/09/2028.
Routes: See Below.
Length: 76.7 km.
Traction: Four V100DB, one G1700 , two shunting locos and one railcar.
Depots: Bhf Vormeppen, Werlte.

The EEB is the current owner and operator of two former private railways: Hümmlinger Kreisbahn (HKB: Lathen–Werlte, 25 km); Meppen–Haselünner Eisenbahn (MHE: Meppen–Essen (Old)). Additionally it covers the Meppen–Meppen Emshafen branch.

ERFURTER BAHN GmbH   EIB

Erfurt, Thüringen.

EVU Licence: Freight & Passenger, 25/10/2010–30/09/2025.
Routes: Erfurt–Gera; Erfurt–Arnstadt–Saalfeld; Jena–Pössneck; Saalfeld–Blankenstein; Gera–Zeulenroda; Gera–Zeitz–Leipzig; Gera–Triptis–Saalfeld; Weimar–Kranichfeld (Diesel Netz Ostthüringen); Meiningen–Schweinfurt Stadt; Gemünden (Main)–Bad Kissingen–Schweinfurt Stadt (Kissinger Stern); Erfurt–Rennsteig.
Traction: Over 40 Stadler RS1 railcars and one Itino railcar; two V100DR.
Depot: Erfurt Ost.

The Erfurter Industrie Bahn is a long established industrial railway and even existed under DDR days. In 1995 this railway changed its function from being the server of several sidings to being a fully-fledged private railway seizing the opportunities that were on offer after the fall of communism. Then came regionalisation and open access giving EIB even greater opportunities. EIB won the contract to provide local train services between Erfurt–Döllstädt–Leinefelde for which it acquired five new Regio Shuttles and later had to get three more. 30/05/1999 saw the new service extended from Leinefelde via Eichenberg to Kassel Wilhelmshöhe. In 2000 EIB joined forces with Hessiche Landesbahn GmbH to run services in the Meiningen area as the Südthuringenbahn GmbH (q.v.). From 03/03/2007 the name was changed to Erfurter Bahn reflecting current operations but interestingly the old initials were retained as the registered VKM. The company now concentrates on its passenger operations. Its first passenger contracts expired in 2013 but it obtained a 12 year contract to run the "Dieselnetz Ostthüringen" 2012–2024, acquiring 37 RS1 railcars and from December 2014 has a contract for 12 years to operate services known as the "Kissinger Stern". For two years from June 2014 EIB is also operating Erfurt to Rennsteig usings its RS1s, some of which have been modified with improved braking for the severe gradients.

ERFURTER BAHNSERVICE GmbH   EBS

Erfurt, Thüringen.
EVU Licence: Freight & Passenger, 14/02/2007–14/02/2022.
Traction: Three V22/23, three V60D, three V100DR, one V170 Nohab, one V180 and two 142s.

Founded in 2006 mainly as a service to provide drivers etc. It later acquired the contract to shunt at the cement works in Karsdorf eventually talking over the depot there previously used by the Karsdorfer Eisenbahn Ges. Infrastructure trains are also worked and there are now some main line workings, its diesel locos being useful for "last mile" work in the area.

ERFURTER GLEISBAU GmbH   EGB

Erfurt, Thüringen.

This company seems to be an EIU but is not registered as such, nor as an EVU. It can only be assumed that it is a leasing company with a locomotive and some draisines which are used by the Thüringer Eisenbahn GmbH (ThE).

erixx GmbH   Erixx

Celle, Niedersachsen.
EVU Licence: Freight & Passenger, 04/11/2011–03/11/2026.
Routes: Hannover–Buchholz and Bremen–Uelzen (Heidekreuz Bahn); Braunschweig–Uelzen, Braunschweig–Bad Harzburg/Goslar, Hannover–Bad Harzburg and Lüneburg–Danneberg (Dieselnetz Niedersachsen Südost).
Traction: 28 Alstom LINT 41 for the Heidekreuz Bahn and a further 28 for the Dieselnetz Niedersachsen Südost, all leased from LNVG.
Depots: Soltau, Uelzen.

This company was set up by the Osthannoversche Eisenbahnen AG (OHE) to acquire contracts for passenger services in the area. It was soon successful, being awarded the contract to run the "Heidekreuz Bahn" from December 2011 for 8 years. Later the marketing name "erixx" was adopted. In 2012 another contract was won for part of the "Dieselnetz Niedersachsen Südost" which runs for 15 years from December 2014.

EUROPOOL – MAX KNAPE GLEISBAU GmbH   EUROPOOL

München, Bayern.

This track engineering company has acquired some of the Class V100.5 that were previously DB 710 9xx. It is believed they have all been rebuilt by ADtranz, probably under sub-contract to RFG at Reichenbach. The firm has many track machines and the four V100s.

FAHRZEUGWERK NIEDERSACHSWERFEN GmbH   FWN

Niedersachswerfen, Thüringen

This is the new title for IGENO at Nordhausen. IGENO declared insolvency in 2005 and was transformed into FWN on 01/01/2006. It is now part of the Villmann group which also owns ITB at Brandenburg. The Nordhausen plant more or less continues as before, maintaining and repairing private locos. Most of the IGENO stock remains on site.

FARGE–VEGESACKER EISENBAHN GmbH   FVE

Bremen.
EVU Licence: Freight, open ended from 19/12/1994.
Route: Bremen-Farge–Bremen-Vegesack.
Length: 10.4 km.
Depot: Bremen-Farge.

What freight traffic remains on this line is now worked by Captrain. However having been freight only since the 1960s the route is now part of the Bremen S-Bahn which is operated by Nord West Bahn.

FRÄNKISCHE MUSEUMS EISENBAHN e.V.   FME

Nürnberg, Bayern.
EVU Licence: Freight & Passenger, 17/01/1996–31/12/2024.
Depot: Nürnberg Nord Ost.

This museum society operates museum trains from Nürnberg Nord Ost. Consequently it has an EVU licence. When locos are spare (i.e. not required for museum trains) those with main line certficates may be used on ballast trains etc.

FREIBERGER EISENBAHNGESELLSCHAFT mbH   FEG

Freiberg, Sachsen.
EVU Licence: Freight & Passenger, 10/01/2001–10/01/2016.
Route: Freiburg (Sachs)–Holzhau.
Length: 31 km.
Traction: Three RS1 DMUs.
Depot: Freiburg.

This company was originally set up by Eurobahn to operate the Freiburg–Holzhau branch, taking over from DB late in 2000 and with a concession to run until 2016. Following the split up of Rhenus Keolis this company is now under Rhenus Veniro.

GET GEORGSMARIENHÜTTE EISENBAHN & TRANSPORT GmbH
GET

Georgsmarienhütte, Niedersachsen.
EVU Licence: Freight & Passenger, 14/01/1997–31/12/2026.
Route: Georgsmarienhütte–Hasbergen.
Length: 7.3 km.
Traction: Five Deutz MG530C diesels.
Depot: Georgsmarienhütte.

GET is Georgsmarienhütten Eisenbahn und Transport. This railway serves the industries in Georgsmarienhütte and once belonged to the steelworks there. Like many other old steelworks towns, times have changed and the blast furnaces closed. Consequently the loco fleet has shrunk. From 1997 DB worked through from Osnabrück Rbf; just the opposite to what has happened elsewhere! The locomotives shunt at the steel works and take traffic to the interchange with DB Schenker. OHE Cargo has recently replaced DBS on trip working from Osnabrück.

GVG VERKEHRSORGANISATION GmbH   GVG

Frankfurt/Main, Hessen.
EVU Licence: Passenger, 31/03/1995–30/06/2023.
Traction: One Class 608 DMU and four Class 109s.

This travel agency company took over the marketing and operation of sleeping car trains from Berlin to Malmö via Mukran–Trelleborg when DB lost interest in the service.

▲ Freight train DGS 69378 is a "runs as required" service conveying cement wagons. It is seen crossing the River Spree on Berlin's outer circle line in the hands of Eisenbahn Gesellschaft Potsdam (EGP) former DR Class E42, 91 80 6142 150 and 6142 128 on 16 May 2014. **Christoph Grimm**

▼ HGK Class 66, 92 80 1266 068, carrying running number DE 668, leads an empty tank train to Duisburg Ruhrort through Roisdorf on 10 August 2012. HGK has subsequently transferred this loco to their marketing arm, RheinCargo (RHC), but the running number DE 668 has been retained.
Matthias Müller

HAFEN & GÜTERVERKEHR KÖLN AG   HGK

Köln, Nordrhein-Westfalen.

EVU Licence: Freight, 13/12/2004–31/12/2019.
Routes: Bonn–Brühl–Köln; Bonn–Wesseling–Köln; Wesseling–Brühl–Berrenrath; Benzelrath–Frechen–Köln-Niehl/Hafen; Nationwide under open access.
Length: 102.2 km.
Traction: Over 40 diesel locos of types G1000, G2000, DE 1002, Class 66, and 20 TRAXX electric locos. Some locomotives are leased, mainly from MRCE.
Depots: Brühl-Vochem, Köln-Deutz Hafen, Köln-Bickendorf.

This company has its origins in Häfen Köln GmbH (HKG), originally just the railway serving the Köln docks. In 1992 the line merged with Köln Frechen Benzelrather Eisenbahn (KFBE) and at the same time took over the freight work from the Köln Bonner Eisenbahn (KBE). Freight traffic is quite heavy with the larger HGK locos working trips into nearby DB yards such as Köln Eifeltor. 102 km of track includes some electrification at 750 V dc used by KVG (ex KBE) services. Open access saw the firm expand rapidly, working all over Germany with several trains going through to Rotterdam. In 2012 HGK formed an alliance with Neuss-Düsseldorfer Häfen GmbH marketed as RheinCargo GmbH.(q.v.) with some locos now appearing in RHC livery.

HAFEN HALLE GmbH   HFH

Halle (Saale), Sachsen-Anhalt.

EVU Licence: None, appears to work under the licences of other companies.
Traction: One each of Classes V180, V232, and 1200D.
Depot: Halle Trofa.

After unification the canal harbour in Halle reverted to ownership by the city which obviously wished to expand. The locos are used on trips from the harbour to the Halle marshalling yards taking wagon load traffic and also acting as a last mile operator for block trains. Some main line work is also understood to take place.

HAFEN KREFELD GmbH & Co. K.G.   RHKE

Krefeld, Nordrhein-Westfalen.

EVU Licence: Freight & Passenger, open ended from 18/01/1996.
Traction: Two G763C, one G1206, one V10B, R42C.
Depot: Krefeld Linn.

The city of Krefeld reorganised the servicing of the harbour lines and founded this company in 2007. The company deals with traffic over the harbour lines offering last mile work to private operators and DB Schenker.

HAMBURG–KÖLN EXPRESS GmbH   HKX

Köln, Nordrhein-Westfalen.

EVU Licence: Freight & Passenger, 28/04/2010–30/04/2025.
Traction: Up to four Class 182s leased as required from MRCE.

Founded in 2008 the principal shareholder is the US Company, Railroad Development Corporation, through its German subsidiary RDC Deutschland GmbH. Their idea is to run trains between Hamburg and Köln; not expensive luxury trains but offering good service to compete with DB. Nine redundant Class 4010 EMUs were purchased from ÖBB as these carriages were considered suitable. However, modernising them and giving them a full overhaul is taking a long time. Principally it is the carriages that are to be used rather than the 4010 power cars themselves.At present three return trips per day are being offered using leased carriages with some strengthening needed at weekends. An innovation in 2014 was introduced through a deal with NOB whereby certain HKX trains ran through to and from Westerland, so restoring the through trains of the 1970s.

HANSEATISCHE EISENBAHN GmbH   HANS

Putlitz, Mecklenburg-Vorpommern.
EVU Licence: Passenger & Freight, 17/12/2013–31/12/2027.

This company is part of the ENON organisation which also owns EGP (q.v.). It was set up in 2014 in order to separate the passenger work from EGP which is now a freight company. Thus it now has responsibility for the following services: Neustrelitz–Mirow; Parchim–Malchow and will probably be taking over Neustadt(Dosse)–Meyenburg from EGP in due course.

HARZER SCHMALSPURBAHNEN   HSB

Wernigerode, Sachsen-Anhalt.
EVU Licence: Freight & Passenger, 24/05/1995–31/12/2022.
Routes: Wernigerode–Nordhausen; Drei Annen Hohne–Brocken; Quedlinburg–Gernrode (Harz)–Hasselfelde; Alexisbad–Harzgerode; Stiege–Eisefelder Talmühle.
Length: 140.4 km.
Depots: Wernigerode, Nordhausen, Gernrode.

After the unification of Germany in 1990 the Harz area Metre gauge lines were sold off - privatised. These lines were originally private railways, being nationalised after WW2 by the communist authorities. As private lines they were known as the Nordhausen–Wernigerode Eisenbahn (NWE) and Gernrode–Harzgerode Eisenbahn (GHE). Upon regaining their private status they are considered now as one railway. The biggest shareholders are Landkreis Harz, Landkreis Nordhausen and the towns of Wernigerode and Nordhausen. The railway's biggest earner is the line to the Brocken mountain peak (1125 metres a.s.l.) which is very busy in the summer and winter tourist seasons. Elsewhere on the lines there is little traffic with school children being the regular passengers. In an attempt to reduce costs some DMUs have been acquired which are adequate for some areas. However the main business will see steam traction for years to come as HSB is gradually overhauling more and more locos. The biggest event in recent years has been the extension of the metre gauge tracks over the former DB line from Gernrode to Quedlinburg. At Nordhausen the line is now linked to the town tramway which has acquired some electro-diesel trams which work through over the HSB to Ilfeld.

It should be noted that several of the 2-10-2Ts have been rebuilt with new frames and cylinders and are in effect new locos. Some locos are on loan to local enthusiast groups.

HAVELLÄNDISCHE EISENBAHN AG   HVLE

Berlin Spandau.
EVU Licence: Freight & Passenger, 27/02/2002–27/02/2017.
Routes: Berlin-Spandau (Gbf)–Johannesstift–Ober Havel and various industrial spurs.
Length: 15.8 km.
Traction: Six V60D, eight modernised V100DR, two Class 246, two Class 285, eight Class 250, three Maxima 40, three Class 185 plus some small shunting locos for use at the depot.
Depots: Johannesstift, Blankenburg.

The HVLE changed its name from Osthävellandische Eisenbahn Berlin-Spandau AG (OHE Sp) 01/01/2006. It was once a much larger network around Berlin but the partition of the city after WW2 gave the OHE-Sp only 18 km of track in the Spandau area of the city. Most work was servicing private sidings from the main line interchange point. After many quiet years, unification and open access brought about bigger opportunities and early in 2000 a V200 was acquired from Poland. The fleet has continued to expand with the acquisition of most of the "Blue Tiger" locomotives. Other traffic won is the movement of limestone on the "Rubelandbahn" in the Harz area whilst nearer to home in Berlin a large part of the Wustermark marshalling yard has been taken over from where trips are worked to the nearby Rail & Logistic Centre which is 75% owned by HVLE. The company also performs the shunting at the Bombardier workshops at Hennigsdorf.

HEAVY HAUL POWER INTERNATIONAL GmbH   HHPI
Erfurt, Thuringen.

EVU Licence: Freight, 09/05/2000–09/05/2015.
Traction: One Class 59 and seven Class 66s; five to seven Powerhaul locos are expected.

Registered in Erfurt, HHPI is descended from DB Foster Yeoman GmbH, established as an independent EVU in 2000 using 59 003 from the UK numbered as 259 003 in Germany. Since then many more locos have been acquired, mostly Class 66s, but at Innotrans 2012 a new GE "Power Haul" locomotive was shown in HHPI colours, although this does not appear to have been accepted in Germany. The company remains busy hauling aggregates and coal over the northern half of Germany. In December 2014 HHPI was expected to start running coal trains from Rotterdam to destinations in Germany such as Bottrop and München using GE Powerhaul diesel locomotives built in Turkey. But these were late arriving from the builder and still had to be fitted with the necessary safety systems. Two prototype locos have been around for sometime to get type acceptance but as this book went to press there was still no news of a starting date.

HEINRICHSMEYER EISENBAHNDIENSTLEITUNGEN UG   HEIN
Trier, Rheinland-Pfalz.

EVU Licence: None, operates using that of Pfalzbahn.
Traction: Four V60D, one V100DB and three 701.

This company appears to be an offshoot of the Hochwaldbahn founded in 2010. It appears to perform local shunting around the Trier area and at Stahlwerk Bous.

HELLERTALBAHN GmbH   HB
Betzdorf(Sieg), Rheinland-Pfalz.

EVU Licence: Freight & Passenger, 13/10/1999–31/12/2015.
Routes: Dillenburg–Haiger–Betzdorf(Sieg).
Length: 35.8 km.
Depot: Bindweide (Westerwaldbahn).

The Hellertalbahn was set up in 1998/99. It is a joint venture between the Hessische Landesbahn (who provide the rolling stock), the Siegener Kreisbahn (responsible for marketing and accounts) and the Westerwaldbahn (responsible for crews and operations). The HB has taken over from DB the local train service Dillenburg–Haiger–Betzdorf. The units are a follow on order after those for BLE, KNE etc. but are Class 525 rather than 508/9. This is believed to be due to these units having first class, second class and toilets. The last three digits are common numbers with the rest of the HLB fleet.

HESSISCHE GÜTERBAHN GmbH   HGB
Buseck-Trohe, Hessen.

EVU Licence: Freight, 24/05/2006–30/04/2021.
Traction: Two V60D, several V100DR and one V180.

As the name infers this company is involved in freight work in Hessen.

HESSISCHE LANDESBAHN Gmbh
HLB BASIS AG
HLB HESSENBAHN Gmbh

HLB
HEB

Frankfurt/Main, Hessen

EVU Licence: HLB GmbH, Freight & Passenger 02/04/2004–31/05/2019; HLB Basis AG: Freight & Passenger 13/02/2007–28/02/2022.
Routes: Butzbach–Pohlgöns 3.1 km; Butzbach Nord–Griedel 3.0 km; Friedberg–Friedrichsdorf 16.0 km; Friedberg–Nidda 25.0 km; Beienheim–Wölfersheim Södel 5 km (Former BLE); Frankfurt/M-Höchst–Königstein 16 km; Ffm-Hochst–Bad Soden 7 km; Friedberg–Friedrichsdorf 16 km; Friedrichsdorf–Brandoberndorf 36.9 km (Former FKE); Kassel-Wilhelmshöhe–Naumburg 32.6 km (Former KNE). Also Giessen–Nidda–Gelnhausen, Friedberg–Hanau, Hanau–Kahl–Schöllkrippen, Giessen–Marburg, Frankfurt/M–Siegen, Limburg–Giessen, Giessen–Fulda and Fulda–Gersfeld have been won from DB Regio.
Traction: 20 VT609, 23 VT646, 33 VT648, six VT642, seven ET427, six ET429 and a few locos.
Depots: Butzbach, Baunatal-Grossenritte, Königstein, Siegen.

The Hessische Landesbahn GmbH (HLB) was founded in 1955 taking over in 1966 the Butzbach–Licher Eisenbahn, Frankfurt–Königstein Eisenbahn, Hersfelder Kreisbahn and Kassel–Naumburg Eisenbahn. These lines though continued to operate under their own identities. More recently the Verkehrsverband Hochtaunaus was also embraced. The HLB is an umbrella organisation for all these lines. The expansion progress can be seen by the following summary:

Awarded a contract in 1999 to run passenger trains from Dillenburg as the Hellertalbahn with the initials HB. This line still retains its own identity.

Early in 2001 Giessen–Nidda–Gelnhausen and from June 2001 Friedberg–Hanau passenger services became operated by HLB.

HLB Hessenbahn GmbH was formed 08/12/2004 taking over the Kahlgrundbahn services with new units based in Butzbach.

In 2005 BLE, FKE, KNE were fused under FKE. The Frankfurt Königstein Eisenbahn AG was registered 20/09/2005, thus BLE and KNE no longer exist as such.

HLB owns 50% of Regionalbahn Kassel (being the former KNE share).

Later another revision saw the main company name come into use as all the railway companies came under HLB Basis AG. Interestingly as noted above two EVU licences still exist.

HLB owns 74.9% of Vectus Verkehrs GmbH, 50% of Cantus Verkehrsgessellschaft mbH, 50.0% of Süd Thüringen Bahn GmbH and 33.3% of Hellertalbahn GmbH.

After a complex reorganisation HLB Basis is now mainly responsible for infrastructure and depots with the main operating company becoming HLB Hessenbahn. More passenger train contracts have recently been won including those noted above from Limburg, Giessen and Fulda. December 2014 saw more routes taken over: Marburg–Stadtallendorf; Limburg–Au; Limburg–Siershahn; Limburg–Wiesbaden/Frankfurt; Au–Siegen–Dillenburg; Siegen–Bad Berleburg; Siegen–Finnentrop–Olpe, whilst December 2015 should see Betzdorf–Haiger and Kassel–Treysa change to Hessenbahn operation. Four FLIRT EMUs have been ordered for the Treysa service. Note that Siegen becomes an important point and a depot is likely to be set up there.

HOLZLOGISTIK UND GÜTERBAHN Gmbh (HLG)   BEBRA

Bebra, Hessen.

EVU Licence: Freight, 23/09/2008–31/12/2023.
Traction: One Class 185 for main line work, one Class 271 and one Class 277 for shunting and tripping.
Depot: Bebra.

A relative newcomer founded in 2007 for the transport of cut timber from Hessen to timber/paper mills in other countries such as Austria and Czech Republic, and spot moves on behalf of other customers. About 150 wagons are leased. Note VKM allocated is BEBRA!

HÖRSELTALBAHN GmbH HTB

Eisenach, Thüringen.

EVU Licence: Freight & Passenger, 03/06/1999–12/10/2024.
Routes: Eisenach area.
Length: 9.2 km.
Depot: Opel werksbahnhof.

This company grew from an industrial shunting activity, firstly under the old DDR at the Wartburg car factory and later at the same place but now for Opel. Privatised, it now serves the Opel factory and other locations in the area around Eisenach.

HSL LOGISTIK GmbH HSL

Hamburg.

EVU Licence: Freight & Passenger, 19/12/2003–31/12/2021.
Traction: 22 locos virtually all leased – three PRIMA diesel and three PRIMA electric locos from Akiem, eight electric locos from SBB Cargo (421/482), six V60D from EGP/WFL, one 290 and one V100DR.

Founded in 2003 this company has experienced steady growth. It provides infrastructure trains, shunting and last mile operations at ports such as Bremen, Hamburg, Rostock as well as inland terminals. Main line work includes oil/petrol and biodiesel transport, block trains of steel products (e.g.wire) and spot traffic in grain and building materials.

HWB VERKEHRSGESELLSCHAFT mbH HWB

Hermeskeil, Rheinland-Pfalz.

EVU Licence: Freight & Passenger, 01/07/2005–31/12/2018.
Depot: Zittau.

This company started off working out of Hermeskeil but has since sold off most of its stock. It retains the depot at Zittau where its remaining stock is maintained as well as locos repaired/ overhauled for other operators.

HzL HOHENZOLLERISCHE LANDESBAHN AG HzL

Hechingen, Baden-Württemberg.

EVU Licence: Freight & Passenger, 26/01/2010–28/02/2025.
Routes: Eyach–Hechingen–Gammertingen–Sigmaringen; Gammertingen–Kleinengstingen; Hanfertal–Sigmaringendorf. Also over the following DB lines: Tübingen–Hechingen–Sigmaringen–Aulendorf; Ulm–Sigmaringen–Tuttlingen; Braunlingen–Donaueschingen–Villingen–Rottweil/ Trossingen Stadt; Rottweil–Tuttlingen–Immendingen–Fridingen; Immendingen–Leipferdingen–Blumberg; Radolfszell–Stockach.
Length: 107.4 km (own infrastructure).
Traction: Two D25B, three D100BB, one G1300BB, two Gravita 15L locomotives; 49 RS1 and four NE81 DMUs.
Depots: Gammertingen, Haigerloch, Immendingen.

The HzL is no newcomer to the scene, being over 100 years old. It has quietly been going about its business in a lovely part of Germany catering for local traffic, both freight and passenger. Open access and Regionalisation opened up further opportunities resulting in HzL getting the contract to provide local services on many DB lines in the area. HzL was one of the first railways to acquire Reggio Shuttles in any large number, hiring them from Rail Charter. VT 44/5 are similar units but numbered differently because they are subsidised by the Tuttlingen area for services from Sigmaringen to Tuttlingen. HzL also operates many seasonal trains for tourists including weekend trains aimed at cyclists. HzL retains some freight traffic.

ILMEBAHN AG ILM
Einbeck, Niedersachsen.
EVU Licence: Freight & Passenger, 26/10/1995–25/10/2025.
Routes: Einbeck Salzderhelden–Einbeck.
Length: 4.4 km.
Traction: One V100DB, one V100DR and a Wismar railbus.
Depot: Einbeck Mitte.

The Ilmebahn is now only half the length it used to be and could be described as a long siding. Most of its own traffic is thus much reduced but it has an arrangement with DB Schenker which generates trip workings in the area around Göttingen.

INDUSTRIETRANSPORTGESELLSCHAFT BRANDENBURG mbH ITB
Brandenburg, Brandenburg.
EVU Licence: Freight, 29/12/1995–31/12/2025.
Routes: Brandenburg steelworks and harbour.
Depot: Brandenburg harbour.

This company started off as the internal shunting provider at the Brandenburg steelworks. It has since acquired the status of an EVU. Besides its traditional work it also serves sidings in the area on behalf of DB Schenker. ITB is part of the Villman group which has works in Nordhausen, Altenburg and Woffleben which are also served.

INFRA LEUNA GmbH LEUNA
Leuna, Sachsen-Anhalt.
EVU Licence: Freight & Passenger, 04/05/2000–31/05/2015.
Routes: Chemical and refinery works in Leuna and Grosskorbetha.
Length: 65 km.
Traction: Four G765C, six G1200, three V100DR and two 228s.
Depot: Leuna, Werk 1.

This organisation has developed from the shunting organisation of the Leuna chemical complex. Under privatisation it has extended into being a provider of Infrastructure services to the industries around Leuna, Grosskorbetha and Merseburg, running ballast trains etc as well as tripping to DB exchange sidings. It later branched out into delivering some trains to final destinations, for which main line locos are leased.

INSELBAHN LANGEOOG IL
Langeoog, Niedersachsen.
EVU Licence: Freight & Passenger, 24/01/1996–13/08/2038.
Route: Bhf. Langeoog–Hafen Langeoog.
Length: 3.0 km.
Gauge: 1000 mm.
Depot: Langeoog.

This island railway is metre gauge and connects the pier head with the town. With only three km of track, the railway was modernised in the 1990s. Most of its surplus railcars were sold to the HSB or museum lines. The locos are listed below as they do not fit into the national register scheme.

No.	Builder, No. & Year	Type	kW	Details	Comments
Kö 1	Schöma 1738/1956	CFL90	88	B DM	
Lok 1	Schöma 5344/1994	CFL250DCL	198	B DH	
Lok 2	Schöma 5345/1994	CFL250DCL	198	B DH	
Lok 3	Schöma 5346/1994	CFL250DCL	198	B DH	
Lok 4	Schöma 5347/1994	CFL250DCL	198	B DH	
Lok 5	Schöma 5348/1994	CFL250DCL	198	B DH	

48

▲ HVLE is a company with a growing portfolio of locomotives. On a wintry 25 January 2013, TRAXX P160DE 92 80 1246 010 with a new VAREO DMU in tow, pauses at Roisdorf to be overtaken by an IC. **Matthias Müller**

▼ In the late 1990s ADtranz produced a design of modern diesel locomotive which became known as the "Blue Tiger". The design was superseded by the TRAXX family and all 11 examples built were subsequently snapped up by private operators. 92 80 1250 007 is one of two examples owned by ITL Eisenbahngesellschaft; it is pictured at Berlin Schönefeld Flughafen on 7 April 2011. **Keith Fender**

INTEGRO VERKEHR GmbH INTEG

Reichenbach (Voghtland), Thüringen.

EVU Licence: Freight & Passenger, 27/01/2009–31/01/2023.
Traction: Two 223s.

Founded in 2008 this small company has links with PRESS and the Deutsches Dampflok Museum in Neuenmarkt Wirsberg. It has regular traffic moving container shuttles and oil trains.

ITL CARGO GmbH
ITL EISENBAHNGESELLSCHAFT mbH ITL

Dresden, Sachsen.

EVU Licence: Freight & Passenger, 08/12/1998–31/12/2028 (but note ITL Cargo has a separate licence for freight and passenger 18/08/2004–31/08/2019).
Routes: Nationwide but particularly in and through Sachsen.
Traction: 52 locos: five V22B, 11 V60D. one V100DB, two V100DR, four V180BB, five 285s, three 232/242, two 250, two 152, 14 185, five 186, with more hired in as necessary.
Depots: Kamenz (former DB depot), Pirna.

Since being established in 1998 this firm, previously Import Transport Logistik (ITL) has grown and grown. Based in the former East Germany the company quickly saw the developing opportunities and has gathered in locos from various sources including lots of former DR examples. In its first five years the firm developed quickly, starting with infrastructure trains using small locos and then getting main line freight traffic requiring more powerful diesels and even electric locos. Traffic to and from Poland and the Czech Republic soon materialised and now there are subsidiary companies in these countries. International traffic grew strongly and so in 2004 another company was created – ITL Cargo GmbH. This is now responsible for organising the traffic flows whilst the original company looks after the workshops and locomotives.

In 2008 an SNCF subsidiary, Transport et Logistique Partenaires S.A., bought 75% of the shares and two years later completely owned the company which is now part of the Captrain empire, conveniently giving SNCF complete access to Germany! Traffic includes chemicals to and from the Netherlands and Czech Republic, intermodal trains from Poland and Czech Republic to North Sea ports in Germany and the Netherlands, car trains, building materials etc.

KAHLGRUND-VERKEHRS-GESELLSCHAFT mbH KVG

Schöllkrippen, Bayern.

EVU Licence: Freight & Passenger, 01/08/2008–31/07/2023.
Route: Schöllkrippen–Kahl am Main.
Length: 30.5 km.
Depot: Schöllkrippen.

Although in Bayern, this line is located just about as far away from München as you can get within the Land - it is closer to Frankfurt/Main. The line is owned by DB (28%), the Bavarian State (67%) and Landkreis Aschaffenburg (5%). However in 2005 DB lost the contract for passenger trains to Hessische Landesbahn who took over on 11/12/2005. The NE 81 railcars were taken over by DB whilst the Desiros went back to Angel Trains Leasing for hire to other operators. DB still has a presence though as the former depot maintains all the DB units used around Aschaffenberg. DB is scheduled to operate the passenger service again from December 2015.

KEOLIS DEUTSCHLAND GmbH & Co KG (EUROBAHN)   ERB

Berlin.

EVU Licence: Freight & Passenger, 29/03/2007–31/03/2022.
Routes:
Hellweg Netz: RB 50 Dortmund–Lunen–Münster; RB 59 Dortmund–Unna–Soest; RB 69 Münster–Hamm–Bielefeld; RB 89 Münster–Hamm–Soest–Paderborn (– Warburg).
Maas–Rhein–Lippe Netz: RE 3 Rhein–Emscher Express, Düsseldorf–Oberhausen–Gelsenkirchen–Dortmund–Hamm; RE 13 Maas–Wupper Express, Venlo–Mönchengladbach–Düsseldorf–Hagen–Hamm.
Dieselnetz Ostwestfalen Lippe: RE 82 Bielefeld–Detmold; RB 67 Bielefeld–Münster; RB 71 Bielefeld–Rahden; RB 73 Bielefeld–Lüttfeld (At Bielefeld RB 67 becomes RB71 and RB73 becomes RE 82).
Teutoburger-Wald Netz: RB 61 Bielefeld–Bad Bentheim–Hengelo (NL); RB 66 Münster–Osnabrück; RB 65 Münster–Rheine; RB 72 Herford–Altenbeken–Paderborn; RE 78 Bielefeld–Minden–Nienburg from December 2017 for 15 years.
Traction. DMUs – nine Talent 3-car; EMUs – 29 FLIRT 4-car and 14 FLIRT 5-car plus two Köfs for depot shunting. Additional units are hired in as required.
Depots: Bielefeld-Sieker (DMUs), Hamm-Hessen (EMUs).

Eurobahn (ERB) is the trading name adopted for services run by Keolis.

Eurobahn started off as a Franco-German organisation owned by VIA-GTI (60%) and BGW/Rhenus Logistik (40%). In 1999 passenger services were reintroduced between Alzey and Kirchheimbolanden after a shut down of 48 years. To get the service off the ground two of the new generation of DMUs were hired from the Bombardier/DWA pool. In 2002 Eurobahn and Verkehrsbetriebe Extertalbahn GmbH obtained an eight year contract to run local trains on the "Weserbahn" (Hildesheim–Löhne) and "Lammetalbahn" (Hildesheim–Bodenburg). 11 LINT 41 (Coradia) DMUs were ordered and are based at the existing Eurobahn depot in Bielefeld. Operations on these lines started 14/12/2003 with an hourly service Monday–Friday and two-hourly at weekends.

From 03/09/2001 Eurobahn was reformed and changed its name to Rhenus Keolis GmbH & Co KG Mainz. The Rhenus group owned 51% and Keolis SA Paris 49%. (This latter firm itself is 48.7% Banque National de Paris and 43.5% SNCF!) Keolis is a merger of VIA-GTI and Carienne. The Eurobahn name is being kept for marketing.

In 2007 the Rhenus Keolis organisation was split into two, becoming Rhenus Veniro GmbH & Co. K.G. and Keolis Deutschland GmbH & Co. K.G. Rhenus Veniro inherited the Alzey line and also the Freiburger Eisenbahn Ges.(q.v.).

On 05/04/2006 Keolis won the contract to operate passenger services on the Hellweg Netz from December 2008 for a period of ten years. 25 Stadler FLIRT EMUs were ordered for this service. Later still Keolis won the contract for the Maas–Rhein–Lippe Netz (RE3, RE13) with effect from December 2009 until December 2025. With this enlargement a new EMU depot was built at Hamm. Four 4-car and 14 5-car FLIRTs were ordered for these services.

More recently another contract has been won for the "Dieselnetz Ostwestfalen-Lippe" (December 2013 to December 2025) for which 14 Talent 3-car DMUs were acquired via Angel Trains Europa, now Alpha Trains. These came from various other operators.

In December 2017 Eurobahn takes over for 15 years various routes in the Teutoburger Wald Netz franchise, most of which are currently operated by Westfalenbahn whose units are expected to transfer to Eurobahn. However, new dual-voltage units will be required for working to Hengelo.

KREISBAHN MANSFELDER LAND Gmbh   KML

Helbra, Sachsen-Anhalt.
EVU Licence: Freight & Passenger, 24/11/1995–01/12/2025.
Routes: Helbra–Klostermansfeld–Wippra 19.9 km, and industrial sidings totalling about 30 km.
Length: 49.9 km.
Traction: Seven V60D, three V22B and four Esslingen DMUs.
Depot: Klostermansfeld.

KML owes its roots to an industrial beginning; it grew out of the works railway for the Mansfeld copper works. With unification and the following privatisation of former state businesses, the railway company was formed first as Mansfeld Transport GmbH (MTG) later becoming KML in 1995. Besides shunting and tripping in the Mansfeld area the company has also taken on passenger work covering the service on the 19.9 km Klostermansfeld–Wippra line as a subcontractor to DB Regio. Locomotives and railcars are maintained at the old works, locomotive depot and repair shop, which trades as MaLoWa (Mansfelder Lokomotiv- und Wagenwerkstatt). The workshops take on a lot of private work specialising in overhauling former DR types for private operators. The Wippra line is expected to close in 2015.

KREISBAHN SIEGEN–WITTGENSTEIN Gmbh   KSW

Siegen, Nordrhein-Westfalen.
EVU Licence: Freight & passenger, open ended from 10/10/1995.
Routes: Siegen–Siegen-Eintracht; Kreuztal–Kreutztal-Buschhütten; Kreuztal–Buschhütten-Siemag; Siegen-Weidenau–Dreis-Tiefenbach; Herdorf–Salchendorf b.N–Pfanneberg.
Length: Circa 20 km.
Traction: One DE1002, one G1000, one G1204, two G1700 and one G2000.
Depot: Siegen-Eintracht.

Previously known as the Siegener Kreisbahn. This company operates various branches around the Siegen and Kreuztal areas including tripping on behalf of DB, last mile and infrastructure work.

LAEGER & WÖSTENHÖFER GmbH & Co KG   LUW

Berlin.
EVU Licence: Freight & Passenger, 23/02/2005–28/02/2020.
Traction: Two Köf and three V60D.

This company dates from 2004 and deals with shunting and trip work.

LAPPWALDBAHN GmbH   LWB

Weferlingen, Sachsen-Anhalt.
EVU Licence: Freight & Passenger, 03/11/1997–31/12/2028.
Routes: Helmstedt–Weferlingen(–Haldensleben).
Length: 51 km.
Traction: Five V60D, three V100DR, two 66 and three 701.
Depots: Oebisfelde (former DB depot).

This company has taken over the Haldensleben–Weferlingen line from DB and negotiated the reopening of the line on to Helmstedt which was achieved in 2009. Infrastructure work is high on their agenda for which they have several diesel shunting locos and also some overhead line units. Building materials (aggregates) are also conveyed.

52

LDS GmbH – LOGISTIK DIENSTLEITUNG UND SERVICE LDS
Eutin, Schleswig-Holstein.
EVU Licence: Freight & Passenger, 28/09/2004–31/12/2019.
Traction: Three V100DR and two G1700.
Another company set up to exploit open access operations – mostly engineering works trains.

LEIPZIGER EISENBAHNVERKEHRSGESELLSCHAFT mbH LEG
Delitzsch, Sachsen.
EVU Licence: Freight & Passenger, 10/10/2003–30/04/2016.
Traction: One 155, four V100DR and two 232.
Depot: Delitzsch.

This organisation was previously known as ASP Schienfahrzeugdiest GmbH & Co. KG (ASP). It was set up to take advantage of trackwork contracts in the former DR areas, no doubt using redundant railway staff! The ASP name came from the founders, André and Sylthe Pietz, but the name was later changed to LEG. Like many similar companies, initial infrastructure work was soon followed by main line work. Traffic handled includes petroleum products on behalf of Transpetrol International.

LEONHARD WEISS GmbH & Co KG EVULW
Göppingen, Baden-Württemberg.
EVU Licence: Freight, 09/05/1996–31/08/2026.
Traction: Two V100DB, two V100DR and 1 Köf.

Leonhard Weiss is a long established engineering and construction company. To move its rail equipment around the coutry it formed is own railway company and aquired its own locomotives.

LOCON LOGISTIK & CONSULTING AG LOCON
Oberuckersee, Brandenburg.
EVU Licence: Freight & Passenger, 02/07/2003–31/12/2017.
Traction: Two 189, three V18B, four V60D, five V100DB, 12 V100DR, one V180, one Maxima 40CC plus hired in 185.
Depot: Pinnow with stabling in Berlin Lichtenberg and elsewhere.

Established in 2002 this company got into trackwork and later became a fully fledged freight EVU. The first locomotives were obtained in late 2003. It seems just to have grown and grown as by 2008 there were 11 locomotives in the fleet and now there are 38, many of which are owned by the company although the electric locos tend to be leased. Traffic handled has more than doubled between 2008 and 2013. Infrastructure work continues but now there are many block trains being worked within Germany and internationally; some trains go to the Netherlands where Locon has now started a Dutch subsidiary.

LOKOMOTION GESELLSCHAFT FÜR SCHIENENTRAKTION mbh
LM

München, Bayern.

EVU Licence: Freight, 28/05/2004–31/05/2019.
Traction: Eight 139, six 185, ten 186, five 189, one 212 and one 333.

Lokomotion is the German EVU involved in running intermodal trains from München to Verona in Italy. The traffic is organised by Kombiverkehr and Bayerische Trailerzug Gmbh. Lokomotion works the trains to and from the Italian border station of Brenner/Brenero, handing over there to locos belonging to Rail Traction Company of Bolzano. But just look at who owns Lokomotion: DB Schenker 30%; RTC 30%; Kombiverkehr 20% and Italian firm STR 20%. No doubt the train drivers are DB Cargo!

Starting with one pair of container trains per day on 16/10/2001, traffic has grown considerably with up to 16 trains a day now traversing the Brenner route. Lokomotion is also working to Italy via the Tauern route and there are now some workings to Slovenia via the Tauern. Locomotion locomotives can appear almost anywhere on spot traffic or leased to other operators. Locomotives appear to maintained by DB Schenker at Nürnberg Rbf depot.

MECKLENBURGISCHE BÄDERBAHN MOLLI Gmbh & Co   MOLLI

Mecklenburg-Vorpommern.

EVU Licence: Freight & Passenger, 28/09/1995–20/02/2021.
Routes: Bad Doberan–Ostseebad Kühlungsborn West.
Length: 15.8 km.
Gauge: 900 mm.
Depots: Ostseebad Kühlungsborn West, Bad Doberan.

This former DR, later DB, narrow gauge line is unusual not only for running through the streets of Bad Doberan but also for its gauge - 900 mm. An early candidate for privatisation, the line was not seen as part of DB and thus reverted to private ownership in 1995. As the name suggests it serves the beach resorts and is thus primarily a summer tourst line but does offer all year round services for the few commuters. Freight traffic ceased in 1969. The locos have reverted to old style DR numbering. Some former industrial diesel locomotives are now located on the line for depot shunting and infrastructure trains.

METRANS RAIL DEUTSCHLAND Gmbh   MTRD

Berlin.

EVU Licence: Freight & Passenger, 20/06/2014–31/08/2020.

Metrans is a subsidiary of Hamburger Hafen und Logistik AG (HHLA) and has started to move its own traffic from Hamburg to places in Europe, especially to its own terminals in in Ceske Trebova and Praha in the Czech Republic. These places alone are linked by 92 trains a week. Additionally Bremerhaven is served with 28 trains a week. Destinations within Germany include Leipzig, Ludwigshafen, München and Nürnberg. It has bought two Class 295s from DB for shunting at Hamburg and is receiving 20 TRAXX MS electric locos which are registered in the Czech Republic as Class 386 but are understood to have Germanz LZB numbers 186 401–420.

METRONOM EISENBAHNGESELLSCHAFT mbH   ME

Uelzen, Niedersachsen.

EVU Licence: Passenger, 22/08/2002–22/08/2017.
Routes: Uelzen–Göttingen; Hamburg–Cuxhaven; Ulzen–Hamburg and Bremen–Hamburg.
ENNO routes: Hannover–Wolfsburg; Wolfsburg–Braunschweig–Hildesheim.
Traction: 29 146 and eight 246.
Depot: Uelzen, Braunschweig.

Metronom was founded to operate the Regio Express passenger services between Uelzen and Göttingen expanding in due course to cover the routes mentioned above. All the trains are push-pull with sets of double-deck carriages. All locomotives and rolling stock are on lease from LNVG. The number of diesel locomotives has been reduced as there was over provision. In 2014 Metronom won the contract for ENNO – E-Netz Niedersachsen Ost. 20 4-car Alstom Coradia Continental EMUs have been ordered which will be class 1440. The units are being purchased by a specially created company, Regionalbahnfahrzeuge Grossraum Braunschweig, which is a subsidiary of Zweckverband Grossraum Braunschweig. Maintenance will be carried out by Alstom at its new base in the former AW Braunschweig. The new contract starts in December 2015 for 10 years.

MINDENER KREISBAHN GmbH   MKB

Minden, Nordrhein-Westfalen.

EVU Licence: Freight & Passenger, 18/06/1996–31/12/2038.
Routes: Minden–Aminghausen 2.0 km; Minden–Hille–Hille Hafen Süd 15.2 km; Minden–Kleinenbremen 11.7 km; Minden–Todtenhausen 8.7 km. Also sidings in Minden to Abstiegshafen 1.3 km, Osthafen 2.5 km and Westhafen 1.0 km.
Length: 45.5 km.
Depot: Minden.

The MKB has been freight only since 1974 but passenger trains run on certain weekends over part of the system operated by the Museums Eisenbahn Minden organisation, often using steam traction. Freight traffic on its own network is now mostly on the dock lines and sidings around Minden. Open access has allowed expansion with container trains going to Bremerhaven, whilst there are chemical trains to other destinations. MKB is part owner of the Westfalenbahn and for the 2015 expansion of Westfalenbahn a new EMU depot is being built on MKB land at Minden.

MITTELDEUTSCHE EISENBAHN GESELLSCHAFT   MEG

Schkopau, Sachsen-Anhalt.

EVU Licence: Freight & Passenger, 12/03/2014–11/03/2029.
Routes: Chemical works complexes at Schkopau and Böhlen; Köthen–Aken and has nationwide operating licence.
Length: 110 km.
Depots: Schkopau.

Previously the railway operation of Buna AG/Chemische Werke Buna AG, the Buna works was part of a large complex of chemical and petro-chemical plants in the Merseburg area. The privatisation of state concerns in the former East Germany saw the internal rail system being set up as an independent operation as a subsidiary of DB Cargo, now DB Schenker! The company is owned by DB Schenker (80%) and Transpetrol GmbH (20%). The smaller MEG locos are used for local trip workings whilst the larger diesel and electric locomotives are on main line duties. In some cases MEG oprerates former DBS services with former DBS locos at a cheaper cost than DBS! Thus MEG can be found working trains that have nothing to do with chemicals (e.g. timber, cars and cement!). Some withdrawn locos have been loaned out to preservation groups but are still owned by MEG. MEG is conducting trials with some of the Alstom battery elctric locomotives for a few years.

MITTELWESERBAHN Gmbh   MWB

Bruchhausen-Vilsen, Niedersachsen.
EVU Licence: Freight & Passenger, 18/10/1999–18/10/2014.
Routes: Nationwide.
Traction: Eight Köf, four V60C, five V100DR, five V100DB, four 140, five G1206, three G1700, two 182, three DE502, plus about seven hired in electric locos from SBB Cargo.
Depot: Bremervörde.

The German preservation society, Deutsche Eisenbahn Verein (DEV), has a narrow gauge line at Bruchhausen Vilsen but also had a standard gauge operation from Hoya. To fall in line with current legislation it formed itself into a proper operating company as an EVU. It soon realised that there was work for its standard gauge shunting locomotives. More work meant the foundation of a separate operating company – MWB. Since then it has gone from strength to strength, the traction figures telling their own story. In 2010 a great change took place when MWB was bought out by another local company – Eisenbahn und Verkehrsbetriebe Elbe-Weser Gmbh (EVB – q.v.). The MWB thus has access to the modern EVB depot whilst EVB for its part has moved its operating staff to work with MWB staff at Bruchhausen Vilsen. Traffic handled is considerable, moving intermodal traffic from coastal and inland ports; wagonload services are offered in co-operation with other EVUs and naturally enough there is infrastructure work which has been a staple traffic from the early days. It owns two electric locos (182s) but hires in many others (It also owns former ÖBB 1020 041 but this is now in need of an overhaul). It is expected that within a year or so MWB will disappear and be fully absorbed into EVB.

MULDENTAL-EISENBAHNVERKEHRSGESELLSCHAFT mbH
MTEG

Meerane, Sachsen.
EVU Licence: Freight & Passenger, 19/01/2001–19/01/2016.
Traction: One V60D, four V100DR, one 189 and the use of preserved 142 001!
Depot: Glauchau.

Founded in 2001 this company has its roots in the 58 3047 preservation group based in Glauchau – another example of railfans grasping the opportunities offered by open access. Staple traffic to start with was infrastructure work but there are now main line trains moving traffic from the Czech Republic (e.g. car trains) and providing shunting and tripping locomotives at various terminals.

MÜLHEIMER VERKEHRSGESELLSCHAFT mbH   MVG

Mülheim/Ruhr, Nordrhein-Westfalen.
EVU Licence: Freight, 05/11/2003–30/11/2018.
Traction: One DHG70C for shunting and up to two hired in trip locos e.g. G1206.

This company services the harbour lines at Mülheim and trips to Ruhr area yards as required.

NAHVERKEHRS SCHLESWIG-HOLSTEIN

Schleswig-Holstein is another land that has set up its own leasing company - Landesverkehrsgesellschaft Schleswig Holstein. Ahead of contracts being placed it has ordered 15 Class 245 multi-engined diesels from Bombardier which will be used on the Hamburg–Westerland route by whichever operator is awarded the contract. This takes effect from December 2015 for 19 years but no announcement has yet been made regarding a new operator.

NATIONAL EXPRESS RAIL GmbH   NXG

Köln, Nordrhein-Westfalen.

EVU Licence: Passenger, 27/05/2013–31/05/2028.
Depot: None; NXG has done a deal with DB for DB to maintain its trains at Düsseldorf, Krefeld and Münster, saving 50 DB Regio jobs!

NXG stands for National Express Group which won the contract in 2013 for two routes in the Ruhr starting in December 2015. These are the Rhein-Münsterland Express (RE7 Rheine–Köln–Krefeld) and the Rhein–Wupper-Bahn (RB48 Bonn–Wuppertal). For these lines 35 Talent 2 EMUs were ordered and the first sets started appearing in mid-2014. National Express is understood to own the Class 403 "Donald Duck" set for use on upmarket excursion trains and has also obtained two Class 113 electric locos so there must be more plans in the pipeline.

As this book went to press it was announced that National Express Rail had won the contract to run the Nürnberg S-Bahn routes for 12 years and would be ordering 38 5-car Regio Panther EMUs from Skoda! Yet another new type for Germany! However, DB Regio has contested the award; a decision is expected during summer 2015.

▲ Many redundant DB Class 212 locos were overhauled at Stendal works prior to commencing a new life with private operators. NBE Rail 92 80 1212 058 is just such an example, resplendent in ex-works condition outside Stendal works on 30 September 2011. Sadly things did not work out so well at NBE and the loco subsequently passed to Metrans Rail Deutschland (MTRD).   **David Hunt**

NBE GROUP GmbH & Co. KG
NBE LOGISTIK GmbH
NBE RAIL GmbH   NBEG

Obernburg & Aschaffenburg, Bayern.

EVU Licence: Freight & Passenger, 15/07/2002–01/08/2017 (NBE Rail); 13/01/2012–31/01/2027 (NBE Logistik).
Traction: 14 V100DB, four V100DR, three V60C, four 225 and two 232.
Depot: Aschaffenburg.

These three companies are all tied in with each other. Nordbayerische Eisenbahn was founded in 2002 and grew rapidly. Because of its size the management decided on a restructuring. There is now a holding company NBE Group and several subsidiary companies of which the two mentioned above deal with the traffic (NBE Logistik) and locomotives (NBE Rail). In effect the last mentioned acts as a leasing company, leasing out locomotives not only to NBE Logistik but to any other company. Traffic handled began with infrastructure trains and now includes block train movements of new cars on a spot basis. Some of the infrastruture trains are no longer local ballast trains but long distance movements of track ballast and sleepers. In 2012 yet another company was formed, NBE Regio being aimed at passenger train contracts which now include Städtebahn Sachsen. It did not stop there as further organisations were established under the NBE umbrella e.g. Rail Time and Rail Time Logistics. However, by mid-2014 it looks as if the company had over-stretched itself and became insolvent. Further separate companies were set up as the owners established Sonata Logistics GmbH and Sonata Rail GmbH, with some of the NBEG locomotives moving to these new companies. Others have been snapped up by other operators.

NEB BETRIEBSGESELLSCHAFT mbH   NEBB

Berlin/Brandenburg.

EVU Licence: Freight & Passenger, 24/03/2005–31/03/2020.
Routes: (Berlin Gesundbrunnen)–Berlin Karow–Basdorf–Gross Schönebeck/Schmachtenhagen; RB 35 Fürtenwalde–Bad Saarow Klinikim; RB 36 Könings Wusterhausen–Beeskow–Frankfurt/Oder; RB 60 Eberswalde–Frankfurt/Oder; RB 61 Schwedt–Angermünde/Prenzlau: RB 63 Eberswalde–Joachimsthal; RB 25 Berlin Lichtenberg–Werneuchen; RB 26 Berlin Lictenberg–Kostrzyn (PL). From December 2015 NEBB takes over from DB, RB 12 Berlin–Templin and RB 54 Berlin–Rheinsberg.
Traction: 10 3-car Talent DMUs and 15 Class 650 DMUs (more units expected in 2015).
Depots: Basdorf.

NEB stands for the Niederbarminer Eisenbahn which today is the infrastructure company and NEBB is the operating company. Besides working over its old home line, in 2006 it obtained the contract to run the Kostrzyn service from Berlin Lichtenberg. Recently two new contracts have been obtained. The first started in December 2014 for ten years for services in part of the "Ostbrandenburg Netz" (R35, R36, R61, R63), some of which have been taken over from ODEG. A year later further services will be taken over (R12, R25, R54) whilst the existing service to Kostrzyn will be retained as part of this group. New Regio Shuttles are intended for the first group of services but in a big surprise move 9 PESA LINK DMUs have been ordered from Poland (this may be a clever ruse as there is talk of the Kostrzyn service being extended further into Poland to Gorzów(Wkp)). These are expected during 2015 allowing a cascade of sets from the December timetable. NEBB units also work from Basdorf into Berlin Gesundbrunnen in the peak hours. This service started as a temporary measure during the S-Bahn crisis of 2009 and has been kept going because of passenger demand.

NEG NORDDEUTSCHE EISENBAHNGESELLSCHAFT NIEBÜLL
GmbH   NEG

Niebüll, Schleswig-Holstein.

EVU Licence: Freight & Passenger 12/03/2004–31/12/2019.
Routes: Niebüll–Dagebüll Hafen.
Length: 26.6 km.
Traction: One V100DB and two DMUs.
Depot: Niebüll.

This company is in effect the old NVAG company which became insolvent in 2003 and was taken over by NEG in 2004. NEG itself was taken over by Luxembourg Railways (CFL) in 2005, the freight arm becoming CFL Cargo Deutschland and the passenger arm NEG Niebüll. Passenger traffic remains as before with DMUs covering the basic service and at times also hauling through IC coaches to Dagebüll harbour.

NESA EISENBAHN-BETRIEBS GESELLSCHAFT NECKAR–
SCHWARZWALD–ALB mbH   NESA

Rottweil, Baden-Württemberg.

EVU Licence: Freight & Passenger, 29/04/1999–30/06/2016.
Depot: Rottweil.
Traction: One 312 and two V100DB.

This company is the operating arm of the preservation group Eisenbahnfreunde Zollernbahn (EFZ). The locos are used on EFZ specials as required but otherwise find use on spot hire contracts in southern Germany.

NEUKÖLLN–MITTENWALDER EISENBAHN-GESELLSCHAFT
NME

Berlin.

EVU Licence: Freight & Passenger, 25/09/90–24/09/2050.
Routes: Berlin Neukölln–Berlin Teltowkanal–Berlin-Britz–Berlin-Rudow Nord.
Length: 8.9 km.
Traction: One M500C, one M700C, one DHG700C and one RC43C.
Depot: Teltowkanal.

This private railway has quietly existed in West Berlin but lost part of its line in the east when the Berlin wall went up. It continued to serve various industrial locations. Traffic includes household waste and oil to a storage site.

NEUSS-DÜSSELDORFER HÄFEN GmbH & Co.KG.
NEUSSER EISENBAHN   NE

Neuss, Nordrhein-Westfalen.

EVU Licence: Freight, 11/03/2004–31/03/2019.
Routes: Various lines in and around Neuss and Düsseldorf including the harbour lines totalling over 100 km.
Traction: One DG1000BBM, three G761C, three G1205, one G1300, one G1700, one G2000, two 145, one 185 and one Kof augmented as required by hired in locos.
Depot: Neuss (Heerdterbuschstrasse).

The principal work of this railway is as its title suggests, servicing the Neuss and Düsseldorf harbour lines for which it is also the EIU. Open access means that coal from the harbours can be taken directly by rail to power stations. Some last mile work is also done in connection with other operators. In 2012 the main company, jointly with Hafen und Güterverkehr Köln (HGK), formed a new company RheinCargo GmbH & Co. KG (RHC).

NIEDERRHEINISCHE VERKEHRSBETRIEBE AG NIAG

Moers, Nordrhein-Westfalen.

EVU Licence: Freight & Passenger, 17/11/1995–31/12/2060.
Routes: Moers–Hoerstgen–Sevelen (20 km); Moers–Rheinberg–Millingen (17 km).
Length: 37 km.
Traction: One G1205, two G1206, three G1700, one DH 1004, two DH 1504, one ME26, one 145, one D25B and one Kof.
Depot: Moers.

NIAG is another predominately harbour railway with very heavy traffic handling some 3.7 million tonnes a year, mostly ore and coal. In 2013/14 NIAG handlled some 6 million tonnes of imported coal, distributing it to power stations in the Ruhr area and even further afield for which some electric locomotives were hired in. The principal owners are now believed to be Rhenus Keolis (51%) and Kreis Wesel (43%). The following two internal use locomotives do not fit into the national numbering system.

No.	Builder, No. & Year	Type	kW	Details	Comments
50	Wind 260149/1998	RW	240	DH	Teletrac at Hafen Orsoy
51	Wind 260184/1999	RW	240	DH	Teletrac at Hafen Orsoy

NORD-OSTSEE-BAHN Gmbh NOB

Kiel, Schleswig-Holstein.

EVU Licence: Freight & Passenger, 19/04/2002–19/04/2017.
Routes: Hamburg (Altona)–Westerland regional services, including Itzehoe–Heide stopping services.
Traction: Four LINT 41H and one Talent DMUs, three ER20 with 5 more leased from MRCE and seven ME26 leased from Vossloh.
Depot: Husum (Veolia depot).

NOB is a Veolia company and has changed over the years since being founded in 2009. It no longer serves Kiel and now concentrates on the "Marschbahn" services to Westerland.

NORDBAHN EISENBAHNGESELLSCHAFT mbH NBE

Kaltenkirchen, Schleswig-Holstein.

EVU Licence: Passenger, 10/12/2002–15/12/2017.
Routes: Bad Oldesloe–Neumünster. From December 2014 extra routes – see below.
Traction: Seven LINT 41 DMUs and eight 6-car and seven 5-car FLIRT EMUs.
Depot: Neumünster Süd/AKN, Hamburg-Tiefsack.

Founded in 2002 this company was then a joint venture between HHA 50% and AKN 50%, but now Benex has replaced HHA. It won the contract for services between Bad Oldesloe and Neumünster for 10 years and recently has had this renewed for another 10 years running through to 2021/22. Another contract started in December 2014 covering services RB 61, Itzehoe to Hamburg Hbf. and RB 71, Wrist/Itzehoe to Hamburg Altona, for which seven 5-car and eight 6-car new FLIRT EMUs have been ordered from Stadler. A new depot is to be established at Hamburg-Tiefsack to service these.

NORDIC RAIL SERVICE GmbH NRS

Lübeck, Schleswig-Holstein.

EVU Licence: Freight & Passenger, 19/07/2004–31/12/2019.
Traction: Two V100DR, one ER20 and one Kof.

Founded in 2004, NRS is a subsidiary of LHG Service Gesellschaft mbH (LHG=Lübecker Hafen Gesellschaft). Originally carrying out wagon repairs it branched out into tripping traffic from Lübeck to the then start of the electrified network in Hamburg. With the extension of electrification this opportunity disappeared, but NRS continues to shunt and trip around the harbour complex and takes advantage of any spot traffic that comes its way.

NORDWESTBAHN GmbH   NWB

Osnabrück, Niedersachsen.

EVU Licence: Freight & Passenger, 10/12/1999–10/12/2029.
Routes: Osnabrück–Wilhelmshafen (170.1 km); Sande–Esens (33.7 km); Hespe–Delmenhorst (–Bremen), (88.4 km); Bremen S-Bahn routes.
Traction: 42 643, 85 648 and 35 440 (17 5-car, 18-3-car).
Depots: Osnabrück Hafen, Dorsten, Bremerhaven-Wulsdorf.

On foundation, the Nordwestbahn was 74% owned by the DEG and 26% by Stadtwerke Osnabrück. DEG subsequently became Connex and later Veolia. It started by winning a contract for services in the Osnabrück area hence the name Nordwestbahn. In 2002 NWB together with TWE won the contract to operate local services from Münster to Bielefeld, Bielefeld to Paderborn, Bielefeld to Altenbeken and Paderborn to Holzminden. 28 3-car Talent DMUs were ordered for these services.

In 2005 it was announced that NWB had won the franchise for the Emscher–Münsterland Netz RE 14 Borken–Dorsten–Essen Hbf, RB 43 Dortmund–Castrop Rauxel–Dortsten and RB 45 Dorsten–Coesfeld, to operate December 2006–December 2018 (except for RB 43 which would only run to December 2008). A new depot was built at Dorsten. Seven further Talent DMUs were ordered.

2008 was a good year for Veolia winning two new contracts. In January it was awarded the contract for the "Niers–Rhein–Emscher Netz" taking over RE 10 and RB 31 from DB and RB 36, RB 44 services from PEG. Then in April 2008 it obtained the contract to run the Bremen S-Bahn services for which 35 Coradia Continental EMUs were acquired. A new depot has been built at Bremerhaven-Wulsdorf. The S-Bahn contract saw passenger services restored to the Farge–Vegesacker route.

More success followed, winning the "Weser Lammental Bahn" RB 77 (2011–2021) and "Diesel Netz Ostwestfalen" (Süd) which includes RB 74, RB 75, RB 84, RB 85 in the Bielefeld/Paderborn/ Osnabrück areas. This contract runs 2013–2025.

NordWestBahn does not own the rolling stock; all of it is leased mostly from Niedersachsen Land which formed its own leasing company (LNVG). Note that that most rolling stock has been built by Alstom in Salzgitter (in Niedersachsen!). There are now over 150 units with NWB and a staff of over 700. Routes covered total over 1000 km.

In 2014 NWB had its contract renewed for services on the Weser Ems Netzes, these being the diesel services from Osnabrück and Bremen to Wilhelmshaven etc. mentioned above.

ORTENAU S-BAHN   OSB

Offenburg, Baden-Württemberg.

EVU Licence: Passenger, 19/11/1997–30/11/2027.
Routes: Offenburg–Hausach–Freudenstadt (63.2 km); Offenburg–Kehl (–Strasbourg) (21.9 km); Offenburg–Oberkirch–Bad Griesbach (37.2 km). All these routes were previously operated by DB. OSB also covers the passenger services on two other routes which are SWEG owned: Achern–Ottenhöfen (10.4 km); Bieberach–Oberharmersbach-Riersbach (10.6 km).
Depot: Ottenhofen. Some maintenance and stabling at Offenburg (DB).

The Ortenau S-Bahn is one of several companies run by Südwestdeutche Verkehrs AG (SWEG q.v.). It was formed at the beginning of the regionalisation process and was awarded the contract for local services around Offenburg. New air-conditioned Regio-Shuttles were ordered being flavour of the month then. Later the contract to run the trains between Hausach and Freundenstadt was obtained so six more RS1s were ordered. The company continues to provide these services and there have been considerable increases in traffic. Its contracts expired at the end of 2014 and SWEG won the renewed contract under its own name so it is possible that the Ortenau S-Bahn is no longer a company in its own right. The VKM is SWEG whilst OSB was the official abbreviation for the subsidiary company.

OSTDEUTSCHE EISENBAHN Gmbh   ODEG

Parchim, Mecklenburg-Vorpommern.
EVU Licence: Freight & Passenger, 02/12/2002–31/12/2017.
Length: 175 km initially.
Traction: 16 445, six 642, six 646 and 36 650.
Depots: Eberswalde, Parchim, Görlitz.

Founded in 2002 as a joint venture between Hamburger Hochbahn AG (HHA) and Pregnitzer Esienbahn GmbH (PEG) to operate several lines in the former DDR. HHA was later replaced by BeNEX Gmbh. Starting off in 2002, ODEG operated the service from Neustrelitz to Hagenow Land and Neustrelitz Süd to Mirow. In 2004 ODEG started operating the Ostbrandenburg-Netz services as follows: OE 25 Berlin Lichtenberg–Tiefensee; OE36 Berlin Lichtenberg–Königs Wusterhausen–Beeskow–Frankfurt/Oder; OE 60 Berlin Lichtenberg–Eberswalde–Frankfurt/Oder; OE 63 Eberswalde–Templin. Some of these routes were lost to NEBB in December 2014. On 19/01/2005 ODEG formed a subsidiary company, Ostdeutsche Instandhaltungsgesellschaft mbH (ODIG), which now runs the depots as a separate organisation. December 2007 saw ODEG take over Fürstenwalde–Bad Saarow–Pieskow for a short period of two years.

On 08/12/2006 ODEG won the ZVON contract for the Spree Neisse Netz lines as follows: Cottbus–Forst; Bischofswerda–Görlitz; Hoyerswerda–Görlitz; Cottbus–Görlitz–Zittau. This contract runs from December 2008 for ten years. Six new Desiros and five Regio Shuttles were ordered for these lines.

Success continued with ODEG beating DB for the contract to run what is now OEX 2 Wismar–Berlin–Cottbus and OEX 4 Stendal–Berlin–Jüterbog, for which double deck KISS EMUs of Class 445 were ordered from Stadler. ODEG then replaced Veolia on the Berlin-Wannsee–Jüterbog route and had its contract for service OE 25 from Berlin Lichtenberg renewed for a further three years. ODEG is also to operate the Stendal–Rathenow–Brandenburg/Berlin-Wannsee service in 2015.

OSTHANNOVERSCHE EISENBAHNEN AG   OHE
OHE CARGO Gmbh   OHEGO

Celle, Niedersachsen.
EVU Licence: Freight & Passenger, 23/10/1995–22/10/2025 (OHE); 23/07/2012–22/07/2027 (OHEGO).
Routes: Celle–Soltau (58.9 km); Celle–Wittingen-Ruhen (85.7 km); Beckedorf–Munster (Örtze) (23.9 km); Beedenbostel–Mariaglück (5.6 km); Soltau–Neunkirchen (12.0 km); Lüneburg–Soltau (57.1 km); Winsen–Hutzel (41.1 km); Winsen–Niedermarschact (18.1 km); Lüneburg–Bleckede (23.8 km).
Length: 333.1 km
Traction: One DG1200BBM, two G1202BB, two G1204BB, three G1600BB, four G2000BB, three 216, one 250, three ER20, three 185, 1 DMU and 6 shunting locos.
Depots: Bleckede (workshops), Celle, Lüneburg.

The OHE is a collection of eight former private railways grouped together, now with headquarters in Celle. Total track distance is over 300 km with some really long branches e.g. Celle–Soltau and Celle–Wittingen. On 01/03/2000 OHE took over operation of the Steinhuder Meer Bahn (StMB). In recent years the change to open access has seen OHE working more and more trains from its system over DB.

Late in 2006 OHE was purchased by Arriva Bachstein GmbH with effect from 01/01/2007. Arriva Deutschland GmbH owns 86% and VB Bachstein GmbH 14%. Arriva later became NETINERA. OHE set up a subsidiary company to run passenger services on the "Heide-Kreuz" routes which is marketed as "Erixx" (q.v.) and has enlarged its operation now with some routes from Braunschweig. Later, for the freight side of the business, OHE Cargo was formed.

▲ Ostdeutsche Eisenbahn operates a growing network of services in the former DDR and became the first private operator to order double-deck EMUs from Stadler, for some of its Berlin routes. 94 80 0445 112, running number ET445.112 is seen arriving at Berlin Ostbahnhof with a Schwerin–Cottbus service on 19 October 2014. **Matthias Müller**

▼ 92 80 1247 901 is one of three prototype diesel Vectron locomotives usually based at Siemens test circuit at Wegberg-Wildenrath. It is seen with a special comprised mainly of TEE stock between Linz (Rhein) and Erpel in the early evening of 18 October 2013. **Matthias Müller**

PBG PREUSSEN BAHN GmbH   PREU

Dresden, Sachsen.

EVU Licence: Freight, 01/03/2005–31/12/2019.
Traction: One hired in 185.

Founded in 2009 this small company took over the operating licence of another firm. It is a 100% subsidiary of Emons Spedition GmbH which uses it to work an intermodal train between Dresden and Hamburg.

PCT PRIVATE CAR TRAIN GmbH   PCT

Wolnzach, Bayern.

EVU Licence: Freight, 09/09/2002–01/08/2017.
Traction: One diesel shunter and five ER20 with up to 10 or more electric locos hired in as required.

This company, founded in 2002, is a 100% subsidiary of ARS Altmann which is a well established company transporting newly built cars around the country. Most traffic is carried on behalf of ARS Altmann, which in 2011 created a car train hub at Bremen Rangierbahnhof utilising spare capacity following DB's withdrawal from wagon load traffic. Car trains from within Germany and other countries come to Bremen with portions for other ports such as Hamburg and Bremerhaven which get sorted and made into outgoing train loads. PCT only has a few of its own locos but leases various diesels for shunting and tripping duties and some 185s for main line work.

POWER RAIL GmbH   POWER

Magdeburg, Sachsen-Anhalt.

EVU Licence: Freight & Passenger, 26/05/2007–21/05/2022.
Traction: One V60D and two ex-CFL 1800.

This small firm is involved with infrastructure trains around Magdeburg.

PRIGNITZER EISENBAHN GmbH   PEG

Putlitz, Brandenburg.

EVU Licence: Freight & Passenger, 27/08/2010–31/12/2025.
Traction: Six 643 (Some already sold off or leased to other operators).

How the mighty are fallen! Ten years ago PEG was one of the largest private operators in the area of the former DDR, but contracts obtained then have expired and no new ones have come along. The freight arm was separated into PEG Cargo which then became EGP (q.v.). The passenger arm was taken over by Arriva which is now NETINERA. Today PEG is fully owned by NETINERA but still has a 50% interest in ODEG.

PRÜF- UND VALIDATIONCENTER WEGBERG-WILDENRATH DER SIEMENS AG RAIL SYSTEMS   PCW

Wegberg-Wildenrath, Nordrhein-Westfalen.

EVU Licence: Freight, 06/11/1999–30/11/2014.
Traction: 4 miscellaneous shunting locos, one ER20 and one 127.

Siemens, for its test centre at Wegberg-Wildenrath, formed its own operating company for the purpose of moving new locomotives and rolling stock from production centres to the testing centre. Basically there are just two main line locomotives for this purpose; the other locomotives are used for shunting and positioning trains at the testing centre.

RAILADVENTURE GmbH RADVE

München, Bayern.

EVU Licence: Freight & Passenger 11/10/2010–11/10/2025.
Traction: One 103 and one 139.

A small company specialising in transport of rolling stock – deliveries from production centres to final customer etc.

RAILDOX GmbH & Co KG RDX

Erfurt, Thüringen.

EVU Licence: Freight & Passenger, 09/07/2008–11/07/2023.
Traction: One 185, one 232 plus hired in 182s from Hupac and other locomotives as required.

Founded in 2005 by a former DB driver who saw that he could do better by organising drivers for private operators and getting his family involved as shareholders. After providing drivers its own EVU licence allowed movement of trains on its own behalf. Locomotives were hired in at first but now it owns a 185 and a 232. Various block trains are worked in Germany, some on behalf of the Austrian firm Salzburger Eisenbahn TransportLogistik GmbH.

RAILFLEX GmbH RF

Ratingen, Nordrhein-Westfalen.

EVU Licence: Freight & Passenger, 23/03/2007–31/03/2022.
Traction: One V100DB plus another hired in from Bochum Dahlhausen museum as required.

A small company located in the Ruhr which has obtained a traffic flow of pulversied coal on behalf of the Chemion concern. It also operates special passenger trains as required.

RAILSYSTEMS RP GmbH RPRS

Hörselberg, Thüringen.

EVU Licence: Freight, 24/04/2012–27/04/2027.
Traction: Eight V60C, three 107 (former DR classification), six V90, one 703 and three 711.

The owner of this company used to be involved in several others such as Adam/MaLowa/Lotrac before deciding to go his own way by forming Railpool Railsystems, later changing it to simply Railsystems but note the VKM remains as RPRS. The firm is growing and has leased the former DB depot in Gotha. The loco fleet has been growing continuously with the main work being infrastructure trains for which OHLE maintenance vehicles have also been obtained.

RAPHAEL HOFMANN GÜTERVERKEHR RHG

This operator came to notice in 2014 and seems to be based in St. Wendel so no doubt some work in the Saar is envisaged. Only one locomotive has come to note.

RBH LOGISTICS GmbH   RBH

Gladbeck, Nordrhein-Westfalen.

EVU Licence: Freight & Passenger, 03/05/2001–30/11/2018.
Traction: 13 E1200, five 140, 30 143, two 145, 16 151, 14 M700C, nine DE501/2, three DHG 1200, five G1204, 24 G1206 and four G2000. (125 total).
Depots: Gladbeck, Dortmund-Mooskamp, Werne.

This company has changed its name several times in recent years as open access came along and the coal industry shrank. Until the turn of the century most people will have known the company by its then initials – RAG – once standing for Ruhrkohle AG. The initials were kept but the company name became RAG Bahn und Hafenbetrieb. Then on 01/10/2004 the railway activities became RBH – RAG Bahn und Hafen GmbH. A big change in 2006 saw the company taken over by DB Railion so it is owned today by DB Schenker which has drafted in many of its own locomotives. On 01/12/2006 the name was changed once again becoming RBH Logistics GmbH where R=Rail, B= Barge and H = Harbour! Most of the coal mines in the Ruhr area are now closed but much is imported through harbours in the area. RBH is deeply involved in moving this coal to power stations in the area and further afield. There is also considerable involvement in oil and chemical block train movements. This explains the acquisition of many former DB main line locomotives. As colleries etc in the Ruhr area reduce, the fleet of smaller locomotives will reduce as well. DB Schenker has now closed the old RAG workshops at Gladbeck and scrapped many surplus locomotives. Maintenance of RBH locos is now carried out at DB Oberhausen Osterfeld Süd depot.

REGENTAL BAHNBETRIEBS GmbH   RBG

Viechtach, Bayern.

EVU Licence: Freight & Passenger, 22/12/1994–31/12/2025.
Routes: See below.
Traction: One Esslingen, two Waggon Union (NE 81) and 25 650 DMUs.
Depots: Viechtach, Lam, Schwandorf, Zwiesel.

Formerly RAG (Regentalbahn AG), the RBG is a much changed organisation with its main operations now being over former DB lines. In 2006 it was taken over by Arriva Deutschland but when Arriva became owned by DB the rail parts in Germany had to be sold off and today NETINERA is the owner, itself part owned by Ferrovie della Stato (FS)!

Besides operating over its own lines RBG has obtained contracts to operate other services. It has operated the "Oberpfalzbahn" since 2001 and has recently had the contract renewed from December 2014 (Schwandorf–Furth im Wald and former RAG lines). Some new "LINK" DMUs have been delivered from PESA (Poland) for this service but at the time of writing these units have not yet been cleared for operation in Germany. It has also operated the "Waldbahn" (Plattling–Bayerische Eisenstein) since 1997 as subcontractor to DB Regio and from December 2013 this contract was renewed but now as a direct contract from Bayern. The same contract (Regionalzüge Ostbayern) also includes Regensburg–Schwandorf–Marktredwitz. The depot at Zwiesel is being modernised/enlarged.

REGIOBAHN BITTERFELD BERLIN GmbH   RBB

Bitterfeld-Wolfen, Sachsen-Anhalt.

EVU Licence: Freight & Passenger, 25/04/1996–20/04/2026.
Depot: Bitterfeld-Wolfen.
Traction: Two 312, one V60D, one V100DB and two G1300BB plus other locos from the Captrain pool.

Founded in 1995 this company grew out of the chemical complex around Bitterfeld and became part of the DEG group which later became Connex, then Veolia and now the company is owned by Captrain. In 2005 Regiobahn Bitterfeld combined with Rail Cargo Berlin, hence the current name and initials. Captrain also took over the former rail4chem and passed on to RBB some of the traffic flows. The smaller locos are still involved in internal traffic in the chemical complex whilst the larger locos and the pool locos undertake the long haul work.

REGIOBAHN FAHRBETRIEBSGESELLSCHAFT mbH   REGIO

Mettmann, Nordrhein-Westfalen.

EVU Licence: Passenger, 01/02/2006–28/02/2021.
Traction: 12 2-car Talent DMUs.
Depot: Mettmann.

Founded in 1992, Regiobahn has operated the local service from Kaarst to Mettmann since 25/09/1999. Kaarst–Neuss and Düsseldorf-Gerresheim–Mettmann are over its own tracks but other sections traverse DB lines. Eight 2-car Talent DMUs started off the service but traffic soon increased by 50%, so much so that the service interval was improved and four more units were obtained. In 2011 the rolling stock and operation was transferred from the founding company, this now being the infrastructure company.

REGIO INFRA SERVICE SACHSEN GmbH   RIS

Chemnitz, Sachsen.

EVU Licence: Freight & Passenger, 06/12/2006–31/10/2021.
Traction: One V100DR and one V60D.
Depot: Chemnitz.

This company was established in 2001 to take over the infrastructure on routes around Chemnitz in preparation for City Bahn Chemnitz. It is now responsible for Stolberg–Alt Chemnitz–Chemnitz Süd, Stolberg–St. Egidien, Hainchen–Niederwiesa and Nossen–Freiberg. Whilst it is mainly an infrastructure undertaking it does use its locomotives for freight traffic over its own infrastructure as well as snow plough trains in winter.

REGIONALBAHN KASSEL GmbH   RBK

Kassel, Hessen.

EVU Licence: Passenger, 26/02/1998–29/02/2028.
Traction: 28 Regio Citadis trams (see below).
Depots: DB Regio Kassel Hbf, KVG Kassel Sandershäuser Strasse.

Regionalbahn Kassel was formed in 1990 to improve local services around Kassel, being a joint venture between Hessische Landesbahn and Kasseler Verkehrsbetrieb GmbH. Later the RBK, then jointly with DB, decided to go for a Karlsruhe type tram system in the Kassel area so a new section of tramway was built linking into the DB terminal station at Kassel Hbf. A prototype system started operating in 2001 on the DB tracks using several trams from the Saarbahn. In 2004 an order was placed with Alstom for 28 Regio Trams of the type Regio Citadis. However, for Kassel there was a different requirement as some diesel-powered vehicles were needed for non-electrified sections. So two types were ordered. 701–718 are Class 452 and are dual-voltage vehicles running on 750V dc and 15 kV ac. 751–760 are Class 689 and are electro-diesel vehicles for the non electrified sections. A subsidiary company has now been formed (Regio Tram Betriebsgesellsschaft) to operate the service, leasing the trams from the parent company. DB Regio owns 51% of this company and RBK the remaining 49%.

The various routes are as follows (RT= RegioTram): RT 3 Kassel–Warburg; RT 4 (Electro-diesel) Kassel–Wolfhagen; RT 5 Kassel–Melsungen; RT 9 Kassel–Treysa. RT9 is transferring to HLB operation in 2015.

REGIONALVERKEHR MÜNSTERLAND GmbH   RVM

Münster, Nordrhein-Westfalen.

EVU Licence: Freight, 31/12/1986–31/12/2031.
Routes: Own tracks Rheine-Altenrheine–Mettingen–Osnabrück-Eversburg (–Osnabrück Rbf); over DB Rheine–Spelle.
Traction: Two DG1200BBM and one G1600BB.
Depot: Rheine Stadtberg.

RVM is the modern day successor to the old Tecklenburger Nordbahn. It is under threat of closure over its old route although still seems to be busy at the Rheine end serving a concrete plant and other local industries.

REGIONALVERKEHR RUHR-LIPPE GmbH   RLG

Soest, Nordrhein-Westfalen.

EVU Licence: Freight, 31/12/1987–31/12/2038.
Routes: Hamm RLG–Vellingshausen; Soest–Soest Süd; Arnsberg–Neheim-Hüsten–Sundern.
Traction: One G1206 and one DG1200BBM.
Depots: Hamm RLG, Neheim-Hüsten.

The RLG was only founded in 1979 but actually goes back further being a name change for what was the Ruhr Lippe Eisenbahn (RLE) with some bits added, not to mention the incorporation of local bus services into the company. Traffic over its own lines has all but disappeared but open access means that it is still in business moving traffic for local customers to and from the Ruhr area.

RENNSTEIGBAHN GmbH & Co KG   RSBG

Stützerbach, Thüringen.

EVU Licence: Freight & Passenger, 17/11/2003–17/11/2018.
Traction: Two V100DB and one 228.

This is an enthusiasts' organisation turned railway operator. It is the EIU for the Ilmenau–Schleusingen–Themar line and has a nationwide open access EVU licence. In effect it is the operating arm of the Verein Dampflokfreunde Mittlerer Rennsteig e.V. It has been successful in obtaining traffic in connection with the timber industry, most of which seems to be spot traffic.

RHEIN-SIEG VERKEHRSGESELLSCHAFT mbH   RSVG

Troisdorf, Nordrhein-Westfalen.

EVU Licence: Freight & Passenger, 29/02/1996–30/09/2021.
Routes: Troisdorf West–Lülsdorf.
Traction: Two G700C.
Depot: Troisdorf-Sieglar.

A freight only line with an interesting street running section in Sieglar which is the reason why locos are fitted with yellow flashing lights!

RHEINCARGO GmbH & Co KG   RHC

Neuss, Nordrhein-Westfalen.

EVU Licence: Freight, 08/08/2012–31/08/2027.
Traction: See HGK and NE.

This is a new company founded in 2012 as a marketing arm for Häfen und Güterverkehr Köln and Neuss-Düsseldorfer Häfen to obtain traffic and make the best use of their combined resources. Quite a few HGK locos are now to be seen carrying RHC as the VKM. Possibly in due course the two companies will be merged as one.

RHEINISCHE EISENBAHN GmbH   RE

Linz/Rhein, Nordrhein-Westfalen.

Traction: Two V100DB, one V60C and one Köf.

Founded in 2002 as a joint venture with the Brohltalbahn, the company today is a 100% subsidiary of Eifelbahn Verkehrsgesellschaft mbH which holds the EVU Licence. Once there was infrastructure work but now it appears that it tends to just act as a leasing company for its four locos.

RHENUS RAIL ST. INGBERT GmbH   RRI

St. Ingbert, Saarland.

EVU Licence: Freight & Passenger, 04/12/1996–31/12//2026.
Traction: 14 diesel shunters of various types, three V100DB, two V100DR and two G1206.
Depots: Homburg, Worms.

A new name but an old company. Going back some years there was once Saarbergwerke and from that came Unisped Spedition und Transportgesellschaft mbh (USS) in 2006. That in turn was taken over by Wincanton Rail GmbH in 2006 and to bring things up to date Wincanton itself was bought out by the present company in 2012. Traffic connected with the steel industry remains important but the company also works the harbour lines in Worms and being based in the Saar deals with various flows to and from France not necessarily connected with steel (e.g. Volvic mineral water), in some cases just providing a driver and not necessarily a locomotive.

RHENUS VENIRO GmbH & Co KG   VEN

Moers, Nordrhein-Westfalen.

EVU Licence: Freight & Passenger, 29/03/2007–31/03/2022.
Routes: Boppard–Emmelshausen (14km); Bullay–Trarben Trarbach.
Depot: Boppard.

This is the splinter organisation from the former Rhenus-Keolis partnership. Veniro inherited two lines – that at Alzey and the Freiberger Eisenbahn Ges. (FEG – q.v.). Since then it has won the contract for the service on the rump Hunrücksbahn from Boppard to Emmelhausen for which a new depot was built at Boppard. In 2014 it lost the Alzey line to Vlexx but gained Bullay–Trarben Trarbach from DB and will operate this line for 15 years using 650s.

ROAD & RAIL SERVICE   ABRRS

Aschersleben, Sachsen-Anhalt.

EVU Licence: Freight, 20/02/2012–31/01/2027.
Traction: One 312 and one V60D.

This is a small company owened by Axel Burkart, hence the VKM ABRRS. Founded in 2009, current work centres around infrastructure trains.

RÖBEL/MÜRITZ EISENBAHN GmbH   RME

Röbel, Mecklenburg-Vorpommern.

EVU Licence: Freight & Passenger, 23/05/2002–31/03/2017.
Traction: Three 312, three V60D and one V100DR.

This company was formed in 1997 by the "Hei Na Ganzlin" preservation group, becoming the operating arm of that organisation allowing main line access with its steam loco and also diesel worked freight along the closed branch Ganzlin to Röbel. The branch line was not a good source of revenue but open access brought a change of mind and the operating company moved to Berlin Lichtenberg former steam depot in 2005, from where advantage was taken of the various works contracts around the Berlin area. Later the old depot was sold/leased to another operator so RME then moved locos to the then closed S-Bahn depot at Berlin-Friedrichsfelde Ost. That was subsequently reopened by DB so it is not clear where the RME locos are now kept. The company now seems rather dormant.

RSE RHEIN-SIEG-EISENBAHN Gmbh RSE

Bonn, Nordrhein-Westfalen.
EVU Licence: Freight & Passenger, 01/07/2005–30/06/2020.
Routes: Bonn Beul–Hangelar (4.6 km).
Traction: Five V60C and four MAN railcars.
Depot: Bonn Beul.

In 1994 some railway enthusiasts, local businesses (i.e. freight forwarders) and various other private individuals formed a new company, Rhein Sieg Eisenbahn Betriebes Gmbh, later adopting the present title. They started by taking over the Bonn Beuel–Hangelar line in 1995 after being upset that DEG had closed it. In 1999 the company started weekend tourist services on the Linz (Rh)–Kalenborn route. RSE holds the operating licenses for several museum line operations e.g. Dieringhausen–Waldbrol. It handles various local traffic flows on behalf of DB Schenker, in effect a last mile service tripping to final destinations for traffic dropped off at Troisdorf.

RST RANGIER SERVICE UND TRANSPORTGESELLSCHAFT mbh RST

St. Ingbert, Saarland.
EVU Licence: Freight, 18/07/2014–31/12/2028.
Traction: 3 small diesel shunting locos.

Founded in 1995 the company acquired shunting duties at Brebach and St. Ingbert which it continues to perform, but also undertakes shunting duties for various firms in the area and in Saarbrücken.

RTS RAIL TRANSPORT SERVICE GERMANY Gmbh RTS

München, Bayern.
EVU Licence: Freight, 14/06/2006–14/06/2021.

This company is a German subsidiary of the Austrian RTS company which itself is a subsidiary of the Swietelsky infrastructure concern. Consequently most work is connected with infrastructure but opportunity is taken for spot traffic in association with the Austrian company. When starting up, RTS was lucky in that another operator Eisenbahnbewachungs GmbH (EBW) became insolvent and so picked up quite a few of its locos which EBW had in fact picked up previously from another infrastructure contractor, TLG!

RÜGENSCHE BÄDERBAHN GmbH & Co (Rasender Roland) RüBB

Putbus, Mecklenburg-Vorpommern.
EVU Licence: Freight & Passenger, 21/12/1995–31/12/2015 (Still listed as issued to Rügensche Kleinbahn!).
Routes: Lauterbach Mole–Putbus (2.5 km, DB Netz); Putbus–Binz Ost–Göhren (26.7 km).
Gauge: 750 mm.
Traction: Mostly steam but with a few diesels.
Depots: Putbus, Göhren.

This narrow gauge line was a private company before WWII but was nationalised under the post-war communist regime. It has now returned to the private sector after a somewhat turbulent time when the ownership was disputed. The line and most locos are owned by Landkreis Rügen with PRESS being the operating company. (99 4011 is owned by PRESS). Since privatisation the line has been extended over the DB standard gauge branch from Putbus to Lauterbach Mole by adding a third running rail. The line is basically a summer tourist line but it does offer all year round service.

RURTALBAHN GmbH   RTB

Düren, Nordrhein-Westfalen.

EVU Licence: Freight & Passenger, 23/10/2003–31/10/2018.
Routes: Düren–Heimbach (RB 21); Düren–Jülich–Linnich (RB 21); Mönchengladbach–Dalheim (RB 39).
Traction: Five 650, 17 654, one vintage railcar and 2 shunting locos for the depot.
Depot: Düren Distelrath.

Previously known as the Dürener Kreisbahn (DKB), the present company dates from 2003 when the passenger rail activities of the DKB became a separate company, Rurtalbahn GmbH. It continues to work over its old lines but also now has a contract to cover trains from Mönchengladbach to Dalheim on behalf of DB Regio.

RURTALBAHN CARGO GmbH   RTBC

Düren, Nordrhein-Westfalen.

EVU Licence: Freight, 07/12/2011–31/12/2026.
Traction: Three 209, three G1206, three G2000, three Class 66, six 185, three 186, five 189, one SBB 482 and hired in locos as required.

The freight part of RTB (see above) was divided into a separate company in 2010. It had already obtained contracts and involvement with trains to and from Rotterdam and now has a subsidiary company there (Rurtalbahn Benelux B.V.). For its trains to Rotterdam diesel locomotives were used at first, but as traffic grew some dual voltage locomotives were hired in although the diesels still appear. Traffic is nationwide, not only going to and from Rotterdam but also to and from German North Sea ports.

SAAR RAIL GmbH   SRG

Völklingen, Saarland.

EVU Licence: Freight, 12/10/2012–31/08/2027.
Traction: Two Gravita 10 diesels and a hired in electric loco.

This is a subsidiary of Saarstahl AG, founded in 2009 to service its own steelworks in Völklingen. It now moves molten steel in torpedo wagons from Dillingen to Völklingen (previously done by DB and even SBB Cargo!) and trips as required between plants in the area.

SAARBAHN GmbH   SBS

Saarbrücken, Saarland.

EVU Licence: Passenger, 01/08/1997–31/03/2027.
Routes: Saarbrücken-Ludwigstrasse–Brebach–Sarreguemines (France); Saarbrücken–Heisweiler Markt(–Lebach).
Electrical Systems: 750 V dc and 15 kV ac 16.7 Hz.
Depot: Saarbrücken-Brebach.

Saarbrücken has decided to follow Karlsruhe and integrate its city transport with the main line network. In the city it is a tramway, outside it is a railway running on former DB/SNCF tracks to Sarreguemines. The initial 15 units have been followed by many more as the system follows the lead of Karlsruhe and extends in all directions! Currrently tramway conditions extend to Brebach and from there train conditions apply on to Sarreguemines. Like Karlsruhe the units are dual-voltage. Extensions to the system are being built with Riegelsberg Süd reached in 2001, Etzenhofen in 2009 and Heusweiler Markt in 2011. The final destination of Lebach was reached in 2014. The fleet has no known EVN but ought to be 94 80 0451 0xx and this is where the units appear in this book.

SÄCHSISCH-BÖHMISCHE EISENBAHNGELLSCHAFT mbH   SBE

Zittau, Sachsen.

EVU Licence: No separate EVU licence appears to have been issued so presumably that of the parent company, HWB, is used.
Routes: Zittau–Seifhennersdorf–Eibau.
Depot: Zittau.

This company started off as a consortium of Sächsisch-Oberlausitzer Eisenbahn Gesellschaft, Hochwaldbahn GmbH and Bohmische Nordbahn (Ceská Sevirni Dráha), set up to operate this former DB line from 19/06/2003. Units from the Hochwaldbahn were used initially. (q.v.); The VT units were hired in from RBG and HWB! However SBE lost its contract when the franchise came up for renewal, as 1960 built railbuses did not meet modern requirements. Instead VBG won the contract using Desiro DMUs. All the SBE units are understood to be stored at Zittau.

No.	Builder, No. & Year	Type	kW	Details	Comments
VT 41	OK 320009/4/1959	515	398	Bo-2 DER	Leased from RBG (VT 09), ex DB 515 511.
VT 42	OK 320010/3/1960	515	398	Bo-2 DER	Leased from RBG (VT 10), ex DB 515 523.

SÄCHSISCHE DAMPFEISENBAHNGESELLSCHAFT mbH   SDG

Annaberg-Buchholz, Sachsen.

EVU Licence: Freight & Passenger, 23/12/1998–29/02/2028.

Oberwiesenthal Line (Fichtelbergbahn)
Route: Cranzahl–Kurort Oberwiesenthal.
Length: 17.4 km.
Depot: Oberwiesenthal.

Freital Hainsberg Line – Weisseritztalbahn
Routes: Freital Hainsberg–Kurort Kipsdorf.
Length: 26.3 km.
Depot: Freital Hainsberg.

Radebeul System (Lössnitzgrundbahn)
Route: Radebeul Ost–Radeburg.
Length: 16.55 km.
Depots: Radebeul Ost, Radeburg.

Previously known as Busverkehr Ober und Westerzgebirge Bahn GmbH (BVO), the current name came into use on 09/05/2007. When DB wanted to rid itself of the 750mm gauge lines in Sachsen there were few takers. One company that did step in was the bus company in Annaberg-Buchholz which bought the line from Cranzahl to Oberwiesenthal (Fichtelbergbahn), taking over on 01/06/1998. Later the firm took over all the remaining DB narrow gauge lines in Sachsen; the Radebeul system on 11/06/2004 and the Freital system 14/09/2004. The last mentioned line had been badly damaged by floods in 2002 and certain guarantees had to be given by the Land. The section to Dippoldiswalde reopened on 13/12/2008 but there is no set date for reopening of the line on to Kurort Kipsdorf, the financial crisis having affected the plans. Work is now underway to restore the line south of Dippoldiswalde which could reopen late in 2015. Heavy repairs to locomotives are carried out at Oberwiesenthal or Meiningen. As locomotives move to and from works they do not always go back to the same system.

SÄCHSISCH-OBERLAUSITZER EISENBAHNGESELLSCHAFT mbH
SOEG

Zittau, Sachsen.
EVU Licence: Freight & Passenger, 15/11/1996–31/08/2026.
Routes: Zittau–Bertsdorf–Kurort Oybin (2.5 km); Bertsdorf–Kurort Jonsdorf (3.5 km).
Gauge: 750 mm.
Depots: Zittau, Bertsdorf.

This former DR narrow gauge line is now owned by the local area with Landkreis Löbau–Zittau having the major stake. The line continues as it always has done with the staple diet being tourist traffic. The company has a freight licence but this is used to cover the operation of a freight train from Löbau bringing coal for the steam locos and uses a locomotive from the preservation society at Löbau.

SBB GmbH
SBB

Konstanz, Baden-Württemberg.
EVU Licence: Passenger, 28/03/2003–31/03/2018.
Traction: Ten SBB 521 and nine SBB 526.

SBB formed a German subsidiary, SBB GmbH, in order to bid for contracts within those parts of Germany close to the Swiss border. It was successful in obtaining two contracts helped by being in the right place at the right time, such as when the Mittel Thurgaubahn went bankrupt leaving the Thurbo operation up in the air, SBB stepped in. The contracts now running are for the Basel–Lörrach–Zell in Wiesental/Weil am Rhein and Konstanz–Radolfzell–Singen–Engen (expires 09/12/2016). Stadler FLIRT units belonging to the parent company are used.

SBB CARGO DEUTSCHLAND GmbH
SBBC

Duisburg, Nordrhein-Westfalen.
EVU Licence: Freight, 17/07/2002–31/07/2017.
Traction: One V100DR, one G1206 and SBB 421 and 482 as required.

This company is a subsidiary of the Swiss company SBB Cargo International. It has drivers based in several major locations (e.g. Mannheim, Köln) and provides shunting duties in some freight yards. The traffic is principally that from Germany to Switzerland and Italy and vice-versa with SBB Cargo locomotives working through from North Germany to Switzerland. As well as intermodal trains there are also oil and chemical trains.

SEEHAFEN KIEL GmbH & Co KG
KIEL

Kiel, Schleswig-Holstein.
EVU Licence: Freight, 28/11/1973–28/11/2023.

As the name suggests this company is responsible for serving the harbour lines in Kiel. It once had its dedicated locomotive fleet but in 2008 it became a part owner of leasing company Northrail and put its own locomotives into the general pool. It is quite possible it is still using its original locos!

SES LOGISTIK GmbH
SES

Ludwiglust, Mecklenburg-Vorpommern.
EVU Licence: Freight, 30/04/2009–31/12/2024.
Traction: One V100DR.

Founded in 2007 this is a small company which uses the former DR depot in Ludwiglust as its base. The main traffic is infrastructure works trains.

SGL SCHIENEN GÜTER LOGISTIK GmbH   SGL

Dachau, Bayern.

EVU Licence: Freight & Passenger, 08/07/2008–31/12/2022.
Traction: Four V100DR, two 221, one 232, two V60D, four 710.9 and three Maxima 40CC.

This is another infrastructure company that has created its own train operating company to move its own trains. The background lies in the Knape track renewals firm. In fact the rebuilt former 710.9s are owned by GSG Knape Gleissanierung. The SGL numbering of locos is similar to that of PRESS where V60.16 is the 16th loco acquired and not the 16th in the class.

SKL UMSCHLAGSERVICE MAGDEBURG GmbH & Co KG   SKLUS

Magdeburg, Sachsen-Anhalt.

EVU Licence: Freight, 07/08/2001–31/08/2016.
Traction: Two 312, one V60DR and one V100DR.

A small company which although having an EVU licence does not seem to do any main line work, instead sticking to shunting and servicing the freight terminal located south east of the Magdeburg Buckau yards.

SLG SPITZKE LOGISTIK GmbH   SLG

Grossbeeren, Berlin.

EVU Licence: Freight, 14/05/2009–31/12/2023.
Traction: Three 312, three V60D, eight V100DR and two G1206.
Depot: Grossbeeren.

Spitzke is a company that has been on the scene since open access started. This particular firm is a subsidiary of the main company, Spitzke SE, which has expanded considerably and has subsidiaries in other countries e.g. Netherlands, Norway. It also has many subsidiaries in the railway infrastructure business. So, besides doing track renewals in Germany the group also gets involved in work in adjoining countries. Thus some of the locos of the Dutch subsidiary are often found working in Germany, the locos being moved around according to workload.

SONATA LOGISTICS GmbH   SONRA

Mücheln, Sachsen-Anhalt.

EVU Licence: Freight, 05/02/2015–31/01/2030.

Sonata seems to be the son of Nord Bayerische Eisenbahn (NBEG). As that company got into financial difficulties in 2014 the Sonata group was formed with a Logistics part and there is also Sonata Rail GmbH. The group also now seems to have Städtebahn Sachsen as part of its portfolio. A developing situation which needs watching in 2015.

STÄDTEBAHN SACHSEN GmbH   STS

Dresden, Sachsen.

EVU Licence: Passenger, 10/12/2010–21/12/2023.
Routes: See below.
Traction: 15 Desiro 2-car DMUs from a variety of sources.

This company is a subsidiary of Städtebahn GmbH which interestingly was jointly owned by Eisenbahn Gesellschaft Potsdam (EGP) and NBE Regio GmbH until June 2013 when EGP sold out to NBE Regio. STS has the contract to run the local trains around Dresden from December 2010 to December 2024 on the following routes: SB 33 Dresden Neustadt–Königsbrück; SB 34 Dresden–Kamenz; SB 71 Pirna–Neustadt (Sachs)–Sebnitz–Bad Schandau; SB 72 Heidenau–Altenberg; SE 19 Dresden–Heidenau–Altenberg (snow/ski service in winter).

STAHLWERKE THÜRINGEN GmbH   SWT

Unterwellenborn, Thüringen.
EVU Licence: Freight, 30/01/2001–30/01/2016.
Traction: Six V100DR with other locos hired in as required.
Depot: Unterwellenborn.

This steelworks has for some years operated local trips in the surrounding area but in 2001 became a fully fledged EVU. It has standard former DR types, most having been modernised in recent years. Not all may be passed for main line work. The works was taken over by the Arcelor company and renamed Arcelor Thüringen GmbH on 20/03/2006, but later reverted to SWT on 05/03/2007. Besides tripping around the works, feeder services conveying scrap etc are also worked from various loading points.

STARKENBERGER BAUSTOFFWERKE GmbH   SBW
(TRIANGULA LOGISTIK GmbH)   TRG

EVU Licence: Freight & Passenger, 14/10/2008–13/10/2023.

This company took over the former Wismut concern in 2014 and acquired an open access licence. Thus, what was previously an industrial operation is now able to operate over the national network and does so, using up its spare capacity. It has five former DB 232s for main line work which have all been re-engined with Caterpillar 3606 engines of 1975 kW, plus two V60D shunting locos. The Wismut concern had a VKM (WIS) but the new mainline operations appear to operate under the Triangula EVU licence.

STAUDEN-VERKEHRS-GmbH   STVG

Augsburg, Bayern.
EVU Licence: Freight & Passenger, 19/02/2004–01/02/2019.

This company grew out of a local railway society. It now operates infrastructure trains as well as running enthusiast specials/tourist trains in the area. Having a passenger licence has been an advantage as one of the Austrian 2143s has been noted working ALEX trains when that operator had a problem.

STOCK-TRANSPORT   STOCK

Bodenheim, Rheinland-Pfalz.
EVU Licence: Freight, 12/05/2004–30/04/2019.
Traction: One 263, one 264 and one 322.

A small company named after its owner, Michael Stock. It has contracts with oil and chemical firms in the Mainz area and is always on the lookout for spot traffic.

SÜD-THÜRINGEN BAHN GmbH   STB

Erfurt, Thüringen.
EVU Licence. Passenger, 04/02/2000–31/12/2016.
Routes: STB 1 Eisenach–Meiningen (60 km); Meiningen–Sonneberg (81 km); STB 2 Wernshausen–Zella Mehlis (30 km); STB 3 Sonneberg–Lauscha–Neuhaus am Rennweg (29 km); STB 4 Erfurt–Arnstadt–Zella Mehlis–Meiningen (86 km); EB 3 Erfurt–Arnstadt–Ilmenau (50 km).
Depots: Former DB Meiningen depot and EB depot in Erfurt.

This is a joint venture between Erfurter Industriebahn and Hessische Landesbahn, each owning 50%. The STB was successful in obtaining the concession to run passenger trains in Thüringen for 15 years from June 2001 on the above lines. 21 Regio Shuttles were ordered which are air-conditioned and are fitted with toilets; the fleet was strengthened soon afterwards with a further six units. STB was then given the job of operating the Erfurt–Ilmenau service on behalf of Erfurter Bahn, so a further batch of RS1 units was delivered in 2002.

▲ Several operators came into being when railway societies decided to make their heritage fleets available for infrastructure trains or hire to other operators. Here, former OBB Class 2143, 92 80 2143 018, on hire from STVG is in charge of an ALEX train from Oberstdorf to Immenstadt, nearing its destination on 20 March 2014. **Matthias Müller**

▼ Vossloh G18 prototype locomotive 92 80 4180 001 stands outside the depot at Moers on 25 May 2014. No series orders have yet been forthcoming for this type of locomotive. **Brian Garvin**

SÜDWESTDEUTSCHE VERKEHRS AG   SWEG

Lahr, Baden-Württemberg.

EVU Licence: It appears SWEG holds just one licence for all its lines valid for freight and passenger services, 21/05/2003–01/06/2018.

Traction: One D65BB, two D75BB, one G1203BB, two 1442 EMUs, one MAN railcar, seven 626 and eight 650.

In 1971 the Mittelbadischen Eisenbahnen AG combined with the south west section of Deutsche Eisenbahn Betriebsgesellschaft to form SWEG, which today is 100% owned by Land Baden-Württemberg. Most of its lines are heavily subsidised branch lines performing a public service to local communities with trains running instead of school buses. The railway services are linked into the SWEG bus network. Each line is listed below. Note that the line from Möckmühl to Dörzbach, which has been closed for several years following storm damage, has been sold to the local community for use as a museum line. SWEG has two subsidiary railway companies: Breisgau S-Bahn GmbH (BSB) and Ortenau S-Bahn GmbH (OSB) which are listed separately.

VERKEHRSBETRIEBE ACHERN–OTTENHÖFEN (AO)

Route: Achern–Ottenhofen.
Depot: Ottenhöfen.

This short branch line connects with the DB at Achern. The depot at Ottenhöfen also services OSB railcars. One SWEG diesel is normally based here for freight traffic.

VERKEHRSBETRIEB BIBERACH–OBERHARMERSBACH (BOH)

Route: Biberach–Zell–Oberharmersbach-Riersbach.
Depot: Oberharmersbach-Riersbach.

The line is now served by OSB units (q.v.).

VERKEHRSBETRIEB ENDINGEN–KAISERSTUHLBAHNEN (KB)

Routes: Breisach–Endingen–Riegel Ort–Riegel (26.4 km); Gottenheim–Bahlingen–Riegel Ort–Endingen (17.5 km).
Depot: Endingen.

This line changed at the end of the 1990s from being in something of a 1960s time-warp into a very modern operation. The line in fact dates back to the 1890s but has changed hands many times with SWEG acquiring it from the Mittelbadische Eisenbahn Gesellschaft in 1971. The depot and workshops have recently been completely rebuilt and expanded to deal with expanding business under regionalisation. The KB depot looks after the BSB units as well as its own. There is some freight traffic in the area so some locomotives are normally based here.

VERKEHRSBETRIEB MECKESHEIM–AGLASTERHAUSEN HÜFFENHARDT (MAH)

Route: Neckarbischofsheim Nord–Hüffenhardt (17.0 km).
Depot: Neckarbischofsheim Nord.

This line has changed fortunes as Meckesheim to Aglasterhausen has passed to DB. SWEG retains the stub to Hüffenhardt as its main workshops are located at Neckarbischofsheim Nord, although there is now some talk of reintroducing a passenger service.

VERKEHRSBETRIEB SCHWARZACH (MEN)

Route: Bühl–Schwarzach–Stollhofen–Greffern/Söllingen.
Depot: Schwarzach (Baden).

The initials are from a previous age when this line was part of a metre gauge network of the Mittelbadischen Eisenbahn and unlike most SWEG lines this one is freight only. Heavy freight traffic is handled as the line receives trainloads of chemicals mostly in tank wagons.

VERKEHRSBETRIEB STAUFEN (MÜNSTERTALBAHN) (MT)

Route: Bad Krozingen–Staufen–Münstertal (11 km).
Depot: Staufen.

In recent years this line has been electrified with SWEG acquiring two Talent 2 EMUs. These tend to stay on the branch filling in between S-Bahn trains from Heidelberg but they do get through to Freiburg on occasional workings.

TEGERNSEE-BAHN BETRIEBSGESELLSCHAFT mbH   TBG

Tegernsee, Bayern.

EVU Licence: Freight & Passenger, 10/10/2007–30/09/2022.
Traction: One Köf.
Depot: Tegernsee.

In the late 1990s the TBG passenger train operations were bought out by BOBY (q.v.) and the TBG loco stock sold. TBG still has an EVU licence but today it is the infrastructure owner and has its own Köf for engineering trains.

TME-TORSTEN MEINCKE EISENBAHN GmbH   TME

Schwerin, Mecklenburg-Vorpommern.

Traction: Three 312 and one V60D.

This firm owns various sidings and lines in the Schwerin area. It has four locomotives for shunting and line inspection duties.

TRANS REGIO DEUTSCHE REGIONALBAHN GmbH   TDR

Koblenz, Rheinland-Pfalz.

EVU Licence: Freight & Passenger, (1999)–19/12/2013–30/06/2015.
Traction: 17 460 and 1 Köf.
Depot: Koblenz-Mosel.

This company was set up in 1999 and was then owned 51% by the Moselbahn (not a railway operator for many years) and 49% by Rheinischen Bahngesellschaft AG Düsseldorf. It started off running trains over several lines in Rheinland-Pfalz using Regio Shuttle DMUs. Meanwhile the Moselbahn backed out and concentrated on its bus business. The company is now a subsidiary of EuRailCo GmbH which itself appears to be a Transdev and Veolia venture. In late 2006 TDR was awarded the contract for the Mittelrheinbahn; Köln–Koblenz and Koblenz–Mainz to run from December 2008 for 15 years. These services are now know as MRB 26 and MRB 32 respectively. On 31/05/2007 it was announced that TDR had purchased the site of the old DB depot in Koblenz (Mosel) and it subsequently built a new depot there for its fleet of Desiro Main Line EMUs, now designated Class 460. Having started operating the Mittelrheinbahn, TDR then lost its diesel services to DB Regio.

TRANSPETROL GmbH

Hamburg.

EVU Licence. Freight & Passenger, 25/10/2007–31/10/2022.

As the name suggests this company is involved with the movement of petroleum trains and chemicals etc. It lets other companies move its traffic but some locomotives do have Transpetrol branding.

TROSSINGEN EISENBAHN GmbH   TE

Trossingen, Baden-Württemberg.

EVU Licence: Passenger, 17/10/2005–30/09/2020.
Electrification System: 600 V dc.
Depot: Trossingen Stadt.

Trossingen lies on the Rottweil–Villingen DB line, but the railway when built by-passed Trossingen itself so that an electric railway was built to connect the town with its "main line" station. In 2003 the line became part of the Ringzug network which is served by HzL DMUs but the line remains electrified and the old electric units do come into traffic from time to time.

No.	Builder, No. & Year	Type	kW	Details	Comments
T 1	MAN 369/1898		2 x 50	Bo ER	
T 3	Essl 19254/1938		4 x 75	Bo-Bo ER	
T 5	Essl 24836/1956		2 x 60	Bo ER	
T 6	Rastatt 21-3/1968		2 x 60	Bo ER	
E 4	AEG 160/1902		2 x 40	Bo E	LINA

TWE BAHNBETRIEBS GmbH
TEUTOBURGER WALD EISENBAHN GmbH   TWE

Gütersloh, Nordrhein-Westfalen.

EVU Licence: Freight, 10/12/2002–31/12/2017.
Routes: Ibbenbüren Ost–Lengerich–Gütersloh Nord–Hövelhof (92.6 km); Brochterbeck–Hafen Saerbeck (7.2 km); Harsewinkel–Harsewinkel West (3.0 km).
Length: 102.8 km.
Traction: One G500C, three V100, five G1203-6 and nine electric locos from the Captrain pool.
Depots: Lengerich Hohne, Gütersloh Nord.

Following the EU lead, Teutoburger Wald Eisenbahn separated its infrastruture and operating into two companies. So TWE Bahnbetriebs is the operating company owned by TWE, which itself is a Captrain subsidiary. Being based in Gütersloh it is not surprising that many of the traffic flows are in and out of the Ruhr area. TWE is quite a surprise having a main line of over 90 km and a couple of short branches, on one of which is a plant manufacturing agricultural equipment; a source of freight traffic for TWE. The depot at Lengerich also has a well equipped workshop handling repairs and maintenance of locos for the Captrain group. Parts of the TWE network are being reviewed with a view to possible closures. Most locomotives are now in the Captrain pool but one vintage railcar remains on home territory.

TX LOGISTIK AG   TXL

Bad Honnef, Nordrhein-Westfalen.

EVU Licence: Freight, 06/12/2001–30/06/2028.
Traction: 12 185 owned plus many 182, 185 and 189 leased, as well as some Swiss 421s. Over 50 locos.

This company started off as KEP Logistik being the EVU for the Eurogate/boxXpress container services. The name changed to Netzwerk Logistic GmbH (Netlog) before becoming more widely known as TX Logistik. In 2003 Trenitalia (FS) bought 15% of the shares and bit by bit has bought all the other shares so that from 2011 the company is a 100% subsidiary of Trenitalia. Not surpringly over the years traffic has increased, its owners of course being very interested in traffic on the north-south routes through Germany, especially trains involving Italy. TX Logistik itself now has subsidiaries in other countries (e.g. Austria, Denmark and Sweden) and has an operators licence valid for the Netherlands.

There are considerable traffic flows as befits what must be the largest private operating company in Germany. Intermodal trains predominate but there are also chemicals, steel and new car flows stretching from Italy to Sweden. TX Logistik is really only concerned with the long haul leaving last mile work and shunting to others including DB Schenker!

USEDOMER EISENBAHN Gbr UEG
Ostseebad Zinnowitz, Mecklenburg-Vorpommern.
EVU Licence: None. Its locos are used by other organisations under the HWB banner.
Traction: One 312, three V60D and one 772.

This organisation seems to hire out its locos and indeed its drivers for works trains, shunting duties etc.

UWE ADAM EVU Gmbh BWESA
Sättelstädt, Thüringen.
EVU Licence: Freight, 02/04/2002–02/04/2017.
Traction: Nine V100DR, two 312 and one ASF.
Depot. Eisenach.

Previously trading as three different organisations, Lotrac took over Adam & MaLoWa Lokvermietungs Gmbh (AML) on 21/12/2004 becoming Lotrac Eisenbahnbetriebsgesellschaft mbH. Uwe Adam EVU GmbH was absorbed 03/09/2007 and it looks as if AMP Bahnlogistik GmbH is now Lotrac as well. Then all change again in December 2008 and the company's name is now Uwe Adam EVU GmbH once again. Traffic is mostly infrastructure related. The old VKMs of ADAM and AML may still be found on locos. More recently some locos have been sold to other operators. The depot at Eisenach is known to be overhauling locomotives from other operators.

VATTENFALL EUROPE MINING AG VE
Spremberg, Brandenburg.
EVU Licence: Freight, 01/09/2006–31/12/2020.
Depot: Schwarze Pumpe.

Technically this is an industrial concern whose locos stay on its own tracks. Of interest is that several of its fleet of V100s are former DR 110 or DB 202 locomotives. Consequently these have been included in the lists as they can often be seen in the exchange sidings at Peitz Ost and Spreewitz.

VECTUS VERKEHRSGESELLSCHAFT mbH VCT
Limburg, Hessen.
EVU Licence: Passenger, 05/04//2004–30/04/2019.
Routes: See below.
Traction: Seven 640, four 646 and 18 648.
Depot: Limburg.

This company was formed in 2003, being 74.9% Hessiche Landesbahn and 25.1% Westerwaldbahn. In 2004 it was successful in obtaining the franchise to run trains on the Westerwald-Taunus Netz. A selection of single and twin LINT DMUs were ordered for the franchise which is for 10 years. Vectus has now lost its contract to HLB Hessenbahn GmbH which will run the lines on a stand alone basis. As all Vectus stock is leased the units will transfer over to the new operator. No new name has been announced. The services all radiate from Limburg and are currently: RB 20 Limburg–Niederhausen; RB 21 Wiesbaden–Niederhausen; RB 25 Limburg–Koblenz; RB 28 Limburg–Au; RB 29 Limburg–Siershahn. The franchise was lost with effect from the December 2014 timetable change, the units changing hands to Hessenbahn GmbH which had also won other contracts from DB. So Vectus is now history but it may be some time before its branding is all removed and the units repainted.

VEOLIA VERKEHR GmbH   VEOLIA
Berlin.

The Veolia story is another rather complicated one. Veolia Verkehr GmbH is a subsidiary of Veolia Transdev S.A. In Germany the background is that the firm was previously Connex Verkehrs Gmbh/DEG Verkehrs GmbH. Deutsche Eisenbahn Gesellschaft was taken over in 1997 by the French CFTA group (60%) and Energie Baden-Württemberg (40%). Now CFTA is part of the Vivendi group and Vivendi has bought out the EnBW share. In 2000 the Connex logo was brought into use. Later Connex changed its name to Veolia Verkehr. There are several subsidiary companies: Veolia Verkehr Niedersachsen/Westfalen GmbH, Veolia Verkehr Regio GmbH and Veolia Verkehr Sachsen Anhalt (Harz–Elbe Express HEX). Details of each line will be found under the respective individual entry. In 2004 the then Connex created a central pool of railcars to allow trains to be strengthened as required. Then, as Connex and later Veolia obtained more franchises, all units were numbered in a common scheme. Veolia will move units between franchises to cover for failures etc so they do not necessarily stay on the line shown. Virtually all the units were acquired via Angel Trains Europa, now Alpha Trains.

VEOLIA VERKEHR REGIO GmbH   VEOLIA
Berlin.

This firm is a 100% subsidiary of Veolia Verkehr GmbH. Veolia is an umbrella organisation for the operation of a growing number of private railway operations in Germany. These are understood to be:

Bayerische Oberlandbahn	BOBY
Bayerische Regiobahn GmbH	BRB
Nord-Ostsee-Bahn	NOB
Nord Westbahn GmbH (64%)	NWB
Ostseeland Verkehr GmbH	OLA
Veolia Verkehr Regio Ost	VVRO
Württembergische Eisenbahn Gesellschaft	WEG

Details of these railways are to be found under their individual entries.

VEOLIA VERKEHR REGIO OST GmbH   VVRO
Leipzig, Sachsen.

EVU Licence: Freight & Passenger, 31/07/2002–31/07/17.
Routes: MRB 113 and 118 – see below.
Traction: Five 642, one 643 and 11 650.

Also called Mitteldeutsche Regiobahn, these initials are use to denote the train services operated: MRB 113 Leipzig–Geithain and MRB 118 Halle–Eilenburg.

VEOLIA VERKEHR SACHSEN-ANHALT GmbH   HEX
Halberstadt, Sachsen-Anhalt.

EVU Licence: Passenger, 08/04/2005–31/03/2020.
Routes: See below.
Traction: Seven 640 and 11 648.
Depot: Units are maintained in part of the Verkehrs Industrie System (VIS) works in Halberstadt.

HEX=Harz Elbe Express. It was started off by Connex in 2004, changing to Veolia in 2006. Services operated are from Magdeburg to Thale/Blankenburg; Halle–Halberstadt–Wernigerode(–Goslar); Halle–Bernburg. Also at weekends there is a Harz–Berlin service.

VERDEN–WALSRODER EISENBAHN GmbH   VWE

Verden (Aller), Niedersachsen.

EVU Licence: Freight & Passenger, 26/10/1995–25/10/2025.
Routes: Verden (Aller) Süd–Stemmen (12.2 km); Walsrode–Hollige (7.2 km).
Traction: One V100DR and one Köf.
Depot: Verden (Aller) Süd.

Verden to Walsode was once a through route but now the middle section is closed. There is still freight traffic on the remaining sections.

VERKEHRSBETRIEBE GRAFSCHAFT HOYA GmbH   VGH

Hoya, Niedersachsen.

EVU licence: Freight & Passenger, 09/11/1995–08/11/2025.
Traction: Two diesel shunters and one railcar.
Depot: Hoya.

The line from Eystrup–Hoya–Syke (37 km) was at one time metre gauge but was converted to standard gauge in the 1950/1960s. Staple traffic at one time was sugar beet but this has died away. In recent years fortunes have changed a little as there is now regular traffic from paper factories located at the eastern end of the line. The railcar is used for excursion traffic.

VERKEHRSBETRIEBE PEINE–SALZGITTER GmbH   VPS

Salzgitter, Niedersachsen.

EVU Licence: Freight & Passenger, 24/01/1996–01/01/2026.
Routes: Salzgitter-Beddingen–Salzgitter-Vosspass and branches to Hütte Nord and Beddingen Hafen; Salzgitter–Immendorf West; other Salgitter area branches (38.2 km); Peine–Ilsede-Broistedt–Salzgitter Engelnstedt (31.3 km).
Traction: 40 530C, five D100BB, six G1700 and four 185.
Depot: Hallendorf.

VPS shunts and trips around the steelwork complexes in Salzgitter and Peine. It also works freights from the works over DB tracks to and from destinations in the area using modern B-B locos. There are also trains to and from the ports and the Ruhr area. It is in the process of re-eqipping its shunting fleet having ordered 40 new G6 locos from Vossloh so the exact fleet details are unclear. VPS hires some electric locos for long distance and heavy trains.

VERKEHRSGESELLSCHAFT LANDKREIS OSNABRÜCK GmbH VLO

Bohmte, Niedersachsen.

EVU Licence: Freight & Passenger, 25/10/2010–08/07/2026.
Traction: One DHG700C and one railcar.
Depot: Bohmte.

VLO operates over what is left of the former Wittlager Kreisbahn. Regular passenger traffic ceased in 1971. The section remaining for freight is from Bohmte to Prussich Oldendorf; it is still possible to ride the line as Museums Eisenbahn Minden runs tourist trains from its base at Prussich Oldendorf.

VERKEHRSVERBUND MITTELSACHSEN GmbH   VMS

Chemnitz, Sachsen.

In preparation for letting franchises in its area, this organisation has ordered 13 3-car and 16 5-car Coradia Continental EMUs from Alstom for delivery in 2016 in time for services to start in May of that year. Services are expected to be RE 3 Dresden–Chemnitz–Hof; RB 30 Dresden–Chemnitz–Zwickau; RB 45 Chemnitz–Riesa–Elsterwerda. A new depot is envisaged in Chemnitz, operated by Alstom.

VETTER BUSUNTERNEHMEN GmbH   VESK

Zörbig, Sachsen-Anhalt.

EVU Licence: Freight & Passenger, 30/01/2002–31/01/2022.
Traction: Three 504.

The closed line from Lutherstadt Wittenberg to Bad Schmiedeberg has for a few years been operated by Vetter as an experiment using some Class 504 diesel railcars. The experiment seems to have been a failure and the units are now spare/stored.

VIAS GmbH   VIAS

Frankfurt/M, Hessen.

EVU Licence: Freight & Passenger, 21/09/2005–30/09/2020.
Routes: See below.
Traction: 26 615, five 427 and 14 428.
Depot: Michelstadt (DMU).

This company was formed in 2005, being 50% Vergehrsgesellschaft Frankfurt/Main and 50% Ruhrtalbahn. VIAS= VIA (Way) and S (Service). The company was formed to bid for, and succeeded in getting, the franchise for the Oldenwaldbahn. 22 ITINO DMUs were ordered for the services and a new depot established. Initially there was to be a staff of 50 including 30 drivers and 10 conductors. All the rolling stock is leased from FAHMA. The fleet of ITINO DMUs was strengthened with the acquisition of another four units in 2009, one of which was earmarked to run a service over the re-opened line from Darmstadt-Eberstadt to Pfungstadt. In 2010 the VGF shares were sold to DSB Deutschland. VIAS must have been considered successful as in 2008 it won the contract to provide the local train service on the right bank of the Rhein choosing Stadler 3-car and 4-car FLIRT EMUs. Diesel routes are Frankfurt/M and Hanau to Eberbach (2005–2015); Darmstadt-Eberstadt–Pfungstadt (2011–2015) and the electric route is Frankfurt/M–Wiesbaden–Rüdesheim–Koblenz–Neuwied (2010-2023).

▲ Resplendent in original livery and carrying original number 217 002, Bahn Tourist Express's flagship locomotive 92 80 1217 002 awaits its next duty at Regensburg Hbf on 6 July 2013.
Matthias Müller

VLEXX GmbH   Vlexx

Mainz, Rheinland-Pfalz.
EVU Licence: Passenger & Freight, 11/02/2014–31/01/2029.
Depot: Mainz.

This is the operating name of the Netinera subsidiary, originally DNSW GmbH, that has won the contract for the Dieselnetzes Südwest. This includes services from Frankfurt/M–Mainz–Saarbrücken and Mainz–Alzey–Kirchheimbolanden and others in the general area. 63 Alstom LINT 54 DMUs were ordered for these trains and a new depot has been built at Mainz Hbf in the area of the old goods depot.

VOGTLANDBAHN-Gmbh   VBG

Neumark, Sachsen.
EVU Licence: Freight & Passenger, 18/03/1998–28/02/2028.
Traction: Five 183, 11 223, 26 642, eight 650, 18 654, one 312 and one G322.
Depots: Neumark, Schwandorf.

Vogtlandbahn is a 100% subsidiary of Regentalbahn AG which itself was owned by Arriva until DB bought Arriva. Today Arriva has been replaced by NETINERA. Starting off in 1996 in western Sachsen (which is where the name Vogtland comes from) with services around Zwickau, it reversed the Karlsruhe model in a way as it took the trains down the street into the town. Services expanded over the years with some trains running through to destinations in the Czech Republic and routes won in northern Bayern. In the Arriva period there were the ALEX trains – Arriva Länder Express. These services have since expanded with ALEX now standing for Allgau Express but this has now become a general brand name as ALEX trains now run München to Lindau/Oberstdorf and München to Hof/Praha! To cater for the southern area workings a new depot has been built at Schwandorf to supplement the one at Neumark. From 2010 for 10 years VBG took over trains in the "Three Countries Corner" around Zittau, running east and west into the Czech Republic. Currently services operated are: Zwickau–Falkenstein–Kraslice–Sokolov (CZ); Zwickau/Gera–Adorf–Cheb–Marktredwitz; Zwickau–Plauen–Hof; München–Lindau/Oberstdorf; München–Regensburg–Hof/Praha; Liberec (CZ)–Zittau–Varnsdorf–Rybniště (CZ). In December 2014 VBG took over from DB the Dresden–Zittau/Görlitz services using the brand name TRILEX and rolling stock released by the new PESA DMUs for the Oberpfalzbahn. However as these units had not been cleared for operation by the EBA some of these services had to be sub-contracted back to DB operation!

VORWOHLE–EMMERTHALER VERKEHRSBETRIEBE GmbH   VEV

Bodenwerder, Niedersachsen.
EVU Licence: Freight & Passenger, 26/10/1995–25/10/2025.
Traction: One 323, one V60D and one 772.

All that is left of this once 32 km line is 4 km at the Emmerthal end that serves a factory. The locos seem to be used to shunt there as traffic is delivered by DB Schenker.

WANNE HERNER-EISENBAHN UND HAFEN GmbH   WHE

Herne, Nordrhein-Westfalen.
EVU Licence: Freight, 21/12/1995–31/03/2026.
Traction: One G1202, two G1204, one G1206, three G1600 and one shunter.
Depot: Wanne Westhafen.

With the decline of the coal industry the WHE has diversified and constructed on its territory a container terminal (Container Terminal Herne GmbH – CTH). Traffic to and from the Osthafen and Westhafen continues whilst the container terminal is now linked to many intermodal services.

WEDLER FRANZ LOGISTIK GmbH & Co KG   WFL

Potsdam, Brandenburg.

EVU Licence: None, operates under the licence of other companies.
Traction: Five 312, nine V60D, eight V100DR, one 228, one 231 and three steam.
Depots: Neubrandenburg, Nossen.

Founded in 2004, the company has a contract to shunt the cement terminal in Berlin-Greifswalder Strasse. It also provides locos for infrastructure trains.

WENDELSTEINBAHN GmbH   WENDEL

Brannenburg, Bayern.

EVU Licence: Freight & Passenger, 30/12/2010–31/12/2025.
Route: Brannenburg–Wendelstein.
Length: 7.7 km.
Gauge: 1000 mm.
Electrical System: 1500 V dc.
Depots: Brannenburg.

This is a typical mountain railway with a short adhesion-worked valley section before the mountain climbing starts using the Strub rack system. The line starts at Brannenburg on the Rosenheim–Kufstein line with the station there at 508 metres asl. The summit station on the Wendelstein is at 1723 metres, the 7.7 km taking 30 minutes.

No.	Builder, No. & Year	Type	kW	Details	Comments
2	Essl 3628/1912		2 x 74	Bo E	Rack
3	Essl 3629/1912		2 x 74	Bo E	Rack
4	Essl 4239/1935		2 x 108	Bo E	Rack
11	SLM 5454/1990	Beh4/4	4 x 253	A1-A1+A1-A1	Rack
12	SLM 5455/1990	Beh4/4	4 x 253	A1-A1+A1-A1	Rack

Note: No. 11 named "Prinzregent Luitpold"; No. 12 named "Otto v. Steinbeis"

WERRA-EISENBAHNVERKEHRSGESELLSCHAFT mbH   WE

Merkers-Kieselbach, Hessen.

EVU Licence: Freight & Passenger, 15/11/2006–15/11/2021.
Traction: One V60D and one 1 V100DB.

A small company with some infrastructure train business and also shunting and tripping in the Bad Salzungen area on behalf of DB Schenker. Note that the company calls itself WEG but the official EVN is WE to avoid a confliction.

WESTERWALDBAHN DES KREISES ALTENKIRCHEN GmbH
WEBA

Steinebach-Bindweide, Rheinland-Pfalz.

EVU Licence: Freight & Passenger, 26/10/1994–10/01/2033.
Traction: Four R30B, two V100 DB and two 628.
Depot: Bindweide.

The Westerwaldbahn is quite an old company having been founded in 1913. Its network has gradually shrunk and was down to two freight only routes when in 1994, under the regionalisation plans, it took over from DB the passenger traffic between Betzdorf and Daaden buying, with help from the Lander, DB unit 628 677 and trailer as well as the line. The remaining part of its old line is Scheuerfeld–Bindweide–Weitefeld. In 2005 it purchased from DB the 33.4 km line from Altenkirchen to Selters and in 2007 rented the DB line from Selters to Siershahn. The reason behind these moves was to serve a factory at Selters which now straddles the line; there is also a scrap dealer at Raubach.

WESTFALENBAHN GmbH WFB

Bielefeld, Nordrhein-Westfalen.

EVU Licence: Freight & Passenger, 10/03/2006–31/03/2021.
Routes: See below.
Traction: 14 427 and five 429.
Depots: Rheine (within Windhoff complex), Minden (from 2015).

This company was formed to bid for passenger franchises in Nordrhein-Westfalen and is a consortium of Abellio (25%), Mindener Kreisbahn (25%), Verkehrsbetriebe Extertal (25%) and mobiel (25%). It was succesful in being awarded the contract for the Teutoburger Wald Netzes for ten years from December 2007. 14 3-car and five 5-car FLIRT EMUs were ordered from Stadler Pankow, being leased via Angel Trains Europa. Services concerned in this contract are RB 61 Bad Bentheim–Bielefeld; RB 65 Münster–Rheine; RB 66 Osnabrück–Münster; RB 72 Herford–Altenbeken–Paderborn. WFB later won another contract for the "Expresslinien Mittelland/Emsland". This will run for 15 years from December 2015. Stadler again got the order for EMUs, this time 15 4-car FLIRT and 13 6-car KISS units for use on the following services: RE trains Münster–Emden; RE trains Rheine/Bielefeld–Braunschweig.

WESTFÄLISCHE LANDES-EISENBAHN GmbH WLE

Lippstadt, Nordrhein-Westfalen.

EVU Licence: Freight & Passenger, from 29/11/1995 until further notice.
Traction: Five shunting locos, seven Deutz main line locos, two 223, two G1204, two G1206, one G1600 and one 189.
Depots: Lippstadt, Beckum, Warstein.
Main Works: Lippstadt Nord.

The WLE is a long established private line dating back to 1883 and is owned by the various communities it serves. Today the main line is Münster–Neubeckum–Lippstadt–Warstein (101.6 km), with Neubeckum–Beckum (6 km) actually owned by DB. Passenger traffic ceased in 1975. The freight traffic remains buoyant despite some factories along the route closing. Warstein has a large brewery from where the beer is sent by intermodal trains to Berlin and München, whilst having mountainous areas on the line there are also shipments of limestone, cement and wood shavings.

WESTSÄCHISCHE EISENBAHNTRANSPORT GESELLSCHAFT mbH WSET

Glauchau, Sachsen.

EVU Licence: Freight, 13/07/2005–31/07/2020.
Traction: One V100DR and 1 hired in Swiss 421.

Founded in 2004 this firm had its sights on the transport of new cars and operates some trains on behalf of Mosolf Automotive Railway Gesellschaft mbH.

WÜRTTEMBERGISCHE EISENBAHN-GESELLSCHAFT mbH WEG

Waiblingen, Baden-Württemberg.

EVU Licence: Freight & Passenger, 07/07/2010–31/08/2025. One licence covers all the lines. WEG however no longer handles freight with what remains being handled by the Captrain group.

The WEG, having had a long history, has changed hands several times more recently. Once part of DEG, the latter was taken over by Connex. Now the owner is Veolia Verkehr Regio GmbH but most of the lines continue to have their own identity. As the name implies it operates several lines in Baden Württemberg. Those still open are:

Nebenbahn Nürtingen–Neuffen (NN)
Zweckverbandes Schönbuchbahn Böblingen–Dettingen (ZVS)
Zweckverbandes Strohgäubahn Korntal–Heimerdingen (ZSB)
Zweckverbandes Verkehrsverband Wieslaftalbahn Schorndorf–Rudersberg Nord–Oberndorf (ZVVW)

NEBENBAHN NÜRTINGEN–NEUFFEN "TALESBAHN" (NN)
Neuffen, Baden-Württemberg.

Traction: Four 650.
Depot: Neuffen.

A short WEG line connecting with DB at Nürtingen on the Plochingen–Tübingen line.

ZWECKVERBAND SCHÖNBUCHBAHN (ZVS)
Böblingen, Baden-Württemberg.

Traction: Eight 650.
Depot: Dettenhausen.

The Schönbuchbahn is a branch line from Böblingen to Dettenhausen, once part of DB which had withdrawn the passenger service in 1965. Freight had just about died away when, in 1988, the local government offices in Böblingen and Tübingen got together with WEG in an attempt to get passenger trains reinstated. They were eventually successful, the leaning to regionalisation just about making their case. DB sold the branch for a nominal 1 DM! Since then the line has been modernised by the local authorities and a new passenger service introduced using Regio Shuttles. The project has been a great success with the number of people travelling far exceeding expectations. The units as delivered had 228 kW engines but these were not powerful enough and have since been replaced by a 257 kW version. Traffic has grown rapidly and by 2001 trains were overcrowded. Platforms have since been extended and now 3-car trains can be operated. To assist this line and others with traffic growth, WEG obtained some more Regio Shuttles and moved various units around the different lines that it operates. The line remains the property of the local authorities but is operated by WEG. Plans for electrification are bring studied.

ZWECKVERBAND "STROHGÄUBAHN" (ZSB)
Ludwigsburg, Baden-Württemberg.

Traction: Seven 650.
Depot: Hemmingen.

This 22 km long branch line, previously called "Nebenbahn Korntal–Weissach", is not far from Stuttgart and has a good amount of commuter traffic with some trains running through to Stuttgart-Feuerbach station to connect into the S-Bahn. However it was not so busy at the Weissach end. Since 2010 the local communities have in fact bought the line, invested in track renewals and rolling stock and handed it over to WEG to run on their behalf. The section of line from Heimerdingen to Weissach has a much reduced service and may be closed. A new workshop/depot has been established at Hemmingen to service the new Regio Shuttles from Stadler.

ZWECKVERBAND VERKEHRSVERBAND WIESLAUFTALBAHN (ZVVW)
Waiblingen, Baden-Württemberg.

Traction: Four 626 and two 650.
Depot: Rudersberg.

This is a similar situation to ZVS. In this case officials from Schorndorf, Rudersberg and elsewhere got together with WEG to take over the closed DB line from Schorndorf to Rudersberg and Welzheim. DB handed it over in 1993 for 1 DM! The line was reopened in 1995. Three NE 81 railcars and trailers were obtained, being one of the last orders for this type of unit before the new generation of units came on the scene. Traffic growth here has also been strong and so RS railcars had to be obtained to provide some back up. The section beyond Rudersberg Oberndorf to Welzheim has not reopened to regular traffic but tourist trains have been run on this section.

ZÜRCHER BAU GmbH   ZBAU
Meissenheim, Baden-Württemberg.

EVU Licence: Freight, 01/02/2013–31/01/2028.

This track contractor works all over Baden Württemberg. Despite the firm dating from 1995 it still only has one locomotive!

2. LEASING COMPANIES

One of the features of the open access railway is the rise in the number of leasing companies which, like the locomotives they own, come in varying sizes; from large companies like Alpha Trains with several hundred locomotives and rolling stock to small firms with just a handful of locomotives.

This is nothing new as there have always been firms that could supply a locomotive at short notice, but this was previously more applicable to industrial concerns. Locomotive builders also usually had locomotives available to cover for ones they have supplied that become defective. Main line railway companies usually had enough spare capacity to move locomotives around from one area to another but the arrival of open access operators created a demand for more locomotives and rolling stock. And so the leasing business entered the big time.

The major leasing companies all have financial backers – indeed shareholders, often banks, that supply the cash to buy the locomotives. These are then leased out on varying terms. The type of lease varies depending on whether a locomotive is needed by an operating company on a long term basis or simply to cover a traffic peak or known short term traffic flow. Some operating companies lease locomotives on a long term basis, sometimes owning them after a set period. One can think of car hire as a comparison – a car can be hired for a short period, going back to the owning company at the end of the hire. A car can also be leased for a longer fixed period and again goes back to the owner at the end of the lease. Alternatively a car can be purchased on hire purchase whereby it becomes yours when all the instalments have been paid. The same applies to locomotive leasing.

Another strange thing is sub-leasing. An operator can approach their usual leasing company for a locomotive when there is nothing available from the leasing company's stock. The leasing company will strike a deal with another leasing company, saving the operator doing a lot of shopping around. Another thing that happens is when a train operating company leases out a locomotive to another operator. In fact the locomotive is quite often sub-leased.

Depending on the type of lease, locomotives may carry the VKM of the leasing company or that of the operating company. They can also carry advertising for the operator but many retain the owning company's livery. Most MRCE locomotives are now black but here again some are in advertising liveries – all taken into account in the leasing deal. The principal leasing companies are:

AKIEM   AK

This company is a subsidiary of SNCF, formed to find work for the many surplus locomotives in the SNCF fleet. Principally, as far as Germany is concerned, Prima locomotives of the 37xxx series are used, getting as far as the Polish border.

ALPHA TRAINS GROUP S.a.r.l.   AT

Based in Luxembourg this firm is descended from the British Rolling Stock Company, Angel Trains. Besides dealing with the British market a subsidiary company was established as Angel Trains International, later known as Angel Trains Europa. Initially the Royal Bank of Scotland was involved but gave up its share and now British, German, Australian and Canadian financial institutions are involved. In 2009 the name was changed from Angel Trains to Alpha Trains. Early in 2014 the locomotives that still belonged to RBS but had been leased on its behalf by Alpha Trains were purchased. So now there is a considerable fleet.

Alpha Trains is divided into two companies:

Alpha Trains Europa stems from Angel Trains Europa and is based in Köln. It is principally involved in passenger rolling stock having bought DMUs and EMUs from Alstom, Bombardier, Siemens and Stadler and leases them to companies such as Arriva, Veolia etc.
Alpha Trains (Locomotives) is basically the former Angel Trains Cargo and is based in Antwerpen. Cargo is the clue here as most of the locomotives are for freight train operators; wagons are also leased. In 2013 there were 230 Alpha Trains locomotives and 137 that were owned by RBS; so in 2015 Alpha Trains has over 360 locomotives on its books. These have come from suppliers such as Bombardier, Classes 145, 185, 186; Siemens ER20 and various types of Mak/Vossloh locomotives, especially G1000, G1206, G1700, G2000.
Two VKMs seem to be in use, ATDE being used for Alpha Trains Europa and ATLD being used for Alpha Trains Locomotives (The DE or D standing for Deutschland).

ALSTOM LOKOMOTIVEN SERVICE Gmbh ALS

After German unification the former DR workshop at Stendal found itself with hundreds of surplus former DR V100s. It started improving them and selling or leasing them to the emerging market. DB then went into partnership with Alstom doing the same work, with Alstom eventually buying up the DB share. Their rebuilding programme for the V100s went on for years and after most of those had been dealt with the works then started modernising or just overhauling former DB V100s. Alstom was also looking to the future. It had built many DMUs for new operators and realised that these trains would need major overhauls in the future, so Stendal works is just what it wanted and is not so far from Salzgitter works. Alstom is now converting some former Class 202s or 298s to battery operation, but in some cases is building new battery electric shunting locomotives for leasing or purchase.

ALTMARK-RAIL Gmbh AMR

This small company in Oebisfelde dates from about 2011 when a railfan bought some former Danish Nohab diesels from Eicholz Eivel and appears to lease them to other operators.

ANLAGEN UND GRUNDSTUCKSVERMIETUNGSGESELLSCHAFT mbH & Co KG AGV

Only a few locomotives were purchased by this company in the early days of open access.

ASCENDOS RAIL LEASING AS

Ascendos Rail Leasing is a subsidiary of CB Rail Sàrl based in Luxembourg and looks after locomotives based in that country and Germany. CB Rail was formed in 2004, taking over the European operations of Porterbrook. Ascendos has Class 66, 145, 185 and ER20 locos plus numerous DMUs and EMUs e.g. Alstom LINT 27 and LINT 41 DMUs and FLIRT 2 and FLIRT 3 EMUs.

BEACON RAIL LEASING LIMITED BRL

This company can be traced back to 2007 as ALLCO, an Australian company soon afterwards changing its name to BTMU, an arm of Mitsubishi. The Beacon Rail name was adopted in 2009. BRL was acquired by Pamplona Capital Management in 2014. It has 77 locomotives, 20 railcars and lots of wagons.

BeNEX Gmbh BX

Founded in 2007 this company is a spin off from the Hamburger Hochbahn AG; BeNEX being understood to mean better networks. Financial partners were soon found and the company appears to have gone from strength to strength. It is involved with several train operating companies such as Agilis, Cantus, Metronom, Nordbahn and ODEG, either part owning the company or owning some of the rolling stock. BeNEX has its own EVU licence: Freight & Passenger, 09/11/2007–30/11/2022.

B UND V LEIPZIG Gmbh BUVL

A relative new comer, this company saw the possibilities that would arise from DB renewing its heaving duty shunting locomotive fleet and making class 290s etc surplus.

COMMERZ REAL MOBILIEN LEASING Gmbh

Mainly involved in providing finance.

DEUTSCHE LEASING · DL

Just like AGV, Deutsche Leasing was involved with the early days of open access, acquiring three 185s but little since.

ELL GERMANY GmbH – EUROPEAN LOCOMOTIVE LEASING · ELOC

A relatively new leasing company based in Wien that seems to have grown very rapidly. It is owned by KKR & Co. LP which is a global investment firm. 50 Vectron locomotives have been ordered from Siemens.

FAHRZEUGBEREITSTELLUNG BADEN-WÜRTTEMBERG GmbH · FBBW

This leasing company was set up to acquire rolling stock for use by train companies operating in Baden-Württemberg.

FAHRZEUGMANAGEMENT REGION FRANKFURT RHEINMAIN GmbH · FAHMA

A similar arrangement to the above for the Frankfurt/Main area.

FAHRZEUG VERMIETUNG DUISBURG GmbH · FVD

A new player on the leasing scene; it has acquired some Austrian 1142s.

HANNOVER MOBILEN LEASING GmbH · HML

Another finance firm involved in the early days of open access having provided the finance for the ALEX 183s and some 185s; owns about 20 locos in total.

KBC LEASE BV LEUVEN (BELGIUM) · KBC

This company provided the finance for some of the DLC/Crossrail 66s.

LANDESNAVERKEHRSGESELLSCHAFT NIEDERSACHSEN mbH · LNVG

The Land of Niedersachsen was one of the first to set up its own leasing company for train operators in the state. Consequently, when a franchise changes hands the trains stay. This is a good arrangement with the Land providing the trains for public transport in the state and able to augment fleets when traffic increases and also able to move units around from one franchise to another should there be a problem with a particular fleet. Interestingly most of the stock purchased tends to be built by Alstom – based in Niedersachsen!

MACQUARIE EUROPEAN RAIL · MER

This is an Australian backed company believed to be descended from Hill Samuel. It took over part of the CB Rail fleet in 2013 with the other part going to Ascendos. CB Rail is understood to have been part of the Lloyds Banking Group. Amongst the locomotive types taken over were EMD 66s, Bombardier TRAXX electric and diesel and some Alstom Primas.

MRCE DISPOLOK GmbH – MITSUI RAIL CAPITAL EUROPE
MRCE/DISPO

This leasing company started off as a subsidiary of Siemens, being originally Siemens Dispolok formed to lease out Siemens built locomotives. In 2006 Dispolok was purchased by Mitsui Rail Capital Europe BV (MRCE) which is a subsidiary of Mitsui & Co. Ltd in Japan. The link with Siemens remains as virtually all locomotives owned are Siemens built. Interestingly MRCE still uses the original VKM – DISPO.

NORTHRAIL GmbH   NRAIL/NTS/KIEL

This is a public-private partnership between Seehafen Kiel GmbH & Co. KG and the investment company Paribus, founded in 2008. Note the Kiel connection with a large number of the locomotives for hire being built in Kiel by Vossloh or Voith. Northrail has two VKMs one for itself as NRAIL and another for a subsidiary NTS – Northrail Technical Services GmbH & Co. KG. Also some locomotives carry the VKM KIEL denoting Seehafen Kiel, which probably represents part of the investment made by that company.

OAK CAPITAL – HAMBURGER EISENBAHN EK   HAEG

Another financial firm getting involved in leasing locomotives; it is understood to have USA backers.

PRIGNITZER LEASING

Thought to be a subsidiary of PEG, it owns some of the locos used by EGP.

RAIL CHARTER FAHRZEUGBEREITSSTELLUNG

This Mannheim based company is a financing arranger. Just look who owns it - 25% HzL, 25% SWEG and 50% ADtranz! It owns all the Regio Shuttles delivered to the railway companies - BSB 9, HzL 22, SWEG 8, OSB 18, DB RAB 20, and 3 spare. It appears that ADtranz is underwriting the purchase of its own units!

RAILPOOL GmbH   RPOOL

Railpool was founded in 2008 with two German banks as backers. Soon some 186s were purchased from Angel Trains which had them stored as it could not find any takers. In May 2014 Oak Tree Capital Management (Los Angeles) bought 50% of the shares and as it already owned some is now the major owner. 45 electric locomotives are owned but increasing as on 25/06/2014, 65 TRAXX electric locomotives were ordered from Bombardier (35 firm, 30 option); a mix of AC2 and MS, the AC2 to be last mile locos which really makes them AC3. There are also some Vectrons on order.

SOCIÉTÉ GÉNÉRALE

Purely a financial company providing the initial cash to obtain stock; it owns most of the BRB VT 200s.

SRI RAIL INVEST GmbH   SRI

A small company still finding its feet but doing well. Founded in 2013/14 by Simon Scherer, it has acquired some 145s and 151s.

SÜDLEASING GmbH   SL

Süd Leasing GmbH is based in Stuttgart and is part of Landesbank Baden Württemberg. It has provided finance for a small amount of rolling stock such as V100s (DB and DR).

SUMITOMO DEUTSCHLAND GmbH

A small number of locomotives have been financed by this firm including SWT 203s and some Locon locomotives.

VOITH TURBO LOKOMOTIVTECHNIK GmbH & Co KG   VTLT

Voith is well known for its transmission gear used on a large percentage of diesel hydraulic locomotives and railcars. A few years ago some former managers with Vossloh changed sides in Kiel and joined the Voith concern which then started to produce locomotives and got the contract to supply new heavy duty shunting locos to DB. It also built some large 3000 and 4000 kW locomotives. Then the bottom fell out of the market as nearly all countries in Europe had renewed their diesel fleets. Voith ended up with locomotives on hand which now form a leasing fleet. Locomotive production has now ceased.

VOSSLOH LOCOMOTIVES GmbH   VL

Vossloh is the locomotive builder but has always had locomotives in stock for sale or lease. Locomotives are built in Kiel but there is a plant in Moers that overhauls Vossloh built locomotives; so there can be short term leases of stock locomotives whilst a client has a locomotive under repair or general overhaul.

▲ Still carrying the markings applied by Voith Turbo Lokomotivtechnik, this is Stock-Transport's powerful Maxima 40CC, 92 80 1264 001 with a train of grain bound for Köln-Eifeltor near Linz on the right bank of the Rhine, on 5 May 2013.   **Matthias Müller**

3. FLEET LISTS

ORDER OF FLEET LISTS

In this new edition the locomotive and railcar fleets are presented in the order of their new European Vehicle Numbers. With more and more private operators using standard locomotives, or in many cases former DB/DR locomotives, it is felt that this is the most convenient way to show the data. The numbering system is explained below but it does not cover everything such as narrow gauge locomotives. As most of the narrow gauge fleets tend to be steam locomotives they have been listed with the standard gauge locomotives and for the sake of simplicity other narrow gauge traction is also listed at the end of the respective sections. But, all narrow gauge diesel locomotives are listed under diesel shunting locos because of their low speed.

EUROPEAN VEHICLE NUMBER & VEHICLE KEEPER MARKING

The European Vehicle Number (EVN) is a refinement of the former UIC full identification number. Because of open access in Europe it is essential that all traction (and indeed all rolling stock) has a European number. The Vehicle Keeper Marking (VKM) has been deemed necessary because of the large number of railway operators in a country following open access and follows the country code. This has helped to simplify matters in Germany as many private operators had duplicate numbers. Now they have a unique EVN as well! This allows all private locomotives to be listed in some sort of order!

Taking electric loco 120 151 as an example its full EVN is 91 80 6120 151-6 D-DB which breaks down as follows:

The first digit is a code for a traction unit with the second digit giving the type of traction. In Germany the types are:

90. Miscellaneous traction – mostly used for steam locomotives e.g. 90 80 0001 509-3 D-PRESS but also hybrid locomotives.
91. Electric Locomotives faster than 99 km/h e.g. 91 80 6186 336-4 D-DB
92. Diesel locomotives faster than 99 km/h e.g. 92 80 1261 036-8 D-DB
93. High speed EMUs e.g. 93 80 5403 027-6 D-DB
94. EMUs e.g. 94 80 0440 106-3 D-AGIL
95. DMUs e.g. 95 80 0650 067-1 D-ODEG
96. Loose trailers (Not used in Germany)
97. Electric shunting locomotives or electric locomotives with maximum speed less than 100 km/h e.g. 97 80 8194 052-7 D-LEG
98. Diesel shunting locomotives or diesel locomotive with maximum speed less than 100 km/h e.g. 98 80 3363 622-2 D-DB
99. Departmental self powered vehicles – includes tamping machines etc. Because of this several DB departmental locomotives have regained their original numbers. Also to note is that vehicles once numbered as DB 701 xxx are shown in this section but under their old numbers as few new numbers are known.

Note that the old UIC railway number (in this case 80 for DB) now stands for the country and not the railway. The railway concerned is indicated at the end as the vehicle keeper. In some cases this might not be a railway but a leasing company.

The following seven digits make up the unique serial number of the locomotive. It will be seen that in most cases the old classification and running number, e.g. 186 336, form part of the new serial number. But in years to come there could be 0186, 1186, 2186 etc with the same running number 336 (This is already happening with the new Class 442 EMUs which have appeared as 442, 1442, 2442 and 9442!). DB in fact selected the leading extra digit in the EVN serial number to keep existing computer check digits the same, but this does not apply to all types, and in particular to DMUs and EMUs. The final number is a computer check digit and is followed by the country code and the VKM.

The full EVN/VKM is shown on the sides of locomotives and vehicles and can be very small as it is a rather long piece of information. For this same reason numbers on the front of locomotives and units only show the basic number without a check digit. With this development check digits have not been shown in the main lists.

(Of the VKMs shown above, DB is self explanatory, AGIL is AGILIS - one of the new private operators whilst ODEG is Ostdeutsche Eisenbahn Gesellschaft. These codes are used in this book to identify the various private operators).

LOCOMOTIVE FLEETS

The locomotive fleets are a very mixed lot as one would expect from numerous private railways. However many locomotives on the different lines are of the same basic type. To meet the needs of the private railways all major German manufacturers produced some standard models, most of these being types not in use on the main lines. In the 1970s the Bundesverband Deutscher Eisenbahnen decided on a series of standard diesel locomotives for use on private lines. Perhaps one manufacturer that should be mentioned in particular is MaK, later Siemens FT and now Vossloh. It has built hundreds of locomotives for industry and private railways, none of which types were built for DB. The MaK B-B single cab diesel now totals more than 1000 examples with the type being continually refined to meet customer needs. This locomotive type has found itself on to several national railway systems such as NS (Class 6400) and Belgian Railways (Class 7700).

CLASSIFICATION OF LOCOMOTIVES

In these lists the locomotives are referred to by their manufacturer's classification such as G1200BB, MG530C etc, or by their DB classification when ex-main line. The classification system is quite simple but does seem to vary from builder to builder; consequently some classifications are still not explained.

In the example of a MaK G1200BB this is broken down as follows:

G   =   Gelenkwelle – cardan shaft
1200 =   1200 horse power
BB   =   B-B wheel arrangement.

A Deutz MG530C is :

M   =   Mittellok i.e. mid horsepower range 300–800 h.p.
G   =   Gelenkwelle – cardan shaft
530   =   530 horse power
C   =   Three axles

Some Deutz descriptions also have an additional suffix of E or M denoting Endführerhaus (end cab) or Mittelführerhaus (middle or centre cab).

WHEEL ARRANGEMENT

For steam locomotives the Whyte notation is the one most British readers will be used to. The number of leading wheels are given, followed by the number of driving wheels and then the trailing wheels. So a 4-6-2 would have two pairs of wheels in front of the driving wheels and another pair behind. Tank locomotives have a T following the wheel arrangement such as 2-6-2T but the type of tank is also shown so there can be ST (Saddle Tank) and WT (Well Tank), but where there is the usual sort of side tank the letter "T" alone is used.

In Continental Europe, different systems applied in different countries with the French counting the number of axles rather than wheels so a 4-6-2 becomes a 231. In Germany a different system applied and was more informative. The number of driving wheels is denoted by a letter where A = 1 axle, B = 2 axles etc whilst numbers were used for the axles before and after the driving wheels so that a 4-6-2 becomes a 2C1. But the system went further so that a superheated locomotive is shown by a letter "h" (heissdampf) and the number of cylinders is also shown so that a superheated 4-6-2 with three cylinders would be shown as a 2C1h3.

Diesel and electric locomotives use the same system as in the UK. A letter denotes the number of axles where A=1, B = 2 etc so that a bogie locomotive would be a B-B but where the axles are individually powered this is denoted by the addition of a letter "o" so that a bogie locomotive with four traction motors would be a Bo-Bo. Where there is a problem is with older shunting locomotives that use coupling rods. The continental system uses a "C" to denote a three axle shunter but in this book where it is known the locomotive has coupling rods it is shown in the Whyte notation as an 0-6-0. Unpowered axles are denoted by a number so that an electric multiple unit with a power bogie under the cab and an unpowered one at the other end is shown as Bo-2.

ACCOMMODATION

Seating accommodation information is given in the format F/S nT (or TD) where F and S represent the number of first and standard class seats respectively and T or TD gives the number of toilets (TD denotes a toilet designated suitable for use by a disabled person). A number in brackets denotes additional tip-up seats. For example 16/48 1T (4) would be a vehicle with 16 first class seats and 48 standard class seats, with 4 additional tip-up seats and a toilet.

▲ Harzer Schmalspurbahn (HSB) 0-4-4-0T 99 5902 rests at Brocken summit on 7 December 2009, with Wernigerode visible down below on the right.   **Brian Garvin**

3.1. CODE 90 80 – STEAM AND MISCELLANEOUS LOCOMOTIVES

This classification has been given to steam locomotives and other types that do not fit into the main scheme. Consequently the new hybrid locomotives built/converted by Alstom have this classification, but not the new last mile electric locomotives built by Bombardier (although one wonders whether new electric locomotives fitted with last mile diesel engines should technically appear here!). As steam locomotives are classified in this series it seems appropriate to include here the narrow gauge steam locos which are not covered by the EVN scheme.

The new numbers for steam locos are listed here but note the locomotives are also listed in the preserved section as most are of course museum locomotives. The lack of consistency can be seen with the new EVNs allocated to Classes 50 and 52; also note that a battery electric railcar appears here as the new EVN system did not consider such units.

3.1.1. STANDARD GAUGE STEAM LOCOMOTIVES

This list gives details of active main line steam locomotives. Locomotives appear in the respective preserved locomotive sections in this book and in German Railways Part 1 but are listed here to shown their computer numbers.

EVN	VKM	Old No.	EVN	VKM	Old No.
0001 066	BYB	01 066	0053 501	DLW	50 3501
0001 118	DME	01 118	0053 545	GfE	50 3545
0001 150	EJS	01 150	0053 552	MH	52 3552
0001 180	BYB	01 180	0053 610	WFL	50 3610
0001 509	PRESS	01 509	0064 289	NESA	64 289
0001 519	NESA	01 519	0064 419	DBK	64 419
0003 155	WFL	03 2155	0064 491	DFS	64 491
0003 204	LDC	03 204	0065 157	BEF	65 1057
0012 066	HDS	01 1066	0070 083	BLV	70 083
0018 201	DME	18 201	0075 118	UEF	75 1118
0018 478	BYB	18 478	0075 998	IBE	131.060
0031 010	HLP	03 1010	0078 468	ETL	78 468
0035 019	LDC	35 1019	0080 106	DBK	80 106
0035 097	MTEG	35 1097	0086 333	WTB	86 333
0038 267	DGEG	38 2267	0088 992	DFS	(9445)
0038 460	LBR	Posen 2455	0088 995	HC	HC 5
0041 150	BYB	41 1150	0089 363	GES	89 363
0044 486	EFSFT	44 1486	0089 977	EBEFW	EFW 1
0044 546	BYB	44 2546	0089 984	EMD	Waldbröl
0044 616	UEF	44 1616	0089 987	KBB	Speyerbach
0050 988	WTB	50 2988	0091 134	PRESS	91 134
0051 077		52 8077	0092 993	GES	11
0051 079	DME	52 8079	0092 995	BEF	Ampflwang
0051 087	SDN	52 8087	0093 960	WTB	93 1360
0051 106	EFSK	52 8106	0094 999	HC	206
0051 131	WFL	52 8131	0095 027	DLHBS	95 027
0051 134	EFBS	52 8134	0515 011	BEM	515 011
0051 154	EMBB	52 8154	2528 168	BYB	52 8168
0051 177	DLFB	52 8177	4111 144	IGEW	41 1144
0052 360	HEV	52 1360	5261 006	VEB	52 6106
0052 409	DME	52 7409	5280 075	IGEW	52 8075
0052 544	HC	52 4544	5280 195	FME	52 8195
0052 596	NESA	52 7596	6510 049	LEG	65 1049
0052 867	HEF	52 4867	8000 010	WAB	10

3.1.2. NARROW GAUGE STEAM LOCOMOTIVES

99.15xx   750 mm Gauge – MEYER   0-4-4-0T (BBn4vt)

A particularly special type of locomotive was built for the Sächsische Staatsbahn which had many narrow gauge lines linking main lines with mountain valleys and resorts. The type IV K is a Meyer locomotive which is different to a Mallet in that the two sets of cylinders face each other. Under unification it was decided that these lines would not form part of the national network so they have been privatised, most becoming part of the Sächsische Dampfeisenbahngesellschaft mbH. It should be noted that many locomotives were "rebuilt" in the 1960s but were in fact new locomotives, the "rebuilding" keeping the accountants happy. Some of the locomotives are still fitted for the "Heberlein Bremse" which was a cable brake connected to the train, pre-dating vacuum brakes.

Built: 1899–1921.   **Gauge:** 750 mm.
Builder: Hartmann.   **Boiler Pressure:** 15 bar.
Wheel Diameter: 760 mm.   **Weight:** 27.4–29.6 tonnes.
Length over Buffers: 9.00 m.   **Cylinders:** (4), 2: 240 x 380 mm.
Maximum Speed: 50 km/h.   2: 370 x 380 mm.

Number	Works No	Built	Location	Notes
99 1561 (Z)	3214	1909	DBGM Mügeln	Ex DB 099 703
99 1564 (Z)	3217	1909	SDG Freital Potschappel	Ex DB 099 705
99 1574	3556	1912	DBGM Mügeln	Ex DB 099 707
99 1584 (Z)	3595	1912	DBGM Mügeln	Ex DB 099 709
99 1594 (Z)	3714	1913	RüBB Glauchau	Ex Norway, ex DR
99 1608	4521	1921	SDG Freital/Radebeul	Ex DB 099 713

99.173x   750 mm Gauge   2-10-2T (1E1h2t)

These locomotives were introduced during the DRG period as a standard locomotive intended to replace most of the Meyers.

Built: 1928–33.   **Gauge:** 750 mm.
Builder: Hartmann (731-741), BMAG (746-762).   **Boiler Pressure:** 14 bar.
Wheel Diameter: 800 mm.   **Weight:** 56.7 tonnes.
Length over Buffers: 10.54 m.   **Cylinders:** (2), 450 x 400 mm.
Maximum Speed: 30 km/h.

Number	Works No	Built	Location	Notes
99 731	4678	1928	SOEG Zittau	Ex DB 099 722
99 1734	4681	1928	SDG Freital	Ex DB 099 723
99 735 (Z)	4682	1928	Oberwiesenthal	Ex DB 099 724
99 1741	4691	1929	Oberwiesenthal	Ex DB 099 725
99 1746	9535	1929	SDG Freital	Ex DB 099 726
99 1747	9536	1929	SDG Nossen	Ex DB 099 727
99 749	9538	1929	SOEG Zittau	Ex DB 099 728
99 750	9539	1929	Grossschönau; plinthed	Ex DB 099 729
99 757 (Z)	10148	1933	SOEG Zittau	Ex DB 099 730
99 758	10149	1933	SOEG Zittau	Ex DB 099 731
99 759	10150	1933	Oberrittersgrün; museum loco	Ex DB 099 732
99 760	10151	1933	SOEG Zittau	Ex DB 099 733
99 1761 (Z)	10152	1933	SDG Cranzahl stored	Ex DB 099 734
99 1762	10153	1933	SDG Oberwiesenthal	Ex DB 099 735

99.177x   750 mm Gauge   2-10-2T (1E1h2t)

These locomotives are a post second world war continuation of the type mentioned above. Since unification many have received new boilers, new frames, new cylinders etc. and are in effect new locomotives!

Built: 1952–57.
Builder: BMAG, LKM.
Wheel Diameter: 800 mm.
Length over Buffers: 10.54 m.
Maximum Speed: 30 km/h.

Gauge: 750 mm.
Boiler Pressure: 14 bar.
Weight: 58 tonnes.
Cylinders: (2), 450 x 400 mm.

Number	Works No	Built	Location	Notes
99 771	32010	1952	SDG Freital	Ex DB 099 736
99 772	32011	1952	SDG Oberwiesenthal	Ex DB 099 737
99 773	32012	1952	SDG Oberwiesenthal	Ex DB 099 738
99 1775 (Z)	32014	1953	SDG Radebeul	Ex DB 099 739
99 1776 (Z)	32015	1953	SDG Oberwiesenthal	Ex DB 099 740
99 1777	32016	1953	SDG Radebeul	Ex DB 099 741
99 1778	32017	1953	SDG Nossen; museum loco	Ex DB 099 742
99 1779 (Z)	32018	1953	SDG Radebeul	Ex DB 099 743
99 1780 (Z)	32019	1953	SDG Freital	Ex DB 099 744
99 1781	32022	1953	RüBB Putbus	Ex DB 099 745
99 1782	32023	1953	RüBB Putbus	Ex DB 099 746
99 783	32024	1953	RüBB Putbus	Ex DB 099 747
99 1784	32025	1953	RüBB Putbus	Ex DB 099 748
99 785	32026	1954	SDG Oberwiesenthal	Ex DB 099 749
99 786 (Z)	32027	1954	SDG Cranzahl	Ex DB 099 750
99 787	132028	1955	SOEG Zittau	Ex DB 099 751
99 1789	132030	1955	SDG Radebeul	Ex DB 099 753
99 1790	132031	1955	SDG Freital; exhibited	Ex DB 099 754
99 1791	132032	1955	SDG	Ex DB 099 755
99 1793	132034	1955	SDG Oberwiesenthal	Ex DB 099 756
99 794 (Z)	132035	1955	SDG Cranzahl	Ex DB 099 757

99 4011   750 mm Gauge   0-8-0T (Dh2t)

This locomotive was obtained by a previous owner of the RüBB and has now been purchased by the current company. It was originally built for the Mansfeld AG, Bergbau- und Hüttenbetrieb, Eisleben No. 7 and passed in due course to the Mansfelder Transport GmbH upon unification. Being designed for hauling heavy freight in an industrial concern it seems quite at home working loaded tourist trains.

Built: 1931.
Builder: OK.
Wheel Diameter:
Length over Buffers: 9.04 m.
Maximum Speed: 30 km/h.

Gauge: 750 mm.
Boiler Pressure: 13 bar.
Weight: 40 tonnes.
Cylinders: (2).

Number	Works No	Built	Notes
"99 4011"	12348	1931	Ex Industry

99.4603   750 mm Gauge   0-4-0WT (Bn2t)

This locomotive was built for L. Moll, a building contractor in München, and was on a plinth until being acquired by Austrian locomotive fans for the Hirschwang–Reichenau line. It was then sold to the previous owner of the RüBB who had it overhauled in Romania and brought it to Putbus. It has now been acquired by the current RüBB owners in lieu of unpaid rent for storage at Putbus. Just what they plan to do with it is not clear. It has a fictitious number; there was a real 99 4603 on the line but it was scrapped in 1966. This locomotive has been made to look like the original.

Built: 1934.
Builder: Henschel.
Wheel Diameter:
Length over Buffers: 6.0 m (approx).
Maximum Speed: 25 km/h.

Gauge: 750 mm.
Boiler Pressure: 13 bar.
Weight: 12.5 tonnes (approx).
Cylinders: (2).

Number	Works No	Built	Notes
"99 4603"	22619	1935	Ex Industry

99.4632   750 mm Gauge   0-8-0WT (Dh2t)

These locomotives were built for the Rügenschen Kleinbahnen and are now happily still working on the remaining part of that system. It is not unknown for them to carry their original numbers 52, 53 Mh.

Built: 1914, 1925.
Builder: Vulcan.
Wheel Diameter: 850 mm.
Length over Buffers: 8.00 m.
Maximum Speed: 30 km/h.

Gauge: 750 mm.
Boiler Pressure: 12 bar.
Weight: 24 tonnes.
Cylinders: (2), 350 x 400 mm.

Number	Works No	Built	Notes
99 4632	2951	1914	Ex DB 099 770
99 4633	3851	1925	Ex DB 099 771

99.4801   750 mm Gauge   2-8-0T (1Dh2t)

Not quite the wheel arrangement one would expect on a narrow gauge line. These locos were built for the Kleinbahnen des Kreises Jerichow. After closure of this network the locos were transferred to Rügen where they remain.

Built: 1938.
Builder: Henschel.
Wheel Diameter: 850 mm.
Length over Buffers: 9.44 m.
Maximum Speed: 45 km/h.

Gauge: 750 mm.
Boiler Pressure: 13 bar.
Weight: 29.7 tonnes.
Cylinders: (2), 360 x 410 mm.

Number	Works No	Built	Notes
99 4801	24367	1938	Ex DB 099 780
99 4802	24368	1938	Ex DB 099 781

99.232x   900 mm Gauge   2-8-2T (1D1h2t)

The "Molli" is the nickname for the narrow gauge line from Bad Doberan to Kuhlungsborn West which for Germany features the unusual gauge of 900 mm. Nationalised under the communist regime, the line is now back in private ownership and has received significant investment; the headline item is a new steam locomotive but not to be dismissed are the extensive modernised facilities at Bad Doberan (new depot and carriage shed). The three original locomotives have all received new frames.

Built: 1932 (2321–3), 2009 (2324).
Builder: OK (2321–3), Meiningen (2324).
Wheel Diameter: 1100 mm.
Length over Buffers: 10.60 m.
Maximum Speed: 50 km/h.

Gauge: 900 mm.
Boiler Pressure: 14 bar.
Weight: 43.68 tonnes.
Cylinders: (2), 380 x 550 mm.

Number	Works No	Built	Notes
99 2321	12400	1932	Ex DB 099 901; new frames 01/2006
99 2322	12401	1932	Ex DB 099 902; new frames 11/2003
99 2323	12402	1932	Ex DB 099 903; new frames –/2006
99 2324	203	2009	

99.233x   900 mm Gauge   0-8-0T (Dh2t)

These locos were originally built for the Wismut AG industrial concern and came into DR stock in 1961. Nowadays they are rarely used and one is in fact normally on display at Kuhlungsborn West station

Built: 1950.
Builder: LKM.
Wheel Diameter: 800 mm.
Length over Buffers: 8.86 m.
Maximum Speed: 35 km/h.

Gauge: 900 mm.
Boiler Pressure: 14 bar.
Weight: 32.4 tonnes.
Cylinders: (2), 370 x 500 mm.

Number	Works No	Built	Notes
99 2331	30011	1951	Ex DB 099 904
99 332	30012	1951	Ex DB 099 905; on display

99.59xx   1000 mm Gauge   0-4-4-0T (BBn4vt)

Built for the Nordhausen–Wernigerode Eisenbahn (NWE), these locomotives remain on home territory. 99 5906 was acquired from the Ruhr–Lippe Eisenbahn in 1920 and is slightly longer. They are usually held at Wernigerode for tourist specials. 99 5903 is reported stored off site on the back of a lorry which takes it to "events" as an advertisement for the line.

Built: 1897–1918.
Builder: Jung (5901–3), Karlsruhe (5906).
Wheel Diameter: 1000 mm.
Length over Buffers: 8.875 m (99 5906 9.40 m).
Maximum Speed: 30 km/h.

Gauge: 1000 mm.
Boiler Pressure: 14 bar.
Weight: 36 tonnes.
Cylinders: (4), 2: 285 x 500 mm.
2: 425 x 500 mm.

Number	Works No	Built	Notes
99 5901	258	1897	NWE 11
99 5902	261	1897	NWE 14 then 12
99 5903	345	1897	NWE 18 then 13; stored
99 5906	2052	1897	NWE 41

99.6001   1000 mm Gauge   2-6-2T (1C1h2t)

Originally NWE 21 it retains its DR number. It was built by Krupp as a prototype standard locomotive for narrow gauge lines but remains a unique example.

Built: 1939.
Builder: Krupp.
Wheel Diameter: 800 mm.
Length over Buffers: 8.91 m.
Maximum Speed: 50 km/h.

Gauge: 1000 mm.
Boiler Pressure: 14 bar.
Weight: 32 tonnes.
Cylinders: (2), 420 x 500 mm.

Number	Works No	Built	Notes
99 6001	1875	1939	NWE 21

99.6101   1000 mm Gauge   0-6-0T (Ch2t)

These locomotives were built for shunting duties. HSB retains one whilst the other is in the hands of a local society.

Built: 1914.
Builder: Henschel.
Wheel Diameter: 800 mm.
Length over Buffers: 7.73 m.
Maximum Speed: 30 km/h.

Gauge: 1000 mm.
Boiler Pressure: 14 bar.
Weight: 32 tonnes.
Cylinders: (2), 400 x 400 mm.

Number	Works No	Built	Notes
99 6101	12879	1914	NWE 6
99 6102	12880	1914	NWE 7

99.72xx   1000 mm Gauge   2-10-2T (1E1h2t)

These massive narrow gauge locomotives can be regarded as a scaled down standard gauge Class 85. 99 7222 is one of the locomotives built for the now closed Eisfeld–Schonbrunn line and was sent to Norway in the second world war, ending up back in Germany and arrived at Wernigerode in 1966. All others were built in the 1950s to replace ageing locomotives. In recent years HSB has had many of the locomotives overhauled at Meiningen works. However, as many of the overhauled locomotives have new boilers, new frames and new cylinders they must surely be new locomotives! The curvaceous nature of the Harzer Schmalspurbahnen lines certainly causes lots of wear and tear. Some of the stored locomotives are awaiting their turn for attention at the Meiningen clinic.

Built: 1931, 1954–56.
Builder: BMAG (99 7222), LKM.
Wheel Diameter: 1000 mm.
Length over Buffers: 11.73 m (99 7222 11.64 m). **Cylinders:** (2), 500 x 500 mm.
Maximum Speed: 45 km/h.

Gauge: 1000 mm.
Boiler Pressure: 14 bar.
Weight: 65.8 tonnes.

Number	Works No	Built	Notes
99 7222	9921	1931	
99 7231 (Z)	134008	1954	Stored, Ilfeld
99 7232	134009	1954	New frames 08/2004
99 7233 (Z)	134010	1954	Stored, Ilfeld
99 7234	134011	1954	New frames 05/2009
99 7235	134012	1954	
99 7236	134013	1955	New frames 7/2008
99 7237	134014	1955	
99 7238 (Z)	134015	1955	Stored, Gernrode
99 7239	134016	1955	New frames 03/2007
99 7240	134017	1955	New frames 04/2013
99 7241	134018	1955	New frames 05/2009
99 7242 (Z)	134019	1955	Stored, Benneckenstein
99 7243	134020	1955	
99 7244 (Z)	134021	1955	Stored, Hasselfelde
99 7245	134022	1955	New frames ?
99 7246 (Z)	134023	1955	Stored, Benneckenstein
99 7247	134024	1956	

3.1.3. HYBRID LOCOMOTIVES

90 80 1001   HYBRID   B-B

Alstom Stendal modernised many of the former DR Class 201/202 diesel locomotives, mostly with improved engines and bogies. The most startling transformation was applied to 202 490 which became 203 701, a prototype hybrid locomotive with diesel and battery power. The batteries are NiCD which provide the main power and are charged up by the 250 kW diesel engine, which can also be used for traction if required. Normal operation is by the batteries which power two inverter-driven three-phase traction motors. Alstom claims a 40% saving in fuel and 60% fewer CO_2 emissions. Alstom is also developing a three-axle version.

Built: 1968–72 for DR.
Builder: LEW.
Rebuilt: Alstom, Stendal 2010–14.
Engine: Deutz 6-cylinder 250 kW.
Transmission: Electric.
Maximum Tractive Effort:
Wheel Diameter: 1000 mm.
Train Heating: None.
Batteries: 600 kW.
Weight: 69 tonnes.
Length over Buffers: 14.24 m.
Maximum Speed:

EVN	Company	Running No	Works No	Built	Notes
1001 001	ALS/MEG	121	13529	1972	Ex ALS 203 701, DB 202 490
1001 002	ALS/MEG	122	11882	1968	Ex ALS 203 702, DB 298 044
1001 003	ALS/MEG	123	11886	1968	Ex ALS 203 703, DB 298 048
1001 004	ALS/MEG	124	11932	1968	Ex ALS 293 704, DB 298 094
1001 005	ALS/MEG	125	11885	1968	Ex ALS 203 705, DB 298 047
1001 006	MHG	2	11884	1968	Ex DB 298 046
1001 007	ALS/VW		11912	1968	Ex DB 298 074
1001 008	ALS/MEG	126	12754	1970	Ex DB 202 290
1001 009	ALS/DBR	LH2	12755	1970	Ex DB 202 291
1001 010	ALS/LEUNA	136	12750	1970	Ex DB 202 286
1001 011	ALS/OHE/VW		12757	1970	Ex DB 202 293

▲ Mitteldeutsche Eisenbahn Gesellschaft (MEG - 80% owned by Deutsche Bahn) was the first private operator to order these former DR Class 201/202 locos, rebuilt as hybrid locomotives by Alstom at Stendal works. Locos 90 80 1001 002-005, running numbers 122-125 (R-L) are pictured at their roll-out event at Schkopau chemical plant on 18 June 2012. **Quintus Vosman**

90 80 1002   ALSTOM H3   Co

Following on from its Hybrid B-B locomotive, Alstom at Stendal has now developed this three-axle version which is of completely new construction but the principal is the same with the batteries charged by the diesel engine. Remote control operation is possible. The first two locomotives are understood to be already employed in the VW car factory at Wolfsburg and consequently stay in private sidings. General approval is expected for the type in the summer of 2015. The DB Regio examples are to be trialled at Nürnberg and Würzburg for up to eight years.

Built: 2014–
Builder: Alstom, Stendal.
Engine: Deutz, TCD12.0 V6 Euro IIIB of 390 kW. **Batteries:** 350 kW NiCd.
Transmission: Electric, 3 TSA 253 kW nose suspended asynchronous traction motors.
Maximum Tractive Effort: 240 kN.   **Weight:** 67.5 tonnes.
Wheel Diameter: 1000 mm.   **Length over Buffers:** 12.80 m.
Maximum Speed: 100 km/h.

EVN	Company	Running No	Works No	Built
1002 001	ALS/VW			2014
1002 002	ALS/VW			2014
1002 003	ALS/VW			2014
1002 004	ALS/DBR			2014
1002 005	ALS/MEG			2014
1002 006	ALS/DBR			2015
1002 007	ALS/DBR			2015
1002 008	ALS/DBR			2015
1002 009	ALS/DBR			
1002 010	ALS/Audi Ingolstadt			
1002 011				
1002 012				
1002 013				

▲ Northrail former ÖBB Class 1142, 91 80 1142 635 hauls the "Hetzerather" special from Rheine to Wittlich through the Mosel valley at Winningen on 14 March 2014.   **Matthias Müller**

3.2. CODE 91 80 – ELECTRIC LOCOMOTIVES WITH MAXIMUM SPEED 100KM/H OR HIGHER

When the EVN numbering scheme was introduced DB decided to prefix its existing locomotives with a 6, thus allowing the check digit to remain the same. Other non-DB electric locomotives obtained by private operators generally have other prefixes.

91 80 0010 Bo-Bo

These locomotives are former SBB Class Re4/4ᴵ

Built: 1946 for SBB.
Builder: SLM (mechanical parts); BBC/MFO/SAAS (electrical parts).
Power Rating: 1830 kW.   **Weight:** 57 tonnes.
Maximum Tractive Effort: 137 kN.   **Maximum Speed:** 125 km/h.
Length over Buffers: 14.70 m.   **Wheel Diameter:** 1040 mm.

EVN	Company	Running No	Works No	Built
0010 006	CBB	10006	3882	1946
0010 008	CBB	10008	3889	1946
0010 019	CBB	10019	3953	1946

91 80 1042 Bo-Bo

Built for ÖBB, this is an unmodified example with rheostatic braking.

Built: 1968.
Builder: SGP (mechanical parts); Elin, Siemens, Brown Boveri (electrical parts).
Power Rating: 4000 kW.   **Weight:** 83.8 tonnes.
Maximum Tractive Effort: 255 kN.   **Maximum Speed:** 150 km/h.
Length over Buffers: 16.22 m.   **Wheel Diameter:** 1250 mm.

EVN	Company	Running No	Works No	Built	Notes
1042 520	CBB	1042 520	18361	1968	Ex ÖBB

91 80 1046 Bo-Bo

Another former ÖBB locomotive type.

Built: 1959.
Builder: SGP Floridsdorf (mechanical parts); Elin, AEG, Siemens (electrical parts).
Power Rating: 1600 kW.   **Weight:** 67 tonnes.
Maximum Tractive Effort: 118 kN.   **Maximum Speed:** 125 km/h.
Length over Buffers: 16.17 m.   **Wheel Diameter:** 1040 mm.

EVN	Company	Running No	Works No	Built	Notes
1046 020	CBB	1046 020	17878	1959	Ex ÖBB
1046 024	CBB	1046 024	17882	1959	Ex ÖBB

91 80 1142 Bo-Bo

These locomotives are former ÖBB main line locomotives of the 1970s modified for push-pull operation in the late 1990s. Being former 1042.5 series they have rheostatic braking.

Built: 1970–74.
Builder: SGP Graz (mechanical parts); Elin, Siemens, Brown Boveri (electrical parts).
Power Rating: 4000 kW.   **Weight:** 83.8 tonnes.
Maximum Tractive Effort: 255 kN.   **Maximum Speed:** 150 km/h.
Length over Buffers: 16.22 m.   **Wheel Diameter:** 1250 mm.

EVN	Company	Running No	Works No	Built	Notes
1142 562	ESGBI	1142 562	67842	1970	Ex ÖBB
1141 578	ESGBI	1141 578	67477	1971	Ex ÖBB
1142 579	NTS/DELTA	1142 579	67478	1971	Ex ÖBB

1142 606	ESGBI	1142 606	69909	1972	Ex ÖBB
1142 635	NTS	1142 635	70689	1974	Ex ÖBB
1142 640	FVD/LM		71115	1974	Ex ÖBB
1142 654	SVG		71129	1975	Ex ÖBB
1142 667	FVD/LM		72281	1975	Ex ÖBB
1142 704	CBB		72832	1977	Ex ÖBB

91 80 6103   Co-Co

A surprise in 2014 was the sale of this loco to Rail Adventure who use it for specialised transfers of new rolling stock around the country and any other work that comes along.

For technical details see Class 103 in German Railways Part 1.

EVN	Company	Works No	Built
6103 222	RAVDE	19635	1973

91 80 6109   Bo-Bo

Built as class E11 passenger locomotives for Deutsche Reichsbahn, these locos became Class 109 upon unification and were soon withdrawn.

Built: 1962–75.
Builder: LEW.
Power Rating: 2920 kW.
Maximum Tractive Effort: 209 kN.
Length over Buffers: 16.26 m.
Weight: 82 tonnes.
Maximum Speed: 120 km/h.
Wheel Diameter: 1350 mm.

EVN	Company	Running No	Works No	Built	Notes
6109 013	GVG	109-2	9904	1962	
6109 026 (Z)	GVG	109-4	9937	1963	
6109 028	EGP	109 028	9939	1963	
6109 030	EGP	E11 030	9941	1963	Ex PE Cargo, ex Ferropolis, ex BKK Bitterfeld 4-1215, ex DR 211 030
6109 073	GVG	109-3	15105	1975	
6109 084	GVG	109-1	15116	1975	

91 80 6110   Bo-Bo

110 511 was a late conversion by Dessau works intended to be a replacement loco for any overhauled locomotive subsequently failing. It was later sold to PRESS who have it advertising National Express! Now three similar locos have also been sold.

For technical details see Classes 110 and 113 in German Railways Part 1.

EVN	Company	Running No	Works No	Built	Notes
6110 491	BTE		19356	1968	
6110 511	PRESS	110 043	18545	1959	Ex 139 134
6113 268	NXG		18927	1963	
6113 309	NXG		19014	1963	

91 80 6127   Bo-Bo

The locomotive that started it all! This is the prototype Euro Sprinter which was in use on DB as Class 127.

Built: 1992.
Builder: Krauss Maffei/Siemens.
Power Rating: 6400 kW.
Maximum Tractive Effort: 300 kN.
Length over Buffers: 19.58 m.
Electric Brake: Rheostatic.
Weight: 84 tonnes.
Maximum Speed: 220 km/h.
Wheel Diameter: 1250 mm.

EVN	Company	Running No	Works No	Built
6127 001	PCW	8	20075	1992

▲ GVG Verkehrsorganisation operate sleeping car services between Berlin and Malmö. Former DR Class E11 91 80 6109 073, running number 109-3, takes empty couchette cars through Berlin Greifswalder Straße en route for stabling and cleaning at Berlin-Lichtenberg on 6 July 2014.

Christoph Grimm

▼ The unique Euro Sprinter locomotive 91 80 6127 001, alias PCW 8, has been retained by Siemens, primarily for transporting other locomotives and multiple units to and from its test centre at Wegberg-Wildenrath. Here it is seen with DB ICE 407 002 in tow, on the way from Mönchengladbach to Nürnberg on 28 March 2014.

Matthias Müller

91 80 6139   Bo-Bo

DB is a part owner of Lokomotion and as part of its investment it provided a batch of Class 139s. Subsequently DB has sold some to other private operators.

For technical details see Class 139 in German Railways Part 1.

EVN	Company	Running No	Works No	Built
6139 133	LM	139 133	18544	1959
6139 135	LM	139 135	18546	1959
6139 177	LM	139 177	3793	1958
6139 213	LM	139 213	18478	1958
6139 260	LM	139 260	18967	1963
6139 285	EGP	139 285	18954	1963
6139 287	BYB	139 287	18956	1963
6139 310	LM	139 310	18839	1964
6139 312	LM	139 312	18841	1964
6139 555	LM	139 555	19069	1964
6139 558	RAVDE	139 558	19072	1965

91 80 6140   Bo-Bo

The mass introduction of Class 185 saw DB disposing of older locomotives. Initially Class 140s went for scrap but with a change of heart many have been sold to private operators, often receiving a main overhaul by DB after sale.

For technical details see Class 140 in German Railways Part 1.

EVN	Company	Running No	Builder	Works No	Built	Notes
6140 002	MWB	140 002	KM	18253	1957	
6140 003	EBM	140 003	KM	18255	1957	
6140 070	EBM	140 070	KM	18244	1957	
6140 184	ELV	140 184	Krp	4103	1960	
6140 438	BYB	140 438	Hens	30669	1963	
6140 543	LM	140 543	Hens	30784	1964	
6140 759	MWB	140 759	Krp	5022	1970	
6140 761	MWB	140 761	Krp	5024	1970	
6140 772	RBH	161	Hens	31444	1970	
6140 774	EVB	140 774	Hens	31446	1970	
6140 789	RBH	162	KM	19516	1971	
6140 797	RBH	164	KM	19524	1971	
6140 798	MWB	140 798	KM	19525	1971	
6140 801	PRESS	165	Hens	31515	1971	Ex RBH 165, ex DB
6140 810	PRESS	140 041	Krp	5103	1971	
6140 815	RBH	163	Krp	5108	1971	
6140 824	EGP	140 824	Krp	5161	1972	
6140 825	PRESS	140 007	Krp	5162	1972	
6140 831	PRESS	140 037	Hens	31612	1972	
6140 834	PRESS	140 042	Hens	31615	1972	
6140 838	ENON/EGP		KM	19554	1972	
6140 845	PRESS	140 008	KM	19561	1972	
6140 848	EVB	140 848	Hens	19564	1972	
6140 851	PRESS	140 038	Hens	31698	1972	
6140 853	EGP/ENON	140 853	Hens	31704	1973	
6140 856	BYB	140 856	Hens	31713	1973	
6140 857	EGP/ENON	140 857	Hens	31697	1972	
6140 866	EVB	140 866	Hens	31711	1973	
6140 868	EVB	140 868	Hens	31714	1973	
6140 870	EVB	140 870	Hens	31716	1973	
6140 876	EGP/ENON	140 876	Hens	31722	1973	

91 80 6142   Bo-Bo

These are former Deutsche Reichsbahn Class E42 (242). Many were acquired by a Swiss private operator but were later snapped up by a German private operator who could use them under "grandfather" rights.

Built: 1962–76.
Builder: LEW.
Power Rating: 2920 kW.
Maximum Tractive Effort: 245 kN.
Length over Buffers: 16.26 m.

Weight: 82 tonnes.
Maximum Speed: 100 km/h.
Wheel Diameter: 1350 mm.

EVN	Company	Running No	Works No	Built	Notes
6142 001	MTEG	142 001	9892	1962	Preserved, but used in traffic
6142 042	DP/EGP	DP 62	10634	1964	Ex SOB 476 012, ex DR 142 042
6142 103	DP/EGP	142 103	11619	1967	Ex Lokoop 477 910, ex DR 142 103
6142 110	EBS	242 110	11626	1967	Ex DP, WAB, TPF, DR 142 110
6142 118	DP/EGP	DP 61	11634	1967	Ex WAB 53, ex Lokoop 477 907, ex DR 142 118
6142 126	DP/EGP	DP 57	11642	1967	Ex Lokoop 477 908, ex DR 142 126
6142 128	DP/EGP	DP 60	11644	1967	Ex WAB 52, ex Lokoop 477 909, ex DR 142 128
6142 130	DP/BYB	DP 68	11646	1967	Ex Lokoop 477 900, ex DR 142 130
6142 132	DP/EGP	DP 53	11648	1967	Ex Lokoop 477 902, ex DR 142 132
6142 133	DP/DLI	59	11649	1967	Ex Lokoop 477 903, ex DR 142 133
6142 134	DP/EGP	DP 52	11755	1968	Ex Lokoop 477 916, ex DR 142 134
6142 145	DP/EBS	142 145	11766	1968	Ex DP 67, ex TPF 417 192, ex DR 142 145
6142 150	DP/EGP	DP 54	11781	1968	Ex Lokoop 477 901, ex DR 142 150
6142 151	TEV	E42 151	11782	1968	Preserved locomotive leased out.
6142 154	DP/EGP	DP 50	11785	1968	Ex Lokoop 477 917, ex DR 142 154
6142 157	DP/EGP	DP 51	11881	1968	Ex Lokoop 477 906, ex DR 142 157
6142 159	DP/EGP	DP 58	12150	1969	Ex WAB 50, ex Lokoop 477 904, ex DR 142 159
6142 191	DP/EGP	DP 55	13623	1972	Ex Lokoop 477 905, ex DR 142 191
6142 199	DP/EGP	142 199	13632	1972	Ex Lokoop 477 912, ex DR 142 199
6142 272 (Z)	DP/EGP	DP 70	15004	1976	Ex Lokoop, ex DR 142 272
6142 287	DP/EGP	DP 56	15421	1976	Ex Lokoop 477 915, ex DR 142 287
6142 288	DP/EGP	142 288	15845	1976	Ex Lokoop 477 914, ex DR 142 288

91 80 6143   Bo-Bo

In Class 143 the Deutsche Reichsbahn introduced this good multi-purpose locomotive. DB allocated all of them to the Regio Sector but with more railcars being introduced and some contracts lost to private operators DB has sold some to subsidiary companies for freight work. The exception is class leader 143 001 (once the "White Lady") which appeared to be the property of ADtranz/Bombardier as it was a prototype. This was later sold to a private operator.

For technical details see Class 143 in German Railways Part 1.

EVN	Company	Running No	Works No	Built	Notes
6143 001	EKO	143 001	16323	1983	
6143 020	MEG	608	18243	1985	
6143 028	RBH	118	18251	1985	
6143 040	RBH	127[II]	18421	1985	
6143 041	RBH	103	18422	1985	
6143 048	RBH	121	18429	1985	
6143 056	RBH	114	18437	1985	
6143 059	RBH	113	18440	1985	
6143 063	RBH	107	18444	1985	
6143 068	RBH	115	18449	1985	
6143 069	RBH	102	18450	1985	
6143 074	RBH	127[I]	18455	1985	
6143 079	RBH	120	17736	1985	

6143 084	RBH	110	18460	1985	
6143 124	RBH	124	18500	1986	
6143 143	RBH	143	18519	1986	
6143 144 (Z)	RBH		18520	1986	Used for spares
6143 173	RBH	134	18922	1986	
6143 175	MEG		18924	1986	
6143 179	MEG	601	18928	1986	
6143 186	RBH	105	18935	1986	
6143 191	RBH	104	18940	1986	
6143 204	MEG	602	18953	1987	
6143 217	RBH	126	18966	1987	
6143 226	RBH	128	18975	1987	
6143 249	RBH	129	20132	1987	
6143 254	RBH	135	20137	1987	
6143 257	MEG	604	20140	1987	
6143 273	RBH	130	20156	1987	
6143 286	RBH	106	20169	1987	
6143 295	RBH	138	20178	1987	
6143 305	RBH	131	19547	1987	
6143 307	RBH	132	19549	1987	
6143 310	MEG	607	19552	1987	
6143 344	MEG	605	19586	1988	
6143 352	RBH	133	19594	1988	
6143 554	RBH	117	18561	1990	
6143 567	RBH		18574	1990	
6143 571	RBH	119	18659	1990	
6143 573	RBH	116	18661	1990	
6143 590 (Z)	RBH		18678	1990	Used for spares
6143 638	RBH	112	20456	1990	
6143 812	RBH	137	20206	1988	
6143 851	MEG	603	20301	1988	
6143 864	MEG	606	20314	1989	
6143 872	RBH	134	20322	1989	
6143 874	RBH	101	20324	1989	
6143 908	RBH	125	20358	1989	
6143 911	RBH	111	20361	1989	
6143 916	RBH	108	20366	1989	
6143 936	RBH	109	20386	1989	
6143 941	RBH	123	20391	1989	
6143 950	RBH	122	20400	1989	

91 80 6145   Bo-Bo

The start of open access in Germany took place just as Class 145 was being built for DB and consequently it was this class that leasing companies started to acquire on behalf of clients. EVNs follow on from the DB series and are gradually replacing the 145 class numbers.

For technical details see Class 145 in German Railways Part 1.

EVN	Company	Running No	Works No	Built	Notes
6145 081	EKO	145 CL 001	33356	1999	
6145 082	EKO	145 CL 002	33366	2000	
6145 083	PRESS	145 023	33370	2000	Ex SBB 481 001, Lokoop 486 651
6145 084	MRCE/LEG	481 002	33375	2000	Ex SBB 481 002, Lokoop 486 652
6145 085	PRESS	145 030	33380	2000	Ex SBB 481 003, Lokoop 486 653
6145 086	MRCE/PCT	145 086	33386	2000	Ex SBB 481 004, Lokoop 486 654
6145 087	SRI/MTRD	145 087	33392	2000	Ex SBB 481 005, Lokoop 486 655
6145 088	SRI/MTRD	145 088	33393	2000	Ex SBB 481 006, Lokoop 486 656
6145 089	AS/HGK	2001	33382	2000	Also numbered 145 CL 011
6145 090	AS/HGK	2002	33821	2000	Also numbered 145 CL 012
6145 091	AS/RHC	145 CL 013	33826	2000	
6145 092	AS/XRAIL	145 CL 014	33828	2000	
6145 093	AS/HGK	2005	33842	2001	Also numbered 145 CL 015
6145 094	MER/CTD-ITL	145 CL 003	33815	2000	

6145 095	MER/CTD-ITL	145 CL 004	33841	2000	
6145 096	AT/XRAIL	145 CL 005	33843	2001	
6145 097	AT/HGK	2015	33844	2001	Also numbered 145 CL 001
6145 098	AT/XRAIL	145 CL 202	33845	2001	Ex RBH 202
6145 099	AT/XRAIL	145 CL 203	33846	2001	
6145 100	AT/XRAIL	145 CL 204	33847	2001	
6145 101	AT/RBH	205	33850	2001	Ex 145 CL 205
6145 102	AT/RBH	206	33849	2001	Ex 145 CL 206
6145 931	AT	145 CL 031	33848	2001	

91 80 6146   Bo-Bo

As with Class 145, leasing companies turned to the passenger equivalent for use on modern push-pull trains.

For technical details see Class 146 in German Railways Part 1.

EVN	Company	Running No	Works No	Built	Names
6146 501	LNVG/ME	146-01	33946	2003	Scheeßel
6146 502	LNVG/ME	146-02	33953	2003	Hansestadt Lüneburg
6146 503	LNVG/ME	146-03	33954	2003	Bienenbüttel
6146 504	LNVG/ME	146-04	33955	2003	Buchholz i. d. Nordheide
6146 505	LNVG/ME	146-05	33956	2003	Rotenburg (Wümme)
6146 506	LNVG/ME	146-06	33957	2003	Winsen
6146 507	LNVG/ME	146-07	33958	2003	Lauenbrück
6146 508	LNVG/ME	146-08	33959	2003	Uelzen
6146 509	LNVG/ME	146-09	33960	2003	Tostedt
6146 510	LNVG/ME	146-10	33961	2003	Bad Bevensen
6146 511	LNVG/ME	146-11	34022	2005	Einbeck
6146 512	LNVG/ME	146-12	34026	2005	Northeim
6146 513	LNVG/ME	146-13	34032	2005	Alfeld
6146 514	LNVG/ME	146-14	34034	2005	Sarstedt
6146 515	LNVG/ME	146-15	34037	2005	Elze
6146 516	LNVG/ME	146-16	34039	2005	Celle
6146 517	LNVG/ME	146-17	34042	2005	Langenhagen
6146 518	LNVG/ME	146-18	34045	2005	Großburgwedel
6146 519	CTD/RBB	146 519	34023	2005	
6146 520	CTD/RBB	146 520	34025	2005	
6146 521	CTD	146 521	34048	2005	
6146 522	CTD	146 522	34051	2005	
6146 531	LNVG/ME	146 531	34091	2007	Seevetal-Maschen
6146 532	LNVG/ME	146 532	34092	2007	Seevetal-Meckelfeld
6146 533	LNVG/ME	146 533	34093	2007	Bardowick
6146 534	LNVG/ME	146 534	34094	2007	
6146 535	LNVG/ME	146 535	34095	2007	Seevetal-Hittfeld
6146 536	LNVG/ME	146 536	34096	2007	
6146 537	LNVG/ME	146 537	34097	2007	Stelle
6146 538	LNVG/ME	146 538	34098	2007	Rosengarten-Klecken
6146 539	LNVG/ME	146 539	34099	2007	
6146 541	ME	146-41	34712	2010	
6146 542	ME	146-42	34711	2010	

91 80 6151   Co-Co

Just like Class 139/140, most of these former DB locos are in use with DB subsidiaries; some have now been acquired by other private operators but the sale of one to Hector Rail seems strange.

For technical details see Class 151 in German Railways Part 1.

EVN	Company	Running No	Builder	Works No	Built
6151 004	RBH	268	Krp	5176	1973
6151 007	EGP		Krp	5179	1973
6151 014	RBH	269	Krp	5256	1973

EVN					
6151 018	LM		Krp	5260	1973
6151 024	RBH	265	Krp	5266	1974
6151 025	RBH	270	KM	19644	1973
6151 033	SRI/EGP	151 033	KM	19652	1974
6151 038	RBH	261	KM	19657	1974
6151 039	SRI/EGP	151 039	KM	19658	1974
6151 056	LM	056	Hens	31799	1974
6151 060	LM	060	Hens	31803	1974
6151 074	LM	074	Hens	31817	1974
6151 078	EGP	151 078	Krp	5328	1975
6151 079	RBH	271	Krp	5329	1975
6151 081	RBH	272	Krp	5331	1975
6151 083	RBH	273	Krp	5333	1975
6151 084	RBH	266	Krp	5334	1975
6151 118	ENON/EGP		Krp	5357	1976
6151 123	RBH	263	Krp	5362	1976
6151 124	SRI/SVG		Krp	5363	1976
6151 127	RBH	274	Hens	32019	1976
6151 143	RBH	264	KM	19811	1976
6151 144	RBH	267	KM	19812	1976
6151 147	RBH	275	KM	19822	1977
6151 151	RBH	276	KM	19826	1977
6151 152	RBH	262	KM	19827	1977
6151 162	S-HECTOR		Krp	5421	1977
6151 170	SRI/EGP	151 170	Hens	32140	1977

91 80 6152   Bo-Bo

Siemens Dispolok leasing company had two Class 152s on its books which have subsequently been sold to ITL.

For technical details see Class 152 in German Railways Part 1.

EVN	Company	Running No	Builder	Works No	Built
6152 196	ITL	152 196	Sie	20448	2000
6152 197	ITL	152 197	Sie	20449	2000

91 80 6155   Co-Co

These former DR/DB locos are mostly in use with DB subsidiary company MEG, but with more being withdrawn by DB other private operators are now snapping them up.

For technical details see Class 155 in German Railways Part 1.

EVN	Company	Running No	Works No	Built
6155 046	MEG	708	15497	1978
6155 049	MEG	709	15500	1978
6155 059	MEG	710	15756	1978
6155 078	LEG	250 078	16338	1979
6155 119	MEG	706[II]	16710	1980
6155 124	MEG	701	16715	1980
6155 137	LEG	250 137	16728	1981
6155 179	MEG	702	17869	1982
6155 184	MEG	703	17874	1982
6155 195	MEG	704	18180	1983
6155 196	MEG	705	18181	1983
6155 198	MEG	706[I]	18183	1983
6155 230	MEG	707	18215	1983
6155 238	INTEG/PRESS	155 045	17194	1984

▲ Owned by SRI Rail Invest and on long-term hire to Eisenbahn Gesellschaft Potsdam (EGP), 91 80 6151 170 passes Mukran with a limestone train from Lancken to Peitz Ost power station on 15 May 2013. **Matthias Müller**

▼ Swedish company Hector Rail uses several Siemens Taurus locomotives with German EVN registrations, some of which are named after characters in the "Toy Story" series of films. 91 80 6182 502, running number 242 502, "Zurg", is seen heading a Padborg to Trier Ehrang freight near Unkel on 16 November 2013. **Matthias Müller**

91 80 6156 {: .left}   Co-Co

91 80 6156   Co-Co

All locos in this former DR class were sold by DB to its MEG subsidiary.

Built: 1991.
Builder: LEW.
Power Rating: 5880 kW.
Maximum Tractive Effort: 210 kN.
Length over Buffers: 19.50 m.

Electric Brake: Rheostatic.
Weight: 120 tonnes.
Maximum Speed: 125 km/h.
Wheel Diameter: 1250 mm.

EVN	Company	Running No	Works No	Built
6156 001	MEG	801	20004	1991
6156 002	MEG	802	20005	1991
6156 003	MEG	803	20006	1991
6156 004	MEG	804	20996	1991

91 80 6180   Bo-Bo

In the last two years DB has sold off all its redundant Class 180 electric locomotives to Czech Operator TSS Cargo. These are now re-entering traffic working container trains through from terminals in the Czech Republic to ports like Bremerhaven. The DB numbers have been retained but the VKM is D-TSSC! So far five locomotives are back in service.

For technical details see Class 180 in German Railways Part 1.

EVN	Company	Running No	Works No	Built
6180 006	TSSC		8787	1991
6180 008	TSSC		8789	1991
6180 011	TSSC		8792	1991
6180 013	TSSC		8794	1991
6180 015	TSSC		8796	1991

91 80 6182   ES64U2   Bo-Bo

The Eurosprinter name became unfashionable after ÖBB ordered large numbers of the type which it called Taurus. The origins of the name are still there in the old classification of ES 64 U2.

For technical details see Class 182 in German Railways Part 1.

EVN	Company	Running No	Works No	Built	Notes/Names
6182 501	MRCE/DBR	ES64U2-001	20557	2001	
6182 502	S-HECTOR	242 502	20558	2001	Zurg
6182 503	S-HECTOR	242 503	20559	2001	Balboa
6182 504	S-HECTOR	242 504	20560	2001	Mr Potato Head
6182 505	MRCE/TXL	ES64U2-005	20561	2001	
6182 506	DB	ES64U2-006	20562	2001	Now sold to DB System Technik
6182 507	MRCE/BOXX	ES64U2-007	20563	2001	
6182 508	MRCE/BOXX	ES64U2-008	20564	2001	
6182 509	MRCE/A-WLC	ES64U2-009	20565	2001	
6182 510	MRCE/TXL	ES64U2-010	20566	2002	
6182 511	MRCE/TXL	ES64U2-011	20567	2002	
6182 512	MRCE/TXL	ES64U2-012	20568	2002	
6182 513	MRCE/TXL	ES64U2-013	20569	2002	
6182 514	MRCE/DB	ES64U2-014	20750	2002	
6182 515	MRCE/BOXX	ES64U2-015	20571	2002	
6182 516	S-HECTOR	242 516	20572	2002	Ferdinand
6182 517	S-HECTOR	242 517	20573	2002	Fitzgerald
6182 518	MRCE/DBR	ES64U2-018	20574	2002	
6182 519	MRCE/DBR	ES64U2-019	20769	2002	
6182 520	MRCE/A-WLC	ES64U2-020	20770	2002	
6182 521	MRCE/A-WLC	ES64U2-021	20771	2002	
6182 522	MRCE/TXL	ES64U2-022	20772	2002	
6182 523	MRCE/A-WLC	ES64U2-023	20773	2002	
6182 524	MRCE/A-WLC	ES64U2-024	20774	2003	
6182 525	MRCE/WLB	ES64U2-025	20775	2003	
6182 526	OLA/HKX	ES64U2-026	20776	2003	

6182 527	MRCE/A-WLC	ES64U2-027	20777	2003	
6182 528	MRCE/TXL	ES64U2-028	20778	2003	
6182 529	MRCE/TXL	ES64U2-029	20781	2003	
6182 530	MRCE/BOXX	ES64U2-030	20782	2003	
6182 531	S-HECTOR	242 531	20446	2000	Ex ES64U2-902; LaMotta
6182 532	S-HECTOR	242 532	20447	2000	Ex ES64U2-903; Lightyear
6182 533	MRCE/TXL	ES64U2-033	21037	2004	
6182 534	OLA/HKX	ES64U2-034	21038	2004	
6182 535	MRCE/A-WLC	ES64U2-035	21039	2004	
6182 536	MRCE/HKX	ES64U2-036	21040	2004	
6182 537	MRCE/A-WLC	ES64U2-037	21041	2004	

6182 538–552 reconfigured to 6182 560–574
6182 553–6182 559 not used

6182 560	MRCE/TXL	ES64U2-060	21052	2004	
6182 561	MRCE/A-LTE	ES64U2-061	21053	2004	
6182 562	MRCE/BOXX	ES64U2-062	21054	2004	
6182 563	MRCE/BOXX	ES64U2-063	21055	2004	
6182 564	MRCE/A-WLC	ES64U2-064	21056	2004	
6182 565	MRCE/BOXX	ES64U2-065	21047	2004	
6182 566	MRCE/A-WLC	ES64U2-066	21048	2004	
6182 567	MRCE/TXL	ES64U2-067	21049	2004	
6182 568	MRCE/A-WLC	ES64U2-068	21050	2004	
6182 569	MRCE/BOXX	ES64U2-069	21051	2004	
6182 570	MRCE/GySEV	ES64U2-070	21042	2004	
6182 571	MRCE/BOXX	ES64U2-071	21043	2004	
6182 572	MRCE/TXL	ES64U2-072	21044	2004	
6182 573	MRCE/LTE	ES64U2-073	21045	2004	
6182 574	MRCE/LTE	ES64U2-074	21046	2004	

6182 575–579 not used

6182 580	MRCE/A-CSV	ES64U2-080	20779	2003
6182 581	MRCE/A-CSV	ES64U2-081	20780	2003
6182 582	MRCE/A-CSV	ES64U2-082	20783	2002
6182 595	MRCE/RDX	ES64U2-095	20784	2002
6182 596	MRCE/BOXX	ES64U2-096	20785	2002
6182 597	MRCE/TXL	ES64U2-097	20786	2002
6182 598	MRCE/TXL	ES64U2-098	20787	2002
6182 599	MRCE/TXL	ES64U2-099	20788	2002
6182 600	HUPAC/A-WLC	ES64U2-100	20445	2000
6182 601	HUPAC/A-WLC	ES64U2-101	20555	2001
6182 602	HUPAC/A-WLC	ES64U2-102	20556	2001
6182 911	MWB	1116 911	20852	2003
6182 912	MWB	1116 912	20892	2003

91 80 6183   ES64U4   Bo-Bo

The multi-voltage Taurus used by ÖBB in Austria as Class 1216 is also used by private operators in Austria and Germany, but the German classification is 6183. See Class 189 for version information.

Built: 2007–11.
Builder: Siemens.
Power Rating: 6400 kW.
Maximum Tractive Effort: 300 kN.
Length over Buffers: 19.28 m.
Weight: 87 tonnes.
Maximum Speed: 230 km/h.
Wheel Diameter: 1150 mm.
Systems: 15 kV AC 16.7 Hz, 25kV AC 50 Hz, 3000 V DC

EVN	Company	Running No	Version	Works No	Built
6183 001	HML/VBG	183 001	G	21130	2007
6183 002	HML/VBG	183 002	G	21132	2007
6183 003	HML/VBG	183 003	G	21134	2007
6183 004	HML/VBG	183 004	G	21522	2007
6183 005	HML/VBG	183 005		21321	2008
6183 500	MGW/A-SETG	183 500		21315	2008

6183 701	A-LOGS	1216 933	VB	21322	2008	
6183 702	A-LOGS	1216 932	VB	21323	2008	
6183 703						
6183 704	A-WLC		VB	21605	2008	
6183 705	A-WLC		VB	21606	2008	
6183 712	A-STBAT	1216 950	VB	21670	2011	
6183 713	A-WLC	1216 955	VB	21671	2011	
6183 714	CZ-AWT		VB	21672	2011	
6183 715						
6183 716						
6183 717	A-STBAT		VB	21675	2011	
6183 718	CZ-AWT		VB	21676	2011	
6183 719	A-CSV		VB	21677	2011	

91 80 6185   TRAXX AC   Bo-Bo

Class 185 is a Bombardier success story and is part of the TRAXX family. TRAXX = Transnational Railway Applications with eXtreme fleXibility. DB ordered 400 locomotives to replace Class 140s but open access was already on the cards resulting in leasing companies ordering the same type with Angel Trains one of the first purchasers. Initially leased locos were numbered in the 185 CL 001 series but soon the 185 5xx numbers came into general use. Class 185 is the dual-voltage alternating current version known as TRAXX F140AC1 the F being for Freight and 140 reflecting the maximum speed whilst 1 denotes the first version. Just where the locomotives can operate depends on them being fitted with the relevant train protection systems and sometimes with different pantographs. Please note that as operating requirements change locomotives are often retro-fitted with different country "packages" to reflect the new requirements. All locomotives are dual voltage as the equipment needed for 25 kV has been installed when built as the extra cost is negligible.

Having started numbering the private locos at 185 501 the series seems to have stopped at 185 717 and then continued at the end of the DB series. Note also that some locomotives are registered outside Germany (e.g. Austria) and are still classed as 185s but have a prefix of 0 rather than 6.

From 185 561 locos are TRAXX F140AC2 – the second version with a modified front end for improved crash resistance.

For technical details see Class 185 in German Railways Part 1.

EVN	Company	Running No	Countries	Works No	Built	Notes/Names
6185 405	S-GC/D-IGE		D DK S	34678	2009	
6185 406	S-GC/D-IGE		D DK S	34688	2009	
6185 407	MRCE/TXL	185 407	D DK S	34961	2011	
6185 408	MRCE/TXL	185 408	D DK S	34965	2011	
6185 409	RDX	185 409	D DK S	34976	2012	
0185 410	Bure Equity/S-RR		D DK S	34977	2012	
0185 411	Bure Equity/S-RR		D DK S	34987	2012	
0185 412	Bure Equity/S-RR		D DK S	34988	2012	
0185 413	Bure Equity/S-RR		D DK S	34989	2012	
0185 414	Bure Equity/S-RR		D DK S	34990	2012	
0185 415	Bure Equity/S-RR		D DK S	34991	2012	
0185 416	Bure Equity/S-RR		D DK S	34992	2012	
6185 417	A-TXL		D A DK S	34993	2013	
6185 418	A-TXL		D A DK S	35060	2013	
6185 419	RDX	185 419		35130	2014	
6185 501	AS/CTD	185 CL 001	D A	33450	2001	
6185 502	AS/CTD	185 CL 002	D A	33452	2001	
6185 503	AS/CTD	185 CL 003	D A	33455	2001	
6185 504	AT/CTD	185 CL 004	D A	33453	2001	
6185 505	AT/CTD	185 CL 005	D A	33451	2001	
6185 506	AT/CTD	185 CL 006	D A	33458	2001	
6185 507	AT/CTD	185 CL 007	D A	33456	2001	
6185 508	AT/VPS	185 CL 008	D A	33477	2002	
6185 509	AT/VPS	185 CL 009	D A	33498	2002	
6185 510	B-RTX		D A	33510	2002	
6185 511	B-RTX		D A	33512	2002	
6185 512	AT/TXL	185 512	D A	33514	2002	

6185 513	AT/EBT	185 513	D A	33516	2002	
6185 514	AT/RHC	185 514	D A	33522	2002	
6185 515	AT/TXL		D A	33523	2002	
6185 516	AT/VPS	185 516	D A	33529	2002	
6185 517	HML/ITL	185 517	D A CH	33531	2002	
6185 518	AT/TXL	185 518	D A	33533	2002	
6185 519	AT/ITL	185 519	D A	33535	2002	
6185 520	AT/CFLDE		D A	33544	2003	
6185 521	AT/HGK	2008	D A	33581	2003	
6185 522	AT/ITL	185 522	D A	33596	2003	
6185 523	AT/HGK	185 523	D A	33601	2003	
6185 524	AT/ITL	185 524	D A	33614	2003	
6185 525	AT/BLSC	185 525	D A CH	33592	2003	
6185 526	AT/HGK	2009	D A CH	33618	2003	
6185 527	AT/LM	185 527	D A CH	33621	2003	
6185 528	AT/A-LTE		D A	33624	2003	
6185 529	AT/A-LTE		D A	33628	2003	Michaela
6185 530	AT/VPS	5601	D A	33633	2004	
6185 531	A-TXL	185 531	D A	33630	2004	
6185 532	HML/CTD	185 532	D A CH	33636	2004	
6185 533	DL/CTD-ITL	185 533	D A CH	33639	2004	
6185 534	AT/CFLDE	185 534	D A	33643	2004	
6185 535	AT/XRAIL	185 535	D A CH	33677	2004	
6185 536	AT/XRAIL	185 536	D A CH	33680	2004	
6185 537	AGV/A-TXL	185 537	D A	33654	2004	
6185 538	AGV/A-TXL	185 538	D A	33657	2004	
6185 539	AGV/A-TXL	185 539	D A	33660	2004	
6185 540	AGV/A-TXL	185 540	D A	33663	2004	
6185 541	HML/CTD-ITL	185 541	D A CH	33720	2005	
6185 542	DL/CTD-ITL	185 542	D A CH	33723	2005	
6185 543	DL/CTD-ITL	185 543	D A CH	33727	2005	
6185 544	MRCE/BOXX		D A CH	33729	2005	
6185 545	MRCE/CTL		D A	33731	2005	
6185 546	MRCE	185 546	D A	33735	2005	
6185 547	MRCE/NIAG	185 547	D A	33733	2005	
6185 548	ITL	185 548	D A	33739	2005	
6185 549	CTD/RBB	185 549	D A CH	33737	2005	
6185 550	CTD/R4C	185 550	D A CH	33741	2005	
6185 551	MRCE/OHE	185 551	D F	33780	2005	
6185 552	MRCE/CFLDE		D F	33781	2005	
6185 553	MRCE/LOCON	185 553	D F	33782	2005	
6185 554	MRCE/NIAG	185 554	D F	33783	2005	
6185 555	MRCE/CTL		D F	33784	2005	
6185 556	MRCE/LOCON		D F	33785	2005	
6185 557	MRCE/CFLDE		D F	33786	2005	

6185 558–560 not used
6185 561 was a test loco for TRAXX F140AC2 and became SBB 482 035

6185 562	ITL	185 562	D A	33745	2005
6185 563	MRCE/LOCON	185 563	D A CH	33765	2005
6185 564	MRCE/BOXX		D A CH	33767	2005
6185 565	MRCE/NIAG		D A CH	33770	2005
6185 566	MRCE/CFLDE		D A CH	33771	2005
6185 567	MRCE/BOXX		D A CH	33773	2005
6185 568	S-HECTOR	241.002	D DK S	33794	2006
6185 569	MRCE/CSV		D A CH	34125	2005
6185 570	MRCE/BOXX		D A CH	34127	2006
6185 571	MRCE/OHEGO		D A CH	34129	2006
6185 572	MRCE/NIAG	185 572	D A CH	34131	2006
6185 573	MRCE		D A CH	34133	2006
6185 574	MRCE/BOXX		D A CH	34135	2006
6185 575	AT/HGK	2010	D A CH	34136	2006
6185 576	AT/XRAIL		D A CH	34137	2006
6185 577	AT/XRAIL		D A CH	34139	2006

6185 578	MER/XRAIL		D A CH	34158	2007	
6185 579	MER/XRAIL		D A CH	34160	2007	
6185 580	MER/XRAIL		D A CH	34162	2007	
6185 581	MER/XRAIL		D A CH	34163	2207	
6185 582	MER/HGK	2051	D A CH	34194	2008	
6185 583	HVLE	E185.01	D A	34193	2008	
6185 584	MER/HGK	2052	D A CH	34196	2008	
6185 585	MER/HGK	2053	D A CH	34199	2008	
6185 586	MER/HGK	2054	D A CH	34200	2008	
6185 587	MER/HGK	2055	D A CH	34204	2008	
6185 588	MER/HGK	2056	D A CH	34207	2008	
6185 589	MER/HGK	2057	D A CH	34210	2008	
6185 590	BRL/XRAIL		D A CH	34216	2008	
6185 591	BRL/XRAIL		D A CH	34218	2008	
6185 592	BRL/XRAIL		D A CH	34220	2008	
6185 593	BRL/XRAIL		D A CH	34222	2008	
6185 594	BRL/XRAIL		D A CH	34225	2008	
6185 595	BRL/XRAIL		D A CH	34233	2008	
6185 596	BRL/XRAIL		D A CH	34246	2008	
6185 597	BRL/XRAIL		D A CH	34251	2008	
6185 598	AK/ITL	185 598	D A CH	34265	2008	
6185 599	BRL/XRAIL		D A CH	34264	2008	
6185 600	BRL/XRAIL		D A CH	34268	2008	
6185 601	BRL/XRAIL		D A CH	34270	2008	
6185 602	BRL/XRAIL		D A CH	34275	2008	
6185 603	AT/HGK	2061	D A	34212	2008	
6185 604	AT/HGK	2062	D A	34214	2008	
6185 605	AT/HGK	2063	D A	34226	2008	
6185 606	AT/HGK	2064	D A	34228	2008	
6185 607	AT		D A H	34234	2008	
6185 608	AT/A-LTE		D A H	34239	2008	
6185 609	AT/A-LTE		D A H	34244	2008	
6185 610[I]	AT		D A H	34249	2008	Now 6185 672
6185 610[II]	AT/TXL		D A H	34653	2009	
6185 611[I]	AT		D A H	34252	2008	Now 6185 673
6185 611[II]	AT/TXL		D A H	34667	2009	
6185 612	AT/PREU	185 612	D A H	34263	2008	
6185 613	AT/A-Ecco Rail		D A H	34271	2009	
6185 614	AT/TXL	185 614	D A H	34272	2008	
6185 615	AT/CTD-ITL	185 615	D A H	34277	2008	
6185 616	AT/LOCON	185 616	D A H	34279	2008	
6185 617	AT/TXL		D A	34248	2008	
6185 618	AT/RHC		D A	34254	2008	
6185 619	AT/MKB	185 619	D A	34257	2008	
6185 620	S-CFL	91 76 0119 001	D A S N	34235	2008	
6185 621	AT/RPOOL-RTBC		D A S N	34231	2008	
6185 622	AT/RPOOL-RTBC		D A S N	34644	2009	
6185 623	AT/RPOOL-RHC		D A S N	34645	2009	
6185 624	AT/RPOOL-RHC		D A S N	34650	2009	
6185 625	AT/RPOOL		D A S N	34654	2009	
6185 626	AT/RPOOL-RHC		D A S N	34656	2009	
6185 627	AT/RPOOL-RHC		D A S N	34661	2009	
6185 628	AT/RPOOL-CN	0119 009	D A S N	34668	2009	
6185 629	AT/RPOOL-CN	0119 010	D A S N	34676	2009	Damaged
6185 630	AT/HGK	2065	D A	34255	2008	
6185 631	AT/HGK	2066	D A	34259	2008	
6185 632	AT/HGK	2067	D A	34261	2008	
6185 633	AT/CTD-ITL	185 633	D A	34283	2009	
6185 634	AT/HLG/BEBRA	185 634	D A	34658	2009	
6185 635	MER/RPOOL-ERS		D A H	34642	2009	
6185 636	AT/RTBC	185 636	D A H	34702	2009	
6185 637	AT/RPOOL-RTBC	185 637	D A H	34701	2009	
6185 638	MER/RPOOL-BOXX	185 638	D A H	34705	2009	
6185 639	MER/RTBC	185 639	D A H	34703	2009	

6185 640	HVLE	E185.02	D A	34281	2009	
6185 641	HVLE	E185.03	D A	34643	2009	
6185 642	HLG		D A S N	34689	2009	
6185 643–648 not used						
6185 649	AK/ITL	185 649	D A H	34706	2009	
6185 650	AK/ITL	185 650	D A H	34695	2009	
6185 651–660 not used						
6185 661	LM	185 661	D A	34669	2009	
6185 662	LM	185 662	D A	34672	2009	
6185 663	LM	185 663	D A	34679	2009	
6185 664	LM	185 664	D A	34684	2009	
6185 665	LM	185 665	D A	34685	2009	
6185 666	LM	185 666	D A	34687	2009	
6185 667–670 not used						
6185 671	RPOOL/N-CN		D A H	34671	2009	
6185 672	RPOOL/RTBC		D A H	34249	2008	Ex 185 610
6185 673	RPOOL/RTBC		D A H	34252	2008	Ex 185 611
6185 674	RPOOL/LM		D A S N	34707	2009	
6185 675	RPOOL		D A S N	34708	2009	
6185 676	RPOOL/RTBC		D A H	34696	2009	
6185 677	RPOOL/PCT	185 677	D A H	34698	2009	
6185 678	RPOOL/N-CL		D A S N	34700	2009	
6185 679	RPOOL/N-CN		D A S N	34680	2009	
6185 680	RPOOL/RTBC	185 680	D A H	34691	2009	
6185 681	RPOOL/SETG	185 681	D A H	34713	2009	
6185 682	RPOOL/N-CL		D A S N	34715	2010	
6185 683	RPOOL/N-CL		D A S N	34719	2010	
6185 684	RPOOL/RTBC	185 684	D A H	34720	2010	
6185 685	RPOOL/N-CL		D A S N	34729	2010	
6185 686	RPOOL/N-CN		D A S N	34742	2010	
6185 687	RPOOL/N-CN		D A S N	34743	2010	
6185 688	RPOOL/N-CL		D A S N	34744	2010	
6185 689	RPOOL/N-CN		D A S N	34745	2011	
6185 690	RPOOL/RTB	185 690	D A H	34746	2011	
6185 691	RPOOL/BEV	185 691	D A H	34747	2011	
6185 692	RPOOL/N-CN		D A S N	34749	2011	
6185 693	RPOOL/S-TXL		D A S N	34750	2011	
6185 694	RPOOL/S-TXL		D A S N	34954	2011	
6185 695	RPOOL		D A S N	34958	2011	
6185 696	RPOOL/BEV		D A S N	34722	2010	
6185 697	RPOOL/BEV		D A S N	34726	2010	
6185 698	RPOOL/N-CL		D A H	34964	2011	
6185 699	RPOOL/N-CL		D A H	34967	2011	
6185 700	RPOOL/N-CL		D A H	34969	2011	
6185 701			D A H			
6185 702			D A H RO			
6185 703			D A H RO			
6185 704	RPOOL/S-TXL		D A S N	34751	2011	
6185 705	RPOOL/S-TXL		D A S N	34753	2011	
6185 706	RPOOL		D A S N	34941	2011	
6185 707	RPOOL/N-CL		D A S N	34943	2011	
6185 708	RPOOL/N-CL		D A S N	34946	2011	
6185 709	RPOOL		D A S N	34949	2011	
6185 710	RPOOL		D A S N	34957	2011	
6185 711	RPOOL		D A S N	34960	2011	
6185 712	RPOOL		D A S N	34962	2011	
6185 713	RPOOL		D A S N	34971	2011	
6185 714	RPOOL		D A S N	34973	2012	
6185 715	RPOOL/S-TXL		D A S N	34974	2012	
6185 716	RPOOL/BOXX		D A H	34190	2007	
6185 717	RPOOL/BOXX		D A H	34242	2008	

91 80 6186　　　　TRAXX MS　　　　Bo-Bo

This is another member of the TRAXX family classed as F140MS where the MS stands for Multi System, being fitted for 1500/3000 V DC and 15/25 kV AC systems and consequently having more pantographs. Originally DB was to have 100 locos of this series but didn't take up the option until much later. Consequently numbering started at 186 101. The series also has some blank numbers which reflect cancelled orders due to the recession. Some of these spare numbers are now being used for new construction. Angel Trains ordered the first batch but these were delivered as recession struck and the locomotives were stored for some time. Angel Trains eventually sold many to Railpool a new leasing company which needed locomotives when Angel Trains still had no demand. Although shown as built at Kassel this is where they are erected. The bodies come from Poland, the bogies from Siegen and electrical equipment from Mannheim and Berlin. Locos 6186 401–420 carry their Czech numbers but have necessarily been allocated German numbers to comply with DB signalling systems.

Built: 2006–
Builder: Bombardier Transportation (Kassel).
Continuous Rating: 5600 kW (4000 kW under 1500 V dc).
Maximum Tractive Effort: 300 kN.
Length over Buffers: 18.90 m.
Systems: 15 kV AC 16.7 Hz; 25 kV AC 50 Hz; 1500/3000 V DC.

Electric Brake: Regenerative.
Weight: 84 tonnes.
Maximum Speed 140 km/h.
Wheel Diameter: 1250 mm.

EVN	Company	Running No	Countries	Works No	Built
6186 101	RPOOL/CH-BLSC		D A CH I NL	34299	2006
6186 102	RPOOL/CH-BLSC		D A CH I NL	34300	2006
6186 103	RPOOL/CH-BLSC		D A CH I NL	34317	2007
6186 104	RPOOL/CH-BLSC		D A CH I NL	34318	2007
6186 105	RPOOL/CH-BLSC		D A CH I NL	34319	2007
6186 106	RPOOL/CH-BLSC		D A CH I NL	34320	2007
6186 107	RPOOL/RTBC	186 107	D A CH I NL	34327	2007
6186 108	RPOOL/CH-BLSC		D A CH I NL	34325	2007
6186 109	RPOOL/CH-BLSC		D A CH I NL	34328	2007
6186 110	RPOOL/RTBC	186 110	D A CH I NL	34330	2007
6186 111	AT/NL-HSA		D A B NL	34303	2006
6186 112	AT/NL-HSA		D A B NL	34304	2206
6186 113	AT/NL-HSA		D A B NL	34302	2006
6186 114	AT/NL-HSA		D A B NL	34310	2007
6186 115	AT/NL-HSA		D A B NL	34309	2007
6186 116	AT/NL-HSA		D A B NL	34311	2007
6186 117	AT/NL-HSA		D A B NL	34321	2007
6186 118	AT/NL-HSA		D A B NL	34322	2007
6186 119	AT/NL-HSA		D A B NL	34323	2007
6186 120	AT/NL-HSA		D A B NL	34331	2007
6186 121	AT/NL-HSA		D A B NL	34339	2007
6186 122	AT/NL-HSA		D A B NL	34342	2007
6186 123	AT/ B-RTX		D A B NL	34312	2007
6186 124	AT/B-B	2802	D A B NL	34313	2007
6186 125	AT/B-B	2803	D A B NL	34316	2007
6186 126	AT/PL-Transchem	91 51 5270 007	D A PL	34305	2007
6186 127	AT/ITL	186 127	D A PL	34306	2007
6186 128	AT/ITL	186 128	D A PL	34334	2007
6186 129	AT/PL-Transchem	91 51 5270 008	D A PL	34335	2007
6186 130 (Z)	AT		D A PL	34338	2007
6186 131	AT/OHE		D A PL	34343	2007
6186 132	AT/PL-Koleje Slaskie	91 51 5270 004	D A PL	34346	2007
6186 133	AT/PL-ITL		D A PL	34347	2007
6186 134	AT/PL-ITL		D A PL	34350	2007
6186 135	AT		D A PL	34351	2007
6186 136	MER/RPOOL-DBF		D A PL	34355	2007
6186 137	MER/RPOOL-DBF		D A PL	34356	2007
6186 138	MER/ITL	186 138	D A PL	34359	2008
6186 139	MER/RPOOL-DBF		D A PL CZ	34360	2008
6186 140	ITL	186 140	D A PL	34366	2008
6186 141	RPOOL/CZ-MTR		D A PL CZ	34367	2008

6186 142	MER/ITL	142	D A B NL	34373	2008
6186 143	RPOOL/H-FLOYD		D A PL CZ	34374	2008
6186 144	MER/NS		D A B NL	34376	2008
6186 145	RPOOL/BEV		D A PL CZ	34377	2008
6186 146	RPOOL/LOTOS		D A PL CZ	34332	2007
6186 147	RPOOL/HSL		D A PL CZ	34336	2007
6186 148	MER/NS		D A B NL	34340	2007
6186 149	MER/NS		D A B NL	34344	2007
6186 150	MER/NL-LOCON		D A B NL	34348	2007

6186 151–160 delivered as 186 901–910.

6186 161	ECR		D B F	34365	2008
6186 162	ECR		D B F	34268	2008
6186 163	ECR		D B F	34430	2008
6186 164	ECR		D B F	34437	2008
6186 165	ECR		D B F	34438	2008
6186 166	ECR		D B F	34443	2008
6186 167	ECR		D B F	34447	2008
6186 168	ECR		D B F	34450	2008
6186 169	ECR		D B F	34454	2008
6186 170	ECR		D B F	34458	2008
6186 171	ECR		D B F	34467	2008
6186 172	ECR		D B F	34469	2008
6186 173	ECR		D B F	34461	2008
6186 174	ECR		D B F	34473	2009
6186 175	ECR		D B F	34475	2009
6186 176	ECR		D B F	34757	2009
6186 177	ECR		D B F	34758	2009
6186 178	ECR		D B F	34759	2009
6186 179	ECR		D B F	34760	2009
6186 180	ECR		D B F	34761	2009
6186 181	RPOOL/RTBC		D A B NL CZ	34411	2008
6186 182	RPOOL/B-B	2861	D A B NL CZ	34412	2008
6186 183	RPOOL/CZ-MTR		D A B NL CZ	34833	2011

▲ Open access has made it easier for freight operators to cover much greater distances, in some cases passing through several countries. Swiss operator BLS Cargo's 91 80 6186 103 is seen at the head of a container train from Melzo in Italy to Venlo in the Netherlands, near Osterspai on 13 March 2014. **Matthias Müller**

6186 184	AK/ITL	186 184	D B F	34463	2009
6186 185	AK/ITL	186 185	D B F	34464	2009
6186 186	AK/CTD		D B F	34470	2009
6186 187	RPOOL/CZ-MTR		D A B NL CZ	34835	2011
6186 188	AK/CTD		D B F		2014
6186 189	AK/CTD		D B F	35117	2014
6186 190	D-AK		D B F		2014
6186 191	D-AK		D B F		2014
6186 192					
6186 193					
6186 194					
6186 195					
6186 196	AT/B-B	2804	D A B NL	34382	2008
6186 197	AT/B-B	2805	D A B NL	34383	2008
6186 198	AT/B-B	2806	D A B NL	34384	2008
6186 199	AT/B-B	2807	D A B NL	34385	2008
6186 200	AT/B-B	2808	D A B NL	34386	2008
6186 201	AT/B-B	2809	D A B NL	34387	2008
6186 202	AT/B-B	2810	D A B NL	34388	2008
6186 203	AT/B-B	2811	D A B NL	34389	2008
6186 204	AT/B-B	2812	D A B NL	34390	2008
6186 205	AT/B-B	2813	D A B NL	34391	2008
6186 206	AT/B-B	2814	D A B NL	34393	2008
6186 207	AT/B-B	2815	D A B NL	34392	2008
6186 208	AT/B-B	2816	D A B NL	34394	2008
6186 209	AT/B-B	2817	D A B NL	34395	2008
6186 210	AT/B-B	2818	D A B NL	34397	2008
6186 211	AT/B-B	2819	D A B NL	34398	2008
6186 212	AT/B-B	2820	D A B NL	34399	2008
6186 213	AT/B-B	2821	D A B NL	34400	2008
6186 214	AT/B-B	2822	D A B NL	34402	2008
6186 215	AT/B-B	2823	D A B NL	34403	2008
6186 216	AT/B-B	2824	D A B NL	34408	2008
6186 217	AT/B-B	2825	D A B NL	34410	2008
6186 218	AT/B-B	2826	D A B NL	34416	2008
6186 219	AT/B-B	2827	D A B NL	34417	2008
6186 220	AT/B-B	2828	D A B NL	34419	2008
6186 221	AT/B-B	2829	D A B NL	34428	2008
6186 222	AT/B-B	2830	D A B NL	34431	2008
6186 223	AT/B-B	2831	D A B NL	34440	2008
6186 224	AT/B-B	2832	D A B NL	34444	2008
6186 225	AT/B-B	2833	D A B NL	34446	2008
6186 226	AT/B-B	2834	D A B NL	34453	2008
6186 227	AT/B-B	2835	D A B NL	34455	2009
6186 228	AT/B-B	2836	D A B NL	34459	2009
6186 229	AT/B-B	2837	D A B NL	34465	2009
6186 230	AT/B-B	2838	D A B NL	34471	2009
6186 231	AT/B-B	2839	D A B NL	34472	2009
6186 232	AT/B-B	2840	D A B NL	34480	2009
6186 233	AT/B-B	2841	D A B NL	34482	2009
6186 234	AT/B-B	2842	D A B NL	34490	2009
6186 235	AT/B-B	2843	D A B NL	34493	2009
6186 236	MER		D A B NL	34436	2009
6186 237	MER/LTE		D A B NL	34441	2009
6186 238	MER/LTE		D A B NL	34447	2009
6186 239	MER		D A B NL	34448	2009
6186 240	MER/RTBC		D A B NL CZ	34457	2009
6186 241	AT		D A PL	34415	2008
6186 242	AT/ITL	186 242	D A PL	34451	2009
6186 243	AT/PL-ORLEN		D A PL	34452	2009
6186 244	AT/PL-ITL		D A PL	34456	2009
6186 245	AT/PL-ITL		D A PL	34474	2009
6186 246	AT/CTD-ITL		D A PL	34477	2009
6186 247	AT/LM		D A PL	34479	2009

6186 248	AT/PL-ORLEN		D A PL	34485	2009	
6186 249	AT/LOCON Benelux		D A PL	34494	2009	
6186 250	AT/PL-ORLEN		D A PL	34495	2009	
6186 251	RPOOL/CH-BLSC		D A CH I NL	34421	2008	186432
6186 252						
6186 253						
6186 254						
6186 255						
6186 256						186435
6186 257						186436
6186 258						
6186 259						
6186 260						
6186 261	D-AK/PL-ORLEN		D A PL		2014	
6186 262	D-AK/PL-ORLEN		D A PL		2014	
6186 263	D-AK/PL-ORLEN		D A PL		2014	
6186 264	D-AK/PL-ORLEN		D A PL		2014	
6186 265	D-AK/PL-CTD		D A PL		2014	
6186 266	D-AK/PL-CTL		D A PL		2014	
6186 267	D-AK		D A PL		2014	
6186 268						
6186 269						
6186 270						
6186 271	RPOOL/LOTOS		D A PL CZ	34766	2010	
6186 272	RPOOL/LOTOS		D A PL CZ	34770	2010	
6186 273	RPOOL/LOTOS		D A PL CZ	34771	2010	
6186 274	RPOOL/LOTOS		D A PL CZ	34781	2010	
6186 275	RPOOL/LOTOS		D A PL CZ	34782	2010	
6186 276	RPOOL/LOTOS		D A PL CZ	34785	2010	
6186 277						
6186 278						
6186 279						
6186 280						
6186 281	RPOOL/LM	186 281	D A I	34460	2009	
6186 282	RPOOL/LM	186 282	D A I	34468	2009	
6186 283	RPOOL/LM	186 283	D A I	34488	2009	
6186 284	RPOOL/LM	186 284	D A I	34756	2009	
6186 285	RPOOL/LM	186 285	D A I	34476	2009	
6186 286	RPOOL/LM	186 286	D A I	34827	2009	
6186 287	RPOOL/LM	186 287	D A I	34828	2009	
6186 288	RPOOL/LM	186 288	D A I	34837	2012	
6186 289	RPOOL/CZ-MTR		D A B NL CZ SK	34841	2011	
6186 290	RPOOL/LM	186 290	D A I	34839	2012	
6186 291	RPOOL/CZ-MTR		D A B NL CZ SK	34840	2012	
6186 292						
6186 293						
6186 294						
6186 295						
6186 296						
6186 297						
6186 298						
6186 299						
6186 300						

6186 301–345 are F-ECR and appear in "French Railways".

6186 346	AT/B-B	2901	D B F	34478	2009
6186 347	AT/B-B	2902	D B F	34483	2009
6186 348	AT/B-B	2903	D B F	34487	2009
6186 349	AT/B-B	2904	D B F	34484	2009
6186 350	AT/B-B	2905	D B F	34481	2009
(6186 401)	CZ/MTR	386 001	D A CZ	35154	2014
(6186 402)	CZ/MTR	386 002	D A CZ	35155	2014
(6186 403)	CZ/MTR	386 003	D A CZ	35156	2014

(6186 404)	CZ/MTR	386 004	D A CZ	35157	2014
(6186 405)	CZ/MTR	386 005	D A CZ	35160	2014
(6186 406)	CZ/MTR	386 006	D A CZ	35145	2014
(6186 407)	CZ/MTR	386 007	D A CZ	35146	2014
(6186 408)	CZ/MTR	386 008	D A CZ	35161	2014
(6186 409)	CZ/MTR	386 009	D A CZ	35149	2014
(6186 410)	CZ/MTR	386 010	D A CZ	35163	2014
(6186 411)	CZ/MTR	386 011	D A CZ	35166	2014
(6186 412)	CZ/MTR	386 012	D A CZ		2014
(6186 413)	CZ/MTR	386 013	D A CZ		2014
(6186 414)	CZ/MTR	386 014	D A CZ SK HU PL	35165	2015
(6186 415)	CZ/MTR	386 015	D A CZ SK HU PL	35168	2015
(6186 416)	CZ/MTR	386 016	D A CZ SK HU PL	35170	2015
(6186 417)	CZ/MTR	386 017	D A CZ	35169	2015
(6186 418)	CZ/MTR	386 018	D A CZ	35171	2015
(6186 419)	CZ/MTR	386 019	D A CZ	35172	2015
(6186 420)	CZ/MTR	386 020	D A CZ	35173	2015
6186 421	RPOOL/RTBC	186 421	D A B NL	35179	2015
6186 422	RPOOL/RTBC		D A B NL	35180	2015
6186 423	RPOOL/MTRD		D A B NL	35181	2015
6186 424	RPOOL/RTBC		D A B NL	35182	2015
6186 430	RPOOL		D A PL NL CZ SK HU		2015
6186 440	LM	440	D A I	35174	2014
6186 441	LM	441	D A I	35175	2014
6186 442	LM	442	D A I	35124	2014
6186 443	LM	443	D A I	35153	2014
6186 444	LM	444	D A I	35178	2014
6186 901	MER/XRAIL		D A CH I	34314	2006
6186 902	MER/XRAIL		D A CH I	34353	2006
6186 903	MER/XRAIL		D A CH I	34354	2006
6186 904	MER/XRAIL		D A CH I	34352	2006
6186 905	MER/XRAIL		D A CH I	34357	2006
6186 906	MER/XRAIL		D A CH I	34358	2008
6186 907	MER/XRAIL		D A CH I	34362	2008
6186 908	MER/XRAIL		D A CH I	34363	2008
6186 909	MER/XRAIL		D A CH I	34370	2008
6186 910	MER/XRAIL		D A CH I	34371	2008

Notes:

6186 123   Ex SNCB 2801
6186 130   Damaged in Poland

6186 140   Scrapped 2012

91 80 6187   TRAXX F140AC3   Bo-Bo

Class 187 is the latest version of the Bombardier TRAXX which can be supplied with a small diesel engine fitted for last mile work and as such it is the TRAXX F140AC3 (third version) or F140AC3LM with the last mile diesel. It is understood that there are also batteries available to add power when away from the overhead wires. Note that the type is designated as an electric locomotive and not a hybrid (Class 90 80). The first locomotives went to private operators and are numbered 187 001 onwards. DB has ordered a large batch which will be 187 101 onwards (not necessarily with last mile diesel).

Built: 2012–
Builder: Bombardier Transportation (Kassel).   **Electric Brake:**
Continuous Rating: 5600 kW.   **Weight:**
Maximum Tractive Effort: **Maximum Speed:**
Length over Buffers: **Wheel Diameter:**
Systems: 15 kV AC 16.7 Hz; 25 kV AC 50 Hz.

EVN	Company	Works No	Built
6187 001	RPOOL/CH-BLSC	34935	2011
6187 002	RPOOL/CH-BLSC	34936	2012
6187 003	RPOOL/CH-BLSC	34937	2012

```
6187 004    RPOOL/CH-BLSC    35055    2014
6187 005    RPOOL/N          35056    2014
6187 006    RPOOL/CH-BLSC    35057    2014
6187 007    RPOOL/CH-BLSC    35058    2014
6187 008    RPOOL/CH-BLSC    35059    2013
6187 009    BTK/DB           35093    2014
6187 010    BTK              35129    2015
6187 011    D-AK             35132    2014
6187 012    D-AK             35133    2014
6187 013    D-AK             35127    2014
6187 014    D-AK             35128    2014
```

91 80 6189   ES64F4   Bo-Bo

This is the Siemens multi-system locomotive of the Euro Sprinter family being classed by Siemens as ES64F4 where ES = Euro Sprinter, 64 = 6400 kW, F = Freight and 4 = four voltages. Up to four pantographs can be fitted. Siemens designates these locomotives as different versions according to the different "country packages" fitted. Where locomotives can work depends not only on them being fitted with the necessary train protection systems but also suitable pantographs which vary between span and fitment (copper or carbon contact strip and whether AC/DC)! To show all these variants would need quite a complex matrix so to simplify things just the countries concerned are listed below. Initially Siemens had its own leasing arm, Siemens Dispolok, but this was sold to a Japanese concern and is now MRCE, but the VKM remains as DISPO! Depending on hiring requirements locomotives may be altered to another version. Good examples of this are some of DB's own locos (Version A, B, C) that are now being converted to operate in Germany, Czech Republic and Poland and are now counted as Version M! When observing these locomotives there is a trap for the unwary. DB sold 189 090-99 to MRCE which became ESF4-990-99, but MRCE already had similar locos ES64F4 090-099 which are 189 990-999!

Versions A, B, C:	Germany
Version D:	Germany, Austria, Italy, Slovenia, Hungary, Romania
Version E:	Germany, Austria, Switzerland, Italy, Netherlands, Slovenia, Hungary, Romania.
Version F:	Switzerland, Italy
Version G:	Sweden
Version H:	Germany, Austria, Poland
Version I:	Italy, Poland
Versions J, K:	Germany, Netherlands
Version L:	Germany, Austria, Switzerland, Italy, Netherlands, Belgium, Slovenia, Hungary, Romania
Version M:	Germany, Austria, Poland, Czech Republic, Slovakia, Hungary, Romania, Slovenia, Croatia
Version N:	
Version O:	Germany, Poland, Netherlands
Version P:	Poland
Version R:	Germany, Austria, Romania

Built: 2003–11.
Builder: Siemens, München-Allach.
Power Rating: 6400 kW.   **Weight:** 86 tonnes.
Maximum Tractive Effort: 300 kN.   **Maximum Speed:** 140 km/h.
Length over Buffers: 19.58 m.   **Wheel Diameter:** 1250 mm.

EVN	Company	Running No	Version	Works No	Built	Notes
6189 090	MRCE/ERS	ES64F4-990	J	21076	2005	
6189 091	MRCE/ERS	ES64F4-991	J	21077	2005	
6189 092	MRCE/LM	ES64F4-992	J	21078	2005	
6189 093	MRCE/SBBCI	ES64F4-993	J	21079	2005	
6189 094	MRCE/NIAG	ES64F4-994	J	21080	2005	
6189 095	MRCE/CTD-NL	ES64F4-995	J	21081	2005	
6189 096	MRCE/SBBCI	ES64F4-996	J	21082	2005	
6189 097	MRCE/LOCON	ES64F4-997	J	21083	2005	
6189 098	MRCE/LOCON	ES64F4-998	J	21084	2005	
6189 099	MRCE/LOCON	ES64F4-999	J	21085	2005	

6189 101	MRCE/A-WLC	ES64F4-101	L	21501	2009
6189 102	MRCE/TXL	ES64F4-102	L	21502	2009
6189 103	MRCE/RTBC	ES64F4-103	L	21503	2009
6189 104	MRCE/CTD	ES64F4-104	L	21505	2009
6189 105	MRCE/A-Eccorail	ES64F4-105	L	21506	2009
6189 106	MRCE/BOXX	ES64F4-106	L	21508	2009
6189 107	MRCE/PL-FPL	ES64F4-107	L	21509	2009
6189 108	MRCE/I-FSTIC	ES64F4-108	L	21511	2009
6189 109	MRCE/ITLB	ES64F4-109	L	21512	2009
6189 110	MRCE/NL-ERS	ES64F4-110	L	21514	2009
6189 111	MRCE/CTD-BCB	ES64F4-111	L	21515	2009
6189 112	MRCE/SBBCI	ES64F4-112	L	21517	2009
6189 113	MRCE/LEG	ES64F4-113	L	21518	2009
6189 114	MRCE/NL-HTRSN	ES64F4-114	L	21520	2009
6189 115	MRCE/TXL	ES64F4-115	L	21521	2009
6189 150	MRCE/AWT	ES64F4-150	M	20758	2004 Ex SBB 474 008, ex 6189 920
6189 151	MRCE/AWT	ES64F4-151	M	21641	2009
6189 152	MRCE/PL-PKP Cargo	ES64F4-152	M	21642	2009
6189 153	MRCE/PL-PKP Cargo	ES64F4-153	M	21643	2009
6189 154	MRCE/PL-PKP Cargo	ES64F4-154	M	21644	2009
6189 155	MRCE/A-LTE	ES64F4-155	M	21645	2009
6189 156	MRCE/A-LTE	ES64F4-156	M	21646	2009
6189 157	MRCE/DBS	ES64F4-157	M	21647	2010
6189 158	MRCE/A-LTE	ES64F4-158	M	21648	2010
6189 159	MRCE/DBS	ES64F4-159	M	21649	2010

▲ Although fitted with a last-mile diesel engine, Class 187 has been allocated the EVN of a high-speed electric locomotive (91 80), rather than that of a hybrid locomotive (90 80). 91 80 6187 007 and 005 are seen at the Velim test circuit in the Czech Republic on 2 July 2014.   **Quintus Vosman**

6189 200	MRCE/ITL	ES64F4-200	O	20719	2004	Ex 6189 906
6189 201	MRCE/FPL	ES64F4-201	O	20980	2004	Ex 6189 911
6189 202	MRCE/ERS	ES64F4-202	O	20986	2004	Ex 6189 913
6189 203	MRCE/TXL	ES64F4-203	O	20986	2004	Ex 6189 919
6189 204 (Z)	MRCE	ES64F4-204	O	21234	2005	Ex 6189 921
6189 205	MRCE/ITL	ES64F4-205	O	21235	2006	Ex 6189 922
6189 206	MRCE/RTBC	ES64F4-206	O	21238	2006	Ex 6189 925
6189 207	MRCE/CTL	ES64F4-207	O	21241	2006	Ex 6189 928
6189 208	MRCE/NL-ERS	ES64F4-208	O	21482	2008	
6189 209	MRCE/CTL	ES64F4-209	O	21246	2006	Ex 6189 933
6189 210	MRCE/NL-ERS	ES64F4-210	O	21483	2008	
6189 211	MRCE/NL-HTRSN	ES64F4-211	O	21484	2008	
6189 212	MRCE/NL-ERS	ES64F4-212	O	21485	2008	
6189 213	MRCE/NL-ERS	ES64F4-213	O	21486	2008	
6189 280	MRCE/TXL	ES64F4-280	K	21487	2008	
6189 281	MRCE/TXL	ES64F4-281	K	21488	2008	
6189 282	MRCE/SBBCI	ES64F4-282	K	21489	2008	
6189 283	MRCE/TXL	ES64F4-283	K	21490	2008	
6189 284	MRCE/TXL	ES64F4-284	K	21491	2009	
6189 285	MRCE/RTBC	ES64F4-285	K	21492	2009	
6189 286	MRCE/NL-ERS	ES64F4-286	K	21493	2009	
6189 287	MRCE/TXL	ES64F4-287	K	21631	2009	
6189 288	MRCE/NL-HTRSN	ES64F4-288	K	21632	2009	
6189 289	MRCE/RTBC	ES64F4-289	K	21633	2009	
6189 290	MRCE/TXL	ES64F4-290	K	21634	2009	
6189 291	MRCE/TXL	ES64F4-291	K	21650	2010	
6189 400	MRCE/IT-CFI	ES64F4-400	I	21242	2006	Ex 6189 929
6189 401	MRCE/IT-NC	ES64F4-401	I	21472	2008	
6189 402	MRCE/IT-NC	ES64F4-402	I	21473	2008	
6189 403	MRCE/IT-OCG	ES64F4-403	I	21474	2008	
6189 404	MRCE/IT-NC	ES64F4-404	I	21475	2008	
6189 405	MRCE/IT-OCG	ES64F4-405	I	21476	2008	
6189 406	MRCE/IT-CFI	ES64F4-406	I	21477	2008	
6189 407	MRCE/IT-CFI	ES64F4-407	I	21494	2009	
6189 408	MRCE/IT-CFI	ES64F4-408	I	21495	2009	
6189 409	MRCE/IT-CFI	ES64F4-409	I	21496	2009	
6189 450	MRCE/PL-ITLPL	ES64F4-450	P	21497	2009	
6189 451	MRCE/PL-LOTOS	ES64F4-451	P	21498	2009	
6189 452	MRCE/PL-LOTOS	ES64F4-452	P	21499	2009	
6189 453	MRCE/WLE	82	P	21500	2009	
6189 454	MRCE/PL-LOTOS	ES64F4-454	P	21504	2009	
6189 455	MRCE/PL-LOTOS	ES64F4-455	P	21507	2009	
6189 456	MRCE/PL-LOTOS	ES64F4-456	P	21510	2009	
6189 457	MRCE/DBS	ES64F4-457	P	21513	2009	
6189 458	MRCE/DBS	ES64F4-458	P	21516	2009	
6189 459	MRCE/PL-CTL	ES64F4-459	P	21519	2009	
6189 601						
6189 700	RO-CTV		R	21609	2009	
6189 701	RO-CTV		R	21610	2009	
6189 800	MTEG	189 800	H2	21608	2008	
6189 801	WLE	81	H2	21611	2009	
6189 802	MRCE/PKP Cargo	ES64F4-802	H2	21616	2010	
6189 803	MRCE/PKP Cargo	ES64F4-803	H2	21619	2011	
6189 804	MRCE/PKP Cargo	ES64F4-804	H2	21620	2011	
6189 805	MRCE/PKP Cargo	ES64F4-805	H2	21624	2011	
6189 806	MRCE/TXL	ES64F4-806	H2	21625	2011	
6189 820	LOCON	501	E	21613	2010	
6189 821	LOCON	502	E	21614	2010	
6189 822	A-STBAT		E	21617	2010	
6189 823	PCW/IT-CFI		E	21627	2011	
6189 824						
6189 825						

6189 840	MRCE/TXL	ES64F4-840	M	21612	2010	
6189 841	MRCE/DBS	ES64F4-841	M	21615	2010	
6189 842	MRCE/PL-PKP Cargo	ES64F4-842	M	21618	2010	
6189 843	MRCE/A-LTE	ES64F4-843	M	21621	2011	
6189 844	MRCE/PL-PKP Cargo	ES64F4-844	M	21622	2010	
6189 845	SK/EXRA	6390 001	M	21623	2011	
6189 901	RTC		D	20680	2003	
6189 902	RTC		D	20683	2003	
6189 903	RTC		D	20669	2002	Ex DB 189 001ᴵ
6189 904	RTC		D	20670	2002	Ex DB 189 002ᴵ
6189 905	RTC		D	20671	2002	Ex DB 189 001ᴵ
6189 906	Renumbered 6189 200					
6189 907	LM	189 907	D	20727	2004	
6189 908	MRCE	ES64F4-008	D	20731	2004	
6189 909	MRCE/TXL	ES64F4-009	D	20735	2004	
6189 910	MRCE	ES64F4-010	D	20724	2004	
6189 911	Renumbered 6189 201					
6189 912	LM	189 912	D	20983	2004	
6189 913	Renumbered 6189 202					
6189 914	LM	189 914	D	20988	2004	
6189 915	MRCE	ES64F4-015	D	20991	2004	
6189 916	MRCE	ES64F4-016	D	20993	2004	
6189 917	LM	189 917	D	21060	2004	
6189 918	LM	189 918	D	21062	2004	
6189 919	Renumbered 6189 203					
6189 920	Renumbered 6189 150					
6189 921	Renumbered 6189 204					
6189 922	Renumbered 6189 205					
6189 923	MRCE/TXL	ES64F4-023	D	21236	2006	
6189 924	MRCE/TXL	ES64F4-024	D	21237	2006	
6189 925	Renumbered 6189 206					
6189 926	MRCE/TXL	ES64F4-026	D	21239	2006	
6189 927	MRCE/LM	ES64F4-027	D	21230	2006	
6189 928	Renumbered 6189 207					
6189 929	Renumbered 6189 400					
6189 930	MRCE/TXL	ES64F4-030	D	21243	2006	
6189 931	MRCE/TXL	ES64F4-031	D	21244	2006	
6189 932	MRCE/I-FSTIC	ES64F4-032	D	21245	2006	
6189 933	Renumbered 6189 209					
6189 934	MRCE	ES64F4-034	D	21478	2009	
6189 935	MRCE/TXL	ES64F4-035	D	21479	2009	
6189 936	MRCE/TXL	ES64F4-036	D	21480	2009	
6189 937	MRCE/OHEGO	ES64F4-037	D	21481	2009	
6189 938	MRCE/TXL	ES64F4-038	D	21650	2010	
6189 982	MRCE/SBBCI	ES64F4-082	E	21635	2009	
6189 983	MRCE/SBBCI	ES64F4-083	E	21636	2009	
6189 984	MRCE/RTBC	ES64F4-084	E	21637	2009	
6189 985	MRCE/IT-ISC	ES64F4-085	E	21638	2009	
6189 986	MRCE/NIAG	ES64F4-086	E	21639	2009	
6189 987	MRCE/IT-ISC	ES64F4-087	E	21640	2009	
6189 988	MRCE/CTD-BCB	ES64F4-088	E	20732	2004	
6189 989	MRCE/RTBC	ES64F4-089	E	20734	2004	
6189 990	MRCE/CTD-BCB	ES64F4-090	E	20736	2004	
6189 991	MRCE/SBBCI	ES64F4-091	E	20739	2004	
6189 992	MRCE/TXL	ES64F4-092	E	20721	2004	
6189 993	MRCE/IT-INRAIL	ES64F4-093	E	20723	2004	
6189 994	MRCE/CTD	ES64F4-094	E	20695	2003	
6189 995	MRCE/TXL	ES64F4-095	E	20698	2003	
6189 996	MRCE/NL-HTRSN	ES64F4-096	E	20701	2003	
6189 997	MRCE/TXL	ES64F4-097	E	20704	2003	
6189 998	MRCE/TXL	ES64F4-098	E	20707	2003	
6189 999	MRCE/IT-NC	ES64F4-099	E	20730	2004	

▲ The most versatile member of the Siemens Euro Sprinter family is the Class 189, available in up to four voltages and with up to four pantographs. Locon Logistik & Consulting (LOCON) 91 80 6189 821 can operate in eight different countries, reflecting the growing operational sphere of that company. It is stabled overnight at Gemünden on 14 September 2012. **Matthias Müller**

▼ The latest Siemens design is the Vectron which is proving very popular with leasing companies. MRCE Dispolok owned 91 80 6193 873, on hire to Hungarian operator Floyd, hauls a train of grain from Hungary to Krefeld at Bonn Beuel on 29 March 2014. **Matthias Müller**

91 80 6193   VECTRON   Bo-Bo

The Vectron family of locomotives can be considered the successor to the Euro Sprinter/Taurus series, the latter having been built during the first ten years of this century. Now Siemens is moving on with a new product and like the Euro Sprinter will be available as AC, AC/DC, DC and even a diesel version – yes the Vectron is also Siemens answer to the Bombardier TRAXX family. Before the last Euro Sprinters had appeared the Vectron was already appearing in 2010 in various experimental versions. The first locomotives were all Siemens demonstrators but by 2013 Railpool and MRCE leasing companies were already snapping up examples as well as relative new comer ELL. DB Schenker Rail Polska ordered some DC only locomotives but most ordered by other operators/leasing companies are for AC versions. At the moment the numbering scheme seems to be very haphazard with multi system (MS) locos mixed up with other types. Locomotives shown as AC are, like the 185s, dual voltage. Of course the idea is that locos can be converted quite easily, but without a proper numbering system who will know what a locomotive is fitted for next week?

Built: 2010–
Builder: Siemens, München-Allach.
Power Rating: 6400 kW.
Maximum Tractive Effort: 300 kN.
Length over Buffers: 18.98 m.

Weight: 88–96 tonnes.
Maximum Speed: 160 (*200) km/h.
Wheel Diameter: 1250 mm.

EVN	Company	Running No	Countries	System	Works No	Built
6193 203	ELOC/RTBC		D A H	AC	21923	2014
6193 204	ELOC/A-CSV		D A H	AC	21928	2014
6193 205	ELOC/CZ-RJ		D A H PL CZ SK	MS	21921	2014
6193 206	ELOC/CZ-RJ		D A H PL CZ SK	MS	21931	2014
6193 207	ELOC/A-LTE		D A H PL CZ SK	MS	21929	2014
6193 208	ELOC/A-LTE		D A H	AC	21920	2014
6193 209	ELOC/SBBCI		D A H	AC	21908	2014
6193 210	ELOC/SBBCI		D A H	AC	21926	2014
6193 211	ELOC/A-ECCO		D A H	AC	21911	2014
6193 212	ELOC/A-ECCO		D A H	AC	21912	2014
6193 213	ELOC/A-WLC		D A H	AC	21914	2014
6193 214	ELOC/CZ-RJ		D A H PL CZ SK	MS	21918	2014
6193 215	ELOC/A-LTE		D A H PL CZ SK	MS	21932	2015
6193 216	ELOC/A-LTE		D A H PL CZ SK	MS	21942	2015
6193 217	ELOC/A-ECCO		D A H	AC	21916	2014
6193 218	ELOC/OHEGO		D A H	AC	21917	2014
6193 219	ELOC/OHEGO		D A H	AC	21907	2014
6193 220	ELOC/CZ-LTB		D A H PL CZ SK RO	MS	21840	2014
6193 221	ELOC/CZ-LTB		D A H PL CZ SK RO	MS	21935	2015
6193 222	ELOC			MS	21956	2015
6193 223	ELOC		D A H	MS	21943	2015
6193 224	ELOC/A-WLC		D A H CZ SK RO	MS	21944	2015
6193 225	ELOC/A-ECCO				21948	2015
6193 226	ELOC			MS	21961	2015
6193 227	ELOC			MS		2015
6193 228	ELOC				21962	2015
6193 229	ELOC			AC	21963	2015
6193 600 *	MRCE/DBFW	X4E-600	D A	AC	21927	2014
6193 601 *	MRCE	X4E-601	D A	AC	21951	2015
6193 602	MRCE/DBS	X4E-602		AC	21952	2015
6193 603	MRCE	X4E-603		AC	21954	2015
6193 801 *	RPOOL/SLG		D A	AC	21772	2012
6193 802 *	RPOOL/A-WLC		D A	AC	21773	2012
6193 803 *	RPOOL/EGOO		D A	AC	21774	2012
6193 804 *	RPOOL/BOXX		D A	AC	21775	2012
6193 805 *	RPOOL/A-WLC		D A	AC	21776	2012
6193 806 *	RPOOL/EVB		D A	AC	21777	2012
6193 810	RPOOL/RTBC		D A H RO	AC	21898	2014
6193 811	RPOOL/A-WLC		D A H RO	AC	21899	2014
6193 812	RPOOL/RTBC		D A H RO	AC	21900	2014

6193 813	RPOOL/A-WLC		D A H RO	AC	21903	2014
6193 814	RPOOL/RTBC		D A H RO	AC	21902	2014
6193 820	ELOC/A-ECCO			MS	21829	2013
6193 821	PCW			MS	21830	2013
6193 822	PCW/LM			MS	21831	2013
6193 823	PCW			MS	21839	2013
6193 831	ELOC/A-SETG		D A H	AC	21844	2014
6193 832	ELOC/RTBC		D A H	AC	21904	2014
6193 840	BOXX		D A	AC	21825	2013
6193 841	BOXX		D A	AC	21826	2013
6193 842	BOXX		D A	AC	21930	2014
6193 843	BOXX		D A	AC	21937	2015
6193 844		D A	AC			
6193 845	MGW/IGE		D A	AC	21913	2014
6193 850	MRCE/BOXX	X4E-850	D A	AC	21824	2013
6193 851	MRCE/BOXX	X4E-851	D A	AC	21827	2013
6193 852	MRCE/BOXX	X4E-852	D A	AC	21842	2013
6193 853	MRCE/BOXX	X4E-853	D A	AC	21843	2013
6193 854	MRCE/DBFW	X4E-854	D A	AC	21891	2013
6193 855	MRCE/PCT	X4E-855	D A	AC	21893	2013
6193 856	MRCE/PCT	X4E-856	D A	AC	21894	2014
6193 857	MRCE/PCT	X4E-857	D A	AC	21895	2014
6193 858	MRCE/PCT	X4E-858	D A	AC	21896	2014
6193 859	MRCE/DBFW	X4E-859	D A	AC	21897	2014
6193 860	MRCE/DBFW	X4E-860	D A	AC	21898	2014
6193 861	MRCE/BOXX	X4E-861	D A	AC	21922	2014
6193 862	MRCE/NIAG	X4E-862	D A	AC	21925	2014
6193 863	MRCE/BOXX	X4E-863	D A	AC	21933	2014
6193 864	MRCE	X4E-864	D A	AC	21941	2015
6193 865 *	MRCE/DBS	X4E-865	D A	AC	21950	2015
6193 866	MRCE					
6193 867	MRCE				21955	2015
6193 868	MRCE					
6193 869	MRCE					
6193 870 *	MRCE/DBS	X4E-870	D A H	AC	21833	2013
6193 871	MRCE/DBFW	X4E-871	D A H	AC	21834	2013
6193 872	MRCE/BEV	X4E-872	D A H	AC	21836	2013
6193 873	MRCE	X4E-873	D A H	AC	21837	2013
6193 874	MRCE/DBS	X4E-874	D A H	AC	21901	2014
6193 875	MRCE/BEV	X4E-875	D A H	AC	21915	2014
6193 876 *	MRCE/BEV	X4E-876	D A H CZ SK RO	AC	21946	2015
6193 877	MRCE/BEV	X4E-877	D A H	AC	21936	2015
6193 878	MRCE/BEV	X4E-878	D A H CZ SK		21940	2015
6193 879 *	MRCE/DBS	X4E-879	D A H CZ SK RO	AC	21945	2015
6193 880	MRCE/BOXX		D A H	AC	21832	2013
6193 881	MRCE/BOXX		D A H	AC	21838	2013
6193 882	BOXX			AC	21938	2015
6193 883	BOXX			AC	21939	2015
1193 890	A-CSV		D A	AC	21919	2013
6193 901	PCW			MS	21691	2010
6193 902	PCW			MS	21694	2010
6193 921	NRAIL/SE-SKJB			AC	21692	2010
6193 922	NRAIL/SE-SKJB			AC	21695	2010
6193 923	PCW/N-CN			AC	21696	2011
6193 924	PCW/N-CN			AC	21697	2011
6193 930	PCW			AC	21905	2015
6193 961	PCW			AC	21699	2013
6193 962[II]	PCW			AC	21700	2013
6193 970	PCW		D A H	AC	21924	2014

1193 971	PCW			AC		2015
1193 980	A-WLC	D A		AC	21934	2014

Notes:

6193 220	Intended as 193 824.		6193 930	Has last mile diesel engine.
6193 840	Originally 193 962.		6193 971	To Finland for tests.
6193 841	Originally 193 963.			

193604

193233

3.3. CODE 92 80 – DIESEL LOCOMOTIVES WITH MAXIMUM SPEED 100KM/H OR HIGHER

92 80 0231 Co-Co DE

A solitary example of the former DR class 231 is now with a private operator, but being classified as 0231 would seem to reflect it is not now in original condition. The data shown however is the original specification

Built: 1973.
Builder: Voroshilovgrad, USSR.
Engine: Kolomna 5D49 of 2208 kW.
Transmission: Electric.
Maximum Tractive Effort: 340 kN.

Train Heating: None.
Wheel Diameter: 1050 mm.
Weight: 120 tonnes.
Length over Buffers: 20.62 m.
Maximum Speed: 100 km/h.

EVN	Company	Running No	Works No	Built	Notes
0231 012	WFL	23	0114	1973	Ex various, ex DR

92 80 0232 Co-Co DE

This series comprises three previously different series grouped together as one. However, it is assumed they are not all quite the same as some are former DR 232s whilst others are former 242s and one is ex USSR. Once again it is assumed they have all been rebuilt in some way. Certainly the 242s were rebuilt by Adtranz/Bombardier with new Caterpillar 3606 engines and this is why they were classed as W232s and not W242s. It is not clear what modification work has been carried out on the later acquisitions.

For principal technical details see Class 232 in German Railways Part 1.

EVN	Company	Running No	Works No	Built	Notes
0232 001	PL-ITL	W232.01	0003	1977	Ex DR 242 003
0232 002	HFH	W232.02	0002	1977	Ex DR 242 002
0232 003	PL	W232.03	0005	1977	Ex DR 242 005
0232 004	PL-ITL	W232.04	0004	1977	Ex DR 242 004
0232 105	PL		0117	1973	Ex various, ex W232.05, ex 231 015
0232 107	SL/NBEG	232 107	0113	1973	Ex various, ex W232 07, ex 231 011; damaged
0232 158	LEG	132 158	0373	1974	Ex Bosnia, ex DB
0232 204	LEG	132 004	0194	1973	Ex Bosnia, ex DB
0232 209	PL-ITL	W232.09	0853	1978	Ex SZD TE109-026; now operating in Poland

92 80 0580   B-B DH

A solitary example of the Gmeinder D100BB in use on HzL

Built: 1985.
Builder: Gmeinder.
Engine: of 1095 kW.
Transmission: Hydraulic.
Maximum Tractive Effort:

Wheel Diameter:
Weight: 72 tonnes.
Length over Buffers:
Maximum Speed: 70 km/h.

EVN	Company	Running No
0580 001	HzL	V 150

92 80 1120   Co-Co

These are former DR V120 locomotives often referred to by their Hungarian classification of M62. Three came into the hands of private operators in Germany although it is understood they are now operating in Poland but may still work into Germany.

Built: 1970–73.
Train Heating: None.
Builder: Voroshilovgrad.
Engine: Kolomna 14 D 40 of 1470 kW.
Transmission: Electric.
Maximum Tractive Effort: 373 kN.

Wheel Diameter: 1050 mm.
Weight: 116 tonnes.
Length over Buffers: 17.55 m.
Maximum Speed: 100 km/h.

EVN	Company	Running No	Works No	Built	Notes
1120 295	PL		1007	1970	Ex LEG V200 295, ASP, ex DR
1120 508	PL		1843	1973	Ex LEG, BKK Geiseltal V200 508
1120 509	PL		1769	1973	Ex LEG, Lokpool V200.009, ex CD 781.545

92 80 1201 & 1202   B-B

The former DR had over 900 V100s and as one would expect with such a large class, modifications took place over the years. The Class 201 locomotives are some of those that remained in original condition when passing into private hands, whereas the Class 202 had been up-rated by DR. The technical data is as built but the new owners may have changed things! Most locomotives have had their train heating removed as their duties are now principally on freight and infrastructure trains. Many locomotives were overhauled by Stendal works before passing to their new owners. Various improvements took place including the fitting of new engines, (often Caterpillar ones) and the removal of train heating. As these locomotives are given the EVN 92 80 etc it is assumed all are now rated at 100 km/h despite some websites having contrary information.

Built: 1964–78.
Builder: LEW.
Engine: See below.
Transmission: Hydraulic.
Maximum Tractive Effort: 206 kN.

Wheel Diameter: 1000 mm.
Weight: 63.7/64 tonnes.
Length over Buffers: 13.94 m (14.24 m 202).
Maximum Speed: 100 km/h.

Engines: There have been many rebuildings with various types of engines and different ratings which are coded as follows:

a	MWJ 12KVD18/21A-3	736 kW	1000 hp	Class 201 original engine
b	MWJ 12KVD18/21AL-4	883 kW	1200 hp	Class 202 original engine
c	MWJ 12KVD18/21A-5	750 kW	1020 hp	Class 298 original engine

d	MWJ	12KVD18/21AL-5	1100 kW	1496 hp	Class 204 original engine	
e	MTU	12U396 TC14	1050 kW	1428 hp	3 locos only!	
f	MTU	12V4000 R10	1240 kW	1686 hp	Class 203 14 locos	
g	CAT	3412 DI-TA	505 kW	686 hp	1 loco VE 110-08	
h1	CAT	3508 DI-TA	736 kW	1000 hp	14 locos	
h2	CAT	3508 DI-TA	773 kW	1050 hp	298s	
h3	CAT	3508 DI-TA	836 kW	1136 hp	7 locos	
h4	CAT	3508 DI-TA	900 kW	1224 hp	7 locos	
j1	CAT	3512 DI-TA	932 kW	1268 hp	21 locos	
j2	CAT	3512 DI-TA	1050 kW	1428 hp	Many	
j3	CAT	3512 DI-TA	1082 kW	1472 hp	Many	
j4	CAT	3512 DI-TA	1140 kW	1550 hp	5 locos	
j5	CAT	3512 DI-TA	1305 kW	1774 hp	Many	

EVN	Engine	Company	Running No	Works No	Built	Notes
1201 004		MHG	1	11212	1966	Ex DB 201 004
1201 171		TSE	110 171	12452	1969	Hamburger Hafen
1201 742	h	ITB	1103	14443	1974	Ex WAB 15, DWU 14, DB 201 742
1201 823	a	RAILS/Redler	16	15095	1975	Ex DB 201 823
1202 219	b	SKLUS	4	12501	1970	Ex ALS, ex DR 202 219
1202 237	j3	MTEG	204 237	12519	1970	Ex ALS, ex DR 202 237
1202 240	j1	EBS	202 240	12522	1970	Ex ADAM 23 *Judy*
1202 241	j1	BWESA/ADAM	22	12523	1970	*Spike*
1202 269	j1	Gleiskraft/DME	202 269	12551	1970	
1202 311	j3	MTEG	204 311	12795	1970	Ex ALS, ex DR 202 311
1202 330	j1	EBM	202 330	12839	1971	
1202 347	j3	MTEG	204 347	12856	1971	Ex ALS, ex DR 202 347
1202 354	j3	MTEG	204 354	12863	1971	Ex ALS, ex DR 202 354
1202 364	j3	EBS	202 364	12873	1971	Once ADAM 21, V203.2, 206 264, 202 364
1202 374	j3	HGB	V100.04	12883	1971	Ex 203 224, 202 374, 203 507, 202 374
1202 423	j5	RRI	101	12932	1972	Ex ALS, ex DR 202 423
1202 459		ADAM	V100 001	14398	1972	Ex NRS V100.001, ex 202 459, damaged
1202 466	j3	EBS	202 466	13505	1972	Ex ADAM 20, V203.1, 206 466, 202 466
1202 481	b	RPE	V100.01	13520	1972	Ex 202 481
1202 488		HGB	V100.03	13527	1972	Ex TLG 16, 202 488
1202 516	b	PRESS	112 516	13555	1973	Loaned to VSE preservation group
1202 520	j1	BUG	V100 03	13559	1973	Ex ADAM 9 *Sebastian*
1202 543		ADAM	202 543	13582	1973	
1202 565	b	PRESS	112 565	13883	1973	ALS, 202 565
1202 586	b	PRESS	204 036	13904	1973	ALS, 202 586
1202 597	j1	EBS	202 597	13915	1973	Ex ADAM 11,
1202 623	f	D-RAILS	3 JENNY	14433	1974	Ex DLI, ex NVAG 203 003 ex DB 202 732
1202 624	f	BSM	203 005	13500	1972	Ex NVAG 203 005 ex DB 202 461
1202 630	j1	MWB	V 1202	13948	1973	202 630
1202 708	b	RIS	112 708	14409	1974	202 708
1202 720	b	RME	202 720	14421	1974	202 720
1202 725	j1	MWB	V 1203	14426	1974	202 725
1202 726	j3	HGB	V100.05	14427	1974	Ex Gmeinder 203 001, KCR/PBSV 15, ALS, DR 202 726
1202 738	j1	EBS	202 738	14439	1974	Ex ADAM 12
1202 743	j1	BWESA/ADAM	10	14444	1974	*Holger*
1202 753	j1	MWB	V 1201	14454	1974	Ex DB 202 753
1202 817	j3	PRESS	204 033	15089	1975	ALS, 202 817
1202 960	j2	HTB	V 143	15395	1976	ex DB 710 960
1202 968	a	ITB	1101	17317	1983	Ex WAB 14, DB 710 968
1202 970		DLI	202 970	16756	1983	WAB 16, DB 710 970

92 80 1203   B-B

Many of the former DR V100s were given major overhauls together with the fitting of new engines. So thorough was the rebuilding at Stendal works that the locomotives were given a new classification of 203. Some locomotives remain the property of Stendal works and are leased by the new operators.

For technical details see Class 203 in German Railways Part 1.

For engine codings see note under 1201 & 1202 above.

EVN	Engine	Company	Running No	Works No	Built	Notes
1203 001	f	SGL	V180.07	12858	1971	Ex 202 349
1203 002	f	DB		14397	1974	Ex 202 696
1203 003	f	SWT	203-28	15240	1976	Ex 202 855
1203 004	f	DPR	203 003	14853	1975	Ex ALS 203 003, DB 202 796
1203 005	f	SGL	V180.08	13887	1973	Ex 202 569
1203 006	f	EFW	203 006	13569	1979	Ex SL, HWB VL 10, EBM 203 005, ALS, ex DB 202 530
1203 007	f	HAEG/Prolok	203 007	14419	1974	Ex various, ex DB 202 718
1203 008	f	BUVL/BSM	203 007	13886	1973	Ex EBM 203 007, ex DB 202 568
1203 012	f	BUVL/LM		14081	1974	Ex HVLE V160.1 ex ALS, ex DR 202 654
1203 013	f	SWT	203-29	14841	1975	Ex ALS, ex 202 784
1203 014	f	BUVL/LM		13905	1973	Ex HVLE V160.2, ex ALS, ex DR 202 587
1203 101	j5	NL-SHTR		15235	1976	Ex 202 850
1203 102	j5	MWB	V 1701	14469	1975	Ex RC 0505, ALS, DR 202 768
1203 103	j5	MWB	V 1702	14891	1975	Ex RC 0506, ALS, DR 202 827
1203 105	j5	HVLE	V160.3	13472	1972	Ex ALS, ex DR 202 433
1203 106	j5	NRS/SGL	V100 004	15234	1976	Ex ALS, ex DR 202 849
1203 107	j5	NRS/SGL	V100 005	13548	1972	Ex ALS, ex DR 202 509
1203 109	j5	HVLE	V160.4	15086	1975	Ex ALS, ex DR 202 814
1203 110	j5	DUD	1701	12860	1971	Ex 202 351
1203 111	j5	ALS/EBM	203 111	14078	1974	Ex 202 651
1203 112	j5	WFL	203 112	14384	1974	Ex 202 683
1203 113	j5	ALS/WFL		12879	1971	Ex ALS, ex DR 202 370
1203 114	j5	WFL	22	12924	1971	Ex ALS, ex DR 202 415
1203 115	j5	EBM	203 115	13489	1972	Ex ALS, ex DB 202 450
1203 116	j5	ALS/SWO-HABA	8	13880	1973	Ex ALS, ex DB 202 562
1203 117	j5	ALS/MEG	203 117	13525	1972	Ex 202 486
1203 118	j5	ALS/WFL		14357	1974	Ex 202 656
1203 119	j5	ALS /MEG	203 119	14417	1974	Ex 202 716
1203 120	j5	ALS/WFL	203 120	14379	1974	Ex 202 678
1203 121	j5	BBL	08	12833	1971	Ex KCR 19, ex DB 202 324
1203 122	j5	BBL	09	13928	1973	Ex KCR 20, ex DB 202 610
1203 123	j5	LOCON	217	12885	1971	Ex RTUL, ex ALS, ex DB 202 376
1203 124	j5	LOCON	218	14420	1974	Ex RTUL, ex ALS, ex DB 202 719
1203 125	j5	ALS/SBBC	203 652	14079	1974	Leased to SBB Cargo Deutschland
1203 126	j5	ALS/RRI	103	13876	1973	Ex ALS, 202 558
1203 127	j5	LDS	3	13563	1973	Ex ALS, 202 524
1203 128	j5	SLG	V100-SP-008	13568	1973	Ex ALS, ex 202 529
1203 129	j5	SLG	V100-SP-009	13567	1973	Ex ALS, ex 202 528
1203 130	j5	DUD	1702	13920	1973	Ex 202 602; Leased to RSBG
1203 131	j5	RRI	102	14390	1974	Ex ALS, ex DB 202 689

1203 135	j5	BLGRT	203 728	14429	1974	Ex Various, ex DB 202 728
1203 136	j5	BLGRT	203 737	14438	1974	Ex Various ex DB 202 737
1203 137	j5	ITL	101	12877	1971	Ex ITLB, ALS, DR 202 368
1203 138	j5	NL-Train Support	TG 102	12878	1971	Ex ALS, ex DB 202 369
1203 139	j5	NL-Train Support	TG 103	14658	1975	Ex ALS, ex DB 202 777
1203 140	j5	NL-Train Support	TG 104	14476	1975	Ex ITLB 104 , ALS, DR 202 775
1203 141	j5	HVLE	V160.09	15076	1975	Ex ALS, ex DR 202 804
1203 142	j5	HVLE	V160.10	15078	1975	Ex ALS, ex DR 202 806
1203 143	j5	HVLE	V160.5	15088	1975	Ex ALS, ex 202 816
1203 144	j5	HVLE	V160.6	14895	1975	Ex ALS, ex 202 831
1203 145	j5	ELL	203 843	15228	1976	Ex DB 202 843
1203 146	j5	SLG	V100-SP-010	15232	1976	Ex ALS, ex 202 847
1203 147	j5	EGOO	V100 egoo 001	12866	1971	Ex DB 202 357
1203 148	j5	BBL	07	12894	1971	Ex DB 202 385
1203 149	j5	ALS/SWT	203 383	12892	1971	Ex DB 202 383
1203 150	j5	HVLE	V160.7	12851	1971	Ex ALS, ex DR 202 342
1203 151	j5	ALS	203 405	12914	1971	Ex DB 202 405
1203 152	j5	ALS/EBM	203 152	15090	1975	Ex ALS, ex 202 818
1203 153	j5	ALS/MEG	203 406	12915	1971	Ex DB 202 406
1203 154	j5	ALS/CLG	203 442	13481	1972	203 442, ex 202 442
1203 155	j5	ALS/CLG	203 443	13482	1972	203 443, ex 202 443
1203 156	j5	BBL	12	13535	1972	203 496, ex 202 496
1203 157	j5	BBL	11	13562	1973	203 523, ex 202 523
1203 158	j5	SGL	V180.13	14359	1974	Ex Kosovo, ex 202 658
1203 159	j5	A-MBS	V10.017	13485	1972	Ex DB 202 446
1203 160	j5	NBEG/ Locon Benelux	203 637	13955	1974	Ex Kosovo, ex DR 202 637
1203 161	j5	SGL	V180.05	13937	1973	Ex 201 619
1203 162	j5	ALS/SONRA	203 162	14843	1975	Ex Kosovo, ex DR 202 786
1203 163	j5	NBEG/ Locon Benelux	203 163	13931	1973	Ex Kosovo, ex DB 202 613
1203 164	j5	ALS/LOCON	219	13877	1973	Ex ALS, ex 203 559, ex 202 559
1203 165	j5	ALS/CLG	203 764	14465	1974	Ex 202 764
1203 166	j5	STRA	203 166	12921	1971	Ex ALS, ex 202 412
	h4	Vattenfall	203-01	15082	1975	Ex 202 810
	h4	Vattenfall	203-02	13900	1973	Ex 202 582
	h4	Vattenfall	203-03	13587	1973	Ex 202 548
	j5	SLG	V10-SP-010	15232	1976	Ex 202 847
	j5	NL-VR	203-1	13578	1973	Ex 202 539
	j5	NL-VR	203-2	14392	1974	Ex 202 691
	j5	NL-VR	203-3	14840	1975	Ex 202 783
	j5	NL-VR	203-4	12922	1971	Ex 202 413
	j5	NL-VR	203-5	13557	1973	Ex 202 518
1203 205	j3	DUD	1401	12828	1970	Ex 202 319
1203 208	j3	DUD	1402	12887	1971	Ex 202 378
1203 211	j3	PRESS	204 010	15388	1976	Ex ALS, ex DB 199 870
1203 212	j3	PRESS	204 011	15229	1976	Ex ALS, ex DB 202 844
1203 213	j3	HGB	V100.01	13892	1973	Ex ALS 203 211, DR 202 573
1203 214	j3	SONRA	V100 006	13896	1973	DUD 1403, ALS, DR 201 577
1203 215	j3	PRESS	204 012	13564	1973	Ex PRESS 204 006, ALS, 202 525
1203 216	j3	PRESS	204 013	13475	1975	ALS 202 436
1203 217	j3	WFL	18	13492	1972	Ex various, ALS, DR 202 453
1203 220	j3	LEG	202 425	12934	1972	Ex 202 425
1203 221	j3	DUD	1404	14436	1974	Ex 202 735
1203 225	j3	PRESS	204 022	12826	1970	202 317
1203 226	j3	BOEG	202 271	12553	1970	Ex ALS, ex DR 202 271
1203 227	j3	LEG	202 327	12836	1971	Ex ALS, ex DR 202 327
1203 228	j3	PRESS	204 031	12835	1971	112 236, ALS 203 505, DR 202 326
1203 229	j3	CLR	202 484	13523	1972	Ex ALS, ex DR 202 484

▲ 92 80 1203 127 is part of a small fleet owned by LDS GmbH, one of the many small companies to have sprung up since the advent of open access. It is seen at the head of a ballast train from Bonn to Köln Eifeltor passing Bornheim on 4 June 2013. **Matthias Müller**

▼ Several former DB Class 211s were substantially rebuilt by On-Rail at Mettmann and reclassified as Class 209. The first such locomotive, 92 80 1209 001, passed to port operator Niederrheinische Verkehrsbetriebe (NIAG) as running number 4. It is pictured stabled at Moers on 1 December 2011. **Brian Garvin**

1203 230	j3	MTEG	202 703	14404	1974	Ex ALS, ex DR 202 703
1203 231	j3	EVULW	203.001 (88514)	12899	1971	ALS 202 390
1203 232	j3	EVULW	203.002 (88515)	12844	1971	ALS 202 335
?	j3	CFLDE	1151	12524	1970	Ex NEG 03, ex ALS, ex DR 202 242
?	j3	CFLDE	1152	12939	1972	Ex NEG 04, ex ALS, ex DR 202 430

1203 300 to 1203 316 are DB

1203 318	j5	ALS/EGOO	203 318	12827	1930	Ex PRESS, Kosovo, DB 202 318
1203 350	j3	PRESS	204 005	12859	1971	Ex DB 202 350
1203 409	j5	SLG	V100 SP 007	13575	1973	Ex ALS, ex 202 536
1203 442		ALS/CLG	203 442	13481	1972	Ex 202 442
1203 443		ALS/CLG	203 443	13482	1972	Ex 202 443
1203 500	j3	RTS	203 500	12549	1970	Ex 203 203, ex 202 267
1203 501	j3	RTS	203 501	12888	1971	Ex 203 204, ex 202 379
1203 558		ALS/CLG	203 558	13876	1973	Ex 202 558
1203 614	j5	LOCON	220	13933	1973	Ex Kosovo, ex DB 202 615
1203 616	j5	HVLE	V160.8	12941	1972	Ex ALS, PRESS, Kosovo, ex DR 202 432
1203 645	j5	BBL	06	14072	1974	Ex 202 645
1203 764		ALS/CLG	203 764	14465	1975	Ex 202 764
1203 841	j5	STRA	203 841	15226	1976	Ex ALS, ex 202 841
1203 915	j3	HTRS/RAR	*Brunhilde*	12774	1970	RAR V1405.2, ex 1200.02, ex ALS, ex DB 202 310

92 80 1204   B-B

This group of locomotives passed from DB with little or no alterations made. Some are still recorded as 80 km/h maximum speed but this is thought to be an error as they would then have to be class 98 80 3204

Built: 1964–78.
Builder: LEW.
Engine: See codings explained under 1201 & 1202 above.
Transmission: Hydraulic.
Maximum Tractive Effort: 222 kN.
Wheel Diameter: 1000 mm.
Weight: 64 tonnes.
Length over Buffers: 14.24 m.
Maximum Speed: 100 km/h.

EVN	Engine	Company	Running No	Works No	Built	Notes
1204 314	j1	PRESS	204 016	12823	1970	Ex ALS, ex DB
1204 358	d	MEG	101	12867	1971	Ex DB
1204 373	j1	LOCON	203	12882	1971	Ex HWB, TSD, DR 202 373
1204 469	d	MEG	104	13508	1972	Ex DB
1204 761	d	MEG	102	14462	1974	Ex DB
1204 774	d	MEG	103	14475	1975	Ex DB; loaned to Wittenberge Museum
1204 860	d	MEG	105	15378	1976	Ex DB
1204 900	a	EBS	201 001	12403	1969	Ex EBW V100.18, ex DR 201 001[II]

92 80 1209   DH 1004   B-B

The On-Rail firm in Mettmann bought several surplus 211s from DB and rebuilt built them into their class DH 1004 which are now classed as 209s. 1209 101 was rebuilt by Henschel.

Built: 1962.
Rebuilt: On Rail, Mettmann 1997–2003.
Engine: MTU 12V396 TC 14 of 1030 kW.
Transmission: Hydraulic, Voith L216rs.
Maximum Tractive Effort:
Wheel Diameter: 950 mm.
Weight: 72 tonnes.
Length over Buffers: 12.1 m.
Maximum Speed: 100 km/h.

EVN	Company	Running No	Builder	Works No	Built	Notes
1209 001	NIAG	4[II]	On Rail	DH1004/1	1997	Ex DB 211 162
1209 002	WEBA	5	On Rail	DH1004/2	1999	Ex DB 211 177
1209 003	SHH	F 6	On Rail	DH1004/3	1999	Ex DB 211 112
1209 004	RTBC	V 104	On Rail	DH1004/4	2000	Ex DB 211 235
1209 005	RTBC	V 105	On Rail	DH1004/5	2001	Ex DB 211 276
1209 006	TWE	V 144	On Rail	DH1004/6	2001	Ex DB 211 293
1209 007	RTBC	V 107	On Rail	DH1004/7	2003	Ex DB 211 104
1209 101	NEG	211 002	Krupp	4343	1961	Ex NVAG DL2, Ex DB 211 233

92 80 1211   B-B

These are all second hand from DB. Once into private hands, details of any modifications carried out since then are difficult to come by. Consequently details given are for as built.

Built: 1958–63.
Builder: As listed.
Engine: MTU MD 12V538 TA or MB 12V493 TZ.
Transmission: Hydraulic, Voith L216rs.
Maximum Tractive Effort: 183 kN.

Wheel Diameter: 950mm.
Weight: 62 tonnes.
Length over Buffers: 12.10 m.
Maximum Speed: 100 km/h.

EVN	Company	Running No	Builder	Works No	Built	Notes
1211 011	EEB	Emsland III	MaK	1000029	1961	
1211 012	EEB	Emsland IV	MaK	1000030	1961	
1211 015	BLP	Wiebe 8	MaK	1000033	1961	
1211 019	ELV	211 019	MaK	1000037	1961	
1211 024	EVB	410 04	MaK	1000042	1961	
1211 030	RAILS	211 030	Jung	13304	1961	Ex RRI 42, BGW, ex DB 211 030
1211 031	NRAIL	(V211 01)	Jung	13305	1961	
1211 041	NESA	V100 1041	Jung	13315	1962	
1211 045	BLP	Wiebe 9	MaK	1000063	1962	
1211 051	EFW	211 051	MaK	1000069	1962	
1211 054	ELV	211 054	MaK	1000072	1962	
1211 061	EVB	410.05	MaK	1000079	1962	
1211 074	EGB	211 074	MaK	1000092	1962	
1211 086	EVB	410.06	MaK	1000104	1962	
1211 125	BE	D 21	KHD	57362	1962	Ex On Rail, ex DB 211 125
1211 160	ITL	111 001	KHD	57397	1962	Ex On Rail, CTTG, DB 211 160
1211 200	DME	V100 1200	Hens	30549	1962	
1211 233	NEG	DL 2	Krp	4343	1961	
1211 237	NTS/MTR		Krp	4347	1961	
1211 252	EVB	410.51	Krp	4362	1962	
1211 271	Redler. 2014 sold to Italy		Krp	4381	1962	Ex RRI 41, Am847 956, BGW, ex DB 211 271
1211 273	BOBY	V 125	Krp	4383	1962	Ex DB 211 273
1211 274	WEBA	07	On Rail	DH1004/8	2003	Ex On Rail, ÖBB 2048 008, DB 211 274
1211 308	EEB	Emsland		18904	1962	
1211 323	EVB	410.01	KM	18919	1962	Ex 285, ex DB
1211 324	EVB	410.03	Jung	13451	1962	Ex 287, ex DB
1211 326	EVB			13453	1962	Used for spares
1211 330	EVB	410.02	Jung	13457	1962	Ex 286, ex DB,
1211 341	BLP	Wiebe 2	Jung	13468	1962	
1211 345	BE	D 25	Jung	13472	1962	
1211 357	GES/EMN	V100 1357	Essl	5293	1962	
1211 365	BYB	V100 1365	Essl	5301	1963	

92 80 1212 B-B

DB sold off several of its 212s to museum lines and some private operators. But upon the mass withdrawal of the class the locos went to Stendal works where they were stored for a while. Along came open access and there was a demand for these medium powered locomotives. Stendal works overhauled and in some cases improved the locomotives but full details are not known.

For principal technical details see Class 212 in German Railways Part 1.

EVN	Company	Running No	Builder	Works No	Built	Notes/Names
1212 007	DGEG	212 007	MaK	1000137	1962	Preserved
1212 009	EGP	V100 2009	MaK	1000139	1962	Privately owned
1212 024	HEIN	212 024	MaK	1000160	1963	JANNIKA
1212 039	RF	212 039	MaK	1001175	1963	Ex LCH 469 001, ex DB
1212 043	AVOLL		MaK	1000179	1963	Ex LCH, ex DB
1212 047	EFW	212 047	MaK	1000183	1963	
1212 052	EFW	212 052	MaK	1000188	1963	
1212 054	P E Leasing/EGP	212 054	MaK	1000190	1963	
1212 055	RAILS	212 055	MaK	1000191	1963	Ex ALS, ex LCH, ex DB
1212 058	MTRD	212 058	MaK	1000194	1963	Ex NBEG (@Hamburg)
1212 060			MaK	1000196	1963	Ex LCH, ex DB. Stored
1212 063	SVG	212 063	MaK	1000199	1963	Ex NBEG, ex NS, ex DB
1212 066	LOCON	213	MaK	1000202	1963	
1212 084	GfE		MaK	1000220	1964	Ex WFB, ex DBK, ex DBM, ex DB
1212 089	BOBY	V 126	MaK	1000225	1964	Ex various, ex DB 212 089
1212 091	VEB	V100 2091	MaK	1000227	1964	
1212 095	LOCON	206	MaK	1000231	1964	Ex ALS, ex DB
1212 100	BYB	212 100	MaK	1000236	1964	
1212 107	BLP	Wiebe 4	Hens	30793	1963	
1212 133	STGBS	V100.01	Hens	30819	1963	Ex ALS, ex DB 212 133
1212 161	BBL	212 161	Hens	30847	1963	Ex ALS, DB 212 161
1212 187	BVM	212 187	MaK	1000334	1965	Ex ALS, ex DB 212 187
1212 192	BLP	Wiebe 3	Jung	13668	1964	
1212 194	EEB	Emsland II	Jung	13670	1964	
1212 242	SVG	212 242	MaK	1000289	1965	Ex NBEG, ex LCH, ex DB
1212 247	MWB	V 1251	MaK	1000294	1965	
1212 249	LM	212 249	MaK	1000296	1965	
1212 256	NBEG	212 256	MaK	1000303	1966	
1212 261	NBEG	212 261	MaK	1000308	1965	
1212 263	LOCON	205	MaK	1000310	1965	Ex ALS, ex DB
1212 267	MTRD	212 267	MaK	1000314	1965	Ex NBEG, ex LCH, ex DB
1212 268	ILM	V100.01	MaK	1000315	1965	
1212 270	NBEG	212 270	MaK	1000317	1965	
1212 272	EGP	212 272	MaK	1000319	1965	
1212 273	RAILS	212 273	MaK	1000320	1963	Ex ALS, ex DB
1212 275	LOCON	210	MaK	1000322	1965	Ex ALS, ex DB
1212 279	EGP	212 279	MaK	1000326	1965	
1212 284	BYB	212 284	MaK	1000331	1965	
1212 285	MWB	V 1253	MaK	1000332	1965	
1212 287	RAILS	212 287	MaK	1000334	1965	Ex BVM
1212 297	RSBG	Caro	MaK	1000344	1965	CARO
1212 299	VEB	V100 2299	MaK	1000346	1965	
1212 309	RE/WEBA	212 309	MaK	1000356	1966	
1212 311	NBEG	212 311	MaK	1000358	1966	
1212 314	EGP	212 314	MaK	1000361	1966	
1212 322	MWB	V 1252	MaK	1000369	1966	
1212 325	EFW	212 325	MaK	1000372	1966	Ex SL, TSD VL 9, Alstom, ex DB
1212 326	DLI	212 326	MaK	1000373	1966	
1212 357	LOCON	208	KHD	57797	1965	Ex ALS, ex DB
1212 358	LOCON	207	KHD	57758	1965	Ex ALS, ex DB
1212 364	NBEG	212 364	KHD	57764	1965	

1212 369	NBEG	212 369	KHD	57769	1965	
1212 370	EFW	212 370	KHD	57770	1965	
1212 371	ALS/NBEF	212 371	KHD	57771	1965	Ex LCH, ex DB.
1212 376	AVOLL/BOEG		KHD	57776	1965	
1212 381	D-STBAT		KHD	57781	1965	Ex EFW, ex DB

92 80 1213   B-B

Class 213 was a small class variant of the Class 212s. For technical details see Class 213 in German Railways Part 1.

EVN	Company	Running No	Builder	Works No	Built	Names	Notes
1213 332	RE	213 332	MaK	1000379	1966		Ex DBG
1213 333	RE	213 333	MaK	1000380	1966		Ex DBG
1213 334	RSBG	213 334	MaK	1000381	1966	MARION	
1213 335	NESA	V100 2335	MaK	1000382	1966		
1213 336	EVG	213 336	MaK	1000383	1966		Ex DBG
1213 337	RE	213 337	MaK	1000384	1966		Ex DBG, for spares?
1213 338	MWB	V 1353	MaK	1000385	1966		
1213 339	WHF/RSBG	213 339	MaK	1000386	1966	DIANA	
1213 340	AVG	465	MaK	1000387	1966		
1213 341	MWB	V 1354	MaK	1000388	1966		

92 80 1214   B-B

Of the numerous Class 212s that ended up stored at Stendal works some were completely modernised and fitted with new Caterpillar engines. The steam heating boilers were removed and replaced by a pre-heating system for the locomotives. Many were sold to private operators but even DB Regio hired some for shunting duties at Nürnberg and Würzburg.

Built: 1963–65.
Builder: As listed.
Engine: Caterpillar 3508 BSC of 970 kW.
Transmission: Hydraulic, Voith Ls216rs.
Maximum Tractive Effort: 176.5 kN.

Wheel Diameter: 950 mm.
Weight: 65 tonnes.
Length over Buffers: 12.10 m.
Maximum Speed: 100 km/h.

EVN	Company	Running No	Builder	Works No	Built	Notes
1214 001	NBEG	214 001	Jung	13673	1964	Ex DB 212 197
1214 002	NBEG	214 002	Jung	13672	1964	Ex DB 212 196
1214 003	LOCON	213	MaK	1000202	1963	Ex ALS, ex DB 212 066
1214 004	SL/LOCON	214	MaK	1000359	1966	Ex DB 212 312
1214 005	SL/LOCON	215ᴵᴵ	MaK	1000297	1965	Ex DB 212 250
1214 006	NBEG	214 006	Hens	30818	1963	Ex DB 212 132
1214 007	SL/LOCON	216ᴵᴵ	Jung	13645	1963	Ex DB 212 169
1214 008	EVULW	214 001 (88519)	MaK	1000301	1965	Ex DB 212 254
1214 009	BBL	02	KHD	57591	1963	Ex DB 212 222
1214 010	EVULW	214 002 (88520)	Jung	13664	1963	Ex DB 212 188
1214 011	NBEG	212 121	Hens	30807	1963	Ex DB 212 121
1214 012	HTRS/RAR	KATHLEEN	KHD	57574	1963	Ex DB 212 205
1214 013	ALS/BBL	04	Hens	30847	1964	Ex SGL V150.05, ex DB 212 161
1214 014	ALS/DBR		Hens	30849	1964	Ex DB 212 163
1214 015	ALS/DBR		MaK	1000306	1965	Ex DB 212 259
1214 016	ALS/DBR		Hens	30838	1964	Ex DB 212 152
1214 017	ALS/DBR		MaK	1000205	1963	Ex DB 212 069
1214 018	ALS/DBR		Hens	30843	1964	Ex DB 212 157
1214 019	HTRS/RAR	ALICIA	Hens	30825	1964	Ex DB 212 139
1214 020	BBL	03	MaK	1000210	1963	Ex DB 212 074; damaged
1214 021	BBL	05	MaK	1000219	1964	Ex DB 212 083
1214 022	ALS/ N-Grenlan Rail		Hens	30809	1963	Ex DB 212 123
1214 023	BBL	10	MaK	1000333	1965	Ex DB 212 286

1214 024	BBL	13	MaK	1000167	1963	Ex DB 212 031
1214 025	BBL	14	MaK	1000166	1963	Ex DB 212 030
1214 026	BBL	15	MaK	1000284	1965	Ex DB 212 237
1214 027	BBL	18	Hens	30795	1963	Ex DB 212 109
1214 028	BBL	20	Mak	1000335	1965	Ex DB 212 288

92 80 1216   B-B

Yet another former DB type, some were modernised by On Rail in 1999–2003, before being sold on to private operators.

Built: 1964–69.
Builder: KHD, Krupp, On Rail.   **Wheel Diameter:** 1000 mm.
Engine: MTU MD 16V 538 TB10 or MB 16V 652 TB 10 of 1415 kW (Original locos); On Rail locos have MTU 12V 4000R20 of 1500 kW.   **Weight:** 77 (*80) tonnes.
Transmission: Hydraulic, Voith L218rs (*L821rs).   **Length over Buffers:** 16.0 m (*16.9 m).
Maximum Tractive Effort: 245 kN.   **Maximum Speed:** 120 km/h.

EVN	Company	Running No	Builder	Works No	Built	Notes
1216 002	RPRS		Krp	4045	1960	
1216 012	BLP	Wiebe 11	Krp	4831	1966	Ex Lokpool, WAB, DB 216 068 but also numbered Wiebe 216 012!
1216 014	* MKB	V 6	OR	DH1504/1	1998	Ex On Rail, ex DB
1216 032	BLP	Wiebe 6	Krp	4665	1965	Ex Italy, ex DB
1216 055	* NIAG	9	OR	DH1504/4	2000	Ex On Rail, ex DB 216 055
1216 111	* NIAG	8	OR	DH1504/3	2000	Ex On Rail, ex DB 216 111
1216 121	* OHE	2000 85	OR	DH1504/6	2002	Ex On Rail, ex DB 216 121
1216 122	BLP	Wiebe 10	KHD	58144	1967	Ex Lokpool, WAB, DB 216 122
1216 123	* OHE	2000 87	OR	DH1504/2	1999	Ex On Rail, ex DB 216 123
1216 158	* OHE	2000 86	OR	DH1504/5	1999	Ex On Rail, ex DB 216 158
1216 224	IGE	216 224	Krp	4885	1968	

92 80 1217   B-B

When DB withdrew all its remaining Class 217s it was not long before private operators started bidding for them. Being fitted with electric train heating, operators of charter trains were quick to snap them up.

For technical details see Class 217 in German Railways Part 1.

EVN	Company	Running No	Builder	Works No	Built
1217 002	BTEX	217 002	Krp	4610	1964
1217 012	PBE		Krp	4947	1968
1217 015	PBE		Krp	4950	1968
1217 017	PBE/RHG		Krp	4952	1968
1217 019	ESG	11	Krp	4954	1968
1217 020	PBE		Krp	4955	1968
1217 021	PBE		Krp	4956	1968

92 80 1218   B-B

Surprisingly, of the large number of 218s that DB had on its books, just three examples have passed into private ownership; remember MEG is a DB subsidiary!

For technical details see Class 218 in German Railways Part 1.

EVN	Company	Running No	Builder	Works No	Built	Notes
1218 006	LWB	225 806	Krp	4963	1968	Ex DB 225 806, ex 218 006
1218 390	MEG	304	MaK	2000112	1975	
1218 399	ELBA	218 399	Krp	5401	1975	

92 80 1219 — B-B

This is a former West German 219: a prototype with electric heating that was withdrawn in 1978 and later sold via a dealer to Italy in 1986. With open access starting it was re-imported as it had "grandfather rights". In 2000 it was overhauled by Gmeinder and fitted with a new Caterpillar engine before passing to EVB.

Built: 1965 (rebuilt 1999/2000).
Builder: KHD.
Engine: Caterpillar 3516B TA-JW of 2000 kW.
Transmission: Hydraulic.
Maximum Tractive Effort:
Wheel Diameter: 1000 mm.
Weight: 76 tonnes.
Length over Buffers: 16.40 m.
Maximum Speed: 120 km/h.

EVN	Company	Running No	Builder	Works No	Built	Notes
1219 001	EVB	420.01	KHD	57846	1965	Ex BGW DH280.01, ex DB

92 80 1220 — B-B

One of the first powerful main line diesels in West Germany was the Class V200, later Class 220. Most were scrapped or sold off to dealers with many ending up in Switzerland and Italy. Just a few have returned to Germany for use with private operators.

Built: 1957.
Builder: As listed.
Engine: MTU MB 12V 493 TZ (2 x 1100 hp).
Transmission: Hydraulic.
Maximum Tractive Effort:
Wheel Diameter: 950 mm.
Weight: 81 tonnes.
Length over Buffers: 18.47 m.
Maximum Speed: 140 km/h.

EVN	Company	Running No	Builder	Works No	Built	Notes
1220 015	BEG	220 015	MaK	2000015	1957	Ex GES, ex SBB, ex DB
1220 017	WLH	V200 017	MaK	2000017	1957	Privately owned, once used by IGE
1220 053	BEG	D 9	KM	18297	1957	Ex EVB 417 01, ex GES, ex SBB, ex DB 220 053

92 80 1221 — B-B

Class 221 is a more powerful version of the Class 220. Upon withdrawal DB sold off many to Greece. Open access and grandfather rights saw most of the Greek locos returned to Germany where they have been overhauled at Neustrelitz works before going into service with private operators. 221 135 is understood to have original engines whilst 221 106 has new Deutz engines; all others have the 1500 kW MTU engine.

Built: 1962–65.
Builder: Krauss Maffei.
Engine: MTU MB 12V652TA(2), MTU 12V4000R41(1500 kW).
Transmission: Hydraulic.
Maximum Tractive Effort:
Wheel Diameter: 950 mm.
Weight: 80 tonnes.
Length over Buffers: 18.44 m.
Maximum Speed: 140 km/h.

EVN	Company	Running No	Builder	Works No	Built	Notes
1221 105	RTS	221 105	KM	18997	1962	Ex OSE 411, ex DB
1221 106	EGP	V270.06	KM	18998	1962	PEG, OSE 412, DB; Deutz engines
1221 112	NETINERA		KM	19004	1963	Ex PEG, ex OSE, ex DB
1221 117	EFW	221 117	KM	19009	1963	Ex PEG, OSE 415, DB
1221 121	SGL	V270.09	KM	19241	1964	Ex OSE 427, ex DB
1221 122	EFW	221 122	KM	19242	1964	Ex PEG, OSE 420, DB
1221 124	SGL	V270.10	KM	19244	1964	Ex OSE 419, ex DB
1221 134	RTS	221 134	KM	19294	1965	Ex OSE 418, ex DB
1221 135	BOEG	221 135	KM	19255	1964	Ex private, ex DB
1221 136	EGP	221 136	KM	19256	1965	Ex Various, OSE 417, DB
1221 145	NETINERA	221 145	KM	19265	1965	Ex PEG, OSE 423, ex DB 221 145
1221 147	BE	D 20	KM	19267	1965	Ex PEG, OSE 416, ex DB 221 147

92 80 1223   SIEMENS EURO RUNNER   Bo-Bo

These locomotives can be considered as the diesel version of the Euro-Sprinter electric locomotive; they were called Euro-Runners by Siemens who built 100 for ÖBB in Austria. At the same time Siemens built some for its then leasing company Dispolok (since sold to MRCE). The first locomotives were given numbers in the ER20 series but as EVNs came into general use the ER numbers faded away. Note that at first some locomotives were given the 253 classification, later altered to 223. When the Allach works was very busy Siemens arranged for a number of 223s to be built at Neustrelitz Works. Missing numbers are where Siemens has started a new batch or where locomotives have actually been sold.

Built: 2003–11.
Builder: Siemens, München Allach or Neustrelitz.
Engine: MTU 16V4000R41 of 2000 kW.
Transmission: Electric.
Maximum Tractive Effort: 235 kN.

Train Heating: Electric.
Wheel Diameter: 1100 mm.
Weight: 80 tonnes.
Length over Buffers: 19.275 m.
Maximum Speed: 140 km/h.

EVN	Company	Running No	Works No	Built	Notes
1223 001	MRCE/NOB	ER20 001	21025	2003	
1223 002	Metrans Danubia	ER20 002	21026	2003	
1223 003	MRCE/SZ	645-003	21027	2003	
1223 004	A-STLB		21028	2003	
1223 005	A-LTE		21029	2003	
1223 006	A-LTE		21030	2004	
1223 007	MRCE/VBG		21031	2004	
1223 008	MRCE/CZ-AWT		21032	2004	
1223 009[i]	A-LTE	92 81 2016 903	21033	2004	
1223 009[ii]	SK-Express Rail	761 101	21181	2005	
1223 010	MRCE/NOB	ER20 010	21034	2004	
1223 011	MRCE/NOB	ER20 011	21148	2005	
1223 012	MRCE/NOB	ER20 012	21149	2005	
1223 013	MRCE/NOB	ER20 013	21151	2005	
1223 014	MRCE/NOB	ER20 014	21152	2005	
1223 015	MRCE/VBG	ER20 015	21153	2005	
1223 031	EVB	420.11	21146	2005	
1223 032	EVB	420.12	21182	2006	
1223 033	EVB	420.13	21150	2006	
1223 034	EVB	420.14	21284	2006	
1223 051	PRESS	253 014	21143	2004	
1223 052	PRESS	253 015	21147	2005	
1223 053	AS/NOB	DE 2000-01	21179	2005	
1223 054	AS/NOB	DE 2000-02	21180	2005	
1223 055	AS/NOB	DE 2000-03	21183	2005	
1223 056	WLE	22	21282	2006	
1223 057	WLE	23	21593	2008	
1223 061	AT/VBG	223 061	21154	2007	
1223 062	AT/VBG	223 062	21157	2007	
1223 063	AT/VBG	223 063	21451	2007	
1223 064	AT/VBG	223 064	21452	2007	
1223 065	AT/VBG	223 065	21453	2007	
1223 066	AT/VBG	223 066	21454	2007	
1223 067	AT/VBG	223 067	21455	2007	
1223 068	AT/VBG	223 068	21456	2007	
1223 069	AT/VBG	223 069	21458	2007	
1223 070	AT/VBG	223 070	21460	2007	
1223 071	AT/VBG	223 071	21461	2007	
1223 072	AT/VBG	223 072	21459	2007	Ex RBG D 09
1223 081	PCW	7	21285	2006	Once ER 20-2007
1223 101	OHE	2700 80	21156	2007	
1223 102	OHE	2700 81	21155	2007	
1223 103	OHE	2700 82	21457	2007	

▲ The brand name ALEX (originally Allgau Express) has been adopted by the Vogtlandbahn and now encompasses many of its services. 92 80 1223 067 in the distinctive ALEX livery waits at München Hbf with a train to Lindau on 2 November 2013.   **Matthias Müller**

▼ Former DSB Nohab MY 1138, now officially 92 80 1227 004, is one of two such locomotives now owned by Cargo Logistik Rail Service. On 20 April 2013 it was stabled at Magdeburg Hafen.
Matthias Müller

1223 141	EGOO	223 141	21597	2009
1223 143	SGL	223 143	21599	2010
1223 144	INTEG/PRESS	223 144	21601	2009
1223 152	INTEG	223 152	21408	2011
1223 153	PCT	223 153	21409	2011
1223 154	PCT	223 154	21410	2011
1223 155	PCT	223 155	21411	2011
1223 156	ENERCON/EGOO	223 156	21681	2011
1223 157	INTEG	223 157	21682	2011
1223 158	PCT	223 158	21683	2011

223147 (handwritten)

92 80 1225   B-B

These locomotives are second hand from DB. For technical details see Class 225 in German Railways Part 1.

*   These locomotives are believed to have reverted to Class 215 designation.

EVN	Company	Running No	Builder	Works No	Built	Notes
1225 001	RPRS	215 001	Krp	4980	1964	
1225 002	NBEG	225 002	Krp	4981	1969	
1225 006	NBEG	225 006	Krp	4985	1969	
1225 015	BBL	19	Krp	5036	1969	Ex LWB
1225 023	EFW		Krp	5044	1970	
1225 025	EFW		Krp	5046	1970	
1225 071	NBEG	225 071	MaK	2000076	1970	
1225 079	NBEG	225 079	MaK	2000084	1971	
1225 082	* AVOLL		MaK	2000087	1971	
1225 086	* RE/EVG	215 086	MaK	2000091	1971	
1225 094	EBM	225 094	Hens	31450	1970	
1225 099	* BBL	17	Hens	31455	1970	
1225 100	* BBL	16	Hens	31456	1970	
1225 101	LWB	225 101	Hens	31457	1970	
1225 133	STGBS	V160.01	Hens	31478	1970	
1225 135	LUW	215 001	Hens	31480	1970	

92 80 1227   DSB MY   A1A-A1A

When open access was in its infancy, would-be operators were looking everywhere for suitable locos especially those that had grandfather rights. Someone remembered that DSB MY diesels were authorised into Germany as part of cross-border operations; DSB had them spare at this time so ten were acquired. And so it is possible for that classic EMD 567C engine sound to be heard around Germany. The number in use varies as the locomotives are starting to show their age!

Built: 1954–65.
Builder: Nohab.
Engine: GM 567C, 16 cyl of 1433 kW.
Transmission: Electric.
Maximum Tractive Effort:
Wheel Diameter:
Weight: 101.6 tonnes.
Length over Buffers: 18.90 m.
Maximum Speed: 133 km/h.

EVN	Company	Running No	Works No	Built	Notes
1227 001		MY 1125	2366	1957	Sold to Hungary
1227 002	AMR	MY 1127	2368	1957	
1227 003	EBS	V170 1131	2372	1957	
1227 004	CLR	MY 1138	2379	1957	
1227 005	BSBS	V170.1142	2383	1958	
1227 006	AMR	MY 1143	2384	1958	
1227 007	EIVEL	1147	2598	1964	
1227 008	AMR	MY 1149	2600	1964	
1227 009	CLR	MY 1151	2602	1965	
1227 010	AMR	MY 1155	2604	1965	

92 80 1228 B-B/C-C

These are former DR V180s, later 118s, and after unification 228s.There were several different batches as the type developed. The V180.0 when improved became the V180.5 series. A further improvement allowed the V180.2-4 batch to be built as C-C wheel arrangement and when modernised, 400 was added to the running numbers. It is thought that all train heating equipment has been removed which is not reflected in the weights shown.

Built: 1962–70.
Builder: LKM. **Wheel Diameter:** 1000 mm.
Engine: 12KVD21-A3 (2 x 736 kW) (B-Bs); 12KVD21AL4 (2 x 883 kW) (C-Cs).
Weight: 79.3/95 tonnes.
Transmission: Hydraulic. **Length over Buffers:** 19.46 m.
Maximum Tractive Effort: **Maximum Speed:** 120 km/h.

EVN	Company	Running No	Works No	Built	Notes
1228 119	ITL	118 001	275106	1965	Ex RBG D 05, DR 228 119
1228 168	BWESA/ADAM	15	275155	1966	Ex DR 228 168
1228 203	HFH	118 203	280003	1966	Ex DR 228 203
1228 321	CLR	228 321	280125	1968	Ex ADAM 8, ex DR 228 731
1228 372	DP/WAB	23	280181	1969	Ex DR 228 372
1228 411	ITB	204	280163	1969	Ex LEUNA
1228 412	ITB	205	280164	1969	Ex LEUNA
1228 501	WFL	20	280113	1968	Ex BUNA 204
1228 502	MEG	201	280110	1968	Ex BUNA 201; Gera Museum
1228 503	MEG	203	280112	1968	Ex BUNA 203; Weimar Museum
1228 504	MEG	202	280111	1968	Ex BUNA 202; Stassfurt Museum
1228 552	ITL	118 002	275052	1964	Ex DR 228 552
1228 585	ITL	118 003	275085	1965	Ex RBG D 06, DR 228 585; plinthed
1228 633	DP/WAB	24	280033	1967	Ex DR 228 633
1228 656	LOCON	301	280056	1967	Ex AML, Falz, ex DR 228 656
1228 705	RSBG		280105	1968	
1228 714	RSBG		280118	1968	
1228 719	EBS		280123	1968	Ex DP/WAB 25, ex DR 228 719
1228 721	CLR	228 321	280125	1968	Ex ADAM 8
1228 731	TEV		280135	1968	TLG 17, BSW Lübeck, DR 118 731; Weimar Museum
1228 742	EBS		280146	1968	Ex TSD, EBM, DB 228 742
1228 748	MEG	206	280152	1968	Ex DB
1228 757	EBS	228 757	280166	1966	Ex DUD 2402, Falz, DB 228 757.
1228 758	RSBG	228 758	280167	1969	
1228 786	MEG	208	280195	1968	Ex DB
1228 788	MEG	205	280197	1969	Ex DB; leased to Weimar Museum
1228 791	MEG	207	280200	1968	Ex DB
1228 792	HGB	V180.01	280201	1969	Ex DB
?	ARCO	2001	280160	1968	Ex LEUNA 201; stored Karsdorf
?	ARCO	2003	280162	1968	Ex LEUNA 203; stored

92 80 1229 C-C

DB got rid of these locomotives to its subsidiary MEG, some locomotives already being loaned to preservation groups! All originally built by U23A. For technical details see Class 229 in German Railways Part 1.

EVN	Company	Running No	Works No	Rebuilt	Notes
1229 120	MEG	301	5656	1992	Ex DB; original works no 24529, built 1982
1229 173	MEG	302	5663	1992	Ex DB; original works no 24815, built 1984
1229 184	MEG		5666	1992	Ex DB; original works no 24826, built 1984; Gera Museum
1229 199	MEG		5670	1992	Ex DB; original works no 24952, built 1985; Weimar Museum

▲ The weekly train of washing machines from a factory in Poland to the German distribution centre in Nauen, Berlin, often employs unusual motive power. On 18 May 2011 Erfurter Bahnservice's former DR Class V180, 92 80 1228 757 was in charge between the Polish border and Nauen. It is seen on Berlin's inner circle line passing Berlin Wedding S-Bahn station. **Christoph Grimm**

▼ Deutsche Gleis- und Tiefbau's former DR V300 "Ludmilla", 92 80 1232 550, heads an empty ballast train near Kerzell on 18 October 2013. **Matthias Müller**

92 80 1230, 1231 & 1232   Co-Co

These are all part of the DR V300 family, also known as Ludmillas. Many 232s are still in use with DB. The 230s were the first type to arrive on DR and are pure freight diesels having no train heating but cleared for 140 km/h. Next came the 231s which again had no train heating but were geared for a maximum of 100 km/h. The 232s became the new standard version with electric train heating.

For technical details see Class 232 in German Railways Part 1.

92 80 1230

EVN	Company	Running No	Works No	Built	Notes
1230 077	RTS	230 077	0099	1972	Ex DB

92 80 1231

EVN	Company	Running No	Works No	Built	Notes
1231 050	SGL		0164	1973	Ex various, ex DR

92 80 1232

EVN	Engine	Company	Running No	Works No	Built	Notes
1232 010		MEG	316	0200	1973	Ex DB
1232 068		MEG	313	0258	1974	Ex DB
1232 088		EFW	232 088	0304	1974	Ex WAB 30, ex Villman, ex DB
1232 103		RDX	232 103	0325	1974	Ex DB via various
1232 109		LEG	232 109	0324	1974	Ex DB
1232 141		WFL		0357	1974	Ex DB
1232 155	CAT 3606	TRG	V300 005	0372	1974	Ex DB
1232 182		LEG	232 182	0400	1975	Ex DB
1232 223		DGT	Lok 11	0437	1975	Ex DB
1232 229		LEG	232 229	0442	1974	
1232 238		LEG		0452	1975	Ex DB
1232 239		MEG	314	0451	1975	Ex DB; can work in Poland
1232 293		EBS		0508	1975	
1232 333		WFL		0547	1976	Ex EWR, ex DB
1232 356		LEG		0591	1976	Ex EWR, ex DB
1232 375		EBM		0610	1976	Ex DB
1232 404	CAT 3606	TRG	V300 001	0636	1976	Ex DB
1232 405	CAT 3606	TRG	V300 002	0640	1976	Ex DB
1232 416		LEG	232 416	0649	1976	Ex DB
1232 429	CAT 3606	TRG	V300 004	0664	1976	Ex DB
1232 446		SGL	V300.18	0681	1976	Ex various, restored with parts from 232 387
1232 489		MEG	315	0724	1976	Ex DB
1232 500		MEG	317	0735	1977	Ex DB; loaned to Wittenberge Museum
1232 550		DGT	Lok 12	0810	1978	Ex DB
1232 673		LEG		0954	1911	Ex DB
1232 684	CAT 3606	TRG	V300 003	0965	1981	Ex DB
1232 690		MEG	318	0971	1981	Ex DB
1232 850		EKO	232 850	0248	1974	DE300.02, DB 232 057

92 80 1240   Mak DE 1024   Co-Co

These locomotives were prototypes from Krupp MaK but no more were built. Used by DB in the Hamburg area they were passed back to the builder who then sold them to HGK. At least one loco is thought to be still operational

Built: 1989–90.
Builder: Krupp MaK Maschinenbau GmbH.   **Wheel Diameter:** 1016 mm.
Engine: MaK 12M282 of 2650 kW.   **Weight:** 120 tonnes.
Transmission: Electric.   **Length over Buffers:** 20.96 m.
Maximum Tractive Effort: 400 kN.   **Maximum Speed:** 160 km/h.

EVN	Company	Running No	Works No	Built	Notes
1240 001	HGK	DE 11	30002	1989	Stored
1240 002	VTLT	DE 12	30003	1989	Stored
1240 003	HGK	DE 13	30004	1989	Overhauled 12/2014

92 80 1241 & 1242   Co-Co

Classes 241 and 242 are the big "Ludmillas". Built for the DR, just a small batch were used at Stralsund on a mixture of duties. Several have been rebuilt and down-graded becoming class 0232 but the Class 1242 loco is understood still to be in original condition.

Built: 1976.
Builder: October Revolution Works, Voroshilovgrad, USSR.   **Wheel Diameter:** 1050 mm.
Engine: Kolomna.   **Weight:** 124.7 tonnes.
Transmission: Electric.   **Length over Buffers:** 20.82 m.
Maximum Tractive Effort: 343 kN.   **Maximum Speed:** 120 km/h.

92 80 1241

EVN	Company	Running No	Works No	Built	Notes
1241 353	EBS		0588	1976	Ex DB

92 80 1242

EVN	Company	Running No	Works No	Built	Notes
1242 001	EKO	42	0001	1976	Ex DR 142 001

92 80 1245   TRAXX P160DE ME   Bo-Bo

In connection with the renewal of the franchise for the Hamburg–Westerland route, Schleswig-Holstein ordered these locomotives which will be leased by the Land to the successful applicant. It is assumed technical details are the same as DB Class 245 – see German Railways Part 1.

EVN	Company	Running No	Works No	Built
1245 201	NRAIL	245 201	35198	2015
1245 202	NRAIL	245 202	35199	2015
1245 203	NRAIL	245 203	35200	2015
1245 204	NRAIL			2015
1245 205	NRAIL			2015
1245 206	NRAIL			2015
1245 207	NRAIL			2015
1245 208	NRAIL			2015
1245 209	NRAIL			2015
1245 210	NRAIL			2015
1245 211	NRAIL			2015
1245 212	NRAIL			2015
1245 213	NRAIL			2015
1245 214	NRAIL			2015
1245 215	NRAIL			2015

92 80 1246   TRAXX P160DE   Bo-Bo

Part of the TRAXX family, this diesel version is only found with private operators. Initially all were with Metronom but after some years experience with the class it was found that three locos could be sold off.

Built: 2006.
Builder: Bombardier, Kassel.   **Wheel Diameter:**
Engine: MTU 16V4000R41 of 2200 kW.   **Weight:** 80 tonnes.
Transmission: Electric.   **Length over Buffers:** 18.90 m.
Maximum Tractive Effort: 270 kN.   **Maximum Speed:** 160 km/h.

EVN	Company	Running No	Works No	Built	Names
1246 001	HVLE	246 001	34301	2006	
1246 002	LNVG/ME	246 002	34307	2006	Buxtehude
1246 003	LNVG/ME	246 003	34308	2006	Cuxhaven
1246 004	LNVG/ME	246 004	34324	2006	Stade
1246 005	LNVG/ME	246 005	34326	2006	Horneburg
1246 006	LNVG/ME	246 006	34329	2006	Hemmoor
1246 007	LNVG/ME	246 007	34333	2006	Himmelpforten
1246 008	LNVG/ME	246 008	34337	2006	Otterndorf
1246 009	LNVG/ME	246 009	34341	2006	
1246 010	HVLE	246 010	34345	2006	
1246 011	IGT	246 011	34349	2006	

92 80 1247 VECTRON DE Bo-Bo

This Siemens product is a diesel-electric version of its Vectron electric locomotives. So far three locomotives have been produced and are going through the usual amount of type testing. No firm orders yet for a production run.

Built: 2010–
Builder: Siemens, München Allach.
Engine: MTU 16V4000R84 of 2400 kW.
Transmission: Electric.
Maximum Tractive Effort: 275 kN.

Wheel Diameter: 1100 mm.
Weight: 81–88 tonnes.
Length over Buffers: 19.98 m.
Maximum Speed: 160 km/h.

EVN	Company	Running No	Works No	Built
1247 901	PCW		21761	2010
1247 902	PCW			
1247 903	PCW		21949	2015

92 80 1250 ADtranz DE-AC33C "Blue Tiger" Co-Co

ADtranz, which preceded Bombardier at Kassel, did a deal with General Electric to build modern diesel electric locomotives. The result was what became known as the Blue Tiger. A prototype was built followed later by a production batch of ten locos under the Bombardier regime, but then the programme was aborted as the TRAXX family was starting to come along.

Built: 1996–2004.
Builder: ADtranz/Bombardier, Kassel.
Engine: GE 7FDL12 of 2460 kW.
Transmission: Electric.
Maximum Tractive Effort: 517 kN.

Wheel Diameter:
Weight: 126 tonnes.
Length over Buffers: 23.41 m.
Maximum Speed: 120 km/h.

EVN	Company	Running No	Builder	Works No	Built	Notes
1250 001	OHE	3300 94	ADtranz	33293	1996	
1250 002	HVLE	V330.1	BT	33831	2003	
1250 003	HVLE	V330.8	BT	33832	2003	Ex OHE 3300 93
1250 004	HVLE	V330.4	BT	33833	2003	Ex MKB V20
1250 005	HVLE	V330.7	BT	33834	2003	Ex OHE 3300 92
1250 006	ITL	250 006	BT	33835	2003	
1250 007	ITL	250 007	BT	33836	2003	
1250 008	HVLE	V330.5	BT	33837	2004	Ex OHE 3300 90
1250 009	HVLE	V330.6	BT	33838	2004	Ex OHE 3300 91
1250 010	HVLE	V330.2	BT	33839	2004	
1250 011	HVLE	V330.3	BT	33840	2004	

92 80 1251   ME26/DE2700   Co-Co

These locomotives can be regarded as a development of the DE 1024 series built by MaK for Norway with a Siemens involvement. However after two years or so in Norway the locomotives were rejected and returned to the builder. In 2000 they were handed over to Siemens Dispolok but within three years they were once again back with the builder, now known as Vossloh. They became a fleet for hire and have seen use with CFL in Luxembourg and other operators but most are now being used by NOB on services out of Hamburg on the Westerland route.

Built: 1996.
Builder: MaK/Siemens.
Engine: MaK 12M282 of 2650 kW.
Transmission: Electric.
Maximum Tractive Effort: 400 kN.

Wheel Diameter: 1060 mm.
Weight: 122 tonnes.
Length over Buffers: 20.96 m.
Maximum Speed: 160 km/h.

EVN	Company	Running No	Works No	Built	Notes
1251 001	VL/NOB	DE2700-01	30005	1996	Ex NSB Di6.661
1251 002	VL/NIAG	DE2700-02	30006	1996	Ex NSB Di6.662
1251 003	VL/NOB	DE2700-03	30007	1996	Ex NSB Di6.663
1251 004	VL/NIAG	DE2700-04	30008	1996	Ex NSB Di6.664
1251 005	VL/LEUNA	DE2700-05	30009	1996	Ex NSB Di6.665
1251 006	VL/NIAG	DE2700-06	30010	1996	Ex NSB Di6.666
1251 007	VL/NOB	DE2700-07	30011	1996	Ex NSB Di6.667
1251 008	VL/NOB	DE2700-08	30012	1996	Ex NSB Di6.668
1251 009	VL/NOB	DE2700-09	30013	1996	Ex NSB Di6.669
1251 010	VL/HLG	DE2700-10	30014	1996	Ex NSB Di6.670
1251 011	VL/NOB	DE2700-11	30015	1996	Ex NSB Di6.671
1251 012	VL/NOB	DE2700-12	30016	1996	Ex NSB Di6.672

▲ Nord-Ostsee-Bahn (NOB) uses a small fleet of MaK DE 2700 locomotives, originally intended for use in Norway but now available for hire from Vossloh Locomotives. 92 80 1251 007, running number DE2700-07, hauls a train from Hamburg Altona to Westerland near Keitum on the Isle of Sylt on 2 June 2014. **Matthias Müller**

92 80 1261   VOITH GRAVITA 10BB   B-B

Voith is well known for its hydraulic transmissions but having received redundant staff from the former MaK works in Kiel decided to go into building locomotives. The Gravita series came along just at the right time as DB was looking for new shunting and trip locos. However the first ten locomotives that went to DB were returned to the builder and are now part of its hire fleet. More locomotives were built for stock and these also became part of the hire fleet. Originally numbered as 260s the EVN given makes them 261s, as are the DB locos.

For technical details see Class 261 in German Railways Part 1.

EVN	Company	Running No	Works No	Built
1261 001	VTLT/NTS/MKB	260 501	10052	2010
1261 002	NTS	260 502	10053	2010
1261 003	NTS/DB	260 503	10054	2010
1261 004	VTLT/N-Baneservice	260 504	10055	2010
1261 005	VTLT/N-Baneservice	260 505	10056	2010
1261 006	NTS	260 506	10057	2010
1261 007	NTS/N-Baneservice	260 507	10058	2010
1261 008	NTS/CLG	260 508	10059	2010
1261 009	NTS/N-CL	260 509	10060	2010
1261 010	NTS/BCB	260 510	10061	2010
1261 300	VTLT/Transpetrol, Hamburg		10003	2008
1261 301	VTLT/DELTA	261 301	10001	2008
1261 302	VTLT/		10002	2008
1261 303	VTLT/RWE Power	490	10004	2010
1261 304	VTLT	261 304	10005	2010
1261 305	SRG	261 305	10006	2010
1261 306	SRG	261 306	10007	2010
1261 307	NRAIL		10008	2011
1261 308	VTLT/SGL		10009	2012
1261 309	VTLT/SGL		10010	2013
1261 310	NTS/CLG		10011	2012
1261 311	VTLT/DBS		10012	2012
1261 312	SHH	F 8	10013	2012
1261 313	VTLT/EGOO		10014	2013
1261 314	VTLT		10015	2013

92 80 1263   VOITH MAXIMA 30CC   C-C

Some of the first locomotives built by Voith were these striking looking heavy haulers given the name of Maxima. However the series has been short lived. Most locomotives are on lease but some might now have been purchased.

Built: 2008–10.
Builder: Voith.
Engine: ABC 12VDZC of 2750 kW.
Transmission: Hydraulic, Voith LS640reU2.
Maximum Tractive Effort: 408 kN.
Wheel Diameter: 1150 mm.
Weight: 126 tonnes.
Length over Buffers: 23.20 m.
Maximum Speed: 120 km/h.

EVN	Company	Running No	Works No	Built
1263 001	VTLT/DWK/RTLOG		30001	2008
1263 002	SGL	V400.11	30002	2009
1263 003	CZ-RCO	92 54 2783 001	30003	2009
1263 004	DWK/		30004	2010
1263 005	DWK/BLP	263 005	30005	2010
1263 006	DWK/SBS		30006	2010

92 80 1264   VOITH MAXIMA 40CC   C-C

At the same time as building the Maxima 30CC an even more powerful version was developed, some of which have actually been purchased. However, after the initial interest no more have been built and Voith is now considering ceasing locomotive production.

Built: 2008–10.
Builder: Voith.
Engine: ABC 16VDZC of 3600 kW.
Transmission: Hydraulic, Voith LS640reU2.
Maximum Tractive Effort: 408 kN.
Wheel Diameter: 1150 mm.
Weight: 135 tonnes.
Length over Buffers: 23.20 m.
Maximum Speed: 120 km/h.

EVN	Company	Running No	Works No	Built	Notes
1264 001	STOCK	264 001	40001	2008	
1264 002	VTLT/SL/TRG	264 002	30018	2008	
1264 003	VTLT/STOCK	264 003	40003	2008	
1264 004	HVLE	V490.1	40004	2008	
1264 005	Structured Lease		40005	2008	
1264 006	NRS	V500.06	40006	2008	Ex SGL
1264 007	DWK		40007	2009	
1264 008	HVLE	V490.3	40008	2009	
1264 009	NRS	V500.14	40009	2009	
1264 010	SGL	V500.17	40010	2010	
1264 011	VTLT/BLP	Wiebe 264 011	40011	2010	
1264 012	HVLE	V490.2	40040	2009	
1264 013	DWK		40041	2009	

92 80 1265   VOITH GRAVITA 15BB   B-B

A more powerful version of the Gravita type. Most locomotives of this type are with DB as Class 265.

For technical details see Class 265 in German Railways Part 1.

EVN	Company	Running No	Works No	Built
1265 300	HzL	V 180	L4-18033	2012
1265 301	HzL	V 181	L4-18034	2013
1265 302	NTS/DELTA		18035	2012
1265 303	NTS/CLG		18036	2012
1265 499	VTLT/EGOO		L04-18001	2011
1265 500	VTLT		L04-18002	2011

92 80 1266   EMD "CLASS 66"   Co-Co

British enthusiasts will be familiar with the Class 66. Two locos intended for EWS in Britain were taken off the production line in Canada and sent to Germany as demonstrator locos, going to HGK in Köln. Open access was starting and powerful diesel locos were needed for freight traffic, especially as some international movements were considered. The type was soon accepted on various European railway systems and examples can now be found in several countries. Apart from a few in Scandinavia all other locos get involved in traffic to, from or through Germany.

The builders classification JT42CWR breaks down as follows: J – loco with two cabs; T – turbocharged engine; 42 – Type 710G engine; C – three axle bogie; W – standard gauge traction motors; R – radial steering bogie. From order 20048653 various improvements were made. These "modified" locos are JT42CWR**M** and have improved cabs, air conditioning and in the case of the 8653 series ETCS has also been fitted on arrival in Europe.

Several locos are currently in France working on new TGV line construction trains. The layout of the fleet list for this class is slightly different showing how the deliveries of the class evolved and also some of the other numbers carried by the locos which may help to cover the period since the last edition of this book was published.

The Class 77 locos ordered by Euro Cargo Rail are not shown in the list as half the class is based in France and since DB Schenker bought ECR the other half of the Class operates in Germany as DB Class 247/266 – see German Railways Part 1.

Note that some locomotives delivered to Continental Europe have been acquired by British operator GBRf whilst some British Freightliner locos have moved to Poland, working with Freightliner Poland. These also work into Germany and have been seen in the Berlin area and around Hamburg.

Built: 1999–2009.
Builder: EMD London, Ontario, Canada.
Engine: JT42CWR; GM 12N-710G3B-EC of 2238 kW.
JT42CWRM; GM 12N-710G3B-T2 of 2238 kW.
Transmission: Electric, 6 GM D43TR traction motors.
Maximum Tractive Effort: 409 kN.

Wheel Diameter: 1120 mm.
Weight: 126 tonnes.
Length over Buffers: 21.35 m.
Maximum Speed: 120 km/h.

Built	Order No	Owner	First No.	Other Nos.	Now	EVN
1999	998101-1	HGK	PB 9902	DE 61	HGK DE 61	92 80 1266 061
1999	998101-2	HGK	PB 9901	DE 62	HGK DE 62	92 80 1266 062
2000	20008212-1	BRL	T 66713		S-Rush Rail	92 74 0066 713
2000	20008212-2	BRL	T 66714	T 66K714	N-Cargo Link	92 74 0066 714
2001	20008254-1	AS	PB 01	R4C PB 01	RTBC V 264	92 80 1266 003
2001	20008254-2	AS	PB 02	R4C PB 02	RHC DE 676	92 80 1266 004
2001	20008254-3	AS	HHPI 29001		RHC DE 687	92 80 1266 005
2001	20008254-4	AS	HHPI 29002	ITL	XRAIL 29002	92 80 1266 006
2001	20008254-5	AS	PB 03	DLC PB 03	XRAIL	92 80 1266 007
2001	20008254-6	AS	PB 04	HGK DE 63	PB 04	92 88 1266 063
2001	20008254-7	AS	PB 05	R4C PB 05	Captrain NL	92 80 1266 009
2001	20008254-8	AS	PB 06	HGK DE 64	RRF PB 06	92 80 1266 064
2001	20008254-9	AS	PB 07	ERS 6601	Captrain BE	92 88 0266 001
2001	20008254-10	AS	PB 08	ERS 6602	XRAIL PB 08	92 88 0266 002
2002	20008254-11	AS	PB 09	ERS 6603	Captrain BE	92 88 0266 003
2002	20008254-12	AS	PB 10	ERS 6604	RTBC V 266	92 80 1266 014
2002	20008254-13	MR	HHPI 29003			92 80 1266 015
2002	20018342-3		FL UK 66608		FPL 66603	92 70 0066 608
2002	20018342-4		FL UK 66609		FPL 66605	92 70 0066 609
2002	20018342-6		FL UK 66611		FPL 66604	92 70 0066 611
2002	20018342-7		FL UK 66612		FPL 66606	92 70 0066 612
2002	20018352-1	BRL	CN 66401	T 66401	Rush Rail	92 76 0309 001
2002	20018352-2	BRL	CN 66402	T 66402	Rush Rail	92 76 0309 002
2002	20018352-3	BRL	CN 66403	T 66403	Cargo Link	92 76 0309 003
2002	20018352-4	BRL	CN 66404	T 66404	Cargo Link	92 76 0309 004
2002	20018352-5	BRL	CN 66405	T 66405	Rush Rail	92 74 0066 405
2002	20018352-6	BRL	CN 66406	T 66406	Rush Rail	92 74 0066 406
2002	20018360-1	AS	PB 11	ERS 6605	Captrain BE	92 80 1266 016
2002	20018360-2	AS	PB 12	DLC PB 12	XRAIL PB 12	92 80 1266 017
2002	20018360-3	AS	PB 13	HGK DE 65	XRAIL PB 13	92 80 1266 018
2002	20018360-4	AS	PB 14	DLC PB 14	XRAIL PB 14	92 80 1266 065
2002	20018360-5	AS	PB 15	HGK DE 66	XRAIL PB 15	92 80 1266 066
2002	20018360-6	AS	PB 16	HGK DE 67	RHC DE 67	92 80 1266 067
2002	20018360-7	AS	PB 17	R4C PB 17	RTBC V 267	92 80 1266 021
2002	20018360-8	AS	PB 18	DLC PB 18	CTD	92 80 1266 022
2002	20018360-9	AS	PB 19	DLC PB 19	HGK 678	92 80 1266 023
2002	20018360-10	AS	PB 20	DLC PB 20	RTX PB 20	92 80 1266 024
2003	20028453-1	BRL	HGK DE 668		RHC DE 668	92 80 1266 068
2003	20028453-2	BRL	HGK DE 669		RHC DE 669	92 80 1266 069
2003	20028453-3	BRL	HGK DE 670		RHC DE 670	92 80 1266 070
2003	20028453-4	BRL	HGK DE 671		RHC DE 671	92 80 1266 071
2003	20028453-5	BRL	HGK DE 672		RHC DE 672	92 80 1266 072
2003	20038513-1	BRL	ER 1	ERS 6606	GBRf 66750	
2003	20038513-2	BRL	ER 2	ERS 6607	LWB 6607	92 80 1266 026
2003	20038513-3	BRL	ER 3	ERS 6608	HHPI 29004	92 80 1266 027
2003	20038513-4	BRL	ER 4	ERS 6609	GBRf 66751	
2003	20038513-5	BRL	ER 5	ERS 6610	HHPI 29005	92 80 1266 029
2003	20038513-6	KBC	ER 6	DLC 6301	XRAIL 6301	92 80 1266 033
2003	20038513-7	KBC	ER 7	DLC 6302	XRAIL 6302	92 80 1266 034
2003	20038513-8	MR	ER 8	ERS 6612	RTX 513-8	92 80 1266 035
2004	20038513-9	MR	ER 9	513-9	ETF 513-9	92 80 1266 036
2004	20038513-10	MR	ER 10	DLC 6303	RHC DE 679	92 80 1266 037

Year	No.	Op	No.	ID4	ID5	ID6
2004	20038545-1	AS	EC1	R4C 66020	ITL 6602	92 80 1266 030
2004	20038545-2	AS	EC2	Railion 266 452	RTX RL 001	92 80 1266 031
2004	20038545-3	AS	EC3	Railion 266 453	RTBC V 270	92 80 1266 032
2004	20038561-1	MR	EM 1	HGK DE 673	FL DE 561-1	92 80 1266 038
2004	20038561-2	MR	EM 2	HGK DE 674	ETF 561-2	92 80 1266 039
2004	20038561-3	MR	EM 3	ERS 6611	ETF 561-3	92 80 1266 040
2004	20038561-4	MR	EM 4	DLC 6304	ETF 561-4	92 80 1266 041
2004	20038561-5	MR	EM 5	HGK DE 680	RHC DE 680	92 80 1266 042
2005	20048653-1	MR	JT 1	HGK DE 675	RHC DE 675	92 80 1266 111
2005	20048653-2	MR	JT 2	ERS 6615	ETF 653-2	92 80 1266 112
2005	20048653-3	MR	JT 3	ERS 6614	RHC DE 682	92 80 1266 113
2005	20048653-4	MR	JT 4	ACTS 653-4	RHC DE 683	92 80 1266 114
2005	20048653-5	MR	JT 5	HTRS 653-5	RRF 653-5	92 80 1266 115
2005	20048653-6	MR	JT 6	ERS 6616		Scrapped 2011
2005	20048653-7	MR	JT 7	ERS 6617	RHC DE 685	92 80 1266 117
2005	20048653-8	MR	JT 8	R4C 653-8	RHC DE 686	92 80 1266 118
2005	20048653-9	MR	JT 9	DLC 6305	ETF 653-09	92 80 1266 119
2005	20048653-10	MR	JT 10	FPL 653-10	RHC DE 684	92 80 1266 120
2006	20058700-01		FL UK 66411		FPL 66013	92 70 0066 411
2006	20058700-02		FL UK 66412		FPL 66015	92 70 0066 412
2006	20058700-07		FL UK 66417		FPL 66014	92 70 0066 417
2006	20058725-1	MER	EU 01	HGK DE 677	XRAIL 6313	92 80 1266 107
2006	20058725-2	AT	EU 02	FPL 66001		92 51 3650 000
2006	20058725-3	AT	EU 03	FPL 66002		92 51 3650 001
2006	20058725-4	AT	EU 04	FPL 66003		92 51 3650 002
2006	20058725-5	AT	EU 05	FPL 66004		92 51 3650 003
2006	20058725-6	MER	EU 06	R4C CB 1000	CT NL CB1000	92 80 1266 105
2006	20058725-7	MER	EU 07	R4C CB 1001	ITL CB 1001	92 80 1266 106
2006	20058725-8	KBC	EU 08	DLC 6306	XRAIL 6306	92 80 1266 101
2006	20058725-9	KBC	EU 09	DLC 6307	XRAIL 6307	92 80 1266 102
2006	20058725-10	KBC	EU 10	DLC 6308	XRAIL 6308	92 80 1266 103
2006	20058725-11	KBC	EU 11	DLC 6309	XRAIL 6309	92 80 1266 104
2006	20058725-12	AT	EU 12	FPL 66005		92 51 3650 004
2006	20058725-13	AT	EU 13	FPL 66006		92 51 3650 005
2006	20058725-14	AT	EU 14	FPL 66007		92 51 3650 006
2006	20058772-1		FL UK			
2006	20058772-2		FL UK 66624	FPL 66602		92 51 3650 014
2006	20058772-3		FL UK 66625	FPL 66601		92 51 3650 013
2006	20058772-4		FL UK 66582	FPL 66009		92 51 3650 014
2006	20058772-5		FL UK 66583	FPL 66010		92 51 3650 011
2006	20058772-6		FL UK 66584	FPL 66011		92 51 3650 012
2006	20058772-7		FL UK			
2006	20058772-8		FL UK 66586	FPL 66008		92 51 3650 009

20068864-1–60 are ECR 77001 - 060

Year	No.	Op	No.	ID4	ID5	ID6
2008	20078920-1	AK	DE 6310F		AK 77504	92 87 0077 504
2008	20078920-2	AK	DE 6311F		AK 77505	92 87 0077 505
2008	20078920-3	AK	DE 6312F		AK 77506	92 87 0077 506
2008	20078920-4	AK	DE 6313F		AK 77507	92 87 0077 507
2009	20078941-1	AK	77501		AK 77501	92 87 0077 501
2009	20078941-2	AK	77502		AK 77502	92 87 0077 502
2009	20078941-3	AK	77503		AK 77503	92 87 0077 503
	20078968-1	FO	DE 6310		XRAIL DE 6310	92 80 1266 280
	20078968-2	FO	DE 6311		XRAIL DE 6311	92 80 1266 281
	20078968-3	FO	DE 6312		XRAIL DE 6312	92 80 1266 282
	20078968-4		DE 6313		GBRf 66748	
	20078968-5	FO	DE 6314			92 80 1266 284
	20078968-6		DE 6315		GBRf 66749	
	20078968-7		DE 6316		GBRf 66747	
2010	20088076-1	BRL	HHPI 29001[II]			92 80 1266 461
2010	20088076-2	To Gabon				
2010	20088076-3	To Gabon				
2010	20088076-4	BRL	HHPI 29002[II]			92 80 1266 464

Names:

92 80 1266 007	Mireille	92 51 3650 000	Willy Brandt
92 80 1266 015	Rhoda Painter	92 80 1266 103	Anja
92 80 1266 017	Marleen	92 80 1266 280	Griet
92 80 1266 018	Ilse	92 80 1266 281	Hana
92 80 1266 027	Dave Meehan	92 80 1266 282	Alix
92 80 1266 029	Ted Gafney	92 80 1266 284	Hanna
92 80 1266 033	Deborah	92 80 1266 461	Hans Cermak
92 80 1266 034	Fredericia	92 80 1266 464	Robert J.G. Savage
92 80 1266 107	Ymke		

92 80 12xx   GE POWERHAUL PH37ACai   Co-Co

This type is the continental profile Freightliner Class 70 but with a full width body, several locomotives having been ordered by HHPI. It was intended to have the locomotives by December 2014 to work coal trains from Amsterdam/Rotterdam into Germany. However the locomotives were not delivered until the last weeks of 2014 and have still to gain acceptance on the Dutch and German networks. It is undertsood that some of the coal trains may run via Belgium and Luxembourg to German destinations so there could be two more countries involved. The locomotives delivered in 2014 plus earlier examples have all congregated at DB Cottbus works to be fitted with the relevant safety systems. Interestingly all the locomotives have been given HHPI style numbers. One locomotive, 29 008 was shown at Innotrans as a demonstrator and has since been replaced by a second 29 008! It is expected there will be some real developments later in 2015.

Built: 2013–14.
Builder: TLMS, Eskisehir, Turkey.
Engine: Powerhaul P616 of 2750 kW.
Transmission: Electric.
Maximum Tractive Effort: 600 kN.

Wheel Diameter:
Weight: 126–132 tonnes.
Length over Buffers: 21.70 m.
Maximum Speed: 120 km/h.

EVN	Company	Running No	Works No	Built
	HHPI	29008^I	001	2012
			002	2012
		29006	003	2013
	HHPI	29008^{II}	004	2013
	HHPI	29009	005	2013
		29010		2014
		29011		2014
		29012		2014
		29013		2014
		29014		2014
		29015	009	2014
		29016	010	2014

92 80 1271   G1000   B-B

Vossloh produced this medium powered locomotive following on the MaK tradition of standard ranges of locomotives with an off centre cab.

Built: 2002–11.
Builder: Vossloh.
Engine: MTU 8V4000 of 1100 kW.
Transmission: Hydraulic, Voith L4r4.
Maximum Tractive Effort:

Wheel Diameter: 1000 mm.
Weight: 72-80 tonnes.
Length over Buffers: 14.13 m.
Maximum Speed: 100 km/h.

EVN	Company	Running No	Works No	Built	Notes
1271 001	KIEL		1001322	2002	
1271 003	VL/CTD/BCB	271 003	1001461	2003	Ex SBB 842 101
1271 004	VL/KSW	V 44	1001462	2003	
1271 005	AT/RHC	271 005	1001463	2003	Ex SBB 842 102
1271 009	AT/WLH		5001530	2004	
1271 011	AT/HTRS		5001532	2004	Ex CFL 1106
1271 013	AT/RHC		5001538	2004	Ex CLG 07, HGK DH 720

1271 014	AT/CTD-RBB		5001539	2004	Ex HGK DH 57
1271 016	AT/F-		5001541	2004	
1271 017	AT/RHC		5001542	2004	Ex HGK DH 721
1271 018	F-VFLI		5001543	2004	
1271 019	EVB	411.51	5001565	2005	
1271 020	SLG/XR	02	5001566	2005	
1271 021	MRCE/NE	09	5001567	2006	Ex CLG
1271 022	MRCE/HGK	DH 49	5001568	2006	
1271 023	VL/MRCE/MVG		5001577	2005	
1271 024	VL/MRCE/NE	500 1578	5001578	2005	
1271 025	NTS/CTD-RBB	271 025	5001782	2008	
1271 026	KIEL/CTD-RBB	271 026	5001783	2008	
1271 027	Hafen Frankfurt	D 2	5001673	2008	
1271 028	HGK	DH 711	5001704	2009	
1271 029	RHC	DH 712	5001832	2009	
1271 030	VL/EVB	411.52	5001849	2008	
1271 031	VL/EVB	411.53	5001894	2009	
1271 033	HGK	DH 713	5001656	2011	
1271 034	HGK	DH 714	5001657	2011	
1271 035	HGK	DH 715	5001659	2011	
1271 036	HGK	DH 716	5001896	2011	
1271 037	HGK	DH 717	5001915	2011	
1271 038	RHC	DH 706	5602134	2014	
1271 039	RHC	DH 707	5602135	2014	
1271 040	RHC	DH 708	5602136	2014	
1271 041	RHC	DH 709	5602136	2014	
1271 911	WLH		1001129	2001	Ex CFL 1503
	VL/CFLDE	1103	5001529	2004	

92 80 1272 & 1273   VOSSLOH G2000   B-B

When the first G2000s came out there was a surprise as outer cabs were provided, but only a small cab at opposite corners of the locomotive – an asymmetrical arrangement. Private operators began to want the locos, but some demanded full width cabs etc. Eventually five versions of the type were built:

G2000.1 Original version with asymmetrical cabs; Class 1273 0xx, Class 1273 1xx.
G2000.2 Left hand driving position for Italy (all in Italy and not included here)
G2000.3 Right hand drive for Germany etc. Some built for Netherlands/Belgium/France; Class 1272
G2000.4 2700 kW version, one loco now in Sweden
G2000.5 2700 kW version for Scandinavia

Built: 2000–08.
Builder: Vossloh.   **Wheel Diameter:** 1000 mm.
Engine: Versions 1, 2, 3, Caterpillar 3516B-HD of 2240 kW; versions 4 & 5, MTU 20V400 R2 of 2700 kW.
Weight: Versions 1, 2, 3, 87.3 tonnes; versions 4 & 5, 90 tonnes.
Transmission: Hydraulic, Voith L620reU2.   **Length over Buffers:** 17.40 m.
Maximum Tractive Effort: **Maximum Speed:** 120 km/h.

1272 0xx. G2000.3

EVN	Company	Running No	Works No	Built	Notes
1272 001	VL		1001456	2004	
1272 002	AT/B-VL		5001699	2008	
1272 010	AT/OHE	V 1460	1001460	2003	

1272 2xx. Germany/Netherlands version

EVN	Company	Running No	Works No	Built	Notes
1272 201	VL/AT/CTD		1001324	2003	
1272 202	VL/WLE	21	1001455	2004	
1272 204	MRCE/RTS	272 204	1001457	2004	
1272 205	MRCE/RTS	272 205	1001458	2004	

1272 4xx. Germany/Netherlands/Belgium version; all are thought to be ETCS equipped.

EVN	Company	Running No	Works No	Built	Notes
1272 401	VL/NL-KV		1001445	2004	
1272 402	AT		1001446	2004	
1272 403	RRF		5001604	2005	
1272 404	AT/OHEGO		5001605	2005	Ex R4C 2006
1272 405	AT/B-RTX		5001606	2005	Ex R4C 2007
1272 406	MRCE		5001607	2005	Ex RTB V 201
1272 407	MRCE/RTS	272 407	5001608	2005	
1272 408	RTBC	V 203	5001752	2008	
1272 409	RTBC	V 204	5001753	2008	
1272 410	RTBC	V 206	5001760	2008	

1272 6xx and 1272 7xx were built for service in Germany/France but all are now in France.

1273 0xx. G2000.1

EVN	Company	Running No	Works No	Built	Notes
1273 001	AT/OHE	V 1028	1001028	2000	
1273 002	AT/RBH	901	1001030	2001	
1273 003	AT/RBH	902	1001031	2001	
1273 004	AT/RBH	903	1001032	2001	
1273 005	VSFT/OHE	V1001-033	1001033	2001	
1273 008	RBH	904	1001036	2001	
1273 009	WLH/HVLE		1001037	2001	Ex RLG 67
1273 012	VL/SPENO		1001040	2002	Ex NE 9
1273 013	AT/OHE	V 1041	1001041	2002	
1273 014	AT		1001042	2002	
1273 016	AT		1001325	2003	
1273 018	VSFT/KSW	V 43	1001327	2002	
1273 019	NL-ERS		1001384	2003	

1273 1xx. Germany/Netherlands version; all are thought to be ETCS equipped.

EVN	Company	Running No	Works No	Built	Notes
1273 101	AT/RF		1001029	2001	ex HGK DH 59
1273 102	AT/KV	1043	1001043	2002	
1273 103	AT/HGK	DH 754	1001039	2002	
1273 104	AT/HGK	DH 753	1001326	2002	
1273 105	AT/HGK	DH 758	1001034	2001	
1273 106	AT/HGK	DH 751	1001035	2001	
1273 107			1001038	2001	

92 80 1275 & 1276   VOSSLOH G1206   B-B

The G1206 is a standard MaK off-centre cab locomotive built over quite a long period and examples are still being turned out. There appear to be about five versions, some having MTU engines and others having Caterpillar engines. Some only have a maximum speed of 80 km/h for use in Ruhr area industrial locations and these appear as class **98 80 0275**! Another batch has been given the EVN 1276, the reason not being clear so the technical details below are assumed to apply. It is not clear which number series have which fittings but the majority of locomotives have Caterpillar engines and the data given is for these locomotives. Adding to the confusion is that some locomotives have gearings giving 60/100 km/h!

Built: 1997–
Builder: MaK, SFT, VSFT, VL.
Engine: Caterpillar 3512B DI-TA, of 1500 kW.
Transmission: Hydraulic, Voith L5r4 zU2.
Maximum Tractive Effort:

Wheel Diameter: 1000 mm.
Weight: 87.3 tonnes.
Length over Buffers: 14.70 m.
Maximum Speed: 100 km/h.

1275 Series

EVN	Company	Running No	Works No	Built	Notes
1275 001	MRCE		5001558	2005	ex RBH 821
1275 002	MRCE		5001563	2005	ex RBH 822
1275 003	MRCE		5001562	2005	ex RBH 823

1275 004	MRCE		5001564	2005	ex RBH 824
1275 005	AVG	461^{III}	5001629	2005	
1275 006	MRCE/RBH	825^{II}	5001569	2006	
1275 007	MRCE/MVG	500 1570	5001570	2006	
1275 008	MRCE/PCT		5001676	2008	
1275 009	MRCE/CTD		5001677	2008	
1275 010	LEUNA	207	5001745	2008	
1275 011	LEUNA	208	5001880	2008	
1275 012	LEUNA	209	5001868	2009	
1275 013	LEUNA	210	5001881	2009	
1275 014	LEUNA	211	5001884	2009	
1275 015	BUVL/DPR	275 015	5001653	2011	
1275 016	BUVL/CFLDE	1510	5001991	2011	
1275 017	NIAG	5^{II}	5001987	2011	
1275 018	NIAG	7^{IV}	5001988	2011	
1275 019	VL/NTS/CLG		5001882	2012	
1275 020	VL/NTS/CTD-RBB		5001989	2012	
1275 021	BUVL		5001990	2012	
1275 022	AT/SBBC		1001114	2000	
1275 101	MWB	V 2101	1001141	2002	Ex RC 0504
1275 102	MWB	V 2102	1001136	2001	Ex RC 0501
1275 103	NRAIL/CLG		1001139	2001	Ex MWB V 2103, Ex RC 0502
1275 104	VSFT/MWB	V 2104	1001140	2002	Ex SR 0501
1275 105	VL/NRAIL/HLG		5001491	2004	Ex MWB V 2105, ex RC 0507
1275 106	WLE	51	1001150	2002	Kreis Warendorf
1275 107	DPR	275 107	5001477	2003	
1275 108	ESGBI	8	5001478	2003	
1275 109	AT/CLG	1130	1001130	2001	
1275 110	AT/CTD		1001119	2001	
1275 111	AT/CTD		1001125	2001	
1275 112	VL/EHG	545	5001556	2004	
1275 113	VL/EHG	546	5001557	2004	
1275 114	VL/EHG	547	5001560	2004	
1275 115	VL/EHG	548	5001501	2004	
1275 116	VL/EHG	549	5001502	2004	
1275 117	ESGBI	1^{II}	1001132	2001	Ex AVG 467
1275 118	RTBC	V 151	5001490	2004	
1275 119	AT/LOCON		1001138	2001	
1275 120	BEBRA		1001123	2001	
	AT/CFLDE	1508	1001127	2001	
1275 210	MEG	210	5001465	2003	
1275 211	MEG	211	Scrapped		
1275 212	MEG	212	5001467	2003	
1275 213	MEG	213	5001468	2003	
1275 214	MEG	214	Scrapped		
1275 215	MEG	215	5001470	2003	
1275 216	MEG	216	5001471	2003	
1275 217	MEG	217	5001472	2003	
1275 218	MEG	218	5001473	2003	
1275 219	MEG	219	5001474	2003	
1275 220	MEG	220	5001500	2004	
1275 221	MEG	221	5001561	2004	
1275 501	VL/HGB	V150.02	5001792	2008	Ex CLG 10
1275 502	VL/HGB	V150.01	5001793	2008	
1275 503	EVB	415.51	5001794	2008	
1275 504	RLG	54	5001639	2008	
1275 505	WLE	53	5001638	2008	Kreis Soest
1275 506	VL/AVG	462^{III}	5001812	2008	
1275 507	VL/AVG	469^{II}	5001815	2008	

1275 610	DH	D 25	5001790	2008	
	DH	D 26	5001789	2009	
1275 612	AT/Captrain NL	1505	5001505	2004	
1275 613	AT/NL-LTE		5001506	2004	
1275 615	MRCE/CH-SERSA		5001508	2004	
1275 618	MRCE/Train Support (NL)	7101	5001553	2005	
1275 619	MRCE		5001554	2005	Overhaul
1275 620	MRCE/CTD		5001555	2005	
1275 621	MRCE/RRI		5001572	2005	ETCS
1275 623	MRCE/Captrain NL	1206L032	5001627	2005	
1275 624	MRCE/RTS		5001510	2006	
1275 625	MRCE/LOCON NL	5001571	5001571	2006	
1275 626	AK		5001509	2006	Now in France
1275 628	MRCE/RTBC	V 152	5001648	2006	
1275 631	DPR	275 631	5001746	2008	
1275 632	AT/LOCON Benelux		5001796	2008	
1275 633	AT/BE	D 27	5001797	2008	
1275 634	AT/NL-Traingroup	TG-105	5001798	2008	
1275 635	WLS/DPR	275 635	5001836	2008	
1275 636	RTBC	V 155	5001652	2009	
1275 637	RTBC	V 156	5001654	2009	
1275 801	RBH		1001022	2000	Ex CFL DE 1509
1275 803	NTS/RAR	275 803	1001012	1999	Ex MRCE, ex RBH 821
1275 804	NRAIL/EHG		1001013	1999	Ex MRCE
1275 805	LPG	275 805	1001014	1999	Ex RAG 823
1275 806	LEUNA	206^{II}	1001015	1999	Ex RAG 824
1275 807	HTRS/RAR	Ronja	1001016	1999	Ex RAR ex RAG 825
1275 808	RHKE	D IV	1001020	2000	
1275 809	AT/LOCON		1001117	2000	Ex CFL 1507
1275	DH	D 23	1001017	1999	Ex NEG 06
1275	DH	D 24	1001018	1999	Ex NEG 07
1275 821	SBBC		1001021	2000	SBB Cargo Deutschland
1275 814	AT/RBH	827	1001023	2000	
1275 815	AT/RBH	828	1001024	2000	
1275 816	AT/CFLDE		1001025	2000	
1275 817	AT/RBH	829	1001026	2000	
1275 818	AT/RBH	830	1001027	2000	
1275 820	AT		1001120	2001	Ex LTE 2150 901
1275 833	AT/CTD-BCB		1001133	2001	
1275 834	EHG	541	1001134	2001	
1275 835	EHG	542	1001135	2001	
1275 837	NTS/WHE	6	1001137	2001	
1275 842	RBG	D05^{II}	1001142	2002	
1275 843	VL/BUVL		5001475	2003	Ex SLG G1206-SP-022
1275 845	EHG	543	1001145	2002	
1275 846	SLG/XR	01	1001382	2003	
1275 848	AT/BE	D26	1001115	2000	Ex CFL 1501
1275 849	AT/L-CFL Cargo		1001116	2000	
1275 850	VL/BUVL		1001383	2003	Ex SLG G1206-SP-021
1275 851	EHG	544	1001151	2002	
1275 867	BUVL/BASF		5001503	2004	
1275 868	BUVL/RBH	834	5001504	2004	
1275 869	RBH	831	5001479	2003	
1275 870	BUVL/BASF		5001499	2004	

1276 Series

EVN	Company	Running No	Works No	Built	Notes
1276 001	AT/CFL		5001513	2007	
1276 002	AT/CFL		5001665	2007	
1276 003	VL/AT/France		5001722	2007	
1276 004	AT/France		5001725	2007	
1276 005	CH-SBBC		5001726	2007	ex MWB V 2106
1276 006	CH-SBBC		5001727	2007	ex MWB V 2107

1276 008	AT/CH-SBBC		5001544	2004	
1276 015	VL/MRCE/RRI	46	5001635	2008	
1276 016	MRCE/CFL		5001636	2008	
1276 018	MRCE/CFL		5001684	2008	
1276 023	VL/MRCE/RRI	47	5001819	2008	
1276 034	MRCE		5001649	2007	Ex CFL 1583
1276 037	MRCE/CFL Cargo	1584	5001731	2007	Ex CFL 1584
1276 038	VL/BASF	MATHIAS	5001552	2008	
1276 039	VL/BASF	ROLAND	5001626	2008	
1276 040	VL/AT/CTD		5001545	2004	
1276 041	RWE	490	5001696	2009	
1276 042	BUVL/CFL Cargo		5001692	2011	
1276 043	HAEG/TXL		5001687	2009	"Beci"
1276 044	HAEG/TXL		5001689	2009	"Tilly"

▲ Vossloh G1206 92 80 1275 103 passes the signalbox at Oberhausen West on 5 June 2013. This loco has seen service with several operators but carries the livery of Northrail, the leasing company that owns it. **Matthias Müller**

92 80 1277   VOSSLOH G1700   B-B

This is basically a development of the MaK G1206, the first batch having many of the dimensions of the G1206 but the G1700-2 version is a more powerful locomotive, longer and features a Caterpillar engine rather than the MTU of the first version. The Swiss Class 843 is a member of this family.

Built: 2001–
Builder: VSFT/VL.
Engine: Caterpillar 3512B-HD of 1700 kW; *MTU 12V40900R20 of 1500 kW.
Weight: 80–88 tonnes.
Transmission: Hydraulic, Voith L620reU2; *L5r4zU2.
Maximum Tractive Effort:

Wheel Diameter: 1000 mm.

Length over Buffers: 15.20 m; *14.70 m.
Maximum Speed: 100 km/h.

G1700-2

EVN	Company	Running No	Works No	Built	Notes
1277 003	HLG/BEBRA	277 003	1001207	2002	
1277 004	AT/NE	208	1001208	2003	Ex VPS 1705
1277 005	AT/VPS	1706	1001212	2003	
1277 011	AT/VPS	1703	5001537	2004	Damaged
1277 015	MRCE/CH-SERSA		5001592	2006	
1277 018	BLP	Wiebe 12	5001679	2007	
1277 030	LDS	277 030	5001713	2008	
1277 031	Schweerbau/LDS	277 031	5001870	2011	
1277 101	A-SETG	V1700.10	1001213	2003	Ex VPS 1701
1277 102	A-SETG	V1700.20	1001214	2003	Ex VPS 1702
1277 401	CH-SERSA		1001210	2003	ex MWB V 2301
1277 402	MWB	V 2302	1001211	2003	
1277 403	CH-SERSA		5001488	2004	ex MWB V 2303
1277 404	MWB	V 2304	5001593	2006	
1277 405	MWB	V 2305	5001721	2007	
1277 406	BHL	20	5001714	2008	
1277 801	HGK				
1277 802	VL/NIAG	31	5001489	2004	Once HGK DH 701
1277 803	VL/NIAG	2	5001534	2004	Once HGK DH 702
1277 804	VL/NIAG	1III	5001535	2004	Ex HGK DH 703
1277 805	VL/NIAG	6II	5001536	2004	Ex HGK DH 704
1277 806	VL/EEB	Emsland V	5001594	2006	Ex HGK DH 705
1277 807	VL/KSW	V 46	5001680	2008	
1277 808	VSFT/MKB	V 19	1001209	2003	
1277 809 *	VSFT/VL		1001113	2001	Ex NE VIII

G1700-1

EVN	Company	Running No	Works No	Built	Notes
1277 902 *	VSFT/KSW	V 42	1001108	2001	
1277 904 *	VSFT/AVG	468	1001112	2003	

92 80 1278   VOSSLOH G800   B-B

This particular type under the Mak classification G800 is better known as the Austrian Class 2070. Just six other locomotives were built and these became Vossloh stock/hire locos.

Built: 2001–02.
Builder: Vossloh.
Engine: Caterpillar 3412E DI-TTA-JW of 738 kW.
Transmission: Hydraulic, Voith L3r4zseU2.
Maximum Tractive Effort:

Wheel Diameter: 1000 mm.
Weight: 72 tonnes.
Length over Buffers: 14.13 m.
Maximum Speed: 100 km/h.

EVN	Company	Running No	Works No	Built
1278 001	Sold to Austria		1001148	2001
1278 002	Sold to Austria		1001149	2001
1278 003	NTS		1001318	2002

1278 004	NTS/CLG		1001319	2002
1278 005	NTS/PCW	6	1001320	2003
1278 006	NTS		1001321	2003

92 80 1280

This locomotive is an original DB V80 re-imported from Italy. It is not clear whether it is for preservation or open access!

Built: 1951.
Builder: MaK.
Engine: MTU MB12V493TZ of 1100 kW.
Transmission: Hydraulic.
Maximum Tractive Effort:

Wheel Diameter: 950 mm.
Weight: 58 tonnes.
Length over Buffers: 12.80 m.
Maximum Speed: 100 km/h.

EVN	Company	Running No	Builder	Works No	Built
1280 007	DP	V80-1	MaK	800002	1951

92 80 1284   EUROLIGHT   Bo-Bo

Vossloh has had a couple of locomotives touring Europe, two of which are registered in Germany but so far there have been no orders for use in this country.

Built: 2010.
Builder: Vossloh Espana.
Engine: Caterpillar C175.
Transmission: Electric, 4 ABB 600 kW traction motors.
Maximum Tractive Effort: 300 kN.

Wheel Diameter: 1100 mm.
Weight: 77 tonnes.
Length over Buffers: 20.32 m.
Maximum Speed: 200 km/h.

EVN	Company	Running No	Works No	Built
1284 001	VE		2603	2010
1284 002	IT-VE	92 83 2284 002	2604	2010

92 80 1285   BOMBARDIER F140DE   Bo-Bo

This type is a diesel version of the TRAXX electric locomotive for freight train use. After some initial interest from German operators few orders have been received. However SNCF was set to have a batch for working between France and Germany; this idea seems to have flopped and locos already built for France are now being offered to German operators.

Built: 2007–13.
Builder: Bombardier, Kassel.
Engine: MTU 16V4000R43L.
Transmission: Electric, 4 x 600 kW traction motors.
Maximum Tractive Effort: 270 kN.

Wheel Diameter: 1250 mm.
Weight: 83 tonnes.
Length over Buffers: 18.90 m.
Maximum Speed: 140 km/h.

Note: There is some confusion surrounding the identities of 1285 110 and 1285 117.

*   Fitted with ETCS and can work in Belgium and the Netherlands

EVN	Company	Running No	Works No	Built	Notes
1285 001	HVLE	285 001	34315	2007	
1285 102	MER/HSL		34361	2007	Ex HVLE *OBERHÄVEL*
1285 103	MER/HSL		34364	2007	
1285 104	MER/HVLE	285 104	34369	2008	
1285 105	MER/HVLE		34372	2008	
1285 106	MER/ITL	285 106	34375	2008	
1285 107	MER/HSL		34378	2008	1/4/13
1285 108	MER/ITL	285 108	34379	2008	
1285 109	MER/ITL	285 109	34380	2008	
1285 110	MER/CTD-ITL		34381	2008	SNCF 476101
1285 111	MER/ITL	285 111	34763	2010	
1285 112 *	RHC	DE 801	34842	2013	Originally for SNCF as 76103
1285 113 *	RHC	DE 802	34843	2013	Originally for SNCF as 76104
1285 114 *	RHC	DE 803	34844	2013	Originally for SNCF as 76105

1285 115	*	RHC	DE 804	34994	2013 Originally for SNCF as 76106
1285 116	*	RHC	DE 805	34995	2013 Originally for SNCF as 76107
1285 117	*	CTD/ITL	285 117	34381	2008 Originally for SNCF; 92 88 0076 108
1285 118	*	CTD/ITL	285 118	34486	2009 Originally for SNCF; 92 88 0076 102
1285 119	*	CTD/ITL	285 119	34996	2013 Originally for SNCF
	*	B-BTK/D-RDX		34997	2013 Originally for SNCF; 92 88 0076 109
	*	D-BTK		34998	2013 Originally for SNCF; 92 88 0076 110; stored
		BTK/SWT		34999	2013 SNCF 76111; 92 88 0076 111
		D-BTK		34462	2009 SNCF 76001; stored
		D-BTK		34492	2009 SNCF 76002; stored
		D-BTK		34762	2010 SNCF 76003; stored
		D-BTK		34838	2013 SNCF 76004; stored

92 80 1293   ADTRANZ REBUILT V100DR   B-B

This class is another rebuild of former DR V100. However they were rebuilt by ADtranz at Kassel; some were given ADtranz order numbers as works numbers, with the original data being lost. Some of this is due to various people acquiring locomotives and destroying the identity so the source could not be traced. During this period ADtranz became Bombardier and this rebuilding work was discontinued; instead the factory concentrated on new construction with the advent of the TRAXX series.

Built: 1970–96, rebuilt 1999–2002.
Builder: LEW.
Engine: Caterpillar, see codes under 92 80 1201.
Transmission: Hydraulic.
Maximum Tractive Effort:
Wheel Diameter: 1000 mm.
Weight: 64 tonnes.
Length over Buffers: 14.24 m.
Maximum Speed: 100 km/h.

EVN	Engine	Company	Running No	Builder	Works No	Built	Notes
1293 001	j2	RTS	293 001	ADtranz	72340	1999	Ex EBW V130.13, TLG 1, ex DR
1293 002	j2	RTS	293 002	ADtranz	73260	2000	Ex EBW V130.14, TLG 8, ex DR
1293 003	j3	RTS	293 003	LEW	12561	1970	Ex EBW V130.15 ex various, ex 202 279
1293 004	j3	RTS	293 004	LEW	13570	1973	Ex various, ex 202 531
1293 005	j2	SES	Georg	LEW	14897	1975	Ex Lokpool, ex DR 201 833
1293 006	e	HGB	V100.02	ADtranz	70120	2001	Ex S&S 293 701 "Nobby", ex Bombardier, ex DR
1293 007	j2	DGT	710 967	ADtranz	17316	1999	Ex 710 967
1293 008	j2	DGT	710 966	ADtranz	72150	1999	Ex ?
1293 009	j2	DGT	710 965	ADtranz	17314	1999	ex 710 965
1293 010	j2	DGT	710 964	ADtranz	17313	1999	Ex 710 964
1293 011	j2	DGT	710 968	ADtranz	72710	1999	Ex ?
1293 501	j2	LDS	1 Grüne Rose	Adtranz	72510	2000	Ex Lokpool/WAB 12.
1293 502	j2	LOCON	211	Adtranz	72520	2000	Ex WAB 13, ex DR
1293 503	j2	LOCON	212	Adtranz	72800	2001	Ex EFW, ex DR
1293 504	j2	RBB	V145	LEW	15381	1976	Now in Switzerland as 5847 904 WRSCH
1293 505	j2	PRESS	293 046	BT	12897	2002	Ex Johanna 03, Captrain V146, ex DR 202 388
1293 506	j2	RBB	V 147		12834	1971	Ex NEB 20, DR 202 388; now in Switzerland as 5847 906 WRSCH
1293 507	j2	Knape GSG/SGL	V150.01	Adtranz	72440	2000	Built as LEW 17310/83
1293 508	j2	Knape GSG/SGL	V150.02	Adtranz	72450	2000	Built as LEW 17311/83
1293 509	j2	Knape GSG/SGL	V150.03	Adtranz	72460	2000	Built as LEW 17312/83

EVN		Company	Running No	Builder	Works No	Built	Notes
1293 510	j2	Knape GSG/SGL	V150.04	Adtranz	72470	2000	Built as LEW 17315/83
1293 511	j2	LDS	6	Adtranz	72350	2000	Ex DR; WEISER BEER
1293 512	j2	ITL	293.01	BT	72540	2002	Ex Bombardier, ex DR 202 xxx
1293 513	j2	ITL	293.02	BT	72550	2002	Ex Bombardier, ex DR 202 xxx
1293 514	j2	BUVL CTD-RBB	293 514	LEW	15084	1975	Ex DR 201 812
1293 515	e	Bayernhafen	293 515	Adtranz	70110	1999	Ex BASF 1003
1293 516	j2	BUVL/DPR	293 516	Adtranz	72030	1999	Ex BASF 1002
1293 881	h3	PRESS	293 021	Adtranz	16375	1996	Ex 201 881; modernised by Adtranz

92 80 1320   V 320   C-C

This was a prototype locomotive used by DB for 14 years before being sold off to the Hersfelder Kreisbahn, who had it for a few years before it was passed on to TWE and then to a dealer who sold it to Italy. When open access started the private operators were looking around for locomotives with grandfather rights and repatriated the V320 from Italy in 1999. It is used by the Wiebe engineering firm for use on its heavy ballast trains but is often leased out on spot hire contracts.

Built: 1962.
Builder: Henschel.
Engine: 2 MTU MB16V652TB of 1900 hp each.
Transmission: Hydraulic, Voith L218vV.
Maximum Tractive Effort: 400 kN.
Wheel Diameter: 1100 mm.
Weight: 128 tonnes.
Length over Buffers: 23 m.
Maximum Speed: 160 km/h.

EVN	Company	Running No	Works No	Built	Notes
1320 001	BLP	Wiebe 7	30400	1962	Ex Italy, ex DB

92 80 2143   ÖBB 2143   B-B

Scratching around for suitable locomotives, the Staudenbahn realised that Austrian 2143s could be used in Germany and acquired some!

Built: 1966.
Builder: SGP.
Engine: SGP T12c of 1100 kW.
Transmission: Hydraulic, Voith L830rU2.
Maximum Tractive Effort: 197 kN.
Wheel Diameter: 950 mm.
Weight: 67 tonnes.
Length over Buffers: 15.76 m.
Maximum Speed: 100 km/h.

EVN	Company	Running No	Works No	Built
2143 006	STVG	2143 006	18344	1966
2143 018	STVG	2143.18	18386	1969
2143 021		2143.21	18389	1970

92 80 4120   VOSSLOH G12   B-B

Built: 2010.
Builder: VL.
Engine: MTU 8V4000R43(L) of 1200 kW.
Transmission: Hydraulic.
Maximum Tractive Effort:
Wheel Diameter: 1000 mm.
Weight: 80–90 tonnnes.
Length over Buffers: 17 m.
Maximum Speed: 100 km/h.

EVN	Company	Running No	Works No	Built
4120 001	D-VL		5001919	2010

92 80 41xx   VOSSLOH DE12   Bo-Bo

Built: 2012–13.
Builder: Vossloh.
Engine: MTU 8V4000R43(L) of 1200 kW.
Transmission: Electric.
Maximum Tractive Effort:

Wheel Diameter: 1000 mm.
Weight: 80–90 tonees.
Length over Buffers: 17 m.
Maximum Speed: 120 km/h.

EVN	Company	Running No	Works No	Built
?	BASF	DE 20	5401961	2013
?	BASF	DE 21	5401962	2013
?		DE 22	5401963	2013
?		DE 23	5401964	2013

92 80 4180   VOSSLOH G18   B-B

The G18 represents a new generation of locomotives from Vossloh. Built in time for Innotrans 2012 there seems to be little interest so far.

Built: 2011.
Builder: Vossloh.
Engine: MTU 12V4000R43(L) of 1800 kW.
Transmission: Hydraulic.
Maximum Tractive Effort:

Wheel Diameter: 1000 mm.
Weight: 80-90 tonnes.
Length over Buffers: 17 m.
Maximum Speed: 100 km/h.

EVN	Company	Running No	Works No	Built
4180 001	D-VL		5001927	2011

92 80 4185   VOSSLOH DE18   Bo-Bo

This class is the diesel electric version of the G18 which has had better luck attracting some orders.

Built: 2010–14.
Builder: Vossloh.
Engine: MTU 12V4000R43(L) of 1800 kW.
Transmission: Electric.
Maximum Tractive Effort:

Wheel Diameter: 1000 mm.
Weight: 80-90 tonnes.
Length over Buffers: 17 m.
Maximum Speed: 120 km/h.

EVN	Company	Running No	Works No	Built
4185 001	D-SPENO		5002018	2012
4185 002				
4185 003	BASF	DE 24	5501984	2013
4185 004	BASF	DE 25	5501985	2013
4185 005				
4185 006	D-EPF		5502012	2014
4185 007	D-EPF		5502019	2014
4185 008				
4185 009	D-EPF		5502073	2014

3.4 CODE 94 80 – ELECTRIC MULTIPLE UNITS

In Germany three principal builders are involved in supplying private operators with electric multiple units: Alstom, Bombardier, and Stadler. Standard products are offered but tailored to the customers' requirements. Consequently there are 2, 3, 4, 5 and even 6-car EMUs with varying seating arrangements, some units being one class only. In some cases there are ticket machines on board and even vending machines for snacks and drinks. All these new trains are air conditioned and where not fitted with passenger information systems and CCTV they are being progressively retro fitted. Many sets have sliding bridge plates to cover the space between train and platform. It is not possible to give individual data for all these variations so just the outline data is given. Note that some companies have given trains their own numbers which are carried on the front with the EVN being on the vehicle sides. However some recent deliveries have trains just carrying one number – the EVN. The Stadler works numbers need a little explanation. There is a works number for the set and one for each vehicle as well!

94 80 0426 STADLER FLIRT 2-SECTION ARTICULATED UNITS

The Stadler FLIRT (**F**linker, **L**eichter, **I**nnovativer, **R**egion **T**riebzug – faster, lighter, innovative regional unit) series of trains is a huge success story for what was a small Swiss train builder. Now it has factories all around Europe and in the former USSR, such has been the demand for these trains. Dutch Railways subsidiary Abellio won the contract for some local services in the Ruhr area ordering a mixture of two and three car EMUs of the FLIRT family. All are leased from Ascendos.

Built: 2006.
Builder–Mechanical Parts: Stadler, Berlin Pankow.
Builder–Electrical Parts: Not quoted.
Wheel Arrangement: Bo-2-2.
Traction Motors: 2 x 500 kW.   **Continuous Rating:** 1000 kW.
Accommodation: 16/68(28) 1TD plus multi-purpose area.
Weight: 76 tonnes.   **Wheel Diameter:** Powered 860 mm, trailing 750 mm.
Length over Couplers: 42.066 m.   **Maximum Speed:** 160 km/h.
Floor Height: 760 mm.   **Maximum Tractive Effort:** 100 kN.

Car 1	Car 2	Company	Unit Number	Works No	Built	Names
426 100	826 100	ABRN	ET22 001	37628	2007	
426 101	826 101	ABRN	ET22 002	37631	2007	Kreuztal
426 102	826 102	ABRN	ET22 003	37634	2007	Essen
426 103	826 103	ABRN	ET22 004	37637	2007	
426 104	826 104	ABRN	ET22 005	37640	2007	
426 105	826 105	ABRN	ET22 006	37643	2007	Siegen
426 106	826 106	ABRN	ET22 007	37646	2007	Iserlohn
426 107	826 107	ABRN	ET22 008	37649	2007	

94 80 0427 STADLER FLIRT 3-SECTION ARTICULATED UNITS

Abellio ordered nine 3-car sets for its Ruhr area services. They are leased from Ascendos.

Built: 2007.
Builder–Mechanical Parts: Stadler, Berlin Pankow.
Builder–Electrical Parts: Not quoted.
Wheel Arrangement: Bo-2-2-Bo.
Traction Motors: 4 x 500 kW.   **Continuous/Maximum Rating:** 2000/2600 kW.
Accommodation: 16/116(45) 1TD plus multi-purpose area.
Weight: 100 tonnes.   **Wheel Diameter:** Powered 860 mm, trailing 750 mm.
Length over Couplers: 58.166 m.   **Maximum Speed:** 160 km/h.
Floor Height: 760 mm.   **Maximum Tractive Effort:** 200 kN.

Car 1	Car 2	Car 3	Company	Unit Number	Works No	Built	Names
427 100	827 100	427 600	ABRN	ET23 001	37652	2007	Altena
427 101	827 101	427 601	ABRN	ET23 002	37656	2007	Märkische Kreis
427 102	827 102	427 602	ABRN	ET23 003	37660	2007	Werdohl

Car 1	Car 2	Car 3	Company	Unit Number	Works No	Built	
427 103	827 103	427 603	ABRN	ET23 004	37664	2007	Hagen
427 104	827 104	427 604	ABRN	ET23 005	37668	2007	Lennestadt
427 105	827 105	427 605	ABRN	ET23 006	37672	2007	Plettenberg
427 106	827 106	427 606	ABRN	ET23 007	37676	2007	
427 107	827 107	427 607	ABRN	ET23 008	37680	2007	Finnentrop
427 108	827 108	427 608	ABRN	ET23 009	37684	2007	Kreis Siegen Wittgenstein

The Westfalenbahn (WFB) also ordered a batch of these units but these vary by having a different seating arrangement and floor height. They are all leased from Alpha Trains. Details as above except:

Accommodation: 16/120(45) 1TD plus multi-purpose area.
Floor Height: 780 mm.

Car 1	Car 2	Car 3	Company	Unit Number	Works No	Built
427 109	827 109	427 609	WFB	ET 001	37545	2007
427 110	827 110	427 610	WFB	ET 002	37549	2007
427 111	827 111	427 611	WFB	ET 003	37553	2007
427 112	827 112	427 612	WFB	ET 004	37557	2007
427 113	827 113	427 613	WFB	ET 005	37561	2007
427 114	827 114	427 614	WFB	ET 006	37565	2007
427 115	827 115	427 615	WFB	ET 007	37569	2007
427 116	827 116	427 616	WFB	ET 008	37573	2007
427 117	827 117	427 617	WFB	ET 009	37577	2007
427 118	827 118	427 618	WFB	ET 010	37581	2007
427 119	827 119	427 619	WFB	ET 011	37585	2007
427 120	827 120	427 620	WFB	ET 012	37589	2007
427 121	827 121	427 621	WFB	ET 013	37593	2007
427 122	827 122	427 622	WFB	ET 014	37597	2007

Hessische Eisenbahn (HEB) ordered three sets which were delivered in 2010 and have wheel arrangement Bo-2-2-1A, so only three traction motors; another four units are on order for delivery in 2015 for the Kassel–Treysa service. Details as 427 100–108 above except:

Wheel Arrangement: Bo-2-2-1A.
Traction Motors: 3 x 500 kW.   **Wheel Diameter:** Powered 870, trailing 750 mm.
Length over Couplers: 58.178 m.   **Floor Height:** 600 mm.

Car 1	Car 2	Car 3	Company	Unit Number	Works No	Built
427 123	827 123	427 623	HEB	427 041	38619	2010
427 124	827 124	427 624	HEB	427 042	38623	2010
427 125	827 125	427 625	HEB	427 043	38627	2010

The Berchesgadener Land Bahn (BLB) also chose Stadler for its trains, again with minor variations to the specification. The units are leased from Alpha Trains. Details as 427 100–108 above except:

Accommodation: 16/120(23) 1TD plus multi-purpose area.
Length over Couplers: 58.178 m.   **Weight:** 101 tonnes.

Car 1	Car 2	Car 3	Company	Unit Number	Works No	Built	Names
427 130	827 130	427 630	BLB	ET 130	38150	2009	
427 131	827 131	427 631	BLB	ET 131	38154	2009	Landkreis Berchesgadener Land
427 132	827 132	427 632	BLB	ET 132	38158	2009	
427 133	827 133	427 633	BLB	ET 133	38162	2009	Markt Berchesgaden
427 134	827 134	427 634	BLB	ET 134	38166	2009	Stadt Freilass

Cantus, which operates in Hessen, ordered both 3-car and 4-car FLIRTS. It was early on the scene and numbered its units as 427 0xx but the EBA has slotted them into the 427 1xx series, the reasoning not being clear. Note that units are numbered in two batches depending on who owns them! Seating is again different as there is no first class. Details as 427 100–108 above except:

Accommodation: –/167(37) 1TD plus multi-purpose area.
Floor Height: 600 mm.

b   Leased from BeNEX
h   Leased from Hannover Mobilen Leasing

Car 1	Car 2	Car 3	Notes	Company	Unit Number	Works No	Built	Names
427 135	827 135	427 635	b	CAN	427 001	37453	2006	
427 136	827 136	427 636	b	CAN	427 002	37457	2006	
427 137	827 137	427 637	b	CAN	427 003	37461	2006	
427 138	827 138	427 638	b	CAN	427 004	37465	2006	
427 139	827 139	427 639	b	CAN	427 005	37469	2006	
427 140	827 140	427 640	b	CAN	427 006	37473	2006	
427 141	827 141	427 641	b	CAN	427 007	37477	2006	
427 142	827 142	427 642	h	CAN	427 051	37481	2006	Kassel
427 143	827 143	427 643	h	CAN	427 052	37585	2006	
427 144	827 144	427 644	h	CAN	427 053	37489	2006	
427 145	827 145	427 645	h	CAN	427 054	37493	2006	
427 146	827 146	427 646	h	CAN	427 055	37497	2006	Alheim
427 147	827 147	427 647	h	CAN	427 056	37501	2006	
427 148	827 148	427 648	h	CAN	427 057	37505	2006	

This small batch for VIAS is similar to the HEB batch above in only having three powered axles. Details as 427 100–108 above except:

Wheel Arrangement: Bo-2-2-1A.
Traction Motors: 3 x 500 kW. **Continuous/Maximum Rating:** 1500/1950 kW.
Accommodation: 16/120(34) 1TD plus multi-purpose area.
Length over Couplers: 58.178 m. **Wheel Diameter:** Powered 870 mm, trailing 750 mm.
Floor Height: 600 mm. **Maximum Tractive Effort:** 150 kN.

Car 1	Car 2	Car 3	Company	Unit Number	Works No	Built
427 149	827 149	427 649	VIAS	ET 301	38667	2010
427 150	827 150	427 650	VIAS	ET 302	38671	2010
427 151	827 151	427 651	VIAS	ET 303	38675	2010
427 152	827 152	427 652	VIAS	ET 304	38679	2010
427 153	827 153	427 653	VIAS	ET 305	38683	2010

94 80 1427 STADLER FLIRT 3-SECTION ARTICULATED UNITS

There must have been a slight design change as these units for the Bayerische Oberlandbahn Meridian services from München received the 1427 designation. Certainly the front end has been redesigned. The wheel arrangement is officially quoted as 1A-2-2-Bo (The opposite way around to those shown here!). Details as 427 100–108 above except:

Wheel Arrangement: 1A-2-2-Bo.
Traction Motors: 3 x 500 kW. **Continuous/Maximum Rating:** 1500/1950 kW.
Accommodation: 8/150 1T 1TD. **Wheel Diameter:** Powered 920, trailing 760 mm.

Car 1	Car 2	Car 3	Company	Unit Number	Works No	Built
1427 001	1827 001	1427 501	BOBY	ET 351	39390	2013
1427 002	1827 002	1427 502	BOBY	ET 352	39394	2013
1427 003	1827 003	1427 503	BOBY	ET 353	39398	2014
1427 004	1827 004	1427 504	BOBY	ET 354	39402	2014
1427 005	1827 005	1427 505	BOBY	ET 355	39406	2014
1427 006	1827 006	1427 506	BOBY	ET 356	39410	2014
1427 007	1827 007	1427 507	BOBY	ET 357	39414	2014

▲ 94 80 0427 103 is a 3-section articulated Stadler FLIRT EMU with running number ET23 004 used by Abellio Rail NRW (ABRN) on services in the Ruhr area. It is seen at Essen Hbf with a "Ruhr Lenne Bahn" RB 40 service to Hagen on 7 June 2008. **Keith Fender**

▼ Another Stadler FLIRT is seen leaving Kaub with a train from Neuwied to Frankfurt Hbf on 29 September 2011. This example is 94 80 0428 145, running number ET 411, a 4-section arrangement used by VIAS for services around Frankfurt/Main. **Matthias Müller**

94 80 0428 STADLER FLIRT 4-SECTION ARTICULATED UNITS

First off the mark for orders of this series was Cantus numbering its units 428 001 etc, but when the full EVN system came in these units were inserted after units built three years later. So the first units listed are from a rather large batch for Eurobahn (ERB) classed as ET5 and ET6. Finally, VIAS acquired some in 2010 for its services from Frankfurt/Main. The data below is for the ERB units. Note the ET5 and ET6 designations refer to operating routes when ordered. All are leased from Alpha Trains.

Built: 2006–12.
Builder–Mechanical Parts: Stadler, Berlin Pankow.
Builder–Electrical Parts: Not quoted.
Wheel Arrangement: Bo-2-2-2-Bo.
Traction Motors: 4x 500 kW.   **Continuous Rating:** 2000 kW.
Accommodation: 16/132(69) 2TD.
Weight: 124 tonnes.   **Wheel Diameter:** Powered 860 mm, trailing 750 mm.
Length over Couplers: 74.276 m.   **Maximum Speed:** 160 km/h.
Floor Height: 780 mm.   **Maximum Tractive Effort:** 200 kN.

Car 1	Car 2	Car 3	Car 4	Company	Unit Number	Works No	Built
428 100	828 300	828 200	428 600	ERB	ET5.01	37994	2008
428 101	828 301	828 201	428 601	ERB	ET5.02	37999	2008
428 102	828 302	828 202	428 602	ERB	ET5.03	38004	2008
428 103	828 303	828 203	428 603	ERB	ET5.04	38009	2008
428 104	828 304	828 204	428 604	ERB	ET5.05	38014	2008
428 105	828 305	828 205	428 605	ERB	ET5.06	38019	2008
428 106	828 306	828 206	428 606	ERB	ET5.07	38024	2008
428 107	828 307	828 207	428 607	ERB	ET5.08	38029	2008
428 108	828 308	828 208	428 608	ERB	ET5.09	38034	2008
428 109	828 309	828 209	428 609	ERB	ET5.10	38039	2008
428 110	828 310	828 210	428 610	ERB	ET5.11	38044	2008
428 111	828 311	828 211	428 611	ERB	ET5.12	38049	2008
428 112	828 312	828 212	428 612	ERB	ET5.13	38054	2008
428 113	828 313	828 213	428 613	ERB	ET5.14	38059	2008
428 114	828 314	828 214	428 614	ERB	ET5.15	38064	2008
428 115	828 315	828 215	428 615	ERB	ET5.16	38069	2008
428 116	828 316	828 216	428 616	ERB	ET5.17	37074	2008
428 117	828 317	828 217	428 617	ERB	ET5.18	38079	2008
428 118	828 318	828 218	428 618	ERB	ET5.19	38084	2008
428 119	828 319	828 219	428 619	ERB	ET5.20	38089	2008
428 120	828 320	828 220	428 620	ERB	ET5.21	38094	2008
428 121	828 321	828 221	428 621	ERB	ET5.22	38099	2008
428 122	828 322	828 222	428 622	ERB	ET5.23	38104	2008
428 123	828 323	828 223	428 623	ERB	ET5.24	38109	2008
428 124	828 324	828 224	428 624	ERB	ET5.25	38114	2008
428 125	828 325	828 225	428 625	ERB	ET6.01	38520	2009
428 126	828 326	828 226	428 626	ERB	ET6.02	38525	2009
428 127	828 327	828 227	428 627	ERB	ET6.03	38530	2009
428 128	828 328	828 228	428 628	ERB	ET6.04	38535	2009

Cantus units are different in that they have no first class. Details as 428 100–128 above except:

Accommodation: –/219(41) 2TD.   **Weight:** 120 tonnes.
Length over Couplers: 74.266 m.   **Floor Height:** 600 mm.

Car 1	Car 2	Car 3	Car 4	Company	Unit Number	Works No	Built	Names
428 129	828 329	828 229	428 629	HHA/CAN	428 001	37510	2006	Eschwege
428 130	828 330	828 230	428 630	HHA/CAN	428 002	37515	2006	
428 131	828 331	828 231	428 631	HHA/CAN	428 003	37520	2006	Bebra
428 132	828 332	828 232	428 632	HHA/CAN	428 051	37525	2006	Kassel
428 133	828 333	828 233	428 633	HHA/CAN	428 052	37530	2006	Rotenburg an der Fulda
428 134	828 334	828 234	428 634	HHA/CAN	428 053	37535	2006	

VIAS units again feature minor changes to the specification. Details as 428 100–128 above except:

Accommodation: 16/176(38) 2TD.
Length over Couplers: 74.278 m.
Wheel Diameter: Powered 870 mm, trailing 750 mm.
Floor Height: 600 mm.

Car 1	Car 2	Car 3	Car 4	Company	Unit Number	Works No	Built	Names
428 135	828 335	828 235	428 635	VIAS	ET 401	38695	2010	
428 136	828 336	828 236	428 636	VIAS	ET 402	38700	2010	
428 137	828 337	828 237	428 637	VIAS	ET 403	38705	2010	
428 138	828 338	828 238	428 638	VIAS	ET 404	38710	2010	
428 139	828 339	828 239	428 639	VIAS	ET 405	38715	2010	
428 140	828 340	828 240	428 640	VIAS	ET 406	38720	2010	Bebra
428 141	828 341	828 241	428 641	VIAS	ET 407	38725	2010	
428 142	828 342	828 242	428 642	VIAS	ET 408	38730	2010	
428 143	828 343	828 243	428 643	VIAS	ET 409	38735	2010	
428 144	828 344	828 244	428 644	VIAS	ET 410	38740	2010	
428 145	828 345	828 245	428 645	VIAS	ET 411	38745	2010	
428 146	828 346	828 246	428 646	VIAS	ET 412	38750	2010	
428 147	828 347	828 247	428 647	VIAS	ET 413	38755	2011	
428 148	828 348	828 248	428 648	VIAS	ET 414	38760	2011	
428 149	828 349	828 249	428 649	HML/CAN	428 007	39158	2012	Bad Hersfeld

94 80 1428　STADLER FLIRT　4-SECTION ARTICULATED UNITS

These new units are for the Westfalenbahn when it takes over the Münster–Emden line services in December 2015. There are some differences to the 0428 series with accommodation being 15/200(50) 1T 1TD. Special mention is made that there are 42 spaces for bicycles. Length is 74.70 m.

Car 1	Car 2	Car 3	Car 4	Company	Unit Number	Works No	Built
1428 101	1828 301	1828 201	1428 601	WFB	ET4.01	40110	2015
1428 102	1828 302	1828 202	1428 602	WFB	ET4.02	40115	2015
1428 103	1828 303	1828 203	1428 603	WFB	ET4.03	40120	2015
1428 104	1828 304	1828 204	1428 604	WFB	ET4.04	40125	2015
1428 105	1828 305	1828 205	1428 605	WFB	ET4.05	40130	2015
1428 106	1828 306	1828 206	1428 606	WFB	ET4.06	40135	2015
1428 107	1828 307	1828 207	1428 607	WFB	ET4.07	40140	2015
1428 108	1828 308	1828 208	1428 608	WFB	ET4.08	40145	2015
1428 109	1828 309	1828 209	1428 609	WFB	ET4.09	40150	2015
1428 110	1828 310	1828 210	1428 610	WFB	ET4.10	40155	2015
1428 111	1828 311	1828 211	1428 611	WFB	ET4.11	40160	2015
1428 112	1828 312	1828 212	1428 612	WFB	ET4.12	40165	2015
1428 113	1828 313	1828 213	1428 613	WFB	ET4.13	40170	2015
1428 114	1828 314	1828 214	1428 614	WFB	ET4.14	40175	2015
1428 115	1828 315	1828 215	1428 615	WFB	ET4.15	40180	2015

94 80 0429　STADLER FLIRT　5-SECTION ARTICULATED UNITS

DB was the first company to order this configuration of unit and classed them as 427s, but must have been chastised by the EBA as it had allocated Class 429 for the type. Consequently, as other companies had received units in the meantime, the DB units are numbered 026-030 despite being built first. The WFB and ERB units are all leased from Alpha Trains. 27 further units are on order for Nordbahn and Abellio, the latter including some dual-voltage units for working into Venlo so ought to have a different classification. Full details are awaited.

Built: 2007–10.
Builder–Mechanical Parts: Stadler, Berlin Pankow.
Builder–Electrical Parts: Not quoted.
Wheel Arrangement: Bo-2-2-2-2-Bo.
Traction Motors: 4 x 500 kW.　**Continuous/Maximum Rating:** 2000/2600 kW.
Accommodation: 16/200(84) 2TD plus multipurpose area.
Weight: 145 tonnes.　**Wheel Diameter:** Powered 860 mm, trailing 750 mm.
Length over Couplers: 90.80 m.　**Maximum Speed:** 160 km/h.
Floor Height: 780 mm.　**Maximum Tractive Effort:** 200 kN.

Car 1	Car 2	Car 3	Car 4	Car 5	Company	Unit Number	Works No	Built
429 001	829 601	829 301	829 001	429 501	WFB	ET 015	37603	2007
429 002	829 602	829 302	829 002	429 502	WFB	ET 016	37609	2007
429 003	829 603	829 303	829 003	429 503	WFB	ET 017	37615	2007
429 004	829 604	829 304	829 004	429 504	WFB	ET 018	37621	2007
429 005	829 605	829 305	829 005	429 505	WFB	ET 019	37627	2007

ERB acquired 14 sets for the Maas–Rhein–Lippe Netz.

Car 1	Car 2	Car 3	Car 4	Car 5	Company	Unit Number	Works No	Built
429 006	829 606	829 306	829 006	429 506	ERB	ET7.01	38436	2009
429 007	829 607	829 307	829 007	429 507	ERB	ET7.02	38442	2009
429 008	829 608	829 308	829 008	429 508	ERB	ET7.03	38448	2010
429 009	829 609	829 309	829 009	429 509	ERB	ET7.04	38454	2010
429 010	829 610	829 310	829 010	429 510	ERB	ET7.05	38460	2010
429 011	829 611	829 311	829 011	429 511	ERB	ET7.06	38466	2010
429 012	829 612	829 312	829 012	429 512	ERB	ET7.07	38472	2010
429 013	829 613	829 313	829 013	429 513	ERB	ET7.08	38478	2010
429 014	829 614	829 314	829 014	429 514	ERB	ET7.09	38484	2010
429 015	829 615	829 315	829 015	429 515	ERB	ET7.10	38490	2010
429 016	829 616	829 316	829 016	429 516	ERB	ET7.11	38496	2010
429 017	829 617	829 317	829 017	429 517	ERB	ET7.12	38502	2010
429 018	829 618	829 318	829 018	429 518	ERB	ET7.13	38508	2010
429 019	829 619	829 319	829 019	429 519	ERB	ET7.14	38514	2010

The HEB units feature minor differences to the specification. Details as 429 001–005 above except:

Accommodation: 16/204(80) 2TD plus multipurpose area.
Wheel Diameter: Powered 860 mm, trailing 750 mm.
Length over Couplers: 90.378 m.   **Floor Height:** 600 mm.

Car 1	Car 2	Car 3	Car 4	Car 5	Company	Unit Number	Works No	Built
429 020	829 620	829 320	829 020	429 520	HEB	429 041	38631	2010
429 021	829 621	829 321	829 021	429 521	HEB	429 042	38637	2010
429 022	829 622	829 322	829 022	429 522	HEB	429 043	38643	2010
429 023	829 623	829 323	829 023	429 523	HEB	429 044	38649	2010
429 024	829 624	829 324	829 024	429 524	HEB	429 045	38655	2010
429 025	829 625	829 325	829 025	429 525	HEB	429 046	39661	2010

94 80 1429 STADLER FLIRT 5-SECTION ARTICULATED UNITS

The Nordbahn acquired FLIRTs for its services from Hamburg but note that here ET5 notes a five car set! Individual cars have letter suffixes e.g. ET5.01 A/C/D/E/B. Details as 429 001–005 above.

Car 1	Car 2	Car 3	Car 4	Car 5	Company	Unit Number	Works No	Built
1429 001	1829 001	1829 301	1829 602	1429 501	NBE	ET5.01	40012	2014
1429 002	1829 002	1829 302	1829 603	1429 502	NBE	ET5.02	40018	2014
1429 003	1829 003	1829 303	1829 604	1429 503	NBE	ET5.03	40024	2014
1429 004	1829 004	1829 304	1829 605	1429 504	NBE	ET5.04	40030	2014
1429 005	1829 005	1829 305	1829 606	1429 505	NBE	ET5.05	40036	2014
1429 006	1829 006	1829 306	1829 607	1429 506	NBE	ET5.06	40042	2014
1429 007	1829 007	1829 307	1829 608	1429 507	NBE	ET5.07	40048	2014

▲ Keolis Deutschland uses the brand name Eurobahn for its services in Germany. Eurobahn 94 80 0429 010, running number ET7.05, is a Stadler FLIRT 5-section articulated EMU; it is seen near Kamen on 25 September 2011 with a train from Hamm to Düsseldorf. **Matthias Müller**

▼ The longest configuration of Stadler FLIRT is this 6-section version used by Bayerische Oberlandbahn (BOBY) on its Meridian branded services. 94 80 1430 003, running number ET 303, approaches Kufstein with a local service from Rosenheim on 28 February 2014. **Robin Ralston**

94 80 1430 STADLER FLIRT 6-SECTION ARTICULATED UNITS

The first order for 6-section units came from the Bayerische Oberland Bahn which now operates them on its Meridian services between München and Salzburg/Kufstein. There is a lift available for wheelchair users but the carriage concerned is not quoted. There are multi-purpose areas at each entrance. The Meridian units are numbered by the operator as ET3xx, the formation is given as ET301.1/3/4/5/6/2 where cars 1 and 2 are the driving cars.

Built: 2013–14.
Builder–Mechanical Parts: Stadler, Berlin Pankow.
Builder–Electrical Parts: Not quoted.
Wheel Arrangement: Bo-2-2-2-2-2-Bo.
Traction Motors: 4x500 kW.　　　　**Continuous Rating:** 2000 kW
Accommodation: 16/317(?) 3T 1TD.
Weight: 174 tonnes.　　　　**Wheel Diameter:** Powered 920 mm, trailing 760 mm.
Length over Couplers: 106.90 m.　　**Maximum Speed:** 160 km/h.
Floor Height: 780 mm.　　　　**Maximum Tractive Effort:** 200 kN.

Car 1	Car 2	Car 3	Car 4	Car 5	Car 6	Co	Unit No	Works No	Built
1430 001	1830 001	1830 301	1830 601	1830 901	1430 501	BOBY	ET 301	39426	2013
1430 002	1830 002	1830 302	1830 602	1830 902	1430 502	BOBY	ET 302	39433	2013
1430 003	1830 003	1830 303	1830 603	1830 903	1430 503	BOBY	ET 303	39440	2013
1430 004	1830 004	1830 304	1830 604	1830 904	1430 504	BOBY	ET 304	39447	2013
1430 005	1830 005	1830 305	1830 605	1830 905	1430 505	BOBY	ET 305	39454	2013
1430 006	1830 006	1830 306	1830 606	1830 906	1430 506	BOBY	ET 306	39461	2013
1430 007	1830 007	1830 307	1830 607	1830 907	1430 507	BOBY	ET 307	39468	2013
1430 008	1830 008	1830 308	1830 608	1830 908	1430 508	BOBY	ET 308	39475	2013
1430 009	1830 009	1830 309	1830 609	1830 909	1430 509	BOBY	ET 309	39482	2013
1430 010	1830 010	1830 310	1830 610	1830 910	1430 510	BOBY	ET 310	39489	2013
1430 011	1830 011	1830 311	1830 611	1830 911	1430 511	BOBY	ET 311	39496	2013
1430 012	1830 012	1830 312	1830 612	1830 912	1430 512	BOBY	ET 312	39503	2013
1430 013	1830 013	1830 313	1830 613	1830 913	1430 513	BOBY	ET 313	39510	2013
1430 014	1830 014	1830 314	1830 614	1830 914	1430 514	BOBY	ET 314	39517	2013
1430 015	1830 015	1830 315	1830 615	1830 915	1430 515	BOBY	ET 315	39524	2013
1430 016	1830 016	1830 316	1830 616	1830 916	1430 516	BOBY	ET 316	39531	2013
1430 017	1830 017	1830 317	1830 617	1830 917	1430 517	BOBY	ET 317	39538	2013
1430 018	1830 018	1830 318	1830 618	1830 918	1430 518	BOBY	ET 318	39545	2013
1430 019	1830 019	1830 319	1830 619	1830 919	1430 519	BOBY	ET 319	39552	2013
1430 020	1830 020	1830 320	1830 620	1830 920	1430 520	BOBY	ET 320	39559	2013
1430 021	1830 021	1830 321	1830 621	1830 921	1430 521	BOBY	ET 321	39566	2013
1430 022	1830 022	1830 322	1830 622	1830 922	1430 522	BOBY	ET 322	39573	2013
1430 023	1830 023	1830 323	1830 623	1830 923	1430 523	BOBY	ET 323	39580	2013
1430 024	1830 024	1830 324	1830 624	1830 924	1430 524	BOBY	ET 324	39587	2013
1430 025	1830 025	1830 325	1830 625	1830 925	1430 525	BOBY	ET 325	39594	2013
1430 026	1830 026	1830 326	1830 626	1830 926	1430 526	BOBY	ET 326	39601	2013
1430 027	1830 027	1830 327	1830 627	1830 927	1430 527	BOBY	ET 327	39608	2013
1430 028	1830 028	1830 328	1830 628	1830 928	1430 528	BOBY	ET 328	39615	2013

Name:

1430 002　　FREILASSING

The next order for 6-section units came from Nordbahn, which uses them for trains between Hamburg and Itzhoe and Hamburg–Wrist–Kellinghusen. This company has used suffixes after the set number to denote the cars e.g. ET6.01 A/C/D/E/F/B. Details as 1430 001–028 above except:

Accommodation: 24/296(?) 1T 1TD.

Car 1	Car 2	Car 3	Car 4	Car 5	Car 6	Co	Unit No	Works No	Built
1430 036	1830 036	1830 336	1830 636	1830 936	1430 536	NBE	ET6.01	40054	2014
1430 037	1830 037	1830 337	1830 637	1830 937	1430 537	NBE	ET6.02	40061	2014
1430 038	1830 038	1830 338	1830 638	1830 938	1430 538	NBE	ET6.03	40068	2014
1430 039	1830 039	1830 339	1830 639	1830 939	1430 539	NBE	ET6.04	40075	2014
1430 040	1830 040	1830 340	1830 640	1830 940	1430 540	NBE	ET6.05	40082	2014
1430 041	1830 041	1830 341	1830 641	1830 941	1430 541	NBE	ET6.06	40089	2014
1430 042	1830 042	1830 342	1830 642	1830 942	1430 542	NBE	ET6.07	40096	2014
1430 043	1830 043	1830 343	1830 643	1830 943	1430 543	NBE	ET6.08	40105	2014

ALSTOM CORADIA CONTINENTAL

Like the other builders, Alstom offers its EMUs in various formations but also has short or long carriages! Otherwise trains are similar as they have to comply with the same regulations about disabled access etc. 3-car, 4-car and 5-car sets have appeared so far.

94 80 0440.1   4-SECTION ARTICULATED UNITS

When Agilis won the contract for services in the Regensburg area it turned to Alstom for it trains, which operate Plattling–Regensburg–Neumarkt (Oberpfalz) and Landshut–Regensburg–Ulm.

Built: 2010–11.
Builder–Mechanical Parts: Alstom.
Builder–Electrical Parts: Alstom.
Wheel Arrangement: Bo-Bo-2-Bo-Bo.
Traction Motors: **Continuous Rating:**
Accommodation:
Weight: **Wheel Diameter:**
Length over Couplers: 74.20 m.   **Maximum Speed:**
Door Step Height: **Maximum Tractive Effort:**

Car 1	Car 2	Car 3	Car 4	Company	Unit Number	Built	Names
440 101	441 101	441 601	440 601	AGIE	ET 101	2010	
440 102	441 102	441 602	440 602	AGIE	ET 102	2010	
440 103	441 103	441 603	440 603	AGIE	ET 103	2010	Abensberg
440 104	441 104	441 604	440 604	AGIE	ET 104	2010	Regensburg
440 105	441 105	441 605	440 605	AGIE	ET 105	2010	
440 106	441 106	441 606	440 606	AGIE	ET 106	2011	Günzburg
440 107	441 107	441 607	440 607	AGIE	ET 107	2011	
440 108	441 108	441 608	440 608	AGIE	ET 108	2011	Ulm

94 80 0440.2   5-SECTION ARTICULATED UNITS

The Nordwestbahn won the contract to run S-Bahn services around Bremen and ordered from Alstom 17 5-car EMUs and 18 3-car EMUs for its four S-Bahn routes radiating from Bremen.

Built: 2010–11.
Builder–Mechanical Parts: Alstom.
Builder–Electrical Parts: Alstom.
Wheel Arrangement: Bo-Bo-2-2-Bo-Bo.
Traction Motors: **Continuous Rating:**
Accommodation:
Weight: **Wheel Diameter:**
Length over Couplers: 87.00 m.   **Maximum Speed:**
Door Step Height: **Maximum Tractive Effort:**

Car 1	Car 2	Car 3	Car 4	Car 5	Company	Unit Number	Built
440 210	441 210	841 210	441 710	440 710	NWB	ET 440 210	2010
440 211	441 211	841 211	441 711	440 711	NWB	ET 440 211	2010
440 212	441 212	841 212	441 712	440 712	NWB	ET 440 212	2010
440 213	441 213	841 213	441 713	440 713	NWB	ET 440 213	2010
440 214	441 214	841 214	441 714	440 714	NWB	ET 440 214	2010
440 215	441 215	841 215	441 715	440 715	NWB	ET 440 215	2010
440 216	441 216	841 216	441 716	440 716	NWB	ET 440 216	2010
440 217	441 217	841 217	441 717	440 717	NWB	ET 440 217	2010
440 218	441 218	841 218	441 718	440 718	NWB	ET 440 218	2011
440 219	441 219	841 219	441 719	440 719	NWB	ET 440 219	2011
440 220	441 220	841 220	441 720	440 720	NWB	ET 440 220	2011
440 221	441 221	841 221	441 721	440 721	NWB	ET 440 221	2011
440 222	441 222	841 222	441 722	440 722	NWB	ET 440 222	2011
440 223	441 223	841 223	441 723	440 723	NWB	ET 440 223	2011
440 224	441 224	841 224	441 724	440 724	NWB	ET 440 224	2011
440 225	441 225	841 225	441 725	440 725	NWB	ET 440 225	2011
440 226	441 226	841 226	441 726	440 726	NWB	ET 440 226	2011

94 80 0440.3/4   3-SECTION ARTICULATED UNITS

Both Nordwestbahn and Agilis ordered 3-car EMUs but they differ as the NWB sets have three powered bogies (440.3) whereas the Agilis units have all bogies powered. (440.4).

Built: 2010–11.
Builder–Mechanical Parts: Alstom.
Builder–Electrical Parts: Alstom.
Wheel Arrangement: Bo-2-Bo-Bo (440.3), Bo-Bo-Bo-Bo (440.4).

Traction Motors:			**Continuous Rating:**		
Accommodation:					
Weight:			**Wheel Diameter:**		
Length over Couplers: 57.80 m.			**Maximum Speed:**		
Door Step Height:			**Maximum Tractive Effort:**		

Car 1	Car 2	Car 3	Company	Unit Number	Built	Names
440 330	441 830	440 830	NWB	ET 440 330	2010	Weserkurier
440 331	441 831	440 831	NWB	ET 440 331	2010	Verkersverbund Bremen Niedersachsen
440 332	441 832	440 832	NWB	ET 440 332	2010	Eisbären Bremerhaven
440 333	441 833	440 833	NWB	ET 440 333	2010	
440 334	441 834	440 834	NWB	ET 440 334	2010	
440 335	441 835	440 835	NWB	ET 440 335	2010	Waterfront Bremen
440 336	441 836	440 836	NWB	ET 440 336	2010	
440 337	441 837	440 837	NWB	ET 440 337	2010	
440 338	441 838	440 838	NWB	ET 440 338	2010	Weserkurier
440 339	441 839	440 839	NWB	ET 440 339	2010	
440 340	441 840	440 840	NWB	ET 440 340	2010	
440 341	441 841	440 841	NWB	ET 440 341	2010	
440 342	441 842	440 842	NWB	ET 440 342	2010	
440 343	441 843	440 843	NWB	ET 440 343	2010	
440 344	441 844	440 844	NWB	ET 440 344	2011	
440 345	441 845	440 845	NWB	ET 440 345	2011	
440 346	441 846	440 846	NWB	ET 440 346	2011	
440 347	441 847	440 847	NWB	ET 440 347	2011	

Car 1	Car 2	Car 3	Company	Unit Number	Built	Names
440 401	441 401	440 901	AGIE	ET 401	2010	Straubing
440 402	441 402	440 902	AGIE	ET 402	2010	Saal a.d.Donau
440 403	441 403	440 903	AGIE	ET 403	2010	Abensberg
440 404	441 404	440 904	AGIE	ET 404	2010	
440 405	441 405	440 905	AGIE	ET 405	2010	
440 406	441 406	440 906	AGIE	ET 406	2010	
440 407	441 407	440 907	AGIE	ET 407	2010	
440 408	441 408	440 908	AGIE	ET 408	2010	Albertus Magnus Stadt Lauingen
440 409	441 409	440 909	AGIE	ET 409	2010	
440 410	441 410	440 910	AGIE	ET 410	2010	
440 411	441 411	440 911	AGIE	ET 411	2010	
440 412	441 412	440 912	AGIE	ET 412	2010	
440 413	441 413	440 913	AGIE	ET 413	2010	
440 414	441 414	440 914	AGIE	ET 414	2010	Regensburg Arkaden
440 415	441 415	440 915	AGIE	ET 415	2010	
440 416	441 416	440 916	AGIE	ET 416	2011	
440 417	441 417	440 917	AGIE	ET 417	2011	
440 418	441 418	440 918	AGIE	ET 418	2011	

98 80 1440.1 4-SECTION ARTICULATED UNITS

Zweckverband Großraum Braunschweig GmbH (ZGB) awarded the contract for electric train services in East Niedersachsen to Metronom. No surprise as this firm is based in Niedersachsen and it was also no surprise that the order for EMUs went to Alstom - also based in Niedersachsen! Apart from the fact that 4-car sets have been ordered the only data that has surfaced is the overall length will be 73.30 m. All units are leased by ZGB.

Car 1	Car 2	Car 3	Car 4	Company	Unit Number	Built
1440 101	1441 101	1441 601	1440 601	ZGB/ME		2015
1440 102	1441 102	1441 602	1440 602	ZGB/ME		2015
1440 103	1441 103	1441 603	1440 603	ZGB/ME		2015
1440 104	1441 104	1441 604	1440 604	ZGB/ME		2015
1440 105	1441 105	1441 605	1440 605	ZGB/ME		2015
1440 106	1441 106	1441 606	1440 606	ZGB/ME		2015
1440 107	1441 107	1441 607	1440 607	ZGB/ME		2015
1440 108	1441 108	1441 608	1440 608	ZGB/ME		2015
1440 109	1441 109	1441 609	1440 609	ZGB/ME	-	2015
1440 110	1441 110	1441 610	1440 610	ZGB/ME		2015
1440 111	1441 111	1441 611	1440 611	ZGB/ME		2015
1440 112	1441 112	1441 612	1440 612	ZGB/ME		2015
1440 113	1441 113	1441 613	1440 613	ZGB/ME		2015
1440 114	1441 114	1441 614	1440 614	ZGB/ME		2015
1440 115	1441 115	1441 615	1440 615	ZGB/ME		2015
1440 116	1441 116	1441 616	1440 616	ZGB/ME		2015
1440 117	1441 117	1441 617	1440 617	ZGB/ME		2015
1440 118	1441 118	1441 618	1440 618	ZGB/ME		2015
1440 119	1441 119	1441 619	1440 619	ZGB/ME		2015
1440 120	1441 120	1441 620	1440 620	ZGB/ME		2015

98 80 1440.2 5-SECTION ARTICULATED UNITS

Alstom has indicated that it is to provide Verkehrsbetriebe Mittelsachsen with 13 3-car and 16 5-car EMUs. These are for use from 2016. Further details are awaited.

Car 1	Car 2	Car 3	Car 4	Car 5	Company	Unit No	Built
1440 201	1441 201	1840 201	1441 701	1440 701	MRB		2015
1440 202	1441 202	1840 202	1441 702	1440 702	MRB		2015
1440 203	1441 203	1840 203	1441 703	1440 703	MRB		2015
1440 204	1441 204	1840 204	1441 704	1440 704	MRB		2015
1440 205	1441 205	1840 205	1441 705	1440 705	MRB		2015
1440 206	1441 206	1840 206	1441 706	1440 706	MRB		2015
1440 207	1441 207	1840 207	1441 707	1440 707	MRB		2015
1440 208	1441 208	1840 208	1441 708	1440 708	MRB		2015
1440 209	1441 209	1840 209	1441 709	1440 709	MRB		2015
1440 210	1441 210	1840 210	1441 710	1440 710	MRB		2015
1440 211	1441 211	1840 211	1441 711	1440 711	MRB		2015
1440 212	1441 212	1840 212	1441 712	1440 712	MRB		2015
1440 213	1441 213	1840 213	1441 713	1440 713	MRB		2015
1440 214	1441 214	1840 214	1441 714	1440 714	MRB		2015
1440 215	1441 215	1840 215	1441 715	1440 715	MRB		2015
1440 216	1441 216	1840 216	1441 716	1440 716	MRB		2015

BOMBARDIER TALENT 2

Talent 2 EMUs from Bombardier are like Alstom Coradia units; a standard product available in 2, 3, 4, and 5-section versions. So far DB Regio has been the largest customer but now private operators are also acquiring these units. Although a standard product, the inclusion of ticket machines, vending machines etc., means each variation needs a separate operating licence. Consequently there have been some delays in getting units into traffic, especially with DB. The authorisation processes have now been revised resulting in units being cleared for service quicker.

94 80 1442.1   3-SECTION ARTICULATED UNITS

The 442 series is the Bombardier Talent 2 EMU, which like those of its competitors can be produced in varying lengths according to customer demand. The 442.1xx are 3-car units up to now delivered only to DB, but other operators are now beginning to receive these sets.

SWEG ordered two 3-car units which surprisingly were numbered completely differently to the other batches then in traffic.

Built: 2013
Builder–Mechanical Parts: Bombardier.
Builder–Electrical Parts: Bombardier.
Wheel Arrangement: Bo-2-2-Bo.
Traction Motors: 4 x 505 kW.   **Continuous/Maximum Rating:** 2200 kW.
Accommodation:
Weight: **Wheel Diameter:**
Length over Couplers: **Maximum Speed:**
Door Step Height: **Maximum Tractive Effort:**

Car 1	Car 2	Car 3	Company	Unit Number	Built
1442 150	1843 150	1442 650	SWEG	ET 150	2013
1442 151	1843 151	1442 651	SWEG	ET 151	2013

▲ Südwestdeutsche Verkehrs (SWEG) obtained two 3-section Bombardier Talent 2 articulated EMUs, principally for working on the Münstertalbahn branch line. 94 80 1442 150, running number ET 150, is seen between Bad Krozingen and Staufen with a train to Münstertal on 25 July 2014. **Matthias Müller**

94 80 9442.1   3-SECTION ARTICULATED UNITS

Abellio has won the contract to run services radiating from Halle and Leipzig as Abellio Rail Mitteldeutschland GmbH. The trains are already appearing for taking over services in December 2015.

Car 1	Car 2	Car 3	Company	Unit Number	Built
9442 101	9843 101	9442 601	ABRM		20
9442 102	9843 102	9442 602	ABRM		20
9442 103	9843 103	9442 603	ABRM		20
9442 104	9843 104	9442 604	ABRM		20
9442 105	9843 105	9442 605	ABRM		20
9442 106	9843 106	9442 606	ABRM		20
9442 107	9843 107	9442 607	ABRM		20
9442 108	9843 108	9442 608	ABRM		20
9442 109	9843 109	9442 609	ABRM		20
9442 110	9843 110	9442 610	ABRM		20
9442 111	9843 111	9442 611	ABRM		20
9442 112	9843 112	9442 612	ABRM		20
9442 113	9843 113	9442 613	ABRM		20
9442 114	9843 114	9442 614	ABRM		20
9442 115	9843 115	9442 615	ABRM		20
9442 116	9843 116	9442 616	ABRM		20
9442 117	9843 117	9442 617	ABRM		20
9442 118	9843 118	9442 618	ABRM		20
9442 119	9843 119	9442 619	ABRM		20
9442 120	9843 120	9442 620	ABRM		20

National Express Rail GmbH has ordered 25 3-car sets for use in the Ruhr area.

Car 1	Car 2	Car 3	Company	Unit Number	Built
9442 151	9843 151	9442 651	NXG		2014
9442 152	9843 152	9442 652	NXG		2014
9442 153	9843 153	9442 653	NXG		2014
9442 154	9843 154	9442 654	NXG		2014
9442 155	9843 155	9442 655	NXG		2014
9442 156	9843 156	9442 656	NXG		2014
9442 157	9843 157	9442 657	NXG		20
9442 158	9843 158	9442 658	NXG		20
9442 159	9843 159	9442 659	NXG		20
9442 160	9843 160	9442 660	NXG		20

94 80 9442.3   5-SECTION ARTICULATED UNITS

Built:
Builder–Mechanical Parts: Bombardier.
Builder–Electrical Parts: Bombardier.
Wheel Arrangement:
Traction Motors: **Continuous/Maximum Rating:**
Accommodation:
Weight: **Wheel Diameter:**
Length over Couplers: **Maximum Speed:**
Door Step Height: **Maximum Tractive Effort:**

Abellio has ordered some 5-car sets for its Mitteldeutschland services.

Car 1	Car 2	Car 3	Car 4	Car 5	Company	Unit Number	Built
9442 301	9843 301	9443 301	9443 801	9442 801	ABRM		20
9442 302	9843 302	9443 302	9443 802	9442 802	ABRM		20
9442 303	9843 303	9443 303	9443 803	9442 803	ABRM		20
9442 304	9843 304	9443 304	9443 804	9442 804	ABRM		20
9442 305	9843 305	9443 305	9443 805	9442 805	ABRM		20
9442 306	9843 306	9443 306	9443 806	9442 806	ABRM		20
9442 307	9843 307	9443 307	9443 807	9442 807	ABRM		20
9442 308	9843 308	9443 308	9443 808	9442 808	ABRM		20

9442 309	9843 309	9443 309	9443 809	9442 809	ABRM		20
9442 310	9843 310	9443 310	9443 810	9442 810	ABRM		20
9442 311	9843 311	9443 311	9443 811	9442 811	ABRM		20
9442 312	9843 312	9443 312	9443 812	9442 812	ABRM		20
9442 313	9843 313	9443 313	9443 813	9442 813	ABRM		20
9442 314	9843 314	9443 314	9443 814	9442 814	ABRM		20
9442 315	9843 315	9443 315	9443 815	9442 815	ABRM		20

National Express for its services in the Ruhr area has also ordered some 5-car sets.

Car 1	Car 2	Car 3	Car 4	Car 5	Company	Unit Number	Built
9442 351	9843 351	9443 351	9443 851	9442 851	NXG		20
9442 352	9843 352	9443 352	9443 852	9442 852	NXG		20
9442 353	9843 353	9443 353	9443 853	9442 853	NXG		20
9442 354	9843 354	9443 354	9443 854	9442 854	NXG		20
9442 355	9843 355	9443 355	9443 855	9442 855	NXG		20
9442 356	9843 356	9443 356	9443 856	9442 856	NXG		20
9442 357	9843 357	9443 357	9443 857	9442 857	NXG		20
9442 358	9843 358	9443 358	9443 858	9442 858	NXG		20
9442 359	9843 359	9443 359	9443 859	9442 859	NXG		20
9442 360	9843 360	9443 360	9443 860	9442 860	NXG		20
9442 361	9843 361	9443 361	9443 861	9442 861	NXG		20
9442 362	9843 362	9443 362	9443 862	9442 862	NXG		20
9442 363	9843 363	9443 363	9443 863	9442 863	NXG		20
9442 364	9843 364	9443 364	9443 864	9442 864	NXG		20
9442 365	9843 365	9443 365	9443 865	9442 865	NXG		20
9442 366	9843 366	9443 366	9443 866	9442 866	NXG		20
9442 367	9843 367	9443 367	9443 867	9442 867	NXG		20
9442 368	9843 368	9443 368	9443 868	9442 868	NXG		20
9442 369	9843 369	9443 369	9443 869	9442 869	NXG		20
9442 370	9843 370	9443 370	9443 870	9442 870	NXG		20

94 80 0445   4-CAR DOUBLE-DECK UNITS

Bombardier produced a prototype double-deck EMU which was tested around Dresden, but the idea did not catch on. The first production double-deck EMUs have come from Stadler which has provided 16 KISS sets for ODEG services through Berlin. The units are of welded aluminium construction and there are two sets of sliding doors per carriage. Sliding bridge plates cover the gap between the train and the platform. There are several multi purpose areas on the lower decks.

Built: 2012.
Builder–Mechanical Parts: Stadler Pankow.
Builder–Electrical Parts: Not quoted.
Wheel Arrangement: 2-Bo + 2-2 + 2-2 + Bo-2.
Traction Motors: 4 x 500 kW.   **Continuous Rating:** 2000 kW.
Accommodation: 24/324(80) 2T 1TD.
Weight: 205.80 tonnes.   **Wheel Diameter:** 920 mm.
Length over Couplers: 105.22 m.   **Maximum Speed:** 160 km/h.
Door Step Height: 600 mm.   **Maximum Tractive Effort:** 200 kN.

b   owned by BeNEX; n: owned by NETINERA

Car 1	Car 2	Car 3	Car 4	Notes	Company	Unit Number	Works No	Built
445 100	446 100	446 600	445 600	b	ODEG	ET445 100	39023	2012
445 101	446 101	446 601	445 601	b	ODEG	ET445 101	39028	2012
445 102	446 102	446 602	445 602	b	ODEG	ET445 102	39033	2012
445 103	446 103	446 603	445 603	b	ODEG	ET445 103	39038	2012
445 104	446 104	446 604	445 604	b	ODEG	ET445 104	39043	2012
445 105	446 105	446 605	445 605	b	ODEG	ET445 105	39048	2012
445 106	446 106	446 606	445 606	b	ODEG	ET445 106	39053	2012
445 107	446 107	446 607	445 607	b	ODEG	ET445 107	39058	2012
445 108	446 108	446 608	445 608	b	ODEG	ET445 108	38983	2012
445 109	446 109	446 609	445 609	n	ODEG	ET445 109	38988	2012
445 110	446 110	446 610	445 610	n	ODEG	ET445 110	38993	2012

445 111	446 111	446 611	445 611	n	ODEG	ET445 111	38998	2012
445 112	446 112	446 612	445 612	n	ODEG	ET445 112	39003	2012
445 113	446 113	446 613	445 613	n	ODEG	ET445 113	39008	2012
445 114	446 114	446 614	445 614	n	ODEG	ET445 114	39013	2012
445 115	446 115	446 615	445 615	n	ODEG	ET445 115	39018	2012

Name:

445 115   Eberswalde

94 80 x445   6-CAR DOUBLE-DECK UNITS

When Westfalenbahn won the contract to run the Braunschweig–Hannover–Minden–Bielefeld/
Rheine service they surprised everyone by ordering 6-car double-deck KISS EMUs from
Stadler. These are due to appear early in 2015 ready for taking over the service at the December
timetable change. Initial data quotes space for 18 bicycles but can be 42 spaces in the summer!
Each carriage has two sets of sliding doors and bridge plates are provided to cover the gap
between train and platform. Further details are awaited.

Built: 2015.
Builder–Mechanical Parts: Stadler Pankow.
Builder–Electrical Parts: Not quoted.
Wheel Arrangement: 2-Bo + 2-2 + Bo-2 + 2-2 + 2-2 + 2-Bo.
Traction Motors: 6 x 500 kW.   **Continuous Rating:** 3000 kW.
Accommodation: 35/523(69) 3T 1TD.
Weight: **Wheel Diameter:**
Length over Couplers: 156.45 m.   **Maximum Speed:** 160 km/h.
Door Step Height: **Maximum Tractive Effort:**

Car 1	Car 2	Car 3	Car 4	Car 5	Car 6	Company	Unit Number	Works No	Built
445 201	xx	xx	xx	xx	445 701	WFB	ET6.01	40315	2015
445 202					445 702	WFB	ET6.02	40322	2015
445 203					445 703	WFB	ET6.03	40329	2015
445 204					445 704	WFB	ET6.04	40336	2015
445 205					445 705	WFB	ET6.05	40343	2015
445 206					445 706	WFB	ET6.06	40350	2015
445 207					445 707	WFB	ET6.07	40357	2015
445 208					445 708	WFB	ET6.08	40364	2015
445 209					445 709	WFB	ET6.09	40371	2015
445 210					445 710	WFB	ET6.10	40378	2015
445 211					445 711	WFB	ET6.11	40385	2015
445 212					445 712	WFB	ET6.12	40392	2015
445 213					445 713	WFB	ET6.13	40399	2015

94 80 0450   GT8-100C/2S
3-SECTION ARTICULATED TRAM-TRAIN UNITS

AVG/Karlsruhe has become well known for its Tram-Train system and indeed was the first major
city to explore such a system, now recognised as the Karlsruhe Model; many other cities are
now contemplating such moves. Quite simply the tram tracks are connected to DB infrastructure
with the Tram-Trains taking over former DB local services. The system has been considerably
extended and late in 2014 the latest extension from Heilbronn to Sinsheim and Neckerelz came
into use. The units are dual voltage and typical trams but special mention must be made that
four have bistro sections! Note that four units are owned by DB; these are listed in German
Railways Part 1.

Built: 1991–95.
Builder: Duewag.
Wheel Arrangement: B-2-2-B.   **Systems:** 750 V DC, 15 kV AC 16.7 Hz.
Traction Motors: 2 x 280 kW DC.   **Continuous/Maximum Rating:**
Accommodation: –/97 (801–808 –/100).
Weight: 73.50 tonnes.   **Wheel Diameter:** 700 mm.
Length over Couplers: 37.61 m.   **Maximum Speed:** 95 km/h.
Door Step Height: 1000 mm.   **Maximum Tractive Effort:**

EVN	Company	Unit Number	Works No	Built
450 801	AVG	801	37554	1991
450 802	AVG	802	37555	1991
450 803	AVG	803	37556	1991
450 804	AVG	804	37557	1991
450 805	AVG	805	37558	1991
450 806	AVG	806	37559	1991
450 807	AVG	807	37560	1991
450 808	AVG	808	37561	1991
450 809	AVG	809	37562	1991
450 810	AVG	810	37563	1991
450 811	AVG	811	38048	1994
450 812	AVG	812	38049	1994
450 813	AVG	813	38050	1994
450 814	AVG	814	38051	1994
450 815	AVG	815	38052	1994

450 816–820 are owned by DB.

EVN	Company	Unit Number	Works No	Built
450 821	AVG	821	38058	1994
450 822	AVG	822	38059	1994
450 823	AVG	823	38060	1994
450 824	AVG	824	38061	1994
450 825	AVG	825	38062	1994
450 826	AVG	826	38063	1994
450 827	AVG	827	38064	1994
450 828	AVG	828	38065	1994
450 829	AVG	829	38066	1994
450 830	AVG	830	38067	1994
450 831	AVG	831	38359	1995
450 832	AVG	832	38360	1995
450 833	AVG	833	38361	1995
450 834	AVG	834	38362	1995
450 835	AVG	835	38363	1995
450 836	AVG	836	38364	1995

94 80 0450   GT8-100D/2S-M
3-SECTION ARTICULATED TRAM-TRAIN UNITS

As the AVG/Karlsruhe system expanded another batch of slightly different units were ordered, with units 845-848 being fitted with bistros! Ticket machines and CCTV have recently been installed in all units.

Built: 1997–2005.
Builder: Duewag/Siemens.
Wheel Arrangement: Bo-2-2-Bo.
Traction Motors: 4 x 127 kW (3 phase asynchronous).
Accommodation: –/100 (845–848 & 900–922 –/85 1T).
Weight: 73.50 tonnes.
Length over Couplers: 37.61 m.
Door Step Height: 580–630 mm.

Systems: 750 V DC, 15 kV AC 16.7 Hz.
Continuous/Maximum Rating:

Wheel Diameter: 740 mm.
Maximum Speed: 100 km/h.
Maximum Tractive Effort:

EVN	Company	Unit Number	Works No	Built
450 837	AVG	837	38602	1997
450 838	AVG	838	38603	1997
450 839	AVG	839	38604	1997
450 840	AVG	840	38605	1997
450 841	AVG	841	38606	1997
450 842	AVG	842	38607	1997
450 843	AVG	843	38608	1997
450 844	AVG	844	38609	1997
450 845	AVG	845	38610	1997
450 846	AVG	846	38611	1997

▲ Karlsruhe is synonymous with the tram-train concept; over 150 vehicles are now in use with Albtal-Verkehrs-Gesellschaft (AVG). Deuwag built 94 80 0450 847, running number 847, passes along Baumeisterstrasse at the corner of Rüpperer Strasse with a line S5 service from Wörth Badepark to Mühlacker on 7 July 2013. This tram-train is one of the four examples to feature an on-board Regio Bistro! **Quintus Vosman**

▼ 94 80 0450 937, running number 937, is a later design of tram-train built for AVG by Bombardier. It is seen in the sidings at Heilbronn Hbf waiting to work to Neckarsulm on 30 May 2014. **Brian Garvin**

450 847	AVG	847	38612	1997
450 848	AVG	848	38613	1997
450 849	AVG	849	38752	1997
450 850	AVG	850	38753	1997
450 851	AVG	851	38754	1997
450 852	AVG	852	38755	1997
450 853	AVG	853	38756	1997
450 854	AVG	854	38757	1997
450 855	AVG	855	38758	1997
450 856	AVG	856	38759	1997
450 857	AVG	857	38760	1997
450 858	AVG	858	38992	1999
450 859	AVG	859	38993	1999
450 860	AVG	860	38994	1999
450 861	AVG	861	38995	1999
450 862	AVG	862	38996	1999
450 863	AVG	863	38997	1999
450 864	AVG	864	38998	1999
450 865	AVG	865	38999	1999
450 866	AVG	866	39000	1999
450 867	AVG	867	39001	1999
450 868	AVG	868	39002	1999
450 869	AVG	869	39003	1999
450 870	AVG	870	39004	1999
450 871	AVG	871	39005	2000
450 872	AVG	872	39316	2000
450 873	AVG	873	39317	2000
450 874	AVG	874	39318	2000
450 875	AVG	875	39319	2000
450 876	AVG	876	39320	2000
450 877	AVG	877	39321	2000
450 878	AVG	878	41670	2002
450 879	AVG	879	41667	2002
450 880	AVG	880	41669	2002
450 881	AVG	881	41671	2002
450 882	AVG	882	41672	2002
450 883	AVG	883	41673	2002
450 884	AVG	884	41668	2002
450 885	AVG	885	41674	2002
450 886	AVG	886	41675	2002
450 887	AVG	887	41676	2002
450 888	AVG	888	41677	2002
450 889	AVG	889	41678	2002
450 890	AVG	890	41780	2002
450 891	AVG	891	41781	2002
450 892	AVG	892	41782	2002
450 893	AVG	893	41783	2002
450 894	AVG	894	41784	2002
450 895	AVG	895	41785	2002
450 896	AVG	896	41786	2002
450 897	AVG	897	41787	2002
450 898	AVG	898	41788	2002
450 899	AVG	899	41789	2002
450 900	AVG	900	42259	2003
450 901	AVG	901	42260	2004
450 902	AVG	902	42261	2004
450 903	AVG	903	42262	2004
450 904	AVG	904	42263	2004
450 905	AVG	905	42264	2004
450 906	AVG	906	42265	2004
450 907	AVG	907	42266	2004
450 908	AVG	908	42267	2004
450 909	AVG	909	42268	2004
450 910	AVG	910	42269	2004

450 911	AVG	911	42270	2004
450 912	AVG	912	43063	2004
450 913	AVG	913	43064	2004
450 914	AVG	914	43065	2004
450 915	AVG	915	43066	2004
450 916	AVG	916	43067	2005
450 917	AVG	917	43068	2005
450 918	AVG	918	43069	2005
450 919	AVG	919	43070	2005
450 920	AVG	920	43071	2005
450 921	AVG	921	43072	2005
450 922	AVG	922	43073	2005

94 80 0450   FLEXITY SWIFT/ET 2010
3-SECTION ARTICULATED TRAM-TRAIN UNITS

AVG Karlrsruhe must have had a change of heart for later extensions of the Tram-Train system as Bombardier became the chosen supplier. However there were problems getting the units authorised for service, this being eventually given in late 2014. Up to 4 units can work together but they are not compatible with the Duewag vehicles apart from being able to couple mechanically. These particular units were ordered for the Heilbronn area.

Built: 2011–13.
Builder: Bombardier, Wien.
Wheel Arrangement: Bo-2-2-Bo.   **Systems:** 750 V DC, 15 kV AC 16.7 Hz.
Traction Motors: 4 x 150 kW (3-phase asynchronous).   **Continuous/Maximum Rating:**
Accommodation: –/84(9) 1T.
Weight: 73.50 tonnes.   **Wheel Diameter:** 740 mm.
Length over Couplers: 37.03 m.   **Maximum Speed:** 100 km/h.
Door Step Height: 550 mm.   **Maximum Tractive Effort:**

EVN	Company	Unit Number	Built	Names
450 923	AVG	923	2012	Karlsruhe
450 924	AVG	924	2012	
450 925	AVG	925	2012	
450 926	AVG	926	2012	
450 927	AVG	927	2012	
450 928	AVG	928	2012	
450 929	AVG	929	2012	
450 930	AVG	930	2012	
450 931	AVG	931	2012	
450 932	AVG	932	2012	
450 933	AVG	933	2012	
450 934	AVG	934	2012	
450 935	AVG	935	2012	
450 936	AVG	936	2012	
450 937	AVG	937	2013	
450 938	AVG	938	2013	
450 939	AVG	939	2013	
450 940	AVG	940	2013	
450 941	AVG	941	2013	
450 942	AVG	942	2013	
450 943	AVG	943	2013	
450 944	AVG	944	2013	Freudenstadt
450 945	AVG	945	2013	
450 946	AVG	946	2013	
450 947	AVG	947	2013	
450 948	AVG	948	2013	
450 949	AVG	949	2013	
450 950	AVG	950	2013	
450 951	AVG	951	2013	
450 952	AVG	952	2013	

94 80 0451   FLEXITY LINK
3-SECTION ARTICULATED TRAM-TRAIN UNITS

The actual EVN for this series of Tram-Train units is not known but this is where logically they ought to fit into the scheme and because the 451 series is blank your compiler has taken the liberty to use this classification. Visitors to the area are asked to check what inscriptions are on the units.

Built: 1996–2000.
Builder–Mechanical Parts: Bombardier Wien Simmering.
Builder–Electrical Parts: Bombardier Wien Simmering.
Wheel Arrangement: Bo + Bo-Bo + Bo.　　　**Systems:** 750 V DC, 15 kV AC 16.7 Hz.
Traction Motors: 8 x 120 kW (3-phase asynchronous).　**Continuous/Maximum Rating:**
Accommodation: –/96.
Weight:　　　　　　　　　　　　　　　　**Wheel Diameter:** 660 mm.
Length over Couplers: 37.87 m.　　　　　**Maximum Speed:** 90 km/h.
Door Step Height:　　　　　　　　　　　**Maximum Tractive Effort:**

EVN	Company	Unit Number	Built
451 001	SBS	1001	1996
451 002	SBS	1002	1996
451 003	SBS	1003	1996
451 004	SBS	1004	1996
451 005	SBS	1005	1996
451 006	SBS	1006	1996
451 007	SBS	1007	1996
451 008	SBS	1008	1996
451 009	SBS	1009	1996
451 010	SBS	1010	1996
451 011	SBS	1011	1996
451 012	SBS	1012	1996
451 013	SBS	1013	1996
451 014	SBS	1014	1996
451 015	SBS	1015	1996
451 016	SBS	1016	2000
451 017	SBS	1017	2000
451 018	SBS	1018	2000
451 019	SBS	1019	2000
451 020	SBS	1020	2000
451 021	SBS	1021	2000
451 022	SBS	1022	2000
451 023	SBS	1023	2000
451 024	SBS	1024	2000
451 025	SBS	1025	2000
451 026	SBS	1026	2000
451 027	SBS	1027	2000
451 028	SBS	1028	2000

94 80 0452   REGIO CITADIS
3-SECTION ARTICULATED TRAM-TRAIN UNITS

The Kassel Regio Tram project was inspired by the Karlsruhe system so that trams can run not only on city streets but also on DB lines in the area. There is one big difference as Kassel has links onto non-electrified DB lines so there is an electro-diesel tram as well (Class 689 q.v.). Up to 4 units can work in multiple. Each unit has four sets of doors and two multi-purpose areas. Ticket machines are also installed.

Built: 2004–05.
Builder: Alstom, Salzgitter.
Wheel Arrangement: Bo-2-2-Bo.　　　　　**Systems:** 750 V DC, 15 kV AC 16.7 Hz.
Traction Motors: 4 x 150 kW.　　　　　　**Continuous/Maximum Rating:**
Accommodation:
Weight: 59.80 tonnes.　　　　　　　　　　**Wheel Diameter:**
Length over Couplers: 36.80 m.　　　　　**Maximum Speed:** 100 km/h.
Door Step Height: 360 mm.　　　　　　　**Maximum Tractive Effort:**

▲ Kassel has followed the example of Karlsruhe and introduced a tram-train network; operator Regionalbahn Kassel (RBK) chose to order Regio Citadis units from Alstom. Unit 94 80 0452 710, running number 710, enters Kassel Hbf on a special working on 29 August 2012. **Brian Garvin**

▼ Trans Regio Deutsche Regionalbahn EMUs 94 80 0460 502 and 515 pass Bornheim, between Bonn and Köln, with a train from Koblenz Hbf to Köln Messe Deutz on 11 April 2012.
Matthias Müller

Car 1	Car 2	Car 3	Company	Unit Number	Built	Names
452 501	852 701	452 701	RBK	701	2005	Hans in Glück
452 502	852 702	452 702	RBK	702	2005	Das Blau Licht
452 503	852 703	452 703	RBK	703	2005	Dornröschen
452 504	852 704	452 704	RBK	704	2005	Der Zertantzen Schuhe
452 505	852 705	452 705	RBK	705	2005	Froschkönig
452 506	852 706	452 706	RBK	706	2005	Hänsel und Gretel
452 507	852 707	452 707	RBK	707	2005	Rapunzel
452 508	852 708	452 708	RBK	708	2005	Der Eisenhans
452 509	852 709	452 709	RBK	709	2005	Der Mond
452 510	852 710	452 710	RBK	710	2005	Fundevogel
452 511	852 711	452 711	RBK	711	2005	Die Sterntaler
452 512	852 712	452 712	RBK	712	2005	Schneeweissen und Rosenrot
452 513	852 713	452 713	RBK	713	2005	Rumpelstilzchen
452 514	852 714	452 714	RBK	714	2005	Rotkäppchen
452 515	852 715	452 715	RBK	715	2005	Aschenputtel
452 516	852 716	452 716	RBK	716	2005	König Drosselbart
452 517	852 717	452 717	RBK	717	2005	Der Zaunkönig
452 518	852 718	452 718	RBK	718	2005	Mariekind

94 80 0460   3-CAR UNITS

This Siemens product is known as Desiro Main Line. In Germany, only Trans Regio Deutsche Regionalbahn GmbH Mittelrheinbahn uses them; 17 units are leased from Alpha Trains. The units are not articulated. They operate over two routes: RB 26 Köln–Andernach–Koblenz and RB 32 Koblenz–Bingen–Mainz.

Built: 2007–09.
Builder–Mechanical Parts: Siemens.
Builder–Electrical Parts: Siemens.
Wheel Arrangement: Bo-Bo + 2-2 + Bo-Bo.
Traction Motors: 8 x 325 kW.   **Continuous/Maximum Rating:**
Accommodation: –/252.
Weight: 132 tonnes.   **Wheel Diameter:**
Length over Couplers: 70.93 m.   **Maximum Speed:** 150 km/h.
Door Step Height: 800 mm.   **Maximum Tractive Effort:** 170 kN.

Car 1	Car 2	Car 3	Company	Unit Number	Works No	Built
460 001	860 001	460 501	AT/TDR	460 001	94371-73	2008
460 002	860 002	460 502	AT/TDR	460 002	94374-76	2008
460 003	860 003	460 503	AT/TDR	460 003	94377-79	2008
460 004	860 004	460 504	AT/TDR	460 004	94381-83	2008
460 005	860 005	460 505	AT/TDR	460 005	94384-86	2008
460 006	860 006	460 506	AT/TDR	460 006	94387-89	2008
460 007	860 007	460 507	AT/TDR	460 007	94390-92	2008
460 008	860 008	460 508	AT/TDR	460 008	94393-95	2008
460 009	860 009	460 509	AT/TDR	460 009	94396-98	2008
460 010	860 010	460 510	AT/TDR	460 010	94399-401	2008
460 011	860 011	460 511	AT/TDR	460 011	94402-04	2008
460 012	860 012	460 512	AT/TDR	460 012	94405-07	2008
460 013	860 013	460 513	AT/TDR	460 013	94408-10	2008
460 014	860 014	460 514	AT/TDR	460 014	94411-13	2008
460 015	860 015	460 515	AT/TDR	460 015	94414-16	2008
460 016	860 016	460 516	AT/TDR	460 016	94417-18	2008
460 017	860 017	460 517	AT/TDR	460 017		2009

3.5 CODE 95 80 – DIESEL MULTIPLE UNITS

95 80 0066   SINGLE CAR

This old railcar is EVB museum stock based at Harsefeld and was previously a Buxthude–Harsefeld unit before going to EVB. The EVN gives away its true identity – former DB VT66 904. Apart from being a 1A-A1 DMR, the technical details need further research.

EVN	Company	Unit Number	Builder	Works No	Built	Notes
0066 904	EVB	VT 175	Wumag	761	1926	Ex DB VT66 904

95 80 0133   VT2E   2-SECTION ARTICULATED UNITS

This class creates a problem in being classed as 0133 while similar units are classed as 0609! Built for AKN Eisenbahn GmbH, the design is derived from the Hamburg Hochbahn DT3 EMUs. The units are used on the AKN lines to the north of Hamburg and are due to be withdrawn from 2015 onwards.

Built: 1976–77.
Builder: LHB.
Wheel Arrangement: Bo-2-Bo.   **Transmission:** Electric.
Engine: 2 MAN D3256 BTYUE or Cummins M11 of 242 kW.
Accommodation: –/88.
Weight: 51.90 tonnes.   **Wheel Diameter:**
Length over Couplers: 30.13 m.   **Maximum Speed:** 88 km/h.
Door Step Height: **Maximum Tractive Effort:**

Car 1	Car 2	Company	Unit Number	Works No	Built	Notes
0133 232	0133 732	AKN	VT2.32	02A/B	1976	
0133 233	0133 733	AKN	VT2.33	03A/B	1976	
0133 234	0133 734	AKN	VT2.34	04A/B	1976	
0133 235	0133 735	AKN	VT2.35	05A/B	1976	
0133 236	0133 736	AKN	VT2.36	16A/06B	1976	VT2 36A ex 2.46A
0133 237	0133 737	AKN	VT2.37	07A/B	1976	
0133 238	0133 738	AKN	VT2.38	08A/B	1976	
0133 239	0133 739	AKN	VT2.39	09A/B	1976	
0133 240	0133 740	AKN	VT2.40	10A/B	1976	
0133 241	0133 741	AKN	VT2.41	11A/B	1976	
0133 242	0133 742	AKN	VT2.42	01A/12B	1976	VT2.42A ex 2.31A
0133 243	0133 743	AKN	VT2.43	13A/B	1977	
0133 244	0133 744	AKN	VT2.44	14A/B	1977	
0133 245	0133 745	AKN	VT2.45	15A/B	1977	
0133 246	0133 746	AKN	VT2.46	06A/16B	1977	VT2.46A ex 36A

95 80 0133   VTA   2-SECTION ARTICULATED UNITS

These units are a later version of the VT2E being longer and having three-phase traction motors. Eight units were rebuilt with third rail pick-up gear to work over Hamburg S-Bahn tracks and are thus electro-diesel units. However, they do not appear to have been reclassified!

Built: 1993.
Builder: LHB.
Wheel Arrangement: Bo-2-Bo.   **Transmission:** Electric.
Engine: 2 Cummins 6 cyl. KTA-19-R2 engines providing a total of 485 kW.
Traction Motors: ABB, 4 x 125 kW asynchronous.
Accommodation: –/96.
Weight: 55.50 tonnes.   **Wheel Diameter:**
Length over Couplers: 32.62 m.   **Maximum Speed:** 105 km/h.
Door Step Height: **Maximum Tractive Effort:**

ED   Electro-diesel.

Car 1	Car 2	Company	Unit Number	Built	Notes
0133 251	0133 751	AKN	VT2.51	1993	ED
0133 252	0133 752	AKN	VT2.52	1993	ED
0133 253	0133 753	AKN	VT2.53	1993	ED
0133 254	0133 754	AKN	VT2.54	1993	ED
0133 255	0133 755	AKN	VT2.55	1993	ED
0133 256	0133 756	AKN	VT2.56	1993	ED
0133 257	0133 757	AKN	VT2.57	1993	ED
0133 258	0133 758	AKN	VT2.58	1993	Ex VGN
0133 259	0133 759	AKN	VT2.59	1993	Ex VGN
0133 260	0133 760	AKN	VT2.60	1993	Ex VGN
0133 261	0133 761	AKN	VT2.61	1993	Ex VGN
0133 262	0133 762	AKN	VT2.62	1993	
0133 263	0133 763	AKN	VT2.63	1993	
0133 264	0133 764	AKN	VT2.64	1993	
0133 265	0133 765	AKN	VT2.65	1993	
0133 266	0133 766	AKN	VT2.66	1993	
0133 267	0133 767	AKN	VT2.67	1993	
0133 268	0133 768	AKN	VT2.68	1993	ED

95 80 0301   MISCELLANEOUS RAILCARS

This series contains railcars that are in effect preserved, but registered with the EBA and thus have EVNs. But what a strange collection! Note that in some cases the EVN incorporates the unit's own number. No technical details for these unfortunately, as further research is needed!

Esslingen railcars: A first series, built 1951–57, includes units with 1A-A1, B-2 and B-B wheel arrangements, overall length of 23.35 m, weight 32–38 tonnes and 80 km/h maximum speed. Seating varies between 71 and 112. Engines are just as varied with two types of Deutz engines, a MAN and a Bussing; these vary between 145 and 220 hp. All units seem to have two engines.

A second series built 1958–61 are all B-B but a little longer at 25.03 m. Weight seems standard at 37.50 tonnes but seating varies between 84 and 98. Three types of Deutz engines and a Daimler Benz give a range of 190 to 270 hp. Each unit has two engines; maximum speed is 85 km/h.

EVN	Company	Unit Number	Builder	Works No	Built	Notes
0301 001	DEV	T 1	Gotha	2550	1936	
0301 005	HzL	VT 5	MAN	145275	1960	
0301 008	HzL	VT 8	MAN	145163	1961	
0301 009	HzL	VT 9	MAN	151129	1966	
0301 010	KML	VT 405	Esslingen	24999	1959	Nurtingen (WEG)
0301 011	KML	VT 407	Esslingen	25628	1961	Ex WEG, ex FKE VT 104
0301 012	KML	VT 408	Esslingen	25001	1959	Ex WEG, ex FKE VT 103
0301 013	AVG	452	Esslingen	25206	1958	Ex SWEG VT 108
	CLBG	VT 103	Esslingen	23499	1952	Ex SWEG
0301 015	WTB	VT 3	Esslingen	23494	1952	Ex HzL
0301 016	PBE	VT 50	Esslingen	23608	1954	Privately owned, ex KVG
0301 017	VBV		MAN			
0301 018	MEM/MKB	VT 01	Dessau	3184	1937	Ex RBG VT 12
0301 020	IGEBA	T 10	Esslingen	23343	1951	Ex ESG, ex WEG VT 402
0301 023	RSE	VT 23	MAN	142782	1956	Ex SWEG VT 23
0301 025	RSE	VT 25	MAN	145166	1960	Ex SWEG VT 25
	CLBG	VT 26	MAN	146643	1962	Ex SWEG VT 26
0301 031	ILM	VT 0511	Wismar	20235	1934	Ex OHE
0301 035	LWB	DTW 1 Anton	Esslingen	23350	1951	
0301 041	RTB	VT 1	Talbot	94821	1952	Ex JKB T 1
0301 121	DHE	VT 121	Wumag	71004	1940	
	VLO	T 3	Wumag		1935	ex GME VT 1
0301 508	TEL	GDT 0515	MaK	508	1954	Ex ACT Italy, ex OHE
0301 511	TEL	GDT 0518	MaK	511	1955	Ex ACT Italy, ex OHE
	EEB	T 1	Talbot	95135	1957	1A-1 DMR
	KML	VT 110	Esslingen	23385	1951	Ex SWEG
	KML	VT 406	Esslingen	25000	1959	Ex FKE VT 102
	OHE	VT 0508	Wismar	20299	1937	
	TWE	T 03	Wegmann	35252	1926	Ex WEG

▲ AKN Eisenbahn 2-section articulated DMU 95 80 0133 246, running number VT2.46, arrives at Elmshorn on 30 September 2008 with a line A3 service from Henstedt-Ulzburg.   **Brian Denton**

▼ The Rhein-Seig-Eisenbahn operates various tourist services in the area around Bonn. One of their MAN railcars, 95 80 0301 025, running number VT 25, is seen outside the shed at Bonn Beuel on 18 June 2013.   **Matthias Müller**

95 80 0302 — MISCELLANEOUS RAILCARS

A similar situation to the previous series. Note that both series have similar units. EVNs have not come to light for some units. No technical details as above.

EVN	Company	Unit Number	Builder	Works No	Built	Notes
0302 001	DEV	T 2	Esslingen	24480	1956	Ex NVAG
	RSE	VT 6	MAN	141756	1955	Ex SWEG VT 6
	DRE	VT 11	MAN	141757	1955	Ex SWEG VT 11
0302 009	RSE	VT 9	MAN	151436	1969	Ex SWEG VT 9
	WB	VT 1	MAN	151187	1966	Ex SWEG
0302 026		VT 26	MAN	146643	1962	Ex SWEG
0302 027	OBEV	VT 11	MAN	151132	1966	Ex SWEG VT 27
0302 028	SWEG	VT 28	MAN	151210	1967	(Endingen)
0303 001	DEV/VGH	T 3	MaK	513	1959	Ex OHE GDT 0520
	ESGBI	VT 11	Esslingen	25058	1958	Ex SWEG VT 112
	RBG	VT 07	Esslingen	23436	1952	Ex BE VT 1
	PBE	VT 50	Esslingen	23608	1954	

95 80 0504 — LVT/S — SINGLE CARS

In the 1990s Germany asked its train manufactures to come up with new types of diesel railcars for regional services. All the then existing firms came up with new ideas for trials and testing. DWA Bautzen produced this single car unit as its contribution. There was a prototype and one series delivery to the Burgenlandbahn, these latter units now being DB Class 672. DWA also produced another four units for lease or sale and it is these that are now classed as 504 (and surprisingly not 672!).

Built: 1998–99.
Builder: DWA Bautzen.
Wheel Arrangement: 1-A.
Engine: Volvo 265 kW.
Accommodation: –/56(5) 1T or –/64(5) 1T.
Weight: 23 tonnes.
Length over Couplers: 16.54 m.
Door Step Height:

Transmission: Mechanical.

Wheel Diameter:
Maximum Speed: 100 km/h.
Maximum Tractive Effort:

EVN	Company	Unit Number	Works No	Built	Notes
0504 001	VESK/EGP	VT 504 001	98-001	1998	
0504 002	VESK/EGP	VT 504 002	98-002	1998	
0504 003		672 919	98-003	1998	(Z)
0504 004		672 920	98-004	1998	(Z)
0504 005	VESK	VT 504 005	98-005	1998	Damaged
0504 006	VESK	VT 504 006	98-006	1998	

95 80 0608 — 2-CAR UNIT

This unit is the survivor of a small batch built for the U.S. Army for high ranking officers travelling around Germany; it received the nickname *"THE GENERAL"*. For many years it could be seen stabled at Heidelberg Hbf. After unification it was acquired by the GVG Tourist organisation for high quality railtours in Germany, but has seen little use in recent years. It is unlikely to see use in the near future as its operating licence has expired.

Built: 1956.
Builder: WMD.
Wheel Arrangement: 2-B.
Engine: 736 kW.
Accommodation:
Weight:
Length over Couplers:
Door Step Height:

Transmission: Hydraulic.

Wheel Diameter: Powered 940 mm, trailing 900 mm.
Maximum Speed: 140 km/h.
Maximum Tractive Effort:

Car 1	Car 2	Company	Unit Number	Works No	Built	Notes
0608 801	0908 801		608 801	1256/7	1956	Ex US Army

95 80 0609   VT/VS 2E   2-SECTION ARTICULATED UNITS

This version is classed as VT/VS because only one powerful diesel engine is provide on one car, but the wheel arrangement is the same so actually the VS is in effect an ET. These units were built for the Frankfurt–Königsteiner Eisenbahn (FKE 8 sets) and the Verkehrsverbund Hochtaunus, otherwise known as Taunusbahn (TSB 12 sets) and originally carried FKE and TSB logos. Today these lines are all part of HLB Hessenbahn GmbH. In 2006–07 units were rebuilt/refurbished by Bombardier.

Built: 1987 & 1992.
Builder: LHB Salzgitter.
Wheel Arrangement: Bo-2-Bo.   **Transmission:** Electric.
Engine: MB OM444LA of 463 kW.
Traction Motors: BBC ERG 2000 4 x 93 kW.
Accommodation: –/96 1T.
Weight: 55 tonnes.
Length over Couplers: 36.62 m.   **Wheel Diameter:**
Door Step Height: **Maximum Speed:** 100 km/h.
                                                    Maximum Tractive Effort:

Car 1	Car 2	Company	Unit Number	Works No	Built	Notes
0609 001	0609 501	HEB	VT 1	01 A/B	1987	Ex FKE
0609 002	0609 502	HEB	VT 2	2 A/B	1987	Ex FKE
0609 003	0609 503	HEB	VT 3	3 A/B	1987	Ex FKE
0609 004	0609 504	HEB	VT 4	4 A/B	1987	Ex FKE
0609 005	0609 505	HEB	VT 5	5 A/B	1987	Ex FKE
0609 006	0609 506	HEB	VT 6	6 A/B	1987	Ex FKE
0609 007	0609 507	HEB	VT 7	7 A/B	1987	Ex FKE
0609 008	0609 508	HEB	VT 8	8 A/B	1987	Ex FKE
0609 009	0609 509	HEB	VT 9	9 A/B	1987	Ex FKE
0609 011	0609 511	VHT/HEB	VT 11	11 A/B	1992	
0609 012	0609 512	VHT/HEB	VT 12	12 A/B	1992	
0609 013	0609 513	VHT/HEB	VT 13	13 A/B	1992	
0609 014	0609 514	VHT/HEB	VT 14	14 A/B	1992	
0609 015	0609 515	VHT/HEB	VT 15	15 A/B	1992	
0609 016	0609 516	VHT/HEB	VT 16	16 A/B	1992	
0609 017	0609 517	VHT/HEB	VT 17	17 A/B	1992	
0609 018	0609 518	VHT/HEB	VT 18	18 A/B	1992	
0609 019	0609 519	VHT/HEB	VT 19	19 A/B	1992	
0609 020	0609 520	VHT/HEB	VT 20	20 A/B	1992	
0609 021	0609 521	VHT/HEB	VT 21	21 A/B	1992	

95 80 0609   INTEGRAL   5-SECTION ARTICULATED UNITS

One of the last trains built by Jenbach was the Integral DMU which was a lightweight articulated DMU of no less than five sections. The only customer has been the Bayerische Oberlandbahn which uses them on routes from München to Bayrischzell, Lengries and Tegernsee with trains made of three units and splitting en route to serve these destinations. Just why these units are classed as 609 is strange as they are nothing like the VT2E units also classed as 609.

Built: 1998–99.
Builder: Integral Verkehrs Technik AG, Jenbach.
Wheel Arrangement: A-A-1-1-1-A.   **Transmission:** Hydraulic.
Engine: Three MAN D2876 LUH of 315 kW.
Accommodation: 12/152 ?T at least 1TD.
Weight: 74 tonnes.
Length over Couplers: 52.99 m.   **Wheel Diameter:**
Door Step Height: 780 mm.   **Maximum Speed:** 160 km/h.
                                                    Maximum Tractive Effort: 112 kN.

EVN	Company	Unit Number	Works No	Built	Names
0609 101	BOBY	VT 101	J3155/01	1998	München
0609 102	BOBY	VT 102	J3155/02	1998	Agatharied
0609 103	BOBY	VT 103	J3155/03	1998	Velley/Darching
0609 104	BOBY	VT 104	J3155/04	1998	Bayrischzell
0609 105	BOBY	VT 105	J3155/05	1998	Reichersbeuren

0609 106	BOBY	VT 106	J3155/06	1998	Hausham
0609 107	BOBY	VT 107	J3155/07	1998	Bad Tölz
0609 108	BOBY	VT 108	J3155/08	1998	Gaissach
0609 109	BOBY	VT 109	J3155/09	1998	Gmund/Tegernsee
0609 110	BOBY	VT 110	J3155/10	1998	Holzkirchen
0609 111	BOBY	VT 111	J3155/11	1998	Tegernsee
0609 112	BOBY	VT 112	J3155/12	1998	Miesbach
0609 113	BOBY	VT 113	J3155/13	1998	Lenggries
0609 114	BOBY	VT 114	J3155/14	1998	Fischbachau
0609 115	BOBY	VT 115	J3155/15	1998	Schaftlach
0609 116	BOBY	VT 116	J3155/16	1998	Schliersee
0609 117	BOBY	VT 117	J3155/17	1999	*Warngau*

95 80 0615   ITINO   2-SECTION ARTICULATED UNITS

The Itino started off as a development of the Adtranz Regio Shuttle DMU, but the consolidations of rolling stock builders saw the Regio Shuttle going to Stadler and the Itino concept to Bombardier. The first units were built in 2002 and went to Sweden. Later some were delivered to VIAS in Germany for services from Frankfurt/M to the Odenwald area, with a small additional batch being produced in 2010 when the line to Pfungstadt was reopened. The only other German operator with this type of unit is the Erfurter Bahn which operates just one – the prototype unit! All the VIAS units were financed by FAHMA.

Built: 2005, 2010 (123-126).
Builder: Bombardier, Hennigsdorf.
Wheel Arrangement: B-2-B.   **Transmission:** Hydraulic.
Engine: Two 12 cylinder MAN D2842LE607 of 500 kW; later two FPT 8 cylinder Vector 8 of 560 kW.
Accommodation: 12/107 1T.
Weight: 61.50 tonnes.   **Wheel Diameter:**
Length over Couplers: 39.47 m.   **Maximum Speed:** 140 km/h.
Door Step Height: **Maximum Tractive Effort:**

Car 1	Car 2	Company	Unit Number	Works No	Built
0615 101	0615 601	VIAS	VT 101	24599/00	2005
0615 102	0615 602	VIAS	VT 102	24601/02	2005
0615 103	0615 603	VIAS	VT 103	24603/04	2005
0615 104	0615 604	VIAS	VT 104	24605/06	2005
0615 105	0615 605	VIAS	VT 105	24607/08	2005
0615 106	0615 606	VIAS	VT 106	24609/10	2005
0615 107	0615 607	VIAS	VT 107	24611/12	2005
0615 108	0615 608	VIAS	VT 108	24613/14	2005
0615 109	0615 609	VIAS	VT 109	24615/16	2005
0615 110	0615 610	VIAS	VT 110	24617/18	2005
0615 111	0615 611	VIAS	VT 111	24619/20	2005
0615 112	0615 612	VIAS	VT 112	24621/22	2005
0615 113	0615 613	VIAS	VT 113	24623/24	2005
0615 114	0615 614	VIAS	VT 114	24625/26	2005
0615 115	0615 615	VIAS	VT 115	24627/28	2005
0615 116	0615 616	VIAS	VT 116	24629/30	2005
0615 117	0615 617	VIAS	VT 117	24631/32	2005
0615 118	0615 618	VIAS	VT 118	24633/34	2005
0615 119	0615 619	VIAS	VT 119	24635/36	2005
0615 120	0615 620	VIAS	VT 120	24637/38	2005
0615 121	0615 621	VIAS	VT 121	24639/40	2005
0615 122	0615 622	VIAS	VT 122	24641/42	2005
0615 123	0615 623	VIAS	VT 123	25272/73	2009
0615 124	0615 624	VIAS	VT 124	25274/75	2009
0615 125	0615 625	VIAS	VT 125	25276/77	2009
0615 126	0615 626	VIAS	VT 126	25278/79	2009

EVN	Company	Unit Number	Works No	Built	Notes
0615 201	EIB	VT 201	23953/54	2004	Itino prototype

▲ The Bayerische Oberlandbahn (BOBY) is the only operator to use these 5-section articulated lightweight DMUs from Jenbach. Units 95 80 0609 102, 110 and 117, running numbers VT 102, 110 and 117, pass München Heimeranplatz with the 1205 München Hbf to Bayrischzell on 28 February 2014.   **Robin Ralston**

▼ 95 80 0615 201, running number VT 201, is the prototype Bombardier Itino DMU. It is now in service with Erfurter Bahn (EIB) and is pictured at Erfurt Hbf on 15 August 2011.   **Keith Fender**

95 80 0620/0621   ALSTOM LINT 81   3-CAR UNITS

These are the Alstom LINT 81 DMUs currently being built. For some years Alstom produced single car units (LINT 27) and articulated two-car units (LINT 41). Now the range has been expanded to LINT 54 and LINT 81; these being two and three-car units without articulation. DB was first off the mark to order some but now private operators are also ordering them with units for Vlexx already in traffic.

For technical details see Classes 620 and 621 in German Railways Part 1.

Car 1	Car 2	Car 3	Company	Unit Number	Built
0620 401	0621 401	0620 901	Vlexx		2014
0620 402	0621 402	0620 902	Vlexx		2014
0620 403	0621 403	0620 903	Vlexx		2014
0620 404	0621 404	0620 904	Vlexx		2014
0620 405	0621 405	0620 905	Vlexx		2014
0620 406	0621 406	0620 906	Vlexx		2014
0620 407	0621 407	0620 907	Vlexx		2014
0620 408	0621 408	0620 908	Vlexx		2014
0620 409	0621 409	0620 909	Vlexx		2014
0620 410	0621 410	0620 910	Vlexx		2014
0620 411	0621 411	0620 911	Vlexx		2014
0620 412	0621 412	0620 912	Vlexx		2014
0620 413	0621 413	0620 913	Vlexx		2014
0620 414	0621 414	0620 914	Vlexx		2014
0620 415	0621 415	0620 915	Vlexx		2014
0620 416	0621 416	0620 916	Vlexx		2014
0620 417	0621 417	0620 917	Vlexx		2014
0620 418	0621 418	0620 918	Vlexx		2014

95 80 0622   ALSTOM LINT 54   2-CAR UNITS

As mentioned above these Alstom 2-car units do not feature articulation and are twin power car sets. DB was again first to order some but now private operators are also getting them with units for Erixx and Vlexx already appearing and more for AKN and NOB expected to appear in 2015.

For technical details see Class 622 in German Railways Part 1.

Car 1	Car 2	Company	Unit Number	Built
0622 201	0622 701	LNVG/Erixx		2013
0622 202	0622 702	LNVG/Erixx		2013
0622 203	0622 703	LNVG/Erixx		2013
0622 204	0622 704	LNVG/Erixx		2013
0622 205	0622 705	LNVG/Erixx		2013
0622 206	0622 706	LNVG/Erixx		2013
0622 207	0622 707	LNVG/Erixx		2014
0622 208	0622 708	LNVG/Erixx		2014
0622 209	0622 709	LNVG/Erixx		2014
0622 210	0622 710	LNVG/Erixx		2014
0622 211	0622 711	LNVG/Erixx		2014
0622 212	0622 712	LNVG/Erixx		2014
0622 213	0622 713	LNVG/Erixx		2014
0622 214	0622 714	LNVG/Erixx		2014
0622 215	0622 715	LNVG/Erixx		2014
0622 216	0622 716	LNVG/Erixx		2014
0622 217	0622 717	LNVG/Erixx		2014
0622 218	0622 718	LNVG/Erixx		2014
0622 219	0622 719	LNVG/Erixx		2014
0622 220	0622 720	LNVG/Erixx		2014
0622 221	0622 721	LNVG/Erixx		2014
0622 222	0622 722	LNVG/Erixx		2014

Car 1	Car 2	Company	Unit Number	Built
0622 223	0622 723	LNVG/Erixx		2014
0622 224	0622 724	LNVG/Erixx		2014
0622 225	0622 725	LNVG/Erixx		2014
0622 226	0622 726	LNVG/Erixx		2014
0622 227	0622 727	LNVG/Erixx		2014
0622 228	0622 728	LNVG/Erixx		2014
0622 401	0622 901	Vlexx		2014
0622 402	0622 902	Vlexx		2014
0622 403	0622 903	Vlexx		2014
0622 404	0622 904	Vlexx		2014
0622 405	0622 905	Vlexx		2014
0622 406	0622 906	Vlexx		2014
0622 407	0622 907	Vlexx		2014
0622 408	0622 908	Vlexx		2014
0622 409	0622 909	Vlexx		2014
0622 410	0622 910	Vlexx		2014
0622 411	0622 911	Vlexx		2014
0622 412	0622 912	Vlexx		2014
0622 413	0622 913	Vlexx		2014
0622 414	0622 914	Vlexx		2014
0622 415	0622 915	Vlexx		2014
0622 416	0622 916	Vlexx		2014
0622 417	0622 917	Vlexx		2014
0622 418	0622 918	Vlexx		2014
0622 419	0622 919	Vlexx		2014
0622 420	0622 920	Vlexx		2014
0622 421	0622 921	Vlexx		2014
0622 422	0622 922	Vlexx		2014
0622 423	0622 923	Vlexx		2014
0622 424	0622 924	Vlexx		2014
0622 425	0622 925	Vlexx		2014
0622 426	0622 926	Vlexx		2014
0622 427	0622 927	Vlexx		2014
0622 428	0622 928	Vlexx		2014
0622 429	0622 929	Vlexx		2014
0622 430	0622 930	Vlexx		2014
0622 431	0622 931	Vlexx		2014
0622 432	0622 932	Vlexx		2014
0622 433	0622 933	Vlexx		2014
0622 434	0622 934	Vlexx		2014
0622 435	0622 935	Vlexx		2014
0622 436	0622 936	Vlexx		2014
0622 437	0622 937	Vlexx		2014
0622 438	0622 938	Vlexx		2014
0622 439	0622 939	Vlexx		2014
0622 440	0622 940	Vlexx		2014
0622 441	0622 941	Vlexx		2014
0622 442	0622 942	Vlexx		2014
0622 443	0622 943	Vlexx		2014
0622 444	0622 944	Vlexx		2014
0622 445	0622 945	Vlexx		2014

95 80 0626   NE 81   SINGLE CARS

These single car units were introduced in 1981 as a standard unit for private operators which at that time were regarded as *Nichtbundeseigenen Eisenbahnen* (Not State Railways), hence the class description of NE 81. They can be regarded as a follow on from the early DB 627s and 628s. The private operators liked these powerful units as they could be used to haul freight wagons, thus saving the costs of a locomotive. They are still in use with some operators, mainly in southern Germany.

Built: 1981–94.
Builder: Waggon Union, Berlin.
Wheel Arrangement: B-B.   **Transmission:** Hydraulic.
Engine: 2 x MAN D2566MTUE of 199 kW or from 1993 2 x MAN D2866 LUE of 250 kW.
Accommodation: –/78 1T (Not all units built with toilets).
Weight: 46 tonnes.   **Wheel Diameter:** 900 mm.
Length over Couplers: 23.90 m.   **Maximum Speed:** 80/100 km/h.
Door Step Height: **Maximum Tractive Effort:**

EVN	Company	Unit Number	Works No	Built	Notes
0626 002	RBG	VT 02	30905	1981	
0626 008	RBG	VT 08	33626	1985	
0626 043	EGP	VT 43	30903	1981	Ex KVG VT 80
0626 044	SAB	VT 411	30902	1981	Ex WEG
0626 120	EGP	VT 120	30895	1981	
0626 121	HzL	VT 121	30896	1981	Ex SWEG
0626 122	SWEG	VT 122	30897	1981	
0626 125	SWEG	VT 125	30900	1981	(Ottenhöfen)
0626 126	SWEG	VT 126	33637	1985	(Endingen)
0626 127	SWEG	VT 127	33638	1985	(Endingen)
0626 128	SWEG	VT 128	36107	1993	Ex BOBFN VT 60; (Endingen)
0626 129	SWEG	VT 129	36108	1993	Ex BOBFN VT 61; (Endingen)
0626 130	SWEG	VT 130	36239	1994	Ex BOBFN VT 62; (Endingen)
0626 141	HzL	VT 41	36100	1993	
0626 142	HzL	VT 42	36101	1993	
0626 143	HzL	VT 43	36102	1993	
0626 410	WEG	VT 410	30901	1981	Münsingen
0626 412	WEG	VT 412	36104	1993	Ottenhöfen
0626 413	WEG	VT 413	36105	1993	Ottenhöfen
0626 420	WEG	VT 420	36234	1994	Korntal
0626 421	WEG	VT 421	36235	1994	Rudersberg
0626 422	WEG	VT 422	36236	1994	Rudersberg
?	KVG	VT 81	30904	1981	Schöllkrippen stored
0626 982	KVG	VT 82	36099	1993	In use with DB (WFB)

95 80 0627   JENBACH 5047   SINGLE CAR

Just one of the single car unit DMUs built by Jenbach as ÖBB class 5047 was exported to Germany for use on the NVAG Niebüll–Dagbüll line.

Built: 1995.
Builder: Jenbach.
Wheel Arrangement: B-2.   **Transmission:** Hydraulic.
Engine: One MTU 12V183TC12 of 419 kW.
Accommodation: 8/54.
Weight: 43.70 tonnes.   **Wheel Diameter:** 840 mm.
Length over Couplers: 25.42 m.   **Maximum Speed:** 120 km/h.
Door Step Height: **Maximum Tractive Effort:**

EVN	Company	Unit Number	Works No	Built	Notes
0627 103	NEG	T 4	3894-103	1995	Ex NVAG

95 80 0628/0629   2-CAR UNITS

Several private operators acquired units similar to DB Classes 628 and 629, either as new or second hand from DB. For technical details see Classes 628 and 629 in German Railways Part 1.

Car 1	Car 2	Company	Unit Number	Builder	Works No	Built	Notes
0628 051	0928 051	HLB/WEBA	628 051	Duewag	91341/2	1994	Ex FKE VT 51
0628 071	0629 071	HEB	VT 71	Duewag	91343/4	1994	Leased to NEG
0628 072	0629 072	HEB	VT 72	Duewag	91345/6	1994	(Z)
0628 150	0928 150	EVB	VT 150	Duewag	90323	1993	Name: Buxtehude
0628 151	0928 151	EVB	VT 151	Duewag	90321	1993	Name: Bremervörde
0628 152	0928 152	EVB	VT 152	Duewag	90325	1993	
0628 153	0928 153	EVB	VT 153	Duewag	90327	1993	Name: Harsefeld
0628 154	0928 154	EVB	VT 154	LHB	135-1	1993	Name: Beverstadt
0628 677	0928 677	WEBA	628 677	Duewag	91285	1994	Ex DB
0629 071		NEG	VT 71	Duewag	91343-44	1995	(Z); Ex FKE
0629 072		HLB/HEB		Duewag	91345-46	1995	(Z)

95 80 0632   PESA LINK II   2-SECTION ARTICULATED UNITS

The Polish firm of PESA received an order from Regentalbahn AG for 12 2-car DMUs for its Oberpfalzbahn network. The prototype was shown at Innotrans 2012. The trains started to arrive in 2014. Meanwhile a further seven units have been ordered by the Niederbarnimer Eisenbahn Geschellschaft for services to Küstrin and Gorzow but numbering details for these units have not been announced. By early March 2015 the Regentalbahn units were still awaiting EBA acceptance of the type; the order was subsequently cancelled. The units are now expected to go to Polish operators with one unit going to Basdorf for Niederbarnimer staff training.

Built: 2014–
Builder: PESA.
Wheel Arrangement: B-2-B.   **Transmission:** Hydrodynamic.
Engine: Two MTU 6H 1800 R85L of 390 kW.
Accommodation: –/124.
Weight: **Wheel Diameter:**
Length over Couplers: 43.73 m.   **Maximum Speed:** 120 km/h.
Door Step Height: **Maximum Tractive Effort:**

Car 1	Car 2	Company	Unit Number	Built
0632 001	0632 501			2014
0632 002	0632 502			2014
0632 003	0632 503			2014
0632 004	0632 504			2014
0632 005	0632 505			2014
0632 006	0632 506			2014
0632 007	0632 507			2014
0632 008	0632 508			2014
0632 009	0632 509			2014
0632 010	0632 510			2014
0632 011	0632 511			2014
0632 012	0632 512			2014

95 80 0633   PESA LINK III   3-SECTION ARTICULATED UNITS

Niederbarnimer Eisenbahn has ordered two of these PESA Link III units which should appear in 2015. DB is also receiving examples of this series. Preliminary data is given below whilst the actual numbering is still to be announced.

Built:
Builder: PESA.
Wheel Arrangement: B-2-2-B.   **Transmission:** Hydrodynamic
Engine: Two MTU 6H 1800 R85L of 565 kW = 1130kW.
Accommodation:
Weight: **Wheel Diameter:**
Length over Couplers: 57.13 m.   **Maximum Speed:** 120 km/h.
Door Step Height: **Maximum Tractive Effort:**

Car 1	Car 2	Car 3	Company	Unit Number	Built
0633					
0633					

95 80 0640   ALSTOM LINT 27   SINGLE CARS

This standard Alstom single unit LINT 27 is used by HEB and HEX. For technical details see Class 640 in German Railways Part 1.

EVN	Company	Unit Number	Built	Names
0640 101	HEB	VT 201	2004	
0640 102	HEB	VT 202	2004	
0640 103	HEB	VT 203	2004	
0640 104	HEB	VT 204	2004	
0640 105	HEB	VT 205	2004	
0640 106	HEB	VT 206	2004	
0640 107	HEB	VT 207	2004	
0640 108	HEB	VT 208	2004	
0640 109	HEB	VT 209	2004	
0640 110	HEB	VT 210	2004	
0640 121	ARL/HEX	VT 870	2005	Langenstein
0640 122	ARL/HEX	VT 871	2005	
0640 123	ARL/HEX	VT 872	2005	
0640 124	ARL/HEX	VT 873	2005	
0640 125	ARL/HEX	VT 874	2005	
0640 126	ARL/HEX	VT 875	2005	
0640 127	ARL/HEX	VT 876	2005	

95 80 0642 DESIRO CLASSIC 2-SECTION ARTICULATED UNITS

The Desiro Classic 2-car unit has been a success story for Siemens with over 300 in use in Germany; DB Regio having 234 and the balance with private operators. Siemens has a unit for its own tests with ETCS (Siemens Trainguard) for which technical details are lacking. Others are similar to the DB Regio units but there may be detail differences.

For technical details see Class 642 in German Railways Part 1.

Car 1	Car 2	Company	Unit Number	Works No	Built	Notes/Names
0642 300	0642 800	PREU	VT1.0	93374/75	2003	TRAINGUARD TEST TRAIN
0642 301	0642 801	VBG	VT 01	92385/86	2000	Kapelle Santa Clara
0642 302	0642 802	VBG	VT 02	92387/88	2000	Gemeinde Pöhl
0642 303	0642 803	VBG	VT 03	92389/90	2000	
0642 304	0642 804	VBG	VT 04	92391/92	2000	Fussballzug
0642 305	0642 805	VBG	VT 05	92393/94	2000	Marienbad / Mariánské Lázne

Car 1	Car 2	Company	Unit Number	Works No	Built	Names
0642 306	0642 806	VBG	VT 06	92395/96	2000	Vogtlandzug
0642 307	0642 807	VBG	VT 07	92397/98	2000	
0642 308	0642 808	VBG	VT 08	92399/00	2000	Gemeinde Neumarkt im Vogtland
0642 309	0642 809	VBG	VT 09	92401/02	2000	Stadt Reichenbach im Vogtland
0642 310	0642 810	VBG	VT 10	93046/47	2002	Stadt Hof
0642 311	0642 811	VBG	VT 11	93048/49	2002	
0642 312	0642 812	VBG	VT 12	93050/51	2002	Landkreis Tirschenreuth
0642 313	0642 813	VBG	VT 13	93052/53	2002	Landkreis Hof
0642 314	0642 814	VBG	VT 14	93054/55	2002	Stadt Neustadt an der Waldnaab
0642 315	0642 815	VBG	VT 15	93056/57	2002	Landkreis Neustadt an der Waldnaab
0642 316	0642 816	VBG	VT 16	93127/28	2002	Stadt Regensburg
0642 317	0642 817	VBG	VT 17	93129/30	2002	Stadt Schwandorf
0642 318	0642 818	VBG	VT 18	92131/32	2002	Stadt Nabburg
0642 319	0642 819	VBG	VT 19	92133/34	2002	Landkreis Wunsiedel im Fichtelgebirge
0642 320	0642 820	VBG	VT 20	92135/36	2002	Landkreis Regensburg
0642 321	0642 821	VBG	VT 21	92137/38	2002	Stadt Weiden
0642 322	0642 822	VBG	VT 22	92139/40	2002	Stadt Plauen
0642 323	0642 823	VBG	VT 23	92141/42	2002	Stadt Zwickau
0642 324	0642 824	VBG	VT 24	92143/44	2002	Vogtlandkreis
0642 325	0642 825	VBG	VT 25	94501/02	2008	Cheb (Eger)
0642 326	0642 826	VBG	VT 26	94503/04	2008	
0642 327	0642 827	AT/STS	642 327	92834-35	2002	Ex DSB MQ 4951/71; VT 600
0642 328	0642 828	AT/STS	642 328	92836-37	2002	Ex DSB MQ 4952/72; VT 601
0642 329	0642 829	AT/STS	642 329	92838-39	2002	Lessingstadt Kamez; Ex DSB MQ 4953/73; VT 602
0642 330	0642 830	AT/STS	642 330	92403-04	2000	Ex KVG VT 2000
0642 331	0642 831	AT/STS	642 331	92854-55	2002	Ex KVG VT 2002
0642 332	0642 832	AT/STS	642 332	93301-02	2003	Ex KVG VT 2003
0642 333	0642 833	AT/STS	642 333	92844-45	2001	Ex LSB VT 561
0642 334	0642 834	AT/STS	642 334	92846-47	2001	Ex LSB VT 562
0642 335	0642 835	AT/MRB	VT 563	92848-49	2001	To Regiojet Slovakia
0642 336	0642 836	AT/OLA	VT 564	92850-51	2001	To Regiojet Slovakia
0642 337	0642 837	AT/OLA	VT 565	92852-53	2001	To Regiojet Slovakia
0642 338	0642 838	AT/MRB	VT 560	92842-43	2001	To Regiojet Slovakia
0642 339	0642 839	AT/STS	VT 610	93147-48	2002	
0642 340	0642 840	AT/STS	VT 611	93149-50	2002	
0642 341	0642 841	AT/STS	VT 612	93151-52	2002	
0642 342	0642 842	AT/STS	VT 613	93153-54	2002	
0642 343	0642 843	AT/STS	VT 614	93155-56	2002	Bierstadt Radeberg
0642 344	0642 844	AT/STS	VT 615	93157-58	2002	To Regiojet Slovakia
0642 345	0642 845	AT/STS	VT 616	93159-60	2002	
0642 346	0642 846	AT/STS	VT 617	93161-62	2002	Rose von Sebnitz
0642 347	0642 847	AT/STS	VT 618	93145-46	2002	To Regiojet Slovakia
0642 401	0642 901	HEB	VT 301	93873-74	2005	
0642 402	0642 902	HEB	VT 302	93875-76	2005	
0642 403	0642 903	HEB	VT 303	93877-78	2005	
0642 404	0642 904	HEB	VT 304	93879-80	2005	
0642 405	0642 905	HEB	VT 305	93881-82	2005	
0642 406	0642 906	HEB	VT 306	93883-84	2005	

Another batch were acquired by ODEG; leased from BeNEX.

Car 1	Car 2	Company	Unit Number	Works No	Built	Names
0642 411	0642 911	BX/ODEG		94653-54	2008	Stadt Görlitz
0642 412	0642 912	BX/ODEG		94655-56	2008	
0642 413	0642 913	BX/ODEG		94657-58	2008	
0642 414	0642 914	BX/ODEG		94659-60	2008	
0642 415	0642 915	BX/ODEG		94561-62	2008	Lausitzer Lieblingsplätze
0642 416	0642 916	BX/ODEG		94563-64	2008	

95 80 0643   TALENT   3-SECTION ARTICULATED UNITS

These units are the same as DB Class 643s, the running numbers all being in one series. As can be seen from the tables below, numerous private operators have them and although some have changed hands as franchises have changed, even the ones in Slovakia are still registered as German units. Although a standard unit, actual seating layouts and ancillary equipment (e.g. ticket machines) may vary between operators. NWB units VT 746 & 747 were originally delivered as two-car units numbered VT 775 and 776 respectively. Similarly sets 643 301–303 had their intermediate cars added later.

For technical details see Class 643 in German Railways Part 1.

Car 1	Car 2	Car 3	Company	Unit No	Works No	Built	Notes/Names
0643 101	0943 101	0643 601	ERB	VT2.01	191300-02	2000	
0643 102	0943 102	0643 602	ERB	VT2.02	191303-05	2000	
0643 103	0943 103	0643 603	ERB	VT2.03	191306-08	2000	
0643 104	0943 104	0643 604	ERB	VT2.04	191309-11	2000	
0643 105	0943 105	0643 605	ERB	VT2.05	191312-14	2000	
0643 106	0943 106	0643 606	ERB	VT2.06	191315-17	2000	
0643 107	0943 107	0643 607	ERB	VT2.07	191395-97	2000	
0643 108	0943 108	0643 608	AT/BOBY	643 108	190633-35	1998	Ex OLA VT 0001
0643 109	0943 109	0643 609	AT/BOBY	643 109	190636-38	1998	Ex OLA VT 0002
0643 110	0943 110	0643 610	AT/BOBY	643 110	190639-41	1998	Ex OLA VT 0003
0643 111	0943 111	0643 611	AT/BOBY	643 111	190642-44	1998	Ex OLA VT 0004
0643 112	0943 112	0643 612	AT/BOBY	643 112	190645-47	1998	Ex OLA VT 0005
0643 113	0943 113	0643 613	AT/BOBY	643 113	190648-50	1998	Ex OLA VT 0006
0643 114	0943 114	0643 614	AT/BOBY	643 114	190651-53	1998	Ex OLA VT 0007
0643 115	0943 115	0643 615	AT/BOBY	643 115	190654-56	1998	Ex OLA VT 0008
0643 116	0943 116	0643 616	AT/BOBY	643 116	190657-59	1998	Ex OLA VT 0009
0643 117	0943 117	0643 617	AT/BOBY	643 117	191342-44	2000	Ex OLA VT 0010
0643 118	0943 118	0643 618	NWB	VT 728	192204-06	2005	Ex NOB VT 728

▲ Bombardier Talent 3-section articulated DMU 95 80 0643 127 has finished its work for Nordwestbahn (NWB) on 3 August 2012 and is stabled for the night at Husum Nord. This Alpha Trains owned unit has subsequently been transferred to Keolis Deutschland – Eurobahn (ERB) and now carries the running number VT 3.05.   **Matthias Müller**

0643 119	0943 119	0643 619	NWB	VT 729	192207-09	2005	Ex NOB VT 729
0643 120	0943 120	0643 620	NOB	VT 730	192210-12	2005	
0643 121	0943 121	0643 621	AT/VVRO		191017-19	1990	Ex OLA VT 0013, ex DME VT01.102
0643 122	0943 122	0643 622	AT/ERB	VT 2.08	191020-22	1999	Ex DME VT01.103
0643 123	0943 123	0643 623	AT/NWB	643 123	191023-25	1999	(Z); ex OLA VT 0012, DME VT01.104
0643 124	0943 124	0643 624	AT/ERB	VT 2.09^{II}	191014-16	1999	Ex DME VT01.101
0643 125	0943 125	0643 625	AT/ERB	VT 3.02	191811-13	2004	Ex NWB VT 721
0643 126	0943 126	0643 626	AT/ERB	VT 3.03	191814-16	2004	Ex NWB VT 722
0643 127	0943 127	0643 627	AT/ERB	VT 3.05	191820-22	2004	Ex NWB VT 724
0643 128	0943 128	0643 628	AT/ERB	VT 3.14	192225-27	2005	Ex BOBY VT 643.19, ex PEG
0643 129	0943 129	0643 629	AT/NWB	VT 643.21	192231-33	2005	
0643 228	0643 728		REGIO	VT 1001	190844-45	1999	Stadt Mettmann
0643 229	0643 729		REGIO	VT 1002	190846-47	1999	Stadt Kaarst
0643 230	0643 730		REGIO	VT 1003	190848-49	1999	Neanderthaler
0643 231	0643 731		REGIO	VT 1004	190850-51	1999	Stadt Neuss
0643 232	0643 732		REGIO	VT 1005	190852-53	1999	Kreis Neuss
0643 233	0643 733		REGIO	VT 1006	190854-55	1999	Düsseldorf
0643 234	0643 734		REGIO	VT 1007	190856-57	1999	Stadt Erkrath
0643 235	0643 735		REGIO	VT 1008	190858-59	1999	Wuppertal
0643 236	0643 736		REGIO	VT 1009	191841-42	1999	Kreis Mettmann
0643 237	0643 737		REGIO	VT 1010	191843-44	1999	Wupper
0643 238	0643 738		REGIO	VT 1011	191845-46	1999	Düssel
0643 239	0643 739		REGIO	VT 1012	191847-48	1999	Nordkanal
0643 240	0643 740		REGIO	VT 643.01	191735-36	2002	Leased to Keolis as ERB VT2.10
0643 241	0643 741		REGIO	VT 643.02	191737-38	2002	Leased to Keolis as ERB VT2.11
0643 271	0643 771		AT/NWB	VT 771	191751-52	2003	
0643 272	0643 772		AT/NWB	VT 772	191753-54	2003	
0643 273	0643 773		AT/NWB	VT 773	191755-56	2003	
0643 274	0643 774		AT/NWB	VT 774	191757-58	2003	
0643 301	0943 301	0643 801	AT/NWB	VT 701	191763-64	2003	Centre car works number 191849
0643 302	0943 302	0643 802	AT/NWB	VT 702	191765-66	2003	Centre car works number 191850
0643 303	0943 303	0643 803	AT/NWB	VT 703	191767-68	2003	Centre car works number 191851
0643 304	0943 304	0643 804	AT/NWB	VT 704	191769-71	2003	
0643 305	0943 305	0643 805	AT/NWB	VT 705	191772-74	2003	
0643 306	0943 306	0643 806	AT/NWB	VT 706	191775-77	2003	
0643 307	0943 307	0643 807	AT/NWB	VT 707	191778-80	2003	
0643 308	0943 308	0643 808	AT/NWB	VT 708	191781-83	2003	
0643 309	0943 309	0643 809	AT/NWB	VT 709	191784-86	2003	
0643 310	0943 310	0643 810	AT/NWB	VT 710	191787-89	2003	
0643 311	0943 311	0643 811	AT/NWB	VT 711	191790-92	2003	
0643 312	0943 312	0643 812	AT/NWB	VT 712	191793-95	2003	
0643 313	0943 313	0643 813	AT/NWB	VT 713	191796-98	2003	
0643 314	0943 314	0643 814	AT/NWB	VT 714	191799-01	2003	
0643 315	0943 315	0643 815	AT/NWB	VT 715	191802-04	2003	
0643 316	0943 316	0643 816	AT/NWB	VT 716	191805-07	2003	
0643 317	0943 317	0643 817	AT/NWB	VT 717	191852-54	2003	
0643 318	0943 318	0643 818	AT/NWB	VT 718	191855-57	2003	
0643 319	0943 319	0643 819	AT/NWB	VT 719	191858-60	2003	
0643 326	0943 326	0643 826	AT/NWB	VT 726	192198-00	2005	
0643 327	0943 327	0643 827	AT/NWB	VT 727	192201-03	2005	
0643 339	0943 339	0643 839	NWB	VT 739	192725-27	2006	
0643 340	0943 340	0643 840	NWB	VT 740	192728-30	2006	
0643 341	0943 341	0643 841	NWB	VT 741	192731-33	2006	

Car 1	Car 2	Car 3	Company	Unit Number	Works No	Built	Notes
0643 342	0943 342	0643 842	NWB	VT 742	192734-36	2006	
0643 343	0943 343	0643 843	NWB	VT 743	192737-39	2006	
0643 344	0943 344	0643 844	NWB	VT 744	192740-42	2006	
0643 345	0943 345	0643 845	NWB	VT 745	192743-45	2007	
0643 346	0943 346	0643 846	NWB	VT 746	191759-60	2003	Centre car added 2007, works no 192746
0643 347	0943 347	0643 847	NWB	VT 747	191761-63	2003	Centre car added 2007, works no 192747
0643 348	0943 348	0643 848	AT/ERB	VT3.01	191808-10	2004	Ex BOBY VT 720
0643 349	0943 349	0643 849	AT/ERB	VT3.04	191817-19	2004	Ex BOBY VT 723
0643 350	0943 350	0643 850	AT/ERB	VT3.06	191823-25	2004	Ex BOBY VT 725
0643 360	0943 360	0643 860	PEG	VT 643.03	191739-41	2003	Leased to Keolis as ERB VT2.12
0643 361	0943 361	0643 861	PEG	VT 643.04	191742-44	2003	
0643 362	0943 362	0643 862	PEG	VT 643.05	191745-47	2003	To Regiojet Slovakia
0643 363	0943 363	0643 863	PEG	VT 643.06	191748-50	2003	To Regiojet Slovakia
0643 364	0943 364	0643 864	AT/ERB	VT3.07	191826-28	2004	Ex PEG VT643.08
0643 365	0943 365	0643 865	AT	VT 643.09	191829-31	2004	To Regiojet Slovakia
0643 366	0943 366	0643 866	AT	VT 643.10	191832-34	2004	To Regiojet Slovakia
0643 367	0943 367	0643 867	AT	VT 643.11	191835-37	2004	To Regiojet Slovakia
0643 368	0943 368	0643 868	AT/ERB	VT3.08	191838-40	2004	Ex PEG VT 643.12
0643 369	0943 369	0643 869	AT/ERB	VT3.09	192180-82	2004	Ex PEG VT 643.13
0643 370	0943 370	0643 870		VT 643.14	192183-85	2004	To Regiojet Slovakia
0643 371	0943 371	0643 871	AT/ERB	VT3.10	192186-88	2004	Ex PEG VT 643.15
0643 372	0943 372	0643 872	AT/ERB	VT3.11	192189-91	2004	Ex PEG VT 643.16
0643 373	0943 373	0643 873	AT/ERB	VT3.12	192192-94	2004	Ex PEG VT 643.17
0643 374	0943 374	0643 874	AT/ERB	VT3.13	192195-97	2004	Ex PEG VT 643.18
0643 404	0943 404	0643 904	AT/NEBB	VT 731	192213-15	2005	
0643 405	0943 405	0643 905	AT/NEBB	VT 732	192216-18	2005	
0643 406	0943 406	0643 906	AT/NEBB	VT 733	192219-21	2005	
0643 407	0943 407	0643 907	AT/NEBB	VT 734	192222-24	2005	
0643 408	0943 408	0643 908	AT/NEBB	VT 735	192473-75	2006	
0643 409	0943 409	0643 909	AT/NEBB	VT 737	192479-81	2006	
0643 410	0943 410	0643 910	AT/NEBB	VT 738	192482-84	2006	
0643 411	0943 411	0643 911	AT/NEBB	VT 643.20	192228-30	2005	
0643 412	0943 412	0643 912	AT/NEBB	VT 736	192476-78	2006	

95 80 0646   STADLER GTW2/6   3-SECTION ARTICULATED UNITS

The Stadler GTW2/6 series production dates from 1997 and like may other Stadler products has been highly successful. As well as the DB owned units, two private operators also have them. Most units have in fact been built in Germany, initially by Bombardier, but later Stadler took over the works at Pankow. The 646 4xx series were all built by the then DWA Bautzen.

For technical details see Class 646 in German Railways Part 1.

Car 1	Car 2	Car 3	Company	Unit Number	Works No	Built
0946 040	0646 040	0946 540	Netinera/ODEG		39191-94	2011
0946 041	0646 041	0946 541	Netinera/ODEG		39195-98	2011
0946 042	0646 042	0946 542	Netinera/ODEG		39199-02	2011
0946 043	0646 043	0946 543	BX/ODEG		39203-06	2011
0946 044	0646 044	0946 544	BX/ODEG		39207-10	2011
0946 045	0646 045	0946 545	BX/ODEG		39211-14	2011
0946 401	0646 401	0946 901	HEB	VT508 101	508001	1999
0946 402	0646 402	0946 902	HEB	VT508 102	508002	1999
0946 403	0646 403	0946 903	HEB	VT508 103	508003	1999
0946 404	0646 404	0946 904	HEB	VT509 104	509001	1999
0946 405	0646 405	0946 905	HEB	VT509 105	509002	1999
0946 406	0646 406	0946 906	HEB	VT509 106	509003	1999
0946 407	0646 407	0946 907	HEB	VT509 107	509004	1999
0946 408	0646 408	0946 908	HEB	VT509 108	509005	1999
0946 409	0646 409	0946 909	HEB	VT509 109	509006	1999
0946 410	0646 410	0946 910	HEB	VT509 110	509007	1999

0946 411	0646 411	0946 911	HEB	VT509 111	509008	1999
0946 412	0646 412	0946 912	HEB	VT509 112	509009	1999
0946 413	0646 413	0946 913	HEB	VT508 113	508004	1999
0946 414	0646 414	0946 914	HEB	VT508 114	508005	1999
0946 415	0646 415	0946 915	HEB	VT508 115	508006	1999
0946 416	0646 416	0946 916	HEB	VT525 116	525001	1999
0946 417	0646 417	0946 917	HEB	VT525 117	525002	1999
0946 418	0646 418	0946 918	HEB	VT525 118	525003	1999
0946 419	0646 419	0946 919	HEB	VT526 119	526001	2000
0946 420	0646 420	0946 920	HEB	VT526 120	526002	2000
0946 421	0646 421	0946 921	HEB	VT526 121	526003	2000
0946 422	0646 422	0946 922	HEB	VT526 122	526004	2000
0946 423	0646 423	0946 923	HEB	VT526 123	526005	2000
0946 424	0646 424	0946 924	HEB	VT526 124	526006	2000
0946 425	0646 425	0946 925	HEB	VT526 125	526007	2000
0946 426	0646 426	0946 926	HEB	VT526 126	526008	2001
0946 427	0646 427	0946 927	HEB	VT526 127	526009	2001
0946 428	0646 428	0946 928	HEB	VT526 128	526010	2001
0946 429	0646 429	0946 929	HEB	VT526 129	526011	2001
0946 430	0646 430	0946 930	HEB	VT526 130	526012	2001

95 80 0648/1648   ALSTOM LINT 41
2-SECTION ARTICULATED UNITS

The Alstom Coradia LINT 41 DMU has been a success story for Alstom; DB operates a sizeable fleet and they are also very popular with private operators, principally in northern Germany as the lists below show. They can also be found in Canada, Denmark and the Netherlands. Amongst the private operators, units have been provided with more powerful engines. The 648 401–410 batch have 2 x 335 kW engines whilst the 648.2xx units with BRB, 648 420-447 and the 1648 series have 2 x 390 kW engines. Note that NWB in particular is gradually dispensing with the old VT numbers and using the shortened EVN as the running number. 0648 420 is the second unit to have carried that number; the first was scrapped following an accident in 2010. 1648 301–306 are due to be delivered during 2015–16. Seven extra units are to appear in 2015 for use on the Eifel–Westerwald–Sieg Netz, whilst in 2016 it is expected that 12 more units will appear for RBG (replacements for PESA LINK) and six for NWB.

For other technical details see Class 648 in German Railways Part 1.

Car 1	Car 2	Company	Unit Number	Built	Notes/Names
0648 010	0648 510	HML/HEB	VT 270	2011	
0648 011	0648 511	HML/HEB	VT 271	2011	
0648 012	0648 512	HML/HEB	VT 272	2011	
0648 013	0648 513	HML/HEB	VT 273	2011	
0648 014	0648 514	HML/HEB	VT 274	2011	
0648 015	0648 515	HML/HEB	VT 275	2011	
0648 016	0648 516	HML/HEB	VT 276	2011	
0648 017	0648 517	HML/HEB	VT 277	2011	
0648 018	0648 518	HML/HEB	VT 278	2011	
0648 019	0648 519	HML/HEB	VT 279	2011	
0648 020	0648 520	HML/HEB	VT 280	2011	
0648 021	0648 521	HML/HEB	VT 281	2011	
0648 022	0648 522	HML/HEB	VT 282	2011	
0648 023	0648 523	HML/HEB	VT 283	2011	
0648 024	0648 524	HML/HEB	VT 284	2011	
0648 025	0648 525	HML/HEB	VT 285	2011	
0648 026	0648 526	HML/HEB	VT 286	2011	
0648 027	0648 527	HML/HEB	VT 287	2011	
0648 028	0648 528	HML/HEB	VT 288	2011	
0648 029	0648 529	HML/HEB	VT 289	2011	
0648 030	0648 530	HML/HEB	VT 290	2011	
0648 031	0648 531	HML/HEB	VT 291	2011	
0648 032	0648 532	HML/HEB	VT 292	2011	
0648 070	0648 570	LNVG/NWB	VT 500	2000	Ex Alstom VT 707

▲ Südwestdeutsche Verkehrs (SWEG) operate a small number of these powerful NE81 single car DMUs built by Waggon Union of Berlin. Dating from 1981, 95 80 0626 125, running number VT 125, stands outside the depot at Ottenhöfen on 25 July 2014. **Matthias Müller**

▼ Abellio Rail NRW (ABRN) 95 80 1648 008, running number VT12 008, leaves Remscheid Lennep with a train from train Wuppertal Hbf to Remscheid Hbf on 29 January 2014. **Matthias Müller**

0648 071	0648 571	LNVG/NWB	VT 501	2000			
0648 072	0648 572	LNVG/NWB	VT 502	2000			
0648 073	0648 573	LNVG/NWB	VT 503	2000			
0648 074	0648 574	LNVG/NWB	VT 504	2000			
0648 075	0648 575	LNVG/NWB	VT 505	2000			
0648 076	0648 576	LNVG/NWB	VT 506	2000			
0648 077	0648 577	LNVG/NWB	VT 507	2000			
0648 078	0648 578	LNVG/NWB	VT 508	2000			
0648 079	0648 579	LNVG/NWB	VT 509	2000			
0648 080	0648 580	LNVG/NWB	VT 510	2000			
0648 081	0648 581	LNVG/NWB	VT 511	2000			
0648 082	0648 582	LNVG/NWB	VT 512	2000			
0648 083	0648 583	LNVG/NWB	VT 513	2000			
0648 084	0648 584	LNVG/NWB	VT 514	2000			
0648 085	0648 585	LNVG/NWB	VT 515	2000			
0648 086	0648 586	LNVG/NWB	VT 516	2000			
0648 087	0648 587	LNVG/NWB	VT 517	2000			
0648 088	0648 588	LNVG/NWB	VT 518	2000			
0648 089	0648 589	LNVG/NWB	VT 519	2000			
0648 090	0648 590	LNVG/NWB	VT 520	2000			
0648 091	0648 591	LNVG/NWB	VT 521	2000			
0648 092	0648 592	LNVG/NWB	VT 522	2000			
0648 093	0648 593	LNVG/NWB	VT 523	2000			
0648 144	0648 644	NBE	VT2.77	2011			
0648 145	0648 645	AKN/NBE	VT2.71	2001			
0648 146	0648 646	AKN/NBE	VT2.72	2001	Dithmarschen		
0648 147	0648 647	AKN/NBE	VT2.73	2001			
0648 148	0648 648	NBE	VT2.74	2001	Segeberg		
0648 149	0648 649	NBE	VT2.75	2001			
0648 150	0648 650	AKN/NBE	VT2.76	2003			
0648 151	0648 651	VCT	VT 251	2004			
0648 152	0648 652	VCT	VT 252	2004			
0648 153	0648 653	VCT	VT 253	2004			
0648 154	0648 654	VCT	VT 254	2004			
0648 155	0648 655	VCT	VT 255	2004			
0648 156	0648 656	VCT	VT 256	2004			
0648 157	0648 657	VCT	VT 257	2004			
0648 158	0648 658	VCT	VT 258	2004			
0648 159	0648 659	VCT	VT 259	2004			
0648 160	0648 660	VCT	VT 260	2004			
0648 161	0648 661	VCT	VT 261	2004			
0648 162	0648 662	VCT	VT 262	2004			
0648 163	0648 663	VCT	VT 263	2004			
0648 164	0648 664	VCT	VT 264	2004			
0648 165	0648 665	VCT	VT 265	2004			
0648 166	0648 666	VCT	VT 266	2004			
0648 167	0648 667	VCT	VT 267	2004			
0648 168	0648 668	VCT	VT 268	2004			
0648 171	0648 671	LNVG/EVB	VT 101	2003			
0648 172	0648 672	LNVG/EVB	VT 102	2003			
0648 173	0648 673	LNVG/EVB	VT 103	2003			
0648 174	0648 674	LNVG/EVB	VT 104	2003			
0648 175	0648 675	LNVG/EVB	VT 105	2003			
0648 176	0648 676	LNVG/EVB	VT 106	2003			
0648 177	0648 677	LNVG/EVB	VT 107	2003			
0648 178	0648 678	LNVG/EVB	VT 108	2003			
0648 179	0648 679	LNVG/EVB	VT 109	2003			
0648 181	0648 681	LNVG/NWB	648 181	2003	Ex ERB	VT 4.01	
0648 182	0648 682	LNVG/NWB	648 182	2003	Ex ERB	VT 4.02	
0648 183	0648 683	LNVG/NWB	648 183	2003	Ex ERB	VT 4.03	
0648 184	0648 684	LNVG/NWB	648 184	2003	Ex ERB	VT 4.04	
0648 185	0648 685	LNVG/NWB	648 185	2003	Ex ERB	VT 4.05	

0648 186	0648 686	LNVG/NWB	648 186	2003	Ex ERB VT 4.06
0648 187	0648 687	LNVG/NWB	648 187	2003	Ex ERB VT 4.07
0648 188	0648 688	LNVG/NWB	648 188	2003	Ex ERB VT 4.08
0648 189	0648 689	LNVG/NWB	648 189	2003	Ex ERB VT 4.09
0648 190	0648 690	LNVG/NWB	648 190	2003	Ex ERB VT 4.10
0648 191	0648 691	LNVG/NWB	648 191	2003	Ex ERB VT 4.11
0648 194	0648 694	LNVG/EVB	VT 110	2003	Ex NWB VT 524
0648 195	0648 695	LNVG/EVB	VT 111	2003	Ex NWB VT 525
0648 196	0648 696	LNVG/EVB	VT 112	2003	Ex NWB VT 526
0648 197	0648 697	LNVG/EVB	VT 113	2003	Ex NWB VT 527
0648 198	0648 698	LNVG/EVB	VT 114	2003	Ex NWB VT 528
0648 199	0648 699	LNVG/NWB	VT 529	2003	
0648 210	0648 710	BRB	VT 210	2008	Augsburg
0648 211	0648 711	BRB	VT 211	2008	Kissing
0648 212	0648 712	BRB	VT 212	2008	Mering
0648 213	0648 713	BRB	VT 213	2008	Merching
0648 214	0648 714	BRB	VT 214	2008	Schmiechen
0648 215	0648 715	BRB	VT 215	2008	Egling
0648 216	0648 716	BRB	VT 216	2008	Geltendorf
0648 217	0648 717	BRB	VT 217	2008	St Otilien
0648 218	0648 718	BRB	VT 218	2008	Schondorf
0648 219	0648 719	BRB	VT 219	2008	Utting
0648 220	0648 720	BRB	VT 220	2008	Diessen
0648 221	0648 721	BRB	VT 221	2008	Raisting
0648 222	0648 722	BRB	VT 222	2008	Weilheim
0648 223	0648 723	BRB	VT 223	2008	Peissenberg
0648 224	0648 724	BRB	VT 224	2008	Hohenpeissenberg
0648 225	0648 725	BRB	VT 225	2008	Peiting
0648 226	0648 726	BRB	VT 226	2008	Schongau
0648 227	0648 727	BRB	VT 227	2008	Friedberg
0648 228	0648 728	BRB	VT 228	2008	Dasing
0648 229	0648 729	BRB	VT 229	2008	Obergriessbach
649 230	0648 730	BRB	VT 230	2008	Aichach
0648 231	0648 731	BRB	VT 231	2008	Kühbach und Radersdorf
0648 232	0648 732	BRB	VT 232	2008	Schrobenhausen
0648 233	0648 733	BRB	VT 233	2008	Ingolstadt
0648 234	0648 734	BRB	VT 234	2008	Eichstätt
0648 235	0648 735	BRB	VT 235	2008	
0648 236	0648 736	BRB	VT 236	2010	
0648 237	0648 737	BRB	VT 237	2010	
0648 278	0648 778	AS/HEX	VT 800	2005	Domschatz Halberstadt
0648 279	0648 779	AS/HEX	VT 801	2005	Saaletal
0648 280	0648 780	AS/HEX	VT 802	2005	
0648 281	0648 781	AS/HEX	VT 803	2005	
0648 282	0648 782	AS/HEX	VT 804	2005	Der Ilsetaler
0648 283	0648 783	AS/HEX	VT 805	2005	
0648 284	0648 784	AS/HEX	VT 806	2005	Das Bodetal. Der Sagenharz
0648 285	0648 785	AS/HEX	VT 807	2005	Wernigerode Brocken Express
0648 286	0648 786	AS/HEX	VT 808	2005	Zoo Halle
0648 287	0648 787	AS/HEX	VT 809	2005	
0648 288	0648 788	AS/HEX	VT 810	2005	Scrapped - accident
0648 289	0648 789	AS/HEX	VT 811	2005	THW Halle
0648 290	0648 790	LNVG/NWB	VT 530	2005	
0648 291	0648 791	LNVG/NWB	VT 531	2005	
0648 292	0648 792	LNVG/NWB	VT 532	2005	
0648 293	0648 793	LNVG/NWB	VT 533	2005	
0648 295	0648 795	OLA	VT 701	2001	(Z)
0648 296	0648 796	NWB	VT 702	2001	Ex OLA
0648 297	0648 797	OLA	VT 703	2001	(Z)
0648 298	0648 798	OLA	VT 704	2001	(Z)
0648 299	0648 799	NWB	VT 705	2001	Ex OLA
0648 300	0648 800	HEX	VT 706	2001	Ex OLA

0648 328	0648 828	ABRN	VT11 001	2005	Bochum
0648 329	0648 829	ABRN	VT11 002	2005	Herne
0648 330	0648 830	ABRN	VT11 003	2005	Gelsenkirchen
0648 361	0648 861	NWB	VT 301	2000	Ex NOB
0648 362	0648 862	NOB	VT 302	2000	
0648 363	0648 863	NWB	VT 303	2000	Ex NOB
0648 364	0648 864	NWB	VT 304	2000	Ex NOB
0648 365	0648 865	NOB	VT 305	2000	
0648 366	0648 866	NOB	VT 306	2000	
0648 367	0648 867	LNVG/NWB	648 367	2000	Ex NOB VT 307
0648 368	0648 868	LNVG/NWB	648 368	2000	Ex NOB VT 308
0648 369	0648 869	LNVG/NWB	648 369	2000	Ex NOB VT 309
0648 370	0648 870	LNVG/NWB	648 370	2010	
0648 371	0648 871	LNVG/NWB	648 371	2010	
0648 372	0648 872	LNVG/NWB	648 372	2010	
0648 373	0648 873	LNVG/NWB	648 373	2010	
0648 374	0648 874	LNVG/NWB	648 374	2010	
0648 375	0648 875	LNVG/NWB	648 375	2010	
0648 376	0648 876	LNVG/NWB	648 376	2010	
0648 377	0648 877	LNVG/NWB	648 377	2010	
0648 378	0648 878	LNVG/NWB	648 378	2010	
0648 379	0648 879	LNVG/NWB	648 379	2010	
0648 401	0648 901	FAHMA/HEB	VT 201	2006	
0648 402	0648 902	FAHMA/HEB	VT 202	2006	
0648 403	0648 903	FAHMA/HEB	VT 203	2006	
0648 404	0648 904	FAHMA/HEB	VT 204	2006	
0648 405	0648 905	FAHMA/HEB	VT 205	2006	
0648 406	0648 906	FAHMA/HEB	VT 206	2006	
0648 407	0648 907	FAHMA/HEB	VT 207	2006	
0648 408	0648 908	FAHMA/HEB	VT 208	2006	
0648 409	0648 909	FAHMA/HEB	VT 209	2006	
0648 410	0648 910	FAHMA/HEB	VT 210	2006	
0648 420	0648 920	LNVG/NWB		2012	
0648 421	0648 921	LNVG/NWB	VT 552	2009	
0648 422	0648 922	LNVG/NWB	VT 553	2009	
0648 423	0648 923	LNVG/NWB	VT 554	2009	
0648 424	0648 924	LNVG/NWB	VT 555	2009	
0648 425	0648 925	LNVG/NWB	VT 556	2009	
0648 426	0648 926	LNVG/NWB	VT 557	2009	
0648 427	0648 927	LNVG/NWB	VT 558	2009	
0648 428	0648 928	LNVG/NWB	VT 559	2009	
0648 429	0648 929	LNVG/NWB	VT 560	2009	
0648 430	0648 930	LNVG/NWB	VT 561	2009	
0648 431	0648 931	LNVG/NWB	VT 562	2009	
0648 432	0648 932	LNVG/NWB	VT 563	2009	
0648 433	0648 933	LNVG/NWB	VT 564	2009	
0648 434	0648 934	LNVG/NWB	VT 565	2009	
0648 435	0648 935	LNVG/NWB	VT 566	2009	
0648 436	0648 936	LNVG/NWB	VT 567	2009	
0648 437	0648 937	LNVG/NWB	VT 568	2009	
0648 438	0648 938	LNVG/NWB	VT 569	2009	
0648 439	0648 939	LNVG/NWB	VT 570	2009	
0648 440	0648 940	LNVG/NWB	VT 571	2009	
0648 441	0648 941	LNVG/NWB	VT 572	2009	
0648 442	0648 942	LNVG/NWB	VT 573	2009	
0648 443	0648 943	LNVG/NWB	VT 574	2009	
0648 444	0648 944	LNVG/NWB	VT 575	2009	
0648 445	0648 945	LNVG/NWB	VT 576	2009	
0648 446	0648 946	LNVG/NWB	VT 577	2009	
0648 447	0648 947	LNVG/NWB	VT 578	2009	
0648 470	0648 970	LNVG/Erixx		2011	
0648 471	0648 971	LNVG/Erixx		2011	

0648 472	0648 972	LNVG/Erixx		2011	
0648 473	0648 973	LNVG/Erixx		2011	
0648 474	0648 974	LNVG/Erixx		2011	
0648 475	0648 975	LNVG/Erixx		2011	
0648 476	0648 976	LNVG/Erixx		2011	
0648 477	0648 977	LNVG/Erixx		2011	
0648 478	0648 978	LNVG/Erixx		2011	
0648 479	0648 979	LNVG/Erixx		2011	
0648 480	0648 980	LNVG/Erixx		2011	
0648 481	0648 981	LNVG/Erixx		2011	
0648 482	0648 982	LNVG/Erixx		2011	
0648 483	0648 983	LNVG/Erixx		2011	
0648 484	0648 984	LNVG/Erixx		2011	
0648 485	0648 985	LNVG/Erixx		2011	
0648 486	0648 986	LNVG/Erixx		2011	
0648 487	0648 987	LNVG/Erixx		2011	
0648 488	0648 988	LNVG/Erixx		2011	
0648 489	0648 989	LNVG/Erixx		2011	
0648 490	0648 990	LNVG/Erixx		2011	
0648 491	0648 991	LNVG/Erixx		2011	
0648 492	0648 992	LNVG/Erixx		2011	
0648 493	0648 993	LNVG/Erixx		2011	
0648 494	0648 994	LNVG/Erixx		2011	
0648 495	0648 995	LNVG/Erixx		2011	
0648 496	0648 996	LNVG/Erixx		2011	
0648 497	0648 997	LNVG/Erixx		2011	
1648 001	1648 501	ABRN	VT12 001	2013	
1648 002	1648 502	ABRN	VT12 002	2013	
1648 003	1648 503	ABRN	VT12 003	2013	
1648 004	1648 504	ABRN	VT12 004	2013	
1648 005	1648 505	ABRN	VT12 005	2013	
1648 006	1648 506	ABRN	VT12 006	2013	
1648 007	1648 507	ABRN	VT12 007	2013	REMSCHEID
1648 008	1648 508	ABRN	VT12 008	2013	
1648 009	1648 509	ABRN	VT12 009	2013	
1648 101	1648 601	HEB/HLB	VT 501	2015	
1648 102	1648 602	HEB/HLB	VT 502	2015	
1648 103	1648 603	HEB/HLB	VT 503	2015	
1648 104	1648 604	HEB/HLB	VT 504	2015	
1648 105	1648 605	HEB/HLB	VT 505	2015	
1648 106	1648 606	HEB/HLB	VT 506	2015	
1648 107	1648 607	HEB/HLB	VT 507	2015	
1648 301	1648 801	LNVG			
1648 302	1648 802	LNVG			
1648 303	1648 803	LNVG			
1648 304	1648 804	LNVG			
1648 305	1648 805	LNVG			
1648 306	1648 806	LNVG			

95 80 0650   REGIO SHUTTLE (RS1)   SINGLE CARS

This is another successful Stadler product although it has its origins with Waggon Union, ADtranz and Bombardier. Because of possible cartel implications, Bombardier was forced to divest itself of the plant in Berlin Wilhelmsruh and it was sold to Stadler. Since 1996 some 500 units have been built for private operators and indeed DB. However there are variations with the length, weight and seating, the principal ones listed in operator order are:

AGIL: Length 25 m.   Accommodation –/76(25) 1T.   Weight 42 tonnes. 2 x 265 kW engines.
BSB: Length 25 m.   Accommodation –/71(?) 1T.   Weight 43 tonnes.
EIB: Length 25.36 m.   Accommodation –/58(12) 1T.   Weight 42 tonnes.
NEBB: Length 25.50 m.   Accommodation –/66(5) 1T.   Weight 42 tonnes.
ODEG: Length 25 m.   Accommodation –/50(20) 1T.   Weight 42 tonnes. 2 x 265 kW engines.
RBG: Length 25.36 m.   Accommodation –/62(8) 1T.   Weight 42 tonnes.
RTB: Length 25 m.   Accommodation –/54(25) 1T.   Weight 42 tonnes. 2 x 265 kW engines.
STB: Length 25.36 m.   Accommodation –/66(5) 1T.   Weight 42 tonnes.
TRDR: Length 25.50 m.   Accommodation –/66(5) 1T.   Weight 42 tonnes.
VBG: Length 25.36 m.   Accommodation –/56(24) 1T.   Weight 42 tonnes. 2 x 265 kW engines.
VEN: Length 25.50 m.   Accommodation –/50(20) 1T.   Weight 44 tonnes. 2 x 265 kW engines.
WEG: Length 25.36 m.   Accommodation –/57(17)   Weight 42 tonnes. 2 x 265 kW engines.

For other technical details see Class 650 in German Railways Part 1.

*   Ex ODEG
@   Tramway fittings
#   Second class only, fitted with IVECO engines.

EVN		Company	Unit No	Works No	Built	Notes/Names
0650 028		FBBW/BSB	VT 001	36606	1998	
0650 029		FBBW/BSB	VT 002	36607	1998	
0650 030		FBBW/BSB	VT 003	36608	1998	
0650 031		FBBW/BSB	VT 004	36609	1998	Wasenweiler
0650 032		FBBW/BSB	VT 005	36610	1998	Ihringen am Kaiserstuhl
0650 033		FBBW/BSB	VT 006	36611	1998	Gottenheim
0650 034		FBBW/BSB	VT 007	36612	1998	Stadt Freiburg im Breisgau
0650 035		FBBW/BSB	VT 008	36613	1998	Breisach - Brücke zu Europa
0650 036		FBBW/BSB	VT 009	36614	1998	Gemeinde March
0650 037		BSB	VT 010	37153	2002	Winden im Elztal
0650 038		BSB	VT 011	37154	2002	Gundelfinden
0650 039		BSB	VT 012	37155	2002	Stadt Elzach
0650 040		BSB	VT 013	37156	2002	Stadt Waldkirch
0650 041		BSB	VT 014	37157	2002	Gutach im Breisach
0650 042		BSB	VT 015	37158	2002	Zwei-Tälerland
0650 043		BSB	VT 016	37159	2002	Denzlingen
0650 044		BSB	VT 017	37160	2002	Stadt Freiburg
0650 045		BSB	VT 018	37161	2002	
0650 046		BSB	VT 019	37162	2002	
0650 047		BSB	VT 020	37400	2005	Landkreis Emmendingen
0650 048		BSB	VT 021	37401	2005	Landkreis Breisgau - Hochschwarzwald
0650 049		CB	VT 511	37128	2002	Stadt Lichtenstein
0650 050		CB	VT 512	37129	2002	Stadt Oelsnitz
0650 051		CB	VT 513	37130	2002	Hohndorf - ein Dorf im Grünen
0650 052		CB	VT 514	37245	2003	
0650 053		CB	VT 515	37270	2004	
0650 054		CB	VT 516	37271	2004	Stadt Hainichen
0650 055		FEG	VT 3.01	36883	2000	Luisa
0650 056		FEG	VT 3.02	36884	2000	Hannah
0650 057		FEG	VT 3.03	36885	2000	Esther
0650 058	*	BX/HLB	VT650.58	37304	2004	Barnimer Eiszeitung
0650 059		BX/ODEG	VT650.59	37293	2004	
0650 060	*	BX/HLB	VT650.60	37294	2004	Frankfurt (Oder)
0650 061	*	BX/HLB	VT650.61	37295	2004	Gemeinde Letschin
0650 062	*	BX/HLB	VT650.62	37296	2004	Amt Schlaubetal
0650 063	*	BX/HLB	VT650.63	37297	2004	Erholungsort Stadt Mülrose

0650 064	*	BX/GWTR	VT650.64	37298	2004	Stadt Storkow (Mark)
0650 065	*	PEG/CD	841.065	37305	2004	Ex ODEG VT650.65
0650 066	*	PEG/RBG	VT650.66	37306	2004	
0650 067	*	PEG/GWTR	VT650.67	37307	2004	Oderbruch Hauptstadt Wriezen
0650 068		PEG/ODEG	VT650.68	37308	2004	Naturparkstadt Biesenthal
0650 069		PEG/ODEG	VT650.69	37292	2004	
0650 070	*	PEG/RBG	VT650.70	37309	2004	
0650 071	*	PEG/EIB	VT650.71	37310	2004	
0650 072	*	PEG/CD	841.072	37311	2004	Ex ODEG VT650.72
0650 073	*	PEG/CD	841.073	37312	2004	Ex ODEG VT650.73
0650 074	*	PEG/CD	841.074	37313	2004	Ex ODEG VT650.74
0650 075		BX/ODEG	VT650.75	37314	2004	
0650 076		BX/ODEG	VT650.76	37315	2004	Schorfheidestadt Joachimsthal
0650 077		BX/ODEG	VT650.77	37316	2004	Eberswaalde
0650 078	*	BX/SWEG	VT650.78	37299	2004	Seelow (Mark)
0650 079	*	BX/SWEG	VT650.79	37300	2004	Erholungsort Wendisch Rietz
0650 080	*	BX/SWEG	VT650.80	37301	2004	Bezirk Lichtenberg von Berlin
0650 081	*	BX/SWEG	VT650.81	37302	2004	Moorheilbad Bad Freienwalde
0650 082	*	BX/SWEG	VT650.82	37303	2004	Königs Wusterhausen
0650 083		HML/ODEG	VT650.83	38120	2009	
0650 084		HML/ODEG	VT650.84	38121	2009	
0650 085	*	NHL/SWEG	VT650.85	38122	2009	
0650 086		PEG/ODEG	VT650.86	37140	2002	Ex VT650.51; Hagenow
0650 087		PEG/ODEG	VT650.87	37141	2002	Ex VT650.52
0650 088		PEG/ODEG	VT650.88	37142	2002	Ex VT650.53; Parchim
0650 089		BX/ODEG	VT650.89	37143	2002	Ex VT650.54
0650 090		BX/ODEG	VT650.90	37144	2002	Ex VT650.55; Müritz Nationalpark
0650 091		BX/ODEG	VT650.91	37145	2002	Ex VT650.56
0650 092		BX/ODEG	VT650.92	37146	2002	Ex VT650.57; Ludwiglust
0650 131		VEN	650 131	36881	2000	Ex VT1.01
0650 132		VEN	650 132	36882	2000	Ex VT1.02
0650 150	@	VBG	VT 50	39351	2011	
0650 151	@	VBG	VT 51	39352	2011	
0650 152	@	VBG	VT 52	39353	2011	Stadt Falkenstein
0650 153	@	VBG	VT 53	39354	2011	Stadt Adorf/V
0650 154	@	VBG	VT 54	39355	2012	
0650 155	@	VBG	VT 55	39356	2012	
0650 156	@	VBG	VT 56	39357	2012	
0650 157	@	VBG	VT 57	39358	2012	Vogtlandkreis
0650 240		EIB	VT 301	39314	2012	Landkreis Saalfeld -Rudolstadt
0650 241		EIB	VT 302	39315	2012	Stadt Zeitz
0650 242		EIB	VT 303	39316	2012	
0650 243		EIB	VT 304	39317	2012	
0650 244		EIB	VT 305	39318	2012	Otto-Dix-Stadt Gera
0650 245		EIB	VT 306	39319	2012	
0650 246		EIB	VT 307	39320	2012	
0650 247		EIB	VT 308	39321	2012	
0650 248		EIB	VT 309	39322	2012	
0650 249		EIB	VT 310	39323	2012	
0650 250		EIB	VT 311	39324	2012	
0650 251		EIB	VT 312	39325	2012	
0650 252		EIB	VT 313	39326	2012	
0650 253		EIB	VT 314	39327	2012	
0650 254		EIB	VT 315	39328	2012	
0650 255		EIB	VT 316	39329	2012	
0650 256		EIB	VT 317	39330	2012	
0650 257		EIB	VT 318	39331	2012	
0650 258		EIB	VT 319	39332	2012	
0650 259		EIB	VT 320	39333	2012	
0650 260		EIB	VT 321	39334	2012	
0650 261		EIB	VT 322	39335	2012	
0650 262		EIB	VT 323	39336	2012	

0650 263	EIB	VT 324	39337	2012	
0650 264	EIB	VT 325	39338	2012	
0650 265	EIB	VT 326	39339	2012	
0650 266	EIB	VT 327	39340	2012	
0650 267	EIB	VT 328	39341	2012	
0650 268	EIB	VT 329	39342	2012	
0650 269	EIB	VT 330	39343	2012	
0650 270	EIB	VT 331	39344	2012	
0650 271	EIB	VT 332	39345	2012	
0650 272	EIB	VT 333	39346	2012	
0650 273	EIB	VT 334	39347	2012	
0650 274	EIB	VT 335	39348	2012	
0650 275	EIB	VT 336	39349	2012	
0650 276	EIB	VT 337	39350	2012	
0650 300	PRESS	650 032	37126	2002	Ex Stadler VT 304
0650 350	VEN	650 350	38545	2011	
0650 351	VEN	650 351	38546	2011	
0650 352	VEN	650 352	38547	2011	
0650 353	BOBFN	VT 63	36782	1998	
0650 354	BOBFN	VT 64	36783	1998	
0650 355	BOBFN	VT 65	36784	1998	
0650 356	BOBFN	VT 66	36785	1998	
0650 357	BOBFN	VT 67	37447	2005	
0650 358	BOBFN	VT 68	37448	2005	
0650 359	BOBFN	VT 69	37449	2005	
0650 361	WEG	VT 361	39306	2012	Korntal
0650 362	WEG	VT 362	39307	2012	Korntal
0650 363	WEG	VT 363	39308	2012	Korntal

▲ The Class 650 Regio Shuttle has been an enormous success for Stadler with over 500 examples built since 1998. Rurtalbahn (RTB) 95 80 0650 740, running number VT 740 dates from 2011; it is seen passing Abenden with a train from Heimbach to Düren on 3 October 2014. **Matthias Müller**

0650 364	WEG	VT 364	39309	2012	Korntal
0650 365	WEG	VT 365	39310	2012	Korntal
0650 366	WEG	VT 366	39311	2012	Korntal
0650 367	WEG	VT 367	39312	2012	Korntal
0650 368	WEG	VT 368	39313	2012	Korntal
0650 380	HzL	VT 251	38541	2009	Landkreis Konstanz
0650 381	HzL	VT 252	38542	2009	Radolfzell
0650 382	HzL	VT 253	38543	2009	Orsingen-Nenzingen
0650 383	HzL	VT 254	38544	2009	Stockach
0650 401	EIB	VT 001	36777	1998	Thüringen Zoopark- Stadt Erfurt
0650 402	EIB	VT 002	36778	1998	Stadt Kassel
0650 403	EIB	VT 003	36779	1998	Stadt Leinefelde
0650 404	EIB	VT 004	36780	1998	Heilbad Heilingenstadt
0650 405	EIB	VT 005	36781	1998	Mühlhausen
0650 406	EIB	VT 006	36786	1998	Ex Adtranz VT 301; Unstrut-Hainich-Kreis
0650 407	EIB	VT 007	36787	1998	Ex Adtranz VT 302; Landskreis Eichsfeld
0650 408	EIB	VT 008	36788	1998	Ex Adtranz VT 303; Stadt Arnstadt
0650 409	EIB	VT 009	36886	2000	Baumkronenpfad Hainich
0650 410	EIB	VT 010	37248	2003	Luftkurort Stützerbach
0650 411	EIB	VT 011	37249	2003	Ilmenau
0650 412	EIB	VT 012	37280	2004	Elgersburg
0650 413	EIB	VT 013	37281	2004	Deutsche Märchenstrasse
0650 414	EIB	VT 014	37282	2004	Theaterstadt Meiningen
0650 415	EIB	VT 015	37283	2004	Hammelburg
0650 416	EIB	VT 016	37284	2004	Stadt Mellrichstadt
0650 417	EIB	VT 017	37285	2004	
0650 418	EIB	VT 018	37286	2004	
0650 419	EIB	VT 019	37287	2004	Gemünden am Main
0650 420	EIB	VT 020	37288	2004	Fränkisches Freilandmuseum Fladungen
0650 421	EIB	VT 021	37289	2004	
0650 422	EIB	VT 022	37378	2004	
0650 423	EIB	VT 023	37379	2004	Landkreis Bad Kissingen
0650 501	STB	VT 101	36899	2000	Stadt Eisenach
0650 502	STB	VT 102	36900	2000	Spielzeugstadt Sonneberg
0650 503	STB	VT 103	36901	2000	Theaterstadt Meiningen
0650 504	STB	VT 104	36902	2000	Wartburg
0650 505	STB	VT 105	36903	2000	Schmalkalden
0650 506	STB	VT 106	36904	2000	Neuhaus am Rennweg
0650 507	STB	VT 107	36905	2000	Johann Sebastian Bach
0650 508	STB	VT 108	36906	2000	Oberhof
0650 509	STB	VT 109	36907	2000	Lutherhaus Eisenach
0650 510	STB	VT 110	36908	2001	Skiarena Silbersattel Steiach (Thür)
0650 511	STB	VT 111	36909	2001	Goetz Höhle Meiningen
0650 512	STB	VT 112	36910	2001	Partner Shuttle Erfurt-Meiningen
0650 513	STB	VT 113	36911	2001	Glasbläserstadt Lauscha
0650 514	STB	VT 114	36912	2001	Bad Salzungen
0650 515	STB	VT 115	36913	2001	Fachwerk und Karnevallsstadt Wasungen
0650 516	STB	VT 116	36914	2001	Themar - Kloster Vessra
0650 517	STB	VT 117	36915	2001	Meininger Dampflokverein
0650 518	STB	VT 118	36916	2001	Porzellenland Rauenstein (Thür)
0650 519	STB	VT 119	36917	2001	Stadt Plaue im Thüringen
0650 520	STB	VT 120	36918	2001	10 Jahre STB 2001-2011
0650 521	STB	VT 121	36919	2001	viba.de
0650 522	STB	VT 122	37121	2001	
0650 523	STB	VT 123	37122	2001	
0650 524	STB	VT 124	37123	2001	
0650 525	STB	VT 125	37124	2001	
0650 526	STB	VT 126	37125	2001	
0650 527	STB	VT 127	37147	2002	

0650 528	STB	VT 128	37148	2002	
0650 529	STB	VT 129	37149	2002	
0650 530	STB	VT 130	37150	2002	
0650 531	STB	VT 131	37151	2002	
0650 532	STB	VT 132	37152	2002	
0650 533 #	AT/NEBB	VT 001	36859	2000	Ex MRB
0650 534 #	AT/NEBB	VT 002	36860	2000	Ex MRB
0650 535 #	AT/NEBB	VT 003	36861	2000	Ex MRB
0650 536 #	AT/NEBB	VT 004	36862	2000	Ex MRB
0650 537 #	AT/NEBB	VT 005	36863	2000	Ex MRB
0650 538 #	AT/NEBB	VT 006	36864	2000	Ex MRB
0650 539 #	AT/NEBB	VT 007	36865	2000	Ex MRB
0650 540 #	AT/NEBB	VT 008	36866	2000	Ex MRB
0650 541 #	AT/NEBB	VT 009	36867	2000	Ex MRB
0650 542 #	AT/NEBB	VT 010	36868	2000	Ex MRB
0650 543 #	AT/NEBB	VT 011	36869	2000	Ex MRB
0650 544 #	AT/NEBB	VT 012	36870	2000	Ex MRB
0650 545 #	AT/NEBB	VT 013	36871	2000	Ex MRB
0650 546 #	AT/NEBB	VT 014	36872	2000	Ex MRB
0650 547 #	AT/NEBB	VT 015	36873	2000	Ex MRB
0650 548 #	AT/NEBB	VT 016	36874	2000	Ex MRB
0650 549 #	AT/NEBB	VT 017	36875	2000	Ex MRB
0650 550 #	AT/NEBB	VT 018	36876	2000	Ex MRB
0650 551 #	AT/NEBB	VT 019	36877	2000	Ex MRB
0650 552 #	AT/NEBB	VT 020	37127	2001	Ex MRB
0650 562	Netinera/VBG	VT 62	37272	2003	Ex PEG VT650.01
0650 563	Netinera/VBG	VT 63	37273	2003	Ex PEG VT650.02
0650 564	Netinera/VBG	VT 64	37274	2003	Ex PEG VT650.03
0650 565	Netinera/VBG	VT 65	37275	2003	Ex PEG VT650.04
0650 566	Netinera/VBG	VT 66	37276	2003	Ex PEG VT650.05
0650 567	Netinera/VBG	VT650.06	37277	2003	Rebuilt 2014 after fire
0650 568	Netinera/VBG	VT650.07	37278	2003	Scrapped 2009 after fire
0650 569	Netinera/VBG	VT 69	37279	2003	
0650 571	FBBW-SWEG/OSB	VT 509	36615	1998	Oberharmersbach
0650 572	FBBW-SWEG/OSB	VT 510	36616	1998	Oberkirch
0650 573	FBBW-SWEG/OSB	VT 511	36617	1998	Kappelrodeck
0650 574	FBBW-SWEG/OSB	VT 512	36618	1998	Oppenau
0650 575	FBBW-SWEG/OSB	VT 513	36619	1998	Achern
0650 576	FBBW-SWEG/OSB	VT 514	36620	1998	Bad Peterstal-Griesbach
0650 577	FBBW-SWEG/OSB	VT 515	36621	1998	Hasalach
0650 578	FBBW-SWEG/OSB	VT 516	36622	1998	Zell am Harmersbach
0650 579	FBBW-SWEG/OSB	VT 517	36623	1998	Steinach
0650 580	FBBW-SWEG/OSB	VT 518	36624	1998	Hausach
0650 581	FBBW-SWEG/OSB	VT 519	36625	1998	Ottenhöfen
0650 582	FBBW-SWEG/OSB	VT 520	36626	1998	Offenburg
0650 583	FBBW-SWEG/OSB	VT 521	36627	1998	Kehl
0650 584	FBBW-SWEG/OSB	VT 522	36628	1998	Gegenbach
0650 585	FBBW-SWEG/OSB	VT 523	36629	1998	Lautenbach
0650 586	FBBW-SWEG/OSB	VT 524	36630	1998	Biberach
0650 587	FBBW-SWEG/OSB	VT 525	36631	1998	Wilstätt
0650 588	FBBW-SWEG/OSB	VT 526	36632	1998	Appenweier
0650 589	SWEG/OSB	VT 527	37392	2005	Wolfach
0650 590	SWEG/OSB	VT 528	37393	2005	Schiltach
0650 591	SWEG/OSB	VT 529	37394	2005	Schenkenzell
0650 592	SWEG/OSB	VT 530	37395	2005	Freundenstadt
0650 593	SWEG/OSB	VT 531	37396	2005	Alpirsbach
0650 594	SWEG/OSB	VT 532	37397	2005	Lossburg Ferienland
0650 595	FBBW/SWEG	VT 501	36555	1997	Endingen
0650 596	FBBW/SWEG	VT 502	36556	1997	Eichstetten
0650 597	FBBW/SWEG	VT 503	36557	1997	Bahlingen
0650 598	FBBW/SWEG	VT 504	36558	1997	Münstertal - Südlicher Schwarzwald
0650 599	FBBW/SWEG	VT 505	36559	1997	Brötzingen

0650 600	FBBW/SWEG	VT 506	36560	1997	Staufen
0650 601	FBBW/SWEG	VT 507	36561	1997	Vogtsburg
0650 602	FBBW/SWEG	VT 508	36562	1997	
0650 603	FBBW/HzL	VT 200	36563	1997	
0650 604	FBBW/HzL	VT 201	36564	1997	
0650 605	FBBW/HzL	VT 202	36565	1997	
0650 606	FBBW/HzL	VT 203	36566	1997	
0650 607	FBBW/HzL	VT 204	36567	1997	
0650 608	FBBW/HzL	VT 205	36568	1997	
0650 609	FBBW/HzL	VT 206	36569	1997	
0650 610	FBBW/HzL	VT 207	36570	1997	
0650 611	FBBW/HzL	VT 208	36571	1997	
0650 612	FBBW/HzL	VT 209	36572	1997	
0650 613	FBBW/HzL	VT 210	36573	1997	
0650 614	FBBW/HzL	VT 211	36574	1997	
0650 615	FBBW/HzL	VT 212	36575	1997	
0650 616	FBBW/HzL	VT 213	36576	1997	
0650 617	FBBW/HzL	VT 214	36577	1997	
0650 618	FBBW/HzL	VT 215	36578	1997	
0650 619	FBBW/HzL	VT 216	36579	1997	
0650 620	FBBW/HzL	VT 217	36580	1997	
0650 621	FBBW/HzL	VT 218	36581	1997	
0650 622	FBBW/HzL	VT 219	36582	1997	
0650 623	FBBW/HzL	VT 220	36583	1997	
0650 624	FBBW/HzL	VT 221	36584	1997	
0650 625	HzL	VT 44	36585	1997	
0650 626	HzL	VT 45	36586	1997	
0650 627	HzL	VT 231	37163	2003	
0650 628	HzL	VT 232	37164	2003	
0650 629	HzL	VT 233	37165	2003	
0650 630	HzL	VT 234	37166	2003	
0650 631	HzL	VT 235	37167	2003	
0650 632	HzL	VT 236	37168	2003	
0650 633	HzL	VT 237	37169	2003	
0650 634	HzL	VT 238	37170	2003	
0650 635	HzL	VT 239	37171	2003	
0650 636	HzL	VT 240	37172	2003	
0650 637	HzL	VT 241	37173	2003	
0650 638	HzL	VT 242	37174	2003	
0650 639	HzL	VT 243	37175	2003	
0650 640	HzL	VT 244	37176	2003	
0650 641	HzL	VT 245	37177	2003	
0650 642	HzL	VT 246	37178	2003	
0650 643	HzL	VT 247	37179	2003	
0650 644	HzL	VT 248	37180	2003	
0650 645	HzL	VT 249	37181	2003	
0650 646	HzL	VT 250	37182	2003	
0650 647	HzL	VT 46	37398	2005	
0650 648	HzL	VT 47	37399	2005	
0650 650	RBG	VT 15	36523	1996	Viechtach
0650 651	RBG	VT 16	36524	1996	Naturpark Bayerische Wald
0650 652	RBG	VT 17	36525	1996	Grafenau
0650 653	RBG	VT 18	36526	1996	Zwiesel
0650 654	RBG	VT 19	36527	1996	Frauenau
0650 655	RBG	VT 20	36604	1997	Deggendorf
0650 656	RBG	VT 21	36605	1997	Stadt Regen
0650 657	RBG	VT 22	36528	1997	Plattling
0650 658	RBG	VT 23	36529	1997	Gotteszell
0650 659	RBG	VT 24	36530	1997	Kinderland Bayerischer Wald
0650 660	RBG	VT 25	36531	1997	Eisenstein
0650 661	RBG	VT 26	36534	1997	Ex ADtranz VT 300; Grenzenlose Waldwildnis
0650 662	RBG	VT 27	37290	2003	

						Based at
0650 663	RBG	VT 28	37291	2003	Železná Ruda	
0650 664	RBG	VT 31	36888	2000		
0650 665	RBG	VT 32	36889	2000		
0650 666	RBG	VT 33	36890	2000		
0650 667	RBG	VT 34	36891	2000		
0650 668	RBG	VT 35	36892	2000		
0650 669	RBG	VT 36	36893	2001	Landkreis Cham	
0650 670	RBG	VT 37	36894	2001		
0650 671	RBG	VT 38	36895	2001		
0650 672	RBG	VT 39	36896	2001	Waldmünchen	
0650 673	RBG	VT 40	36897	2001	Bad Kötzing	
0650 674	RBG	VT 41	36898	2001		
						Based at
0650 680	WEG	VT 414	36456	1996		Korntal
0650 681	WEG	VT 415	36457	1996	Schaichtal	Dettenhausen
0650 682	WEG	VT 416	36458	1997		Dettenhausen
0650 683	WEG	VT 423	36554	1997	Schönbuch	Dettenhausen
0650 684	WEG	VT 430	36559	1996	Dettenhausen	Dettenhausen
0650 685	WEG	VT 431	36560	1996	Weil im Schönbuch	Dettenhausen
0650 686	WEG	VT 432	36561	1996	Holzgerlingen	Dettenhausen
0650 687	WEG	VT 433	36562	1996	Böblingen	Dettenhausen
0650 688	WEG	VT 440	36846	2000		Rudersberg
0650 689	WEG	VT 441	36847	2000		Rudersberg
0650 690	WEG	VT 442	36848	2000	Katja	Nürtingen
0650 691	WEG	VT 445	36878	2000	Alice	Nürtingen
0650 692	WEG	VT 446	36879	2000	Agnes	Nürtingen
0650 693	WEG	VT 447	36880	2000	Maren	Nürtingen
0650 701	AGIL		38816	2010		
0650 702	AGIL		38817	2010		
0650 703	AGIL		38818	2010		
0650 704	AGIL		38819	2010		
0650 705	AGIL		38820	2010	Neuenmarkt Wirsberg	
0650 706	AGIL		38821	2010		
0650 707	AGIL		38822	2010		
0650 708	AGIL		38823	2010		
0650 709	AGIL		38824	2010		
0650 710	AGIL		38825	2010		
0650 711	AGIL		38826	2011		
0650 712	AGIL		38827	2011	Helmbrechts	
0650 713	AGIL		38828	2011		
0650 714	AGIL		38829	2011		
0650 715	AGIL		38830	2011	Naila	
0650 716	AGIL		38831	2011	Münchberg	
0650 717	AGIL		38832	2011		
0650 718	AGIL		38833	2011		
0650 719	AGIL		38834	2011		
0650 720	AGIL		38835	2011	Coburg	
0650 721	AGIL		38836	2011		
0650 722	AGIL		38837	2011		
0650 723	AGIL		38838	2011		
0650 724	AGIL		38839	2011	Bad Rodach	
0650 725	AGIL		38840	2011		
0650 726	AGIL		38841	2011		
0650 727	AGIL		38842	2011		
0650 728	AGIL		38843	2011		
0650 729	AGIL		38844	2011		
0650 730	AGIL		38845	2011		
0650 731	AGIL		38846	2011		
0650 732	AGIL		38847	2011		
0650 733	AGIL		38848	2011		
0650 734	AGIL		38849	2011		
0650 735	AGIL		38850	2011		
0650 736	AGIL		38851	2011		

0650 737	AGIL		38852	2011	
0650 738	AGIL		38853	2011	
0650 739	BeNEX/ODEG		38978	2011	Bad Saarow
0650 740	RTB	VT 740	38979	2011	
0650 741	RTB	VT 741	38980	2011	
0650 742	RTB	VT 742	38981	2011	
0650 743	RTB	VT 743	38982	2011	
0650 744	RTB	VT 744	38983	2011	
0650 745	BOBFN	VT 70		2013	
0650 746	BOBFN	VT 71		2013	
0650 997	KVG	VT 97	36603	1997	In use with DB

95 80 0654   REGIO SPRINTER (RVT)
3-SECTION ARTICULATED UNITS

Mention has been made of the project in the early 1990s for German industry to introduce a new generation of diesel trains for regional service. One of the first was the Regio Sprinter or Regional Verbrennungs Triebwagen (RVT) delivered by Duewag, later Siemens. These 3-section units only went to three companies (two in Germany and one in Denmark) before the type was replaced by the Siemens Desiro. The Rurtalbahn was the first company to order units when it was known as the Dürener Kreisbahn with the Vogtlandbahn following later. The Rurtalbahn seems to have ordered far too many and units are often to be found on loan to other companies. The Vogtlandbahn has some units fitted out to conform with tramway operation for working along the street into Zwickau.

Built: 1995–97.
Builder: Duewag.
Wheel Arrangement: A-2-A.   **Transmission:** Mechanical.
Engine: 2 MAN D2865 LUH05 of 198 kW (RTB), 2 x 228 kW (VBG).
Accommodation: –/74(10) 1T (RTB), –/77(3) 1T (VBG).
Weight: 49.20 tonnes.   **Wheel Diameter:**
Length over Couplers: 24.80 m (RTB), 25.17 m (VBG).   **Maximum Speed:** 120 km/h.
Door Step Height: 530 mm.   **Maximum Tractive Effort:**

@   Tramway fittings

EVN	Company	Unit Number	Works No	Built	Names
0654 001	RTB	6.001	91345	1995	
0654 002	RTB	6.002	91346	1995	
0654 003	RTB	6.003	91347	1995	
0654 004	RTB	6.004	91348	1995	
0654 005	RTB	6.005	91349	1995	Krause Outlet
0654 006	RTB	6.006	91350	1995	
0654 007	RTB	6.007	91351	1995	
0654 008	RTB	6.008	91352	1995	Ottmar Alt Sprinter
0654 009	RTB	6.009	91353	1995	
0654 010	RTB	6.010	91354	1995	
0654 011	RTB	6.011	91355	1995	
0654 012	RTB	6.012	91356	1995	
0654 013	RTB	6.013	91357	1995	
0654 014	RTB	6.014	91358	1995	
0654 015	RTB	6.015	91359	1995	
0654 016	RTB	6.016	91360	1995	
0654 017	RTB	6.017	91572	1995	
0654 031	VBG	VT 31	91482	1996	Stadt Klingenthal
0654 032	VBG	VT 32	91483	1996	
0654 033	VBG	VT 33	91484	1996	Karlovy Vary / Karlsbad
0654 034	VBG	VT 34	91485	1996	Stadt Auerbach im Vogtland

0654 035	VBG	VT 35	91486	1996
0654 036	VBG	VT 36	91487	1996
0654 037	VBG	VT 37	91488	1996
0654 038	VBG	VT 38	91489	1996
0654 039 @	VBG	VT 39	91693	1997
0654 040 @	VBG	VT 40	91694	1997
0654 041 @	VBG	VT 41	91695	1997
0654 042 @	VBG	VT 42	91696	1997
0654 043 @	VBG	VT 43	91697	1997
0654 044 @	VBG	VT 44	91698	1997
0654 045 @	VBG	VT 45	91699	1997
0654 046 @	VBG	VT 46	91700	1997
0654 047 @	VBG	VT 47	91701	1997
0654 048 @	VBG	VT 48	91702	1997

95 80 0670 — SINGLE CARS

Class 670 is rather unique in being a double deck single car unit! Built by DWA in Dessau and Ammendorf, only seven were produced - a demonstrator unit and six for DB, before interest was lost in the project. In fact DB had a lot of problems with the units and returned them all in 2001 to the builders which by then had been taken over by Bombardier. Today a few still see some use.

Built: 1995–96.
Builder: DWA Dessau/Ammendorf.
Wheel Arrangement: 1-A.
Engine: MTU 6V183 TD 13 of 250 kW.
Accommodation: –/78.
Weight: 34.25 tonnes.
Length over Couplers: 16.332 m.
Door Step Height: 600 mm.

Transmission: Hydromechanical.

Wheel Diameter:
Maximum Speed: 100 km/h.
Maximum Tractive Effort:

EVN	Company	Unit Number	Works No	Built	Notes
0670 001	FBE	670.1	1.571/1	1996	
0670 002	KSR	670 002	1.571/2	1996	
0670 003	DVE	VT670.003	1.571/6	1996	Ex 670 006
0670 004	DVE	VT670.004	1.571/5	1996	Ex 670 005
0670 006	EGP	VT 670.3	1.572/3	1996	Ex 670 003
0670 007	EGP	VT 670.4	1.571/4	1996	Ex 670 004

95 80 0689   REGIO CITADIS
3-SECTION ARTICULATED TRAM-TRAIN UNITS

The Regio Tram Kassel has something making it different from other systems as it has some hybrid trams which under EBA classification are included in the diesel series. Within the city the units operate at the tramway voltage but at Kassel Hbf the diesel engines are started up and the tram goes forward under diesel-electric power. There is one engine mounted on the roof of the driving cars which also contain a fuel tank.

Built: 2004–05.
Builder: Alstom, Salzgitter.
Wheel Arrangement: Bo-2-2-Bo.
Engine: (2).
Traction Motors: 4 x 150 kW.
Accommodation: –/84(6).
Weight: 63.40 tonnes.
Length over Couplers: 36.80 m.
Door Step Height: 360 mm.

Systems: 750 V DC/Diesel-electric.

Continuous/Maximum Rating:

Wheel Diameter:
Maximum Speed: 100 km/h.
Maximum Tractive Effort:

Car 1	Car 2	Car 3	Company	Unit Number	Built	Names
689 551	989 751	689 751	RBK	751	2005	Die Gänsermagd
689 552	989 752	689 752	RBK	752	2005	Die Zwölf Brüder
689 553	989 753	689 753	RBK	753	2005	Der Treue Johannes
689 554	989 754	689 754	RBK	754	2005	Jorinde und Joringel
689 555	989 755	689 755	RBK	755	2005	Der Krautesel
689 556	989 756	689 756	RBK	756	2005	Up Reisen Gohn
689 557	989 757	689 757	RBK	757	2005	Scheewittchen
689 558	989 758	689 758	RBK	758	2005	Allerleirauh
689 559	989 759	689 759	RBK	759	2005	Frau Holle
689 560	989 760	689 760	RBK	760	2005	Brüderchen und Schwesterchen

95 80 0771 SINGLE CARS

These lightweight railbuses were the DR equivalent of the DB Class 795. They did not have buffers and operated with a trailer car which had to be run round at terminating stations. 70 were built for use on light branch lines with easy gradients.

Built: 1957–64 for DR.
Builder: VEB Waggonbau Bautzen.
Wheel Arrangement: 1-A. **Transmission:** Mechanical.
Engine: Rosslau 6 KVD 18 HRW of 134 kW. **Wheel Diameter:** 900 mm.
Accommodation: –/54 1T. **Maximum Speed:** 90 km/h.
Weight: 19.30 tonnnes. **Length over Couplers:** 13.55 m.
Door Step Height: **Maximum Tractive Effort:**

EVN	Company	Unit Number	Works No	Built	Notes
0771 056	BSV	171 056	26	1964	

95 80 0772 SINGLE CARS

A development of Class 771, the 772 has multiple working connections and normally worked with a driving trailer. A more powerful engine needed the frames strengthening so the weight is higher.

Built: 1965–68 for DR.
Builder: VEB Waggonbau (Bautzen 772.0), Görlitz (772.1).
Wheel Arrangement: 1-A. **Transmission:** Mechanical.
Engine: Rosslau 6 VD 18/15-1 HRW of 134 kW. **Wheel Diameter:** 900 mm.
Accommodation: –/54 1T. **Maximum Speed:** 90 km/h.
Weight: 19.40/22.10 tonnes. **Length over Couplers:** 13.55 m.
Door Step Height: **Maximum Tractive Effort:**

EVN	Company	Unit Number	Builder	Works No	Built	Notes/Names
0772 001	VHN	772 001	Btz	8	1964	Hafenbahn Neustrelitz
0772 002	BSV	772 106	Gör	6	1968	
0772 003	BSV	772 150	Gör	50	1968	
0772 004	BSV	772 155	Gör	55	1968	
0772 005	BSV	772 162	Gör	62	1968	
0772 006	BSV	772 312	Btz	5	1963	Ex 771 012
0772 007	BSV	772 367	Btz	37	1964	Ex 771 067
0772 132	KSR	172 132	Gör	32	1968	
0772 149	KSR	172 149	Gör	49	1968	
0772 155	VEV	172 155	Gör	55	1968	Traditionsgemeinschaft Ferkeltaxe
0772 171	KSR	172 171	Gör	71	1968	
0772 173	UEG	772 173	Gör	73	1968	
0772 332	LDC	772 332	Btz	25	1963	Erlebnispark Teichland Ex 771 032
0772 339	BSV	772 139	Gör	39	1968	
0772 342	LDC	772 342	Btz	11	1964	Teichland Express Ex 771 042
0772 345	EBS	772 345	Btz	15	1964	Ex 771 045
0772 414	VEV	VT22.001	Gör	14	1968	Ex 772 114

95 80 0795   SINGLE CAR

This lightweight series of diesel railbuses introduced in the early 1950s allowed many branch lines to remain open. The units do not have normal buffing gear and thus normally ran with dedicated trailers of Class 995 which were loose trailers.

Built: 1954–56.
Builder: MAN.
Wheel Arrangement: 1-A.
Engine: One Büssing of 112 kW.
Accommodation: –/57 1T.
Weight: 11.5–13.9 tonnes.
Length over Couplers: 10.65–13.298 m.
Door Step Height:

Transmission: Mechanical.

Wheel Diameter: 900 mm.
Maximum Speed: 90 km/h.
Maximum Tractive Effort:

EVN	Company	Unit Number	Works No	Built
0795 396	BEF	795 396	140894	1954
0795 398	HGK	VT 1	140896	1954
0795 626	VEB	VT 95 9626	141712	1955

95 80 0796/0798   SINGLE CAR

This railbus series is a more powerful version of Class 795 being fitted with two engines and normal buffing gear. When door controls were added for driver only operation the classification was altered to 796 but the running number remained the same.

Built: 1955–62.
Builder: Various, as shown.
Wheel Arrangement: A-A.
Engine: 2 x 112 kW.
Accommodation: –/56 IT.
Weight: 27 tonnes.
Length over Couplers: 13.95 m.
Door Step Height:

Transmission: Mechanical.

Wheel Diameter:
Maximum Speed: 90 km/h.
Maximum Tractive Effort:

EVN	Company	Unit No	Builder	Works No	Built	Notes
0796 625	NESA/EFZ		Uer	61980	1956	
0796 690	EVG	796 690	Uer	66577	1960	
0796 724	SBE	VT 53	MAN	145115	1960	(Z)
0796 667	EVB	VT 166	WMD	1307	1960	Spare parts
0796 757	SBE	VT 51	WMD	1297	1962	(Z)
0796 760	EVG	796 760	WMD	1300	1960	
0796 784	VEB	796 784	MAN	145566	1961	
0796 785	VEB	VT 52	MAN	146567	1961	(Z)
0796 802	EVG	796 802	MAN		1961	
0796 825	PBE	798 825	MAN	146607	1962	
0796 826	EVB	VT 168	MAN	146608	1962	
0796 828	EVB	VT 169	MAN	146610	1962	Ex EFW, ex EBG, ex DB
0798 007	WEMEG	VT 27	Uer	68639	1961	Ex EBOE VT3.07, AKN, DKB VT 211
0798 307	DRE		MAN	146595	1962	Ex 798 813, 728 001, AKN VT3.07
0798 308	AKN	V 3.08	Uer	68640	1961	
0798 309	AKN	V 3.09	Uer	72837	1967	
0798 469	DNV		SGP	78200	1965	Ex ÖBB 5081 561
0798 514	EEB	0798 514	Uer	60254	1955	Now HKB T 2
0798 538	DP	T 1	WMD	1221	1955	Ex PEG, ex DB
0798 576	EVG	VT 56	WMD	1212	1956	(Z); Ex DKB VT 202, ex DB
0798 585	HGK	VT 2	WMD	1221	1956	
0798 592	DRE	798-01	WMD	1226	1956	Ex DKB VT 204, ex DB
0798 598	EVG	798 598	WMD		1956	
0798 610	ENON/EGP	798 610	Uer	61965	1956	
0798 622	PBE	798 622	Uer	61977	1956	
0798 644	DP	T 3	Uer	61999	1956	Ex PEG, ex DB
0798 667	ENON/EGP	798 667	Uer	66552	1959	Ex PEG T11, ex DB
0798 670	VEB	798 670	Uer		1959	

0798 698	PEG	T 5	Uer	66570	1960	Stored
0798 701	PEG	T 12	Uer	66605	1960	Stored
0798 723	DP	T 9	MAN	145114	1960	Ex PEG, ex DB
0798 751	SBE	VT 58	WMD	1291	1960	(Z); Ex DB
0798 767	EVB	VT 166	WMD	1307	1955	
0798 808	VEB	VT 57	MAN	146590	1962	(Z); Ex DKB 208, ex DB
0798 813	Wiesentalbahn		MAN	146595	1962	
0798 818	PBE	798 818	MAN	146600	1962	Hired from DB Museum
0798 829	OEF	798 829	MAN	146611	1962	

▲ In the 1990s the Regio Sprinter was Deuwag's response to Germany's requirement for a new generation of DMUs. The type did not meet with universal success; only two German operators placed fleet orders. Rurtalbahn 95 80 0654 004, running number 6.004, is seen near Binsfeld with a special train from Düren to Zülpich on 3 October 2014. **Matthias Müller**

NARROW GAUGE RAILCARS

This railcar was built for the Gernrode–Harzgerode Eisenbahn and in effect has never left its home line being today part of the Harzer Schmanlspurbahn. It is in effect preserved and used for special charters etc.

Built: 1933.
Builder: Dessau.
Wheel Arrangement: A-1.
Engine: 66 kW.
Weight: 12.5 tonnes.
Length over Couplers: 8.60 m.

Gauge: 1000 mm.

Accommodation:
Transmission: Mechanical.
Wheel Diameter: 700 mm.
Maximum Speed: 30 km/h.

EVN	Company	Unit Number	Works No	Built
187 001	HSB	GHE T1	3046	1933

These railcars have an interesting history as they originated with the Kreis Altenaer Eisenbahn and then went to the Inselbahn Langeoog system in 1961, being acquired by the Harzer Schmalspurbahn in 1996. During 2014 both units were rebuilt at Miraustrasse GmbH, Hennigsdorf. A new unspecified type of MAN engine has been fitted and the transmission altered to Voith Hydraulic.

Built: 1955.
Builder: Talbot.
Wheel Arrangement: 1A-A1.
Engine: MAN.
Weight: 28.20 tonnes.
Length over Couplers: 16.20 m.

Accommodation: –/65.
Transmission: Hydraulic.
Wheel Diameter: 650 mm.
Maximum Speed: 50 km/h.

EVN	Company	Unit Number	Works No	Built	Notes
187 011	HSB		97519	1955	Ex IL VT 1, KAE VT 1
187 013	HSB		97520	1955	Ex IL VT 4, KAE VT 2

This is another railcar that has travelled around. Originally with the Zell–Todtnau system, when that closed it moved on to the WEG Amstetten–Laichingen line in 1968. Closure there saw it going to Inselbahn Langeoog in 1976, from where it was acquired by HSB in 1995.

Built: 1955.
Builder: Fuchs.
Wheel Arrangement: B-B.
Engine: Two 155 kW.
Weight: 34.20 tonnes.
Length over Couplers: 16.13 m.

Accommodation: –/48.
Transmission: Hydraulic.
Wheel Diameter: 850 mm.
Maximum Speed: 60 km/h.

EVN	Company	Unit Number	Works No	Built	Notes
187 012	HSB		9107	1955	Ex MEG T 15

After unification the HSB wanted some new railcars and this prototype was supplied by DB Wittenberge carriage works.

Built: 1996.
Builder: DB Wittenberge.
Wheel Arrangement: B-2.
Engine: 242 kW.
Weight: 32 tonnes.
Length over Couplers: 16.05 m.

Accommodation: –/49 1T.
Transmission: Hydraulic.
Wheel Diameter: 720 mm.
Maximum Speed: 50 km/h.

EVN	Company	Unit Number	Built
187 015	HSB		1996

After testing 187 015 for some years HSB decided to order a few more, but this time it was the DB carriage works in Halberstadt that got the job.

Built: 1999.
Builder: DB Halberstadt.
Wheel Arrangement: B-2.
Engine: 254 kW.
Weight: 30. Tonnes.
Length over Couplers: 17.30 m.

Accommodation: –/24 (20) 1T.
Transmission: Hydraulic.
Wheel Diameter: 720 mm.
Maximum Speed: 50 km/h.

EVN	Company	Unit Number	Works No	Built
187 016	HSB		1	1999
187 017	HSB		2	1999
187 018	HSB		3	1999
187 019	HSB		4	1999

This is another of the original railcars being former Nordhausen–Wernigerode T 3.

Built: 1940.
Builder: Wismar.
Wheel Arrangement: Bo-Bo.
Engine: 345 kW.
Weight: 34.50 tonnes.
Length over Couplers: 15.60 m.

Accommodation:
Transmission: Electric, BBC.
Wheel Diameter: 800 mm.
Maximum Speed: 60km/h.

EVN	Company	Unit Number	Built
187 025	HSB	NWE T 3	1940

▲ RBH Logistics 97 80 1200 011 hauls a raft of electric locomotives out of the depot at Gladbeck West on 30 August 2012. **Brian Garvin**

3.6. CODE 97 80 - ELECTRIC LOCOMOTIVES WITH MAXIMUM SPEED LESS THAN 100 KM/H

This code has little use as it was originally intended for electric shunting locomotives, but with some private operators using former DB 194s and RBH having some trip locomotives the coding is still in use.

97 80 1200   1200   Bo-Bo

These locomotives were built by Henschel for use on the coal railways of Ruhrkohle AG which later became RBH Logistics and is now a DB subsidiary. Intended for shunting and trip working a lot of this type of work has disappeared and what remains can be covered by RBH using second hand DB locos. Consequently as 1200s wear out they are being withdrawn. Two have been preserved. The class was in effect the forerunner of Austrian Class 1063.

Built: 1976, 1984.
Builder: Henschel.
Traction Motors: 4 x kW.
Maximum Tractive Effort: 330 kN.
Length over Buffers: 15 m.

Weight: 88 tonnes.
Maximum Speed: 100 km/h.
Wheel Diameter: 1100 mm.

EVN	Company	Running No	Works No	Built	Notes
1200 011	RBH	011	32774	1984	RAG 011
1200 013	RBH	013	32776	1984	RAG 013
1200 016	RBH	016	32829	1984	RAG 016

97 80 8194   E94   Co-Co

When open access started, few locomotives were available to private operators. Fortunately some operators managed to get hold of locomotives that had "grandfather rights" from preservation societies. This included some E94 electric locomotives and some former ÖBB 1020s which are the same class.

Built: 1940-45, 1954-56.
Builder–Mechanical Parts: Henschel, Krauss Maffei, Krupp, WLF.
Builder–Electrical Parts: AEG, SSW.
Power Rating: 3000 kW.
Maximum Tractive Effort: 363 kN.
Length over Buffers: 18.60 m.

Weight: 118.70 tonnes.
Maximum Speed: 90 km/h.
Wheel Diameter: 1250 mm.

EVN	Company	Running No	Builder	Works No	Built	Notes
8194 051	PBE	194 051	AEG	5330	1941	Owned by Singen Stadt
8194 052	LEG	254 052	AEG	5331	1941	Ex DR; now loaned to Lokschuppen 1905 Freilassing
8194 095	MWB	194 095	AEG	5720	1943	Ex ÖBB 1020 034; spares loco
8194 103	A-SLB		AEG	5728	1943	Ex MWB, ex ÖBB 1020 041
8194 158	RAILU	194 158	AEG	5865	1945	
8194 192	BYB	194 192	KM	18185	1956	Ex DB
8194 580	RAILU	194 178	KM	18192	1955	Ex DB

3.7 CODE 98 80 - DIESEL LOCOMOTIVES MAXIMUM SPEED LESS THAN 100 KM/H

This group of locomotives consists mainly of shunting locomotives but also includes trip locomotives which by way of being medium powered fall into this category. Many of the shunting locomotives are of types built specially for industrial users and some of the technical details are vague. The EVN for some types is not known as the locos concerned do not stray from their own line. An educated guess has been used to place such locos in a logical place. Note that some odd locomotive types tend to have their class designation starting with "0" but that most former DB types retain the DB prefix of 3.

98 80 0xxx   HF130C   0-6-0DH

The HF in the type designation stands for Herres Feldbahn, 130 the power rating and C for 3 axles. This locomotive was originally of 750 mm gauge but converted to standard gauge in 1947.

Built: 1944.
Builder: Gmeinder.
Engine: **Wheel Diameter:**
Transmission: Hydraulic.   **Weight:**
Maximum Tractive Effort: **Length over Buffers:**
                                 Maximum Speed:

EVN	Company	Running No	Works No	Built
	OHE	0607	4196	1944

98 80 0xxx   MB9N   B

A small industrial type shunting locomotive.

Built: 1971.
Builder: OK Dortmund.
Engine: 250 hp.   **Wheel Diameter:**
Transmission: Hydraulic.   **Weight:** 32 tonnes.
Maximum Tractive Effort: **Length over Buffers:** 7.24 m.
                                 Maximum Speed:

EVN	Company	Running No	Works No	Built
	HABA	5	26727	1971

98 80 0112   MBB1200N   B-B

Built originally for the Hoesch Hüttenwerke AG in Dortmund, it later passed to the Dortmunder Eisenbahn.

Built: 1975.
Builder: OK Dortmund.
Engine: **Wheel Diameter:**
Transmission: Hydraulic.   **Weight:**
Maximum Tractive Effort: **Length over Buffers:**
                                 Maximum Speed:

EVN	Company	Running No	Works No	Built
0112 001	DE	804	26814	1975

98 80 0125   MB170N   B

Built for industrial users in the Ruhr, 26744 was actually preserved by a group in Hamm, but in 1998 it was sold to the WLE.

Built: 1973.
Builder: OK Dortmund.
Engine:
Transmission: Hydraulic.
Maximum Tractive Effort:
Wheel Diameter:
Weight:
Length over Buffers:
Maximum Speed:

EVN	Company	Running No	Works No	Built
0125 001	WLE	07	26745	1973
0125 002	WLE	06	26744	1973

98 80 0128   MB280N   B

Another industrial type that is now in use with a private operator.

Built: 1973.
Builder: OK Dortmund.
Engine:
Transmission: Hydraulic.
Maximum Tractive Effort:
Wheel Diameter:
Weight:
Length over Buffers:
Maximum Speed:

EVN	Company	Running No	Works No	Built	Notes
0128	RST	2	26775	1972	Ex industry
0128	RST	3	26736	1972	Ex industry

98 80 0170   MC700N   C

It appears only nine locomotives of this type were built with most of them still in use.

Built: 1971–79.
Builder: OK Dortmund.
Engine: 515 kW.
Transmission: Hydraulic.
Maximum Tractive Effort:
Wheel Diameter:
Weight:
Length over Buffers:
Maximum Speed:

EVN	Company	Running No	Works No	Built	Notes/Names
	DH	R 21	26711	1971	
	DE	751	26817	1976	Ex Hoesch 751
0170 011	DE	752	26818	1976	Ex Hoesch 752
0170 012	BSM	80	26880	1979	MAX
0170 013	BSM	81	26881	1979	MORITZ
0170 014	EH	756	26893	1978	

98 80 0212   G 1300   B-B

The 212 designation reveals that this type is related to the DB Class 212. MaK built 10 locos based on the DB V100 for private operators with two going to the Swedish Nora Bergslags Järnväg and eight to German operators with TWE having three. One of the Swedish locos is now in Germany having also worked in Denmark!

Built: 1964–69.
Builder: MaK.
Wheel Diameter:
Engine: MA301FAK of 957 kW (1300 hp).
Transmission: Hydraulic, Voith L216rsb.
Maximum Tractive Effort:
Weight: 64–72 tonnes.
Length over Buffers: 12.61 m.
Maximum Speed: 54–79 km/h.

EVN	Company	Running No	Works No	Built	Notes
0212 901	RAILS	Lok 1	1000243	1964	Ex EKML 105
0212 902	NE	V	1000244	1965	Ex MaK, OHJ 46, NBJ 25
0212 903	RRI	40	1000245	1965	Ex HEG V32

0212 905	HzL	V 122	1000247	1964	Now preserved
0212 906	RAILS	Lok 2	1000248	1966	Ex OHJ T 45
0212 907	TWE	V 131	1000255	1968	
0212 908	TWE	V 132	1000256	1968	
0212 909	RBB	V 133	1000257	1968	Ex TWE
0212 910	HzL	V 124	1000258	1969	

98 80 0236 — V 36 — 0-6-0

Again the designation gives away that these are V36 type locos, but ones that were never in DB stock. Built for wartime use these locos ended up with private operators. The technical data is for standard locos but engines and transmissions may have changed.

Built: 1940–58.
Builder: Various.
Engine: KHD V6M436.
Transmission: Hydraulic.
Maximum Tractive Effort:
Wheel Diameter: 1100 mm.
Weight: 38–41 tonnes.
Length over Buffers: 9.20 m.
Maximum Speed: 55 km/h.

EVN	Company	Running No	Builder	Works No	Built	Notes
0236 127	KBB	V36 127	BMAG	11254	1941	Ex BASF D 18
0236 299	EBEFW	V2	BMAG	11458	1942	Zuckerfabrik Wetterau
0236	DLI	3	OK	21341	1940	Ex Industry

98 80 0261 — G 1100 BB — B-B

This type from MaK was built specially for industrial and private operators and was a development of the G850, hence the works numbers in the 800xxx range. 17 were built and most are still in service, but the example numbered as 021 is strange.

Built: 1969–78.
Builder: MaK.
Engine: MaK 6M282AK of 810 kW (1100 hp).
Transmission: Hydraulic, Voith L520r or L5r4.
Maximum Tractive Effort:
Wheel Diameter: 1000 mm.
Weight: 68–80 tonnes.
Length over Buffers: 12.20 m.
Maximum Speed: 36–60 km/h.

EVN	Company	Running No	Works No	Built	Notes
0261 001	IGB	DL 9	800162	1968	Ex Behala 11
0261 005	AKN	V2.017	800167	1970	
0261 011	BE	D 22	800180	1972	
0261 021	CFLDE	02	800190	1978	Ex LSG, SK2

98 80 0262 — G761/762/763C — C

Basically an industrial shunting locomotive, some have ended up with private operators. Of the three types there were 18 G761, three G762 and 27 G763, built with minor variations in the technical specification. Consequently they are all grouped together.

Built: 1978–93.
Builder: MaK.
Wheel Diameter: 1000 mm.
Engine: MTU 6V331TC11 of 470 kW or 6V331TC12 of 500 kW (G761); MTU 8V331TC11 of 600 kW (G762); MTU 6V396TC13 of 560 kW (G763). **Weight:** 54–66 tonnes.
Transmission: Hydraulic, Voith L4r4zU2 (G761/2), L3r4U2 (G763). **Length over Buffers:** 9.87 m.
Maximum Tractive Effort: Max. Speed: 30–55 km/h (G761/2); 32–40 km/h (G763).

EVN	Company	Running No	Works No	Built	Notes
	DE	730	700023	1978	Ex Krupp
0262 004	NE	II	700025	1978	
0262 005	DPR	7	700026	1978	Ex HAFAG 7
	DE	731	700027	1978	Ex Krupp
	DE	734	700028	1979	Ex Krupp
	DE	735	700029	1979	Ex Krupp
	DE	733	700031	1979	Ex Krupp
	DE	736	700032	1979	Ex Krupp
	DE	737	700033	1979	Ex Krupp

	NE	10	700060	1982	
0262 018	NE	III	700061	1982	
	RHKE	D I	700069	1982	
	RHKE	D II	700070	1982	
	VL		700075	1985	Off lease
	VL/CLG	Bayer 108	700088	1985	
0262 217	VGH	22	700093	1989	Ex KSW V 31
	VL/CLG	Bayer 110	700094	1990	
	VL		700110	1993	Ex KSW V33

98 80 0263   G700C   C

This is another shunting locomotive intended originally for the steel industry but now in use with many operators. The running numbers seem to be based on the original order built.

Built: 1966–76.
Builder: MaK.
Engine: MaK, 6M282A of 515 kW (700 hp).
Transmission: Hydrauic, Voith L4r4.
Maximum Tractive Effort:
Wheel Diameter: 1000 mm.
Weight: 50–60 tonnes.
Length over Buffers: 9.86 m.
Maximum Speed: 40–48 km/h.

EVN	Company	Running No	Works No	Built	Notes
	MVG	35	500046	1967	
	RSVG	3	500053	1970	
	RSVG	4	500058	1972	
	EVB	306 51	500068	1975	
0263 007	NTS/WHE		500054	1970	
0263 008	KIEL	263 008	500057	1972	
0263 013	NTS/NIAG	11	500075	1975	Ex SWK V 6

98 80 0264   G765   C

The G765 is the follow on type from G763 with the first going to private operators and later examples going into industrial service.

Built: 1993–94.
Builder: Mak/SFT.
Engine: MWM TBD234BV12(1993), MTU6V39612TC (1994), CAT 3412 DI-TA (1994) all of 560 kW.
Weight: 60–66 tonnes.
Transmission: Hydraulic, Voith L3r4U2.
Maximum Tractive Effort: 194 kN.
Wheel Diameter: 1000 mm.
Length over Buffers: 10.35 m.
Maximum Speed: 40–47 km/h.

EVN	Company	Running No	Works No	Built	Notes
0264 001	EH	771	700106	1993	ex HKM Duisburg 80
0264 002	EH	772	700107	1993	ex HKM Duisburg 81
0264 003	LEUNA	181	700108	1993	
0264 004	LEUNA	182	700109	1994	
0264 005	HTB	V 71	700112	1994	
0264 007	LEUNA	183	700114	1994	
0264 008	LEUNA	184	700115	1994	

98 80 0265   MaK G320B   B

The classification would appear to be intended for private operators' locomotives similar to DB V65. Indeed, a scrapped example was such a loco but the only example that has now come to light is this one which is a completely different type of loco. Others exist in industrial use.

Built:
Builder: MaK.
Engine: MB 846 Ab of 259 kW (350 hp).
Transmission: Hydrauic, Voith L320 U.
Maximum Tractive Effort:
Wheel Diameter: 1000 mm.
Weight: 36–40 tonnes.
Length over Buffers: 8.45 m.
Maximum Speed: 40–48 km/h.

EVN	Company	Running No	Works No	Built	Notes
0265 010	RTBC	V 35	220090	1968	Ex DKB V 35

▲ Open access has seen some older classes return to front line service thanks to their "grandfather" operating rights. RAILU's 97 80 8194 580, running number 194 178 is just such a loco, seen passing Bornheim with a tank train from Ingolstadt to Neuss Gbf on 6 June 2013. **Matthias Müller**

▼ Mittelweserbahn (MWB) 98 80 0273 007, running number V 1001 (on the right) stands next to 92 80 1203 107, running number V 1802 at Hamburg Walthershof harbour on 12 May 2012. The latter has since moved to SGL and now carries a different running number. **Matthias Müller**

98 80 0266   G500C   C

This class is similar to the G700.

Built: 1966–75.
Builder: MaK.
Engine: Mak 6M282 of 390 kW (530 hp).
Transmission: Hydraulic, Voith L4r4.
Maximum Tractive Effort:

Wheel Diameter: 1000 mm.
Weight: 55–60 tonnes.
Length over Buffers: 9.86 m.
Maximum Speed: 35–43 km/h.

EVN	Company	Running No	Works No	Built
0266 001	EVB	304.51	500041	1966
0266 003	NTS		500045	1967
	TWE	V 51	500071	1974

98 80 0270   G1202BB   B-B

In the late 1970s MaK started developing a series of medium powered bogie diesel locomotive with off centre cabs for industrial and private operators. The prototype was the G 1201 (one loco) and the first production type the G 1202 with 12 locos built, the first four being 945 kW and the remaining eight 1000 kW; production then changed to the next version.

Built: 1978–80.
Builder: MaK.
Engine: MTU 12V331TC11 of 945 kw, 12V33TC12 of 100kW.
Transmission: Hydraulic, Voith L5rU2.
Maximum Tractive Effort:

Wheel Diameter: 1000 mm.
Weight: 72–88 tonnes.
Length over Buffers: 12.50 m.
Maximum Speed: 40–75 km/h.

EVN	Company	Running No	Works No	Built	Notes/Names
0270 002	NTS				
0270 003	HAEG/CLG	270 003	1000782	1978	Ex Unirail, ex NIAG 6
	WHE	25	1000783	1979	
0270 008	OHE	1400.01	1000786	1979	
0270 009	OHE	1500.02	1000788	1979	Was 1400.02 but re-engined
0270 010	RBG	D 03	1000789	1980	
0270 011	BE	D 23	1000790	1980	Landkreis Graftschaft Bentheim
0270 012	RBG	D 04	1000791	1980	

98 80 0271   DE 501/2   Co

As the maker's class description signifies, these are diesel electric locomotives featuring three-phase traction that were delivered principally to industrial users to replace first generation diesel locomotives. Some of the DE 502 locos have MTU 6V396TC13 engines giving 560 kW output.

Built: 1980–82.
Builder: MaK.
Engine: MTU 6V331TC12 of 500 kW or MWM TBD234V12 of 510 kW.
Weight: 60–66 tonnes.
Transmission: Electric (BBC).
Maximum Tractive Effort:

Wheel Diameter: 1000 mm.
Length over Buffers: 9.87 m.
Maximum Speed: 45 km/h.

DE 501

EVN	Company	Running No	Works No	Built	Notes
	RBH	551	700039	1980	(Z)
	EH	766	700040	1980	ex Krupp 79
	RBH	557	700047	1981	
	EH	761	700043	1981	
0271 007	EH	762	700045	1981	ex HKM Duisburg 71
0271 008	EH	767	700046	1981	ex HKM Duisburg 73
	RBH	557	700047	1981	ex Krupp 84
	EH	763	700048	1981	(Z)
					ex HKM Duisburg 76

0271 012	EH	764	700050	1981	ex HKM Duisburg 77
	RBH	558	700051	1981	
	EH	765	700052	1981	ex HKM Duisburg 79
	RBH	552	700053	1981	(Z)
	RBH	553	700054	1981	
	RBH	554	700055	1981	
	RBH	555	700056	1981	
	RBH	556	700057	1982	

DE 502

EVN	Company	Running No	Works No	Built	Notes
0271 101	MWB	V 761	700077	1985	Zeche Sophia Jacoba 14
0271 102	BUVL/DPR	271 102	700078	1984	Ex WHE 29
0271 103	BUVL/DPR	271 103	700079	1984	DE 502
0271 104	VL		700080	1985	
0271 105	CH	Panlog 847 804	700081	1985	
0271 106	MWB	V 762	700082	1987	Zeche Sophia Jacoba 15
	BASF	D36	700083	1987	
	BASF	D37	700084	1987	
0271 109	MWB	V 763	700085	1989	Zeche Sophia Jacoba 16
	RBH	561	700095	1989	
	RBH	562	700096	1989	
	RBH	563	700097	1989	
	RBH	564	700098	1989	

98 80 0272   DE 1002   Bo-Bo

Following on from the building of shunting locos with three phase transmission it was not long before this bogie line locomotive appeared. 25 were built for private operators, principally in the Köln area where most of them are still at work. HGK is changing to RHC.

Built: 1982–93.
Builder: MaK.   **Wheel Diameter:**
Engine: MTU 12V396TC13 of 1120 kW or MWM TBD604BV12 of 1320 kW.
Weight: 80–100 tonnes (MTU engine) or 90 tonnes (MWM motor).
Transmission: Electric, BBC/ABB three phase.   **Length over Buffers:** 13.00 m.
Maximum Tractive Effort: **Maximum Speed:** 90 km/h.

EVN	Company	Running No	Works No	Built	Notes/Names
0272 001	NTS	V2.022	1000792	1982	Ex AKN V2.022
0272 002	NTS		1000781	1978	Ex NIAG 5
0272 003		V2.023	1000794	1983	Ex AKN V2.023
0272 004	BE	D 24	1000795	1983	Neuenhaus-Veldhausen
0272 005	NTS	V2.024	1000829	1982	Ex AKN V2.024
0272 006	NTS	V2.021	1000830	1985	Ex AKN V2.021
0272 007	HLB	831	1000831	1988	Ex HEG
0272 008	KSW	V 41	1000832	1987	Ex HEG 832
0272 009	HGK	DE 71	1000833	1987	
0272 010	HGK	DE 72	1000834	1987	
0272 011	HGK	DE 93	1000835	1987	Ex KBE DE 83
0272 012	HGK	DE 74	1000836	1987	
0272 013	HGK	DE 75	1000837	1987	
0272 014	HGK	DE 91	1000838	1987	Ex KFBE DE 91
0272 015	HGK	DE 76	1000839	1987	
0272 016	HGK	DE 73	1000840	1987	
0272 017	HGK	DE 94	1000841	1987	Ex KFBE DE 94
0272 018	HGK	DE 92	1000842	1987	Ex KFBE DE 95
0272 019	HGK	DE 81	1000882	1993	ATBL
0272 020	HGK	DE 82	1000883	1993	ATBL
0272 021	HGK	DE 83	1000884	1993	ATBL
0272 022	HGK	DE 84	1000885	1993	
0272 023	HGK	DE 85	1000886	1993	
0272 024	HGK	DE 86	1000887	1993	

98 80 0273 — G 1203 BB — B-B

After the G1201 and 1202, along came the 1203 having a different MTU engine. A further six locos were built with Cummins engines but these were all exported to Gabon. Note the MTU engine has eight cylinders but is practically as powerful as the 12 cylinder version in the G 1202.

Built: 1982–91.
Builder: MaK.
Wheel Diameter: 1000 mm.
Engine: MTU8V396TC13 of 745kW.
Transmission: Hydraulic, L4r4zU2.
Maximum Tractive Effort:

Weight: 70–100 tonnes.
Length over Buffers: 12.50 m.
Maximum Speed: 33–70 km/h.

EVN	Company	Running No	Works No	Built	Notes
0273 001	AVG	464	1000799	1982	Ex VKP V103
0273 003	SWEG	V 100	1000801	1982	Endingen
0273 004	CTD/TWE		1000802	1982	Ex DE 821, HÜSA, AVG 462, SWEG
V101					
0273 005	MWB	273 005	1000803	1982	ex RCN 0901
0273 006	NRAIL/CLG		1000804	1983	Ex RLG 66
0273 007	MWB	V 1001	1000805	1983	Ex RC 0503, MKB V 4
0273 009	NRAIL/CLG		1000809	1983	Ex RLG 67
	DE	811	1000848	1990	
	DE	812	1000849	1990	
	VL	Bayer 2	1000850	1990	
0273 018	MKB	V 5	1000852	1991	
0273 019	NTS/NRS		1000853	1991	ex SK 4

98 80 0274 — G 1205 BB — B-B

This series has two sub groups. The first 12 locos built were for Eisenbahn und Hafen and featured a Caterpillar engine and low gearing for heavy haulage. Later deliveries changed to MTU engines which were now even more powerful. Overall length is slightly longer.

Built: 1991–97.
Builder: MaK.
Wheel Diameter: 1000 mm.
Engine: CAT 3512 DI-TA of 1120 kW (* MTU 12V396TC14 of 1180 kW).
Weight: 88 tonnes.
Transmission: Hydraulic, Voith L5r4U2.
Maximum Tractive Effort:

Length over Buffers: 12.80 m.
Maximum Speed: 60 (* 80) km/h.

EVN		Company	Running No	Works No	Built	Notes
0274 066		EHG	EHG 521	1000854	1991	
0274 067		EHG	EHG 522	1000855	1991	
0274 068		EHG	EHG 523	1000856	1991	
0274 069		EHG	EHG 524	1000857	1991	
0274 070		EHG	EHG 525	1000858	1991	
0274 071		EHG	EHG 526	1000859	1991	
0274 072		EHG	EHG 527	1000860	1992	
0274 073		EHG	EHG 528	1000861	1992	
0274 074		EHG	EHG 531	1000862	1992	
0274 075		EHG	EHG 532	1000863	1992	
0274 076		EHG	EHG 533	1000864	1992	
0274 077		EHG	EHG 534	1000865	1992	
0274 101	*	ESGBI	7[II]	1000875	1992	Ex VKP V 155
0274 102	*	NE	VI	1000890	1993	
0274 103	*	KIEL		1000892	1993	Ex OHE 150006
0274 104	*	KIEL		1000893	1993	Ex OHE 150007
0274 106	*	NIAG	3	1000894	1993	
0274 107	*	TWE	V 156	1000895	1994	
0274 108	*	TWE	V 157	1000896	1994	
	*	NE	12	1000897	1995	
0274 110	*	NE	VII	1000906	1997	

98 80 0275   G1206-2 BB   B-B

Steelworks in the Ruhr needed some heavy duty shunting and trip locomotives and Vossloh's answer was a modified G1206 classified as G1206-2 BB.

Built: 2007–11.
Builder: Vossloh.
Engine: CAT 3508B DI-TA of 920 kW.
Transmission: Hydraulic, Voith L4r4 zeU2.
Maximum Tractive Effort:

Wheel Diameter: 1000 mm.
Weight: 87.30 tonnes.
Length over Buffers: 14.70 m.
Maximum Speed: 50 km/h.

EVN	Company	Running No	Works No	Built
0275 601	EH	601	5001738	2007
0275 602	EH	602	5001739	2007
0275 603	EH	603	5001740	2007
0275 604	EH	604	5001741	2007
0275 605	EH	605	5001742	2008
0275 606	EH	606	5001743	2008
0275 607	EH	607	5001744	2008
0275 608	DH	D 25	5001790	2008
0275 609	VL/RUHRO		5001791	2008
0275 611	DH	D 26	5001789	2009

98 80 0275   G1206 BB   B-B

These are standard Mak off-centre cab trip engines specially turned out for work in the Ruhr industrial area. They differ from their main line classed variation (92 80 1275) having a lower maximum speed and weighing a few tonnes more. The G1206 MaK bogie locomotive was developed during the period when MaK became Siemens Fahrzeug Technik and later Vossloh. The type has been a huge success story for the works in Kiel with the first deliveries going to Ruhr area industrial railways and then becoming such a popular loco that many private German operators wanted them; in particular, what could be called the main line version (92 80 1275).

Built: 1997–2000.
Builder: SFT/VSFT.
Engine: 800s – MTU 16V396 TC14 of 1500 kW; 900s – MTU 12V4000 R20 of 1500 kW.
Weight: 90 tonnes.
Transmission: Hydraulic, Voith L5r4 zU2.
Maximum Tractive Effort:

Wheel Diameter: 1000 mm
Length over Buffers: 14.70 m.
Maximum Speed: 80 km/h.

EVN	Company	Running No	Builder	Works No	Built	Notes
0275 801	RBH	801	SFT	1000900	1997	Ex RAG
0275 802	RBH	802	SFT	1000901	1997	Ex RAG
0275 803	RBH	803	SFT	1000902	1997	Ex RAG
0275 804	RBH	804	SFT	1000903	1997	Ex RAG
0275 805	RBH	805	SFT	1000904	1997	Ex RAG
0275 806	RBH	806	SFT	1000905	1997	Ex RAG
0275 807	RBH	807	VSFT	1000913	1998	Ex RAG
0275 808	RBH	808	VSFT	1000914	1998	Ex RAG
0275 809	RBH	809	VSFT	1000915	1998	Ex RAG
0275 810	RBH	810	VSFT	1000916	1998	Ex RAG
0275 811	RBH	811	VSFT	1000917	1998	Ex RAG
0275 901						
0275 902	DE	401	VSFT	1001008	1999	
0275 903	DE	402	VSFT	1001009	1999	
0275 904	DE	403	VSFT	1001010	1999	
0275 905	DE	404	VSFT	1001011	2000	

98 80 0276　　　　　G1204 BB　　　　　B-B

The development of MTU engines caused MaK to change the designation of the G 12xx series to G 1204; otherwise the locomotives look identical to earlier versions.

Built: 1981–91.
Builder: MaK.
Engine: MTU 12V396TC13 of 1120 kW.
Transmission: Hydraulic, Voith L5r4U2.
Maximum Tractive Effort:

Wheel Diameter: 1000 mm.
Weight: 72–88 tonnes.
Length over Buffers: 12.50 m.
Maximum Speed: 42-80 km/h.

EVN	Company	Running No	Works No	Built	Notes/Names
0276 001	WLE	71	1000796	1981	LIPPSTADT
	RBH	674	1000797	1982	Ex RAG
0276 003	HAEG/MVG	276 003	1000798	1982	Ex Unirail, ex NIAG 1
0276 004	WLE	72	1000806	1982	BECKUM
	RBH	676	1000807	1983	
0276 006	RBH	677	1000812	1983	
	WHE	27	1000813	1983	
0276 008	OHE	1500 03	1000814	1984	
0276 009	RBH	678	1000815	1984	
	WHE	28	1000816	1984	
0276 011	RBH	673	1000817	1984	Ex RAG
0276 013	HAEG/Prolok	276 013	1000820	1985	Ex Unirail, ex NIAG 2
0276 015	OHE	1500 04	1000822	1985	
0276 016	KSW	V 45	1000866	1991	Ex VL, ex SERSA 847 953 BETTINA

98 80 0279　　　　　G 6　　　　　C

In 2008 Vossloh produced the prototype for a modern three-axle shunting locomotive, having spotted a need for such locos after a gap in production for many years. Indeed it was rather obvious that locos produced in the 1960s and 1970s needed replacing. This prototype was allocated Class 0279 but the production series is now class 0650.

Built: 2008.
Builder: Vossloh.
Engine:
Transmission: Hydraulic, Voith L3r4zeU2 or L3r4zseU2.
Maximum Tractive Effort:

Wheel Diameter: 1000 mm.
Weight: 60–67.50 tonnes.
Length over Buffers: 10.35 or 10.79 m.
Maximum Speed: 35–80 km/h.

EVN	Company	Running No	Works No	Built
0279 001	VL		5001844	2008

98 80 0421　　　　　DG2000CCM　　　　　C-C

Built:
Builder: KHD.
Engine:
Transmission:
Maximum Tractive Effort:

Wheel Diameter:
Weight:
Length over Buffers:
Maximum Speed:

EVN	Company	Running No	Works No	Built	Notes/Names
0421 001	HEB	DG 201	57877	1965	KNE DE 20
0421 002	HEB	DG 202	56955	1959	KNE, KFBE V 82
0421 003	WLE	30	57651	1964	Ex OHE; Helmut Ellinger
	WLE	34	56288	1956	Damaged
	WLE	37	58251	1970	Ex DE stored
0421 006	WLE	38	58252	1970	Ex DE
0421 007	VTLT/WHE		57649	1963	Ex OHE 2000.91
	VTLT		57650	1964	Ex OHE 2000.92

▲ 98 80 0276 008, Running number 150003, is a MaK G1204 design operated by Osthannoversche Eisenbahn (OHE). It is seen shunting at Wunstorf station on 3 June 2014. **Brian Garvin**

▼ As part of its testing regime, Vossloh Locomotives hired 98 80 0650 107 to DB Regio for shunting at Berlin Lichtenberg. It is pictured between duties on 6 September 2012. **Matthias Müller**

98 80 0423   DG1000BB   B-B

This is rather strange as one loco seems to be classified differently to other similar locos which are 98 80 3422. Please see that designation for details

EVN	Company	Running No	Works No	Built	Notes
0423 004	WLE	40	58254	1970	ex Klöckner Hütte, Bremen

98 80 0424   DG1200BB   B-B

Built: 1961.
Builder: KHD.   **Wheel Diameter:** 1000 mm.
Engine: **Weight:**
Transmission: **Length over Buffers:**
Maximum Tractive Effort: **Maximum Speed:**

EVN	Company	Running No	Works No	Built
0424 001	OHE	1200 65	57273	1962

98 80 0505   MH05   C

In 1984 Krauss Maffei introduced this class as a new series of shunting locomotives, with just a few being built each year until the class totalled 43. The first 13 locos have MTU engines whilst the remainder have Caterpillar ones.

Built: 1984–2001.
Builder: Krauss Maffei.   **Wheel Diameter:** 1000 mm.
Engine: MTU6V396TC12 of 525 kW or CAT 3412E DI-TTA JW of 522 kW.
Weight: 60–66 tonnes.
Transmission: Hydraulic, Voith L3r4U2.   **Length over Buffers:** 9.86 m.
Maximum Tractive Effort: **Maximum Speed:** 45 km/h.

EVN	Company	Running No	Works No	Built
0505 004	LUTRA	HAKON 22	19927	1984
	DH	R 22	20076	1993
0505 009	HFM	D 1	20079	1994
0505 011	HFM	D 8	20044	1992
0505 013	HFM	D 9	20077	1993
0505 101	EH	851	20329	1997
0505 102	EH	852	20330	1997
0505 103	EH	853	20331	1997
0505 104	EH	854	20332	1997
0505 105	EH	855	20333	1997
0505 106	EH	856	20334	1997
0505 107	EH	857	20335	1997
0505 108	EH	858	20336	1997
0505 109	EH	859	20337	1998
0505 110	EH	860	20338	1998
0505 111	EH	861	20339	1998
0505 112	EH	862	20340	1998
0505 113	EH	863	20341	1998
	DH	D 18	20342	1998
0505 114	EH	864	20343	1998
0505 116	EH	865	20344	1998
0505 117	EH	866	20345	1998
0505 118	EH	867	20346	1998
	EH	876	20347	1998

0505 121	EH	868	20440	1999
0505 122	EH	869	20441	1999
	EH	870	20442	1999
0505 124	EH	872	20451	2000
0505 125	EH	871	20444	1999
0505 126	LEUNA	191	20450	2000
0505 128	EH	874	20452	2001
0505 129	EH	875	20453	2001
0505 130	EH	873	20454	2001

98 80 0506   ME05   Co

Krauss Maffei, as well as producing a diesel hydraulic shunting locomotive, caused some surprise by also offering a diesel electric version. A surprise is that as well as the usual centre cab version, it was also offered with cabs at each end which Dortmunder Eisenbahn in particular found very useful.

Built: 1981–88.
Builder: Krauss Maffei.
Engine: MTU 6V396TC12 of 500 kW.
Transmission Electric, BBC.
Maximum Tractive Effort:

Wheel Diameter: 1000 mm.
Weight: 75 tonnes.
Length over Buffers: 10 m.
Maximum Speed: 50 km/h.

EVN	Company	Running No	Works No	Built	Notes
	VPS	701	19885	1982	
0506 006	VPS	703	19887	1982	
	DE	765	19888	1982	Cab each end
	DE	766	19889	1982	Cab each end
	DE	767	19890	1982	Cab each end
	DE	768	19891	1982	Cab each end
	DE	769	19892	1982	Cab each end
0506 009	VPS	706	19914	1984	
	DH	Z 1	19915	1984	
	DH	R 3	19917	1985	
0506 051	WLH	71	19815	1975	Ex NE I, Leased to NE
	DE	770	19970	1988	Cab each end
	DE	771	19971	1988	Cab each end
	DE	772	19972	1988	Cab each end
	DE	773	19973	1988	Cab each end

98 80 0550   DE500C   Co

Gmeinder also built some three-axle diesel shunters but did not attract any large orders. The arrival of a large number of Vossloh G6 locomotives with BASF would suggest those may have finished working with that company.

Built: 1981–91.
Builder: Gmeinder.
Engine:
Transmission:
Maximum Tractive Effort:

Wheel Diameter:
Weight:
Length over Buffers:
Maximum Speed:

EVN	Company	Running No	Works No	Built	Notes
	BASF	D50	5686	1990	
	BASF	D51	5687	1990	
	BASF	D52	5688	1990	
0550 007	BE	D 5	5692	1990	Ex MVG 8
	BASF	D53	5693	1991	
	BASF	D54	5694	1991	
	BASF	D55	5698	1992	

98 80 0551   DH500   C

Just like Krauss Maffei, Gmeinder also produced three-axle shunting locomotives in hydraulic and diesel electric versions.

Built:
Builder: Gmeinder.
Engine:
Transmission:
Maximum Tractive Effort:

Wheel Diameter:
Weight:
Length over Buffers:
Maximum Speed:

EVN	Company	Running No	Works No	Built	Notes
	RRI	19	5281	1964	Ex RAG 414
	RRI	415	5282	1964	Ex RAG 415
0551 005	RRI	21	5278	1963	Ex RAG 412
0551 014	RRI	20	5376	1965	Ex RAG 416

98 80 xxxx   D05B   B

Built:
Builder: Gmeinder.
Engine:
Transmission:
Maximum Tractive Effort:

Wheel Diameter:
Weight:
Length over Buffers:
Maximum Speed:

EVN	Company	Running No	Works No	Built	Notes
	WLE	15	5373	1965	Ex EH 201

98 80 0554   D25B   B

Gmeinder produced this small diesel shunting locomotive for use by customers wanting a small but powerful locomotive.

Built: 1972–85.
Builder: Gmeinder.
Engine: 380 kW.
Transmission: Hydraulic.
Maximum Tractive Effort: 145 kN.

Wheel Diameter: 1000 mm.
Weight: 45 tonnes.
Length over Buffers: 8.24 m.
Maximum Speed: 15 km/h.

EVN	Company	Running No	Works No	Built	Notes
0554 001	NIAG	12	5471	1972	
	WINR	2	5476	1972	
	HzL	V 24	5491	1972	Ex SWEG V23-01
	HzL	V 34	5651	1985	
	BASF	D4	5547	1976	

98 80 xxxx   D65BB   B-B

Built: 1959.
Builder: Gmeinder.
Engine: 480 kW.
Transmission: Hydraulic.
Maximum Tractive Effort:

Wheel Diameter: 950 mm.
Weight: 56–68 tonnes.
Length over Buffers: 10.24 m.
Maximum Speed:

EVN	Company	Running No	Works No	Built
	SWEG	V70-01	5117	1959

98 80 0575   D75BB   B-B

Built: 1982–89.
Builder: Gmeinder.
Engine: 1000 kW.
Transmission: Hydraulic.
Maximum Tractive Effort:
Wheel Diameter: 1000 mm.
Weight: 72 tonnes.
Length over Buffers: 12 m.
Maximum Speed:

EVN	Company	Running No	Works No	Built
	BASF	D42	5614	1982
0575 002	SWEG	V102	5647	1985
0575 003	SWEG	V103	5648	1985
	BASF	D43	5689	1989

98 80 0580   D100BB   B-B

Built: 1985–2000.
Builder: Gmeinder.
Engine: MTU 12V396TC 13 of 1100 kW or 12V400R20 of 1500 kW.
Weight: 72–80 tonnes.
Transmission: Hydraulic.
Maximum Tractive Effort:
Wheel Diameter: 1000 mm.
Length over Buffers: 13.09 m.
Maximum Speed: 70–110 km/h.

EVN	Company	Running No	Works No	Built	Notes
0580 001	HzL	V 150	5649	1985	
0580 002	HzL	V 151	5650	1985	
0580 003	VPS	1501	5690	1990	
0580 004	VPS	1502	5691	1990	
0580 005	HzL	V 152	5701	1992	
0580 006	RBW	486	5706	1993	
0580 007	VPS	1503	5707	1993	
0580 008	VPS	1301	5708	1993	2014 to Müller Gleisbau (CH).
0580 009	VPS	1302	5733	1996	2014 to Müller Gleisbau (CH).
0580 010	VPS	1303	5734	1996	2014 to Müller Gleisbau (CH).
0580 011	VPS	1504	5739	2000	
0580 012	VPS	1505	5740	2000	

98 80 0650   G 6   C

Just why the classification of the G 6 was changed from 0279 to 0650 lies somewhere in the offices of the EBA as the base number 650 xxx could be a DMU, but of course the full number with the 98 tells us it is a diesel shunter. There have been two big purchasers for the type – BASF Ludwigshafen and VPS Salzgitter. Others have gone to Vossloh itself for leasing to possible customers (including DB which has several) or to Northrail, a leasing company located on Vossloh's doorstep.

Built: 2009–
Builder: Vossloh.
Engine:
Transmission: Hydraulic, Voith L3r4zeU2 or L3r4zseU2.
Maximum Tractive Effort:
Wheel Diameter: 1000 mm.
Weight: 60–67.5 tonnes.
Length over Buffers: 10.35 or 10.79 m.
Maximum Speed: 35–80 km/h.

EVN	Company	Running No	Works No	Built	Notes/Names
0650 001	VPS	601	5001905	2011	
0650 002	VPS	602	5001910	2011	
0650 003	VPS	603	5001914	2011	
0650 004	CTD-DE		5001918	2011	Ex VPS 604
0650 005	VPS	605	5001944	2011	
0650 006	CTD-DE		5001941	2011	Ex VPS 606
0650 007	CTD-DE		5001945	2011	Ex VPS 607

0650 008	VPS	608		5001946	2011
0650 009	VPS	609		5001934	2011
0650 010	VPS	610		5001947	2012
0650 011	VPS	611		5001948	2012
0650 012	VPS	612		5001949	2012
0650 013	VPS	613		5001950	2012
0650 014	VPS	614		5001951	2012
0650 015	VPS	615		5001952	2012
0650 016	VPS	616		5001953	2012
0650 017	VPS	617		5001954	2012
0650 018	VPS	618		5001955	2012
0650 019	VPS	619		5102025	2013
0650 020	VPS	620		5102026	2013
0650 021	VPS	621		5102027	2013
0650 022	VPS	622		5102028	2013
0650 023	VPS	623		5102029	2013
0650 024	VPS	624		5102030	2013
0650 025	VPS	625		5102031	2013
0650 026	VPS	626		5102032	2013
0650 027	VPS	627		5102033	2014
0650 028	VPS	628		5102034	2014
0650 029	VPS	629		5102035	2014
0650 030	VPS	630		5102036	2014
0650 031	VPS	631		5102037	2014
0650 032	VPS	632		5102038	2014
0650 033	VPS	633		5102039	2014
0650 034	VPS	634		5102040	2014
0650 035	VPS	635		5102041	2014
0650 036	VPS	636		5102042	2014
0650 037	VPS	637		5102043	2014
0650 038	VPS	638		5102044	2014
0650 039	VPS	639		5102045	2014
0650 040	VPS	640		5102046	2014
	BASF	G1		5102047	2013
	BASF	G2		5102048	2013
	BASF	G3		5102049	2013
	BASF	G4		5102050	2013
	BASF	G5		5102051	2013
	BASF	G6		5102052	2013
	BASF	G7		5102053	2013
	BASF	G8		5102054	2013
	BASF	G9		5102055	2013
	BASF	G10		5102056	2013
	BASF	G11		5102057	2013
	BASF	G12		5102058	2013
	BASF	G13		5102059	2013
	BASF	G14		5102060	2013
	BASF	G15		5102061	2013
	BASF	G16		5102062	2013
0650 076	HAEG			5001859	2010
0650 077	VL/PCT		0650 077	5001908	2011
0650 100	VL/CTD			5101982	2013
0650 101			Zellstoff Stendal 6	5001858	2009
0650 102	NRAIL/BASF			5001860	2010	REINER
0650 103	VL/BASF			5001861	2010	BETTINA
0650 104	VL/BASF			5001862	2010	At Antwerpen
0650 106			Zellstoff Stendal 7	5101992	2011
0650 107	VL/DBR Berlin			5001986	2011
0650 108	NRS/DB Cottbus			5101993	2011
0650 109	VL/PL Kolej Baltycka			5001957	2012
0650 110	VL			5001958	2012
0650 115	VL/PCT			5102066	2013
0650 116	NRAIL/CLG			5102067	2013	At Ingolstadt

0650 117	Slovenia	5102064	2013	
0650 118	PCT		2013	At Milbertshofen
0650 119	VL	5102092	2014	
0650 120				
0650 121	VL/NIAG	5102091	2014	
0650 122	VL	5102099	2014	
0650 123	VL	5102107	2014	
0650 300	CZ Ostrava	5101978	2012	
0650 301	VL/DBR	5101980	2012	
0650 302	Sweden	5101981	2013	
0650 303	VL/NIAG	5102106	2014	

98 80 0991   CGF250 DVR

Built: 1991.
Builder: Schöma.
Engine:
Transmission:
Maximum Tractive Effort:

Wheel Diameter:
Weight:
Length over Buffers:
Maximum Speed:

EVN	Company	Running No	Works No	Built
0991 001	DHE	9	5173	1991

98 80 3107   V 75   Bo-Bo

This class is the same as the former DR V 75; indeed one former DR loco is listed. It is of course the ČKD T435.0 type of which 20 were delivered to the DR. When open access started some operators acquired some of this type from industrial concerns in the Czech Republic as the class had grandfather rights in Germany. The V 75 designation reflected the 750 hp rating.

Built: 1961–65.
Builder: ČKD.
Engine: ČKD 6S310DR of 551 kW.
Transmission: Electric.
Maximum Tractive Effort:

Wheel Diameter: 1000 mm.
Weight: 61 tonnes.
Length over Buffers: 12.56 m.
Maximum Speed: 60 km/h.

EVN	Company	Running No	Works No	Built	Notes
3107 018	RPRS	107 018	5698	1962	Ex Arco, KEG, ex DR 107 018
3107 513	RPRS	107 513	6808	1965	Ex Arco 4070.51, ex KEG, ex Kladno (CZ) 721 513
3107 554	RPRS	T435 0554	5075	1961	Ex Arco, ex KEG, ex CZ

98 80 3201/3202   V100DR   B-B

These classifications reflect that some former DR 201/202 series, mostly modernised at Stendal works, did not receive improved bogies and consequently have a maximum speed of 80 km/h. Some German sources quote some locomotives as 100 km/h but either they or the EBA are wrong as a 100 km/h speed would put them into the 92 series. So for this book it is assumed the EBA classification is correct and all locos in these classes are 80 km/h! (Except the Vattenfall locos which are 65 km/h.)

For Technical details and engine types see 92 80 1201 etc.

EVN	Engine	Company	Running No	Works No	Built	Notes
3201 004	h3	MHG	1	11212	1966	Ex DR 201 004
3201 019	a	RAILS	201 019	11228	1967	Ex DR 201 019
3201 025	a	SEM	110 025	11234	1967	

▲ Ostsächsische Eisenbahnfreunde (OSEF) owned **98 80 3202 331** carries its original DR red livery and original number **112 331**. On 19 October 2013 it is working an OSEF special train near Heinersbrück (north east of Cottbus) on the Vattenfall operated Kohleverbindungsbahn system.
Keith Fender

▼ Westfälische Landes-Eisenbahn **98 80 3423 005**, running number **44**, stands at the WLE depot at Lippstadt on 23 July 2014.
Matthias Müller

3201 026	a	NETINERA	WL 2	11455	1967	Ex DR 201 026. Neustrelitz
3201 028	a	ITB	54	11457	1957	Ex DR 201 028
3201 067	a	AHG	4	11905	1968	Ex DR 110 067 via Industry
3201 068	a	ENON	201 068	11906	1968	
3201 070	a	RAILS	18	11908	1968	
	a	NL-Railpro	V100 093	11931	1968	
3201 101	a	WFL	18	11939	1968	
3201 110	h1	HTB		12409	1969	Ex V100-BUG-01, ex Laubag 110-10, DR 110 108
	h1	Vattenfall	110-12	12418	1969	Ex DR 110 117
	h1	Vattenfall	110-09	12422	1969	Ex DR 110 121
	h1	Vattenfall	110-07	12432	1969	Ex DR 110-131
	h1	Vattenfall	110-06	12439	1969	Ex DR 110 138
	h1	Vattenfall	110-03	12447	1969	Ex DR 110 146
	h1	Vattenfall	110-11	12449	1969	Ex DR 110 148
	g		110-08	12460	1969	Ex DR 110 159
3201 171	c	TSE	110 171	12452	1969	Ex DB
3201 211	a	LOCON	201	12493	1970	AMP 6, ex DR 201 211
3201 222	a	LOCON	202	12504	1970	Ex various, ex DR 201 222
3201 308		LWB	V100-121	12772	1970	Ex DR 201 308
3201 380	a	UBB	201 380	12889	1971	Ex DR
3201 792	a	UBB	201 792	14849	1975	Ex DR
3201 865	a	EBS	V100-120	15383	1976	Ex LWB, ex DR 201 865
3201 878	e	LOCON	209	16372	1977	Ex Lokpool, ex DR 201 878
3202 057	b	EBS	202 057	11895	1968	Ex LWB V100-121
3202 066	b	A-SETG	V100.01	11904	1968	Ex KCL 01, ex KCR PBSV 12, DR 202 066
3202 078	b	BWESA/ADAM	202 078	11916	1968	Stored
3202 098	j1	AHG	01	11936	1968	
3202 109	b	ALS		12410	1969	Stored
3202 144	b	ALS		12445	1969	Stored
3202 166	b	ALS		12467	1969	Stored
3202 167	b	ALS		12468	1969	Stored
3202 209	b	ALS		12491	1970	Stored
3202 220	b	ALS	202 220	12502	1970	Stored
		PRESS	204 031	12518	1970	Ex DB 202 326
3202 248	b	ALS		12530	1970	
3202 264	b	WFL	17	12546	1970	Ex ALS 203 504, DR 202 264
3202 265	j3	VWE	DL 3	12547	1970	Also quoted as 3202 655!
3202 266	b	ALS		12548	1970	Stored
3202 287	h4	A-SETG	V100.02	12751	1970	Ex KCL/KCR 11, PBSV, DR 202 287
3202 294	b	ALS		12758	1970	Stored
3202 297	b	ALS		12761	1970	Stored
3202 299	b	ITB	88	12763	1970	Ex DR 202 299
3202 302	b	ILM	V100 02	12766	1970	Ex DR 202 302
3202 331	b	OSEF	112 331	12840	1971	
	j5	SLG	V100-SP-006	12849	1971	Ex 202 340; now in NL
3202 347		MTEG	204 347	12856	1971	Ex DR 202 347
3202 354		MTEG	204 354	12863	1971	Ex DR 202 354
3202 427	a	ALS	202 427	12936	1972	Stored
3202 439	j3	PRESS	204 009	13478	1972	Ex Johanna 05, ex NRS V100 002, ex 202 439
3202 453		WFL	16	13492	1973	Ex various, ex ALS 203 502, ex DR 202 483
3202 457		DBM Halle		13496	1972	
3202 458	b	RAILS	202 458	13497	1972	Ex DR

3202 459	j3	BWESA/ADAM	24	13498	1972	Ex NRS V100 001
3202 483	b	WFL	24	13522	1972	Ex various incl. 203 502, DR 202 483
3202 487	b	EBS	202 487	13526	1972	Ex LWB V100-122
3202 488	b	HGB	V100.03	13527	1972	Ex TLG 16 ex DR
3202 494	b	A-SETG	03	13533	1972	Ex KCL/KCR 16, PBSV, 202 494
3202 500	a	DLI	202 970	16756	1983	Ex 710 970
3202 501	j3	BUG	V100-BUG-02	17729	1983	Ex ADAM 19, ARCO, KEG 1001
3202 535		HAEG/Prolok	202 535	17732	1938	Ex KTG 1
3202 536		SLG	V100-SP-007	13575	1973	
3202 543		BWESA/ADAM	202 543	13582	1973	
3202 547	b	EGP	202 547	13586	1973	Ex V100SP002, DR 202 547
3202 563	b	DLW Meiningen	202 563	13881	1973	
3202 594	b	ALS		13912	1973	Stored
3202 646	b	EGB	202 646	14073	1974	Stored
3202 648	b	ALS		14075	1974	Stored
3202 674	b	ALS		14375	1974	Stored
3202 677	h3	SLG	V100 SP 003	14378	1998	Ex 202 677
3202 690	j5	SLG	V100 SP 004	14391	1974	Ex 202 690; now in NL
3202 722	b	ALS		14423	1974	Stored
3202 744	j5	SLG	V100 SP 005	14445	1974	Ex 202 744; now in NL
3202 746	j1	PRESS	293 026	14447	1974	ALS 202 001, DR 202 746
3202 778	j3	DPR	202 001	14659	1975	Ex 202 778
3202 787	b	A-SETG	04	14844	1975	Ex KCL/KCR 18, PBSV, ALS 203 503, 202 787
3202 811	j3	PRESS	204 044	15083	1975	Ex Johanna 04, NRS V100 003
3202 822	j3	WFL	15	15094	1975	Ex various, ex DR
3202 846	j1	SLG	V100 SP 001	15231	1976	Ex 202 846
3202 885	b	EGB	202 885	16379	1978	Loaned to SEM Chemnitz
3202 960		HTB	V 143	15395	1976	Ex DB 710 960
3202 970		DLI	202 970	16756	1983	Ex DB 710 970

98 80 3236   V36   0-6-0

This classification is for V36 diesel shunters that were previously in DB stock. For technical details see 98 80 0236.

EVN	Company	Running No	Builder	Works No	Built	Notes
3236 204	DP	8 / V36 204	BMAG	10991	1939	Ex preservation, ex DB
3236 237	DEV	V36 005	KHD	47179	1944	Ex DB
3236 255	DP	9 / 236 255	MaK	2012	1948	Ex industrial, ex DB

98 80 xxxx   G321B   B

MaK built 15 of these small shunters, mostly for industrial use. The two locomotives that have come to notice do not appear to have EVNs, presumably because they do not venture away from their own system.

Built: 1981–93.
Builder: MaK.
Engine: KHD F12L413F of 246 kW.
Transmission: Hydraulic, L2r2.
Maximum Tractive Effort:

Wheel Diameter: 1000 mm.
Weight: 32–44 tonnes.
Length over Buffers: 7.24 m.
Maximum Speed: 22–36 km/h.

EVN	Company	Running No	Works No	Built
	HGK	V 21	220105	1981
	HGK	V 22	220106	1981

98 80 3262   240B   0-4-0

A standard small shunting locomotive mostly used in industry but a few remain in service with private operators.

Built: 1954–65.
Builder: MaK.
Engine: MaK MS24 of 177 kW.
Transmission: Hydraulic, Voith L33yUb.
Maximum Tractive Effort:

Wheel Diameter: 950 mm.
Weight: 28–33 tonnes.
Length over Buffers: 7.70 m.
Maximum Speed: 56 km/h.

EVN	Company	Running No	Works No	Built	Notes
	EIVEL	Lok 02	220095	1962	Ex Bayer Brunsbüttel 1
3262 005	TEL	V 9	220022	1954	Ex AKN V2.009
3262 011	BE	D 12	220028	1957	
3262 049	VEF	DL 4			

98 80 3263   240C   0-6-0

A three-axle version of the preceding class; 14 were built.

Built: 1955–62.
Builder: MaK.
Engine: MaK MS24 of 177 kW.
Transmission: Hydraulic, Voith L33yUb.
Maximum Tractive Effort:

Wheel Diameter: 950 mm.
Weight: 29–36 tonnes.
Length over Buffers: 7.70 m.
Maximum Speed: 56 km/h.

EVN	Company	Running No	Works No	Built
3263 009	KIEL	Seehafen Kiel 3	220059	1960

▲ BEG 98 80 3295 049 is pictured at Brohl Gbf on 1 November 2014 where it is stabled for the weekend. This locomotive is one of just three EVN registered examples built by Jung, the majority being built by MaK. **Matthias Müller**

98 80 3265   600D   0-8-0

This series has the 3265 classification based on the DB V65, 265 series. However there are several sub-series as besides the 600D there are 650, 800, 1000 and 1200, but all have one thing in common – they are all 0-8-0s. The basic data is given and at the start of each sub-section differences are given.

Built: 1953–61.
Builder: MaK.
Engine: MaK MS301A of 442 kW (600 hp).
Transmission: Hydraulic, Voith L37zUb.
Maximum Tractive Effort:
Wheel Diameter: 1250 mm.
Weight: 54–66 tonnes.
Length over Buffers: 11.36 m.
Maximum Speed: 59–68 km/h.

3265 1xx. These are shorter, being 10.6 m.

EVN	Company	Running No	Works No	Built	Notes
3265 101	VBV	V2.004	500004	1953	
3265 103	TEL	V46-01	500013	1955	Ex EVB V280
3265 201	DME	V 62	600129	1956	
3265 202	BEG	INGE	600139	1958	Ex RCT, TWE, AEE

3265 3xx. The 650D series rated at 478 kW (650 hp).

3265 301	HC	V 15	600148	1957	Ex KBE V15
3265 303	STVG	V65-12	600154	1959	Ex ESG 1, ex TBG V65.12
3265 304	VGH	21	600155	1959	Ex OHE 600.21

3265 4xx. The 800D series rated at 589 kW (800 hp), length 10.6 m and speed 60–80 km/h.

3265 401	SEH	800 011	800011	1954	

3265 6xx. The 1200D series with engine MaK MA302BK of 884 kW (1200 hp), weight 60–80 tonnes and speed 66–87 km/h.

3265 601	HAEG	265 601	1000016	1959	Ex OHE V1200 51
3265 602	DME	V 122	1000057	1961	
3265 603	HFH	265 603	1000156	1963	Ex OHE V1200 54

98 80 3270   V 20   0-4-0

These small diesel shunters were built for military service during WW2. About 30 locos came into DB service being given the V20 description which later became 270.

Built: 1940–41.
Builder: BMAG.
Engine: KHD A6M324 or MaK MDS24 of 200 hp.
Transmission: Hydraulic.
Maximum Tractive Effort:
Wheel Diameter: 1100 mm.
Weight: 27 tonnes.
Length over Buffers: 8 m.
Maximum Speed: 55 km/h.

EVN	Company	Running No	Builder	Works No	Built	Notes
3270 046	SEM	V 262	BMAG	39643	1943	Ex StMB 262
3270 049	TEL/DL	00601	KHD	11399	1941	Ex NME, OHE

98 80 3290   V90   B-B

This type description is for former DB 290s that have been sold on to private operators. All built by MaK except 3290 189, built by KHD. For technical details see Class 290 in German Railways Part 1.

*   Built by KHD, other MaK.

EVN	Company	Running No	Works No	Built
3290 003	RPRS		1000261	1964
3290 008	RPRS		1000266	1964
3290 127	RPRS/HSL	290 127	1000458	1968
3290 189 *	RPRS	290 189	58359	1969
3290 502	LCH		1000260	1964
3290 518	LCH		1000276	1964
3290 535	LCH		1000408	1967
3290 536	LCH		1000409	1967

98 80 3291   291   B-B

This type description is for former DB 291s that have been sold to private operators. For technical details see Class 291 in German Railways Part 1.

EVN	Company	Running No	Works No	Built	Notes
3291 034	RPRS		1000716	1975	
3291 035	RPRS		1000717	1975	
3291 037	RPRS		1000719	1975	
3291 971	NTS/DELTA		1000492	1972	Ex OHE 1200.77
3291 972	NTS/Bugdoll Gleisbau		1000516	1971	Ex OHE 1200.76
	WLE	62	1000599	1974	

98 80 3293   V100.4   B-B

The V100.4 designation came from the builders as various types of the DR V100 were built. The V100.4 was for heavy duty shunting and tripping as opposed to the first V100s which were branch line passenger and freight locos. Some of these locos are original V100.4s but many are ordinary V100s upgraded at Stendal works by being fitted with new engines and having their steam heating boilers removed. Even ADtranz got involved before it became too busy with its TRAXX locomotives. Hardly any locomotives are now in original condition so the technical details given reflect the rebuilt state. Some German sources quote that various rebuilt locos have a maximum speed of 100 km/h but this is thought to be erroneous as such locos would be classed 92 80 1293. See 92 80 1201 etc for explanation of engine codings. Works numbers in the 72xxx series are ADtranz rebuild numbers.

Built: 1973–83.
Builder: LEW, Rebuilt by ADtranz or Stendal.   **Wheel Diameter:** 1000 mm.
Engine: CAT 3508 DI-TA of 773–900kW or 3512 DI-TA of 932–1140 kW.
Weight:
Transmission: Hydraulic.   **Length over Buffers:** 15.24 m.
Maximum Tractive Effort: **Maximum Speed:** 80 km/h.

EVN	Engine	Max Speed	Company	Running No	Works No	Built	Notes
3293 001	a	65	RTS	V100.17	17851	1982	Ex PCK V100.4.17
3293 002	j2	80	RDX		16672	1981	Ex BTE 1001, Ex Laubag 110-01
3293 016		72	OTDTL	293 016	16327	1981	Ex PRESS 293 016, ex DWU 13, ex CZ 745 527
3293 021	a	65	WFL	12	16580	1981	Ex EIB 21, CZ 745 580
3293 022	a	65	MTEG	293 022	16584	1981	Ex SWT 22
3293 023	h1	65	MTEG	293 023	17849	1982	Ex SWT 23
3293 024	j2	(100)	EIB	20	16383	1978	Ex DR 110 889
3293 025	j2	(100)	EIB	22	72570	2000	Ex TLG, ex DR
3293 026			WFL	12	16580	1981	Ex various, CZ 745 580
3293 060	j2	(100)	EKO	60	16384	1978	Lokpool, DB 201 890
3293 061	j2	80	EKO	61	17850	1982	Ex LEUNA 135
3293 062	j2	80	EKO	62	17852	1982	
3293 063	j2	(100)	EKO	63	13936	1973	201 618
3293 064	j2	80	EKO	64	17730	1983	
3293 065	j2	80	EKO	65	17733	1983	
3293 828	j2	(100)	AULOC	41	14892	1975	Ex DB 201 828
3293 884	j2	(100)	AULOC	42	16378	1978	Ex DB 201 884
3293 891	j2	(100)	AULOC	43	16385	1978	Ex DB 199 891
3293 900	j2	(100)	CTD-RBB	V 141	15382	1976	Ex DB 201 864
3293 901	j2	72	CTD-RBB	V 142	17728	1983	Ex EKO 63
3293 902	a	65	RAILS/Redler	14	16328	1981	Ex ARCO/KEG 1003
3293 903	j3	80	AULOC	46	16581	1981	Ex Infra Leuna 131
3293 904	h4	80	LEUNA	132	16582	1981	
3293 905	h4	80	LEUNA	135ᴵᴵ	16583	1981	Ex EKO 61
3293 906	h4	80	LEUNA	133	16676	1981	
3293 907	j3	80	AULOC	45	16677	1981	Ex Infra Leuna 134

3293 908	j2	(100)	AULOC	44	72580	2000	Ex ??
3293 909	j1	80	ITB	(1102)	16675	1981	Ex PCK Schwedt
							V100-16
	h1	65	Vattenfall	110-02	17731	1983	Ex Laubag
	h1	65	Vattenfall	110-04	16671	1981	Ex Laubag
	h1	65	Vattenfall	110-05	17727	1983	Ex Laubag

98 80 3294   294   B-B

These locomotives are DB 294s sold to private operators. For technical details see Class 294 in German Railways Part 1.

EVN	Company	Running No	Builder	Works No	Built
3294 096	RPRS		KHD	58326	1968

98 80 3295   295   B-B

These locomotives are DB 295s sold to private operators or similar locos built by MaK for private operators. For technical details see Class 295 in German Railways Part 1.

*   Built by Jung, all others by MaK.

EVN	Company	Running No	Works No	Built	Notes/Names
3295 014	BUVL/DPR	295 014	1000696	1975	
3295 015	BUVL		1000697	1975	
3295 017	BUVL		1000699	1975	
3295 020	BUVL		1000702	1975	
3295 023	RPRS		1000705	1975	
3295 024	BUVL/ABEG		1000706	1975	(Hamburg)
3295 025	BUVL/ABEG		1000707	1975	(Hamburg)
3295 026	BUVL/ABEG		1000708	1975	(Hamburg)
3295 027	BUVL/DPR	295 027	1000709	1975	
3295 028	BUVL		1000710	1975	
3295 029	BUVL		1000711	1975	
3295 030	BUVL		1000712	1975	
3295 045 *	BUVL		14209	1975	
3295 048 *	BUVL/BOEG		14212	1975	Leased from EAH
3295 049 *	BEG		14213	1976	
3295 057	BOEG	295 057	1000730	1976	Wrongly carries VKM BEG
3295 061	BUVL		1000734	1976	
3295 064	BUVL		1000737	1976	
3295 069	RPRS/RNE		1000742	1977	
3295 073	BUVL		1000746	1977	
3295 079	ISL	2	1000752	1977	Infraserv Logistics Frankfurt/M
3295 081	EHB	HABA 9	1000754	1977	SWO Stadtwerk Osnabruck
3295 082	MTRD (Hamburg)		1000755	1977	PRAHA
3295 084	EHB	HABA 10	1000757	1977	SWO Stadtwerk Osnabruck
3295 088	RPRS		1000761	1978	
3295 091	MTRD (Hamburg)		1000764	1978	
3295 092	MTRD (Hamburg)		1000765	1978	HAMBURG
3295 095	AGLVG		1000768	1978	Ex RPRS
3295 097	ISL		1000770	1978	Infraserv Logistics Frankfurt/M
3295 100	ISL	3	1000773	1978	Infraserv Logistics Frankfurt/M
3295 950	OHE	1600 73	1000517	1971	
3295 951	OHE	1600 74	1000518	1972	
3295 952	OHE	1600 75	1000597	1975	
3295 953	RVM	61	1000596	1974	Kreis Soest
3295 954	WLE	62	1000598	1975	Leased to RVM
3295 955	DE	022	1000599	1975	
3295 956	DE	023	1000600	1975	
3295 957	DE	024	1000601	1975	
3295 958	DE	026	1000602	1975	
3295 960	DE	027	1000774	1976	

3295 961	DE	028	1000775	1976	
	WHE	22	1000776	1978	
	WHE	23	1000777	1978	
3295 964	WHE	24	1000778	1978	
3295 970	NTS		1000492	1972	Aluminium Norf, Neuss

98 80 3298   298   B-B

These are DB Class 298s sold to private operators after an upgrade overhaul at Stendal works where new Caterpillar engines were fitted making them similar to DB 298.3 (CAT 3508 DI-TA 773 kW). For technical details see Class 298 in German Railways Part 1.

EVN	Company	Running No	Works No	Built	Notes
3298 050	SWT	298-30	11888	1968	Ex DB
3298 052	MEG	112	11890	1968	Ex DB
3298 085	SWT	298-31	11923	1968	Ex DB
3298 088	MEG	113	11926	1968	Ex DB
3298 102	MEG	111	11940	1968	Ex DB
3298 130	SWT	298-24	12431	1969	Ex DB
3298 135	SWT	298-25	12436	1969	Ex DB
3298 151	MEG	114	12472	1969	Ex DB
3298 301	MEG	115	16678	1981	Ex DB

98 80 3309   N4b/V10B   0-4-0

LKM built hundreds of these small shunting locos for use in DDR industries. A few have found their way into the hands of open access operators. It appears two different types have been grouped into this series.

Built: 1958–70.
Builder: LKM.
Engine:
Transmission: Mechanical.
Maximum Tractive Effort:

Wheel Diameter:
Weight:
Length over Buffers:
Maximum Speed:

EVN	Variant	Company	Running No	Works No	Built	Notes
3309 001	Type N4b	EBS		251255	1958	
3309 503	Type V10B	WFL	7	252115	1960	Ex EFZ, ex NVA
		RHKE	D V	252537	1970	

98 80 3310   Kö II   B

The DR had many Kö II locomotives which were given the class number 100 and after unification became Class 310. Thus the classification 3310 gives an indication of the heritage. Those numbered below 800 have mechanical transmission with above 800 numbers having hydraulic transmission.

Built: 1933–44.
Builder: Various.
Engine: 6KVD14.5SRW of 92 kW.
Transmission: Mechanical or Hydraulic.
Maximum Tractive Effort:

Wheel Diameter: 850 mm.
Weight: 16 tonnes.
Length over Buffers: 6.392 m.
Maximum Speed: 30 km/h.

EVN	Company	Running No	Builder	Works No	Built	Notes
3310 275	PBE	310 275	OK	20269	1934	
3310 278	PBE	310 278	OK	20272	1933	Privately owned
3310 441	FWN		Jung	5643	1934	Ex IGENO, ex DR
3310 634	MBBKB		BMAG	10288	1934	
3310 802	DP	110	BMAG	11501	1942	Ex DR 310 802
3310 821	FWN		KHD	47377	1944	Ex IGENO, ex DR
3310 912	HEF	Kö 5712	BMAG	11494	1940	
3310 950	DP	Kö 5750	DWK	655	1939	Ex DR 310 950

98 80 3311 — V15B, V18B — 0-4-0

The original type given DB designation 311 was the Kö I but the EVN seems to cover this type and the two mentioned above. Perhaps just a convenient slot into which several small types could be placed? The DR 101s were given this class number as DB no longer had any of the originals still in stock but there were some in industry and preservation so some confusion is understandable.

Built: 1960–74.
Builder: LKM.
Engine: 6KVD18SRW of132kW.
Transmission: Hydraulic.
Maximum Tractive Effort: 66 kN.

Wheel Diameter: 900 mm.
Weight: 21.50 tonnes.
Length over Buffers: 6.94 m.
Maximum Speed: 37 km/h.

EVN	Company	Running No	Builder	Works No	Built	Notes
3311 009	HEIN	VL 3		253010	1960	Ex DR
3311 101	LOCON	007		261350	1964	Ex Hamburger Aluminium Werke, ex BKK Brieske
	LOCON			261399	1964	Ex DDR Industry
3311 227	WAB	311 227	Wind	310	1936	Ex industry ex DB
3311 260	BEF	Ko 0260	Gmdr	1621	1936	
3311 350	WFL	2		261333	1969	Ex Industry
3311 501	ABRRS	V22-307		262505	1974	
3311 535	CFLDE	311 009		261312	1963	Ex FLEX, ex Preservation ex DR 101 535
3311 559	BEF	V15 2082		261135	1962	numbered locally as V22 2082
3311 620	ITB	205[II]		261131	1962	Ex DB
3311 699	ATL	1		261397	1964	Ex DB
	AHG	1		261213	1962	Ex industry
	DLI			261548	1967	Ex industry
	ELS	311 CL 914		261465	1965	
	EGP	V22.02		261386	1964	Ex HKW Guben 5
	ELBA			261336	1964	Ex IFA ? 2

EVN	Company	Running No	Builder	Works No	Built	Notes
3311 900	EVB	V 224	KHD	55534	1953	Ex BHE

98 80 3312 — V22/23 — 0-4-0

The former East German Classes V22 and V23 are grouped together here with former DR 102.0 and 102.1 series. Even so, two locos in this grouping are V18s but these could have been rebuilt to V23 standards.

Built: 1962–78.
Builder: LKM.
Engine: 6KVD18/15-1SRW of 132kW.
Transmission: Hydraulic.
Maximum Tractive Effort: 66 kN.

Wheel Diameter: 1000 mm.
Weight: 24 tonnes.
Length over Buffers: 6.94 m (312.1 8.0 m).
Maximum Speed: 35/40 km/h.

EVN	Company	Running No	Works No	Built	Notes
3312 001	PRESS	312 002	262607	1967	HKW Dresden 1
3312 002	DP/WAB	2	261184	1962	Ex DR 311 665
3312 003	DP	4	262349	1971	Ex Nickelhütte St. Egidien
3312 004	EGP		262350	1971	Ex DP/WAB 3, Ex Nickelhütte St. Egidien
3312 005	DP/WAB	102	262351	1971	Ex Nickelhütte St. Egidien
3312 006	DP/WAB	1	262634	1976	Ex Materiallager Wittenhagen
3312 007	DP/WAB	103	252506	1974	Ex DDR Industry
3312 008	EGP	V22.02	261386	1964	Ex DDR Industry
3312 012	RBB	33	262603	1975	Ex DDR Industry
3312 013	SLG	V22-SP-030	262216	1969	Ex DDR Industry
3312 014	SLG	V22-SP-031	262136	1968	Ex DDR Industry
3312 015	SLG	V22-SP-032	262256	1969	Ex DDR Industry

3312 021	AHG	02	262337	1971	Ex DDR Industry
3312 030	OST	312 030	262064	1968	Ex DR via industry
3312 031	KML	19	262246	1970	Ex MTG
3312 033	WFL	4	262471	1983	Ex Industry; leased to ELS
3312 034	WFL	11	262140	1969	Ex Industry; leased to ELS
3312 035	WFL	13	262557	1975	Ex Industry
3312 037	RME	4	262071	1978	Ex DR
3312 038	SKLUS	1	262665	1976	Ex DDR Industry
3312 039	SKLUS	2	262265	1970	Ex DDR Industry
3312 040	ABG		262076	1968	Ex RAW Dessau, RAW Potsdam, ex DR
3312 041	NESA	V22 519	262625	1976	Ex NVA
3312 046	RME	5	262095	1968	Ex DR
3312 048	NFG/Scholtz Espenhain		262624	1976	
3312 055	TME	1	262104	1968	Ex DR
3312 056	TME	2	262418	1973	Ex DDR Industry
3312 057	TME	2	262518	1973	Ex DDR Industry
3312 066		312 066	262115	1968	Kley's Bau GmbH
3312 069	CLR	312 069	262173	1968	Ex MHG 21
3312 071	EBS		262120	1968	Ex DDR Industry
3312 079	ITB	2	262128	1968	Ex IGENO
	WFL	2	261333	1969	Ex industry; leased to SETG at Schwedt
	EGP	V22 03	262305	1971	Ex industry in Riesa
	EGP	V22 01	262340	1971	Ex PE Cargo, ex industry Calbe 14
	EBS	102 002	262200	1969	Ex DDR Industry
	EBS	V22 002	262567	1965	Ex DDR Industry
	HVLE	V22.1	262533	1974	Ex Bombardier/ADtranz/ LEW 3
	TME	4	262168	1969	Ex DDR Industry
	WFL	12	262289	1971	Ex DDR Industry
	Vattenfall	102-03	262651	1975	Ex Laubag
	Vattenfall	102-13	262529	1974	Ex Laubag
	Vattenfall	102-30	262621	1975	Ex Laubag
	Vattenfall	102-32	262477	1973	Ex Laubag
	LOCON		262300	1972	(Z); Ex DDR Industry
3312 101	BWESA/ADAM	16	265063	1970	Ex 312 163
3312 102	Stendal Works	WL 2	265002	1970	
3312 103	HVLE	V22.1	262533	1974	Ex Bombardier, ADtranz, LEW 3
3312 108	ITB	203			?? Unknown
3312 109	ZF Anklam Werklok		262369	1972	
3312 113	EBS	312 113	265013	1970	Ex DR
3312 117	ADAM	312 117	265017	1970	
3312 124	NETINERA		265024	1970	Neustrelitz
3312 145	RME	312 145	265045	1970	
3312 150	VBG	WL 1	265050	1970	Neumark shunter
3312 162	ITB	3	265062	1970	ex IGENO
3312 163	ADAM	16	265063	1970	Hektor; Eisenach shunter
3312 166	Stendal Works		265066	1970	
3312 167	BUVL/Delitzsch Works		265067	1970	
3312 183	HCM	102 183	265083	1970	
3312 188	IGDA		265088	1970	
3312 195	FWN	5	265095	1970	Ex IGENO
3312 200	IGEW		265100	1970	
3312 208	RBG	D 08^{II}	265108	1970	Ex DR
3312 242	ABG		265142	1970	Ex RAW Dessau, ex DR
3312 251	RBG	102 251	265151	1970	Ex DR
3312 253	UEG	102 253	265153	1970	Ex DR
3312 254	ALS	312 254	265074	1970	Ex ASLVG 01 ex DR 312 174
3312 287	ITL	102 004	261128	1962	Ex Materialwerke Schwepnitz
3312 501	EBS	312 002	362200	1969	Ex SEM 102 002

AHG	3	262495	1974	Ex Industry
Bahnlog	V22.1	262630	1976	
CLR		262173	1969	Ex MHG 21
ITB	205	262174	1969	Ex Industry
ITL	102 001	262367	1972	Ex Elbe Kies 3
ITL	102 002	262466	1973	Ex Papierfabrik Greiz; scrapped in 2013
ITL	102 003	262364	1972	Ex VEB Gummiwerke Watterhausen
ITL	102 005	262490	1974	Ex Materialwerke Schwepnitz
KML	13	262292	1971	Ex MTG
KML	16	262161	1967	Ex MTG
MHG	21	262005	1967	Ex DDR industry
RBB	33	262603	1975	Ex Thyssen halle
RBB	34	262422	1972	Ex Industry
ABRRS	V22-306	262505	1974	Ex Industry
RME	1	262291	1973	Ex Industry

98 80 3322   DB 322   B

DB disposed of all its Class 322 shunters many years ago, with some going to industry and others into preservation. They have been grouped again in order of their former DB numbers.

Built: 1933–60.
Builder: Various.
Engine: KHD A6M517 or Kaelble GN130S of 92 kw.
Transmission: Hydraulic, Voith.
Maximum Tractive Effort: 39.2 kN.

Wheel Diameter: 850 mm.
Weight: 16–17 tonnes.
Length over Buffers: 6.45 m.
Maximum Speed: 30 km/h.

EVN	Company	Running No	Builder	Works No	Built	Notes
3322 160	DIEBM		KHD	12759	1935	Ex DB
3322 182	EBN	Köf 6128	Gmdr	4677	1951	DB via Industry
3322 520	NTS		Gmdr	5103	1959	Ex DB via various
3322 605	BEF	Köf 4280	KM	15416	1934	Ex DB via Industry
3322 607	PBE	322 607	KM	15429	1934	Leased to STOCK
3322 637	INNR	322 637	KM	15382	1933	Ex DB via Industry
3322 640	PBE		Gmdr	4811	1954	Ex DB via Industry
3322 642	EEB	D 10	Krupp	1373	1934	Ex DB
3322 660	WTB	322 660	Krupp	1382	1934	Ex DB via Industry

98 80 3323   DB 323   B

These small DB shunters have always found favour with industrial concerns and branch line operators. Technical details as for 98 80 3322

EVN	Company	Running No	Builder	Works No	Built	Notes/Names
3323 052	DIEBM		KHD	47350	1944	
3323 075	NTS		Gmdr	4691	1952	EMMA
3323 104	DP	5	KHD	57014	1959	Ex Industrial, ex DB 323 104
3323 133	AVOLL	323 133	KHD	57278	1959	Ex various, ex DB
3323 143	KIEL/SK	5	KHD	57288	1959	
3323 146	IGEBA	323 146	KHD	57291	1959	Ex DB via industry
3323 149	EVG	323 149	KHD	57294	1959	
3323 166	BLP	Wiebe 5	OK	26005	1959	
3323 173	DIEBM		OK	26012	1959	
3323 210	DP	6	KHD	57312	1960	Ex industrial, ex DB 323 210
3323 216	DP	11	KHD	57318	1960	EMMA; Ex industrial, ex DB 323 216
3323 270	KIEL		OK	26051	1960	
3323 325	LWB		KHD	57328	1960	

3323 351	EVG	323 351	KHD	57931	1965	
3323 486	RBG		Jung	5492	1934	
3323 574	VEV	V2-01	Gmdr	4885	1956	
3323 627	BVM	323 627	Gmdr	5015	1958	
3323 639	BLP	Wiebe 1	Gmdr	5027	1958	Ex DB
3323 680	BYB	Köf 6498	Gmdr	5132	1959	Ex DB
3323 681	RAILS	Köf 6499	Gmdr	5133	1959	
3323 686	DUD	121	Gmdr	5138	1959	Ex DB via industry
(323 687)	Unirail		Gmdr	5139	1959	Ex DB via industry
3323 697	SDN Neuoffingen		Jung	13137	1959	
3323 699	CLBG	323 699	Jung	13139	1959	
3323 711	DP	7"	Gmdr	5004	1957	Ex industrial Tm 134 in Switzerland, ex DB
3323 714	IGEBA	323 714	Gmdr	5148	1960	Ex DB
3323 718	HAEG/NIAG		Gmdr	5152	1960	
3323 719	IGEBA	323 719	Gmdr	5153	1960	Ex DB via industry
3323 751	BLP	Wiebe 14	Gmdr	5185	1960	Ex DEW V14, ex industry, ex DB
3323 771	IGEBA	323 771	Gmdr	5205	1960	Ex DB via industry
3323 784	Infraserv, Wiesbaden		Jung	13137	1959	
3323 808	INNR	323 808	Jung	13176	1960	Ex DB via industry
3323 829	STVG	Kof 6759	Jung	13197	1960	Ex DB via industry
3323 837	HAEG		Jung	13205	1960	
3323 850	TWE	323 850	Jung	13218	1960	
3323 912	ESGBI	5	KM	15444	1934	Ex DB 323 912
3323 939	HAEG/NIAG	323 939	Gmdr	4671	1951	"Tom"
3323 942	HE Mannheim		Gmdr	4788	1953	
3323 951	Unirail		KM	15386	1933	Ex DB via industry
3323 958	FME Nurnberg		Gmdr	4812	1954	
3323 963	EVULW		Gmdr	5108	1959	EMMA; Ex DB 323 963
3323 970	BE	D 13	OK	20975	1938	Ex DB 323 970
3323 972	EVG Linz		KHD	10911	1934	

98 80 3332   DB 332   B

The more modern Köfs have, like their predecessors, followed them into industrial and private use. For technical details see Class 332 in German Railways Part 1.

EVN	Company	Running No	Builder	Works No	Built	Notes/Names
3332 002	MWB	V 241	Gmdr	5121	1960	
3332 008	DP	332 008	OK	26303	1962	Ex MWB V 244, ex DB
3332 010	DP	332 010	OK	26305	1962	Ex industry, ex DB 332 010
3332 011	WLH/RBSA	25	OK	26306	1962	Ex DB 332 011
3332 028	DHE	10	Gmdr	5266	1963	Ex MWB V 245, ex DB
3332 030	NEWAG		Jung	13572	1963	ex MWB V 246, ex DB
3332 032	EBN		Jung	13574	1963	Ex DB, leased to HLG/BEBRA
3332 046	ESGBI	3	Jung	13630	1963	
3332 050	LUW	332-001	Gmdr	5291	1963	MWB 248, ex DB
3332 068	IGE	332 068	Gmdr	5309	1964	(Passau)
3332 081	RNE		OK	26319	1963	
3332 090	ERB	V 249	OK	26328	1963	Ex MWB
3332 092	BYB		OK	26330	1963	
3332 093	ERB		OK	26331	1963	Hamm shunter
3332 095	VPS	201	OK	26333	1963	
3332 098	AKO	Köf 11 098	OK	26336	1963	
3332 103	BE	D 2	OK	26341	1964	to Eisenbahnbedarf Bad Nauheim
3332 109	VEB	332-CL-109	OK	26347	1964	Museum lok
3332 115	MWB	V 247	OK	26353	1964	
3332 128	PBE		OK	26365	1964	Museum Lok Mannheim

3332 136	BEF	Köf 11 036	OK	26373	1964	Museum Lok Basdorf
3332 144	DP	332 144	OK	26381	1965	Ex industry ex DB 332 144
3332 152	ZBAU	11000050	OK	26389	1965	
3332 153	NRS	332 153	OK	26390	1965	
3332 161	ABRN	V 1	Jung	13747	1964	
3332 169	NEWAG		Jung	13782	1964	Ex MWB V 250, ex DB
3332 178	DP	332 178	Jung	13791	1964	Ex industry ex DB 332 178
3332 189	EBN	V332.01	Jung	13802	1964	
3332 204	LUW	332-002	Gmdr	5344	1963	Various, ex DB
3332 210	TBG	332-15	Gmdr	5350	1965	OTTOKAR II
3332 215	WTBB	332 215	Gmdr	5355	1965	
3332 218			Gmdr	5384	1965	Stored
3332 240	PBE		Gmdr	5406	1966	
3332 271	FME		Jung	13916	1966	
3332 288	ITB	101	OK	26403	1965	
3332 289	MWB	V 243	OK	26404	1965	
3332 298			OK	26413	1965	
3332 312	ESGBI	4	OK	26427	1966	
3332 801	BOBY	V23 001	Gmdr	5124	1959	Ex WEG V23, ex DB 332 801
3332 901	RE	332 901	Gmdr	5304	1964	

98 80 3333/3335   DB 333   B

For technical details see Classes 333/335 in German Railways Part 1.

EVN	Company	Running No	Builder	Works No	Built	Notes/Names
3333 096	DIEBM		OK	26455	1969	
3333 172	MWB	V 254	OK	26481	1975	
3333 682	NTS		OK	26491	1975	
3333 674	BSM	74	OK	26483	1975	Ex DB
3333 716	LM	333 716	OK	26926	1977	Ex DB
3333 902	DP	332 902	Ruhr	3575	1958	Ex MGB Tm 4973, ex FO, ex DB, ex Kerkerbach 19
3335 013	RNE		Jung	14053	1968	
3335 026	LUW		Jung	14066	1968	
3335 038	HAEG		Gmdr	5440	1968	Anja; leased to EuroMaint, Kaiserslautern
3335 045	NTS		Gmdr	5441	1968	
3335 053	VWE		Gmdr	5449	1969	MARS
3335 059	MWB/NOB	V255	Gmdr	5455	1969	
3335 063	MWB	V253	Gmdr	5459	1969	Leased to STS
3335 064	EVB	202 51	Gmdr	5460	1969	
3335 069	TDR	335 069	Gmdr	5465	1969	
3335 099	BE	D 4	OK	26548	1968	
3335 106	NTS/NOB		Gmdr	5496	1973	
3335 123	DIEBM		Jung	14177	1973	
3335 126	NRAIL		Jung	14180	1973	
3335 127	DIEBM		Jung	14181	1973	
3335 130	DIEBM		Jung	14184	1973	
3335 139	SHH		Jung	14193	1974	
3335 143	KIEL/NOB	335 143	Gmdr	5506	1974	
3335 167	LUW		OK	26476	1974	
3335 212	MWB	V 252	OK	26922	1977	
3335 218	LUW	335 201	OK	26923	1977	
3335 219	RHC	DH 111	OK	26929	1977	Ex NE 11[II]
3335 231	SHH	F21	OK	26941	1977	
3335 245	MWB	V 251	Gmdr	5532	1977	

▲ Delmenhorst-Harpstedter Eisenbahn (DHE) Köf 98 80 3332 028 is one of the many former DB Class 332 locomotives that have found their way to private operators. It stands at Harpstedt on 6 July 2008. **Keith Fender**

▼ Former DR V60, 98 80 3345 227, still carrying running V60 08 although now in the hands of Eisenbahn Gesellschaft Potsdam, is seen at Magdeburg yard on 29 September 2011. **David Hunt**

98 80 3345/3346/3347   DR V60D   0-8-0

After Unification there were lots of spare shunting locos in the former DDR which private operators soon acquired - many for spare parts or waiting for better days. For technical details see Classes 345–347 in German Railways Part 1.

*   built by LKM, all others LEW.

EVN	Company	Running No	Works No	Built	Notes/Names
3345 023	HEIN	VL 15	15125	1976	GISELA; Ex HWB, ex DR
3345 028	LOCON	101	15151	1976	Ex BUG V60BUG003, ex DR 345 028
3345 029	EBS	V60.02	13749	1973	Ex EIVEL V60-02
3345 030	NSW		15153	1976	Natursteinwerke Weiland
3345 033	RME	345 033	15156	1975	Ex DB
3345 037	PRESS		15160	1976	Spares
3345 050	LWB	V60-104	14889	1976	Ex DB
	WFL	25?	15584	1977	Ex DDR industry
3345 055	HEIN	VL 16	15586	1977	Brigette; Ex HWB, ex DR
3345 061	HCM/EGP	345 061	15592	1977	Sold to industry, Blankenstein (Saale)
3345 067	LOCON	103	15598	1977	Ex BUG V60BUG001, ex DR 345 067
3345 072	MEG	84	15603	1977	Ex DB; loaned to Wittenberge museum
3345 091	PRESS	346 025	16566	1979	Ex DB
3345 095	LWB	V60-106	16570	1979	Ex DB
3345 100	UEG	345 100	16987	1980	
3345 104	LWB	V60-105	17411	1980	Ex DB
3345 112	HVLE	V60.3	17793	1980	Ex DR 345 112
3345 113	HVLE	V60.4	17794	1980	Ex DR 345 113
3345 116	OST	345 116	17797	1980	Ex DR via industry
3345 119	RIS	345 119	17564	1981	
3345 128	UEG	345 128	17573	1981	
3345 133	MEG	85	17578	1981	Ex DB
3345 137	SKLUS	3	17582	1981	Ex DB
3345 152	MEG	86	17678	1981	
3345 159	DLI	345 159	17685	1982	
3345 161	HGB	V60.01	17687	1982	Ex BUG V60-BUG-02, DR 345 161
3345 165	DLI	345 165	17691	1982	
3345 201	SLG	V60-SP-013	11258	1971	Ex DDR Industry
3345 202					
3345 203	SLG	V60-SP-015	16966	1979	Ex DDR Industry
3345 204	SLG	V60-SP-014	12686	1970	Ex DDR Industry
3345 205	EGP	V60.03	12383	1969	Ex Raillogic V60.01, ex DDR industry; leased to PCT
3345 206	TWE	V 68	16575	1979	Leased to HTB
3345 207	PRESS	346 001	11977	1968	Ex KUSS 1
3345 208	PRESS	346 003	16956	1980	Ex MEG 06
3345 209	PRESS	346 004	15693	1979	Ex CZ 716 601
3345 210	PRESS	346 014	14824	1975	Ex Mibrag Di441-65-B4
3345 211	PRESS	346 018	15360	1976	Ex Espenhain Di472-65-B4
3345 212	PRESS	346 019	13784	1973	Ex Industrial
3345 213	PRESS	346 020	15200	1976	Ex Industrial
3345 214	PRESS		13751	1973	Spares; Ex LEUNA 174
3345 215	PRESS		13768	1973	Spares; Ex RBB 23
3345 216	PRESS		16962	1980	Spares loco
3345 217	DP	19	14197	1871	Ex Kaliwerk Merkers
3345 218	DP	20	14816	1975	Ex Laubag 106-03
3345 219	EGP/DP	21	12945	1971	Spares; Ex Kaliwerk Merkers 12
3345 220	EGP/DP	22	15609	1977	Spares; Ex Laubag 106-02
3345 221	LEG/WE	345 970	15572	1977	Ex LEG, ex Wismut V60.10

3345 224	HVLE	345 107	17419	1980	
3345 225	KNAUF	WL 4	15669	1979	
3345 226	KNAUF	WL 3	16973	1980	
3345 227	EGP	V60.08	11028	1965	Ex PE Cargo, ex LMBV 26
3345 228	CLR	345 228	17641	1982	Ex BBL 01, HWB VL 6 ex Czech Industry
3345 229	RBB	24	14193	1974	Ex VEB Bitterfeld 24
3345 230	EGP	V60.01	15147	1976	Ex PEG Cargo, PCK V60.41; leased to HSL
3345 231	EGP	V60.02	11026	1965	Ex PEG Cargo
3345 234	DP/WAB	105	13765	1973	Ex DDR Industry
3345 235	DP/WAB	104	12736	1970	Ex Wismut V60-13
3345 237	RTS	345 237	15673	1979	Ex EBW V60.05, DDR Industry
3345 240	FME	V60 11011	11011	1965	
3345 243	HGB	V60.02	16965	1980	Ex TLG 15, KEG 006, Zement Karsdorf
3345 244	RPRS	346 12 400	12400	1969	
3345 245	DLI	345 159	17685	1982	Ex DR
3345 247	DLI	345 165	17691	1982	Ex DR
3345 248	DLI	63	14320	1974	Ex MEG 63, ex DB 346 933
3345 250	EBS	106 250	12243	1969	Ex BWESA/ADAM 2, ex Industrial
3345 251	KML	5	13766	1976	Ex Industrial
3345 252	KML	7	13826	1973	Ex EHW Thale
3345 253	KML	8	16572	1979	Ex Kali Steinsalz, Stassfurt
3345 254	KML	9	16681	1979	Ex Kali Steinsalz, Stassfurt
3345 259	WFL	1	15369	1976	Ex Industrial; scrapped 2012
3345 260	WFL	3	18102	1983	Ex Industrial
3345 261	LOCON	104	14579	1975	Ex V60BUG05, DR 346 967
3345 263	MHG	3	15365	1976	Ex Industrial
3345 266	ITB	6	14198	1974	
3345 268	ITB	627	16578	1979	Ex Brandenburg steelworks
3345 269?	ITB	628	16464	1980	Ex Brandenburg steelworks
3345 270?	ITB	629	17594	1981	Ex Brandenburg steelworks
3345 271	ITB	630	17595	1981	Ex Brandenburg steelworks
3345 272	ITB	631	13333	1972	
3345 273	ITB	7	17586	1981	Ex RBB 29 ex industry
3345 275	RAN	V60 001	16698	1979	Ex DDR Industry
3345 280	ITL	106 002	10944	1965	Ex BKK Bitterfeld Di230-65-B4
3345 281	ITL	106 003	11319	1966	Ex MaLoWa 3
3345 282	ITL	106 006	16576	1979	Ex Edelstahlwerke Freital
3345 283	ITL	106 007	16970	1980	Ex DREWAG 2
3345 284	CTD-ITL	106 008	14536	1975	Ex DREWAG 1
3345 285	ITL	106 010	13810	1973	Wacker Chemie Nünchritz
3345 289	WFL	19	15137	1976	Ex DDR Industry
3345 290	LTH	106-001	12244	1969	VKM is DDR!
3345 296	SGL	V60.16	15355	1976	Ex Kali Bischofferode 2
3345 297	TSE		15196	1976	
3345 362	MEG	2	17801	1980	Ex Regis-Breitingen
3345 363	MEG	3	13755	1973	Ex Böhlen 3
3345 364	MEG	4	11010	1965	Ex Böhlen 4
3345 365	MEG	5	10765	1966	Ex Böhlen 5
3345 368	MEG	68	13750	1973	Ex Buna
3345 371	MEG	69	15197	1976	Ex Buna
3345 372	MEG	70	15352	1976	Ex Buna
3345 373	MEG	71	15363	1976	Ex Buna
3345 375	MEG	75	15607	1977	Ex Buna
3345 376	MEG	76	16573	1979	Ex Buna
3345 377	MEG	77	16682	1979	Ex Buna
3345 378	MEG	78	15671	1979	Ex Buna
3345 380	RAILS/Redler	13	13778	1973	Ex industrial V60.03
3345 382	HTRS/RAR	V655.02	12255	1969	Ex 346 545

3345 383	HTRS/RAR	V655.03	13760	1973	Ex RAR, ex EKO 32
3345 384	SGL	V60.12	13297	1971	Ex RAR V650.04, DR 346 784
3345 385	HTRS/RAR	V655.05	17639	1982	Ex MWB V643, ex CZ 716.530
3345 387	LUW	346-001	18002	1982	MWB V 641; ex CZ; leased to MHG
3345 388	LUW	346-002	15633	1978	OSE 106 642, ex Industrial
3345 392	ITB	622	13827	1973	Ex PBSV 08
3345 393	DP	18	13866	1973	Ex ITB
3345 397	BUVL/LM	V60 001	17694	1983	Ex NRS, ex Industry
3345 400	EGP	V60.05	13860	1974	Ex HWB VL 4
3345 401	TME	3	16969	1980	Ex Hermeskeil, ex Umformwerk Erfurt 1
3345 900	HVLE	V60.6	15580	1977	Ex Bombardier 2, ADtranz, LEW
3345 901	HTS Emmerich Hafen		17697	1982	Ex RAILS V60.02, ex KEG 608
3345 970	PRESS	346 024	14194	1974	
	AMP/ADAM	1	18008	1982	
	ADAM	13	11344	1967	
3346 006	LOCON	102	12233	1969	NVAG 346 006, RAW Halle 5
3346 015	BEF	106 238	12669	1973	
3346 034	LDC	V60 001	12362	1969	
3346 171 *	LUTRA/HAKON	12	270156	1963	Ex industry Di390-65-B4
3346 177 *	TSE		270162	1970	
3346 248	EKO	47	10939	1965	Ex DR
3346 302	ITL	106 001	11020	1965	Ex DR 346 302
3346 391	HVLE	V60.5	11672	1967	Ex Bombardier 1, EKO 48, RBG D 08, DR 346 391
3346 501	LUW	346-003	14186	1974	Ex EIB
3346 502	EBS	346 502	16691	1979	Ex Plattenwerk Vogelsdorf.
3346 522	ITB	625^{II}	12292	1968	Ex DB
3346 545	HTRS/RAR	V655.02	12255	1969	Ex RAR, ex DB
3346 560	CLR	346 560	12315	1969	Ex DB Services, DR 346 560
3346 590	POWER	346 590	12363	1969	Ex EKO 35; scrapped 2013
3346 601	EBS	346 601	17591	1981	Ex SEM Chemnitz 106 897
3346 603	EBS	346 603	12261	1968	Ex ARCO 5061.51
3346 613	AKO	V60 15613	15613	1977	Ex PBSV
3346 659	WFL	14	12630	1970	Ex DR; leased to HSL
3346 674	WFL	5^{II}	12647	1970	Ex MEG 80 ex DR 346 674; leased to HSL
3346 685	WFL	10	12660	1970	Ex DB; leased to BPRM
3346 692	WFL		12667	1970	Ex DB for spares. Ex MEG 81, ex DB
3346 727	WFL	8	12988	1971	Ex MEG 82, ex DR
3346 738	ITL	106 004^{II}	12999	1971	Ex DR 346 738
3346 756	MTEG	346 756	13787	1973	Ex ESTEG 19, not DR
3346 799	ITL	106 005^{II}	13316	1971	Ex DR 346 799
3346 816	ITB	631	13333	1971	Ex BUG V60BUG04, ex DB
3346 820	DEBG		13352	1972	
3346 823	HVLE	V60.1	13362	1972	Ex DR 346 823
3346 824	UEG	106 824	13737	1972	
3346 826	LUW	346 004	16996	1981	Ex HSL V60.04, ex CZ 716 522
3346 828	HTS, Stuttgart Hafen		13867	1974	Ex HSL V60.03, ex industry
3346 833	HVLE	V60.02	13819	1973	
3346 852	WFL	9	13847	1973	Ex DR
3346 891	DLI	346 891	14141	1974	Ex DR
3346 920	DLI	346 920	14214	1974	Ex WEBA, ex DR
3346 931	WFL	6^{II}	14284	1974	Ex MEG 6, ex DR
3346 933	DLI	63	14320	1974	Ex MEG 63

3346 962 (Z)	DLI	346 962	14574	1975	
3346 967	LOCON	104	14579	1975	Ex V60BUG05, ex DB 346 967
3346 970	ABRRS	346 970	16359	1980	Ex DDR Industry
3346 971	HEIN	VL 5	11975	1967	MERSEBURG
3346 972	DME/Gleiskraft	-	11416	1967	Wismut V60.09; "RONNEBURG"
3346 973	DME/Gleiskraft		11418	1967	Wismut V60.08; "BEERWALDE"
3346 980	RME	346 980	14592	1975	Ex DB
3346 988	HVLE	V60.7	14600	1975	Ex DR
	ARCO	5061.01	16574	1979	
	ARCO	5061.03	16687	1979	
	ARCO	5061.04	13757	1973	
	ARCO	5061.17	14818	1975	
	ARCO	5061.20	15684	1979	
	ARCO	5061.51	10870	1964	
	ARCO	(ex Lotrac 3)	13347	1972	
	DLI	156 21	15621	1977	Ex industry
	DLI	V60 06	17589	1981	Ex EIB 6
	EBS	2	12261	1969	Ex DDR Industry
	EBS		15611	1979	
	EGP	V60.04	16696	1979	Ex PE Cargo, ex HKW Guben 9
	HSL	V60.02	17697	1983	Ex Waggonbau Bautzen
	HTRS/RAR	V655.05	17639	1982	Ex RAR, MWB, CZ 716 530
*	ITB	6	270036	1962	Ex Hafenbahn Brandenurg 6
	ITB	625	15367	1976	Ex Brandenburg steelworks
	ITB	632I	15130	1976	Ex DDR Industry
	ITB	632II	11964	1968	Ex Brandenburg steelworks 615
	ITB	633	11740	1968	Ex MHG 4
	ITL	106 004I	10943	1965	Ex Sprotta 3
	ITL	106 005II	16680	1979	Ex Binnenhafen Mittel Elbe
*	KML	1	270161	1964	Stored
	KML	2	11040	1965	Stored
	KML	6	15620	1977	Stored
	LWB	V60-100	16363	1978	Ex Industry
	LWB	V60-103	15674	1979	Ex Industry
	RME	V60-101	18122	1983	Ex Industry
	PCW	1	17417	1980	Ex Industry
		V60.02	13749	1973	Ex Laubag 106-01 was with EIVEL
		03	14836	1975	Ex Laubag 106-03 was with EIVEL
	RAILS	12	18112	1983	Ex Kali Rossleben 2
	RAILS	V60 030	11030	1966	Ex Schwenk Zement
	RAILS	V60.1	12670	1970	Ex Kali Bernburg 3
	RAILS	V60.2	13777	1973	Ex Kali Merkers 13
	RTS		17416	1980	Ex Ex EBW, TLG 4, EBG 6, BUNA 79
	TME	3	16969	1980	Ex Umformtechnik Erfurt 1
	RAILS	13	13778	1973	Ex Kali Zielitz 4
	SBW	WL 14	13743	1973	
	SBW	WL 15	13869	1974	
	SLG	V60-SP-011	13746	1973	Stored
	SLG	V60-SP-012	15202	1976	Stored
*	VEV	V 9	270160	1963	Ex DDR Industry
3347 079	FHS/BPRM	347 079	15659	1978	Ex DB
3347 096	FHS/BPRM	347 096	16571	1979	Ex DB
3347 975	FHS/BPRM	347 975	14587	1975	Ex DB

98 80 3352   G322/G400   B

The G322 was built for Danish State Railways where it was class MK. With the rationalisation of wagon load services some locomotives became spare and were snapped up by German firms. The continuation of the design became the G400.

Built: 1996–98 (G322), 2003 (G400).
Builder: SFT/Vossloh.
Engine: MTU 8V183TD13 of 390 kW.
Transmission: Hydraulic, Voith L2r4zseU2.
Maximum Tractive Effort:

Wheel Diameter: 1000 mm.
Weight: 40 tonnes.
Length over Buffers: 9.40 m.
Maximum Speed: 60 (G322), 70 (G400) km/h.

EVN	Company	Running No	Builder	Works No	Built	Notes
3352 001	NTS/VBG	352 001	SFT	220139	1996	Schwandorf shunter
3352 002	NTS/NRS	352 002	SFT	220120	1996	Ex MWB V 601, ex VL, ex DSB MK 601
3352 003	OHE	600.25	SFT	220121	1996	Ex VL, ex DSB MK 602. Normally Metronom depot shunter at Uelzen
	NTS	322 220 123	SFT	220123	1996	Ex DSB MK 604
	NTS	322 220 124	SFT	220124	1996	Ex DSB MK 605
	NTS	322 220 125	SFT	220125	1996	Ex DSB MK 606
	NTS	322 220 126	SFT	220126	1997	Ex DSB MK 607
	NTS	322 220 127	SFT	220127	1997	Ex DSB MK 608
	NTS	322 220 130	SFT	220130	1997	Ex DSB MK 611
	NTS	322 220 131	SFT	220131	1997	Ex DSB MK 612
3352 101	NTS		VL	1001300	2003	
3352 102	NTS/DB		VL	1001301	2003	
3352 103	NTS/DB		VL	1001302	2003	
3352 104				1001303	2003	
3352 105	VL/DB	352 105		1001304	2003	

98 80 3360–3365   DB V60C   0-6-0

These classes are all former DB V60 shunters. For technical details see Classes 360–365 in German Railways Part 1.

98 80 3360

EVN	Company	Running No	Builder	Works No	Built	Notes
3360 106	PCT	260 106	MaK	600026	1956	
3360 109	RE	260 109	MaK	600029	1956	
3360 114	DFS	V60 114	MaK	600034	1956	
3360 152	DPR	360 152	MaK	600073	1957	Stored
3360 159	BLG	260 159	MaK	600080	1957	
3360 215	DPR	360 315	Henschel	29295	1956	
3360 239	BLG	260 239	Henschel	29319	1956	
3360 311	INNR	260 311	KHD	56714	1957	
3360 312	BLG	260 312	KHD	56715	1957	
3360 318	DPR	360 318	KHD	56721	1957	Stored
3360 335	EMN	V360.02	Essl	5176	1957	
3360 366	DIEBM		Jung	12496	1957	
3360 413	ETG	V360 01	Mak	600171	1958	
3360 555	MWB	V 662	Krupp	3978	1960	
3360 572	MWB	V 663	Krupp	3995	1960	
3360 573	BEG	D 6	Krupp	3996	1960	
3360 577	PBE/DME	360 577	KM	18631	1960	
3360 608	BOEG	360 608	Krupp	4031	1960	Ex MWB V664, ex DB 360 608
3360 749	MWB	V 661	Henschel	30038	1959	
3360 770	EFW	260 770	Henschel	30059	1960	
3360 773	STWB	260 773	Henschel	30062	1960	
3360 782	DPR	360 782	Henschel	30071	1960	Stored

3360 783	DPR	360 783	Henschel	30072	1960	Stored
3360 860	BYB	V60 860	KM	18622	1960	on loan to Bahnpark Augsburg
3360 869	PBE	360 869	KM	18631	1960	

98 80 3361

EVN	Company	Running No	Builder	Works No	Built	Notes
3361 157	RRI		Krupp	4477	1962	
3361 197	DPR	361 197	Krupp	4517	1963	Stored
3361 234	ELV	V60 1234	MaK	600470	1963	Ex VEV, DB Museum, DB
3361 663	ELV	V60 663	MaK	600252	1959	Ex HWB VL 14, TSD 361 663, DB 361 663
3361 671	AVOLL	261 671	MaK	600260	1959	Ex EBN
3361 687	EFRN		MaK	600276	1959	
3361 841	HABA	7	KM	18603	1959	

98 80 3362

EVN	Company	Running No	Builder	Works No	Built	Notes
3362 407	BYB		MaK	600165	1959	
3362 544	PRESS		Krupp	3967	1960	Spares
3362 556	DGT		Krupp	3979	1060	
3362 562	PRESS		Krupp	3985	1960	Spares
3362 787	NRS	362 787	Henschel	30076	1960	Ex RPRS, ex DB
3362 798	HSL	362 798	Henschel	30087	1960	
3362 799	PRESS	362 040	Henschel	30088	1960	
3362 806	PRESS		Henschel	30095	1960	Spares
3362 848	BYB	362 848	KM	18610	1960	
3362 874	HSL	362 874	KM	18636	1960	(Augsburg)
3362 879	PRESS	362 034	KM	18641	1960	
3363 883	ESG		KM	18645	1960	
3362 888	BYB	362 888	KM	18650	1960	
3362 911	STWB	362 911	MaK	600358	1961	
3362 915	PRESS	362 035	MaK	600362	1961	
3362 937	PRESS		MaK	600384	1961	

98 80 3363

EVN	Company	Running No	Builder	Works No	Built	Notes
3363 043	PRESS	363 028	Essl	5271	1959	
3363 121	RPRS		MaK	600436	1963	
3363 137			MaK	600452	1963	
3363 151	RPRS		Krupp	4471	1962	
3363 159	PRESS	363 027	Krupp	4479	1962	
3363 162	EBM	363 162	Krupp	4482	1962	
3363 170	RPRS	363 170	Krupp	4490	1963	
3363 171	RPRS		Krupp	4491	1963	
3363 180	BTEX	363 180	Krupp	4500	1963	
3363 186	PRESS		Krupp	4506	1963	
3363 196	STGBS		Krupp	4516	1963	
3363 198	SGL		Krupp	4518	1963	
3363 212	BYB	363 212	Krupp	4624	1963	
3363 230	STGBS		Krupp	4642	1963	
3363 621	ESGBI	6"	MaK	600210	1959	
3363 638	PRESS	363 039	MaK	600227	1959	
3363 661	BYB	363 661	MaK	600250	1960	
3363 664	SGL	V60.14	MaK	600253	1959	
3363 666	RPRS	363 666	MaK	600255	1959	
3363 675	PRESS		MaK	600264	1959	
3363 680	RHG	261 680	MaK	600269	1959	
3363 685	RPRS		MaK	600274	1959	
3363 688	RPRS	363 688	MaK	600277	1959	
3363 689	SVG		MaK	600278	1959	
3363 698	PRESS	363 029	MaK	600287	1960	
3363 713			MaK	600302	1960	
3363 714	PRESS	363 006	MaK	600303	1960	
3363 717	RPRS	363 717	MaK	600306	1960	Spares

3363 734	MWB	V666	MaK	600323	1960
3363 736	PRESS		MaK	600325	1960
3363 815	PEF		Henschel	30104	1960

98 80 3364

EVN	Company	Running No	Builder	Works No	Built	Notes
3364 403	NBEG	364 403	MaK	600161	1959	
3364 428	RSE	364CL428	MaK	600186	1959	
3364 514	ELBA	364 514	Krupp	3937	1959	
3364 524	JW		Krupp	3947	1959	Spares
3364 531	BVM	364 531	Krupp	3954	1959	
3364 569	BYB	364 569	Krupp	3992	1960	
3364 578	JW	Johanna 02	Krupp	4001	1960	
3364 611	INNR	364 611	Krupp	4034	1960	
3364 762	RSE	364 762	Henschel	30051	1960	
3364 778	ESGBI	9	Henschel	30067	1960	
3364 786	DP	264 786	Henschel	30075	1960	
3364 847	ELBA	364 847	KM	18609	1959	Ex Johanna 01
3364 850	SWA	364 850	KM	18612	1960	
3364 851	JW		KM	18613	1960	Spares
3364 869	PBE/HEIN	364 869	KM	18631	1960	
3364 890	PBE	364 890	KM	18652	1960	Spares

98 80 3365

EVN	Company	Running No	Builder	Works No	Built	Notes
3365 108	ESGBI	2^{II}	MaK	600423	1963	
3365 109	RSE	365 109	MaK	600424	1963	
3365 120	STAV		MaK	600435	1963	Ex EBM V365.03
3365 130	MWB	V 665	MaK	600445	1963	
3365 131	RSE	365 131	MaK	600446	1963	
3365 140	VEB	V60 1140	MaK	600455	1963	
3365 145	GKL/ELG	365 145	MaK	600460	1963	
3365 148	RPRS	365 148	MaK	600463	1963	Spares; sold to Lokservice Sascha Dehn
3365 184	VEB	V60 1184	Krupp	4504	1963	
3365 205	PRESS		Krupp	4615	1963	Spares
3365 208	ESGBI	10	Krupp	4620	1963	
3365 214	BYB	365 214	Krupp	4626	1960	
3365 217	RSE	365 217	Krupp	4629	1963	
3365 221	BLW		Krupp	4633	1963	
3365 227	NBEG	365 227	Krupp	4639	1963	
3365 695	AVOLL		MaK	600284	1960	
3365 733	RSE	365 733	MaK	600322	1960	

98 80 3420   MG530C   C

A former industrial shunter; one locomotive is now with an EVU but others remain working in industry.

Built: 1965–70.
Builder: KHD.
Engine: Deutz T8M625 of 530 hp.
Transmission: Hydraulic, Voith L37Ab.
Maximum Tractive Effort:
Wheel Diameter: 1050 mm.
Weight: 54 tonnes.
Length over Buffers: 9.88 m.
Maximum Speed: 33 km/h.

EVN	Company	Running No	Works No	Built	Notes
3420 001	WLE	05	57876	1970	ex Klöckner Hütte, Bremen
	GET	2	57802	1965	
	GET	5	57805	1965	
	GET	6	57806	1965	
	GET	7	57807	1965	
	GET	8	57808	1965	

98 80 3421   KHD MS800D   0-8-0

Just one locomotive of this type has come to notice and no EVN seems to have been issued/reported, but this is where your compiler thinks it ought to fit. Technical details still being sought.

EVN	Company	Running No	Works No	Built	Notes
	EEB	Hümmling	56459	1957	Ex Klöckner Hagen-Haspe 1

98 80 3422   KHD DG1000BBM   B-B

This is the KHD version of the off-centre cab bogie locomotive for branch line and trip working duties. Several locomotives of this type have come to light and judging by the reported EVNs there ought to be more somewhere!

Built: 1959–68.
Builder: KHD.
Engine: T12M265 of 736 kW.
Transmission: Hydraulic, L306r.
Maximum Tractive Effort:

Wheel Diameter: 1000 mm.
Weight: 64–80 tonnes.
Length over Buffers: 13.30 m.
Maximum Speed: 70 km/h.

EVN	Company	Running No	Works No	Built	Notes
3422 003	EBO		57250	1961	Ex Die Lei, ex OHE 1200 69
	WLE	36	57419	1962	
3422 006	OHE	1200 68	57465	1962	
3422 013	NE	IV^{II}	57801	1964	Ex GET 1

98 80 3423   KHD DG1200BBM   B-B

A slightly more powerful locomotive than the preceding one but technical details are mostly the same; built 1960–66.

EVN	Company	Running No	Works No	Built	Notes
3423 001	OHE	1200 71	57100	1960	
3423 002	ASLVG	V90 002	57101	1960	Ex OHE 1200 72
3423 003	WLE	36	57419	1962	
3423 005	WLE	44	57190	1961	
3423 008	RLG	68	57466	1962	
3423 010	ORME	D 7			
	DLI	DH 35	57541	1963	Ex HGK DH 35, KBE 37
3423 013	RVM	28	57672	1964	KFBE 73
3423 014	RVM	45	57673	1964	KFBE 74
3423 016	DLI	112	57982	1966	Ex HGK DH 37, KFBE 75

98 80 3424   KHD DG1600BBM   B-B

This is another class whose EVN has not come to light. There were three locomotives built for the WLE and one still survives but its days must be numbered. No technical details have come to light.

EVN	Company	Running No	Works No	Built
	WLE	31	56594	1957

98 80 34xx   KHD KG130B   B

Just one of these small shunters has come to light and as it does not appear to work off its own system, no EVN has come to light either.

Built: 1966.
Builder: KHD.
Engine: Deutz A6L714 of 130 hp.
Transmission: Hydraulic, Deutz DHG H4G.
Maximum Tractive Effort:

Wheel Diameter:
Weight: 14 tonnes.
Length over Buffers: 5.39 m.
Maximum Speed:

EVN	Company	Running No	Works No	Built
	RTB	6.301.1	57884	1966

98 80 3425   KHD KS230B   0-4-0

With this class there is an allocated EVN class number but none have yet to be reported. A typical 1950s light shunting locomotive.

Built: 1953–61.
Builder: KHD.
Engine: A122L714 of 230 hp.
Transmission: Hydraulic, Voith L33y.
Maximum Tractive Effort:

Wheel Diameter:
Weight: 20 tonnes.
Length over Buffers: 7.31 m.
Maximum Speed: 32 km/h.

EVN	Company	Running No	Works No	Built	Notes
	HGK	V 4	55545	1953	ex KFBE V 3
	OHE	230 42	57201	1961	
	OHE	230 43	57202	1961	

98 80 xxxx   KHD KG230B   B

This is the cardan shaft version of the preceding class but no EVN has come to notice.

Built: 1964–67.
Builder: KHD.
Engine: A122L714 of 230 hp.
Transmission: Hydraulic, Voith L33y.
Maximum Tractive Effort:

Wheel Diameter:
Weight: 26–36 tonnes.
Length over Buffers: 8.03 m.
Maximum Speed: 30 km/h.

EVN	Company	Running No	Works No	Built	Notes
	PCT	01	57718	1964	Ex Weserport Bremerhavn 18
	AMR	884 048	57832	1965	Ex Volkswagen 884 048
	HVLE	Lok 1	58216	1967	

98 80 3432   KHD KS55B   0-4-0

Just a couple of these small industrial shunters have come to notice.

Built: 1952–63.
Builder: KHD.
Engine: A4L514 of 55 hp.
Transmission: Mechanical.
Maximum Tractive Effort:

Wheel Diameter:
Weight: 12–14 tonnes.
Length over Buffers: 5.73 m.
Maximum Speed: 12 km/h.

EVN	Company	Running No	Works No	Built
	WHE	12	55334	1952
3432 501	TEL	2	57675	1963

98 80 3433   KHD KK140B   B

A solitary locomotive has been found that slots into this EVN series.

Built: 1965.
Builder: KHD.
Engine: AL6L614/714 of 140 hp.
Transmission: Hydraulic, Voith L33y.
Maximum Tractive Effort:

Wheel Diameter:
Weight: 20 tonnes.
Length over Buffers: 6.51 m.
Maximum Speed: 35 km/h.

EVN	Company	Running No	Works No	Built
	HTRS/RAR	V140.01	57788	1965

98 80 3434   KHD A8L614R   0-4-0

Built: 1958.
Builder: KHD.
Engine: A8L614R of 90 hp.
Transmission: Hydraulic.
Maximum Tractive Effort:

Wheel Diameter:
Weight: 22 tonnes.
Length over Buffers:
Maximum Speed: 54 km/h.

EVN	Company	Running No	Works No	Built	Notes
	RRI	3	56761	1958	Ex SBW 3

98 80 xxxx   KHD A6M324R   0-4-0

Another small shunting locomotive from the Köln builder.

Built: 1942.
Builder: KHD.
Engine: A6M324R of 235 hp.
Transmission:
Maximum Tractive Effort:

Wheel Diameter:
Weight: 38–45 tonnes.
Length over Buffers:
Maximum Speed: 30 km/h.

EVN	Company	Running No	Works No	Built	Notes
	STVG	V20 050	36656	1942	Ex MAN 2

98 80 3439   KHD KG275B   B

The KHD factory had a large catalogue of diesel shunting locomotives with something available in most horse power ranges.

Built: 1963–68.
Builder: KHD.
Engine: BA12L714 of 275 hp.
Transmission: Hydraulic, Voith L213.
Maximum Tractive Effort:

Wheel Diameter:
Weight: 32–36 tonnes.
Length over Buffers: 8.03 m.
Maximum Speed: 46 km/h.

EVN	Company	Running No	Works No	Built
3439 002	EEB	L2^{II}	57504	1962

98 80 3440   KHD T4M625R   0-4-0

This small shunting locomotive has EVN 3440 181 which leads one to think there may be more!

Built: 1961.
Builder: KHD.
Engine: T4M625R of 225 hp.
Transmission:
Maximum Tractive Effort:

Wheel Diameter:
Weight: 28 tonnes.
Length over Buffers:
Maximum Speed: 50 km/h.

EVN	Company	Running No	Works No	Built	Notes
3440 181	TEL	230.41	57200	1961	Ex OHE

98 80 3443   KHD MS430C   0-6-0

Another class with just one example known appropriate to the EVN numbering scheme.

Built: 1961.
Builder: KHD.
Engine: A8M528 of 430 hp.
Transmission: Hydraulic, Voith L24A.
Maximum Tractive Effort:

Wheel Diameter:
Weight: 45 tonnes.
Length over Buffers: 9.84 m.
Maximum Speed: 64 km/h.

EVN	Company	Running No	Works No	Built	Notes
	ESGBI		57205	1961	Ex Bosch 2

98 80 3504   ML440C   0-6-0

A standard type from Krauss Maffei with quite a few built and several survivors coming into the EVN numbering.

Built: 1956–57.
Builder: Krauss Maffei.
Engine: MAN W8V 17.5/22A of 440 hp.
Transmission: Hydraulic, Voith L37V.
Maximum Tractive Effort:

Wheel Diameter: 1100 mm.
Weight: 43–54 tonnes.
Length over Buffers: 8.70 m.
Maximum Speed: 55 km/h.

EVN	Company	Running No	Works No	Built
	AULOC	AL 21	18325	1956
3504 107	AULOC	AL 22	18326	1956
	AULOC	AL 23	18327	1956
3504 109	AULOC	AL 24	18328	1956
	AULOC	AL 25	18329	1956
	AULOC	AL 26	18383	1956
3504 121	EFW	4	18352	1957
	STVG	V 6	18355	1957

98 80 35xx   ML500C   C

No EVN has come to light for this locomotive which has been slotted in where the compiler thinks it ought to be.

Built: 1966.
Builder: Krauss Maffei.
Engine:
Transmission:
Maximum Tractive Effort:

Wheel Diameter:
Weight:
Length over Buffers:
Maximum Speed:

EVN	Company	Running No	Works No	Built	Notes
	RRI	9	19293	1966	Ex SBW 9

98 80 3507   M700C, ML700C   C

This is a medium powered shunter from Krauss Maffei with many examples used in industry.

Built: 1962–79.
Builder: Krauss Maffei.
Engine:
Transmission:
Maximum Tractive Effort:

Wheel Diameter:
Weight:
Length over Buffers:
Maximum Speed:

EVN	Company	Running No	Works No	Built	Notes
3507 002	RAILS		18847	1962	Ex DE 702
3507 004	IGB	DL 8	18849	1962	Ex ON RAIL, DE
	NME	ML 00605	19086	1965	
	RRI	10	19087	1965	Ex SBW 10
3507 014	IGB	DL 7	19088	1963	Ex ON RAIL, RAG 531

BASF	D34	19697	1974
RBH	510	19730	1974
RBH	512	19679	1973
RBH	513	19680	1973
RBH	515	19689	1974
RBH	517	19688	1973
RBH	519	19729	1974
RBH	570	19693	1974
RBH	572	19685	1973 (Z)
RBH	573	19681	1973
RBH	575	19686	1973
RBH	577	19684	1973
RBH	578	19682	1973
RBH	579	19683	1973
RBH	580	19691	1974
RBH	581	19731	1974 (Z)
RBH	584	19692	1974
RBH	585	19733	1975
RBH	586	19677	1973
WEBA	6	19454	1968
BHL	1	19874	1979
BHL	3	19699	1973

98 80 3508   M 800   B-B

A small class of eight industrial shunters.

Built: 1966–67.
Builder: Krauss Maffei.
Engine:
Transmission:
Maximum Tractive Effort:
Wheel Diameter:
Weight:
Length over Buffers:
Maximum Speed:

EVN	Company	Running No	Works No	Built	Notes
	BHL	10	19289	1966	Ex HOAG 210
	EH	571	19290	1966	Ex 262, ex HOAG 211
3508 003	EH	572	19291	1966	Ex 263, ex HOAG 212
3508 004	EH	573	19292	1966	Ex 264, ex HOAG 213
3508 005	EH	574	19325	1967	Ex 265, ex HOAG 214
			19326	1967	Ex 266, ex HOAG 215
			19327	1967	Ex 267, ex HOAG 216

98 80 3509   M500C/ML500C   C

Another type built mainly for industrial use.

Built: 1963–77.
Builder:
Engine:
Transmission:
Maximum Tractive Effort:
Wheel Diameter:
Weight:
Length over Buffers:
Maximum Speed:

EVN	Company	Running No	Works No	Built	Notes
	SAB	V50 001	18356	1957	
	NME	ML 00613	19091	1965	
	HGK	V 27	19295	1971	
3509 014	RRI	12	19585	1972	
3509 017	AVG	463	19819	1975	Ex Krupp Stahl

98 80 3512 — M1200BB — B-B

Mostly used in the Ruhr industries, two examples of this class ended up further south but are now owned by Northrail and could be on lease anywhere in the country.

Built: 1972–78.
Builder: Krauss Maffei.
Engine:
Transmission:
Maximum Tractive Effort:

Wheel Diameter:
Weight:
Length over Buffers:
Maximum Speed:

EVN	Company	Running No	Works No	Built	Notes
3512 001	EHG	501	19573	1972	Ex EH 281
3512 002	EH	502	19574	1972	Ex EH 282
3512 003	EH	503	19575	1972	Ex EH 283
3512 004	EHG	504	19576	1972	Ex EH 284
3512 005	EHG	505	19578	1972	Ex EH 285
3512 006	EH	506	19579	1972	Ex EH 286
3512 007	EH	507	19580	1972	Ex EH 287
3512 008	EH	508	19581	1972	Ex EH 288
3512 010	VTLT		19855	1978	Ex HzL V 118
3512 011	VTLT/Prolok		19856	1978	Ex HzL V 119

98 80 3602 — DH240B — 0-4-0

These are the smallest of the Henschel shunting locos that have come to notice and may now be withdrawn.

Built: 1952–57.
Builder: Henschel.
Engine: MWM RSH518A of 240 hp.
Transmission: Hydraulic, Voith L33yU.
Maximum Tractive Effort:

Wheel Diameter: 1150 mm.
Weight: 28–30 tonnes.
Length over Buffers: 7.54 m.
Maximum Speed: 60 km/h.

EVN	Company	Running No	Works No	Built
	ARCO	5021.03	29704	1958
	ARCO	5021.04	29703	1958

98 80 36xx — DH360C — 0-6-0

Built: 1951–66.
Builder: Henschel.
Engine: Henschel 12V1416 of 265kW/360hp.
Transmission:
Maximum Tractive Effort:

Wheel Diameter:
Weight:
Length over Buffers:
Maximum Speed: 30/60 km/h.

EVN	Company	Running No	Works No	Built	Notes
	BYB	350 001	26750	1960	
	RRI	5	27105	1958	
	EVB	274	28641	1956	Ex WZTE

98 80 36xx — DH440C — 0-6-0

Another 0-6-0 shunting loco from Henschel; three locos of this type became DSB MH 201-3.

Built: 1958–60.
Builder: Henschel.
Engine: MAN W8V17.5/22A of 324kW/440 hp.
Transmission: Hydraulic, Voith L37U.
Maximum Tractive Effort:

Wheel Diameter:
Weight: 40.50 tonnes.
Length over Buffers: 9.44 m.
Maximum Speed: 60 km/h.

EVN	Company	Running No	Works No	Built
	DH	D 7	30014	1959
	DH	D 9	30260	1960

98 80 36xx — DH500C — 0-6-0

Just one locomotive of this type has come to notice but no EVN has been reported.

Built: 1959–71.
Builder: Henschel.
Engine: Mercedes Benz MB836Bb of 500 hp.
Transmission: Hydraulic.
Maximum Tractive Effort:

Wheel Diameter: 1250 mm.
Weight: 54 tonnes.
Length over Buffers: 8.90 m.
Maximum Speed: 30/60 km/h.

EVN	Company	Running No	Works No	Built
	DH	D 14	29963	1959
	ARCO	5051.01	30264	1960

98 80 3605 — DE500C — Co

A small class of shunting locos built for use in the steel industry.

Built: 1982–84.
Builder: Henschel.
Engine:
Transmission: Electric, three-phase.
Maximum Tractive Effort:

Wheel Diameter:
Weight:
Length over Buffers:
Maximum Speed:

EVN	Company	Running No	Works No	Built
3605 005	EH	703	32563	1983
	DH	R 4	32566	1983

98 80 3606 — DHG500C — C

A relatively large class of shunting locos for the coal and steel industries.

Built: 1963–76.
Builder: Henschel.
Engine: Henschel 12V1416 of 368kW/500hp.
Transmission: Hydraulic.
Maximum Tractive Effort:

Wheel Diameter:
Weight:
Length over Buffers: 9.90 m.
Maximum Speed: 30/50 km/h.

EVN	Company	Running No	Works No	Built	Notes
	RBH	434	31189	1966	
	RBH	440	30573	1963	Ex RAG
	RBH	446	30855	1963	(Z); Ex RAG
	RBH	453	31183	1966	Ex RAG
	RBH	475	31074	1965	Ex RAG
	DH	D 10	31245	1967	
	DH	D 11	31238	1967	
	DH	D 16	31112	1965	

98 80 3607 — DHG700C — C

Another class built for industrial use. As only 55 locos were built those numbered as 3607 1xx must have been rebuilt or modified in some way.

Built: 1973–85.
Builder: Henschel.
Engine: Henschel of 507kW/690 hp.
Transmission: Hydraulic.
Maximum Tractive Effort:

Wheel Diameter:
Weight:
Length over Buffers: 9.84 m.
Maximum Speed: 37 km/h.

EVN	Company	Running No	Works No	Built	Notes
	MVG	9	30859	1964	Ex RAG 546
	RBH	523	31468	1970	
	RRI	11	31681	1973	Ex SBW 11
	RRI	13	31866	1976	Ex SBW 13

	RRI	14	31997	1978	Ex SBW 14
3607 039	RRI	16	32476	1981	Ex SBW 16
3607 046	WLH/RBSA	70	32558	1981	Ex NME 00607
	NME	ML 00606	32559	1981	Ex Edelstahlwerke Witten 3
3607 048	IGB	DL 6	32560	1982	Ex Edelstahlwerke Witten 4
3607 049	RRI	17	32561	1982	Ex SBW 17
3607 051	RRI	18	32721	1982	Ex SBW 18
3607 103	WLH/RBSA	57	31195	1966	Ex RAG 522
3607 115	VLO	2	31567	1972	

98 80 3612   DHG1200   B-B

A bogie locomotive built for industry; many were exported.

Built: 1966–75.
Builder: Henschel.
Engine: ? of 883 kW/1200hp.
Transmission: Hydraulic.
Maximum Tractive Effort:

Wheel Diameter:
Weight: 88 tonnes.
Length over Buffers: 13.74 m.
Maximum Speed:

EVN	Company	Running No	Works No	Built	Notes
3612 102	EH	511	31576	1973	
	DE	801	31950	1975	Ex Hoesch 801
3612 109	DE	802	31951	1975	Ex Hoesch 802
3612 110	DE	803	31952	1975	Ex Hoesch 803
	RBH	640	31178	1966	Ex RAG
	RBH	641	31179	1966	Ex RAG

▲ Railsystems RP 98 80 3362 787 heads south from Hürth-Kalscheuren with a crane in tow on 30 March 2013. This loco has subsequently moved to Nordic Rail Services. **Matthias Müller**

98 80 3651   1100BB   B-B

This is the LHB bogie diesel for heavy industry.

Built: 1967.
Builder: LHB.
Engine:
Transmission:
Maximum Tractive Effort:

Wheel Diameter: 1100 mm.
Weight: 80 tonnes.
Length over Buffers: 13.90 m.
Maximum Speed: 77 km/h.

EVN	Company	Running No	Works No	Built	Notes
3651 001	VPS	1101	3139	1967	Stored
3651 002	VPS	1102	3140	1967	Stored

98 80 3653   530C   C

This is the LHB medium powered shunting locomotive. The Peine-Salzgitter concern was a good customer being on the builder's doorstep but with recent deliveries of Vossloh G6 shunting locos it is expected most of the old locos may have ended up in the blast furnaces.

Built: 1964–66.
Builder: LHB.
Engine: MTU 6V396TC12 of 386 kW/525 hp.
Transmission: Hydraulic.
Maximum Tractive Effort:

Wheel Diameter: 950 mm.
Weight: 54 tonnes.
Length over Buffers: 9.50 m.
Maximum Speed: 40 km/h.

EVN	Company	Running No	Works No	Built	Notes
3653 501	WLH	50	3103	1964	Ex VPS 501
3653 502	VPS	502	3114	1964	
3653 503	VPS	503	3115	1964	
3653 504	VPS	504	3116	1964	
3653 506	VPS	506	3133	1966	
3653 507	VPS	507	3134	1966	
3653 509	VPS	509	3153	1972	
3653 510	VPS	510	3154	1972	
3653 511	VPS	511	3155	1972	
3653 512	VPS	512	3156	1972	
3653 513	VPS	513	3157	1972	
3653 514	VPS	514	3158	1972	
3653 515	VPS	515	3095	1964	
3653 516	VPS	516	3096	1964	
3653 517	VPS	517	3098	1964	
3653 518	VPS	518	3101	1964	
3653 519	VPS	519	3102	1964	
3653 520	VPS	520	3104	1964	
3653 521	VPS	521	3108	1964	
3653 522	VPS	522	3109	1964	
3653 523	VPS	523	3110	1965	
3653 524	VPS	524	3111	1965	
3653 525	VPS	525	3112	1965	
3653 526	VPS	526	3113	1965	
3653 527	WLH	55	3123	1966	Ex VPS 527
3653 528	VPS	528	3124	1966	
3653 529	VPS	529	3125	1966	
3653 530	WLH	51	3126	1966	Ex VPS 530
3653 531	VPS	531	3127	1966	
3653 532	VPS	532	3128	1966	
3653 533	VPS	533	3129	1966	
3653 534	VPS	534	3130	1966	
3653 535	VPS	535	3131	1966	
3653 536	VPS	536	3145	1966	
3653 537	VPS	537	3151	1972	

EVN	Company	Running No	Works No	Built	Notes
3653 538	VPS	538	3152	1972	
3653 539	VPS	539	3097	1964	
3653 540	VPS	540	3099	1964	
3653 541	VPS	541	3100	1964	
3653 542	VPS	542	3105	1964	
3653 543	VPS	543	3106	1964	
3653 544	OHE	544	3135	1966	
		600 24	3136	1966	Ex VPS 545

98 80 3654   S200   B

With one example this class is a bit of a mystery with no technical data available.

EVN	Company	Running No	Works No	Built
3654 001	TEL	5	3087	1963

98 80 3716   SNOWPLOUGH

Just why this snowplough has been given a 98 classification is not clear as it is a departmental vehicle and should have appeared in the 99 series.

EVN	Company	Running No	Builder	Works No	Built	Notes
3716 501	MTEG	716 501	Rolba		1980	Ex DR Rotary Snowplough

98 80 39xx   RK8B   B

The Jung built shunting engines appear in the 39xx series but no EVN has been noted for this locomotive.

Built: 1964–72.
Builder: Jung.
Engine: MB Type OM321 of 80 hp.
Transmission: Hydraulic, Voith RS 14 y.
Maximum Tractive Effort:
Wheel Diameter: 850 mm.
Weight: 15 tonnes.
Length over Buffers: 5.77 m.
Maximum Speed: 15 km/h.

EVN	Company	Running No	Works No	Built
	BEG	D 8	14128	1972

98 80 3942   R42C   0-6-0

Jung produced this type as its medium-powered shunting locomotive. 32 were built, of which a few are still in service.

Built: 1955–62.
Builder: Jung.
Engine: MAN W8V 17.5/22A of 324 kW/440 hp.
Transmission: Hydraulic, Voith L37 A.
Maximum Tractive Effort:
Wheel Diameter: 1100 mm.
Weight: 45 tonnes.
Length over Buffers: 9.285 m.
Maximum Speed: 60 km/h.

EVN	Company	Running No	Works No	Built	Notes
3942 018	EFBS/Siegener Krsb	11	13119	1960	
3942 019	EBN	17	13286	1961	HLB Basis, BLE 17
3942 024	EBN	13	13408	1961	HLB Basis, BLE 13
	RHKE	D VI	13430	1962	

98 80 3944   R30B   0-4-0

Interestingly, the remaining locos of this type are all located in what could be called Jung's backyard. 17 were built, some of which were exported.

Built: 1955–59.
Builder: Jung.
Engine: Deutz T4M625 of 260 hp.
Transmission: Hydraulic, Voith L24 U.
Maximum Tractive Effort:
Wheel Diameter: 1000 mm.
Weight: 24–30 tonnes.
Length over Buffers: 7.68 m.
Maximum Speed: 23/46 km/h.

EVN	Company	Running No	Works No	Built
3944 001	WEBA	V26.1	12102	1956
	WEBA	V26.2	12103	1956
3944 005	WEBA	V26.3	12748	1957
	WEBA	V26.4	12997	1959

98 80 39xx   R30C   0-6-0

A three-axle version of the R30B. Only 11 were built.

Built: 1956–62.
Builder: Jung.
Engine: MAN W6V17, 5/22A of 325 hp.
Transmission: Hydraulic, Voith L24 V.
Maximum Tractive Effort:
Wheel Diameter: 1000 mm.
Weight: 36–39 tonnes.
Length over Buffers: 8.10 m.
Maximum Speed: 50 km/h.

EVN	Company	Running No	Works No	Built	Notes
	HEIN	VL 2	12991	1958	ex AAE

98 80 39xx   R43C   C

With only five built, two locomotives have come to light but no EVN is known

Built: 1970–75.
Builder: Jung.
Engine: MTU 6R362 of 400 hp.
Transmission: Hydraulic, Voith L2r3 U.
Maximum Tractive Effort:
Wheel Diameter: 950 mm.
Weight: 48–51 tonnes.
Length over Buffers: 8.64 m.
Maximum Speed: 40 km/h.

EVN	Company	Running No	Works No	Built	Notes
	NME	ML 00612	14040	1970	
	RST	5	14041	1970	Ex Stadtwerke Düsseldorf 3

98 80 39xx   R60D   0-8-0

Another small class with five locos built and at least two surviving.

Built: 1955–66.
Builder: Jung.
Engine: MAN W6V22/30A of 650 hp.
Transmission: Hydraulic, Voith L37zA(b).
Maximum Tractive Effort:
Wheel Diameter: 1100 mm.
Weight: 60 tonnes.
Length over Buffers: 9.90 m.
Maximum Speed: 60 km/h.

EVN	Company	Running No	Works No	Built
	HVLE	DL 5	13712	1963
	HVLE	DL 6	13931	1966

98 80 3953 — MG530C — C

Built: 1965.
Builder: Jenbach.
Engine:
Transmission:
Maximum Tractive Effort:

Wheel Diameter:
Weight:
Length over Buffers:
Maximum Speed:

EVN	Company	Running No	Works No	Built
3953 001	EHG	751	3680059	1965

NARROW GAUGE DIESEL LOCOMOTIVES

HF130C — 0-6-0 DH

Many narrow gauge diesel locomotives were built for wartime use, some passing on in peacetime to state railways etc. This locomotive ended up on the DR becoming Köf 6001 then 100 901.

Built: 1944–46.
Gauge: 750 mm.
Builder: Gmeinder.
Engine: KHD A 6 M 517 of 77 kW.
Transmission: Hydraulic.
Maximum Tractive Effort:

Wheel Diameter: 680 mm.
Weight: 16.50 tonnes.
Length over Buffers: 5.35 m.
Maximum Speed: 20 km/h.

No.	Operator	Works No	Built	Notes
199 002	RüBB	4205	1944	Ex DB 399 703, ex Köf 6003

V10C — 0-6-0 DM

This type is one of many standard products from the LKM works for public and industrial lines and can be found in different versions for the different gauges

Built: 1962–64.
Gauge: 750/900/1000 mm.
Builder: LKM.
Engine: 6KVD 14.5 SRL of 75 kW.
Transmission: Mechanical.
Maximum Tractive Effort: 4 kN.

Wheel Diameter: 1000 mm.
Weight: 16 tonnes.
Length over Buffers: 5.40 m.
Maximum Speed: 24km/h.

No.	Operator	Gauge	Works No	Built	Notes
199 005	HSB	1000mm	250352	1964	(Z)
199 006	HSB	1000mm	250353	1964	(Z)
199 008	PRESS	750mm	250310	1962	
199 009	PRESS	750mm	250337	1964	
199 014	MBB	900mm	250284	1962	
199 015	MBB	900mm	250292	1962	
199 016	MBB	900mm	250288	1962	
199 017	MBB	900mm	250287	1962	

Ns4 0-6-0

199 032 was originally built for 600 mm gauge industrial use; it was later re-gauged to 750 mm gauge for further industrial service before becoming DR 199 008 and later DB 399 702. It was acquired by the privatised Döllnitzbahn in 1993.

Built: 1957.
Gauge: 750 mm.
Builder: LKM.
Engine: 66 kW.
Transmission: Mechanical.
Maximum Tractive Effort:

Wheel Diameter:
Weight: 14.60 tonnes.
Length over Buffers: 5.34 m.
Maximum Speed: 24 km/h.

No.	Operator	Works No	Built	Notes
199 007	PRESS	250029	1957	
199 032	DBGM	250027	1957	Ex DB 399 702, DR 199 008

Kö II B

Formerly standard gauge, the DR rebuilt several of its small shunting locomotives for use on 1000 mm gauge lines.

Built: 1934–35.
Gauge: 1000 mm.
Builder: BMAG, Jung.
Engine: MWJ 4 KVD 18 SRW of 92kW.
Transmission: Mechanical.
Maximum Tractive Effort:

Wheel Diameter:
Weight: 16 tonnes.
Length over Buffers: 6.392 m.
Maximum Speed: 30 km/h.

No.	Operator	Builder	Works No	Built	Notes
199 010	HSB	BMAG	10224	1934	(Z); Ex DR 100 325
199 011	HSB	Jung	5668	1935	Ex DR 100 639
199 012	HSB	BMAG	10164	1934	(Z); Ex DR 100 213

▲ **199 031** is one of two former ÖBB Class 2091 narrow gauge diesels acquired for the Döllnitzbahn. It is seen waiting at Oschatz on 14 August 2012. **Keith Fender**

L30H 0-6-0

This locomotive was imported from Poland to provide back up cover on an otherwise steam operated line.

Built: 1980.
Gauge: 750 mm.
Builder: U23A.
Engine: MB836B.
Transmission: Hydraulic.
Maximum Tractive Effort:

Wheel Diameter:
Weight: 24 tonnes.
Length over Buffers: 7.10 m.
Maximum Speed: 25 km/h.

No.	Operator	Works No	Built	Notes
199 013	SOEG	24060	1980	Ex Poland Lyd2-103

L45H B-B

These locomotives were imported from Poland and Romania to provide back up motive power on the narrow gauge lines in Sachsen. This was after unification when costs of running ballast trains etc had to be reduced.

Built: 1969–73.
Gauge: 750 mm.
Builder: U23A.
Engine: MB836Bb of 450 hp.
Transmission: Hydraulic.
Maximum Tractive Effort:

Wheel Diameter: 750 mm.
Weight: 32 tonnes.
Length over Buffers: 10.24 m.
Maximum Speed: 36 km/h.

No.	Operator	Works No	Built	Notes
199 018	SOEG	21888	1973	Ex CFR 87-0029
L45H-083	SDG	24972	1985	Ex Industry Romania
L45H-084	SDG	24973	1985	Ex Industry Romania
L45H-358	SDG	20850	1969	Ex PKP Lxd2-358
87-0024	SDG			Ex CFR
87-0027	SDG			Ex CFR

2091 1-Bo-1

After many years in use on narrow gauge lines in Austria, these locomotives were acquired second hand from ÖBB for the privatised line at Oschatz.

Built: 1940.
Gauge: 750 mm.
Builder: Simmering.
Engine: SGP R8 of 154 kW.
Transmission: Electric.
Maximum Tractive Effort: 35 kN.

Wheel Diameter: 820 mm.
Weight: 22 tonnes.
Length over Buffers: 10.80 m.
Maximum Speed: 50km/h.

No.	Operator	Works No	Built	Notes
199 030	DBGM	66765	1940	Ex ÖBB 2091.10
199 031	DBGM	66767	1940	Ex ÖBB 2091.12

L18DH 0-6-0

Imported from Poland where the closure of narrow gauge lines meant there was surplus motive power available.

Built: 1981.
Gauge: 750 mm.
Builder: U23A.
Engine: MB836B of 300 hp.
Transmission: Hydraulic.
Maximum Tractive Effort:

Wheel Diameter: 1000 mm.
Weight: 24 tonnes.
Length over Buffers: 7.10 m.
Maximum Speed: 25 km/h.

No.	Operator	Works No	Built	Notes
199 033	DBGM	24378	1981	Ex Poland Industrial Lyd2-71
199 034	DBGM	24059	1981	Ex EBG, ex Poland Industrial Lyd2-102

V30C 0-6-0

This locomotive was a prototype for a series of locos exported to Indonesia which were of 1067 mm gauge. The prototype was built as 1000mm gauge and tested on the Harz narrow gauge system. It remained there afterwards becoming DR V30 01 and later 103 901, 199 001, 399 001.

Built: 1966.
Gauge: 1000 mm.
Builder: LKM.
Wheel Diameter: 850 mm.
Engine: ER6VD1815 of 243 kW.
Transmission: Hydraulic.
Maximum Tractive Effort:

Weight: 30 tonnes.
Length over Buffers: 8.20 m.
Maximum Speed: 30 km/h.

No.	Operator	Works No	Built	Notes
199 301	HSB	263001	1966	(Z)

V100 DR C-C

In an effort to replace the steam locomotives on its narrow gauge lines in the Harz Mountains, DR Stendal works rebuilt several standard gauge B-B diesel locos into 1000 mm gauge C-C locomotives in the 1988–90 period. Upon privatisation the Harzer Schmalspurbahn decided to keep steam locomotives going and sold off several of the diesels but kept six for itself; only a couple are in normal use.

Built: 1976–78.
Gauge: 1000 mm.
Builder: LEW.
Engine: 12 KVD18/21 AL-4 of 883 kW.
Transmission: Hydraulic.
Maximum Tractive Effort:

Wheel Diameter:
Weight: 60 tonnes.
Length over Buffers: 14.24 m.
Maximum Speed: 50 km/h.

No.	Operator	Works No	Built	Notes
199 861	HSB	15379	1976	
199 871	HSB	15389	1976	(Z)
199 872	HSB	15390	1976	
199 874	HSB	15392	1976	
194 877	HSB	16371	1978	(Z)
199 892	HSB	16386	1978	(Z)

V51/251   B-B

Built new for the DB narrow gauges lines in Baden Württemberg, this loco is a kind of scaled-down DB V100. It was sold to the Austrian Steiermärkische Landesbahn in 1971 where it became VL 21. In 1998/99 it was sold via dealers to the now privatised Rügensche Bäderbahn where it remains in use. The engine quoted is as first built. It may well now have a different one.
Built: 1964.
Gauge: 750 mm.
Builder: Gmeinder.   **Wheel Diameter:** 850 mm.
Engine: 2 x MWM TRHS 518 A.   **Weight:** 39 tonnes.
Transmission: Hydraulic.   **Length over Buffers:** 9.81 m.
Maximum Tractive Effort: 12 kN.   **Maximum Speed:** 40 km/h.

No.	Operator	Works No	Built
251 901	RüBB	5327	1964

3.8. CODE 99 80 – DEPARTMENTAL VEHICLES

This group contains a few types that are well known, such as the overhead line vehicles, but it also encompasses all departmental stock such as tamping machines and other on-track plant including road/rail vehicles! It is not intended to list all those sort of vehicles which deserve a book of their own. The numbering presents a problem in as much as some straightforward numbering has been reported whereby the new number includes the old but there have been reports of completely new numbers in the 99 80 91xx etc series. A lot of the 701/702s have their numbers on a small white data panel on the side of the vehicle which is impossible to read once work stained. Note that DB is still giving "old style" numbers to new equipment; witness the new Kirow crane displayed at Innotrans in 2014 carrying 732 001 as well as a 99 series number.

For technical details please see Departmental Vehicles in German Railways Part 1.

EVN	Company	Running No	Builder	Works No	Built	Notes
	HEIN	701 005		1101	1955	Stored
	HEIN	701 007		1102	1955	Stored
	DLI	701 008	WMD	1103	1955	Stored
1701 014	BVM	701 014	WMD	1238	1957	
	DLI	701 021	WMD	1246	1957	Stored
1701 031	BVM	701 031	WMD	1275	1958	
	HEIN	701 032	WMD	1276	1958	Spares
1701 045	LWB	TVT 2	WMD	1463	1962	
	DLI	701 046	WMD	1464	1962	97 98 01 501 17-7?
	DLI	701 048	WMD	1470	1962	
	EMN	701 052	WMD	1467	1962	
	DLI	701 058	WMD	1466	1962	Stored
701 064	ELL	TVT 2	WMD	1462	1962	
701 066	ELL	TVT 3	WMD	1417	1962	
	LDS	701 071	WMD	1491	1963	
	EMN	701 072	WMD	1495	1963	
	HWB	701 073	WMD	1490	1963	
	DLI	701 074	WMD	1487	1963	97 98 01 502 17-5
1701 076	BVM	701 076	WMD	1486	1963	
	LWB	TVT 2	WMD	1500	1963	Ex DB 701 080
	DLI	701 082	WMD	1502	1963	97 98 01 503 17-3
	DLI	701 088	WMD	1492	1963	
	RNE	701 097	WMD	1516	1964	
1701 098	LWB	TVT 1	WMD	1511	1964	
	AVOLL	701 099	WMD	1512	1964	
1701 100	ELL	TVT 1	WMD	1513	1964	
	DLI	701 101	WMD	1509	1964	Stored
	DLI	701 103	WMD	1506	1964	Stored
	NETINERA	701 108	WMD	1522	1964	Neustrelitz
	RNE	701 110	WMD	1518	1954	
	DLI	701 118	Uer	72826	1967	
	HEIN	701 120	Uer	72834	1968	Spares

	DLI	701 127	Uer	72833	1968	97 98 01 509 17-0
	DLI	701 128	Uer	72830	1967	97 98 01 505 17-8
	HEIN	701 130	Uer	72829	1967	
	DLI	701 140	WMD	1554	1971	97 98 01 504 17-1
	HWB	701 141	WMD	1555	1971	
	HWB	701 142	WMD	1556	1971	
	LDS	701 145	WMD	1559	1971	
	EMN	701 152	MBB	09002	1972	
	DLI	701 158	MBB	9008	1973	Stored
1701 162	LWB	TVT 3	MBB	9012	1973	ex 701 162
	DLI	702 042	WMD	1458	1962	Stored
	PBE	702 050	WMD	1483	1962	
	DLI	702 123	Uerdingen	72827	1967	Stored
	DLI	702 124	Uerdingen	72831	1967	Stored
1702 129	BVM	702 129	Uerdingen	72828	1968	Spares
1702 131	AVG	480	WMD	1525	1969	Stored; Ex DB 702 131
	DLI	702 135	WMD	1529	1969	Stored
	DLI	702 136	WMD	1550	1970	Stored
	RPRS	703 007	Windhoff	2418	1996	Ex DB
	AVG	703 009	Windhoff	2420	1996	Ex DB
	RPRS	711 002	Windhoff	2428	1996	Ex DB
	RPRS	711 006	Windhoff	2432	1996	Ex DB
	RPRS	711 007	Windhoff	2433	1996	Ex DB
	RPRS	711 009	Windhoff	2435	1996	Ex DB
	RPRS	711 011	Windhoff	2437	1996	Ex DB
(716 501)	MTEG	716 501	Rolba	95521360	1981	
	HEIN	724 002	Uer	59453	1954	Ex DB ex 795 471
	HEIN	727 001	Uer	57105	1952	Ex DB ex 795 113

▲ The unique narrow gauge V51/251, 251 901 is seen shunting at Putbus on the Isle of Rügen on 12 May 2013.
Matthias Müller

4. RAILWAY MUSEUMS AND MUSEUM LINES

The lists in this section are arranged in alphabetical order of the Länder and then of places within that Länder. A selection of tramway museums and garden/park railways is also included. At locations where there is a running line with regular services, the Kursbuch der Deutschen Museums Eisenbahnen (KME) timetable number is shown. This publication appears each year and is indispensable when planning visits to German Museum lines. In 2015 Eisenbahn Kurier took over compilation and publication of this book and completely revamped it. The new references are included here.

Perhaps the greatest differences between preservation in Germany and in the UK are that few groups in Germany own their own line and that few lines operate mid-week. A glance at the operating dates shows that a month of Sundays is required to ride many of the lines! To help with planning trips websites are shown for most operations. We strongly advise these should be consulted to ascertain actual operating dates. Early in 2015 many websites were still showing 2014 data and nothing for the forthcoming year. Do check the websites!

Where numbers of traction types are shown, this refers to the total number likely to be found at each location and not just those listed in this book.

BADEN-WÜRTTEMBERG

Amstetten–Gerstetten. 20 km.   BW 18

www.uef-lokalbahn.de

Ulmer Eisenbahnfreunde. UEF Lokalbahn Amstetten–Gerstetten e.V. (LAG). This is a former WEG line closed in 1996; since then UEF has taken it over and runs museum trains on various Sundays between May and October, but not usually the same Sundays as on its narrow gauge operation from Amstetten.

2 steam, 3 diesel, 1 railcar.

Amstetten–Oppingen. 5.7 km. 1000 mm gauge.   BW 16c

www.albbaehnle.de

Museumsbahn Amstetten–Oppingen. This former WEG line used to run through to Laichingen but closed in 1986. Local fans including Ulmer Eisenbahnfreunde saved a short section. Operations are on various Sundays May–October.

2 steam, 3 diesel, 1 railcar.

Böblingen–Dettenhausen. 17 km.   BW 14c

www.ges-ev.de

A relatively new operation by the Stuttgart group GES. Steam trains run occasionally. Check the website for operating days.

Blumberg–Weizen. 26 km.   BW 25

www.stadt-blumberg.de or www.sauschwaenzlebahn.de

Wutachtalbahn. This interesting line was a German strategic line avoiding Swiss territory and was kept in good order for many years under NATO instructions. Now it is a museum line and has some spectacular viaducts and even a spiral. Recently there has been some falling out between the enthusiasts that provided the volunteer labour and the local councils that owned the line. Apparently the enthusiasts not only owned the operating locos but also the shed at Fützen. The line belongs to the local authorities who have now taken over the operation but will presumably have to find some motive power. The enthusiast group now calls itself Dampfbahn Schwarzwald–Bodensee and has been leasing out its locos. Check website for latest information.

5 steam, 2 diesel, 1 railcar.

Crailsheim. DBK Historische Bahn.

This organistaion used to be based at Gaildorf West as Dampfbahn Kochertal (hence DBK) but when that line closed it moved to Crailsheim. Trains run on lines in the greater area especially from Schorndorf. At Crailsheim the intention is to restore the old loco depot to all its former glory. A 23 metre turntable has been acquired from Reichenbach. One to watch!

6 steam, 5 diesel, 1 railcar.

Dörzbach. 750 mm gauge.   BW 06

www.jagsttalbahn.de

Jagsttalbahnfreunde. Regretably this line is still sleeping not having operated for many years after flood damage. Work continues at the depot at Dörzbach but when operations will restart is still a matter of conjecture.

2 steam, 3 diesel, 2 railcars.

Eschach-Seifertshofen.

Schwäbisches Bauern und Technik Museum. This private museum has collections of farming machinery, old cars, fire engines etc. and a railway section. Open daily 10.00–17.00.

3 steam, 5 diesel, 1 battery electric.

Ettlingen–Bad Herrnalb. 19 km.   BW 16a

www.albtalbahn-dampfzug.de

Albtalbahn. Ulmer Eisenbahnfreunde (UEF) run steam trains over the Albtalbahn from Ettlingen Stadt usually on the last Sunday of the month May–October.

3 steam, 1 diesel.

Freiburg in Breisgau. 1000 mm gauge.

Freiburger Verkehrs AG. The city of Freiburg has a tram network with a few nostalgic trams available for excursions and charters.

6 trams.

Heidelberg. 1000 mm gauge.

Heidelberger Strassen und Bergbahn AG. The local tramway has three historic trams, one of which is available for excursions.

Heilbronn.   BW 07

www.eisenbahnmuseum-heilbronn.de

Süddeutsches Eisenbahn Museum, Heilbronn (SEH). This centre has grown and grown with Ulmer Eisenbahnfreunde using it as a major base especially for flagship loco 01 1066. Open Saturdays, Sundays and holidays March–October 10.00–18.00.

24 steam, 18 diesel, 2 electric.

Horb. Eisenbahn Erlebniswelt. BW 08

www.eisenbahn-erlebniswelt.de

Quite a new location but growing at an impressive rate. In effect groups that were in Stuttgart have had to find a new home because of the redevelopment programme there. The area south of Horb station, which was a former marshalling yard, has been cleared and a large museum building erected. Normally open Saturday, Sunday and holidays April–October 11.00–17.00 plus Tuesday–Friday in local school holiday periods in the summer.

2 steam, 8 electric, 6 diesel, 6 EMU, 6 DMU.

Kandern–Haltingen. 13 km. BW 26

www.kandertalbahn.de

Kandertalbahn. Eurovapor have operated museum trains over this private line for more than 40 years. Trains normally run on Sundays May–October with one round trip in the morning and two in the afternoon, meaning that the line can be traversed from either end. Haltingen is on the DB main line from Freiburg to Basel.

3 steam, 2 diesel, 1 railcar.

Karlsruhe. 2 .7 km. 600 mm gauge. BW 05b

Schlossgartenbahn. A lesser known park railway that has been operating with steam since 1967. Trains run at weekends May to October and daily in the summer. Normally trains only run in the afternoon and only with steam haulage at weekends when the weather is fine.

1 steam, 1 diesel.

Karlsruhe.

Verkehrsbetriebe Karlsruhe. The tramway company has five nostalgic trams available for excursions and charters.

Karlsruhe–Baiersbronn. Circa 71 km. BW 16b

Ulmer Eisenbahnfreunde and AVG have a long-standing degree of co-operation which enables UEF/AVG to operate steam trains on the AVG managed line to Baiersbronn, usually on the first Sunday of the month June–September using a loco from the UEF collection.

Korntal–Weissach. 22.5 km. BW 14a

www.ges-ev.de

Gesellschaft zur Erhaltung von Schienfahrzeugen (GES). GES operate steam trains on this private line on various Sundays May to September. Check website for operations as the line is subject to major engineering works.

Kornwestheim.

BSW Freizeitgruppe IG E93 07. This BSW group looks after not only E93 07 but also E94 279. Only the E94 is currently in operational condition.

Kornwestheim.

Gesellschaft zur Erhaltung von Schienfahrzeugen (GES). The main base for this society used to be in the DB depot at Kornwestheim but is now at an old wagon shop in the nearby rangierbahnhof. Active locos here are used on the line from Korntal.

5 steam, 1 electric, 7 diesel.

Mannheim.

Landesmuseum fur Technik und Arbeit in Mannheim (LTA) now known as Technoseum. This town museum includes a railway section. 89 312 "steams" most days operating as a fireless or indeed compressed air locomotive, so as to not pollute the inside of the museum. One of the Class 202 diesels that pioneered three-phase motors is also on show. Open Tuesday–Sunday 10.00–17.00 (20.00 Wednesday).

3 steam, 4 diesel.

Mannheim. 1000 mm gauge.

Oberrheinische Eisenbahn Gesellschaft (OEG). This railway has restored a 1928 twin set for excursions.

Mannheim-Friedrichsfeld Süd.

www.historische-eisenbahn.ma.de

Located at the Heidelberg end of the vast marshalling yard in a former departmental depot, Historische Eisenbahn Mannheim e. V. has been steadily building up its collection. Check website for opening days.

1 electric, 11 diesel, 2 DMU.

Marxzell.

Fahrzeugmuseum Reichert. This private museum opened in the late 1960s and is somewhat run down and very small compared to Sinsheim and Speyer. Four gauges are represented.

4 steam, 3 diesel, 5 trams.

Münsingen. Schwäbische Alb Bahn.

This organisation runs DMU services on Sundays and holidays May–October over part of the HzL with connecting specials from Ulm.

2 diesel, 6 DMU.

Neckarbischofsheim–Hüffenhardt. 17 km. BW 20

www.krebsbachtal-bahn.de

Krebsbachtalbahn. On Sundays and holidays May–late October railcar services operate over this SWEG line.

Neresheim–Sägmühle. 3 km. 1000 mm gauge. BW 23

www.hmb-ev.de

Hartsfeld Museumsbahn (HMB). This society has preserved some locomotives and stock of the closed metre gauge line from Aalen to Dillingen. The section between Neresheim and Sägmühle has been reopened. The line operates on selected days May–October. See website for actual days.

2 steam, 1 diesel, 2 DMU.

Nürtingen–Neuffen. 8.9 km. BW 14b

www.ges-ev.de

Gesellschaft zur Erhaltung von Schienfahrzeugen (GES). This Stuttgart/Kornwestheim based society operates over this private line on the third Sunday of the month June to October using locos from the Kornwestheim pool. First and last trains often start/terminate at Ludwigsburg and run over the Stuttgart avoiding line.

Oberharmersbach. Badische Lokaleisenbahn AG. (ex Ottenhöfen). BW 17

The group that operated trains from Achern to Ottenhöfen for some 40 years has had to find a new home and during 2014/15 was transferring to this new location which is on a SWEG branch line. It is exected that operations will be similar with steam trains running on two Sundays a month.

2 steam, 1 diesel.

Ochsenhausen–Warthausen. 19 km. 750 mm gauge. BW 01

www.oechsle-bahn.de

This line is classed as a historic monument and has quickly established itself as a traditional German narrow gauge line. 2015 will see its Mallet 0-4-4-0T back in traffic so a visit could be well worthwhile. It operates every Sunday May–mid October but also the first and third Saturdays in those months and Thursdays July–September. Services start at the main line end at 10.30 easily allowing connections from major centres.

3 steam, 2 diesel.

Reutlingen.

Freunde der Zahnradbahn Honau–Lichtenstein e.V. (ZHL). There used to be a rack railway here and this society hopes to reopen it! It has not only managed to get hold of some of the DB Class 797 railcars but also has restored rack steam loco 97 501 to operation.

1 steam, 3 diesel, 4 DMU.

Riegel–Breisach. 26 km. BW 24

www.rebenbummler.de

Kaiserstuhlbahn/Eisenbahnfreunde Breisgau (EFB). Museum trains operate over the local private railway one weekend a month May–October, sometimes with a hired in DBK steam locomotive when its own is out of service.

1 steam, 2 diesel, 1 DMU.

Rottweil.

Eisenbahnfreunde Zollernbahn (EFZ). A very active society running excursion trains over the local DB and HzL networks and now based here rather than Tübingen.

3 steam, 1 diesel.

Schorndorf–Rudersberg–Welzheim. 22.9 km. BW 19

www.dbkev.de

Dampfbahn Kochertal (DBK). This Crailsheim based group operates steam trains on this line on selected weekends during the year, often using 64 419.

Seebrugg. IG 3 Seenbahn. BW 10

A new organisation, already finding some success in this highly scenic area. Steam trains have been run using EFZ or Dampfbahn Schwarzwald–Bodensee locomotives.

1 electric, 2 diesel.

Sinsheim. BW 13

www.technik-museum.de

Auto und Technik Museum (ATM). This museum is similar to the one at Speyer and is just as excellent. Allow a lot of time for a visit as there is plenty to see here, not only for the railfan but transport enthusiasts in general will find much of interest. A station (halt) has been opened to serve the museum and when last visited trains from here went through to Speyer, thus making both easily accessible in a day - if there is enough time. Do not miss the military section as there is a camouflaged Class 52 in there!

9 steam, 4 electric, 1 diesel.

Stuttgart.

BSW Freizeit Gruppe. Stuttgart railway staff have pledged to look after 612 506/7. The Class 612 unit has proved successful on railtours in the area and of course is not restricted to where the catenary goes. Currently the unit needs an overhaul.

1 railcar set.

Stuttgart, Parkeisenbahn Killesberg. 381 mm gauge. BW 12

Few people seem to be aware that Stuttgart has a park railway with two lovely Krauss Maffei pacifics from 1950. There is daily operation in the afternoons May to September but steam is not necessarily used every day. This particularly applies to early and late season and bad weather days. During 2014 it acquired another 4-6-2 from Spain.

3 steam, 2 diesel.

Stuttgart-Bad Constatt. BW 11a & 11b

Strassenbahnwelt. A good collection of Stuttgart area trams are housed here. Several are in working order and on Saturdays can be found working on two routes. On the last Saturday of the month they run between Stuttgart (Innenstadt) and the museum whilst the second Saturday of the month sees a circular route operated from the museum. Naturally the museum is also open on these days.

33 trams.

Triberg. BW 04

www.dasferienland.de

For some years now this town has supported the running of steam trains over the Black Forest line with its various tunnels. Eisenbahnfreunde Zollernbahn normally provide the locos and stock. Check website for the latest information.

Tuttlingen.

Deutsche Dampflok Museum, Tuttlingen. This is located in the small roundhouse south of the station. It is believed to be open most Sundays. Most locomotives are from the DR fleet and in an "as received" condition.

26 steam, 6 diesel.

Ulm.

Strassenbahn Nostalgie Ulm has a 1000 mm gauge tramway and there are a few old vehicles which usually operate on the last Sunday of the month May–October.

4 trams.

BAYERN

Augsburg. Bahnpark.   BY 05a & 05b

www.bahnpark-augsburg.eu

Located in the former DB locomotive depot which has become a state monument, an early idea was to have some international locomotives exhibited here. This was a good move as lots of publicity has been generated and high ranking officials from countries concerned have attended events. Money has started to be made available to restore to working order one of the turntables and roof repairs are in hand. Open 10.30–17.00 on first Sunday of the month May–October. Steam trips are organised on certain days in the summer. Check website for details.

10 steam, 12 electric. 5 diesel, 2 DMU, 1 EMU.

Augsburg.

Freunde der Augsburger Strassenbahn. The supporting group has since 1985 helped to restore some of the 1000 mm gauge trams which are available for excursions and charters.

12 trams.

Bad Endorf–Obing am See. 18.5 km.   BY 18

Bad Endorf is on the München–Salzburg main line from where a branch heads northwards; this was closed by DB some years ago and the local society Chiemgauer Lokalbahn has taken it over, running excursion trains on Sundays and holidays May–October.

5 diesel, 1 railcar.

Bayerisch Eisenstein.   BY 09 & 10

www.localbahnverein.de

Bayerische Localbahn Verein (BLV). The old roundhouse here is a listed building so what better place to have a railway museum! BLV have several locos here with local connections to either private lines or industry; some steam excursions operate from Bayerische Eisenstein. Open most days April–November except Mondays in the fringe season. Steam trips often run to Zwiesel during one week in August. Check website!

9 steam, 1 electric, 3 diesel, 3 railcars.

Ebermannstadt–Beringersmuhle. 16 km.   BY 04

www.dfs.ebermannstadt.de

Dampfbahn Frankische Schweiz (DFS). Formed in the late 1970s, this group started running trains over the line in 1983. Trains operate most Sundays May–October but steam operation is variable with the last return trip booked for a diesel.

3 steam, 5 diesel, 1 battery electric, 2 railcars.

Eggmühl–Langquaid. 11 km.   BY 06

www.laabertalbahn.de

Laabertalbahn. Located south of Regensburg, this branch line is now owned by the community. Four return trips operate on occasional dates in the summer season.

Fladungen–Mellrichstadt. 18 km.   BY 11

www.freilandmuseum-fladungen.de

Frankische Freilandmuseum Fladungen. Trains usually operate on the first and third Sundays May–early October.

3 steam, 3 diesel.

Freilassing. Lokwelt.

www.lokwelt.freilassing.de

This new museum is located in the old DB roundhouse and is well worth a visit. There is an international collection with locos from Austria, Switzerland and the former Jugoslavia, hence the name Lokwelt. Open Fridays, Saturday and Sundays 10.00–17.00 all year and daily except Mondays 1 July–mid September.

3 steam, 8 electric, 5 diesel, 2 railcars.

Heroldsbach-Parkeisenbahn. 2.1 km.

Freizeitpark Schloss Thurn has a 600 mm gauge railway which Is believed to operate daily May–August and other occasional dates fringing the season.

2 steam.

Kiefersfelden–Wachtl. 5 km. 900 mm gauge.   BY 13

www.wachtl-bahn.de

Tourist trains run on this 900 mm gauge electrified line which was built to serve a cement works. It straddles the border with Austria near Kufstein. It operates Saturday afternoons and all day Sunday late June to the end of September.

Landshut–Neuhausen. 14 km.   BY 12d

www.bayerbahn.de

Special trains run on this line on the first Sunday of the month May–October but not in August.

Lichtenfels.

The old DB roundhouse is now officially an annexe to the DB Museum and not open to the public except for special open days.

2 steam, 4 electric, 6 diesel, 3 railcars.

München.

Deutsches Museum. A railway section can be found in this museum which is normally open daily 09.00–17.00 throughout the year.

4 steam, 4 electric, 1 steam railcar, 3 EMU, 4 trams.

München.

Freunde des Münchner Trambahnmuseums e.V. (FMTM). München has a large tramway network and naturally there is a supporting group and some historic vehicles.

13 trams.

Neuenmarkt Wirsberg.   BY 02a & 02b

www.dampflokmuseum.de

Deutsches Dampflok Museum (DDM). The DDM collection dates from the 1970s and is housed in a redundant loco shed and wagon shop; it includes some rare items such as 10 001. Locomotives are steamed over various weekends and there are also special events. Open Tuesday–Sunday and holidays 10.00–17.00 but closes at 15.00 November–March. Operates local trips in the summer up the famous "Schiefe Ebene" using a mix of traction.

26 steam, 2 electric, 6 diesel (1435 mm), and 9 steam, 11 diesel (600mm).

Nordhalben–Steinwiesen. 11 km.   BY 07

www.rodachtalbahn.de

Eisenbahnfreunde Rodachtalbahn operates a railbus set over this remote line close to the Thüringen border. Four round trips operate on Sundays and holidays 1 May to end of October.

Nördlingen.   BY 12a, 12b & 12c

www.bayerisches-eisenbahnmuseum.de

Bayerische Eisenbahn Museum (BEM). Founded in 1969 as Eisenbahn Club München (ECM), the club obtained more and more material and needed a bigger site than was available in München. Then DB closed its Nördlingen depot and BEM was formed when ECM transferred to its new home in Nördlingen. Now BEM has formed an operating company to run trains under open access on main lines. Not only that, they have obtained from DB (in association with local government) the line from Nördlingen to Dombühl and also to Gunzenhausen and operate services over these lines on a rotating basis. Dombühl line trains run as far as Feuchtwagen (42 km) on the last Sunday of the month May–October. Gunzenhausen (39 km) trains run on the second Sunday of the month May–October. The museum is open on Tuesday to Saturday, May to September 12.00–16.00 and Sundays and holidays, May–September 10.00–17.00. Check the website for alterations.

33 steam, 10 electric, 2 battery electric, 18 diesel, 2 railcars, 1 battery electric railcar.

Nürnberg.   BY 01

Verkehrsmuseum Nürnberg. The museum dates back to Bayerische Staatsbahn times and as the name implies is not only concerned with railways. The railway section became in recent times the DB Museum. When visiting the museum do not forget the annexe on the other side of the road and retain your ticket for this. Indeed retain your railway ticket to Nürnberg and get a reduced price admission ticket! Open Tuesday–Sundays 09.00–17.00 (Sundays 10.00–18.00) throughout the year.

8 steam, 6 electric.

Nürnberg.

DB Bw. Nürnberg Rangierbahnhof. Following the fire at Nürnberg West depot, the recent modernisation at the Rbf depot has left a roundhouse free which has become a museum store. Not open to the public.

2 steam, 6 electric, 2 diesel.

Nürnberg.

Freunde der Nürnberg–Fürther Strassenbahn. Based in the old depot at St. Peter this group has been preserving and restoring trams for over twenty years. The depot is open the first weekend of each month (except January) 10.00–18.00. Historic trams operate on Line 5 from the Hbf. 9 trams are active.

18 trams.

Nürnberg.

Frankische Museums Eisenbahn (FME). This group dates from 1985; the year of the DB 150 Celebrations. Today they are based in industrial sidings close to Nürnberg Nord Ost station. No main line excursions at the moment as running certificates have expired.

1 steam, 13 diesel.

Passau.

Passauer Eisenbahnfreunde (PEF). This group has taken over the former DB depot, where it carries out work on its rolling stock and locomotives.

1 steam, 5 diesel, 2 railcars.

Passau–Freyung. 49.5 km.   BY 17

www.ilztalbahn.eu

Ilztalbahn GmbH. A relatively new operation on a line that used to run into Czechoslovakia. Operates Saturdays, Sundays and holidays early may to late October. With such a long line two trains operate.

Prien–Stock. 1.7 km. 1000 mm gauge.   BY 14

www.chiemsee-schiffarht.de

This is no museum line but a small railway doing the job it has done for over 120 years connecting the main line railway at Prien with the harbour at Stock. The line operates daily May–September. Beware the steam tram locomotive has a backup similar looking loco which is a diesel replica!

Selb.

www.muecselb.de

Modell und Eisenbahnclub Selb/Rehau. Formed in the 1970s this group has its home in the old sub-shed at Selb, which unfortunately is now too small for the collection so some locomotives are kept outside in the open. The museum is normally open on a Saturday afternoon but check website.

2 steam, 1 electric, 9 diesel.

Seligenstadt–Volkach-Astheim. 10.1 km.   BY 16

www.mainschleifenbahn.de

Mainschleifenbahn. Located close to Würzburg this branch line goes from the main line down to the River Main and is popular with tourists. It operates Sundays and holidays May to October and also on Saturdays mid September to the end of October using a railbus set.

Viechtach–Gotteszell. 25 km.   BY 08

www.wanderbahn.de

The Bayerische Lokomotive und Waggonsocietät operate Regentalbahn DMUs over this delightful line on certain Sundays from the end of June to early September, with two return trips in the fringe months and three return trips in the peak tourist months of July and August.

2 DMU.

Würzburg.

BSW Gruppe Historische Fahrzeuge, Würzburg. From its base at Zell yard 52 7409 is used on excursions in the area.

2 steam, 7 diesel.

BERLIN & BRANDENBURG

Berlin.   BE/BB 05

www.sdtmb.de

Deutsches Technik Museum. This excellent museum is located in the former locomotive depot for Berlin Anhalter Bahnhof. Everything has been restored – locomotives and buildings alike. Surplus stock is stored elsewhere off the site. The museum is open Tuesday–Sunday throughout the year except 1 May. Open 09.00–17.30 Tuesday–Friday, 10.00–18.00 Saturday, Sunday and holidays.

20 steam, 13 electric, 12 diesel, 4 EMU, 1 railcar.

Berlin. 600 mm gauge.   BE/BB 01

www.parkeisenbahn.de

Berliner Parkeisenbahn. Wuhlheide. 600 mm gauge. What was once a pioneer railway is now regarded as a park railway. It operates in the afternoon daily (except Mondays and Fridays) April–October but check the website.

4 steam, 11 diesel.

Berlin.   BE/BB 04

www.hisb.de

S-Bahn Berlin GmbH and Historische S-Bahn Berlin. The main company and a supporting group have restored some of the old Berlin S-Bahn cars. Some 18 sets have been saved and many are operational allowing tourist trains to run throughout the year. Much stock is held at Erkner depot and visits can be made on certain days 11.00–18.00. Watch out for trips on the fourth Saturday of each month.

Berlin-Schöneweide.

The Dampflokfreunde Berlin has taken over most of the former DR locomotive depot site. Excursions are run regularly (Berlin macht Dampf) and there are open days at the depot from time to time.

5 steam, 5 diesel, 1 railcar.

Basdorf. — BE/BB 03

www.berliner-eisenbahnfreunde.de

Berliner Eisenbahnfreunde has its museum collection in part of the old NEB depot at Basdorf from where it runs excursions from time to time over part of the old NEB between Berlin Wilhelmsruher Damm and Basdorf. The museum at Basdorf is open each Saturday March–October.

2 steam, 7 diesel, 1 railcar.

Belzig.

Eisenbahnfreunde Hoher Flaming. This small group started in 1994 by restoring a Köf and then went on to acquire more locos as DR types became spare. No operating line.

2 steam, 4 diesel.

Buckow–Müncheberg. 4.9 km. — BE/BB 06

www.bkb-info.de

Museumsbahn Buckower Kleinbahn.This group has taken over the former DR branch line from Müncheberg to Buckow which is electrified at 740 V dc. Trains run on Saturdays, Sundays and holidays May to October.

3 diesel, 4 EMU, 3 trams.

Cottbus.

Lausitzer Dampflok Club (LDC). This club started by restoring 03 204 then went on to acquire more locos. Slowly growing and operates main line excursions several times each year.

3 steam, 3 diesel, 2 railcars.

Cottbus. Park Railway. 600 mm gauge. — BE/BB 09

This is another former pioneer railway now a park railway. It operates at weekends April–September but also Tuesday–Friday, May–August. Steam operation is normally only at weekends and public/school holidays.

2 steam, 7 diesel.

Falkenberg/Elster.

One of the old locomotive depots at Falkenberg is now a private museum. It is owned by the same person that owns Hermeskeil. Open days take place a few weekends each year. Most locos are in "as received" condition.

54 steam, 1 electric, 26 diesel.

Finsterwalde–Crinitz. 16.95 km. — BE/BB 11

www.niederlausitzer-museumseisenbahn.de

Niederlausitzer Museumseisenbahn. Founded in 1995 and usually operates on the first Sunday of the month in June/July/August, but on the third Sunday in May and September. The main depot is at Kleinbahren.

2 steam, 7 diesel, 1 railcar.

Gramzow. BE/BB 07

www.eisenbahnmuseumgramzow.de

Brandenburgisches Museum für Klein und Privatbahnen. A splendid museum has been established here since 1992 opening to the public in 1996. It is usually open 10.00–17.00 Tuesday–Sunday, May–October.

3 steam, 1 electric, 4 diesel, 2 railcars.

Lindenberg–Mesendorf. 8 km. 750 mm gauge. BE/BB 10

www.pollo.de

Prignitzer Kleinbahn Museum. This 750 mm line, a recent addition to the preservation scene, is still growing. A working steam loco is usually brought in for specials in May, otherwise operation is diesel. Operates on the first weekend of the month May to October.

1 steam, 5 diesel, 1 railcar.

Mildenberg. 4.5 km. 630 mm gauge. BE/BB 08

www.ziegeleipark.de

A narrow gauge tourist line operates at this former brickworks site April–October, normally with diesel traction. However a steam train runs on the first weekend of the month.

Wreizen.

Eisenbahn Museum Oderland has been established in the old DR depot at this country junction, but little has been heard of it in recent years.

1 electric, 24 diesel.

HESSEN

Bad Nauheim–Munzenberg. 20.1 km. HE 08

www.ef-wetterau.de

Eisenbahnfreunde Wetterau e.V. run excursion trains on the first and third Sunday April–October.

1 steam, 4 diesel.

Bad Orb–Wächtersbach. 6.5 km. 600 mm gauge. HE 11

www.bad-orb.info

Operates on Sundays and holidays April–October, but not necessarily in May. Check website. One morning and two afternoon round trips.

Borken.

www.braunkohle-bergbaumuseum.de

Nordhessisches Braunkohle Bergbaumuseum. As the name suggests this museum is devoted to the mining of brown coal (lignite). Gauges of 600, 900 and 1435 mm are represented. Open Easter to October 14.00–17.00 (not Mondays). In winter open only on Sunday afternoons.

1 steam, 2 electric, 4 electro-diesel, 5 diesel.

Darmstadt.   HE 10a & 10b

www.bahnwelt.de

Eisenbahnmuseum Darmstadt Kranichstein. The location is the former DB depot of Darmstadt Kranichstein which is easily accessible from the nearby station of that name opposite the site. The museum is open 10.00–16.00 every Sunday and some Wednesdays April–September. Occasional specials are operated over lines in the area.

13 steam, 3 electric, 15 diesel, 1 EMU, 4 railcars.

Darmstadt. Town tramway. 1000 mm gauge.   HE 13

www.historische-heag-fahrzeuge.de

A DME metre gauge steam locomotive runs over the town tramway at weekends during May, June and September. Operating dates do vary. The tramway also has 8 trams listed as historic vehicles.

Frankfurt am Main. Eiserner Steg–Mainkur/Griesheim. 11 km.
HE 02

www.frankfurt-historischeeisenbahn.de

Historische Eisenbahn Frankfurt. This group runs trains along industrial lines alongside the river and into nearby DB interchanges. The only access is believed to be at Eisener Tor. Operating dates are rather irregular. 01 118 is often used on main line excursions in the area.

2 steam, 4 diesel, 1 railcar.

Frankfurt am Main. 600 mm gauge.   HE 03

www.feldbahn-ffm.de

Frankfurter Feldbahnmuseum. The museum is not too far away from the old FF2 depot along Am Romerhof. A connection from the narrow gauge depot/museum into the nearby Rebstockpark allows an operating line of about 1.5 km. There is an excellent standard of restoration by a small but dedicated band of Feldbahn fans! The museum is open every first Saturday of the month 14.00–17.00 and the first Friday 17.00–19.00 and of course on operating days. Limited operating dates, see website for details.

16 steam, 27 diesel, 3 battery electric, 1 compressed air.

Frankfurt am Main.   HE 01

Verkehrsmuseum Schwanheim. This tramway museum at Rheinlandstrasse 132 is excellent and is open Saturdays, Sundays and holidays throughout the year. Nostaligic trams run throughout the year.

1 steam, 17 trams.

Giessen.

Oberhessisches Eisenbahnfreunde e.V. (OEF). This is a BSW group from the local DB depot at Giessen preserving railbuses for excursions in the area.

3 diesel, 7 railcars.

Hanau.

www.museumseisenbahn-hanau.de

Museums Eisenbahn Hanau is based in the former DB depot. Excursion trains are run over DB lines several times a year.

3 steam, 9 diesel.

Kassel–Naumberg. 33 km.   HE 05

www.hessencourrier.de

Hessencourier e.V. This organisation runs trains over the private line from Kassel to Naumburg. There are depots at both ends of the line. Trains usually run at least one Siunday each month April–October.

5 steam, 4 diesel.

Kassel.

IG Nahverkehrsbetrieb Kassel. The city has trams and an active tramway society. A museum has been set up in the depot at Hollandische Strasse.

9 trams.

Solms Oberbiel. 600 mm gauge.   HE 12

www.foederverein-grube-fortuna.de

Feld und Grubenbahnmuseum, Besucherbergwerk Fortuna. This iron ore mine closed about 1983 and is now a tourist attraction with the railway used to take people on sightseeing tours. Open Tuesday–Sunday, April to October.

7 steam, 2 electric, 47 diesel, 4 battery electric, 1 compressed air.

Treysa.   HE 06

www.eftreysa.de

Eisenbahnfreunde Schwalm Knulll. Based in the old depot at Treysa, this group runs trains several times a year over lines in the area but their steam locomotive is now out of ticket so operations may be restricted.

2 steam, 7 diesel, 1 battery-electric.

Wiesbaden–Dolzheim–Bad Schwalbach–Hohenstein. 23.9 km.
HE 09

www.aartalbahn.de

Nassauische Touristik bahn e.V. (NTB). Operations suspended because of a damaged bridge.

2 steam, 6 diesel.

MECKLENBURG-VORPOMMERN

Bad Doberan–Ostseebad Kühlungsborn. 900 mm gauge. 15.4 km.   MV 04

www.molli-bahn.de

This is a former DR narrow gauge line and remains open for business but now privatised. Noted for its street running in Bad Doberan. All year round regular interval service.

Klütz–Reppenhagen. 4.5 km. 600 mm gauge.   MV 01b

www.stiftung-deutsche-kleinbahnen.de

The Klützer Kleinbahn is located on a former standard gauge branch line. Operations started in 2014. More locos are expected to arrive. Open April–October but not at weekends. See website.

4 steam, 2 diesel.

Pasewalk.   MV 02

www.lokschuppen-pomerania.de

Eisenbahnerlebniszentrum. This is located in the roundhouse close to the station. Open daily 10.00–18.00, April–October.

3 steam, 3 diesel, 1 battery electric.

Prora.   MV 01a

www.etm-ruegen.de

Eisenbahn und Technikmuseum, Prora. This museum is located in a former army base close to Prora station. Also accessible by bus from Binz. Open daily April–October, 10.00–17.00.

12 steam, 3 electric, 24 diesel, 2 battery electric, 10 trams.

Schwerin.   MV 03

www.mef-schwerin.de

Mecklenburgische Eisenbahnfreunde Schwerin and DB Museum. At the old DR depot the local staff have formed a BSW Group to look after what were previously DR Tradition Loks and now belong to DB Museum.

5 steam, 9 diesel, 1 railcar.

Schwichtenberg–Uhlenhorst. 2.4 km. 600 mm gauge.   MV 05

www.mpsb.de

Mecklenburg Pommersche Schmalspurbahn. Operates weekends and holidays May–October, trains starting at 14.00.

Wismar.   MV 06

Eisenbahnfreunde Wismar. This group is developing the rather derelict old roundhouse into a railway museum. Not all stock may be on site.

4 diesel, 1 railcar.

NIEDERSACHSEN & BREMEN

Almstedt. NI/HB 19

www.almetalbahn-online.de

Arge Historische Eisenbahn e.V. This group now only has an 800 metre demonstration line. There are occasional open days when footplate rides may be given.

1 steam, 10 diesel.

Bad Bederkesa–Bremerhaven Fischereihafen. Circa 20 km. NI/HB 23

www.museumsbahn-bremerhaven-bederkesa.de

Museumsbahn Bremerhaven–Bederkesa normally operates on the first and third Sundays of the month, May–October. There are three round trips so a return trip from the Bremerhaven end should not be a problem as trains call at the Hbf.

6 diesel.

Borkum. 900 mm gauge.

Borkumer Kleinbahn und Dampfschiffart GmbH operates the railway on this island and for the last few years has included a regular steam hauled train service. This usually runs in the afternoon. Besides the reconditioned steam loco there is also a vintage Wismar railcar.

1 steam, 1 railcar.

Bornum–Derneburg. 15.7 km. NI/HB 21

www.dampfzug-betriebs-gemeinschaft.de

Dampfzug Betriebs Gemeinschaft e.V. (DBG) operate about four times over this route in the season July–October using a loco from their pool which could be steam or diesel.

Braunschweig. NI/HB 11b

www.eisenbahnerlebnis.de or www.lokpark.de

Verein Braunschweiger Verkehrsfreunde, Borsigstrasse 2 (old loco works). This group has its collection based in part of the old locomotive works. On open days a garden railway often operates. Public excursions are operated in the area. Open first Saturday of the month April–October, 13.30–17.00.

4 steam, 18 diesel, 2 railcars.

Braunschweig–Wittmar/Asse. NI/HB 11a

www.asse-bummler.de

Verein Braunschweiger Verkehrsfreunde operate excursions on this route four or five times a year using stock from their collection.

Bremen–Bremervörde–Stade. Circa 90 km. NI/HB 28

www.evb-elbe-weser.de or www.moorexpress.net

The EVB runs excursions over these lines on Saturdays and Sundays from May to October using vintage stock.

Bremen–Kirchhucting–Leeste–Thedinghausen. 25 km. NI/HB 09

www.pingelheini.de

Kleinbahn Leeste operates diesel trains on about six Sundays between early May and late September.

2 diesel.

Bruchhausen Vilsen–Asendorf. 8 km. 1000mm gauge. NI/HB 07

www.museumseisenbahn.de

Deutsche Eisenbahn Verein (DEV) operates what is Germany's oldest preservation line using a wonderful selection of beautifully restored locomotives and rolling stock. It operates on Saturdays, Sundays and public holidays May to October, usually running one morning and three afternoon round trips.

7 steam, 5 diesel, 8 railcars.

Buxtehude–Harsefeld. 14.8 km. NI/HB 06

Buxtehuder–Harsefelder Eisenbahnfreunde operate a 1926 vintage railcar over the line on the second Sunday of the month May–September, performing four round trips.

1 railcar.

Cloppenburg–Friesoythe.

www.museumseisenbahn-friesoythe-cloppenburg.de

This line has been operating trains for ten years now but is still little known. The website should be consulted as sometimes trains operate from one end and sometimes from the other end!

Deinste–Lütjenkamp. 2 km. 600 mm gauge. NI/HB 02

www.kleinbahn-deinste.de

A typical feldbahn railway which operates on the third Sunday of the month May–September, with trains running 10.40–16.40.

1 steam, numerous diesel.

Eystrup–Bruchhausen Vilsen–Syke. 36.7 km. NI/HB 08

www.kaffkieker.de

DEV have a standard gauge operation over this VGH line. It operates first and third Sundays early May to end September. Based at Hoya the railcar performs two complete round trips each day.

1 diesel, 2 railcars.

Harpstedt–Delmenhorst Süd. 22 km. NI/HB 05

www.jan-harpstedt.de

The Delmenhorst Harpstedter Eisenbahnfreunde operates three return trips over the Harpstedt to Delmenhorst line on operating days, usually the first and third Sundays May–September. The last return trip often operates with a DMU.

2 steam, 4 diesel, 2 railcars.

Lüneburg–Bleckede. 23 km.   NI/HB 04a

www.heide-express.de

Tourist trains run over this normally freight-only OHE line on the first and third Sundays, April–mid September.

Lüneburg West–Bispingen. 39.5 km.   NI/HB 03

www.heide-express.de

Touristik Eisenbahn Lüneburger Heide GmbH. The full run only takes place a few times each year, otherwise there are numerous shorter workings over this and other OHE lines – see website.

5 diesel, 3 railcars.

Meppen–Essen(Old). 51 km.   NI/HB 10

Eisenbahnfreunde Hasetal-Haselünne eV., based in Haselünne. A very busy line with many cyclists taking advantage of the baggage car and the buffet car! Operates on various weekends through the season.

1 steam, 3 diesel.

Norden–Dornum. 17 km.   NI/HB 20

www.mkoev.de

Museumseisenbahn Küstenbahn Ostfriesland e V. This group runs trains on most Sundays June–end October plus occasional early season workings. See website for details.

5 diesel.

Oldenburg–Ocholt. 23 km.   NI/HB 22

www.mas-online.de

Museumseisenbahn Ammerland–Saterland uses Ocholt as its base for operating railcars over this line. Check website for details.

3 railcars.

Osnabrück.   NI/HB 26

www.osnabruecker-damflokfreunde.de

Osnabrück Dampflokfreunde. This group operates trains two or three times a year from Osnabrück Hbf to Zeche Piesberg. Trains also run to local events in the greater Osnabrück area.

3 steam, 9 diesel, 1 railcar.

Rinteln Nord–Stadthagen West. 20.4 km.   NI/HB 15

www.der-schaumburger-ferst.de

An interesting cross country line which operates usually on the second or third Sunday of the month March–November using a railbus set. However steam trains are planned for early September. Check the website!

Salzgitter.

Linke Hofmann Busch museum. This private museum can be visited by prior arrangement. It contains several locomotives and rolling stock built by the firm. There has been talk of it opening to the public.

4 steam, 1 battery electric, 1 EMU, 1 railcar, 2 trams.

Salzgitter Bad–Borssum. 15 km.   NI/HB 17

www.dg41096.de

Dampflokgemeinschaft 41 096 e.V. This group is based at Klein Mahner and operates only three or four times a year.

2 steam, 10 diesel, 1 railcar.

Sehnde-Wehmingen.   NI/HB 29

www.wehmingen.de

Hannoversches Strassenbahn Museum (HSM). This museum has a large collection of trams, of which 12 are operational and many more under restoration. Trams are not only from Hannover but other places in Germany. The museum is open Sundays and holidays April–October, 11.00–17.00.

65 trams.

Soltau–Döhle. 30 km.   NI/HB 13

www.soltau.de

Soltau Touristik operate an old Wismar railcar over this line on Sundays, July–September.

Verden–Stemmen. 12 km.   NI/HB 14

www.kleinbahnbezirk.de

Verdener Eisenbahnfreunde/Kleinbahn Verden-Walsrode e.V. operate on the first Sunday of the month, May–October.

6 diesel, 2 railcars.

Vienenburg.   NI/HB 18

www.eisenbahnmuseum-vienenburg.de

Eisenbahnmuseum Vienenburg. This is located at Vienenburg station with most exhibits outside but museum officially open Thursday–Sunday through the year.

1 steam, 3 diesel.

Walsrode–Bomlitz. 8 km.   NI/HB 04c

www.heide-express.de

For 2015 there are three operating days when railcars traverse this freight only line.

Walsrode-Hollige–Altenboitzen. 2.7 km.   NI/HB 16

www.boehmetal-kleinbahn.de

This group offers draisine trips but also has a diesel locomotive and visiting steam locomotives. Check the website for what is happening as it operates most weekends April–November and Saturdays only at other times.

Werlte–Lathen. 25.2 km.

Museumseisenbahn Hummlinger Kreisbahn e.V. Service understood to be suspended.
2 railcars.

Wilhelmshaven.   NI/HB 12

www.wilhelmshaven-touristik.de

A new operation in the Wilhelmshaven area is to operate using the railbus from the Hummlinger
Kreisbahn. On some Saturdays or Sundays there is a 90 minute trip from Bohnenburg bei
Hooksiel into Wilhelmshaven. This appears to start on the freight only line that goes north of the
city. It should be possible to do a round trip from Wilhelmshaven by using the 12.00 departure
from there. See the website or the Museums Kursbuch for details.

Winsen Süd–Salzhausen–Amelinghausen–Sottorf. 55 km.

Winsen Süd–Niedermarsehacht. 17 km.   NI/HB 04b

www.heide-express.de

Touristik Eisenbahn Lüneburger Heide GmbH (TELH). These are some of the numerous TELH
operations over OHE lines. Trains usually run once a month, June to September.

NORDRHEIN-WESTFALEN

Alsdorf.

Berbaumuseum Wurmrevier e.V. A new museum is being established at Alsdorf which will have a railway section associated with the local mining industry.

2 steam, 2 diesel.

Bochum Dalhausen.   NW 08

www.eisenbahnmuseum-bochum.de

Deutsche Gesellschaft fur Eisenbahngeschichte (DGEG). This society used to have three sites around the country but now there are only two. Consequently a few extra items are now on show here. To meet current laws the museum is now known as Stiftung Eisenbahnmuseum Bochum. Located in a former DB depot the site has quite a few sidings and so extra storage buildings have been built on the site. A DMU shuttle operates from the station to the museum. Museum trains operate from Hattingen to Wengern Ost (22 km). A Feldbahn line has been constructed on the site. The museum is open Tuesday–Friday, Sundays and holidays 10.00–17.00 (last entry 16.00).

14 steam, 3 electric 12 diesel, 1 battery electric, 1 EMU, 4 railcars, 1 battery electric railcar.

Bochum Dahlhausen–Hattingen–Hagen. 36 km.   NW 09

www.ruhrtalbahn.de

This is a DGEG operation from their museum at Bochum Dahlhausen operating as the Ruhrtalbahn. Steam trains run on the first Sunday of the month, April–October, with railcars also running on Fridays and Sundays, May–October.

Bösingfeld–Barntrup. 11.2 km.   NW 04

www.landeseisenbahn-lippe.de

Landeseisenbahn Lippe e. V. runs excursion trains over the Extertalbahn line using a mixture of traction. This is another line where the website should be checked for operating days.

2 steam, 2 electric, 2 diesel.

Dieringhausen.   NW 11

Eisenbahn Museum Dieringhausen. This museum is located in the former DB roundhouse at Dieringhausen; it expanded quite a lot in the 1990s, obtaining locomotives from the eastern part of the country. However, in recent years quite a few locomotives have moved away or have been sold. Open each weekend 10.00–17.00.

9 steam, 3 electric, 11 diesel, 2 battery electric, 1 railcar.

Dieringhausen–Oberwiehl. 16 km.   NW 11

www.wiehltalbahn.de

Stock from Dieringhausen museum is used on this line on various dates April–October; steam and diesel. Check website for details.

Dortmund. Westfalisches Industriemuseum.

This industrial museum is located in a former coal mine site which has retained many of the buildings and has a selection of locomotives etc. associated with the industrial past of the area. Open daily except Monday 10.00–18.00.

9 steam, 7 diesel, numerous narrow gauge mining locos.

Düren–Euskirchen. 29.8 km.   NW 27

www.igrurtalbah.de www.rurtalbahn.de www.boerdeexpress.de

The Rurtalbahn operates regular excursion trains over this scenic freight only line every weekend, April to the end of the year using its own DMUs. There are four round trips at three hour intervals.

Eslohe.   NW 17

www.museum-eslohe.de

Maschinen und Heimatmuseum. What started as a small private collection has grown and grown and includes lots of machinery and some locomotives. 600 mm, 1000 mm and 1435 mm gauges are represented. Operates over a short display circuit on the first and third Saturday, April–October.

4 steam, 2 diesel.

Essen Kupferdreh–Haus Scheppen. 3.3 km.   NW 12

www.hespertalbahn.de

Verein zur Erhaltung des Hespertalbahn e.V. operates trains over this former colliery line on most Sundays May–September.

4 steam, 6 diesel.

Geilenkirchen–Gillrath–Schierwaldenrath. Selfkantbahn. 5.5 km. 1000 mm gauge.   NW 16

www.selfkantbahn.de

Interessengengemeinschaft Historischer Schienenverkehr has, over the last 40 years, restored to a high standard locomotives and rolling stock from various narrow gauge lines. It operates every Sunday, May to September and alternate Saturdays.

9 steam, 4 diesel, 3 electric railcars, 4 diesel railcars.

Gelsenkirchen.

Freunde des Bahnbetriebswerks Bismarck. The old DB depot is a listed building and consequently is attracting preservation groups.

6 steam, 1 electric, 10 diesel, 2 DMU.

Gutersloh. 600 mm gauge.   NW 02

www.dampfkleinbahn.de

Dampfkleinbahn Muhlenstroth e. V. operate this short line (circa 1 km) around a park. It is a purpose built line. Check website for operating days which are infrequent.

11 steam, 9 diesel, 1 battery electric.

Gütersloh-Nord–Versmold–Bad Laer. 32.1 km.   NW 05a

www.eisenbahn-tradition.de

On three Sundays in the year Eisenbahn Tradition runs two return trips over this freight only part of the TWE usually steam hauled with a Class 78 4-6-4T.

Hamm–Lippborg. 18.7 km. NW 06

www.museumseisenbahn-hamm.de

Hammer Eisenbahnfreunde operate trains over this RLE route three or four times a year. Check website for actual operations.

3 steam, 7 diesel.

Hellenthal–Kall. 17.2 km. NW 26

www.oleftalbahn.de

On Sundays and holidays May–October a MAN railbus does four round trips on this freight only line. The line known as the Oleftalbahn has a preservation order on it and is understood to be quite scenic.

Huinghausen–Plettenberg. 3.5 km. 1000 mm gauge. NW 18

www.sauerlaende-kleinbahn.de

Markische Museums Eisenbahn e.V. Operates May to September usually on the first and third Sundays. Check website.

4 steam, 3 diesel, 1 railcar.

Köln-Nippes. Rheinisches Industriebahn Museum. NW 15

www.rimkoeln.de

This museum is located in the old DB depot of Köln Nippes in the Lengerich area of the city at the north end of the old Köln Nippes freight yard (now ICE/S-Bahn depot). The museum is open once a month April–September. Eight gauges are represented here – 600, 700, 750, 785, 800, 900, 1000 and 1435 mm!

10 steam, 2 electric, 16 diesel, 4 battery electric, 1 EMU and lots of narrow gauge diesels!

Krefeld St Tonis–Hülser Berg. 13.6 km. NW 19

www.swk.de

Stadtische Werk Krefeld AG. This industrial line operates tourist trains over its own network on Sundays and holidays, May–September.

1 steam.

Minden Oberstadt–Hille. 13.4 km. NW 01b

Minden Oberstadt–Kleinenbremen. 14.8 km. NW 01b

www.museumseisenbahn-minden.de

Museums Eisenbahn Minden operates these lines from its Minden base with trains running on numerous Sundays, May–October. Check website for actual dates.

4 steam, 6 diesel.

Oberhausen.

Dampflok Arge Oberhausen have their base at the old wagon shops at Oberhausen Osterfeld Süd. It is a BSW group looking after its own loco and some from the national collection. Excursions are organised sporadically.

3 steam, 12 diesel.

Oekoven. 600 mm gauge. NW 13

www.gillbachbahn.de

Feld und Werkbahnmuseum. A museum line close to the DB station with a short demonstration line. Operates first Sunday of the month, May–October and other special occasions (e.g. Santa Specials).

5 steam, 5 electric, 35 diesel, 1 battery electric, 1 railcar.

Osnabrück–Mettingen. 21.6 km. NW 05b

www.eisenbahn-tradition.de

On three Sundays a year Eisenbahn Tradition operates steam trains over this freight only line. In 2015 these were in May, July and November. Check the website for actual operating dates.

Prussich Oldendorf–Bohmte. 16 km. NW 01a

www.museumseisenbahn-minden.de

Museums Eisenbahn Minden (MEM) operates this line on occasional dates April–October. The depot is at Prussisch Oldendorf with the first train going out to Bohmte allowing easy access from Osnabrück. The 4 km section from Prussisch Oldendorf to Holzhausen is temporarily closed.

3 steam, 3 diesel, 3 railcars.

Rahden–Uchte. 25.3 km. NW 07

www.museumsbahn-rahden.de

Museumsbahn Rahden operates over this line with railcars once a month, June–October.

1 diesel, 2 railcars.

Siegen. Eisenbahnmuseum Siegen. NW 28

www.sem-siegen.de

Südwestfälisches Eisenbahnmuseum. Located in the former DB roundhouse. Opens last Sunday in the month, March–November.

5 steam, 3 electric, 6 diesel.

Wanne Eickel. Emschertalmuseum.

An open air small collection of locos and trams associated with the area.

2 steam, 1 electric, 1 diesel, 4 trams.

Wesel Hafenbahn. 7 km. NW 03

www.hsw-wesel.de

Historische Schienenverkehr Wesel operates occasional trains over the harbour lines at Wesel. Check website for actual dates.

1 steam, 3 diesel.

Wuppertal–Kohlfurth. 1000 mm gauge. NW 14

www.bmb-wuppertal.de

Strassenbahnmuseum der Bergischen Museumsbahnen (BMB). Another tramway museum open 11.00–17.00 Saturdays throughout the year and Sundays and holidays May–October. 5 trams are active.

22 trams.

RHEINLAND-PFALZ

Brohl–Engeln. 17.5 km. 1000mm gauge. RP/SL 05

www.vulcan-express.de

IG Brohltal Schmalspureisenbahn (IBS). This is a supporting organisation for the Brohtalbahn. Steam and diesel excursions are operated at weekends plus holidays May–October, Tuesday and Thursday May to October, and Wednesday and Friday June to end September. Many "Santa Specials" operate in December. 2015 will see the return to steam of the Mallet 0-4-4-0T; watch out for announcements.

2 steam, 4 diesel, 1 railcar.

Gerolstein.

www.eifelquerbahn.de

Vulcan-Eifelbahn-Bahn Betriebsgesellschaft mbH. Like many preservation groups, what was a club or society has had to change into a company to comply with new legislation. Gerolstein depot (a historical monument) is the operating base for excursions to Daun and Kaisersesch which use a mixture of steam and diesel traction. Services operate weekends and holidays April–October, but in peak summer (July and August) there is also a Monday–Friday service.

1 steam, 6 diesel, 6 railcars.

Hermeskeil. RP/SL 06

Eisenbahn Museum Hermeskeil. A private museum set up in an old DB depot by Bernd Falz who started acquiring locos as long ago as the 1970s. The collection was moved to Hermeskeil in the 1980s and considerably enlarged when DR locos became available after the Berlin Wall came down. Many of the steam locos are ex stationary boiler use and are in "as received" condition. Open weekends April, May, September 10.00–16.00; daily June, July, August 10.00–16.00.

41 steam, 4 electric, 13 diesel.

Koblenz Lützel. DB Museum. RP/SL 08

www.dbmuseum-koblenz.de

This is an old DB locomotive depot latterly used as a wagon shop. It is now an official annexe of the DB Museum. There has been considerable expansion as diesels and electrics from the 1950/60s have been withdrawn. A large roof has been erected over the outside exhibits to give some form of protection. Open April–December on Saturdays 10.00–16.00 but in July and August open daily except Monday 10.00–17.00.

4 steam, 25 electric, 14 diesel, 2 DMU.

Lambrecht–Elmstein. "Kuckuksbähnel". 13 km. RP/SL 01

www.eisenbahnmuseum-neustadt.de

DGEG Neustadt/Weinstrasse locos and stock are used for tourist trains over this pleasant line on various weekends in the season. The first and last trains originate/terminate at Neustadt/W. Check website for actual operating days.

Linz–Kalenborn. 8.8 km. RP/SL 07

www.zugtouren.de

Eifelbahn Verkehrsgesellschaft mbH. An hourly railbus service operates at weekends from Easter to December; there is a limited service on Wednesdays during the local summer holiday period.

3 railbuses plus trailers.

Neustadt/Weinstrasse. RP/SL 02

www.eisenbahnmuseum-neustadt.de

Eisenbahn Museum Neustadt. This museum is run by DGEG; located close to Neustadt/ Weinstrasse station it is an old loco depot. In 1999 the society obtained use of a more modern loco depot when DB gave up using a small roundhouse nearby. So DGEG now has extended territory including the old mechanical signalbox that straddles the running lines. The museum is also the operating base for running trains on the line from Lambrecht. The museum is open Saturdays, Sundays and holidays 10.00–16.00, Tuesday–Friday 10.00–13.00. Closed on Sundays in January and February.

13 steam, 3 electric, 11 diesel, 1 railcar.

Speyer.

www.technik-museum.de

Technik Museum, Speyer. This museum opened in the early 1990s and is excellent. Owned by the same people that run the museum at Sinsheim, both can be visited quite easily using the local train services. However such is the nature of the museums that a whole day could be spent at either. The railway collection is only one part of several themes in the museum which cover all forms of transport and also have military sections. Allow a lot of time! To get to the museum from Speyer station, take the bus! Open daily 09.00–18.00.

14 steam, 3 electric, 8 diesel.

▲ Südwestdeutsche Verkehrs (SWEG) 0-4-0T No 20 has arrived at Ottenhöfen on 9 May 2010 with the 1745 from Achern. **Keith Fender**

SAARLAND

Merzig Ost–Delborner Mühle. 16.4 km.   RP/SL 04

www.museumsbahn-losheim.de

Museumseisenbahnclub Losheim (MECL). This group runs trains over part of the old Merzig–Buschfelder Eisenbahn between Merzig Ost and Delborner Mühle. Trains run once a month, April–October, but there are some extra operating days – see website. The depot is at Losheim; trains returning to Merzig spend twenty minutes there.

4 steam, 6 diesel.

Schwarzerden–Ottweiler. 21 km.   RP/SL 12

www.ostertalbahn.de

Diesel trains operate May–October, usually on the first and third Sundays with one morning and two afternoon return trips.

2 steam, 4 diesel.

SACHSEN

Adorf.   SN 29

www.bwadorf.de

Vogtländische Eisenbahn Verein, Adorf e.V. (VEA). Bahnbetriebswerk Adorf. This group is based at the old DR roundhouse in Adorf. Opens occasional days per month and special trains run just as frequently. Consult the website!

3 steam, 10 diesel, 1 battery electric.

Bad Schandau–Lichtenhainer Wasserfall. "Kirnitzschtalbahn".
1000 mm gauge.   SN 08

This delightful metre gauge tramway operates alongside the road and uses trams from various systems. It is open April–October. There are four historic vehicles available for charter, but the "normal" trams date from the 1960s!

3 trams and 1 trailer (not including the normal fleet).

Chemnitz. 600 mm gauge.   SN 30

www.parkeisenbahn-chemnitz.de

Parkeisenbahn, Kuchwaldring 24. Operates in the afternoon on Tuesday–Sunday, April–October. Steam usually operates on one weekend a month.

1 steam, 4 diesel, 1 battery electric.

Chemnitz.   SN 28

www.sem-chemnitz.de

Sächsiches Eisenbahnmuseum, Chemnitz Hilbersdorf. Bw Hilbersdorf is a listed building as it retains much of its Sachsen beginnings. It was in use for steam traction until quite late and consequently has retained full steam facilities including a large coaling plant. With the closure of the nearby marshalling yard the depot was redundant and the fans moved in to make a museum out of it. Some interesting locomotives can be found there including a few Sachsen types and many industrial locos with local connections. Open every weekend, April–November.

22 steam, 3 electric, 22 diesel, 3 battery electric, 4 railcars; also 4 steam and 17 diesel on the narrow gauge line.

Chemnitz.

Strassenbahnfreunde Chemnitz. The Chemnitz tramway network was unusual in having two gauges 1435 mm and most unusually 925 mm! The museum collection is kept at the Kappel depot and can usually be seen by local arrangement. Only a short section of 925 mm gauge track remains for museum operation.

9 trams.

Cranzahl–Kurort Oberwiesenthal. 17 km. 750 mm gauge. SN 24

www.fichtelbergbahn.de

This is no preserved railway but a normal operating line – the Fichtelbergbahn being one of several run by what is now called the Sächsische Dampfeisenbahngesellschaft. What is more it now uses the facilities at Oberwiesenthal to overhaul locos from other lines under its control. Operates daily with up to six round trips in high season – normally all are steam hauled.

Dresden.   SN 05

www.verkehrsmuseum-dresden.de

Verkehrsmuseum Dresden (VMD). This museum is located within the city and naturally has railway and tramway sections. The VMD also owns many other locos which are spread around the former DDR as there is no space for them at the museum. Many are at Bw Dresden Altstadt (q.v.). The museum is open Tuesday–Sunday all year 10.00–17.00.

4 steam, 1 electric, 5 trams.

Dresden.   SN 16

www.igbwdresden-altstadt.de

Bw Dresden Altstadt. This depot was in DDR times planned to be an annexe of the VMD but now is an annexe of the DB Museum. In early spring each year the Dresden Dampflokfest brings large crowds to the depot. The site is not as large as previously as a new DB Regio depot has swallowed up quite a slice. Additionally the old workshops belong to the VMD and are rarely opened.

13 steam, 1 electric, 8 diesel, 1 railcar, 2 trams.

Dresden. Parkeisenbahn. 5.6 km. 381 mm gauge.   SN 09

www.schloesser-dresden.de

Alongside Wien Prater this must be one of the best known park railways in Europe. An intensive service can operate at times with the railway open Tuesday–Sunday, 10.00–18.00, May to October but also on Mondays 13.00–18.00 in July and August. Special events often take place.

2 steam, 2 battery electric.

Dresden. Strassenbahn Museum.   SN 04

www.strassenbahnmuseum-dresden.de

When visiting the Dresden area do not forget the tramway museum! Check the website for opening dates and times.

Freital Hainsberg–Dippoldiswalde. 15 km. 750mm gauge. SN 17

www.weisseritztalbahn.com

Weisseritztalbahn. This narrow gauge line is another operated by Sächsische Dampfeisenbahngesellschaft with steam hauled regular service trains. The line used to go much further to Kurort Kipsdorf (km 26.1) but much of the infrastructure was damaged by floods; happily, rebuilding the last section is now underway and full operation might resume in 2015. There are six return trips per day on the section that remains open. Normal steam operation.

Glauchau.

BSW Freizeitgruppe IG 58 3047. Based in the old DR loco depot, this group has several locos to look after; excursions operate from time to time.

5 steam, 3 electric, 6 diesel.

Görlitz. 665 m line. 600 mm gauge.   SN 20

www.goerlitzerparkeisenbahn.de

Görlitzer Oldtimer Parkseisenbahn. A park railway that operates weekends and holidays April–October, with trains also running on Wednesdays in July and August.

Herrenleite. 600 mm gauge.   SN 10

www.feldbahnmuseum-herrenleite.de

The feldbahn fans have amassed a huge collection at this former oil works. Over 100 narrow gauge locomotives including two steam. Open Saturday afternoons June–September but check website for any extra events.

Jöhstadt–Steinbach. 7.8 km. 750 mm gauge.   SN 15

www.pressnitztalbahn.de

IG Pressnitztalbahn. This society actually got going in DDR times but has really prospered since unification. Their objective is to preserve part of the Wolkenstein–Jöhstadt narrow gauge line which was closed in the mid 1980s – a line that used Sachsen Meyers until closure. The group forged ahead after unification restoring first the depot at Jöhstadt and then laying track back towards Wolkenstein. Now 8 km has been laid to the former station of Steinbach which is the limit of the line. First class work has been done with the group setting a high standard of restoration. The line operates with steam most weekends May to September, but diesels may substitute early and late season.

7 steam, 4 diesel.

Klingenthal.

Eisenbahnfreunde Klingenthal. This little group has a small local museum at Klingenthal station.

1 diesel, 1 tram.

Leipzig.

BSW Kultur und Freizeit Gruppe "Historische Ellok". A group of DB staff at Bw Leipzig Hbf West look after what were once the depot's "Tradition Loks". Some of these are usually exhibited at Leipzig Hbf station.

1 steam, 3 electric, 1 DMU.

Leipzig–Auensee. 381 mm gauge.   SN 06

www.parkeisenbahn-auensee-leipzig.de

The Auensee Park railway has a circuit of about 2 km. It operates May to October daily in the afternoon 14.00–18.00 (10.00–18.00 Sundays and holidays). Trains do not operate in bad weather! This line is another one with a Krauss Pacific but you have to be lucky to catch it working.

1 steam, 1 battery electric.

Leipzig-Möckern.   SN 07

www.strassenbahnmuseum.de

Historische Strassenbahnhof Leipzig-Möckern. The city of Leipzig has a large tramway network and naturally has some historic vehicles. The Möchern depot usually has a few open days during the year. The historic trams normally operate on the third Sunday of the month from outside the Hauptbahnhof or indeed from Möchern depot 09.00–17.00.

22 trams (10 in working order).

Leipzig-Plagwitz   SN 25

www.dampflokmuseum.de

Eisenbahnmuseum Bayerische Bahnhof (EMBB). This society is quite active often running excursions from its base at Leipzig Plagwitz depot. See website for actual open day dates.

2 steam, 4 diesel.

Löbau.   SN 18

www.osef.de

Ostsächsiche Eisenbahnfreunde (OSEF) was founded in the early 1990s and has its base at the old DR loco depot in Löbau. Some excursion trains operate each year and open days are held; otherwise open each Wednesday 09.00–14.00.

3 steam, 12 diesel, 1 battery electric, 1 railbus.

Nossen.

BSW Freizeitgruppe IG Dampflok, Nossen. This society was formed after unification at the depot that used to look after 23 1113, once a "Traditions Lok". When local branch lines lost their passenger services the depot became available as a base. A few open days are held each year, but enthusiasts will probably find someone working there on a Saturday. The depot is now home to several operating locos including 03 155 and 50 3610.

8 steam, 6 diesel.

Oelsnitz.

Bergbaumuseum. A mining museum with a collection of industrial locomotives of various gauges. The only steam loco is a DR Class 52.8.

1 steam, 3 electric, 1 diesel, 1 battery electric.

Oelsnitz.

Lugauer Eisenbahnfreunde (LEF). Based at the former DR sub-shed, this small society has some small ex-DR shunting locos and several Ferkeltaxes!

6 diesel, 1 railbus.

Oschatz–Mügeln–Glossen. 16.1 km. 750mm gauge.   SN 21

www.doellnitzbahn.de

A preservation society helps to run steam excursions over this private railway usually on the last Sunday of the month April–September, but check latest information on the website. Steam can occasionally be found in use on regular trains during the week when diesels are not available.

Plauen. 1000 mm gauge.

Strassenbahnnostalgie. Some vintage cars from the Plauen tramway have been saved; the oldest in use dating from 1905.

4 trams.

▲ Preserved OHE DMU, GDT 0518 works a "Heide Express" excursion on 24 April 2010.

Keith Fender

Radebeul Ost–Radeburg. 16.6 km. 750 mm gauge. SN 11a & 11b

www.loessnitzgrundbahn.de

The Traditionsbahn Radebeul runs vintage trains on this line which is now owned by SDG. These are usually in addition to the regular service timetable. Normal steam operation.

Rittersgrün.

www.ssmo.de

Sächsisches Schmalspur Museum, Rittersgrün. This museum dates from DDR days when the narrow gauge line here was closed in the early 1970s. The collection has expanded since unification and is well worth a visit. The diesels are all ex-industry. A park railway has also been created. Open Tuesday–Friday, April–October, 10.00–14.00 and Saturdays and Sundays 10.00–16.00.

3 steam, 8 diesel.

Schönberg–Schleitz-West. 16 km. TH 07

www.wiesenttatalbahn.de

Wiesentatalbahn. This branch line is where to find DR nostalgia of a different sort as some trains are worked by Ferkeltaxe railbuses. Usually operates on the second and fourth Sunday of the month, April–October.

Schönheide–Stützengrün. 750 mm gauge. 4.5 km. SN 12

www.museumsbahn-schoenheide.de

Museumsbahn Schönheide/Carlsfeld. The Sachsen narrow gauge lines were always loved by fans in the DDR and as can be seen from these pages, several groups are ensuring that Sachsen Meyers and the Heberleinbremse will not be forgotten. This group has saved part of the old Wilkau Hasslau–Carlsfeld narrow gauge line that had Meyers in use until it closed in the mid 1970s. The original depot in Schönheide Mitte has been restored. Trains operate on at least one weekend per month. Check website for actual dates.

3 steam, 1 diesel.

Schwarzenberg. SN 27

www.vse-eisenbahnmuseum-schwarzenberg.de

Eisenbahn Museum Schwarzenberg, Verein der Sächsische Eisenbahnfreunde (VSE). Another post unification success story helped along in the early days by a series of successful plandampfs. Located in a typical roundhouse the museum is open Monday–Friday 10.00–14.00, weekends and holidays 10.00–17.00 (November–March 10.00–14.00). Railtours and festival days are held.

6 steam, 12 diesel, 1 battery electric.

Schwarzenberg–Annaberg Buchholz. 26.7 km. SN 26

www.erzgebirgische-aussichtsbahn.de

The VSE at Schwarzenberg operate trains over the Erzgebirgische Aussichtsbahn (EAB) on behalf of the local tourist organisations. On one weekend a month May–October steam or railbus trains run over this highly scenic route which rarely sees any other trains.

Weisswasser–Bad Muskau/Kromlau. 18.8 km. 600 mm gauge.
SN 23

www.waldeisenbahn.de

Waldeisenbahn Muskau (WEM) was a forest line that passed into DR ownership. Two of the original steam locos and much original rolling stock survive but have been joined by a large number of second-hand industrial diesel locos made spare after unification. Trains run each weekend May–October but steam-hauled usually only on the first weekend of the month. In the holiday periods (early July–mid August) trains also run on Thursday and Friday. There is an excellent museum at Weisswasser.

4 steam, 35 diesel.

Zittau–Kurort Oybin/Kurort Jonsdorf. 12.8 km. 750 mm gauge.
SN 01

www.soeg-zittau.de

Not a museum line but a real live railway doing what it has done since opening; taking tourists to the spas in the mountains. All year normal steam operation.

Zwickau.

Strassenbahn Nostalgie. This town has a metre gauge tramway and local fans have obtained and restored two historic trams to working order.

2 trams.

SACHSEN-ANHALT

Aschersleben.

Eisenbahn Club Aschersleben. This group has taken over part of the old DR depot. Restricted opening but usually someone is there at weekends.

10 diesel.

Aschersleben.

Deutsches Werkbahn Museum. Located with Eisenbahn Club Aschersleben, this group moved here from Hannover.

5 steam, 1 electric, 18 diesel, 2 electro-diesel, 1 battery electric.

Blankenburg (Harz)–Rübeland. 14.2 km.   ST 04

www.arbeitsgemeinschaft-ruebelandbahn.de

This group now operates 95 027 over part of the Rübelandbahn and is also looking after one of the line's original locos 95 6676. Operations are limited to one weekend a month but not July and September.

Dessau.

www.dwe-web.info

Förderverein Dessau–Wörlitzer Museumsbahn. This line runs between the places named using some of the double-deck railcars built in Dessau as well as loco-hauled trains. Operations in 2014 were daily April–October.

1 steam, 6 diesel, 3 EMU, 3 DMU.

Gräfenhainchen.

Ferropolis Bergbau und Erlebisbahn. This museum is located at one of the old lignite centres. It had many locomotives and rolling stock associated with the mining of brown coal, but it is understood many items have been scrapped in recent years. Apart from the mining equipment the main interest now seems to centre on running trolley rides around the site.

1 steam, 14 electric, 10 diesel, 3 battery electric plus many narrow gauge items.

Halle. DB Museum.   ST 11

One of the roundhouses at the old Halle P depot is now an outpost of the DB Museum. It is open on Saturday mornings throught the year except over the Christmas and New Year period.

5 steam, 7 electric, 6 diesel, 2 railcars.

Halle.

Hallesche Strassenbahnfreunde. When in Halle remember the trams! There is a museum depot at Seebener Strasse 191 and historic trams run on tours of the town. The museum is open on Saturdays May to October.

18 trams.

Halle. 600 mm gauge.   ST 12

Park Railway. Another former Pioneerbahn. It is located on the Peissnitzinsel.

4 diesel, 3 battery electric.

Harzer Schmalspurbahn. 1000 mm gauge.   ST 01a, 01b & 01c

www.hsb-wr.de

The main centre for the line is Wernigerode where the main depot and workshops are located, but there are outstations at Gernrode and Nordhausen (Thüringen). All year round steam operation including the fantastic run up to the summit station of Brocken (1124 metres above sea level) from Wernigerode (234 m asl). The mainstay of the service is hauled by 2-10-2Ts but the 0-4-4-0 Mallets are often in use as well. Lots of special events for which the website should be consulted.

Hettstedt.

Mansfeld Museum. This museum deals with the history of mining in the area and has a railway section as the mines had narrow gauge networks.

1 steam, 3 diesel, 1 battery electric.

Klostermansfeld (Benndorf). 10 km. 750 mm gauge.   ST 03

www.bergwerksbahn.de

Mansfelder Bergwerksbahnverein (MBB). This society has managed to save part of the old mining railway network and restored some locomotives. It has also bought a Gr type 0-8-0 from Estonia, a few of which used to work here many years ago. Operates on Saturdays May–October with steam normally operating on the first Saturday of the month, but there are occasional extra days.

2 steam, 2 diesel.

Loburg–Altengrabow. 12 km.   ST 02a & 02b

www.dampfzug-betriebs-gemeinschaft.de

Arbeitskreis Loburger Bahn and Dampfzug Betriebsgemeinschaft (DBG) have come together to set up a museum depot and line at Loburg. DBG is a former West Germany society that has moved east. It is not clear whether all DBG stock is at Loburg but the totals include it. Operates on occasional Saturdays in the summer. The loco collection can be visited by prior arrangement on Monday–Friday mornings.

2 steam, 10 diesel.

Magdeburg.

Magdeburger Eisenbahnfreunde was formed about 1995 and has a base in the harbour lines area.

1 steam, 5 diesel, 1 railcar.

Magdeburg.

This is another city with trams. There are six historic trams, the oldest dating from 1898.

Magdeburgerforth. 750mm.   ST 05

www.kj-1.de

This is a relatively new operation by the Traditionsverein Kleinbahnen des Kreises Jerichow I e.v. gradually taking off and may even have an operating steam locomotive this year. Operations are probably only in station limits but if in the area it is worth checking out.

Naumburg.   ST 06

www.naumburger-strassenbahn.de or www.ringbahn-naumburg.de

This town has a tramway and it would appear some active enthusiasts as some trams have been acquired from various other towns and cities. About three have been restored. Operating days are Saturday, Sunday and holidays April–October.

8 trams.

Stassfurt.   ST 08

www.eisenbahnfreunde-stassfurt.de

Traditions Bahnbetriebswerk Stassfurt. The roundhouse and sidings have been taken over by this group and turned into a museum which is open on Saturdays 10.00–15.30 (except when a holiday). There are some special weekends in June and September with locos in steam and perhaps some railtours around the area.

13 steam, 1 electric, 13 diesel, 1 railcar.

Wittenberge. ST 09

www.dampflokfreunde-salzwedel.de

The old locomotive depot is now home to two groups – Verein Historische Lokshuppen Wittenberge and Dampflokfreunde Salzwedel. The latter group were forced to leave the depot at Salzwedel and have now settled in at Wittenberge. Open Saturdays April–October, 10.00–17.00.

8 steam, 12 diesel.

SCHLESWIG-HOLSTEIN

Aumühle. SH/HH 03

www.vvm-museumsbahn.de

There is a VVM depot and workshop here which is open to the public every Sunday 11.00–17.00.

3 steam, 5 diesel, 2 EMU, 1 DMU.

Bergedorf Süd–Geesthacht–Krummel. 15.7 km. SH/HH 04

www.geesthachter-eisenbahn.de

Arbeitsgemeinschaft Geesthachter Eisenbahn runs trains over what is part of the AKN and an industrial branch, on various weekends in May, June, September and October plus other occasional dates.

3 steam, 3 diesel, 1 railcar.

Kappeln–Süderbrarup. 14.6 km. SH/HH 02

www.angelner-dampeisenbahn.de

Angeln Bahn and Freunde des Schienenverkehrs Flensburg e V. Former SJ and DSB locos are operated over the lines of Verkehrsbetriebe des Kreises Schleswig-Flensburg. Trains operate most Sundays May–September, with a Wednesday offering in the peak season.

2 steam, 6 diesel, 1 railcar.

Lübeck.

Historische Eisenbahnfahrzeuge Lübeck e. V. This group looks after several locos and stock on behalf of DB Museum.

2 diesel.

Neumünster.

The old DB depot here was an outpost of DB Museum but some years ago the site was sold and all locos and stock dispersed around the country. However it now appears that the new owner has refurbished the site but for what purpose is not clear.

Schönberger Strand–Kiel. 24.1km. SH/HH 01

www.vvm-museumsbahn.de

Verein Verkehrsamateure und Museumsbahn, Hamburg (VVM). Operates Saturdays and Sundays May–December with varying levels of service.

3 steam, 1 electric, 6 diesel, 1 EMU, 2 railcars, 18 trams.

THÜRINGEN

Arnstadt.   TH 06

www.ebm-arnstadt.de

Historisches Bw Arnstadt. Arnstadt depot was planned to be a steam centre by the DR where it would be the Traditions Bw for the area. However DB has no remit for this sort of operation so the local BSW group and others got together to form a society to save the depot and locos. Open Wednesday–Sunday 10.00–16.00 (17.00 Saturday and Sunday).

8 steam, 11 diesel, 2 battery electric.

Eisenach.

IG Werrabahn. This group started out at Gerstungen but lost the use of the depot there. They now seem to have a base in Eisenach but some of their stock is still stored on the Hersfelder Kreisbahn line.

2 steam, 1 diesel.

Erfurt.

This is another city with a tramway. Three museum trams reported to be here.

Georgenthal.   TH 03

www.hirzbergbahn.de

IG Hirzbergbahn e.V. is another new group set up since unification and still gathering stock. It is understood that there is a demonstration line at least within the confines of the station. It is still in the early stages of development. Consult website for any open days.

1 steam, 4 diesel.

Gera.

The local tramway has three museum trams.

Gera.

Eisenbahnwelt e.V. This group has taken over the old depot in Gera.

3 steam, 1 diesel.

Heiligenstadt.

Heiligenstadter Eisenbahnverein. This small society has collected some interesting exhibits which are displayed or stored at Heilgenstadt Ost station.

1 steam, 5 diesel, 1 battery electric.

Ilmenau.   TH 02

www.schaubergwerk-langewiesen.de

Museum fur Bergbau and Feldbahntechnik. A mining museum open April to November Tuesday–Friday 09.00–16.00, Saturday, Sunday and holidays 10.00–18.00. Two demonstration lines, one of which goes into the mine.

80 feldbahn locomotives.

Ilmenau–Themar.   TH 01

www.rennsteigbahn.de

Dampfbahnfreunde Mittlerer Rennsteig e.V. Irregular operations over lines in the area; the working steam locomotive is being overhauled. Check website for details of current operations.

4 steam, 2 diesel.

Meuselwitz–Regis Breitingen. 14 km. 900 mm gauge.   TH 05

www.kohlebahnen.de

Kohlebahn Haselbach. Excursion trains are run over this coal railway. The old DR depot at Meuselwitz has been incorporated into the system and now has tracks of standard and narrow gauge. Both ends of the line have some locomotives on display. Operates most Sundays, April–October. Check the website.

5 steam, 2 electric, 9 diesel.

Nordhausen.

When visiting the Harz narrow gauge lines remember that Nordhausen has a tramway with three historic vehicles.

Weimar.   TH 04

www.thueringen-eisenbahnverein.de

Thüringen Eisenbahnverein. This group is based in the old DR depot at Weimar and has concentrated on preserving electric locomotives, although the collection has expanded. Open March–November Tuesday–Friday 08.00–14.00, and weekends by arrangement except for special events. Check website.

2 steam, 15 electric, 12 diesel, 8 battery electric, 1 railcar.

▲ The Bayerisches Eisenbahnmuseum in the former DB shed at Nördlingen is home to a large collection of heritage steam, diesel and electric locomotives. 1918 built S 3/6 Pacific 3673 has the EVN 90 80 0018 478, incorporating its German operating number 18 478. It stands outside the museum on 13 June 2009.   **Keith Fender**

5. PRESERVED LOCOMOTIVES & MULTIPLE UNITS OF PRIVATE RAILWAYS

A good selection of locomotives and units has survived from the private railways. Where lines closed many years ago there is often a plinth as a momento. Others have moved from their normal areas into museum collections around the country or elswhere. But they have been saved!

The current status of motive power is indicated as follows:

M	Museum, on display (not active)
MA	Museum, active
MR	Museum, under repair
MS	Museum, stored
P	Plinthed
S	Stored

5.1 STEAM LOCOMOTIVES

Gauge	Railway	No.	Type	Built	Status	Location etc.
1000	AVG	7s	0-4-4-0T	1898	M	Bruchhausen Vilsen
900	Borkumer Kleinbahn	I	0-4-0WT	1938	MA	Borkum
900	Borkumer Kleinbahn	II	0-4-0WT	1937	P	Bevern
1000	Klb. Bremen – Tarmstedt	1	0-6-0T	1899	P	Bremen
1435	BE	22	0-6-0WT	1925	P	Nordhorn
1435	BLE	16	0-6-0T	1901	MS	Almstedt
1435	BLE	146	2-6-0T	1941	MA	Bochum Dahlhausen
1000	Brohltalbahn	Sm 11	0-4-4-0T	1906	MA	Brohl
1435	DEG	184	0-8-0T	1946	MA	Darmstadt
1435	DHE	4	0-6-0T	1925	MS	Haaksbergen, Netherlands
1000	Drachenfelsbahn	2	0-4-2RT	1927	P	Königswinter
1000	Dürener Eisenbahn	4	0-4-0T	1899	MA	Schierwaldenrath
1435	FKE	262	2-8-2T	1954	MR	WTB, Blumberg
1435	HzL	11	0-8-0T	1911	MA	Neuffen
1435	HzL	16	0-8-0T	1928	M	Erlebniswelt, Horb
1435	Julicher Kreisbahn	152	2-6-0T	1927	MA	Haaksbergen, Netherlands
1000	Klb. Hoya-Syke-Asendorf	31	0-6-0T	1899	MS	Asendorf
1000	Klb. Hoya-Syke-Asendorf	33	0-6-0T	1899	P	Bruchhausen Vilsen
1000	KAE	13	0-6-0T	1907	P	Altena
1000	KAE	15	0-6-0T	1911	MA	Bruchhausen Vilsen
1000	KAE	22	0-6-0T	1930	M	Ludenscheid
1435	KFBE	21	0-8-0T	1915	M	Marrum (NL)
1435	KNE	206	0-10-0T	1941	MA	Kassel
1435	LAG	FÜSSEN	0-6-0T	1889	M	Nördlingen
1435	Lb. Lam – Kotzting Schwarzeck 4		0-8-0T	1928	M	Bayerisch Eisenstein
1000	MEG	46	0-4-0T	1897	MS	Schierwaldenrath
1000	MEG	101	0-4-0T	1949	MA	Schierwaldenrath
1000	OEG	56	0-4-0T	1886	M	Mannheim
1000	OEG	102	0-4-0Tm	1891	M	Mannheim
750	Klb. Philippsheim – Binsfeld 1		0-6-0T	1899	M	Gerolstein
750	Klb. Philippsheim – Binsfeld 2		0-6-0T	1899	P	Binsfeld
1435	Marburger Kreisbahn	1	0-6-0T	1904	MA	Bad Nauheim
1000	Nassauische Klb	16	0-6-0T	1900	P	Nastätten
1435	RAG	01	0-6-0WT	1890	M	Bayerisch Eisenstein
1435	RAG	03	0-6-0T	1923	M	Bayerisch Eisenstein
1435	RAG	04	0-8-0T	1927	M	Bayerisch Eisenstein
1435	RAG	05	0-8-0T	1927	M	Bayerisch Eisenstein
785	RSE	53	2-8-2T	1944	M	Asbach
1435	SWEG	7	0-4-0T	1907	MR	Kandern
1435	SWEG	20	0-6-0WT	1928	MA	Oberharmersbach
1435	SWEG	23	0-6-0WT	1897	P	Zell Unterharmersbach

750	SWEG	24	0-6-0T	1929	MR	Dörzbach
1435	SWEG	28	0-6-0WT	1900	MA	Oberharmersbach
1435	SWEG	30	0-6-0T	1904	MA	Kandern
750	SWEG	152	0-10-0T	1952	S	Ingolstadt
1435	SWEG	384	0-8-0T	1927	MA	Endingen
1435	SWEG	394	0-8-0T	1917	P	Rust/Lahr
1435	TAG	7	2-8-2T	1936	MR	Landshut
1435	TAG	8	2-6-4T	1942	M	Nördlingen
1435	TWE	154	2-6-0T	1940	MA	Mariembourg, Belgium
1000	WEG (AL)	2s	0-6-0T	1901	M	Amstetten
1435	Wiesloch – Waldorf	14	0-6-0WT	1902	MA	Fladungen
1000	WNB	11	0-4-0T	1913	MS	Neresheim
1000	WNB	12	0-4-0T	1913	MA	Neresheim
1000	Zell-Todtnau	74	0-6-0T	1888	M	Bochum Dahlhausen
1000	Zell-Todtnau	104	0-6-6-0T	1925	M	Chaulin, Switzerland
1000	Zell-Todtnau	105	0-4-4-0T	1918	M	Chaulin, Switzerland

5.2 ELECTRIC LOCOMOTIVES

Gauge	Railway	No.	Type	Built	Status	Location etc.
1000	AVG	2	Bo-Bo E	1910	P	Karlsruhe
1000	BZB	2	Bo E	1929	P	Garmisch Partenkirchen
1000	BZB	3	Bo E	1929	M	München
1435	EH	83	Bo-Bo BE	1929	M	Duisburg Herborn
1435	EH	103	Bo-Bo ED	1955	M	Duisburg Herborn
1435	EH	107	Bo-Bo ED	1957	M	Aschersleben
1435	EH	116	Bo-Bo ED	1959	M	Aschersleben
1435	EH	118	Bo-Bo ED	1961	M	Köln Nippes
1435	EH	159	Bo-Bo ED	19xx	M	Oberhausen
1435	EH	162/385	Bo-Bo ED	1971	P	Moers
1435	EH	183	Bo-Bo ED	1977	M	Duisburg Herborn
1435	EH	345	Bo-Bo BE	1949	P	Duisburg Marxloh
1435	EH	346	Bo-Bo BE	1929	M	Wanne Eickel
1435	EH	348	Bo BE	1919	M	Dieringhausen
1435	EH	389	Bo-Bo ED	1955	M	Hattingen
1435	KBE	E 3	Bo-Bo E	1950	MS	Brühl Vochem
1435	RBH	E1200 003	Bo-Bo E	1976	M	Bochum Dahlhausen
1435	TE	E 4	Bo E	1902	M	Trossingen

5.3 DIESEL LOCOMOTIVES

Gauge	Railway	No.	Type	Built	Status	Location etc.
1435	AKN	V2.003	0-8-0DH	1953	MA	Wiesbaden
1435	AKN	V2.004	0-8-0 DH	1953	M	Braunschweig
1435	AKN	V2.011	B DM	1935	MA	Schönberg
1435	Bad Orber Klb.	V 11	0-6-0 DH	1959	M	DME Darmstadt
1435	Bad Orber Klb.	V 12	0-6-0 DH	1959	M	DME Darmstadt
1435	BE	D 10	B DM	1941	MS	Stadskanal, Netherlands
1435	BE	D 12ˡ	0-4-0 DH	1956	MR	Neuenhaus
1435	BHE	223	B DM	1916	P	Hannover
1435	BHE	224	0-4-0 DM	1953	M	Harsefeld
1435	BHE	276	C DH	1941	MS	Hanau
1435	Bielefeld Krsb.	10	0-4-0 DM	1939	M	Bad Oeynhausen
1435	Birkenfelder Eb	-	0-6-0 DH	1956	MS	Krefeld
1435	BLE	V 13	0-6-0 DH	1961	MR	Butzbach
1435	BLE	V 17	0-6-0 DH	1961	MR	Butzbach
1000	Borkumer Kleinbahn.	Emden	Bo DE	1942	MA	Bruchhausen Vilsen
1435	DHE	7	0-6-0 DM	1955	MS	Loburg
1435	DHE	222	0-4-0 DM	1935	MS	Harpstedt

1435	DHE	273	C DH	1956	MR	Harpstedt
1435	DKB	T 1	B DM	1966	P	Düren
1435	EEB	L 3	D DM	1957	MR	Haslünne
1435	EH	244	C DH	1961	MR	Simpelveld, Netherlands
1435	EH	259	B DH	1957	MR	Essen
1435	EKO	34	0-8-0 DH	1969	MS	Cottbus
1435	Euskirchener Krsb	21	B DM	1957	M	Bruchhausen Vilsen
1435	EVB	277	0-6-0 DH	1955	MS	Walburg
1435	EVB	280	0-8-0 DH	1953	MA	Lüneburg
1000	Geilenkirchener Krsb	V 11	B DM	1955	MR	Schierwaldenrath
1435	GME	11	C DH	1952	MS	Bad Nauheim
1435	HEG	VT 52	A-A DMR	1959	S	Wilburstetten
1435	HGK	V 3	0-4-0 DH	1953	MS	Brühl Vochem
1435	HKB	L1	0-6-0 DH	1955	M	Heiligenstadt
1435	HzL	V 23	0-4-0 DH	1958	M	Erlebniswelt, Horb
1435	HzL	V 25	0-4-0 DH	1954	M	Erlebniswelt, Horb
1435	HzL	V 81	0-8-0 DH	1957	M	Erlebniswelt, Horb
1435	HzL	V 122	B-B DH	1963	MA	SHE Heilbronn
1435	Ilmebahn	V60.03	0-8-0 DH	1953	MS	Brauschweig
1435	Ilmebahn	V65.02	0-8-0 DH	1963	MS	Bad Bederkesa
1435	KBE	V 15	0-8-0 DH	1957	MA	Kassel
1435	KFBE	V 2	B DM	1946	MS	Köln Nippes
1435	KFBE	V 6	0-4-0 DH	1957	MR	Wesel
1435	Kleinbahn Leeste	1	B DH	1947	MS	Stuttgart
1435	Klb. Lüchow–Schmarsau	205	0-4-0 DM	1941	MS	Almstedt
1000	Inselbahn Langeoog	Ko 1	4w DM	1937	M	Schierwaldenrath
1000	Inselbahn Langeoog	Ko 2	4w DM	1937	P	Langeoog
1000	Inselbahn Spiekeroog	V 2	B DM	1940	MS	Harlesei
1000	Inselbahn Spiekeroog	V 4	B DM	1957	M	Bruchhausen Vilsen
1435	Merzig-Buschfelder Eb	V 51	0-6-0 DH	1959	MA	Losheim
1435	Merzig-Buschfelder Eb	V 52	0-6-0 DH	1959	MA	Losheim
1435	MEG	201	C-C DH	1968	MA	Gera
1435	MKB	V 5	B DH	1936	MS	Minden
1435	MKB	V 8	0-6-0 DH	1941	MR	Minden
1435	MKB	V 9	0-6-0 DH	1940	MS	Braunschweig
1435	NME	ML 0601	0-4-0 DH	1941	MA	Lüneburg
1435	NVAG	DL 1	0-4-0 DM	1956	MS	Tonder, Denmark
1435	OHE	0602	0-4-0 DH	1941	M	Bayerisch Eisenstein
1435	OHE	0603	0-4-0 DH	1938	M	Wittenberge
1435	OHE	0604	0-4-0 DM	1935	MA	Wittenberge
1435	OHE	0605	0-4-0 DM	1942	MA	Wittenberge
1435	OHE	0606	0-4-0 DH	1957	MA	Wittenberge
1435	OHE	800 011	0-8-0 DH	1953	MA	SHE Heilbronn
1435	OHE	1200 54	0-8-0 DH	1963	M	Wittenberge
1000	Rendsburger Krsb	V 11	B DH	1941	MA	Bruchhausen Vilsen
1435	RLE	D 52	0-4-0 DM	1954	MR	Hamm
785	RSE	V 13	B DM	1960	M	Asbach
1435	RStE	V 31	0-6-0 DH	1941	MA	Stadthagen
1435	RVM	29	0-8-0 DH	1958	MA	Wiesbaden
1435	SKB	11	0-6-0 DH	1960	M	Siegen
1435	StMB	V 33	0-6-0 DH	1955	MR	Neuenhaus
1435	StMB	DL 262	0-4-0 DH	1943	MR	SHE Heilbronn
1435	StMB	263	0-4-0 DH	1954	MA	Neuenhaus
750	SWEG	V22.01	B DH	1965	MA	Ochsenhausen
750	SWEG	V 22.02	B DH	1965	MS	Dörzbach
750	SWEG	V 22.03	B DH	1953	MS	Dörzbach
1435	SWEG	V29.01	BB DH	1952	MA	Bruchhausen Vilsen
1435	SWEG	V34.04	0-6-0 DH	1956	MA	Endingen
1000	Sylter Inselbahn	V 14	B DM	1937	MA	Schierwaldenrath
1435	Klb. Vechta–Cloppenburg	V22.03	4w DH	1961	MR	Loburg
1435	VGH	V36 006	0-6-0 DH	1950	MA	Bad Bederkesa
1435	VKSF	34	0-6-0 DH	1956	MR	Aschersleben
1435	VPS	015	0-4-0 DM	1953	MR	Salzgitter
1435	VPS	017	0-4-0 DM	1954	P	Salzgitter

1435	VPS	018	B DM	1954	MA	Passau
1435	VPS	151	C DH	1957	M	Salzgitter
1435	VPS	209	B DM	1965	MR	Salzgitter
1435	VPS	210	B DH	1965	MS	Salzgitter
1435	VPS	701	Co DE	1982	M	Gross Ilsede
1435	VWE	V 2	B DH	1947	MR	Stemmen
1435	VWE	DL 4	0-4-0 DH	1964	MR	Stemmen
1435	WEG	V 62	0-8-0 DH	1956	MA	DME Darmstadt
1435	WEG	V 122	0-8-0 DH	1961	MA	DME Darmstadt
1435	Wittlager Kreisbahn	DL 2	C DH	1958	MS	Preussisch Oldendorf
1435	WLE	VL 0601	B DH	1954	MS	Stadtlohn
1435	WLE	VL 0603	B DH	1946	MR	Minden
1435	WLE	VL 0604	B DH	1948	MA	Münster

5.4 EMUs

Gauge	Railway	No.	Type	Built	Status	Location etc.
1000	BZB	11	Bo ERR	1929	M	München
1000	BZB	13	Bo ERR	1929	P	Garmisch Partenkirchen
1435	KBE	ET 57	Bo22Bo ER	1956	MS	Köln Nippes
1435	KBE	ET 201	Bo-Bo ER	1960	MS	Brühl Vochem
1000	OEG	1	A1-A1 ER	1914	M	Schierwaldenrath
1000	OEG	37	1A-A1 ER	1914	M	Schierwaldenrath
1435	TE	ET 1	Bo ER	1898	M	Trossingen
1435	TE	T 6	Bo ER	1968	P	Schewenningen

5.5 DMUs

Gauge	Railway	No.	Type	Built	Status	Location etc.
1435	AKN	VT2.09	A-1 DMR	1951	MR	Aumühle
1435	AKN	VT3.07	A-A DMR	1962	MA	Kaltenkirchen
1435	AKN	VT3.08	A-A DMR	1961	MA	Kaltenkirchen
1435	AKN	VT3.09	A-A DMR	1967	MA	Kaltenkirchen
1435	AVG	VT 451	1A-A1 DHR	1959	MR	Braunschweig
1435	BHE	T 175	1A-A1 DR	1926	M	Harsefeld
900	Borkumer Kleinbahn	VT 1	A-1 PMR	1940	MA	Borkum
750	Borkumer Kleinbahn	T 2	A-1 PMR	1939	S	Kanzach
1435	BOE	T 101	A-1 DMR	1934	MS	Wunstorf
1435	BOE	VT 162	B-B DMR	1950	MS	Braunschweig
1435	BOE	T 164	1A-A1 DHR	1955	MA	Zeven
1435	BOE	T 170	B-2 DHR	1959	MA	Zeven
1435	BTh	VT 2	A-A DMR	1936	MA	Bochum Dahlhausen
1435	DHE	T 121	A-A DHR	1940	MA	Harpstedt
1435	DHE	T 148	A-A PMR	1936	MA	Haaksbergen, NL
1435	EBOE	VT3.04	B-2 DHR	1959	MS	Elmshorn
1435	EBOE	VT 27	A-1 DHR	1961	MA	Essen
1435	EEB	VT 1	A-1 DMR	1957	MR	Werlte
1435	EVB	VT 175	1A-A1 DMR	1926	MA	Harsefeld
1435	HEG	VT 50	A-1 DMR	1955	M	Hattingen
1435	HEG	VT 52	A-A DMR	1959	MS	Nordlingen
1435	HKB	VT 3	1A-A1 DHR	1955	MS	Beekbergen, NL
1435	HzL	VT 3	1A-A1 DHR	1952	MA	Fützen
1435	HzL	VT 5	A-A DHR	1960	MA	Münsingen
1435	HzL	VT 6	A-A DHR	1962	MS	Mittenwalde
1435	HzL	VT 7	A-A DHR	1962	MS	Mittenwalde
1435	HzL	VT 8	A-A DHR	1961	MA	Münsingen
1435	HzL	VT 9	A-A DHR	1966	MA	Münsingen
1000	Inselbahn Juist	T 1	1A-A1 DMR	1950	MR	Plettenberg
1000	Inselbahn Juist	T 2	1A-A1 DMR	1949	MA	Bruchhausen Vilsen

1000	Inselbahn Langeoog	VT 2	1A-A1 DMR	1950	MA	Schierwaldenrath
1435	KBEF	VT 11	1-A DMR	1955	P	Frechen
1435	Klb. Lüchow – Schmarsau	VT 1	A-A PMR	1941	MA	Darmstadt
1435	Klb. Lüchow – Schmarsau	VT 141	A-A DMR	1933	MR	Loburg
1435	KVG	VT 50	1A-A1 DHR	1954	MS	Worms
1435	Merzig-Buschfelder Eb.	105	A-A DHR	1956	P	Muhlen
1000	MEG	T 7	A-A DMR	1939	MS	Schierwaldenrath
1000	MEG	T 13	A-A DMR	1941	MR	Schierwaldenrath
1435	MKB	T 7	A-1 DMR	1931	MR	Ebermannstadt
1435	MKB	VT 9	A-1 D R	1953	M	Treignes, Belgium
1435	Moerser Kreisbahn	VT 10	2-B DMR	1923	M	Hoorn, Netherlands
1435	Moerser Kreisbahn	T 22	A-1 DHR	1953	MA	Rahden
1435	OHE	DT 502	A-1 DMR	1934	MS	Stemmen
1435	OHE	DT 0504	A-1 DMR	1933	MA	Lüneburg
1435	OHE	VT 508	A-A PMR	1937	MA	Soltau
1435	OHE	VT 509	A-A PMR	1936	MA	Schönberg
1435	OHE	VT 0510	A-1 DMR	1938	MR	Stemmen
1435	OHE	DT 511	1-A DMR	1934	MA	Soltau
1435	OHE	GDT 0514	1A-A1 DHR	1959	MR	Gütersloh
1435	OHE	GDT 0515	1A-A1 DHR	1954	MR	Lüneburg
1435	OHE	GDT 0516	1A-A1 DHR	1959	MR	Gütersloh
1435	OHE	GDT 0518	1A-A1 DHR	1955	MR	Lüneburg
1435	OHE	VT 0521	1A-A1 DMR	1959	M	Braunschweig
1435	OHE	GDT 0522	1A-A1 DHR	1959	MR	Gütersloh
1435	RAG	VT 01	1A-A1 DHR	1938	MR	Dessau
1435	RAG	VT 07	A-1 DMR	1939	M	Bayerisch Eisenstein
1435	RAG	VT 18	A-1 DMR	1937	MR	Darmstadt
1435	RAG	VT 19	A-1 DMR	1937	MA	Ebermannstadt
1435	Schleswiger Kreisbahn	VT 2	A-1 DMR	1925	M	Mariembourg, Belgium
1435	SWEG	VT 3	Bo DHR	1928	MA	Kandern
1435	SWEG	VT 5	A-1 DMR	1932	MA	Darmstadt
1435	SWEG	VT 11	B-2 D R	1958	M	Erlebniswelt, Horb
1435	SWEG	(V) T 21	Bo DR	1930	MR	Endingen
1435	SWEG	VT 24	A-1 D R	1925	MA	Schönberg
1435	SWEG	VT 27	A-A DMR	1966	MA	Bielefeld
1435	SWEG	VT 103	1A-A1 DMR	1952	MA	Orbing
1435	SWEG	VT 114	1A-A1 DMR	1952	MR	Crailsheim
750	SWEG	VT 300	1A-A1 DMR	1941	MS	Dörzbach
750	SWEG	VT 303	1A-A1 DMR	1935	MS	Dörzbach
1000	StMB	VT 41	A-A PMR	1932	MA	Bruchhausen Vilsen
1000	Sylter Inselbahn	LT 4	A-1 DMR	1953	M	Sehnde
1000	Sylter Inselbahn	T 23	B-2 DMR	1925	MS	Bruchhausen Vilsen
1435	VEV		A-1 DMR	1952	P	Boffzen
1435	VEV	VT 2	A-1 DMR	1960	MS	Wunstorf
1435	VGH	T 1	A-1 DMR	1936	MA	Bruchhausen Vilsen
1435	VGH	T 2	Bo DER	1953	MR	Wathlingen
1435	VGH	T 4	B-2 DMR	1926	MR	Ocholt
1435	VLO	T 3	A-1 DMR	1935	MR	Preussisch Oldendorf
1435	VPS	VT 4	A-1 DMR	1957	MR	Salzgitter
1435	VPS	VT40 901			MR	Salzgitter
1435	WEG	VT 06	B DHR	1956	MR	Gerstetten
1435	WEG	VT 09		1963	MR	Cloppenburg
1000	WEG	VT 30	Bo-Bo DER	1956	MA	Brohl
1000	WEG	VT 33	B-2 DMR	1934	MA	Neresheim
1000	WEG	VT 34	1A-B DMR	1937	MS	Amstetten
1435	WEG	VT 36		1956	M	Erlebniswelt, Horb
1000	WEG	VT 37	B-B DHR	1960	MR	Neresheim
1435	WEG	VT 401	1A-A1 DMR	1928	MR	Halle
1435	WEG	VT 402	1A-A1DMR	1951	MS	Neuoffingen
1435	WEG	VT 410	B-B DHR	1981	MA	Münsingen
1435	WEG	VT 411	B-B DHR	1981	MA	Münsingen
1435	WZTE	VT 145	A-A DMR	1937	MS	Preussich Oldendorf

APPENDIX I. ABBREVIATIONS

Page numbers denote where further details of the company concerned can be found in this book.

Page No.

Abbr.	Page No.	Name
A		Austria
AAE		Ahaus Alstätter Eisenbahn GmbH
ABEG	20	Anhaltinisch-Brandenburgische Eisenbahngesellschaft mbH
ABG		Anhaltische Bahngesellschaft
ABRM	17	Abellio Rail Mitteldeutschland GmbH
ABRN	17	Abellio Rail NRW GmbH
ABRRS	68	Road & Rail Service
ADAM		Sylvia & Uwe Adam Transport
AEE		Ahaus-Enscheder Eisenbahn
AGIE	18	Agilis Eisenbahngesellschaft mbH & Co. KG.
AGIL	18	Agilis Verkersgesellschaft mbH & Co. KG.
AGV	88	Anlagen und Grundstucksvermietungsgesellschaft mbH & Co. KG.
AHG	19	AHG Industry GmbH & Co KG
AK	87	Akiem (leasing arm of French Railways).
AKN	19	AKN Eisenbahn AG
ALEX		Allgau-Express
ALS	88	Alstom Lokomotiven Service GmbH
AML		Adam & MaLoWa Lokvermietung GmbH
AMP		AMP Bahnlogistik
AMR	88	Altmark-Rail GmbH
ARCO	20	Arco Transportation GmbH
ARL		AR Logistic Consulting GmbH
AS	88	Ascendos Rail Leasing
ASLVG	21	A.V.G. Ascherlebener Verkehrsgesellschaft mbH
AT	87	Alpha Trains
ATBL		Automatische Trein Beinvloeding. (Train protection system)
ATL	20	Ammendorfer Transport und Logistik GmbH
AULOC	20	Augsburger Localbahn GmbH
AVG	19	Albtal-Verkehrs-Gesellschaft mbH
AVOLL		Aggerbahn Andreas Voll
AW		Ausbesserungswerk
AWT		Advanced World Transport
B		Belgium
B-B		Belgian Railways
BASF	21	BASF AG – factories in Ludwigshafen & Antwerpen
BBL	23	BBL Logistik GmbH
BCB	22	Bayerische CargoBahn GmbH
BE		Belgium
BE	24	Betheimer Eisenbahn
BEBRA	45	Holzlogisik & Güterbahn GmbH (HLG)
BEF		Berliner Eisenbahn Freunde
BEG	27	Brohltal-Schmalspureisenbahn Betriebs-GmbH
BEM		Bayerisches Eisenbahnmuseum
BEV	26	Rudolf Bräunert – Bräunert Eisenbahnverkehr GmbH & Co KG
BGW		Bahn Gesellschaft Waldhof AG
BHE		Bremische Hafeneisenbahn
BHE		Buxtehude-Harsefelder Eisenbahn
BHL	23	BEHALA-Berliner Hafen- und Lagerhausgesellschaft mbH
BK	26	Borkumer Kleinbahn und Dampfschiffart GmbH
BKK		Braun Kohle Kombinat
BLB	24	Berchtesgadener Land Bahn GmbH
BLE		Butzbach-Licher Eisenbahn
BLG		BLG AutoRail GmbH
BLGRT	24	BLG RailTec GmbH
BLP	25	BLP Wiebe Logistik GmbH
BLSC		BLS Cargo
BLV		Bayerische Localbahnverein e.V.
BLW		Blöss Lokdienste

BOBFN	25	Bodensee-Oberschwaben-Bahn
BOBY	22	Bayerische Oberlandbahn GmbH
BOE		Bremervörde-Osterholzer Eisenbahn
BOEG	25	Bocholter Eisenbahngesellschaft mbH
BOXX	26	BoxXpress.de GmbH
BPRM	21	Baltic Port Rail Mukran GmbH
BRB	22	Bayerische Regiobahn GmbH
BRL	88	Beacon Rail Leasing Limited
BSB	27	Breisgau S-Bahn GmbH
BSBS		BSBS Braunschweiger Bahn Service GmbH
BSM	21	Bahnen der Stadt Monheim GmbH
BSW		Bundesbahn Sozialwerk
BTE		Bremen-Thedinghausener Eisenbahn GmbH
BTEX	21	Bahn Touristik Express GmbH
BTh		Bremen-Thedinghauser Eisenbahn
BTK		Bombardier Transportation Kassel
BUG	27	BUG Verkehrsbau AG
BUK		Bossdorf & Kerstan GmbH
BUNA		Buna Werke, Schkopau
BUVL	88	B und V Leipzig GmbH
BVM		BSM GmbH
Bw		Bahnbetriebswerke
BWESA	79	Uwe Adam EVU GmbH
BX	88	BeNEX GmbH
BYB	23	BayernBahn Betriebsgesellschaft mbH
BZB	22	Bayerische Zugspitzbahn Bergbahn AG
CAN	28	Cantus Verkersgesellschaft mbH
CB	31	City Bahn Chemnitz GmbH
CBB	30	Centralbahn AG
CBR		ÇB Rail GmbH
CD		Çeske Dráhy a.s.
CFI		Compagnia Ferroviaria Italiana SrL
CFL		Soc. Nat. des Chemins de Fer Luxembourgeois
CFLDE	30	CFL Cargo Deutschland GmbH
CFR		Compania Nationala de Cai Ferate Romania
CH		Switzerland
CL		Cargo Link, Norway
CLBG		Chiemgauer Lokalbahn
CLG	30	Chemion Logistik GmbH - Bahnbetriebe
CLR	28	Cargo Logistik Rail Service GmbH
CN		Cargo Net, Norway
CR	28	Cargo Rail GmbH
CSV		CargoServ GmbH (Austria)
CTD	28	Captrain Deutschland GmbH
CTL	31	CTL Logistics GmbH
CTV		Cargo Trans Vagon S.A. Romania
CZ		Czech Republic
D		Deutschland
DB		Deutsche Bahn
DBF		DB Fernverkehr
DBFW		DB Fahrwegdienste GmbH, Berlin
DBGM	33	Döllnitzbahn GmbH
DBK		Dampf Bahn Kochertal
DBM		DB Museum
DBR		DB Regio
DBS		DB Schenker
DDR		Deutsche Demoktratische Republik
DE	33	Dortmunder Eisenbahn GmbH
DEBG		Dampfzug-Betriebs-Gemeinschaft e.V
DEG		Deutsche Eisenbahn-Gesellschaft
DELTA	32	DeltaRail GmbH
DEV		Deutsche Eisenbahn Verein e.V.
DEW		Dampfeisenbahn Weserbergland e.V.
DFS		Dampfbahn Fränkische Schweiz e. V.

DGEG		DGEG Bahnen & Reisen Bochum AG
DGT		Deutsche Gleis- und Tiefbau
DH		Dillinger Hütte
DHE	32	Delmenhorst-Harpstedter Eisenbahn GmbH
DIEBM		Die Bahnmeisterei
DK		Denmark
DKB		Dürener Kreisbahn
DL	89	Deutsche Leasing
DLC		Dillen & Le Jeune Cargo NV, Belgium. (→ Crossrail).
DLFB		Dampflokfreunde Berlin
DLI	32	Die-Lei GmbH
DLW	31	Dampflokwerk Meiningen
DME		Deutsche -Museums-Eisenbahn GmbH (Also used for Gleiskraft)
DNV		DNV-Verlag/DNV Touristik GmbH
DP	32	DP Deutsche Privatbahn GmbH
DPR	33	Duisport Rail GmbH
DR		Deutsche Reichsbahn
DRE		Deutsche Regional-Eisenbahn
DREWAG		Dresden Wasser
DRG		Deutsche Reichsbahn-Gesellschaft
DSB		Danske Statsbaner
DUD	31	D & D Eisenbahngesellschaft GmbH
DVE		Dessauer Verkehrs- und Eisenbahngesellschaft mbH
DWK		DWK GmbH
DWU		Deponie Wirtschaft Umweltschutztechnik GmbH
EAH		Eisenbahn Anlagen Handel GmbH
EBA		Eisenbahn-Bundesamt
EBEFW		Eisenbahnfreunde Wetterau e.V
EBG		Eisenbahn-Betriebsgesellschaft
EBM	37	Eisenbahnbetriebsgesellschaft Mittelrhein mbH - EBM Cargo GmbH
EBN		Eisenbahnbedarf Bad Nauheim
EBO		Eisenbahnbedarf Bad Orb
EBOE		Elmshorn–Barmstedt–Oldesloer Eisenbahn
EBS	39	Erfurter Bahnservice GmbH
EBT		Emons Bahntransporte GmbH
EBW		Eisenbahnbewachungs-GmbH
ECCO		ECCO Rail GmbH
ECR		Euro Cargo Rail
EEB	38	Emsländische Eisenbahn GmbH
EFBS		Eisenbahnfreunde Betzdorf e.V.
EFRN		Freunde der 212 001-2 e.V
EFSFT		Eisenbahnfreunden Strassfurt
EFSK		Eisenbahnfreunde Schwalm–Knüll e.V.
EFW	34	EfW-Verkehrsgesellschaft mbH
EFZ		Eisenbahnfreunde Zollernbahn
EGB	39	Erfurter Gleisbau GmbH
EGOO	38	Eisenbahngesellschaft Ostfriesland-Oldenburg mbH
EGP	35	Eisenbahn-Gesellschaft Potsdam mbH
EH	36	ThyssenKrupp Steel Europe AG (ex Eisenbahn & Hafen)
EHB/HABA	34	EHB Eisenbahn und Hafenbetriebsgesellschaft GmbH Region Osnabrück mbH
EHG	36	EH Güterverkehr GmbH
EIB	38	Erfurter Bahn GmbH
EIU		Eisenbahn Infrastrukture Unternehmen
EIVEL	34	Eichholz Eivel GmbH
EJS		Eisenbahnsiftung Joachim Schmidt
EKO	20	ArcelorMittal Eisenhüttenstadt Transport GmbH
EKML		Eisenbahn Köln–Mülheim–Leverkusen
ELBA	38	ELBA Logistik GmbH
ELG	35	Eisenbahn Logistik Gesellschaft – ELG GmbH
ELL	35	Eisenbahn Logistik Leipzig GmbH
ELOC	89	ELL Germany GmbH – European Locomotive Leasing
ELS	35	ELS Eisenbahn Logistik und Service GmbH
ELV	36	Eisenbahn Logistik Vienenburg (Willrich & Mühlberg GbR)

EMBB		Eisenbahnmuseum Bayerischer Bahnhof zu Leipzig
EMN	37	Eisenbahnbetriebe Mittlerer Neckar GmbH
ENERCON		Enercon GmbH
ENON		ENON GmbH & Co. K.G.
EPF		Europorte France
ERB	50	Keolis Deutschland GmbH & Co KG – Eurobahn
Erixx	39	erixx GmbH
ERS		ERS Railways
ESG		Eisenbahn- und Sonderwagen-Betriebsgesellschaft mbH
ESGBI	36	Eisenbahn-Service-Gesellschaft mbH
ETCS		European Train Control System
ETF		Eurovia Traveau Ferroviaires. (France)
ETG		Eisenbahn-Technik Gesellschaft
EUROPOOL	39	Europool – Max Knape Gleisbau GmbH
EVB	34	Eisenbahnen und Verkehrsbetriebe Elbe-Weser GmbH
EVG		Eifelbahn Verkehrsgesellschaft
EVU		Eisenbahn Verkehrs Unternehmen
EVULW	52	Leonhard Weiss GmbH & Co KG
EWR		East West Railways
EXRA		Express Rail
F		France
FAHMA	89	Fahrzeugmanagement Region Frankfurt Rheinmain GmbH
FBBW	89	Fahrzeugbereitstellung Baden-Württemberg GmbH
FBE		Ferropolis Bergbau und Erlebnisbahn.
FEG	40	Freiberger Eisenbahngesellschaft mbH
FEVE		Ferrocarriles de Vía Estrecha
FFS		Funk Fern Steurung
FHS		Fahr Hafen Sassnitz
FKE		Frankfurt–Königstein Eisenbahn
FL		Freightliner
FLOYD		FLOYD ZRt. (Hungary)
FME	40	Fränkische Museums-Eisenbahn e.V
FO		Fortis
FPL		Freightliner Poland
FS		Ferrovie dello Stato Italiane
FSTIC		FS Trenitalia Cargo
FVD	89	Fahrzeug Vermietung Duisburg GmbH
FVE	40	Farge-Vegesacker Eisenbahn GmbH
FWN	39	Fahrzeugewerk Niedersachswerfen GmbH
GBRf		GB Railfreight
GC		Green Cargo
GDT		Grossraum Diesel Triebwagen
GES		Gesellschaft zur Erhaltung von Schienenfahrzeugen Stuttgart e.V.
GET	40	GET Georgsmarienhütte Eisenbahn und Transport GmbH
GfE		GfE Gesellschaft für Eisenbahnbetrieb mbH
GHE		Gernrode–Harzgerode Eisenbahn
GKL		G.K. Lokservice GbR, Duisburg
GVG	40	GVG Verkehrsorganisation GmbH
GWTR		GW Train Regio, Czech Republic
GySEV		Györ-Sopron-Ebenfurti Vasut Részvénytarsasag (Hungary)
H		Hungary
HABA		Hafenbahn Osnabrück GmbH
HAEG	90	Oak Capital – Hamburger Eisenbahn eK
HAFAG		Hafen AG – Duisburg Ruhrorter Häfen AG
HAKON		Binnenhafen Königs Wusterhausen
HANS	43	Hanseatische Eisenbahn GmbH
HB	44	HellertalBahn GmbH
HC		Hessencourier e.V
HCM		Hans Christian Müller
HDS		Historischer Dampfschnellzug
HE		Historische Eisenbahn
HEB	45	HLB Hessenbahn GmbH
HECTOR		Hector Rail AB (Sweden)
HEF		Historiche Eisenbahn Frankfurt e.V.

HEIN	44	Heinrichsmeyer Eisenbahndienstleitungen UG
HEX	80	Veolia Verkehr Sachsen-Anhalt GmbH
HFH	42	Hafen Halle GmbH
HFM		Hafen Magdeburg
HGB	44	Hessische Güterbahn GmbH
HGK	42	Häfen und Güterverkehr Köln AG
HHA		Hamburger Hochbahn AG
HHPI	44	Heavy Haul Power International GmbH
HKB		Museumseisenbahn Hümmlinger Kreisbahn e.V.
HKM		Hüttenwerke Krupp Mannesmann
HKW		Heiz Kraft Werk
HKX	42	Hamburg–Köln Express
HLB	45	Hessische Landesbahn - HLB Basis AG
HLG		Holz Logistik & Güterbahn
HML	89	Hannover Mobilen Leasing GmbH
HSA		High Speed Alliance
HSB	43	Harzer Schmalspurbahnen
HSL	46	HSL Logistik GmbH
HTB	46	Hörseltalbahn GmbH
HTRSD		Husa Transportation Railway Services – HTRS Süd GmbH
HTRSN		HTRSN Nederland bv
HTS		HTS Kassel
HUPAC		Hupac SA
HÜSA		HÜSA Bahntechnik GmbH
HVLE	43	Havelländische Eisenbahn AG
HWB	46	HWB Verkehrsgesellschaft mbH
HzL	46	Hohenzollerische Landesbahn AG
I		Italy
IFA		IFA Automobilwerke Ludwigsfelde
IG		Interessengesellschaft
IGB		Industriebahn-Gesellschaft Berlin
IGDA		IG Bw Dresden-Altstadt e.V.
IGE		IGE Internationale Gesellschaft für Eisenbahnverkehr GmbH & Co. KG
IGEBA		IGeBa- Ingeniergesellschaft Bahn MbH
IGENO		IGENO Schienfahrzeug Nordhausen
IGEW		IGE "Werrabahn Eisenach" e.V
IGT		Inbetriebnahmegesellschaft Transporttechnik mbH
IL	47	Inselbahn Langeoog
ILM	47	Ilmebahn AG
INNR		Innrail Eisenbahndienstleistugen UG
INRAIL		In Rail (Italy)
INTEG	49	IntEgro Verkehr GmbH
ISC		Interporto Servizio Cargo S.p.A.
ISL		Infraserv Logistics Frankfurt/M
IT		Italy
ITB	47	Industrietransportgesellschaft Brandenburg mbH
ITL	49	ITL Eisenbahngesellschaft mbH – ITL Cargo GmbH
ITLB		ITL Benelux
ITLPL		ITL Poland
JW		Johann Walthelm GmbH
KAE		Kreis Altenaer Eisenbahn
KBB		Deutsche Gesellschaft für Eisenbahngeschichte e.V
KBC	89	KBC Lease BV Leuven (Belgium)
KBE		Köln-Bonner Eisenbahn
KBEF		Köln-Bonner Eisenbahnfreunde e.V.
KCL		KUBE CON Logistics GmbH
KCR		KUBE CON Rail GmbH
KEG		Karsdorfer Eisenbahngesellschaft mbH
KFBE		Köln–Frechen–Benzelrather Eisenbahn
KIEL	72	Seehafen Kiel GmbH & Co KG
KME		Kursbuch der Deutschen Museums-Eisenbahnen
KML	51	Kreisbahn Mansfelder Land GmbH
KNAUF		Knauf Deutsche Gipswerke. KG
KNE		Kassel-Naumburger Eisenbahn AG

KSR		Köstner-Schienenbusreisen
KSW	51	Kreisbahn Siegen–Wittgenstein GmbH
KTG		Kali Transport
KV		Kombi Verkehr
KVG	49	Kahlgrund-Verkehrs-Gesellschaft mbH
L		Luxembourg
LAG		Lokalbahn AG
Laubag		Lausitzer Braunkohle AG
LCH		Logistik Center Hungaria GmbH
LDC		Lausitzer Dampflok Club e.V
LDS	52	LDS GmbH – Logistik Dienstleistung und Service
LEG	52	Leipziger Eisenbahnverkehrsgesellschaft mbH
LEUNA	47	Infra Leuna GmbH
LM	53	Lokomotion Gesellschaft für Schienentraktion mbH
LNVG	89	Landesnahverkersgesellschaft Niedersachsen mbH
LOCON	52	LOCON Logistik & Consulting AG
LOGS		Logistik Service GmbH
Lokoop		Defunct Swiss Leasing Company
LOKOTRAIN		LokoTrain s.r.o.
LOTOS		LOTOS Kolej Sp. z o.o.
LPG		Locomotive Pool GmbH
LSB		Lausitzer Bahn
LSG		Lokomotiv Service Gesellschaft
LTE		LTE Logistik und Transport GmbH
LTH		LTH Transportlogistik GmbH
LUTRA		LUTRA GmbH – Mittelbrandenburgische Hafengesellschaft
LUW	51	Laeger & Wöstenhöfer GmbH & Co KG
LWB	51	Lappwaldbahn GmbH
LZB		Linienzugbeeinflussung (cab signalling system)
MBB		Mecklenburgische Bäderbahn Molli GmbH & Co
MBBKB		Buckower Kleinbahn-Eisenbahnverein Märkische Schweiz e.V
MBS		Montafonerbahn Bludenz–Schruns
ME	54	metronom Eisenbahngesellschaft mbH
MEG	54	Mitteldeutsche Eisenbahn Gesellschaft
MEM		Museums Eisenbahn Minden
MER	89	Macquarie European Rail
MGB		Matterhorn Gotthard Bahn
MGW		mgw Service GmbH & Co. KG
MHG		Magdeburger hafenbahn gesellschaft
MKB	54	Mindener Kreisbahnen GmbH
MOLLI	53	Mecklenburgische Bäderbahn Molli GmbH & Co
MR		short version of MRCE
MRB		Mitteldeutsche Regio Bahn
MRCE	90	MRCE Dispolok GmbH – Mitsui Rail Capital Europe
MTEG	55	Muldental-Eisenbahnverkehrsgesellschaft mbH
MTG		Mansfeld Transport GmbH, Lutherstadt Eilsleben
MTR		Metrans Rail
MTRD	53	Metrans Rail Deutchland GmbH
MVG	55	Mülheimer Verkersgesellschaft mbH
MWB	55	Mittelweserbahn GmbH
N		Norway
NBE	59	Nordbahn Eisenbahngesellschaft mbH
NBEG	57	NBE Group GmbH & Co KG - Nordbayerische Eisenbahn GmbH
NBJ		Nora Bergslags Järnvägar (Sweden)
NC		Nord Cargo
NE	58	Neuss-Düsseldorfer Häfen Gmbh & Co KG – Neusser Eisenbahn
NEB		Niederbarnimer Eisenbahn
NEBB	57	NEB Betriebsgesellschaft mbH
NEG	58	Norddeutsche Eisenbahngesellschaft Niebüll GmbH
NESA	58	NeSA Eisenbahn-Betriebsgesellschaft Neckar–Schwarzwald–Alb mbH
NETINERA		Subsidiary of Train Italia and previously Arriva Deutschland.
NEWAG		Newag GmbH & Co. K.G. Oberhausen
NFG		NFG Bahnservice GmbH
NIAG	59	Niederrheinische Verkehrsbetriebe AG

NL		Netherlands
NME	58	Neukölln-Mittenwalder Eisenbahn-Gesellschaft
NOB	59	Nord-Ostsee-Bahn GmbH
NRAIL	90	Northrail GmbH
NRS	59	Nordic Rail Service GmbH
NS		Nederlandse Spoorwegen
NSB		Norges Statsbaner BA
NSW		Natursteinwerke Weiland
NTS	90	Northrail Technical Service GmbH & Co KG
NVA		National Volks Armee
NVAG		Nordfriesische Verkehrsbetriebe A.G.
NWB	60	NordWestBahn Gmbh
NWE		Nordhausen Wernigerode Eisenbahn
NXG	56	National Express Rail GmbH
ÖBB		Österreichische Bundesbahnen
OBEV		Osning Bahn e.V.
OCG		Oceanogate Italia s.p.a.
ODEG	61	Ostdeutsche Eisenbahn GmbH
OEG		Oberrheinische Eisenbahngesellschaft AG
OHE	61	Osthannoversche Eisenbahnen AG
OHEGO	61	OHE Cargo GmbH
OHJ		Odsherreds Jernbane (Denmark)
OHLE		Overhead Line Equipment
OLA		Ostseeland Verkehr GmbH
ORLEN		ORLEN KolTrans Sp. z o.o. (Poland)
ORME		On Rail Gesellschaft für Eisenbahnausrüstung und Zubehör mbH
OSB	60	Ortenau S-Bahn
OSE		Organismos Sidirodromun Ellados (Greek Railways)
OSEF		Ostsächsische Eisenbahnfreunde e.V
OST		Lok-Ost, Olaf Still, Stassfurt
PB		Porterbrook
PBE		Pfalzbahn Eisenbahnbetriebsgesellschaft mbH
PBSV		Planung & Bau von Sicherungs und Verkehrsanlagen (→KUBE)
PCK		PCK Raffinerie, Stendell
PCT	63	PCT Private Car Train GmbH
PCW	63	Prüf- und Validationcenter Wegberg-Wildenrath der Siemens AG Rail Systems
PEF		Passauer Eisenbahnfreunde
PEG	63	Prignitzer Eisenbahn GmbH
PKP		Polskie Koleje Panstwowe
PL		Poland
POWER	63	Power Rail GmbH
PRESS	37	Eisenbahn-Bau- und Betriebsgesellschaft Pressnitztalbahn mbH
PREU	63	PBG Preussen Bahn GmbH
Prolok		Prolok GmbH, Straupitz. (now insolvent)
R4C		Ruhr Oel GmbH
RADVE	64	RailAdventure GmbH
RAG		Ruhrkohle A.G.
RAILS		Rail & Service
RAILU		Rail 4U-Eisenbahndienstleistungen
RAN		Railservice Alexander Neubauer
RAR		Rent-A-Rail Eisenbahn Service
RAW		Reichsbahn Ausbesserungs Werk
RBB	65	Regiobahn Bitterfeld Berlin GmbH
RBG	65	Regental Bahnbetriebs-GmbH
RBH	65	RBH Logistics GmbH
RBK	66	Regionalbahn Kassel GmbH
RBSA		RBS Reuschling Bahn und Service GmbH
RBW		Rhein Braun Werke
RC		Rail Centre
RCN		RCN Rail Center Nürnberg GmbH & Co Kg
RCO		Railco (Czech Republic)
RCT		Royal Corps of Transport
RDX	64	Raildox GmbH & Co KG

RE	67	Rheinische Eisenbahn GmbH
Redler		Redler Service (=RAILS)
REGIO	66	Regiobahn Fahrbetriebsgesellschaft mbH
RF	64	Railflex GmbH
RHC	67	RheinCargo GmbH & Co KG
RHEB		Rheinhessische Eisenbahn
RHG	64	Raphael Hofmann Güterverkehr
RHKE	42	Hafen Krefeld GmbH & Co KG
RIS	66	Regio Infra Service Sachsen GmbH
RJ		Regio Jet
RLE		Ruhr-Lippe Eisenbahn
RLG	67	Regionalverkehr Ruhr-Lippe GmbH
RME	68	Röbel/Müritz Eisenbahn GmbH
RNE		RNE Rhein-Neckar-Eisenbahserviceges ellschaft mbH
RO		Romania
RPE		RP Eisenbahn
RPOOL	90	Railpool GmbH
RPRS	64	Railsystems RP GmbH
RR		Rush Rail
RRF		Rotterdam Rail Feeding
RRI	68	Rhenus Rail St. Ingbert GmbH
RSBG	67	Rennsteigbahn GmbH & Co KG
RSE	69	Rhein-Sieg-Eisenbahn GmbH
RST	69	RST Rangier Service und Transportgesellschaft mbH
RStE		Rinteln-Stadthagener Eisenbahn-Gesellschaft
RSVG	67	Rhein-Sieg Verkehrsgesellschaft mbH
RTB	70	Rurtalbahn GmbH
RTBC	70	Rurtalbahn Cargo GmbH
RTC		Rail Traction Company (Italy)
RTLOG		Rail Time Logistics GmbH
RTS	69	RTS Rail Transport Service Germany GmbH
RTX		Railtraxx BVBA (BE)
RTUL		Rail Technology & Logistics GmbH
RUHRO		Ruhr Oel GmbH
RüBB	69	Rügensche Bäderbahn GmbH & Co. (Rasender Roland)
RVM	66	Regionalverkehr Münsterland GmbH
RWE		RWE Umwelt Westsachsen GmbH
S		Sweden
SAB		Schwäbische Alb -Bahn e.V
SBB	72	Schweizerische Bundesbahnen - SBB GmbH
SBBC	72	SBB Cargo Deutschland GmbH
SBBCI		SBB Cargo International
SBE	71	Sächsisch-Böhmische-Eisenbahngesellschaft mbH
SBS	70	Saarbahn GmbH
SBW	74	Starkenberger Baustoffwerke GmbH (formerly Wismut)
SDG	71	SDG Sächsische Dampfeisenbahngesellschaft mbH
SDN		Schwaben Dampf Neuoffingen
SEH		Süddeutsche Eisenbahn Museum, Heilbronn
SEM		Sächsisches Eisenbahnmuseum Chemnitz-Hilbersdorf e.V
SERSA		Sersa Group Management AG
SES	72	SES Logistik GmbH
SETG		Salzburger Eisenbahn Transportlogistik GmbH (Austria)
SGL	73	SGL Schienen Güter Logistik GmbH
SHH		Städtischen Häfen Hannover
SHTR		Shunter Tractie B.V. (Netherlands)
SJ		Statens Järnvägar (Swedish Railways)
SK		Slovakia
SK		Seehafen Kiel
SKB		Siegener Kreisbahn
SKJB		Skandinaviska Jernbanor AB
SKLUS	73	SKL Umschlagservice Magdeburg GmbH & Co KG
SKW		SKW Stickstoffwerke Piesteritz GmbH
SL	91	SüdLeasing GmbH
SLB		Salzburger Lokalbahn

SLG	73	SLG Spitzke Logistik GmbH
SNCF		Société Nationale des Chemins de Fer Français
SOEG	72	Sächsisch-Oberlausitzer Eisenbahngesellschaft mbH
SONRA	73	Sonata Rail GmbH
SPENO		Speno International S.A.
SRI	90	SRI Rail Invest GmbH
SRG	70	Saar Rail GmbH
STAV		STAV GmbH
STB	74	Süd-Thüringen Bahn GmbH
STBAT		Steiermarkbahn Transport & Logistik GmbH
STGBS		Stuttgarter Bahnservice Ltd.
STLB		Steiermärkische Landesbahnen
StMB		Steinhider Meer Bahn
STOCK	74	Stock-Transport
STRA		Strabag AG (Austria)
STS	73	Städtebahn Sachsen GmbH
STVG	74	Stauden-Verkehrs-GmbH
STWB		Steigerwaldbahn
SVG		Schienenverkehrsgesellschaft mbH
SWA		Stadtwerke Andernach GmbH
SWEG	76	Südwestdeutsche Verkehrs AG
SWK		SWK Mobil GmbH (Stadtwerke Krefeld)
SWO		Stadtwerke Osnabrück
SWT	74	Stahlwerke Thüringen GmbH
SZD		Sovetskaya Zwiznaja Doroga (Soviet Railways)
TAG		Tegernsee-Bahn
TBG	77	Tegernsee-Bahn Betriebsgesellschaft mbH
TDR	77	Trans Regio Deutsche Regionalbahn GmbH
TE	78	Trossingen Eisenbahn GmbH
TEL		Touristik-Eisenbahn Lüneburger Heide GmbH
TEV		Thüringer Eisenbahnverein Weimar e.V.
TLG		Transport und Logistik GmbH
TME	77	TME-Torsten Meincke Eisenbahn GmbH
TPF		Transports Publics Fribourgeois
TRG	74	TRIANGULA Logistik GmbH
TSD		Transport-Schienen-Dienst GmbH
TSE		Thomas Speich Eisenbahndienstleistungen
TSSC		TSS Cargo (CZ)
TWE	78	TWE Bahnbetriebs GmbH – Teutoburger Wald Eisenbahn GmbH
TXL	78	TX Logistik AG
UBB		Usedomer Bäder-Bahn
UEF		Ulmer Eisenbahnfreunde
UEG	79	Usedomer Eisenbahn GbR
Unirail		Unirail Schienfahrzeuge GmbH (dealer)
US		United States of America
VBG	83	Vogtlandbahn-GmbH
VBV		Verein Braunschweiger Verkehrsfreunde e.V
VCT	79	Vectus Verkehrsgesellschaft mbH
VE	79	Vattenfall Europe Mining AG
VE		Vossloh Espana
VEB		Vulkan Eifel bahn
VEF		VEF Kleinbahn Verden-Walsrode e.V.
VEN	68	Rhenus Veniro GmbH & Co KG
VEOLIA	80	Veolia Verkehr GmbH - Veolia Verkehr Regio GmbH
VESK	82	Vetter Busunternehmen GmbH
VEV	83	Vorwohle–Emmerthaler Verkehrsbetriebe GmbH
VFLI		Voies Ferrées Locales et Industrielles (France)
VGH	81	Verkehrsbetriebe Grafschaft Hoya GmbH
VGN		Verkehrs Gesellschaft Norderstedt
VHN		Verein Hafenbahn Neustrelitz
VHT		Verkehrsverband Hochtaunus
VIAS	82	VIAS GmbH
VKM		Vehicle Keeper Marking
VKP		Verkehrsbetriebe Kreis Plön GmbH

VKSF		Verkehrsbetriebe des Kreises Schleswig-Flensburg
VL	91	Vossloh Locomotives GmbH
Vlexx	83	Vlexx GmbH
VLO	81	Verkehrsgesellschaft Landkreis Osnabrück GmbH
VMS	81	Verkehrsverbund Mittelsachsen GmbH
VPS	81	Verkehrsbetriebe Peine–Salzgitter GmbH
VR		Volker Rail
VSE		Verein Sächsischer Eisenbahnfreunde e.V
VSFT		Vossloh Schienenfahrzeug-Technik GmbH
VTLT	91	Voith Turbo Lokomotivtechnik GmbH & Co KG
VVM		Verein Verkehsamateure und Museumsbahn e.V
VVRO	80	Veolia Verkehr Regio Ost GmbH
VW		Volkswagen Werk
VWE	81	Verden–Walsroder Eisenbahn GmbH
WAB		Westfälische Almetalbahn
WB		Wiehltalbahn GmbH
WE	84	Werra-Eisenbahnverkersgesellschaft mbH
WEBA	84	Westerwaldbahn der Kreises Altenkirchen GmbH
WEG	85	Württembergische Eisenbahn-Gesellschaft mbH
WEMEG		Westmecklenburgische Eisenbahngesellschaft mbH
WENDEL	84	Wendelsteinbahn GmbH
WFB	85	WestfalenBahn GmbH
WFL	84	Wedler Franz Logistik GmbH & Co KG
WHE	83	Wanne-Herner Eisenbahn und Hafen GmbH
WHF		Wald-Holz-Forst Gbr
WINR		Wincanton Rail GmbH
WL		Werklok
WLB		Wiener Lokalbahnen AG
WLC		Wiener Lokalbahnen Cargo GmbH
WLE	85	Westfälische Landes-Eisenbahn GmbH
WLH		Westfälische Lokomotiv Fabrik Karl Reuschling GmbH & Co KG
WLS		Waltheim Logistik & Service GmbH
WNB		Würtembergische Nebenbahnen
WSET	85	Westsächsische Eisenbahntransport Gesellschaft mbH
WTB		Stadt Blumberg-Wutachtalbahn
WZTE		Wilstedt–Zeven–Tostedter Eisenbahn
XR		Xaver Riebel Gleisbau GmbH
XRAIL		Crossrail
(Z)		Stored
ZBAU	86	Zürcher Bau GmbH
ZF		Zukker Fabriek
ZGB		Zweckverband Grossraum Braunschweig
ZVON		Zweckverband Verkehrsverbund Oberlausitz-Niederschlesien

APPENDIX II. BUILDERS

ADtranz	ABB Daimler Benz Transportation, Kasse, later Bombardier Transportation
AEG	Allgemeine Elektrizitäts Gesellschaft, Hennigsdorf (bei Berlin), Germany
Alstom	Générale de Constructions Electriques et Mechaniques Alstom, Belfort, France, later Alstom Transportation; now has a plant in Germany at Salzgitter.
BBC	Brown Boveri et Cie, Baden, Switzerland and Mannheim, Germany
BMAG	Berliner Maschinenbau AG, vorm. L. Schwartzkopff, Berlin-Wildau, Germany
BT	Bombardier Transportation, Hennigsdorf for railcars, Kassel for locomotives.
Btz	Waggonbau Bautzen GmbH and later companies
CKD	Ceskomoravska Kolbeen Danek A.S., Praha, Czechoslovakia (now Czech Republic)
Dessau	Dessauer Waggonfabrik AG, Dessau, Germany
Deutz	Motoren Fabrik Deutz AG, Köln, Germany; see also KHD
Duewag	Düsseldorfer Waggonfabrik AG, Düsseldorf, Germany
DWA	Deutsche Waggonbau AG, works at Bautzen, Berlin, Görlitz, Halle-Ammendorf, later Bombardier Transportation
DWK	Deutsche Werke, Kiel AG, Kiel-Friedrichsort, Germany.

EMD	General Motors/EMD, London, Ontario, Canada
Essl	Maschinenfabrik Esslingen, Esslingen am Neckar, Germany
Fuchs	H. Fuchs Waggonfabrik AG, Heidelberg-Kirchheim, Germany
Gmdr	Gmeinder & Co GmbH, Lokomotiven u Maschinenfabrik, Mosbach, Germany
Görl	Waggon und Maschinenbau AG, Görlitz
Gotha	Gothaer Waggonfabrik AG, Gotha, Germany.
Halberstadt	Former DR carriage works in Halberstadt, Germany
Hartmann	Sachsiches Maschinenfabrik vormals Richard Hartmann AG, Chemnitz, Germany
Hens	Henschel & Sohn GmbH, Kassel, Germany.
JW	Jenbacher Werke AG, Jenbach in Tirol, Austria
Jung	Arn. Jung Lokomotivfabrik GmbH, Jungenthal bei Kirchberg an der Sieg, Germany
Karlsruhe	Maschinenfabrik Karlsruhe AG
KHD	Motoren Fabrik Deutz AG, Köln (until 1930); Humboldt Deutz Motoren AG Köln (1930-1938); Klockner Humboldt Deutz, AG, Köln,(Deutz und Kalk), Germany (1938-)
KM	Krauss Maffei AG, München- Allach, Germany, later Siemens
KrMu	Lokomotivfabrik Krauss Krauss & Co, München, Germany
Krp	Friedrich Krupp Maschinenfabrik, Essen, Germany.
LEW	VEB Lokomotivbau Elektrotechnische Werke "Hans Beimler" Berlin-Hennigsdorf
LHB	Linke Hofmann Busch, Breslau, Germany (1928-1930); Linke Hofmann Busch, Salzgitter-Watenstadt, Germany (1949-), later Alstom
LKM	VEB Lokomotivbau und Bahnbedarf, Potsdam-Babelsberg, East Germany
Lugansk	Vorshilovgradskij Teplovozstroiteniy Zavod, Lugansk, USSR (Now Ukraine)
MaK	Maschinenbau Kiel GmbH, Kiel-Friedrichsort, Germany, later SFT, then VSFT
MAN	Maschinefabrik Augsburg - Nürnberg
MBB	Messerschmidt Bölkow Blohm GmbH, München and Donauwörth
Meiningen	Reichsbahn Ausbesserungswerk, Meiningen, East Germany
Nohab	Nydqvist och Holm AB, (Nohab) Trollhättan, Sweden.
OK	Orenstein & Koppel, Berlin-Drewitz, Germany (until 1938); Orenstein & Koppel & Lubecker Maschinenbau AG, Dortmund-Dorsfeld, Germany (1950-)
OR	On Rail Gesellschaft für Eisenbahnausrüstung und Zuberhör mbH, Mettmann, Germany
PESA	Pojazdy Szynowe Pesa Bydgoszcz, Bydgoszcz, Poland
Schöma	Christoph Schöttler Maschinenfabrik GmbH, Diepholz
SGP	Simmering Graz Pauker AG, plants in Graz, Wien Floridsdorf and Simmering.
Sie	Siemens Schuckterwerke, Berlin-Siemenstadt, Nürnberg & Erlangen, Germany; now mostly Krefeld-Uerdingen (units) and München Allach (Locomotives)
SFT	Siemens Schienenfahrzeugtechnik GmbH, Kiel, Germany, later VSFT
Simm	Simmeringer Maschinen und Waggonbau, AG, Wien, Austria
Skoda	Skoda Transportation, Plzen, CZ.
SLM	Schweizerische Lokomotiv und Maschinenfabrik, Winterthur, Switzerland
Stadler	Stadler Fahrzeug AG Berlin, later Stadler Pankow GmbH
Talbot	Waggonfabrik Talbot, Aachen, Germany.
TLMS	Türkiye Lokomotif ve Motor Sanayii A.S. (Tülomsaş) Eskisehir, Turkey.
U23A	Uzinele 23 August, Bucuresti, Romania. (former Malaxa works)
Uer	Waggonfabrik Uerdingen AG, Krefeld-Uerdingen & Dusseldorf, Germany
VE	Vossloh España
VL	Vossloh, Kiel, former MaK plant
VSFT	Vossloh Schienenfahrzeugtechnik GmbH, Kiel, Germany
VTLT	Voith Turbo Lokomotivtechnik GmbH & Co. KG.
Vulcan	Stettiner Maschinenbau Aktien Gesellschaft Vulcan, Abt. Lokomotivbau, Stettin-Bredow, Germany
WagU	Waggon Union GmbH, Berlin, later Stadler
Wegmann	Wegmann & Co. Kassel-Rothenditmold, Germany.
Wind	Rheiner Maschinenfabrik Windhoff AG, Rheine (Westfalen), Germany
Wismar	Eisenbahn-Verkehrsmittel AG, Waggonfabrik Wismar, Wismar, Germany.
Wittenberge	Former DR carriage works in Wittenberge, Germany
WMD	Waggon und Maschinenbau GmbH, Donauwörth, Germany
Wumag	Waggon und Maschinenbau, Görlitz, Germany.